Operating Systems: A Spiral Approach

Ramez Elmasri, Professor
University of Texas, Arlington

A. Gil Carrick, Lecturer
Formerly of the University of Texas, Arlington

David Levine, Senior Lecturer
University of Texas, Arlington

Boston   Burr Ridge, IL   Dubuque, IA   New York   San Francisco   St. Louis
Bangkok   Bogotá   Caracas   Kuala Lumpur   Lisbon   London   Madrid   Mexico City
Milan   Montreal   New Delhi   Santiago   Seoul   Singapore   Sydney   Taipei   Toronto

Higher Education

OPERATING SYSTEMS: A SPIRAL APPROACH

Published by McGraw-Hill, a business unit of The McGraw-Hill Companies, Inc., 1221 Avenue of the
Americas, New York, NY 10020. Copyright © 2010 by The McGraw-Hill Companies, Inc. All rights
reserved. No part of this publication may be reproduced or distributed in any form or by any means,
or stored in a database or retrieval system, without the prior written consent of The McGraw-Hill
Companies, Inc., including, but not limited to, in any network or other electronic storage or transmission,
or broadcast for distance learning.

Some ancillaries, including electronic and print components, may not be available to customers outside the
United States.

This book is printed on acid-free paper.

1 2 3 4 5 6 7 8 9 0 DOC/DOC 0 9

ISBN 978–0–07–244981–5
MHID 0–07–244981–0

Global Publisher: *Raghothaman Srinivasan*
Director of Development: *Kristine Tibbetts*
Senior Marketing Manager: *Curt Reynolds*
Project Manager: *Joyce Watters*
Senior Production Supervisor: *Kara Kudronowicz*
Senior Media Project Manager: *Jodi K. Banowetz*
Associate Design Coordinator: *Brenda A. Rolwes*
Cover Designer: *Studio Montage, St. Louis, Missouri*
(USE) Cover Image: © *Getty Images*
Compositor: *Laserwords Private Limited*
Typeface: *10/12 Times Roman*
Printer: *R. R. Donnelley Crawfordsville, IN*

Library of Congress Cataloging-in-Publication Data

Elmasri, Ramez.
    Operating systems : a spiral approach / Ramez Elmasri, A. Gil Carrick, David Levine. —1st ed.
       p. cm.
    Includes index.
    ISBN 978–0–07–244981–5 — ISBN 0–07–244981–0 (hard copy : alk. paper)
    1. Operating systems (Computers)—Textbooks. I. Carrick, A. Gil. II. Levine, David (David E.) III. Title.
    QA76.76.O63E4865 2010
    005.4'3—dc22
                                                                                                    2008051735

www.mhhe.com

Dedication

"To peace, knowledge, and freedom."

—Ramez Elmasri

"To Judith, whose limited patience was strongly tested."

—Gil Carrick

"To close family and friends."

—David Levine

Table of Contents

Preface

WHY WE WROTE YET ANOTHER OPERATING SYSTEMS BOOK

We have long felt that the traditional approach to teaching about Operating Systems (OSs) was not the best approach. The purpose of this book is to support a different approach to this task. When studying any complex domain of knowledge, the order in which one learns the hierarchy of principles, laws, ideas, and concepts can make the process easier or more difficult. The most common technique is to partition the subject into major topics and then study each one in great detail. For OSs, this has traditionally meant that after a brief introduction to some terms and an overview, a student studied isolated topics in depth—processes and process management, then memory management, then file systems, and so on. We can call this a depth-oriented approach or a vertical approach. After learning a great mass of unrelated details in these isolated topic areas, the student then examined case studies, examples of real OSs, and finally saw how the different topics fit together to make a real OS.

We believe that a better model is that followed by children when learning a language: learn a few words, a little grammar, a little sentence structure, and then cycle (or spiral) through; more words, more grammar, more sentence structure. By continuing to spiral through the same sequence, the complexity of the language is mastered. We can call this a breadth-oriented or spiral approach.

We have taken this approach to the subject of OSs. The first few chapters give some basic background and definitions. We then begin to describe a very simple OS in a simple system—early PCs—and evolve toward more complex systems with more features: first limited background tasks (such as simultaneous printing), then multitasking, and so on. In each case we try to show how the increasing requirements caused each system to be designed the way it was. This is not specifically a historical order of OS development. Rather, we choose a representative system at each complexity level in order to see how the different OS components interact with and influence one another. It is our belief that this approach will give the student a greater appreciation of how the various features of each level of OS were put together.

Part of the motivation for this approach has to do with why Computing Science students are told they must study OSs at all. It is highly unlikely that many of these students will work on the development of OSs. However, virtually every system that they do work on will run on top of an OS, though perhaps a very few will work on embedded systems with no OS. For the rest of them, the OS will stand between the applications and the hardware, and failure to thoroughly understand the nature of the OS will mean that these applications will be underperforming at best and hazardous at worst. We believe that our approach will lead students to a better understanding of the entire architecture of modern OSs than does the traditional approach.

THE ORGANIZATION OF THE BOOK

In Part 1 of the book we give some general background information. This information will cover basic principles of OSs and show several different views of an OS. It will also include an overview of typical computer hardware that an OS controls. Another chapter addresses such basic concepts as processes, multiprogramming, time sharing, resource management, and different approaches to OS architecture.

Then in Part 2 of the book, we will cover five types of operating systems in increasing order of complexity, our spiral approach, as follows:

1. A simple single-process OS (CPM)
2. A more complex OS (Palm OS), which allows simple system multitasking
3. An OS with full multitasking for a single user (Apple Mac OS, pre-OS X)
4. An OS that supports multiple users (Linux)
5. A distributed OS (mostly Globus)

In each case we have selected an OS that is typical of the class on which to base the discussion so as to make it more concrete. This selection was made with an eye to practicality. We first discuss simple systems in terms of process, memory, file, and I/O management, and then (slowly) move to more complex systems, gradually introducing such concepts as multitasking, time sharing, networking, security, and other issues. Occasionally we will also mention other well-known OSs that are examples of a class, such as MS-DOS in Chapter 3 and the Symbian OS in Chapter 4.

In Parts 3–5 of the book, we move to an in-depth approach of covering each OS topic in more detail: from processes to memory management to file systems. We also discuss many recent issues in operating systems: threading, object orientation, security, and approaches to parallel and distributed systems. In these chapters we revisit the sample systems discussed in Part 2 and explain the mechanisms in more detail, especially for the modern OSs.

In Part 6 we look more closely at several OSs in what are typically called case studies. Now that we know more about the details, we look at some systems in more depth and see how some features were implemented. In two cases we are revisiting more closely OSs that were covered in Part 2.

An appendix covers basic computer hardware architecture for those institutions that do not require such a course as a prerequisite for an Operating Systems course. It can also be used as a reference for those who need to review a specific topic.

THE STYLE OF THE BOOK

- We use a conversational style to avoid boring the students with excessive pedantry.
- We avoid the use of excessive formalisms. A more formal presentation is provided where needed. This choice stems from our belief that most students will not develop OSs, but rather will use them to support applications.

- We use the normal, accepted terms but also discuss alternative terms when no accepted standard terminology exists or where other terms were used historically.
- We discuss algorithmic solutions as opposed to listing actual code since students at different schools will have been exposed to different languages.
- For each OS that is treated separately, whether in the spiral section or in the case studies, we include some history of the industry at the time, and sometimes the key companies or individuals involved. This follows from our basic belief that a student can understand OSs better if they are placed in a meaningful context.
- We cover modern OSs found in devices not conventionally regarded as computers since the students use these devices every day and have an operational familiarity with them.
- Frequent figures are incorporated as an aid to those who learn best visually rather than by reading sequences of words.
- Each chapter ends with a set of questions that a student can use to assess the level of understanding of the material in the chapter.
- Projects are outlined for many chapters, which can be used by the instructor to ground the students' understanding in reality.

The Authors

We have been teaching OS classes for quite a few years using other materials. We have developed this text because we felt the need for a different methodology. We all have served on the faculty of the Department of Computer Science and Engineering at the University of Texas at Arlington (UTA).

Ramez Elmasri is a Professor at the University of Texas at Arlington. He received his BS in Electrical Engineering from Alexandria University, Egypt, in 1972, and his MS and PhD degrees in Computer Science at Stanford University in 1980. His current research interests are in sensor networks and RFID, mediators for bioinformatics data, query personalization, and systems integration. He is the lead co-author of the textbook "Fundamentals of Database Systems," now in its 5th Edition. His previous research covered various aspects of databases, conceptual modeling, and distributed systems.

A. Gil Carrick was formerly a Lecturer at UTA and is now retired from teaching. He received his BS in Electronics Technology from the University of Houston in 1970 and his MSCS in 2000 from the University of Texas at Arlington. He is a member of Upsilon Pi Epsilon, the Computer Science Honor Society. His career spans the information technology industry: end-user organizations, hardware manufacturers, software publishers, third-party maintenance, universities, and R&D firms. He has written for professional journals and edited IT books, primarily in the networking field. In his career he has used all the operating systems discussed in this text and many others besides.

David Levine has been teaching courses in operating systems, software engineering, networking, and computer architecture. His research interests include mobile computing, mobile objects, and distributed computing and he has presented the results of this research in recent publications and several international conferences. He enjoys discussing Operating Systems, talking about current research with students and reading about new OS advances.

HOW TO USE THIS BOOK—FOR INSTRUCTORS

This text is intended to be used for a one-semester undergraduate course in Operating Systems, probably in the junior or senior year. The first part of the book is designed to consolidate basic background information necessary for the following chapters. Chapter 1 sets the discussion and gives some historical perspective. The instructor can skim this chapter and decide what to include. The appendix is a brief look at fairly modern hardware architectures. If a course in hardware is not a prerequisite for this course, then this appendix could be included. Chapter 2 defines some simple terms used in OSs and offers some more perspective on the larger topic of OS design. Again, an instructor can review this chapter and select different parts to include or exclude.

Part 2 begins the spiral approach. We believe this is a significant portion of the book. Here the student is gradually introduced to a series of OSs with more complex goals. These increasingly more complex goals lead to increasingly more complex OSs. Only two of these chapters are not normal topics in OS texts—Chapter 4 on a single-user multitasking operating system and Chapter 7 on a distributed operating system. They could be left out at the instructor's discretion, but more and more students will be working in such environments as users and as programmers.

Part 3 begins the in-depth chapters. Each chapter is fairly independent of the others, though Chapters 12 and 13 are strongly related. Beginning with Chapter 14 the individual chapters can probably be left out if the topic is the major subject of another course that the students will be required to take.

Notes about the bibliographies: The chapters in Part 3 all include a bibliography section. The reference papers that are cited are widely regarded as being seminal papers or good summaries. They may cover material that is not covered in the text. If an instructor or a student is looking for material to provide a better understanding of a given topic, then they are suggested reading.

HOW TO USE THIS BOOK—FOR STUDENTS

For students the most important thing about using this text is to understand how one learns best. There are many pathways to get information into the brain. The book itself directly addresses two of these pathways. There is obviously the text for those who learn best through reading the words and the illustrations for those who are more visually oriented. When you attend the lectures you will hear the instructor talk about the material. This is for those who learn best through hearing words. At the same time, the instructor will probably use visual aids such as the PowerPoint slides that are available for the text. Again, this is to the benefit of those who learn best by reading the words and seeing the illustrations. Some students learn best from mechanical skills, so the process of outlining the material or making study notes works well for those students.

Also presented in the book at the end of each chapter are questions about the material. These questions are designed such that a student who has a reasonable grasp of the material should be able to answer the question.

As new information is presented to the brain it takes a certain amount of time to link with other information already there. But the brain gets much information during the day that is not significant and therefore it does not retain it. Only when presented with the same or similar material again a short time later will the brain retain a significant amount of the information. The more different mechanisms that are used and the more times the information is repeated, the stronger the retention of the material. So the best method is to use all these methods combined, focusing on what works best for you. What we have found works well for most students is the following sequence:

- Print the slides to be covered in the next section, with several slides per page.
- Read the assigned material in the text. Note questions on the slide printouts.
- Come to class and listen to the instructor, amplifying any notes, especially things the instructor says that are not in the text. (Those points are favorite issues for the instructor and they tend to show up on exams.)
- Ask questions about things that are unclear.
- When it is time to review the material for an exam, go over the slides. If there are points that are unclear, go back to the text to fill them in. If any questions remain, then contact the instructor or teaching assistants.
- The review questions can be studied at any time the student finds convenient.

AVAILABLE RESOURCES FOR INSTRUCTORS

The text is supported by a website with separate sections for instructors and students.

- Supplements to the text will be made from time to time as the need presents itself.
- A set of suggested projects will be available for instructors. Most of these projects will have been used by the authors. They should be sufficiently rich and OS independent that they can be readily adapted to fit any situation. They are not based on any specific package that the instructor, students, or assistants will have to master in order to work the labs.
- PowerPoint slides are provided for the students to use, as described earlier. Instructors are encouraged to modify these presentations to fit their needs. Acknowledgement of their source is requested.
- Review question answers are provided for the instructors in order that they not be embarrassed by not knowing some arcane point the authors thought was important.
- A current list of errata will be maintained on the website.
- Reference to web resources are provided for many chapters, but the web is very volatile. The website for the book will contain an up-to-date set of web references.

ACKNOWLEDGMENTS

This text has actually been developing for longer than we would like to remember. The people at McGraw-Hill have been exceptionally patient with us. In particular, we would like to thank the following folks with McGraw-Hill: Melinda Bilecki, Kay Brimeyer, Brenda Rolwes, Kara Kudronowicz, Faye Schilling, and Raghu Srinivasan. We would also like to thank Alan Apt and Emily Lupash, who were our editors when we started working on the book. Finally, we also thank Erika Jordan and Laura Patchkofsky with Pine Tree Composition.

The chapter on Windows Vista was reviewed by Dave Probert of Microsoft. He provided valuable feedback on some items we had only been able to speculate on and brought several problems to our attention. His participation was arranged by Arkady Retik, also with Microsoft Corporation. Two chapters were reviewed by our fellow faculty members at University of Texas, Arlington. These included Yonghe Liu who reviewed the chapter on networking and Matthew Wright who reviewed the chapter on protection and security. Another faculty member, Bahram Khalili, used drafts of the text in his OS class. Naturally any remaining problems are our responsibility and not theirs.

We have used drafts of these materials in our teaching for several years and we wish to thank all our students for their feedback. In particular we wish to thank the following students: Zaher Naarane, Phil Renner, William Peacock, Wes Parish, Kyle D. Witt, David M. Connelly, and Scott Purdy.

REMAINING ERRORS

One difficulty with working on a project with multiple authors is that with the best of intentions, one of the writers can alter a bit of text that he himself did not write, thinking that he is clearing up some minor point, but actually altering the meaning in some subtle but important way. Accordingly, you may find minor errors in the text. Naturally these errors were not the fault of the original author, who doubtless wrote the original text correctly, but were introduced by another well-meaning author who was not as familiar with the material.

Still, such errors may be present, and we must deal with them. So, if you do find errors, we would be very happy to know about them. We will publish any errata, fix them in the next edition, determine who is to blame, and deal with the offending authors appropriately.

Part 1

Operating Systems Overview and Background

In this part:

This part of the book contains two chapters. Chapter 1 gives a basic explanation about what an Operating System (or OS for short) is. It explains how the OS provides services to users and programmers. These services make it possible to utilize a computer without having to deal with the low-level, arcane details, but rather, being allowed to concentrate on the problem(s) to be solved. Such problems may be anything, including not only the things we normally consider computing activities, but also activities such as playing games, dynamically generating art, and monitoring the performance of an automobile engine.

Chapter 2 provides an initial high-level look at OS concepts, components, and architecture. General terms are introduced that a student will need to know in order to study the series of increasingly more complex OSs that are presented in Part 2.

Chapter 1

Getting Started

In this chapter:

Operating systems are at the heart of every computer. The **Operating System** (or **OS** for short) provides services to users and programmers that make it possible to utilize a computer without having to deal with the low-level, difficult-to-use hardware commands. It provides relatively uniform interfaces to access the extremely wide variety of devices that a computer interacts with, from input/output devices such as printers and digital cameras, to wired and wireless network components that allow computers to communicate. It allows users to create, manage, and organize different types of files. In addition, most modern OSs provide graphical user interfaces (GUIs) to allow a relatively easy-to-use interface for computer users.

In this opening chapter, we start in Section 1.1 with a brief introduction to show how important an Operating System is and how they are used not only in computers but also in many types of electronic devices that we all use in our daily routines. Section 1.2 is a more technical look at why even simple devices contain an Operating System. Then in Section 1.3 we discuss the different views of what an Operating System does by looking at the Operating System from two perspectives: the user's perspective and the system's perspective. We also discuss the requirements that each type of user has for the Operating System. Section 1.3 next gives a few simple examples to illustrate some sequences of functions that an Operating System goes through to perform seemingly simple user requests. In Section 1.4 we present some basic terminology and concepts, and give some figures to illustrate typical components for a simple Operating System. We give a brief historical perspective in Section 1.5 and conclude with a chapter summary in Section 1.6.

1.1 INTRODUCTION

For many years, OSs were viewed by most people as uninteresting—except for OS programmers and computer "nerds." Because of a number of high-profile cases, OSs have occasionally become front-page news in recent years. Suddenly, the OS is seen by some as controlling all computing. There are very strongly felt opinions about what constitutes good versus bad OSs. There is also quite a bit of disagreement about what functionality should be provided by the OS. While many people (and some courts!) believe that one company dominates the OS market, others say that the OS is increasingly unimportant—the **Internet browser** *is* the OS. In fact, there is a very wide variety of types of OSs, and OSs exist at some level on every conceivable computing device, including some that may surprise many people.

For example, handheld personal digital assistants (**PDA**s) have very capable, complex, and flexible OSs. Most electronic devices that have some intelligence have complex, yet easy-to-use OSs and system software to control them. The OS that was once thought of as the arcane world of process management and memory management techniques is now occasionally a conversation topic in cafés, bars, and computer stores. Many people now seem to be experts—or at least have an opinion—on OSs.

(Perhaps) Surprising places to find an OS:

Personal digital assistants

Cable TV controller boxes

Electronic games

Copiers

Fax machines

Remote controls

Cellular telephones

Automobile engines

Digital cameras

While we also have our opinions, we try to get behind the hype—generated by marketing and salespeople as well as millions of opinionated users—in order to explain the real systems. We also throw in our own opinions when needed and explain why we hold these beliefs. We give many examples of currently used systems to demonstrate concepts and show what is good and bad about the various systems. We try to avoid the so-called religious issues, such as: Which is the better OS: **Windows** or **Mac-OS?** Or are **UNIX** and its variations such as **Linux** better than both? Instead, we point out how these systems came about and what they provide to users and programmers.

Increasingly, certain parts of the OS—particularly those handling user and application program interaction—are visible to users and programmers and often may be critical in marketing a computer or electronic—or even mechanical—device. Buyers are becoming very critical and have higher expectations of what the OS should provide them. More than ever before, the system must not only provide new features and be easier to use but it must also support those old features and applications that we are used to. Of course, as we add new devices—video devices and disks, high fidelity sound, and wireless networking, for example—we want the system to easily adapt to and handle those devices. In fact, a good OS architecture should even allow the connection of new devices that were not yet available and may not even have been thought of when the OS was created!

1.2 WHAT ARE OPERATING SYSTEMS ALL ABOUT?

In this section, we give a simple example—a simple handheld game system—to illustrate some of the basic functionalities that an OS should provide.

Think about a handheld electronic game system, one that is very cheap but has a small screen, a few buttons, and several games. Although this game system might not require an OS, it probably has one. The main reason is to consolidate the common functions needed by the various games installed on the game system.

The games typically have some common parts. For example, each game needs to get some input from the buttons, and to display something on the screen. While those actions sound easy, they do require some not-so-simple software programming. Getting the input from a button—that sounds easy. Well, except that the user may push two buttons at once—what then? It is also likely that a cheap game does not use sophisticated and expensive buttons, so there is electronic noise that may distort the signal coming in—how should the games deal with that? The easy solution is to handle each of these common issues in one, single place. For example, all button pushes can be read in, have any noise cleaned up, and so forth in a single software routine. Having a single *read-the-button* software routine has the advantage of providing a consistent user interface—all games treat button input in the same way. It also allows the routine to occupy space in only one place in system memory instead of occupying space in each individual game. And where should that *read-the-button* software routine be placed? It should be in the OS—where every game that needs to read a button can call this routine.

The OS should also handle unexpected events. For example, a user may quit a game in the middle (when losing) and start another game. No reboot of the game system should be necessary. The user's need to switch from game to game (task to task) is natural and expected. In fact, users (5-year-olds) may push buttons at unexpected times and the screen should continue to be updated (refreshed) while the game is being played—even while waiting for a button to be pushed. This is called **asynchronicity,** which can be defined informally as the occurrence of events at random or unexpected times—a very important feature in even simple systems like a handheld game.

Several important OS concepts are part of this game system: When a game is started, some part of its software may be loaded into memory, whereas other parts may have been preloaded in ROM (read-only memory) or fixed memory[1]; dynamic memory is reserved for use by the game and is initialized; timers may be set. All on a cheap (but fun) game! What more does one expect from an OS?

1.3 USER VERSUS SYSTEM VIEW OF AN OS

You have probably heard the old adage; "There are two sides to every question." (Maybe that should be "two *or more* sides.") The idea is that trying to look at some question from different perspectives often helps our understanding. One of the important methods to learning something new is to view it from different perspectives. For an OS, the two most important perspectives are the **user view** and the **system view.**

The user view pertains to how users or programs—programs are the main users of the OS—utilize the OS; for example, how a program reads a keystroke. The system view pertains to how the OS software actually does the required action—how it gets keystrokes, separates out special ones like *shift,* and makes them available to the user or program. We present OS facilities, concepts, and techniques from both user and system points of view throughout the book. First, we elaborate on the different types of users and their views of the OS.

1.3.1 Users' views and types of users

The term **user** is often too vague—especially for persons whose role in computing is so critical—so it is important to first describe the various types of users. Trying to pin down the role of a user of an OS is not simple. There are various types of users. We primarily want to distinguish among end users, application programmers, system programmers and system administrators. Table 1.1 lists some of the most important concerns about what the OS should provide for each of the three main types of users. Of course, there is some overlap among these concerns. We are merely trying to show how those viewpoints sometimes diverge. Further complicating the issue is that sometimes users fit into several of the roles or even all of them. Such users often find themselves having conflicting needs.

Application Users (or End Users)—this group includes all of us, people who use (or run) application or system programs. When we use a word processor, a web browser, an email system, or a multimedia viewer, we are a user of that application. As users, we expect a quick, reliable response (to keystrokes or mouse movement), a consistent user view (each type of command—such as scrolling or quitting an application—should be done in a similar manner), and other features that depend on each specific type of OS. Other needs are listed in Table 1.1. In general, this group of users is most often called simply *users,* or sometimes **end users.**

Application Programmers—this group includes the people who write application programs, such as word processors or email systems. Programmers are very demanding of the OS: "How do I read and write to a file?", "How do I get a user's keystroke?", and "How do I display this box?" are typical questions programmers

---
[1] We define these terms in Chapters 2 and 3.

TABLE 1.1   **Concerns of Various User Classes**

End Users	Easy to use and learn
	Adapts to user's style of doing things
	Lively response to input
	Provides lots of visual cues
	Free of unpleasant surprises (e.g., deleting a file without warning)
	Uniform ways to do the same thing (e.g., moving an icon or scrolling down a window—in different places)
	Alternative ways to do one thing (e.g., some users like to use the mouse, others like to use the keyboard)
Application Programmers	Easy to access low-level OS calls by programs (e.g., reading keystrokes, drawing to the screen, getting mouse position)
	Provide a consistent programmer view of the system
	Easy to use higher-level OS facilities and services (e.g., creating new windows, or reading from and writing to the network)
	Portability to other platforms
Systems Programmers	Easy to create correct programs
	Easy to debug incorrect programs
	Easy to maintain programs
	Easy to expand existing programs
System Managers and Administrators	Easy addition or removal of devices such as disks, scanners, multimedia accessories, and network connections
	Provide OS security services to protect the users, system, and data files
	Easy to upgrade to new OS versions
	Easy to create and manage user accounts
	Average response is good and predictable
	System is affordable

ask when learning to use a new OS. The facilities that the OS provide are the programmers' view of the OS. Sometimes they are called system calls or an API (application program interface). They may also appear as language library functions or sometimes just as packages of classes. Programmers also want the software they develop to be easily ported to other platforms.

Systems Programmers—these are the people who write software—either programs or components—that is closely tied to the OS. A utility that shows the status of the computer's network connection or an installable driver for a piece of hardware are examples of systems programs. Systems programmers need to have a detailed understanding of the internal functioning of the OS. In many cases, systems programs need to access special OS data structures or privileged system calls. While OS designers sometimes are concerned with portability to other platforms, often they are not—they are charged with developing a specific set of functions for a specific platform and portability is not a concern.

System Administrators—this group includes the people who manage computer facilities, and hence are responsible for installing and upgrading the OS, as well as other systems programs and utilities. They are also responsible for creating and managing user accounts, and for protecting the system. They need to have a detailed understanding of how the OS is installed and upgraded, and how it interacts with other programs and utilities. They must also understand the security and authorization features of the OS in order to protect their system and users effectively.

1.3.2 System view

The system view refers to *how the OS actually provides services.* In other words, it refers to the internal workings of the OS. This is a less common view. Often only a few people, the OS designers and implementers, understand or care about the internal workings of an OS. Indeed this information is often considered secret by companies that produce and sell OSs commercially. Sometimes the overall workings of major parts of the system—management of files, running of programs, or handling of memory—may be described to help programmers understand the use of those subsystems. In some cases, the whole source code for an OS is available. Such systems are known as **open source** systems.[2]

The majority of this book is concerned with the *how*—how does the system run a program, create a file, or display a graphic. To understand the actual "how"—the internal details—we describe algorithms and competing methods for implementing OS functions. We now illustrate the system view (or views) with two examples: tracking mouse and cursor movement, and managing file operations. Although these examples may seem a bit complex, they serve to illustrate how the OS is involved in practically all actions that are performed by a computer user.

1.3.3 An example: moving a mouse (and mouse cursor)

While the movement of a mouse pointer (or cursor) on a screen by moving the mouse (or some other **pointing device** such as a pad or trackball) seems straightforward, it illustrates the many views of an OS. Figure 1.1 illustrates this process. When the pointing device is moved, it generates a hardware event called an **interrupt,** which the OS handles. The OS notes the movements of the mouse in terms of some hardware-specific units—that is, rather than millimeters or inches the readings are in number of pulses generated. This is the **low-level system view.** The actual software reading the mouse movements is part of the OS, and is called a **mouse device driver.** This device driver reads the low-level mouse movement information and another part of the OS interprets it so that it can be converted into a **higher-level system view,** such as screen coordinates reflecting the mouse movements.

On the "other side" or view is the question, What does the user see? The **user's view** is that the cursor will smoothly move on the screen and that as the mouse moves greater distances faster, the screen movement will appear faster too. In between these

---
[2] The Linux OS is a well-known example of an open source operating system.

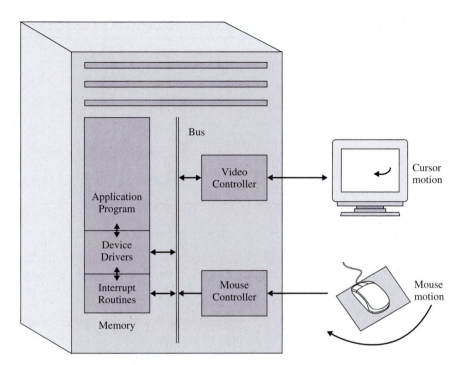

FIGURE 1.1
The cursor tracking
mouse motion.

views is the **application programmers' view,** How do I get the mouse movement information in order to use it and display it in my application? Another issue is how this information on mouse movements is presented to the application programmer. This is the higher-level system view mentioned earlier.

And to complete these views a bit let us return to the system's view, Which application gets this mouse movement if there are multiple open windows? The mouse movements may need to be queued up if there are multiple movements before the application retrieves them. The movements may even be lost if the OS is busy doing other things—for example, loading a Web page through a network connection—and cannot receive the device driver's input in a timely manner.

1.3.4 Another (bigger) example: Files

Sometimes the most critical **end user's view** of an OS is the file system—in particular, file names. Can file names contain spaces? How long can they be? Are upper- and lowercase letters allowed? Are they treated as different or the same characters? How about non-English characters or punctuation? An OS may even be called good or bad simply because long file names are not used or the difference between upper- and lowercase characters is not distinguished.

In the **application programmer's view,** the file system is a frequently used, critical part of the system. It provides commands for creating a new file, using an existing file, reading or appending data to a file, and other file operations. There may even be several different types of files provided by the system. The **system**

TABLE 1.2   **The Steps in Copying a File from a CD to a Hard Disk**

Check for file on CD

Check for file on hard disk—confirm overwrite

Create file name in hard disk directory

Find space for file on hard disk

Read data sectors from CD

Write data sectors to hard disk

Update hard disk directory

Update hard drive space information

Do all this in seconds (or less!)

view of the file system is so large it is usually divided into subparts: file naming and name manipulation (directory services), file services such as locating and mapping a file name to its data (file allocation and storage), trying to keep parts of open files in main memory to speed up access to its data (file buffering and caching), and the actual management of the storage devices (disk scheduling).

For example, suppose that a user types the name of a file to be copied from a CD to a hard disk. The program may first need to see whether that file exists on the CD, and if it would overwrite a file with that name on the hard disk. The OS then needs to create an entry for the file in the hard disk directory, find space on the hard disk for storing the data, and find and get the data from the CD, which has been recorded in pieces (sectors) that will be copied. And all this should be done in a few seconds or even a fraction of a second! See Table 1.2.

1.4 SOME OS TERMS, BASIC CONCEPTS, AND ILLUSTRATIONS

We now list and define some important OS concepts and terms. Then we give some diagrams to illustrate these concepts.

1.4.1 Basic terminology

Operating System (or just **System**). Although we can give different definitions based on the different views of an OS, the following informal definition is a good starting point: The OS is a collection of one or more software modules that manages and controls the resources of a computer or other computing or electronic device, and gives users and programs an interface to utilize these resources. The managed resources include memory, processor, files, input or output devices, and so on.

Device.   A device is a piece of hardware connected to the main computer system hardware. Hard disks, DVDs, and video monitors are typical devices managed by an OS. Many devices have a special electronic (hardware) interface, called a **device controller,** which helps connect a device or a group of similar devices to a computer system. Examples include hard disk controllers and video monitor controllers. There are many types of hard disk controllers that usually follow industry standards such as SCSI, SATA, and other common but cryptic acronyms. Device controllers are the hardware glue that connects devices to the main computer system hardware, usually through a **bus.**

Device driver.   A device driver is a software routine that is part of the OS, and is used to communicate with and control a device through its device controller.

Kernel.   This term usually refers to that part of the OS that implements basic functionality and is always present in memory. In some cases the entire OS is created as one monolithic entity and this entire unit is called the kernel.

Service.   Services are functions that the OS kernel provides to users, mostly through APIs via OS calls. These services can be conveniently grouped into categories based on their functionality, for example, file manipulation services (create, read, copy), memory allocation services (get, free), or miscellaneous services (get system time). The key to a programmer's understanding a system is to understand the OS services it provides.

Utility.   These are programs that are not part of the OS core (or kernel), but work closely with the kernel to provide ease of use or access to system information. A **shell** or **command interpreter** is an example of a utility. The shell utility provides a user interface to many system services. For example, user requests such as listing file names in a directory, running a program, or exiting (logging out), may all be handled by the shell. The shell may invoke other utilities to actually do the work; for example, directory file listing is sometimes a utility program itself.

1.4.2 How about some pictures?

Figure 1.2 is a simplified view of a small personal computer showing some basic devices connected to the computer memory and CPU (processor). The OS program (or kernel) will include various device drivers that handle the peripherals (devices) of the system under CPU control. For example, part of the contents of memory may be transferred to the video controller to be displayed on the monitor, or the contents of a part of the disk (a sector) may be transferred to the disk controller and eventually to memory (for a disk read operation).

Figure 1.3 is a simplistic view of part of an OS. The OS controls (or manages) the system resources: it controls the disks, keyboards, video monitor, and other devices. It controls allocation of memory and use of the CPU by deciding which program gets to run. It provides services to the shell and other programs through the use of system calls. It also provides an abstraction of the hardware by hiding complex details of hardware devices from programs.

Figure 1.3, a common one used to illustrate OSs, is a logical view, not a physical one. For example, the OS kernel physically resides inside the memory unit and it is running (executing) on the CPU. Thus, the arrows between the kernel—which is software—and the devices—which are hardware—represent a logical control, not physical.

FIGURE 1.2

Hardware: A very simplistic view of a small personal computer.

(Note: This picture is *too* simple. In reality there are often multiple buses, say between video and memory. We will get to more detailed pictures in the Appendix.)

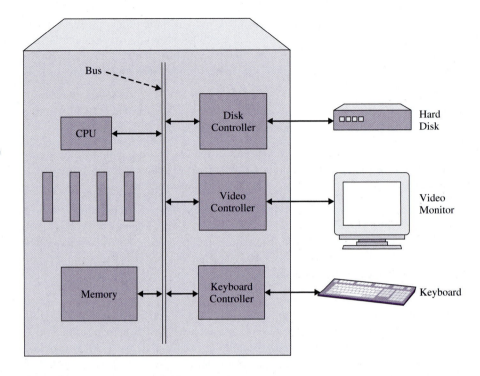

FIGURE 1.3

A simplistic view of the OS software in relationship to hardware.

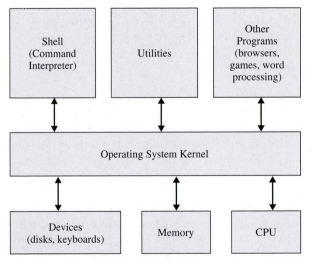

Figure 1.4 represents a layered view of the OS, where the outermost circle represents the utilities/applications layer that accesses the OS kernel layer, which in turn manages access to the hardware layer.

1.4.3 Closer to reality: A personal computer OS

Figure 1.5 shows more detail of a simple OS for a personal computer or PC. The OS has two additional components that were not shown in Figure 1.3: **device drivers**

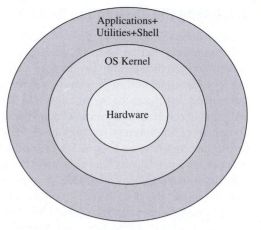

FIGURE 1.4
A layered view
of an OS.

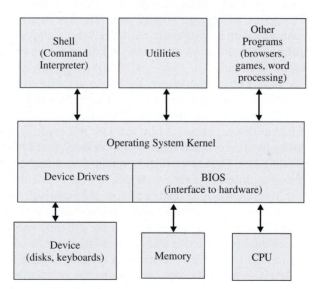

FIGURE 1.5
The PC (small
system) model
of an OS.

and a **BIOS** (**Basic Input/Output System**). The BIOS abstracts the hardware—that is, the BIOS manages common devices, such as keyboards, basic video, and the system clock. This allows the main or higher-level part of the OS to deal with all devices of the same type—for example, all keyboards—in the same way. Thus, the OS kernel does not change whether a keyboard has 88 keys, 112 keys, or some other number, or even in cases where keys may not appear where they might on different keyboards because of different language characters or accent keys. Device drivers also provide a similar abstraction to similar devices. For example, a DVD device driver can be supplied by a device manufacturer to provide an abstract or common view of the DVD device to the OS, so that the OS does not have to vary with every idiosyncrasy of DVD drives, regardless of the manufacturer.

The next section elaborates further on why it is important to provide abstraction layers when designing an OS.

1.4.4 Why the abstraction layers?

Good question. Early in the days of personal computers, computer hobbyists had fun assembling and building the hardware and getting simple programs to work, usually written in assembly language or machine language. This was a good learning tool for some, but programming was very tedious. But people wanted to enjoy the experience of writing more interesting and therefore larger and more complex programs. So better tools were needed. These tools include easy-to-use editors and compilers or interpreters for high-level languages. For end users, the desire was to use the computer as a business or productivity tool. These users needed word processing, spreadsheets, and communication software. Certainly there were many very dissimilar computer hardware systems being built. But there were also a number of similar, but not identical, computers, built by many manufacturers. These systems might either have the same CPU from the same CPU manufacturer, or use a compatible CPU that had the same instruction set. However, they may have video devices that were quite different. For example, one system might have a terminal-like device attached to a serial port, whereas another might have a built-in video controller with many capabilities for advanced graphics. Keyboards would typically differ in function keys or "arrow" or cursor movement keys, with other keys being added or missing.

In order for programmers to be able to create programs that would run on these different systems with minor or no changes required to the program when moving it to a different system, the OS provided the same interface to the hardware for all the different devices supported by that OS. For instance, a program could read a keystroke from a keyboard regardless of what type of keyboard it was by a system call to read a key. The OS would take care of translating the keys which were in different places on different keyboards or which were coded differently.

To avoid the complexity and cost of having different versions of the OS for different keyboards, different video monitors, different disks, and so forth, the OS was split into a part that was adapted to the different hardware devices (the BIOS and device drivers) and a part that remained the same for all hardware (shown as the kernel in Figure 1.5). This technique of dividing complicated work into several **layers,** or **levels,** is an established software technique used in large and complex software systems including OSs. Thus, adapting an OS to a new compatible computer system with different devices involved changing (or writing) a BIOS but using the same module for the rest of the kernel and the same programs and utilities. This was a very attractive idea for everyone—users, manufacturers, and OS writers.

A problem arose when a computer peripheral manufacturer (e.g., a video card manufacturer) designed a new device and wanted to sell it to users so they could upgrade their computer to newer hardware designs. Often the existing BIOS in the computer was installed in ROM (read only memory) and would be difficult and expensive to replace. The solution to this problem was the creation of a modifiable BIOS by allowing device drivers to be loadable at the time the OS was loaded into memory. Having BIOS code that could be replaced when the system was booted allows adding new features to the computer or replacing features in the BIOS with new software and perhaps supporting new functions on existing hardware.

1.5 A SMALL HISTORICAL DIVERSION

We close this chapter with a historical perspective on how OSs were developed, and the different views about what type of functionality should be included in an OS. We give a more detailed historical timeline of OS development at the end of Chapter 3, after we have introduced some additional concepts.

1.5.1 Origins of operating systems

Before personal computers there were of course many larger computers. Early on these machines were very large and very expensive, but by modern standards primitive, and there were few programmers. Programs were limited in their capabilities because main memory was quite small, the CPU processors were very slow, and only a few simple input and output devices existed. A typical early computer system may have had a few thousand words[3] of main memory, a processor that executed several thousand instructions per second, and a Teletype[4] device for input/output. The limited capabilities of these early computers required very careful and well-thought-out programs which were mostly written in the basic machine code of the computer, machine language or assembly language.

These programs were amazing in that in a few hundred or thousand machine instructions they accomplished a tremendous amount of work. But they all faced similar needs: How can a program print some output? How can a program get loaded into memory to begin execution? These needs—the need to load programs into memory, to run a program, to get input and produce output—were the impetus for creating early OSs. At those early times the few programmers on a system knew each other and would share routines (program code) that had been debugged to simplify the job of programming. These shared routines (e.g., "print the value in register A on the Teletype") would eventually be combined into a *library* that could be combined (linked) with an application program to form a complete running program.

These early computers were **single-user** systems. That is to say that only one user—and one program—could run at any one time. Typically programmers would reserve the use of the computer in small blocks of time—perhaps increments of 10–15 minutes. A programmer would use this time to run or debug a program. Because computers were expensive and computer time was very valuable, often bigger blocks of time were available only in the middle of the night or early in the morning when things were quieter, few managers were around, and one could get much more done than in the daytime. This tradition, started in the early days of computing, is one of the few that has lasted until today!

The programs, once written and assembled, were linked or bound with utility routines for input, output, mathematical functions,[5] printout formatting, and other

---

[3] A **word** was typically six characters, but differed from system to system.

[4] A **Teletype** is an electromechanical printer and keyboard, built for telegraphy, that could print or type at a speed of a dozen or so characters per second.

[5] Early computer hardware often did not have instructions for complex mathematical and even arithmetic operations—for example, long division—so these operations were implemented in software utility routines.

FIGURE 1.6

An application program with a loader and OS-like utilities.

common tasks, into an executable program ready to be loaded into memory and run. The program might be stored on punched paper tape or punched cards. The computer hardware would know how to start reading from the input device, but it would only load the first card or the first block of the tape. So that block had to include a small routine that would be able to load the rest of the application into memory. This short routine is called a **loader.** The loader would in turn read the programmer's executable program and put it and the needed utility routines into memory at a specified location, usually either the first memory address or some special fixed location. Then it would transfer execution—by a branch or "subroutine" call—to the program it had loaded. The loadable program tape or card deck might look as illustrated in Figure 1.6.[6] The END delimiter tells that loader that there are no more routines to be loaded since there might be data records following the routines.

As programmers had time to develop more utility routines, the loader grew more sophisticated. Loaders were soon able to load programs that had been translated (compiled) from higher-level programming languages. As the size of loaders, utility routines, and users' programs grew, the card decks or paper tapes became very large (and it became unfortunately common to drop a card deck or tear a paper tape). These loaders and utility routines would become the beginnings of early OSs, which were then often called **monitors.**

1.5.2 What should an Operating System do (or what should it support)?

From the early days of computing until today there has been a fierce debate—ranging from polite discussion to a political or almost religious argument—about what an OS should do. The two extreme views of this debate could be called the maximalist view and the minimalist view. The maximalist view argues that the OS should include as much functionality as possible, whereas the minimalist view is that only the most basic functionality should be part of the OS. From the early systems, the question started: "Should all the routines for input and output be included in my program? I don't even read from the card reader." Including too many routines—any that are not necessary—makes the memory available for my program smaller, and it is too small to begin with. How can one get just what one needs? Mathematical routines such as programs for performing floating-point arithmetic could be done once in the OS rather than separately included in each user's program. But then every program incurred the overhead of the extra memory occupied by these routines in the OS, even programs like accounting applications that did not use floating point arithmetic.

---

[6] This type of loader is often known as a **bootstrap loader.**

In more recent times the debate concerning what to include in an OS continues. For example, a user-friendly OS interface is now commonly considered to have a pointing device—such as a mouse, trackball, or pad—and some type of screen windowing with pull-down menus. Whether that interface should be a part of the OS—thus giving all applications a similar "look and feel," or part of the shell—to allow each user to decide the particular look they want is one of the current issues of the debate about what the OS should include.

To be fair, like many hotly contested issues, both maximalist and minimalist sides have a point. The historical trends are not clear. Newer OSs have been in some cases smaller, simpler, and more configurable and in other cases exactly the opposite—larger, more functional, and more constraining. This issue of what functionality should go where (in the OS kernel or not) has created different design possibilities for OSs, as we discuss further in Chapter 2.

1.6 SUMMARY

In this chapter, we first introduced some of the basic functionality of operating systems. We gave a few simple examples to illustrate why OSs are so important. Then we discussed the different views of what an OS does by looking at the OS from two perspectives: the user's perspective and the system's perspective. We then presented some basic terminology and concepts, and provided some figures to illustrate typical components of simple OSs. Next we began to look at a few architectures that are commonly used to actually create OSs and discussed the very idea of abstraction that is so fundamental to the successful design of OSs. We concluded with a brief historical perspective on the origins of OSs.

The next chapter gives an overview of the major components of an OS and discusses the architecture alternatives in more detail.

REVIEW QUESTIONS

1.1 Give a one-sentence definition of an OS.

1.2 Since most of us are not going to be writing an OS, why do we need to know anything about them?

1.3 Give three reasons why a simple device such as a handheld electronic game probably contains an OS.

1.4 What is the primary difference between a user view of an OS and a system view?

1.5 What are the four different classes of users that were discussed, and what aspects of an OS are they mostly interested in?

1.6 The chapter discussed how the different users are supported from the system view. Two examples were presented, moving a mouse and file systems. Consider another aspect of an OS and discuss how the system view works to support the three different classes of users.

1.7 Should OSs be proprietary so that the manufacturers will be able to make enough profit to continue their development or should the internals and specifications of OSs be open for all users to know?*

1.8 With respect to the study of OSs, how is a controller best defined?

1.9 What is the general principle of abstraction?

1.10 What are some of the reasons why we want abstraction in an OS?

1.11 Distinguish between an OS and a kernel.

1.12 Describe briefly the origins of OSs on the early large mainframe systems.

1.13 Should the characteristics of a windowing interface—the factors that determine its look and feel—be a part of the OS kernel or part of the command shell?

---

* Note to instructors: Don't use this question as part of the class unless you have nothing else to talk about for the day.

Chapter 2

Operating System Concepts, Components, and Architectures

In this chapter:

In this chapter, we discuss in general what the operating system does, and give an overview of OS concepts and components so that a student has some overall perspective about OSs. We also discuss some common techniques employed in nearly all OSs.

To gain some understanding of how the OS is involved in practically all system operations, we start in Section 2.1 with a simple user scenario and describe some of the actions within the scenario that are undertaken by the OS. In Section 2.2 we give an overview of the main types of system resources that the OS manages. These resources include the processor (CPU), main memory, I/O devices, and files. We then give an overview of the major OS modules, and the services that each module provides. These include the process management and CPU scheduling module, the memory management module, the file system module, and the I/O management and disk scheduling module. These may or may not be implemented as separate modules in any particular OS, but looking at each of these separately makes it easier to explain OS concepts.

Then in Section 2.3 we define the concept of a process, which is central to what the OS does, and describe the states of a process and some of the information that the OS maintains about each process. A process (sometimes called job or task)[1] is basically an executing program, and the OS manages system resources on behalf of the processes. In Section 2.4 we discuss the characteristics of different types of OSs, from systems that can run or execute a single process at a time, to those that manage concurrently executing processes, to time sharing and distributed systems.

In Section 2.5 we present some of the different architectural approaches that have been taken for OS construction. These include monolithic OS, microkernels, and layered architectures. We then describe some implementation techniques that are used repeatedly by various OS modules in Section 2.6. These include the queues that are maintained by multitasking OSs to keep track of the jobs that are waiting to acquire resources or to have certain services performed. For example, processes could be waiting for disk I/O or CPU time or printing services. We also describe interrupts and how they are handled in some detail, object-oriented OS design, and virtual machines. Section 2.7 gives a philosophical discussion concerning what functionality should be part of an OS. Finally, in Section 2.8 we summarize this chapter.

2.1 INTRODUCTION: WHAT DOES THE OS DO?

In this section, we go over a small example scenario, in order to see how the OS is involved in nearly every aspect of computing. Consider the following simple user scenario:

A user wants to type a small note to himself.[2] Coming into work this morning he heard a radio advertisement that his favorite music group is coming to town, and he wants to have a reminder to buy tickets and invite some friends. So he starts a scheduling program (or possibly a text editor or a word processing program), types in his reminder, saves the document, and exits. The user could have used a PDA (personal digital assistant), a Windows-based system (e.g., Mac, MS Windows or Linux with a GUI-based text editor), or simply a text-based command shell such as UNIX. Let's assume he is using a GUI-based text editor to write a separate note and save it as a file. Regardless of the type of system used, this scenario caused the OS to create, manage, and terminate software components to accomplish the work. When the user started the editor or some other program he created a **process** (also called **task** or **job**).[3] A process is basically a program in **execution.** A process may be waiting to run, currently running, waiting for something to happen, or finishing. Some of the events that a process may be waiting for include a keystroke from the user, or some data to be read from a disk drive or to be supplied by another program.

Before a process can be started, the executable program file (binary) that will be run must be brought into main memory. This is usually loaded from a disk or some

---

[1] The terms *job* and *task* are used to refer to the same concepts in some of the literature, and to different concepts in other literature. We discuss this as needed in the footnotes.

[2] For grammatical simplicity, this text will assume the user is a male.

[3] Starting a program is sometimes called instantiating, executing, loading, or running the program.

electronic memory such as a flash drive. Several major OS activities are needed to accomplish this. First, a portion of main memory is needed to hold the program's executable code. Additional memory is needed for the program's data, variables, and temporary storage. In our example, the data would be the entry that the user is creating in the memo file. These activities to allocate memory are part of the **memory management** that the OS must do. Often several programs may be in memory at the same time. The OS memory manager module controls which processes are placed into memory, where they are placed, and how much memory each is given. **Process management**—deciding which process gets to run, for how long, and perhaps at what priority (or level of importance)—is another key management activity of the OS, usually handled in part by the OS CPU scheduler.

Once the editor process is running, it needs to accept some keystrokes and display what has been typed on the screen. Even if the device is a PDA with no keyboard, characters are input and accepted by the OS in some manner. Acquiring keystrokes or characters and displaying those characters on the screen are done in a series of steps through the **I/O and device management** component of the OS.

When our user hits a key, he enters a character that must be read by the system. The device—in this case a keyboard—inputs the information about the raw key action. This information—the row and column of the key's position on the keyboard and whether it was pressed or released—is stored in a temporary buffer. In a PDA or PC, there may be a special keyboard controller chip that saves the key action information and then sends an interrupt to the processor. The processor may have its own keyboard device controller in addition to the controller chip on the keyboard. The interrupt causes the CPU to stop the process that is running. This may be done immediately if the CPU is doing lower priority work, or it may be done later if the CPU had been doing higher priority work. Then an interrupt service routine is started by the OS to handle the keyboard action. The interrupt service routine is a part of the interrupt handling and device control in the OS. This processing is repeated for each character typed. The character must be sent to the editor process and displayed on the screen—another action that goes through the OS. In this case, an output operation to the video monitor is performed.

When our user finishes typing his note, he saves his note as a file. This may involve moving a pointing device such as a mouse to point to the file menu on the screen. The mouse movement and clicking are handled first by a device controller—which tracks the mouse coordinates and sends them to the OS. The mouse tracking icon (e.g., an arrow) must be moved and displayed on the monitor display screen—another output to the screen. When the mouse button is clicked, the controller sends that information to the OS, which forwards the coordinates where the clicking occurred to the windowing system that is managing the user interface. The windowing system will have information concerning which window is currently active and the positions of various buttons and other icons within that window. Using this information, it will match the coordinates of the cursor when the user clicked the mouse button to the particular screen button icon (or symbol) that was "clicked." The windowing system that handles user interaction is usually quite complex. It is considered by some to be a **systems program,** separate from the OS, and by others to be an integral part of the OS (see Section 2.7 for a discussion on what is and is not part of the OS).

Continuing with our scenario, our user may now choose a directory called "personal notes" within which he wants to store his file. This brings into play the **file management** component of the OS. When the user selects the directory (e.g., by double-clicking on a folder icon), this causes the OS file manager to take several actions. First, it must open the directory by retrieving the directory information from the OS internal tables. The directory information includes the names of files (and possibly other directories) stored under this directory as well as where the directory is stored on disk. The user must then type a file name such as "concert_remind," and the file system will check to make sure that no existing file in that directory has the same name. It may then invoke the disk space allocation module to find an area of free space on disk to store the file. Finally, the OS file manager will create a file entry in the directory to contain the information about the new file such as its name, file type, and disk location.

As we can see from this very simple example, the OS is involved in practically every aspect of user and program interaction—from low-level actions such as processing keyboard strokes and mouse movements, to resource allocation algorithms such as allocating memory space and processor time, to higher-level actions such as managing file names and directories. We describe how the OS handles all these various tasks throughout this book.

2.2 RESOURCES MANAGED BY THE OS AND MAJOR OS MODULES

A major role of an OS is the management of the system resources, so this section covers the main types of resources that the OS manages. Then it covers a conceptual view of a typical OS, showing the major OS modules, the resources that each module manages, and the services and functions that each module provides.

2.2.1 Types of resources managed by an OS

This section first addresses some of the major resources managed by a typical OS. These resources are CPUs (processors), main memory and caches, secondary storage, and I/O devices at the lowest level, and file system and user interface at a higher level. The OS also manages network access and provides security to protect the various resources it is managing.

CPU

The OS needs to schedule which process to run on each CPU at any point in time. In older single-process systems, this is very simple because only one process will be memory resident so the OS would mainly be responsible for starting the memory-resident process by giving it control of the CPU. However, even in such a simple system, the OS must do other tasks such as setting up any memory protection registers and switching to user execution mode before giving the process control of the CPU.

In multitasking systems, managing the CPU resource is quite complex since multiple processes will be memory resident. It may be further complicated by having multiple CPUs in the system. The OS will maintain various queues of processes. The queue most relevant to CPU scheduling is called the **ready queue,** which contains all processes that are ready to execute. If processes have different priorities a separate ready queue may exist for each priority level. Each process is typically given control of the CPU for a maximum period of time, called a **time quantum.** If the time quantum expires before the process finishes execution, a timer interrupt would initiate an OS process called **context switching** that would switch CPU control to another process. We discuss how the OS manages the CPU resource and CPU scheduling algorithms in detail in Chapter 9.

Main memory and caches

The OS needs to assign memory space to a process before it can execute. The executable code of a program will typically be stored on hard disk (or some other secondary storage medium). When a user or program wants to execute a disk-resident program, the OS must locate the program code file on disk and it must allocate enough memory space to hold an initial part of the program. Since many programs are quite large, the OS might load only part of the program from the disk. One of the main memory management functions is to allocate initial memory space to a process, and perhaps to load additional parts of the program from disk as the process needs them. If all memory space is full, the memory management module of the OS must **swap out** some of the memory-resident information so it can load additional portions needed by the process. We discuss memory management techniques in Chapters 10 and 11.

Secondary storage

Another important resource managed by the OS is secondary storage, which is typically hard disk. Most program code files and data files are stored on hard disk until there is a request to load some parts of them into main memory. Whenever a process requires data or code that are not in memory, a request is sent to the disk scheduling module of the OS. The OS would typically suspend the requesting process until the required data are read into memory. In a multitasking system, there could be many requests to read (load into memory) and write (store to disk) disk data. The OS typically maintains one or more queues for the disk read and write requests, and uses various algorithms to optimize the servicing of these requests. We discuss disk scheduling in Chapter 14 as part of our discussion of I/O management.

I/O devices

The OS must also control and manage the various input and output devices connected to a computer system.[4] The OS will include modules called **device drivers** that control access to these devices. Since there are many different types of I/O devices and users often add new I/O devices to their systems, modern OSs have the capability to detect new hardware and install the appropriate device drivers dynamically. A device driver handles low-level interaction with the device controllers, and presents a higher-level view of the I/O devices to the rest of the OS. That way, the OS can handle similar devices in an abstract, uniform way. We discuss I/O management in Chapter 12.

---

[4] It is not uncommon to consider disk management as part of I/O management since both disks and I/O devices either input (read) or output (write) bytes to/from main memory.

File systems

The resources discussed so far are considered low level because they are all hardware resources. The OS also manages higher-level resources that are created through software. One of the main such resources is the **file system.** The file system is an OS module that provides a higher-level interface that allows users and programs to create, delete, modify, open, close, and apply other operations to various types of files. The simplest type of file is just a sequence of bytes. More complex file structures are possible—for example, structuring file contents into records. The file system allows users to give names to files, to organize the files into directories, to protect files, and to access those files using the various file operations. We discuss file management in more detail in Chapter 12.

User interfaces

Many modern OSs include another high-level component to handle user interaction. This includes the functionality for creating and managing windows on a computer screen to allow users to interact with the system. By having such a component in the OS, the user can access various resources in a uniform way. For example, access to the directory of the file system or to Internet documents would be handled through a uniform interface.[5] We discuss user interfaces in various chapters throughout the book.

Network access

Another resource that the OS manages is network access to allow users and programs on one computer to access other services and devices on a computer network. An OS can provide both low- and high-level functionality for network access. An example of low-level functionality is the capability given to a program to create network ports and to connect to a port on another machine. An example of high-level functionality is the capability to access a remote file. We will discuss networks and distributed systems in Chapters 15 and 17.

Providing protection and security

The OS also provides mechanisms to protect the various resources from unauthorized access, as well as security techniques to allow the system administrators to enforce their security policies. The simplest type of security is access authorization through passwords, but generally this is not sufficient. We will discuss security and protection in Chapter 16.

2.2.2 Major modules of an OS

Figure 2.1 is an illustration of some of the major modules of an OS at an abstract level. Not surprisingly, many of these modules correspond closely to the resources that are being managed. Other modules provide common support functions used by several other modules. The modules provide functions that are accessed by system users and programs as well as by the other OS modules. Some functionality is restricted so that it can only be accessed in privileged mode by other OS modules—for example, device

---

[5] As we mentioned earlier, user interfaces are sometimes considered to be part of the systems programs rather than an integral part of the OS.

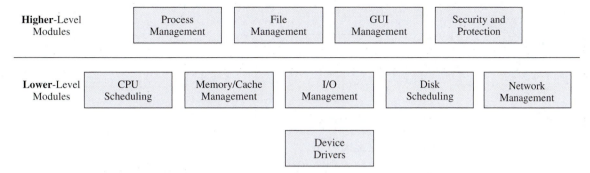

FIGURE 2.1 The major OS modules.

driver functions are often restricted to OS access. Other functionality is available to OS modules, users, and application programs—for example, file system functions.

In Figure 2.1, we do not show how the OS modules interact with one another. This is because the types of interactions depend on the particular architecture used to implement the OS. For example, in a **layered architecture,** the modules would be separated into layers. Generally, modules at one level would call the functions provided by the modules at either the same level or at lower levels. On the other hand, in an **object-oriented architecture,** each module would be implemented as one or more objects with services, and any object can invoke the services provided by other objects. In a **monolithic architecture,** all modules would be implemented as one giant program. We discuss the most common OS architectures in a later section.

2.3 THE PROCESS CONCEPT AND OS PROCESS INFORMATION

We now introduce the concept of a process, as it is central to presenting OS concepts. First, we define what a process is, and describe the various states that a process can go through and the types of events that cause process state transitions. Next, we discuss the types of information that an OS must maintain on each process in order to manage processes and resources. We also introduce the concept of a PCB (process control block), the data structure that the OS maintains to keep track of each process. Finally, we categorize various types of processes.

2.3.1 Process definition and process states

A **process** is a running or executing program. To be a process, a program needs to have been started by the OS. However, a process is not necessarily running all the time during its existence—for example, it may be waiting for I/O (say, a key to be pressed) or it may be waiting for the OS to assign it some resource (say, a block of RAM). Every process has a particular sequence of execution, and hence a **program counter** that specifies the location of the next instruction to be executed. It will also have various resources allocated to it by the OS. For example, it will need some **memory space** in which to store all or part of its program code and data (such as

FIGURE 2.2

Simplified diagram
of process states
and transitions.

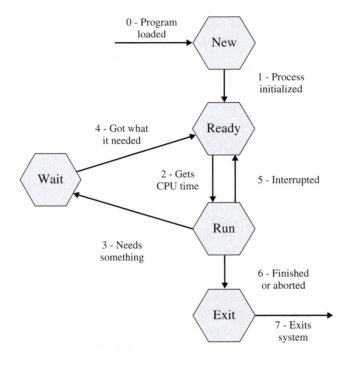

program variables). It will almost certainly be accessing files, so it will probably
have some **open files** associated with it. A process has also been called a **job**[6] or a
task, and we use these terms interchangeably.

Once a process is created, it may be in one of several states: *running* (if it has
control of the CPU), *ready to run* (if other processes currently are using all of the
CPUs), *waiting* (for some event to occur), and so on. The typical states that a process can go through are illustrated in Figure 2.2, which is called a **state transition
diagram.** The **nodes** (shown as hexagons) in Figure 2.2 represent **process states,**
and the **directed edges** (arrows) represent **state transitions.** We now discuss these
states, and the events that cause state transitions.[7]

State transition 0 (zero) creates a new process, which can be caused by one of
the following events:

1. A running OS process may create or spawn a new process. For example, when
   an interactive user logs onto a computer system, the OS process that handles
   logins typically creates a new process to handle user interaction and commands.
   The OS may also create new processes to handle some OS functions such as an
   interrupt handler or error handler process.

---

[6] The term **job** historically referred to a sequence of control that may invoke various tasks using a
language called **JCL,** or **Job Control Language.** This interpretation is primarily used in older batch
systems.

[7] This state diagram is typical, but for any particular OS there may be other states that the OS designers
want to distinguish among, so one might see fewer or more states internally and in the documentation.

2. A user process may also create another process by calling the OS function for new process creation. For example, a Web browser might create a new process to run an external "plug-in" module to handle a particular type of multimedia content accessed on a website.

3. When a job is started by the OS as a scheduled event (e.g., a "cron" job on a UNIX system), the OS creates a process to execute that job.

As a new process is being created, it is in the **new** state. The OS must build the table that will hold information about the process (see Section 2.2.2), allocate necessary resources (e.g., memory to hold the program), locate the program executable file and any initial data needed by the process, and execute the appropriate routines to load the initial parts of the process into memory. State transition 1 in Figure 2.2 shows that the OS moves a process from the new state to the **ready** state, which indicates that the process is now ready to execute. Note that before this transition can occur the OS must be ready to add a new process—for example, some OSs may have a maximum number of allowed processes at a given time and hence would not permit a new process to be added if the maximum is already reached. In a large mainframe system or cluster system there might also be resource requirements that the job must have available before it can run—perhaps a specific I/O device or a certain number of CPUs. After all this initialization has occurred, the process can be moved to the ready state.

Even after a process is in the ready state, it does not start executing until the OS gives it control of the CPU. This is state transition 2 in Figure 2.2. The process is now executing, and is in the **running** state. If there is more than one process in the ready state, the part of the OS that chooses one of those to execute is called the *CPU scheduler* or *process scheduler*. We discuss process scheduling in detail in Chapter 9.

If a process executes until its end or has an error or exception that causes the OS to abort it, these events—a process reaching its end or having a fatal error—will cause state transition 6 in Figure 2.2. This leads a process to the **terminated** state, at which point the OS will do cleanup operations on the process—for example, delete the process information and data structures and free up the process memory and other resources. When this cleanup is completed, this indicates state transition 7 in Figure 2.2, which causes the process to exit the system.

Two other state transitions may occur when a process is in its running state— transitions 3 and 5 in Figure 2.2. State transition 3 occurs if the process requires some resource that is not available or if it needs some I/O to occur—for example, waiting for a keystroke or reading from a file—before it can continue processing. This leads a process to the **wait** or **blocked** state. A process remains in the wait state until the resource it needs is allocated to it or its I/O request is completed, at which point state transition 4 occurs to move the process from the wait state back to the ready state. On the other hand, state transition 5 from running state directly to ready state typically occurs when the OS decides to suspend the process because it has more urgent processes to run. This may be because of a timer or some other kind of interrupt, which can occur for various reasons. The most common reason is to allocate the CPU to another process because of the CPU scheduling algorithm, as we describe in Chapter 8.

2.3.2 Process information maintained by the OS

To keep track of a process, the OS typically assigns to it a unique **process identifier** (or **process ID**). It also creates a data structure called a **process control block** (or **PCB**) to keep track of the process information, such as the process ID, resources it is using or requesting, its priority, its access rights to various system resources or files, and so on. The PCB will also include references to other OS data structures that include information on how to locate the memory space and open files being utilized by the process. For processes not in the running state, the PCB will save information on the hardware **processor state** for the process, such as the values stored in the program counter register and other processor registers. This information is needed to restart the process when it moves back to the running state. Figure 2.3 illustrates some of the information that is typically kept in a process control block.

The information on open files that the process is using is typically kept in a separate OS data structure, which is created and used by the OS file manager module (see Chapter 12). The information on which areas of memory are occupied by the process is usually kept in page tables or limit registers that are created and used by the OS memory management module (see Chapters 10 and 11). Both these tables are referenced from the PCB data structure. Additional information, such as the process priority level, and a reference to the security or protection levels of the process (see Chapter 16) will also be included in the PCB.

2.3.3 Types of processes and execution modes

We can categorize processes into several types:

1. User or application processes. These are processes that are executing application programs on behalf of a user. Examples include a process that is running an accounting program or a database transaction or a computer game.

FIGURE 2.3
Information the OS maintains in a process control block.

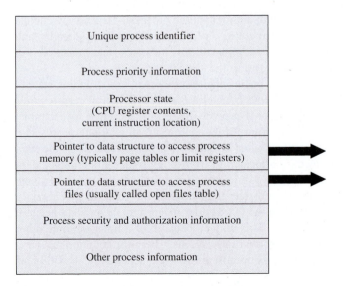

2. Systems program processes. These are other application programs that perform a common system service rather than a specific end-user service. Such programs often interact closely with the OS and need special information about interfaces and system structures such as the layout of a relocatable program module or an executable program file. Examples include programming language compilers and program development environments. Other programs such as Internet browsers, windowing user interfaces, and OS shell programs are considered by some to be in this category, and by others to be part of the OS itself (see Section 2.7).

3. OS processes. These are also known as daemons and are processes that are executing OS services and functions. Examples include memory management, process scheduling, device control, interrupt handling, file services, and network services.

Almost all processors have two execution modes for processes: privileged mode and nonprivileged or regular (user) mode. OS kernel processes typically execute in **privileged mode**—also known as **supervisor mode, kernel mode,** or **monitor mode**—allowing them to execute all types of hardware operations and to access all of memory and I/O devices. Other processes execute in **user mode,** which prohibits them from executing some commands such as low-level I/O commands. User mode also brings in the hardware memory protection mechanism, so that a process can only access memory within its predefined memory space. This protects the rest of memory—used by the OS and other processes—from erroneous or malicious access to their memory space that may damage their data or program code.

2.4 FUNCTIONAL CLASSES OF OSs

There are many different types of OSs. Some OSs are quite restricted and provide limited services and functions, whereas other OSs are very complex, and provide many services and a wide range of functionality. We now give a brief overview of five types of OSs: single-user, multitasking, time-sharing, distributed, and real-time systems.

2.4.1 Single-user single-tasking OS

A **single-user single-tasking** OS runs a single process at a time. The first OSs were of this type, as were OSs for early personal computers such as CP/M and earlier versions of MS-DOS. Similar OSs may be found today in systems with limited resources such as embedded systems. Such an OS is not as complex as the other OSs we discuss below. However, there are still a lot of details and issues that it must handle. The main services it provides would be handling I/O and starting and terminating programs. Memory management would be fairly simple since only the OS and one process reside in memory at any particular time. There would be no need for CPU scheduling. Following our spiral approach, we describe the basic services and functionality provided by a single-user OS in Chapter 3. We use primarily CP/M as an example to illustrate how these concepts were implemented in a real system. We also mention MS-DOS from time to time since it dominated the OS market for quite some time.

2.4.2 Multitasking OS

The next level in OS complexity is a **multitasking** or **multiprogramming** OS. Such an OS will control multiple processes running concurrently. Hence, it must have a CPU scheduling component to choose which of the ready processes to run next. The majority of modern-day computers support multitasking. One of the initial reasons for creating multitasking OSs was to improve processor utilization by keeping the CPU busy while I/O is performed. In a single-tasking system, if the single running process requests I/O and needed to wait for the operation to complete, then the CPU would remain idle until the I/O request was completed. By having several processes ready to execute in memory, the CPU can switch to running another process while I/O is performed. Changing from running one process to running another is known as **context switching.** But there is a high cost for a context switch. The entire CPU state must be saved so that it can be restored when the process is later restarted. Basically, when a running process—say process A—requests I/O that can be handled by an I/O controller, the OS CPU scheduler module would check to see if there are any processes in the ready state. If there are, one of the ready processes—say, process B—will be selected based on the CPU scheduling algorithm. The OS will save the processor state of process A (in A's PCB) and load the processor state of process B (from B's PCB) into the appropriate CPU registers. The OS will then give control of the CPU to process B, which moves to the running state, while process A moves to the waiting (or blocked) state until the I/O operation is complete.

Multitasking is now available in most computer OSs, including personal computers. Even though a PC typically has a single interactive user, that user can create multiple tasks. For example, if there are multiple windows on the display screen, each is often handled by a separate task or process. In addition, other tasks may be running in the background. Some early multitasking OSs could handle only batch jobs—which were loaded on disk in bulk through card readers or other old-fashioned I/O devices. Many current systems handle both batch jobs and interactive jobs. Interactive jobs are processes that handle a user interacting directly with the computer through mouse, keyboard, video monitor display, and other interactive I/O devices.

We can further distinguish between two types of multitasking OSs: those that usually interact with a **single user** and those that support **multiple interactive users.** Single-user multitasking systems include most modern PCs that support windowing. In such systems it is common that one user is interacting with the system but that the user may have several tasks started simultaneously. For example, the user may have an email program, a text editor, and a Web browser, all open at the same time, each in a separate window. The task that has the current user focus is called the foreground task, while the others are called background tasks. The other type of multitasking system handles multiple interactive users concurrently, and hence is called a time-sharing OS. We discuss these next.

In our spiral approach part we describe two examples of single-user multitasking OSs: an OS for a handheld Palm Pilot device in Chapter 4 and the Mac OS from Apple in Chapter 5.

2.4.3 Time-sharing OS and servers

A **multiuser** or **time-sharing OS** also supports multitasking, but a large number of the tasks (processes) running are handling users interacting with the machine. These were called time-sharing systems because the computer time was "shared" by the many interactive concurrent users. In terms of OS internals, the main difference between interactive and batch processes is in their response requirements. Interactive jobs typically support many short interactions, and require that the system respond rapidly to each interaction. But quick response to interactive users' requirements calls for a high level of context switching and this introduces a lot of nonproductive overhead. Batch jobs, on the other hand, have no live user so rapid response is not a requirement. Therefore, less context switching is needed and more time is spent on productive computing. A time-sharing OS will support both interactive and batch jobs and will typically give higher priorities for interactive jobs. Early time-sharing systems in the 1960s and 1970s, such as IBM's OS 360 TSO[8] and Honeywell's MULTICS, supported large numbers of interactive users, which were all logged in to the same system through dumb monitors and terminals. This was because terminals cost many orders of magnitudes less than the computer system itself in those days.

As the price of hardware and processors was being dramatically reduced, the need for time sharing declined. In modern computing the new generation of systems that can be considered to be the successors of interactive time-sharing systems are the systems that are used in file, database, and Web servers. **File servers** and **database servers** handle requests for file and database access from tens to thousands of users. Instead of being located at dumb terminals attached to processes running on the server, the users are working at PCs or workstations and the service requests are coming to the server through the network. Large database servers are often called **transaction processing systems,** because they handle very many user transactions per second. **Web servers** handle requests for Web documents, and often retrieve some of the document information from database servers. Database and Web servers require OSs that can handle hundreds of concurrent processes.

2.4.4 Network and distributed OS

Most computers today are either permanently connected to a network, or are equipped so that they can be connected and disconnected from some type of network. This allows information and resource sharing among multiple machines, and requires that the OS provide additional functionality for these network connections. This additional functionality can be categorized into two main levels:

1. **Low-level network access services.** The OS will typically include additional functionality to set up network connections, and to send and receive messages between the connected machines.
2. **Higher-level services.** Users want to be able to connect to other machines to browse through information, download files (text, pictures, songs) or programs of

---

[8] OS 360 TSO stands for Operating System 360 Time Sharing Option.

various types, or access databases. This is typically done through Web browsers or specialized services, such as **telnet** for logging on to remote machines or **ftp** for file transfer. As we mentioned earlier, these services are considered by some to be independent systems programs and by others to be part of the OS.

The standard network protocols actually provide several levels of service, from the basic hardware level to the user interaction level, as we will see in Chapter 15. Separately from the network connection, a distributed OS can provide a wide spectrum of capabilities. A very basic distributed OS, sometimes called a **network OS,** provides the capability to connect from a machine where the user is logged in—called the **client**—to a remote machine—called the **server,** and to access the remote server. However, the client user must know the name or address of the specific machine they want to access. Most current systems provide at least this level of service. For example, telnet and ftp services fall in this category.

At the other end of the spectrum, a completely general **distributed OS** may allow a user logged in at a client machine to transparently access all possible services and files they are authorized to access without even knowing where they reside. The OS itself will keep directory information to locate any desired file or service, and to connect to the appropriate machine. This is known as **location transparency.** The files and services may be physically replicated on multiple systems so the OS would choose the copy that is most easily or most efficiently accessible—known as **replication transparency.**[9] The OS could also do **dynamic load balancing** to choose a machine that is not heavily loaded when choosing a server. Such OSs would obviously be very complicated, and hence do not yet exist except in the realm of special-purpose systems or research prototypes!

Between the two ends of the spectrum, one can consider many types of distributed OSs that can provide more than the minimum capabilities but less than the full wish list of capabilities.

2.4.5 Real-time OS

Real-time OSs are multitasking systems that have the additional requirement of time deadlines for completing some or all of their tasks. Two types of deadlines are:

1. **Hard deadlines.** A task with a hard deadline of, say, n milliseconds *must* be completed within n milliseconds of submission; otherwise, it would be useless and there may be very bad consequences for missing the deadline. Examples of such tasks include industrial control tasks in a steel mill or an oil refinery, or a task in a weapons guidance system.
2. **Soft deadlines.** A process with a soft deadline of n milliseconds *should* be completed within n milliseconds of submission; however, the deadline may be missed without catastrophic consequences. An example could be a task to update the display in a virtual reality game as the user moves about.

Hard real-time OSs have scheduling algorithms that take into account the deadline of each process and its estimated running time when deciding which process to run

---

[9] There are many additional transparency levels that a distributed OS can achieve; see Chapter 17.

next. These OSs are mainly used in embedded systems that are found in devices such as aircraft or process control systems, where a software process that makes a crucial decision must be completed within its specified deadline. Soft real-time systems, on the other hand, only need to give high priority to the tasks that have been designated as real-time tasks. So most current OSs—for example, Windows 2000 or Solaris—provide soft real-time support.

Unfortunately, most of the techniques that have evolved to give smooth average response in most OSs are based on statistical decision making. These techniques will not work in a hard real-time system. Such systems require unique algorithms for scheduling time-critical events. As a result, we will not spend much time discussing such systems. They are best treated separately.

2.5 ARCHITECTURAL APPROACHES TO BUILDING AN OS

2.5.1 Monolithic single-kernel OS approach

The first OSs were written as a single program. This approach to building the OS is called the **kernel** or **monolithic kernel** approach, and was illustrated in Figure 1.3. As the monolithic kernel OS included more functionality its size grew, in some cases from a few thousand bytes to many millions of bytes. With limited and expensive memory, the OS size overhead (the percentage of main memory occupied by the OS) was considered too large. This bloated OS not only occupied memory, but like most large programs, the OS was less efficient than a more minimal system, had more bugs, and was difficult to maintain, either to add features or to fix bugs. This led OS designers to develop OSs based on a more modular, layered design.

2.5.2 Layered OS approach

The modular approach that was developed was a **layered architecture.** The OS would be divided into modules that were limited to a specific function such as processor scheduling or memory management. The modules were grouped into layers of increasing abstraction—each layer provides a more abstract view of the system and relies on the services of the layers below it. The layered approach would hide the peculiarities and details of handling hardware devices, and provide a common abstract view to the rest of the OS. Thus, when new devices entered the marketplace, new device drivers could be added to the kernel without drastically affecting the other OS modules, which provide memory management, processor scheduling, and the file system interface. This is illustrated in a very rudimentary way in Figure 2.4.

This approach can be extended to implement an OS with several layers. One variation would allow modules at layer n to call only the modules in the next lower layer $n-1$. Another variation would allow modules at layer n to call modules at any of the lower layers ($n-1, n-2,$ and so on). A further variation would allow level n modules to interact with other level n modules, in addition to lower-level modules. Because of the difficulty of separating complex OS functionality into multiple layers, usually

FIGURE 2.4
Layered model of
an Operating System.

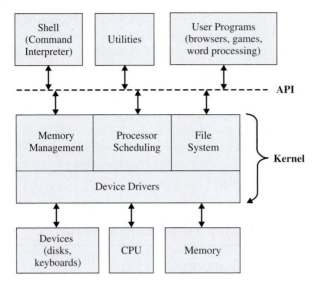

only two or three layers are used in practice. We examine more specific instances
of layered designs in later chapters. Most modern OSs are built on a layered architecture. However some OS programmers felt that the layered approach was not sufficient, and that OS design should return to a minimum amount of code in the kernel
and the concept of microkernel.

2.5.3 Microkernel OS approach

The **microkernel** approach is illustrated in Figure 2.5. Here only basic functionality, usually the interfaces to the various types of device drivers, is included in the
microkernel. Specifically, the only code in these modules is code that must run in
supervisor mode because it actually uses privileged resources such as protected
instructions or accesses memory not in the kernel space. The remainder of the OS
functions are still part of the resident OS, but they run in user mode rather than
protected mode. Code running in protected mode literally can do anything, so an
error in this code can do more damage than code running in user mode. So the
theory of the microkernel is that the benefits to this approach arise partly from the
fact that the amount of code that is running in supervisor mode is smaller, making
them more robust. It also makes them easier to inspect for flaws. Also, the extra
design effort required makes it more probable that the implementation will be correct. Finally, it is easier to port a small microkernel to a new platform than it is to
port a large, layered, but monolithic kernel. On the other hand, a microkernel must
make use of interrupts to make the necessary calls from the user mode portions
of the OS to the supervisor mode portions. These interrupts will often necessitate
context switches. Critics of the microkernel approach say that this makes a microkernel OS run more slowly. (It should be noted that this issue is not resolved in the
OS community.)

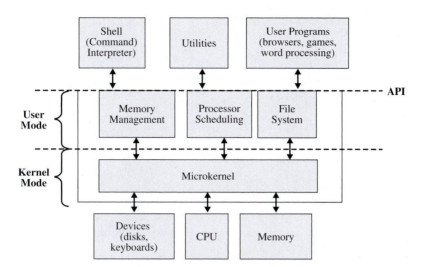

FIGURE 2.5
Microkernel model
of an Operating
System.

2.6 SOME OS IMPLEMENTATION TECHNIQUES AND ISSUES

As we discussed in Sections 2.2 and 2.5, an OS is a complex software system with many modules and components. As with any such system, there will be many data structures and algorithms implemented within a typical OS. In this section, we discuss a few implementation techniques that are part of most or all OSs. These subjects include the normal method used for handling interrupts, queues and data structure used in many OS components, an object-oriented approach to OS implementation, and the topic of Virtual Machines.

2.6.1 Interrupt handling using interrupt vectors

As we have already mentioned several times, an **interrupt** is a mechanism used by an OS to signal to the system that some high-priority event has occurred that requires immediate attention. Many interrupt events are associated with I/O. Some of these typical interrupt events are signaling that a disk block read or write has been completed, signaling that a mouse button has been clicked, or signaling that a keyboard button has been pressed. As we can see, most of these interrupts correspond to some hardware action. The hardware associates with each interrupt event a particular interrupt number. The interrupting controller typically places this interrupt number in an interrupt register when the corresponding event occurs. Depending on the particular type of interrupt event, the OS has to take certain actions. The question that comes up is, How can the OS efficiently determine which particular interrupt event has occurred, and how does it start up the appropriate process that services that interrupt?

The normal technique for interrupt handling uses a data structure called an **interrupt vector** (see Figure 2.6). The vector has one entry for each interrupt number. That entry contains the memory address of the interrupt service routine for that type of interrupt. The interrupt number placed in the interrupt register is used as an index into the interrupt vector. The interrupt vector entry is picked up by the hardware as

FIGURE 2.6

An interrupt vector
for handling
interrupts.

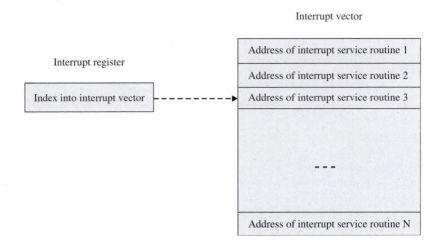

an address and the hardware effectively calls the appropriate interrupt routine as a subroutine. When the interrupt routine is finished it will simply return from the call, resuming the process that was interrupted.

In a small embedded system with only a few I/O devices the hardware may not provide an interrupt system. The alternative is known as a **status-driven** system. In such a system the application (or the OS) is mostly a large loop. It will check the status of each device in turn to see whether it needs servicing.

2.6.2 System calls

Application programs normally need to use data and services managed by the OS. For example, OSs typically manage all the hardware devices on the system, such as sound cards, and applications are not allowed to access them directly. Also, applications may need to communicate between one another and the OS has to act as an intermediary.

Any normal application needs such abilities and the way it asks the OS for services is by using a **system call.** A system call is much like any other function call. First, the application will load certain registers with information describing the service required and then will execute a system call instruction. However, instead of directly calling a section of code that will do the function, the system call instruction will usually cause an interrupt, which the OS will handle. The OS will perform the requested service and then return control to the application. This mechanism also allows the OS to implement some security by first checking to see if the application is allowed to access the resource in the requested way.

Generally, application development systems provide a library that loads as part of application programs. This library handles the details of passing information to the kernel and executing the system call instruction. Having this function provided by the library reduces the strength of the connection between the operating system and the application and make the application more portable.

2.6.3 Queues and tables

An OS manages many data structures to accomplish its tasks. Two of the common data structures used are tables and queues. Tables are used to store information about various objects that the OS manages. For example, the PCB, described in Section 2.2, is an example of a table that the OS maintains to keep track of the information associated with each process. Another frequently found table is the **page table,** which is used to keep track of the address space of a process when the hardware supports paged memory (see Chapter 11). The OS will maintain one PCB and one page table for each process. Another typical table is the **open files table,** which keeps an entry for each file open in the system.

The OS also maintains a number of queues to keep track of information that is ordered in some way. Each resource that can be shared by multiple processes would need a queue to hold service requests for that resource. For example, since multiple processes may need to read and write disk pages, the OS maintains a **disk scheduling queue** that has a list of processes waiting for disk I/O. Requests for printer services may be maintained in a **printer queue.** A list of processes that are ready to run can be maintained in a **ready process queue.**

Many of these "queues" are not strictly speaking queues at all since a queue is always managed on a first-in-first-out (FIFO) basis. But the scheduling algorithm that utilizes the queue determines the order of entries in a queue. For example, if the policy of choosing which process to run next were a priority policy, the scheduler for the ready process queue would implement that policy. In the FIFO case each new entry is placed at the end of the queue. When the CPU needs to execute a new process, it would remove an entry from the beginning of the queue for processing. As we will see, there are various ways for organizing queues depending on the particular requirements for each type of queue.

Each entry in a queue must contain all the information that the OS needs to determine the action that must be taken. For example, each ready queue entry may contain a pointer to the PCB of a ready process. By accessing the PCB through the pointer, the OS can retrieve the needed process information.

2.6.4 Object-oriented approach

One approach to OS development is to use the principles and practices developed for object-oriented software engineering and apply them to OS design and implementation. In this approach, each OS module would be designed as a collection of **objects** and each object will include **methods** that are provided as services to other parts of the OS or to application programs. Building the OS with objects provides the many advantages of object-oriented software engineering, such as encapsulation of object data structures, separating an interface from its implementation, extensibility and ease of reuse of objects, and many other advantages. In simpler terms, the key feature of an object is that the internal structure of an object is hidden and any access to the data contained in an object is through the methods of the object. This makes it less likely that an application can misuse an object and cause problems for other modules.

There have been several attempts at making an OS that is object oriented, most notably the NEXTSTEP OS from NeXT and BeOS from Be Inc. A few research projects have created—most notably Choices, Athene, Syllable, TAJ, and JNode—an OS written in Java. But it seems that there is no major OS that is truly based on objects. Usually a kernel module is written in C or assembler and a library provides an API of object-oriented interfaces that can be invoked in most high-level languages that provide support for objects. Windows NT is typical of such OSs. Data structures that are internal to a single module are not objects.

2.6.5 Virtual machines

Yet another approach to OS design is the technique of using a software emulator for abstracting or **virtualizing** a total system (devices, CPU, and memory). This concept is referred to as a **virtual machine** (**VM**). One prime reason for VMs is that it allows the different emulation environments to be protected from one another so that a crash in one program does not crash others. The system design being abstracted can be either an actual hardware design or an idealized application virtual machine.

Hardware virtual machines

In this approach, a program or kernel subsystem will provide a software emulation of an actual hardware machine. There are two different sorts of such emulation, one in which the host hardware system itself is being emulated and another where another CPU is being emulated. The latter sort was traditionally developed by a manufacturer to assist the migration of customers from an older system to a newer one by providing a program that would emulate the older system. Various emulation packages were created by IBM, for example, to help customers migrating from the 1401 systems, then in common use, to the 360 series. In such cases the emulation is usually done by an application program running in user mode.

Emulation of the host machine is often used to allow multiple OS kernels to run simultaneously, as illustrated in Figure 2.7. In such cases the emulation is done by the kernel of a special **host OS.** This model allows one or more OS kernels to run on top of a virtual machine layer as **guest OSs.** The VM layer creates an interface that abstracts the hardware, so that each kernel believes that it alone is running on the hardware. Kernels may be from different OSs or may be different instances of the same OS.[10] One of the prime difficulties in the VM model is to create a VM that accurately emulates the hardware—so that kernels may run on a VM the same way they ran directly on the real hardware (only slower, because they are actually sharing the hardware with other kernels). One of the first, if not *the* first, such emulation packages was created by IBM for a modified version of the 360 model 40 and was known as CP-40. It ran multiple instances of client operating systems—particularly CMS, the Cambridge Monitor System. That early package has been reimplemented several times and the current version, **z/VM,** runs on their z9 series of mainframes.

---

[10] In fact, the VM concept was created in part (by IBM) to allow OS programmers to test a kernel, since even if the kernel being debugged crashed, other kernels would continue to run.

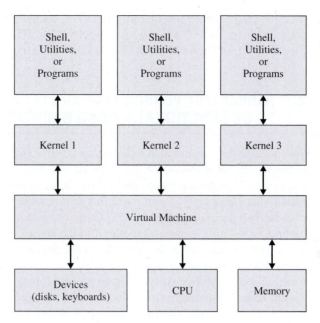

FIGURE 2.7
A hardware virtual machine.

VM systems are becoming quite common now. As one can easily imagine, having one OS run on top of another OS is not terribly efficient. So contemporary VM OSs are usually running a slightly modified version of the guest OS that is aware that it is running in a VM environment and does things in a slightly different way so that the VM emulation can be more efficient. In addition, newer CPUs often have additional instructions and other features that assist in virtualization.

Application virtual machines

It is now common to apply the term *virtual machine* (VM) to any software that creates an abstraction of a machine. Sometimes the machine being emulated is not an actual CPU but rather is an idealized machine specification designed to support either a specific language or a broad class of languages. Such systems are sometimes known as **application virtual machines.** One early such design was known as the **p-code** system and was designed by the University of California San Diego to support their Pascal system. A VM that is currently very popular is the **Java virtual machine** (**JVM**), which creates an abstract machine that runs Java programs. Sometimes the JVM runs as a separate package that enables the execution of Java programs. In other cases the VM emulation may be internal to another program such as a Web browser. In such cases the Java programs are more restricted in what they are allowed to do. Another such package is the **Common Language Runtime** (**CLR**) created by Microsoft for support of their .net architecture. In this case the abstract machine was designed for supporting a broad class of languages rather than a single language.

Since emulation of a virtual machine can be somewhat inefficient, code created to run in an application virtual machine can usually also be compiled into native machine code so that it will run faster. This technique is known as **just-in-time** compilation, or **JIT.** The binary code produced by JIT compilation is normally discarded after execution but it can also be saved permanently for later reuse.

2.7 MINIMALIST VERSUS MAXIMALIST APPROACHES TO OS FUNCTIONALITY AND BACKWARD COMPATIBILITY

We conclude this chapter with a discussion on what functionality should be included in the OS. In other words, what exactly should the OS do? That is a big question. Let us take a somewhat philosophical look at it. At one end of the spectrum is the **minimalist** philosophy—only those things that really must go into the kernel (or microkernel) are included in the OS. Other components may be added into library routines or as "user" programs (not part of the kernel, but usually not written by the user). At the other end of the spectrum is the **maximalist** philosophy—to put most of the commonly used services in the OS. For example, if a maximalist philosophy were adopted, a service such as screen window management would be included in the OS kernel, since almost everyone uses this service.

Minimalists argue that their approach allows each user to choose what they want. For example, a user may pick from a large group of window managers, and in fact may pick two or more if desired. This makes it easier to select components and build the desired configuration. A user may even write new components. Minimalists also argue that this approach makes the OS modules easy to design and program, and easier to debug. They often say that the resulting system is more "elegant" or "cleaner."

Maximalists will counterargue that user choice in some fundamental areas is a problem—it is *too* flexible. They say a common *"look and feel"* for common applications functions such as scroll bars, menus, and moving a cursor allow for a more consistent usage and more satisfied users. This makes it easier for users to know the basics of how applications work and creates consistency among applications. They contend that common functions such as drawing on a screen, moving a mouse, and menus, are used by almost every application program and should be accomplished in one place efficiently and consistently—the OS. They will claim that some functions may be done more efficiently in the OS and other functions—for example, security features—*must* be done in the kernel.

In reality very few OSs really are minimalist or maximalist—as in most arguments the choice is made by a big dose of the "real world" injected into the discussion. For example, if we examine OSs for handheld small computers (personal digital assistants), many of these real-world issues affect the design choices. These issues include very limited memory, and hence making as many functions available in the OS as possible in order to use less memory in the applications by sharing routines. Another issue was to make a common look and feel, but to include only the most commonly needed routines so that not everyone needs to pay the price of extra memory use for infrequently used services.

2.7.1 **Backward compatibility**

One last issue, that of backward compatibility, is the price of success. This issue has caused more difficulty for OS system designers and implementers than can possibly be imagined.[11] **Backward compatibility** is the ability to run old application programs on newer versions of the OS. This ability is a selling point of almost every new version of any OS—in fact, even new OSs that have *no* previous versions may claim to be able to run applications done for *other* (popular) OSs without change— *transparently.* Note that this means that the executable program (the binary code) must run unchanged on the new system.

Some systems claim that the new system is "source code compatible"—that the source code for the application must be recompiled, but not necessarily changed, to move from old to new system. This does not help someone who purchased a program and has only the executable! Not only does this require that every new version of the OS contain all services in the previous versions—they must work the same way, even though newer services doing the same or similar things may be more efficient and more secure. One of the most horrible problems is that even bugs—those that may have been discovered—must remain since some applications may have taken advantage (used features!) of those bugs. For example, a famous bug in Microsoft DOS that allowed one to truncate the size of a file—make a file size *shrink*—has remained for decades in many versions of the OS—even through Windows—because in the original "buggy" version, there was no other way to truncate files. It had been fixed in a version soon afterward, but to allow compatibility with already existing executable, it was fixed as an extension—a new service. The old service remained "buggy." (Compatibility issues are sometimes hidden under the famous statement: "It's not a bug—it's a feature!")

2.7.2 **User optimization versus hardware optimization**

One final point: Personal computers have stood the traditional goals of OSs on their head. Until PCs came along, one of the chief goals of an OS was to optimize the utilization of a bunch of very expensive hardware. This meant using every bit of expensive memory (leading to the infamous Y2K bug), every instruction cycle of the slow CPU, and every sector of the limited-capacity, expensive disk drive. Once the level of integration of the circuitry made it fairly cheap to produce a personal computer, the most expensive part of the total system became the unit sitting in front of the monitor, not the unit sitting behind it. This means that the OS needs to be very responsive to the keyboard and to update the screen displays as fast and as smoothly as possible, even if that means using the CPU in a less efficient manner. GUIs are a good example. They would most likely be much less common if we were still using only mainframe systems that cost a million dollars each.

---

[11] After all, how difficult is it just to leave old code in the system?

2.8 SUMMARY

In this chapter, we started with a simple user scenario and described some of the actions within the scenario that are undertaken by the OS. We then gave an overview of the main types of system resources that the OS manages, and discussed the major OS modules. Then we defined the process concept, which is central to what the OS does, and described the states of a process and some of the information that the OS maintains about each process. We then discussed the characteristics of different types of OSs, from systems that can execute a single process at a time to those that manage concurrently executing processes to time-sharing and distributed systems.

Following that, we presented some of the different architectural approaches that have been taken for constructing an OS. These include monolithic OS, microkernels, and layered architectures. We discussed some of the common data structures that an OS maintains, namely interrupt vectors and queues, object-oriented systems, and virtual machines. Finally, we concluded with a philosophical discussion on the minimalist versus maximalist approaches to OS functionality.

BIBLIOGRAPHY

Bach, M. J., *The Design of the UNIX Operating System.* Englewood Cliffs, NJ: Prentice Hall, 1986.

Beck, M. et al., *Linux Kernel Programming,* 3rd ed., Reading, MA: Addison-Wesley, 2002.

Hayes, J. P., *Computer Architecture and Organization.* New York: McGraw-Hill, 1978.

Lewis, R., and B. Fishman, *Mac OS in a Nutshell.* Sebastopol, CA: O'Reilly Media, 2000.

Russinovich, M. E., and D. A. Solomon, *Microsoft Windows Internals,* 4th ed. Redmond, WA: Microsoft Press, 2005.

WEB RESOURCES

http://developer.apple.com/technotes/

http://www-03.ibm.com/systems/z/os/zos/index.html (IBM mainframe OSs)

http://www.academicresourcecenter.net/curriculum/ pfv.aspx?ID=7387 (Microsoft® Windows® Internals, Fourth Edition: Microsoft Windows Server™ 2003, Windows XP, and Windows 2000 by Russinovich, M.E., and D.A. Solomon)

http://www.linux.org (the home of Linux kernel development)

http://www.kernel.org (a repository of historic kernel sources)

http://www.osdata.com (Operating System technical comparison)

http://www.tldp.org (The Linux Documentation Project)

REVIEW QUESTIONS

2.1 What are some of the types of resources that an OS must manage?

2.2 What is the difference between a program and a process?

2.3 What are the states that a process can be in?

2.4 How many processes can be in the run state at the same time?

2.5 What sort of events can cause a transition from the run state to the terminate state?

2.6 Name at least a few things that a process might be waiting on.

2.7 Some information stored in a PCB is not always kept current. What are some examples of such information?

2.8 Give examples of the three types of processes: user, system, and OS.

2.9 The chapter discussed five different overall design types for OSs. What design types do these examples belong in?

    a. OSs in handheld computers and PDAs

    b. UNIX

    c. Novell Netware

    d. VCRs

    e. Automobile engine

2.10 If we are writing applications, what are some of the reasons that we need an OS to manage the hardware for us?

2.11 What are some of the reasons why we divide an OS into separate modules?

2.12 What is a "microkernel" OS?

2.13 Generally speaking, object-oriented programming is less efficient than procedural programming. Why would we want to use a less efficient tool to make an OS?

2.14 When an OS gets an interrupt from a device, what mechanism does it usually use to select the code to handle the interrupt?

2.15 How does an application ask the OS to do something?

2.16 True or false? The evolution of OSs has resulted in the present state in which most modern OSs are virtual machine OSs.

2.17 What are the two modern software virtual machine architectures?

2.18 Do you feel that an OS should include many common system functions or that it should contain only a minimum level of functions, leaving as much as possible to be in additional layers and libraries? Justify your answer.

2.19 What is the most standard OS API that applications can be designed around?

Part 2

Building Operating Systems Incrementally: A Breadth-Oriented Spiral Approach

In this part:

Part 2 of this book is the part that makes the book different from others. Other books tend to treat a series of separate topics concerning different aspects of typical OS in depth, but isolated from one another. Instead, this part of the book presents a series of chapters that treat selected operating systems to show how operating systems were forced to evolve as the underlying hardware evolved and the expectations and demands of users grew. The systems that were selected all run on a personal computer of some sort. This choice was deliberate. It was based partly on the belief that such computers will be familiar to most students, perhaps having seen many of these machines and OSs before. They are also the systems that students are most likely to have access to, at least the more modern systems. At the same time, the evolution of the OSs for personal computers paralleled that of OSs for larger machines. As a result, examples exist of personal computer OSs that range from the most primitive to the most complex. Many of these OSs are also available on larger machines, including some of the largest mainframes available today.

Part 2 consists of five chapters. Chapter 3 discusses an early personal computer OS, CP/M. This is a single-user, single-tasking OS with no graphical user interface, or GUI. It supported only a flat file system. As such, it was very similar to many of the early mainframe OSs such as IBSYS for the IBM 709x series. We show all of the basic mechanisms required of the OS in these simple systems. These mechanisms include separation of the kernel from the OS and file system support.

In Chapter 4 we look at an OS that introduces two additional concepts: the idea of running multiple programs at the same time and the use of a GUI. The OS that is covered is the Palm OS, used in many PDAs and cellular phones. These two additional requirements necessitate additional OS mechanisms to support them, most notably the idea of CPU abstraction and a process control block. PDAs and cell phone systems usually do not have secondary storage devices, but they still have the concept of a file system because the metaphor is so familiar to application programmers. They do have a GUI, but the use of the screen is limited by its very small size. We discuss the impact these two restrictions had on the design of the OS.

The OS series discussed in Chapter 5 introduces additional requirements. It is the Macintosh OS series, and it was designed from the start with secondary storage in mind. The evolution of this family is interesting in that it is in itself an example of a spiral evolution. The only feature that the MAC OS initially offered that was not discussed in the Palm OS was that the MAC OS GUI could have overlapping windows. It was still a single-user system and had a flat file system, just as did CP/M and the Palm OS. However, as the MAC OS evolved, Apple added many new features such as multitasking, a hierarchical file system, multiple users (though not concurrently), multiple CPUs, and eventually a virtual memory system. Each of these mechanisms is discussed in turn, and the virtual memory topic leads naturally into the next chapter.

Chapter 6 covers Linux as an example of an OS that has been ported to many different hardware platforms ranging from embedded systems to real-time systems to supercomputers. The main distinction made here for Linux is that it was designed with the assumption of multiple users at multiple terminals. In order to provide this functionality an OS must provide more protection mechanisms in the OS, and especially in the file system. Linux is also an example of an open source OS, and this distinction is explored in this chapter as well. A later portion of the book covers Linux in greater detail.

Chapter 7 explores the issues that arise when an OS is designed that spans multiple computer systems. Often, such systems cross administrative domains. Almost certainly the policies and interests of the institutions involved are not the same. Indeed, they may even conflict with one another. Still, the institutions involved have found some common interests that compel them to establish systems that cross such boundaries, and GLOBUS is used in this chapter to illustrate some of the issues involved. Other systems are discussed as well.

Chapter **3**

A Simple, Single-Process Operating System

In this chapter:

We now start the "spiral" part of the book, where each chapter discusses a type of operating system based on a particular real OS. We start with a real but simple OS with limited capability and discuss progressively more complex OSs in the following chapters. We base most of our presentation in this chapter on the features of an early personal computer operating system—CP/M—and the hardware commonly used to run this system. We discuss how these OSs were designed as well as the rationale behind the design. Although these systems were single-process, limited functionality systems, they provided sufficient power for hundreds of applications to be written for millions of personal computers. Thus, they provide a good practical example of a simple operating system. The issues discussed in this chapter—such as I/O management, the file system, and memory and process management—are expanded upon in subsequent chapters as more complex operating systems are introduced. However, we start here with a basis: real but simple functionality.

This chapter is organized as follows. Section 3.1 describes the predecessors of simple operating systems, called monitors, and discusses how they evolved into early operating systems because of the need for standardization. In Section 3.2, we describe the characteristics of the early PC systems for which this type of OS was used. Then we discuss how input/output was managed in such an early OS in Section 3.3, followed by description of the file system in Section 3.4, and process and memory management in Section 3.5.

The systems of this era were quite limited—they ran only one user application at a time. Process management was initially limited to loading and starting a particular application program. Late in the life of CP/M a background printing function was added. This facility was the beginning of the concept of multiprocessing as it is carried out in more modern OSs. Memory management in the OS was limited to which part of memory to use for the OS, the interrupt vector, the user program, the program data, and so on. But because memory was quite limited, large programs often did not fit completely into memory or were limited in the amount of data they could handle. It was necessary for an application programmer to break down such programs into sections, and to replace one section in memory with another as needed. This memory management technique, known as **overlays,** is discussed in Section 3.5. Again, these techniques foreshadow the more complex memory management techniques found in a modern OS.

3.1 INTRODUCTION: MONITORS AND CP/M

We start this section with a discussion on why a need emerged for a PC operating system. The predecessors of these OSs were called **monitors,**[1] and had very limited capabilities. There was no standard for monitors—each manufacturer of early PC systems used to write their own monitor program, which had unique commands and conventions. This variety meant that early application programs had to be rewritten for each monitor.

3.1.1 Introduction to monitors: The predecessors of simple OSs

When personal computing was young and single-chip microprocessors made it possible to build small, relatively inexpensive computers, there was a software crisis. The advent of cheap microprocessors allowed small startup companies to sell kits for home hobbyists who wanted to build their own computer. These kits typically contained a circuit board, a microprocessor, some memory, and some additional device controller chips. The additional chips were for controlling various input and output devices—for example, cassette tapes, floppy disks, external video terminals, and printers. There were a large number of companies selling PC kits. At first they were, by any standard, very limited. In early systems of this type, memory size was one to four kilobytes—or sometimes even less. Application programs were written in machine language or assembly language. There was typically no operating system. Instead, there was a small **monitor program** usually stored in **ROM**—read-only memory—that would allow an application to do simple, common tasks, such as:

- output a character to a device such as a video display or Teletype
- get a character from the keyboard device
- save the contents of all or part of memory to a cassette tape or floppy disk
- restore memory from a saved image on tape or disk
- print a character to the printer

The monitor did only these basic tasks and not much else.

---

[1] We are talking about a software module that is a precursor to an OS, not a video display terminal, sometimes also called a monitor and often used on computers.

An application program could print a character (e.g., a "1") on the **console**—a video display or Teletype—by calling the monitor using the following steps:

1. Put the character in a specific register as specified by the monitor (assume that this is register E). In this case, the value 31 Hex (the ASCII value of "1") is placed in register E.
2. Select a particular monitor function, in this case, the "print a character" function, which has value 2. Place the number corresponding to the selected monitor function in register C.
3. Finally, a call to the monitor is executed through Interrupt 5. This would cause the monitor to execute the print function called for by the function code stored in register C using the character stored in register E.
4. After the monitor outputs the character, it returns a status code in register A that indicates OK or not OK. Not OK indicated some exceptional condition such as a device that is not responding or illegal values for some of the parameters to the function. The application should look at the status code in register A to determine an appropriate action in case of errors. Typical early applications did not always check for errors because there was little they could do for most errors anyway.

3.1.2 Why CP/M? What was the software crisis?

There were many companies building computer kits, and each had to provide the software for a small monitor. These monitors were not large in terms of memory requirements—a few hundred or a few thousand bytes. Typically, a monitor provided only a dozen functions or so, but these functions required time and expertise to develop, debug, and build. Even worse, there was no standard monitor or interface to a monitor. Each manufacturer simply implemented whatever functions they imagined that programmers wanted. For example, passing parameters to functions might use registers in one monitor. In another monitor, the parameters might be passed in memory locations. They might use some combination of both methods in a third monitor. This created a problem for application programming. How could a program be written that was **portable**—that is, it would run on different manufacturer's computers?[2] Because of the different monitor programs, application programs would need to be specially written for each manufacturer's computers. This situation led to the development of **CP/M** (**Control Program/Monitor**). Created for microcomputers based on the Intel 8080/8085 CPU circuits, it was initially the product of one person, Gary Kildall of Digital Research, Inc.

3.1.3 Components of CP/M

CP/M (Control Program/Monitor) was written to allow software developers, users, and manufacturers to have one single, simple, standard interface. The hardware devices would be isolated from the operating system by a layer of software: the **BIOS** (**Basic Input/Output System**). This BIOS would be similar to a monitor but with standard

---

[2] Since the early application programs were written in machine language, the CPUs had to be identical, or at least compatible—that is, one CPU's instruction set had to be a superset of the other.

specified functions and interfaces. Each manufacturer would adapt the BIOS to the set of devices included with their particular machine.[3] The interface to the BIOS, however, was the same, no matter how the underlying devices might work. Porting CP/M to a new system consisted mostly of writing the BIOS routines for the hardware.

The core of the operating system was called the **BDOS (Basic Disk Operating System)**. It was what we call the kernel today. It would be independent of the hardware and would call the more primitive services in the BIOS. The BDOS software would be the same for any system that CP/M was to run on. This kind of standardized interface that provides general system functions but hides the messy hardware details is called an **abstraction.** We refer to the technique of abstraction many times in this book.

The last part of the OS was a user interface to the operating system called the **CCP (console command processor)**. The other commands that the CCP executed were mostly programs on the disk. These three components of a CP/M operating system were quite small. Each component was 2,000–4,000 bytes in size and all of CP/M fit on a few sectors of a floppy disk for booting the computer.

The existence of a de facto standard in CP/M encouraged software writers to develop application software for personal computers built by a wide variety of manufacturers. The software could support many input and output devices—such as different capacity floppy disks, hard disks, and video terminals. Applications did not need to be custom written for each type of computer. There were hundreds of programs written within a very short time. For programmers there were text editors, compilers for many programming languages, and debuggers. There were word processors, accounting packages, simple file systems, games, and many other programs written that created a booming market for personal computers. And since the operating system was well designed, with a clearly specified interface at each layer, there were several replacements for the CCP that offered different interfaces.

When IBM decided to enter the personal computing market, the decision was initially made to use the well-established CP/M standard. Since the CPU for the IBM PC (Intel 8088) was not exactly compatible to the CP/M-80—which was based on Intel 8080 and Zilog Z-80 processors—some small modifications were made. The IBM hardware was well known and specific, so the BIOS could take advantage of those characteristics.[4]

In the following sections, we take the liberty of abstracting the hardware of early IBM PCs and CP/M computers. Our purpose is not to teach CP/M, but rather to use it as an example to illustrate the features and functionality of a simple OS.

3.2 CHARACTERISTICS OF A SIMPLE PC SYSTEM

Early PC systems consisted of a main circuit board—the **motherboard** of the PC. The motherboard had a microprocessor chip (CPU), some random access memory (RAM), a ROM memory that contained the BIOS, and several other integrated

---

[3] It was also possible for a hobbyist user to do this adaptation, since instructions and examples came with the software. Even something as simple as adding memory to a system required recreating the BIOS.

[4] In the end, IBM adopted the MS/DOS operating system—developed by Microsoft—for their PC.

circuits (ICs) that interfaced these chips together. The motherboard had some slots to insert additional expansion circuit boards—called **cards** in early PC terminology. These cards included a video controller that was connected to a video monitor by plugging the monitor's cable into the video controller card. Other expansion cards could include additional RAM and floppy disk and hard disk controllers. User input/output was through a video monitor and keyboard. The keyboard was plugged directly into the motherboard, which had a keyboard controller chip built in. There was also a simple clock or timer chip on the motherboard.

A simple system schematic view of the typical hardware components in an early PC computer system is illustrated in Figure 3.1. Some of the characteristics of this type of system that had major effects on the design of the operating system were the following:

1. **Main memory was quite limited in size.** This led to the OS design decision that a single application program would be loaded into memory at a time. Because the CP/M OS was quite small, it would be permanently placed in memory. This includes the loader, interrupt handler, and device drivers. If an application program did not fit into the remaining available memory, the application would have to be written so that it is divided into sections that individually fit in memory. When a new section is needed, a memory management technique known as **overlays** could be used by the application to replace the old section with the new one.

2. **Disk format was standardized.** The disk block size and format was fixed for both floppy and hard disks in early PCs. This led to a standardized file system design that was based on the standard disk format.

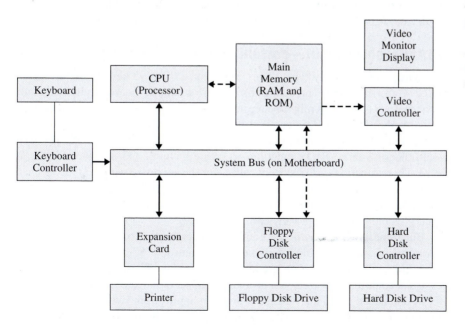

FIGURE 3.1
Hardware components in an early PC system.

3. **Interrupt handling was mainly for I/O devices.** Since one application would be running at a time, there was no need for switching between applications. No CPU scheduling was needed in the OS. The main types of interrupts were for handling I/O devices.

3.3 INPUT/OUTPUT MANAGEMENT

I/O handling was limited in early OSs since the types of I/O devices were quite limited compared to the wide variety available nowadays. Most application programs for early PCs needed the following I/O services:

1. Read characters from the keyboard.
2. Write characters to the video screen.
3. Print a character to the printer.
4. Utilize the disk file system to create a new file, read and write to the file, and close a file.

One problem for many programs was the lack of flexibility in handling keyboard input and screen output. Because there were many different companies making computer hardware that worked differently, the OS tried to provide a standard way of dealing with these differences.

Another problem was performance: executing some I/O commands by direct calls to the BIOS or the hardware was often much faster and more flexible than calling the appropriate OS command. This led to a tradeoff between **portability**—if application designers used only OS calls to perform I/O—versus the flexibility and higher speed that was possible if application designers used direct calls to BIOS and hardware functions. As an example, we discuss these tradeoffs with respect to the two most common I/O devices in early systems: keyboard for input and video monitor for output.

3.3.1 Keyboard input—Portability versus flexibility

Keyboards came in many types. They might have 65 to 95 keys placed in different places on the keyboard. The data transferred from the keyboard might be serialized or parallel and characters might be represented by seven or eight bits. How could this be standardized? The BIOS was customized for each type of keyboard, but would provide the same set of BIOS interface functions to the rest of the OS. The BDOS would then use those BIOS functions to create a simple OS interface for the keyboard. These functions—OS system calls—for the keyboard were: (1) read a character from the keyboard and (2) check if a key has been pressed. For many applications this was adequate. If an application used these standard functions for its keyboard input, it would be portable to any computer system.

But some applications needed additional flexibility. For example, a word processor may want to use "modified" keys—a "control + S" might save the file, and a "control + C" might pop up a command list menu. These special keystrokes or keystroke combinations created a problem because they were not recognized by the BDOS and hence could not be passed on to an application. Even worse, some combinations like "control + C" might be interpreted by the BIOS or BDOS and cause some OS action such as a reboot. In this case, it would obviously not pass the keystroke combination to the application.

Applications that wanted additional flexibility to handle the keyboard so that combinations of keystrokes had meaning to the application bypassed the BDOS. This was trivial to do. It might mean simply reading keys from the BIOS rather than the BDOS, or even reading keys directly from the keyboard hardware (actually the keyboard interface chip). It was easy to bypass the operating system (BDOS) because in early systems there was no memory protection. Any application could address any part of memory. It was just as easy to use BIOS calls as to use BDOS calls, and the BDOS call would not do what was needed by the application. The problem with this approach is that programs would not be portable anymore, especially if the application went directly to the hardware.

3.3.2 Video monitor output—Portability versus functionality and performance

The screen—or **video monitor**—posed even more significant problems. First, the functions available through the BDOS and BIOS interface functions was rather limited. There were many features of video systems that could not be used directly by the simple OS system calls. For example, one could not use color, write multiple "pages" of video memory to simulate motion by rapidly displaying a series of images, or move the cursor independently of writing to the screen. Second, and even more critical, screen output using BDOS was very slow. Many applications would write characters directly to the screen memory and access the video controller hardware directly. Many applications would also move the cursor using BIOS calls. The main reason for bypassing BDOS was to improve application performance.

Writing directly to video memory provided not only more functionality but was also much faster than going through an OS system call. Depending on the programming language used, it could be 100 times faster or even more! Bypassing the OS to display characters created the same type of portability problems that bypassing the keyboard did. But the performance benefits were so significant that many application programs ignored portability to improve performance. This was especially true of game programs, which always tried to wring every possible ounce of performance out of the hardware. Games have always driven the rapid progress of PC hardware development.

For example, to put a white-colored "+" on a black screen background required a call to a single machine instruction: "Move 0F800, 2B07." Writing text directly to video memory was relatively straightforward. Video memory began at location 0F800 Hex, which corresponded to the first visible character on the upper left corner of the screen. It was followed by the **video attributes** of that character. In the case of a color adapter this was 8 bits of information: 3 bits of color information for the foreground[5]; 3 bits of background color; one bit for "high intensity foreground" (bright); and the last bit for blinking the character. So the character "+" ("2B" ASCII) was written to the screen at location upper left corner (F800) and was set to a foreground

---

[5] Color was specified using 1 bit each for red, green, and blue; white is all 3 bits as 1's.

FIGURE 3.2
A floppy disk
for early PCs.

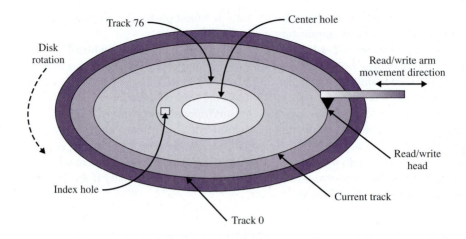

of white ("7") on a black ("0") background. A black character on a white background would simply have the attribute "70."

3.4 DISK MANAGEMENT AND THE FILE SYSTEM

Since so many applications bypassed the keyboard and video OS system calls, what did the OS really provide? One of the main services that such an early OS provided was a standard and portable file system. About 75% of OS system calls were disk file related. In this section, we discuss the file system for CP/M but first we describe the disk system that is the basis for the file system.

3.4.1 The Disk System

In early PC systems, there was a standard for the hardware disk devices for use with the file system—the 8-inch floppy, illustrated in Figure 3.2. This floppy had a hole in the middle where the floppy disk drive would position it on a spindle. The spindle is connected to a disk drive motor that would spin the disk at 360 revolutions per minute. The standard disk had 77 **tracks** numbered from track 0 at the outside track furthest from the hole to track 76 at the innermost track. Tracks were concentric circles—each track began and ended equidistant from the center hole. A track contained 26 **sectors** (sometimes called **blocks**), the first sector numbered 1 and the last sector 26.[6] Each sector contained 128 bytes of data, plus some control information, such as which sector number it was. Floppy disks were two-sided, with the sides numbered, not surprisingly, 0 and 1. There was a small hole called the **index hole** near the center hole that was used by the disk controller to find out where the first sector of each track was. Since all tracks had 26 sectors, the tracks were longer on the outside and shorter on the inside, but each track held the same amount of data.[7]

---

[6] Tracks started at 0, but sectors started at 1.

[7] This is no longer true in modern hard disks.

The disk system was comprised of the **disk drive** and **disk controller.** The disk drive held and rotated the disk media (a floppy disk), which actually contained the stored data. The disk controller was usually built on to the computer's motherboard or on a circuit card plugged into the motherboard. Disk drives can move a **disk head**—which contains read and write magnetic sensors—from track to track. To read any individual sector on a track, the drive must wait for the sector to rotate under the disk head.

A disk controller can take commands to read or write a sector or multiple sectors on a given track and on a given side of the disk. When the disk drive head movement motor moved the head it might sometimes miss (go to the wrong track). The controller would notice this (each sector of each track has the track number on it) and would reposition the disk head correctly. Sometimes sectors may be incorrectly read and again the disk controller would notice this and try to read again. The controller would also reorient itself to start looking for sectors on tracks starting after the index hole rotates around. All of these activities are invisible to the OS or even the BIOS. They are implemented either at the hardware level of the disk controller itself or on the software controlling the specialized processor on the disk controller. This software embedded in ROMs on controllers is often known as **firmware.**

Such a standard disk for early PC systems contained: 77 (tracks) * 26 (sectors per track) * 128 (bytes per sector) * 2 (sides) = 512,512 bytes of raw data (500 Kbytes), after being formatted by the OS. **Disk formatting** is the process of writing control information on the disk to divide the disk tracks into sectors. This standard disk was used as the basis for implementing the OS file system for PCs, which we discuss in the next section.

3.4.2 The File System

The OS had a simple file system built on top of the BIOS to store user and system files. A part of the system files that can be stored on a disk contain the binary OS code itself. In addition, each disk has a directory that stores information about all files stored on the disk, their sizes, the physical disk locations (sectors) where they are stored, and so on. The files stored on disk may contain any of the following types of data:

- application-produced data (documents, spreadsheets, source code)
- application program executables (binary code)
- directory information (the names of the files, date created, location—where it is stored on the disk)
- the binary executable of the operating system (the OS executable, used to load or "boot" the OS)

To accommodate the different types of information stored on a disk, each physical disk is divided into three areas for a BIOS file system, as shown in Figure 3.3:

- a **reserved area,** where the OS executable is placed (also called the **disk boot area**)
- the **file directory area** containing entries with information about each file stored on disk

FIGURE 3.3
Typical CP/M file
system layout.

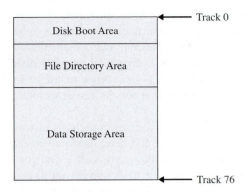

- the **data storage area** for data and program files, which occupies the remainder of the disk and is the largest part of the disk.

The BIOS has a built-in table that gives the size of each of these areas. We now discuss the contents of each of these areas in more detail.

Disk boot area

The simplest part of the file system is this reserved area, which holds the OS binary for booting the PC. This area is not visible from the file system—it has no directory entry and no name. The loadable image of the BIOS, BDOS, and CCP are written in this area, sector-by-sector, track-by-track, starting at track 0, sector 1. These are not part of any "file." They simply occupy the first few tracks of a disk. The BIOS is usually 2 KB, the BDOS is 3.5 KB, and the CCP is 2 KB, so together the OS binaries occupy the first three tracks.

When the computer is turned on or rebooted a small program in ROM is run that copies the OS executable image from disk to memory and then starts executing this program—the Operating System. This is called **booting** or **OS loading.**[8]

File directory area

The size of the directory area is fixed and is recorded in a table in the BIOS. For a floppy disk the directory holds up to 64 entries of 32 bytes each.[9] A disk directory entry layout is shown in Figure 3.4. Each entry in a directory contains the following:

1. A *user number.* This is actually a group number from 0 to 15, which allows multiple users or groups to share a disk and collect their files into a group. Notice that there are actually no subdirectories—all files are in one directory. Group numbers provide an illusion of having single-level subdirectories. In effect these are virtual subdirectories.
2. A *file name and file type.* These may be considered as one item, which is 1–8 characters of file name and 0–3 characters of file type—often called **8.3 file**

---

[8] In modern PCs, a similar booting is usually done from the hard disk rather than a floppy. The hard disk is usually preloaded with an OS by the PC manufacturer.

[9] For hard disks, it is of course much larger.

User Number - 1
File Name - 8
File Type - 3
Extent Counter - 2
Reserved - 1
Number of records - 1
Allocation - 16

FIGURE 3.4
CP/M file directory entry.

names. If the actual file names are smaller than 8.3 they are padded with spaces. Not all characters are allowed in file names. A period is used to separate the file name and type (e.g., MYFILE.DOC) but is not stored in the directory, so using periods or spaces is not allowed. While utility programs that come with the OS do not allow illegal names, the OS calls that an application program uses to create, open, or rename a file do not actually check the names, so an application can create files that may not be accessible to other programs.

3. An *extent counter.* An extent is the portion of a file controlled by one directory entry. If a file takes up more blocks than can be pointed to by one directory entry it is given additional directory entries. The extent is set to zero for the first part of the file and then is sequentially numbered for each of the remaining parts of the file. Large files will have multiple directory entries with the same file name but different file extent numbers and a different group of allocation pointers in each entry. Since files may be deleted and their directory entries reused, the extents may not be in order in the directory.

4. The *number of records.* This is actually the number of 128-byte records used in this extent. If the count is 080x, this extent is full and there may be another one on the disk. File lengths are rounded up to the nearest 128 bytes, so applications had to know how much data was really in the last record. This lead to the convention of a Control-Z character to mark the end of a text file.

5. An *allocation map.* This is a group of numbers of (or pointers to) the disk blocks that contain the data for the file. There are eight pointers of 16 bits each. Each value points to a sector on the disk that contains part of the file. If the file is so small that it contains fewer than eight sectors, then the unused pointers are set to zero. If the file is too large and eight sectors are not enough to contain the file's data, then an additional extent is allocated and another directory entry filled in. On some systems there were 16 pointers of eight bytes each. Such inconsistencies were one of the main problems that restricted the growth of CP/M.

Data storage area

The data storage area contains the data blocks for the files. For the system to access a file, the user or application program would provide the file name and the file system would search the disk directory to determine if a file with that name was stored on the disk. If the file name was found, the directory entry would have the addresses of the sectors where the file was stored, so the file data could be accessed.

Note: Actually, the disk structure is just a bit more complicated. If you count up the total number of file pointers as described above, in all files, 64 (directory entries) * 8 (file pointers per entry) gives 512 sectors, but there are more sectors (77 * 26 = 2002) on a floppy disk! This would not allow one to use most of the floppy space. So, in reality, rather than pointing to an individual sector, sectors are grouped together into **allocation blocks,** which are consecutive sectors grouped together. The size of these allocation blocks is determined by the size of the disk, but in typical early floppies it is eight sectors, or 1024 bytes. So in reality each directory entry points to up to eight allocation blocks of 1024 bytes each.

Here are a few observations about and limitations of this file system structure:

- There are no dates or times in the directory.
- There is no explicit file size entry, so the file size must be calculated roughly from the number of pointers in its directory entry and possible extents.
- There is only a single directory with no subdirectories, but group numbers give the illusion of a one-level subdirectory.
- A file must be stored entirely on one disk.
- If the directory is full, so is the disk. The directory is a fixed size, so only 64 files or fewer can be stored on a floppy disk.

An Observation: One of the biggest complaints against CP/M was the 8.3 file names, something that should have been relatively easy to fix. Directory entries, where file names are stored, are 32 bytes long. They could have easily been lengthened to 48- or 64-byte directory entries, allowing 23.3 or even 40.3 names. But the original design was simple, and the designer did not want to use too much disk space for the directory. The design compromise was made to minimize the disk space (and memory space) for each directory entry. This was particularly important for floppy disks where the file contents and directory entries together were a few hundred kilobytes.

3.5 PROCESS AND MEMORY MANAGEMENT

In the more complex OSs that we will study later, the topics of process and memory management are covered first since processes correspond to what a user wants to get done, so they are of primary importance. But in this simple OS, process management and memory management are rather limited, since only one program at a time is executing. And the issues of hardware abstraction and file systems were therefore more significant.

Still, even with this limited functionality, there are several process and memory issues that the OS must handle. First, we discuss the typical flow during program execution. Then we discuss command processing. Finally, we discuss memory management and an overlay technique that can be used when the program to be created is larger than the main memory space available.

3.5.1 **Creating and executing an application program**

An application program is usually written by typing the program language instructions into a text editor. It is then compiled or assembled (or both) and finally linked together with library routines using a link editor. This results in a **program image** file that is ready to be loaded into memory and run. The program image has been given many names, for example **program executable, program binary,** or **runnable program.** After a few rounds of debugging this program is ready for use.

In order for a program to begin running, its executable binary code file must be loaded into memory. This loading process is usually done by the CCP. The CCP is itself an application program that provides a few **built-in functions**—for example, the "DIR" command gives a directory listing of all files, and the "ERA" command erases a file or a group of files. CCP accomplishes its work by making only BDOS calls—it never calls the BIOS or hardware directly. This makes the BDOS more easily portable to a new hardware system. When a name is entered to the CCP, it first looks to see if it is the name of a built-in command. If so, then that command is executed. If the name is not that of a built-in command, then the CCP tries to find an executable program file on the disk with that name. If one exists, then the contents of that file are loaded into memory and the program starts running. There was a special code in the program header that would identify the file as being an executable program. Alternatively the command the user entered might name a text file that was a string of commands that the CCP should read and execute one at a time. These were called **subfiles** in CP/M after the standard extension ".sub," which was the second part of the file name. Command files of this sort are commonly known as **scripts** or **batch** files.

In CP/M, normal application programs are always loaded into RAM beginning at address 0100 Hex. Having a fixed load address for all programs makes it easy for compilers and linkers to create executables, since the program starting address will be known in advance.

Programs typically need additional memory for static data—for example, predefined fixed-size data such as static strings. In addition, a stack is needed for dynamic data—for example, temporary variables. The predefined static data are loaded into memory following the loading of the program binary file. Additional memory following static data is reserved for other data. Figure 3.5 illustrates the general memory map for the various parts of an executing program.

The stack is initially placed at the highest location in memory that is just below the OS code. The stack grows in memory toward lower memory addresses (see Figure 3.5). After loading is complete, the OS calls the first instruction of the program as though it were calling a subroutine. The program executes until it has finished its work, at which time control simply returns to the CCP program that loaded it. The CCP might still be in memory, but if it is not then it is simply reloaded from the disk. As a program executes it may use all available memory anytime it wants to except for reserved memory containing the OS or parts of the OS.

The process executes from start to finish. If it requires I/O, the CPU will remain idle until the required I/O is completed. For example, the process may wait for user input from the keyboard. For large programs that do not fit entirely in memory, the

FIGURE 3.5

Typical memory contents when executing a program.

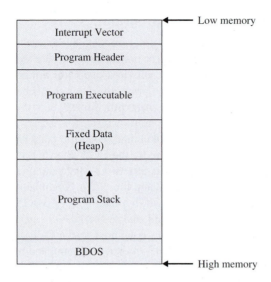

Many users prefer additional functions or a different "look and feel," menus or graphics, for instance. It was fairly common to replace the CCP with a shell more suited to a one's likes. In many OSs one has a choice of several different shells. Writing a command processor or shell is a fun exercise. But like many programs, as you and others use it, it will need new and more complex functions added, such as recalling past commands or the ability to chain commands together.

program code is typically divided into several segments that are brought into memory separately. When one segment calls a function whose code is not in memory, a technique called memory overlay is used to bring in the new code segment in place of the other code segment currently in memory. Implementing overlays was left up to the application program, though it usually had some assistance from the application libraries. We discuss this technique further in Section 3.5.3.

3.5.2 Command processing via the CCP

In our simple OS the CCP is a program pretty much like any other. The CCP is perhaps better structured than some programs since it only uses OS system calls and never bypasses the OS. In other OSs, the component similar to the CCP is sometimes called a **shell** or **command interpreter.** A user can directly invoke CCP commands by typing a CCP command or the name of an executable program file. Still another name for this kind of command interpreter is **command line interface,** since each command is entered on a screen line and is submitted to the command interpreter when the user presses the <carriage return> or <enter> key. The CCP was linked to load in high memory just under the BDOS. When a program was finished running, it would exit by returning control to the BDOS, which would check to see if the CCP was still intact in the memory. If it was, then the BDOS would return control to the CCP without reloading it.

Many users prefer additional functions or a different "look and feel," menus or graphics, for instance. It was fairly common to replace the CCP with a shell more suited to a one's likes. In many OSs one has a choice of several different shells. Writing a command processor or shell is a fun exercise. But like many programs, as you and others use it, it will need new and more complex functions added, such as recalling past commands or the ability to chain commands together.

3.5.3 **Memory management**

As we discussed in Section 3.5.1, the basic handling of memory by the CP/M OS is quite simple. All programs are loaded at a fixed address in memory. Programs are divided into two parts: (1) the program executable code and (2) fixed (static) data—such as constant values in the program, character strings, and so forth.

The software that copies these two parts into memory from disk is called a **loader,** and is a part of the CCP command processor. A program also needs some **stack** space to store temporary variables, pass parameters to called subroutines, and return data from those routines. The stack was placed at the highest location in memory, immediately below the OS itself. This allowed the stack to "grow" downward in memory and not "collide" with the program data—unless no more memory is available. Figure 3.5 illustrates this memory structure.

But CP/M had no provision for detecting a collision between the stack and fixed data. Such an occurrence would usually either crash the program or produce strange results because the CPU had no memory management registers for memory protection. Such memory overwriting bugs were difficult to find and fix and occurred frequently on CP/M systems.

For programs written in some high-level programming languages—for instance, Pascal or C—there is a large pool of memory that can be dynamically allocated and returned called the **heap.** The heap was set aside by the loader, but managed by routines in the high-level language runtime libraries. Not all programs used a heap. If there was one, it would be located in memory between the fixed data and the stack.

A **program header** was located in memory immediately preceding the executable binary code. The program header contained pointers to memory addresses where the stack is located and where the fixed data is located. It also contained a pointer to strings passed as parameters to the program when the user typed the command and supplied arguments to the program. For example, if a user entered a command to run a text editor, the command line would probably also include the name of the file to be edited.

Why was the OS located in the highest part of memory rather than in low memory? Because CP/M systems did not all have the same amount of memory. Some computers might have 32 KB of memory, others 48 or 64 KB. So the operating system would be generated (configured) to occupy the highest locations in memory, leaving a fixed address—always 100 Hex—to load programs. If the OS became larger it would start at a lower address in memory, but not force any program to change addresses, although a user program would have less memory remaining in which to run. This meant that when the OS was upgraded to a new version it was not necessary to relink all the application programs.

3.5.4 **Overlays**

The maximum size of memory in a CP/M system was constrained by the amount of memory that the CPU could address. Initially, this was 64 KB but some later versions of the CPU allowed more memory and some computers had additional hardware added to provide "banks" of memory that could be mapped into memory spaces by program control. What happened if a program would not fit in the available space? This problem had been an issue since the earliest days of computers.

Of course, programs that manipulated large amounts of data could keep some of the data on disk, rather than in memory, bringing in only what was needed at a given time. But what could be done about programs whose binary code was large? Those programs could similarly bring in only those parts of the program needed for some part of the processing. These parts or programs would "overlay" each other in the same locations in memory and were called **overlays.** Programs that had large amounts of code would be divided into a main part of the program and other program sections. The main part of the program would always reside in memory. Those sections of the program that were only needed sometimes would be brought into memory as overlays that replaced other sections. Typical candidates for overlays were some large computations or error-handling routines.

The programmer would have to identify those parts of the program that should be grouped together into an overlay. When designing overlays, it is important to avoid one overlay calling into a different overlay that would take the place of the first one in memory. The actual loading of overlays was done by the programming language runtime library, which used CP/M system calls to load an overlay. The programmer would indicate to the compiler which parts of a program—which functions and procedures—would be in each overlay, and the compiler produced the loadable overlay code. Figure 3.6 illustrates these concepts. Here, a program has one main part and three overlays. Only one of the overlays would be in memory at any particular time.

An example of a program that might use overlays is an assembler. The source program is typically read twice. During the first pass the assembler is building a symbol table and allocating space for both code and data. Then the source program is reread and the actual code generation takes place. Now the assembler has sufficient information to generate the instructions and fill in the addresses they reference. Clearly these two passes over the source program do not reference one another directly and can thus overlay one another. In this case there are often at least two other

FIGURE 3.6

Overlays in memory when executing a program.

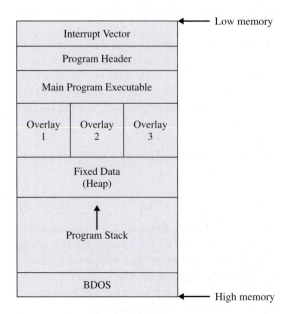

possible overlays. One would be an initialization phase that takes in the user control options, opens the input file, allocates the symbol table, and so on. A second might be providing additional printed output about the file such as a listing of the generated code with the user comments. While that full assembler might run in a large machine without overlays, smaller machines might not be able to run it. In addition, the size of the source program that can be handled is limited by the storage space for the symbol table, so that an overlaid assembler can handle much larger programs.

3.5.5 **Processes and basic multitasking**

Even in early systems with limited memory and slow processors, users wanted to do some work in parallel. One very common request was the ability to print a file in a **background process** while editing (or playing a game) in a **foreground process.** This processing of printing while allowing another foreground program to run was a very widely requested feature. Printers were slow, and starting a print job and then leaving your computer printing and walking away for 30 minutes or an hour was very boring, and wasteful of a most valuable resource—a person's time. This was especially true if something went wrong and the user returned 30 minutes later to find that the printer was waiting for user attention.

CP/M's solution was a background printing process. A small program was loaded into memory at the highest location of memory, immediately below the OS. This program initialized itself and then returned control to the CCP, allowing another program to run. When a user wanted to print in the background, the name of the file to print was passed to the background print handler. This would print a little bit of the file—a line or two—whenever it got control. The background process would typically get control any time a foreground process did a system call, or possibly by setting a timer and causing an interrupt of the foreground process.

Background printing gave the appearance of the computer doing two things at once, something called multitasking. The background print handler would allow only printing in the background, and nothing else. Users liked the idea of doing work in parallel, especially input and output that was very slow, like printing on early printers. We will see that all newer OSs, even those on very small devices, have some sort of multitasking facility.

3.6 SUMMARY

In this chapter, we presented the typical components of a simple OS with limited capability. We based our presentation on the features of an early personal computer operating system, CP/M, and the basic hardware of early PC systems. We started by describing the predecessors of simple operating systems, called monitors, and discussed how they evolved into early operating systems because of the need for standardization. We then described the characteristics of the

early PC systems for which this type of OS was used. Next, we discussed how input/output was managed in such an early OS. We saw that application programs often ignored the use of standardized I/O functions provided by the OS to achieve better performance and more flexibility.

We then continued with a description of the file system in such a simple OS, and the standard disk devices that the file system was based on. We then moved on to discuss process and memory management. We saw, that a program binary was always loaded starting at a fixed predefined memory location because only one program was in memory at a time. Other parts of memory stored the OS binaries and fixed program data. A stack area was reserved for storing dynamic data. We discussed the techniques of overlays for large programs that could not fit in memory. Overlays allowed programmers to divide a program into sections that would replace one another in memory when needed. Finally, we discussed an early example of multitasking—that of background printing.

BIBLIOGRAPHY

Barbier, K., *CP/M Solutions.* Englewood Cliffs, NJ: Prentice-Hall, 1985.

Barbier, K., *CP/M Techniques.* Englewood Cliffs, NJ: Prentice-Hall, 1984.

Cortesi, D. E., *Inside CP/M: A Guide for Users and Programmers with CP/M-86 and MP/M2.* Austin, TX: Holt, Rinehart and Winston, 1982.

Dwyer, T. A., and M. Critchfield, *CP/M and the Personal Computer.* Reading, MA: Addison-Wesley, 1983.

WEB RESOURCES

http://www.digitalresearch.biz/ (the creators of CP/M)

http://www.seasip.demon.co.uk/Cpm/ (outsider archive site)

http://www.osdata.com (Operating System technical comparison)

http://www.pcworld.com/article/id,18693-page, 3-c,harddrives/article.html (hard disk characteristics)

REVIEW QUESTIONS

3.1 What kinds of limited functions did early PC monitor programs provide?

3.2 What kind of error checking was done on the arguments to the calls to the monitor program? What was the likely result?

3.3 In the PC era there were a multitude of small startup hardware vendors and all of their users were clamoring for software. What was the characteristic of early monitors in this environment that led to the development of a real OS?

3.4 What was the overriding characteristic of the hardware systems that CP/M and MS-DOS were designed to run on and what were some of the design decisions that were made as a result?

3.5 The basic I/O needs of early programs were fairly modest. Some applications, however, had somewhat more complex needs. In many cases the functions provided by the monitor were much slower than equivalent functions that were in the BIOS code. What did the application programmers do when the functions the OS provided hid the functions that the application needed or were so slow that the performance of the application was unacceptable? What problems did that cause?

3.6 Besides the keyboard and video, what was the other major I/O system that was very important in the early OSs?

3.7 To the command interpreter, most of the commands that a user types are executed by finding a program on the disk with that name and running it. A few commands are not mapped to programs on the disk. Where do they reside?

3.8 On a floppy disk (or a hard disk) the heads on all of the surfaces will be in the same relative position over the surfaces measured in from the outside of the disk. As the disk rotates a certain portion of a surface will pass under each head. What is that portion of the surface called? That portion is divided up into smaller pieces. Those pieces are the smallest addressable portion of the disk. What are these pieces called?

3.9 CP/M divided the contents of a floppy disk into three parts. What were these three parts?

3.10 Why does the CP/M OS reside in high memory instead of low memory?

3.11 True or false? Overlays are an obsolete technique used when system memories were very small and are no longer used in modern systems.

3.12 While CP/M did not allow true application multiprocessing, it did allow one sort of background processing. What was that?

Chapter 4

A Single-User Multitasking Operating System

In this chapter:

In this chapter we discuss a more complex class of operating systems than the one discussed in Chapter 3, and one that is considerably more modern. We look at the Palm Operating System[1] developed by Palm, Inc. The CP/M system, which was covered in the previous chapter, originally supported only one program (or process) at a time. Toward the end of its major period of use it was extended to include functions such as background printing. In contrast, the Palm OS was designed from the outset to support the execution of several processes at the same time.

We start this chapter in Section 4.1 with an overview of Palm OS and some background about the underpinnings of the kernel. There are several other OSs in

---

[1] The OS functions described in this chapter cover releases of the Palm OS prior to release 5. Release 5 is a different OS and supports a different CPU. We feel that there will continue to be a class of devices and corresponding OSs that will function at approximately the level described, so we have not changed the material to correspond to the later versions. The functions covered in this chapter are probably more representative of the functions that students will find in similar low-end OSs for some time to come. For example, as nanotechnology evolves, it is quite likely that such machines will often contain computer systems that will require an OS and there will be no secondary storage. Furthermore, it currently seems likely that rotating data storage devices may soon be a thing of the past, and that most new computers will have vast amounts of primary storage and some removable tertiary storage but no secondary storage. Thus, all OSs might function like this OS at some point.

this class, most notably EPOC by Symbian™ and scaled-down versions of Linux and Windows NT. The latter is called the Windows Mobile (formerly the Pocket PC) OS. At the end of the chapter we look at these other OSs and also some more recent developments in this highly dynamic field. The Palm OS was developed for small handheld devices called **personal digital assistants (PDAs)** or **personal information managers (PIMs)** that are typically used by a single user to keep track of personal schedules, contacts, and to-do lists or to access email or the World Wide Web while on the move. These OSs are now used in cellular phones that have much of the same functionality as a PDA. The Palm OS usually runs only a few applications at a time, and can concurrently run some OS processes in parallel with the small number of applications. Thus, it supports a limited number of concurrently executing tasks. It provides more features than the single-tasking type of OS described in Chapter 3. It also serves to illustrate a modern version of a simple OS.

In Section 4.2 we discuss some unusual hardware characteristics of the handheld computers that use the Palm OS. These special characteristics force the choices of some of the decisions made in the Palm OS design. In the CP/M world we saw at the very end the introduction of multiple programs in memory at the same time, providing such functions as pop-up windows and background printing. The Palm OS has much more complex multiprogramming, so in Section 4.3 we discuss the scheduling of application processes and OS tasks in the Palm OS.

When multiple programs are running in a system at the same time, memory management becomes more complex. A program can no longer assume that it can use all the memory there is. The OS must take on the responsibility of allocating sections of memory to applications as they ask for it. It must therefore track the memory used by each application and recover it when the application ends. Therefore, Section 4.4 moves on to discuss memory management. Section 4.5 covers the organization of files in the Palm OS, and Section 4.6 covers the basic I/O functions that the Palm OS provides.

Early PDAs were text based to a large extent, though many had special icons or small portions of the screen that had graphics capabilities. Now such devices always have graphics-oriented displays. CP/M was a text-based OS, so in this chapter we also introduce some simple characteristics of a graphical user interface, or GUI. All modern OSs include support for a GUI, though they are not always intrinsic to the OS itself. Programs on a CP/M system assumed that they were in total control of the system, so they were designed to interact in a certain way. Programs that work in a GUI have to cope with events that occur asynchronously to the main flow of the program. So this chapter also introduces event-oriented programming. Section 4.7 describes the display subsystem and Section 4.8 first discusses event-oriented programming and then describes the design of a typical Palm OS application. We conclude with a chapter summary in Section 4.9.

Later in the book we cover a few more advanced features of the Palm OS and similar systems. Chapter 20 discusses several interesting subsystems in the Palm OS and explains the nature of the cross-development systems needed to develop programs for such a limited environment. It also covers some of the developments in later releases of the Palm OS.

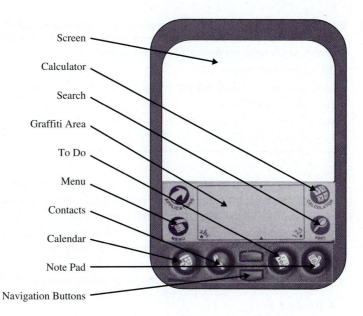

Screen
Calculator
Search
Graffiti Area
To Do
Menu
Contacts
Calendar
Note Pad
Navigation Buttons

FIGURE 4.1
A Palm Pilot.

4.1 INTRODUCTION: A SIMPLE MULTITASKING SYSTEM

The Palm OS was developed by Palm, Inc. for use with their small handheld comput-ers. A typical unit is shown in Figure 4.1. This platform has become very popular. Several hardware manufacturers have produced devices that conform to this tech-nology, including Handspring, Sony, and IBM. The same OS is also used in several cellular telephones, including the Treo and the Samsung 500. The environment in which Palm OS runs has several characteristics that are unusual compared to most general-purpose computers or PCs. These characteristics forced some unusual deci-sions to be made when developing the OS. However, these characteristics are typical in many systems that will be seen more and more in the future, so that far from being a distraction, these characteristics will actually be quite important to current and future OS architects. These characteristics also limit the design goals of the OS so that it is only a little more complex than the single-process OSs covered in Chapter 3. They are summarized in Table 4.1.

The first of these unusual characteristics arises from the fact that these handheld computers are grown-up versions of the PDAs that preceded them. They are designed to give top priority to servicing the interface with the user—so much so that the OS is actually built on top of a real-time kernel that Palm, Inc. licensed from another vendor.[2] For example, this real-time kernel allows the system to support the use of a stylus to "write" on a small section of the liquid crystal display (LCD) screen. The screen is touch sensitive, and touching the screen (preferably with the stylus) will cause an interrupt that will give the coordinates of the touched screen location to a

---

[2] That system is the AMX™ Multitasking Executive from KADAK Products Limited.

TABLE 4.1   Unusual Characteristics of the Palm OS

Real-time OS tasks but non-real-time applications

All solid state memory

Low power to conserve batteries

Single-window GUI

Multiple text input options

Expansion through plug-ins

routine that will track the movement of the stylus across the screen. The OS attempts to read and interpret the handwriting in real time—this is known in the Palm OS as **Graffiti input.**[3] While the OS is handling this real-time task, it also allows a few applications to be running on the machine at the same time. Having multiple applications as well as the real-time kernel running concurrently necessitates a **multitasking** or **multiprogramming** system design.

The Palm OS is designed for supporting applications such as the following:

- Reading email
- Keeping track of contacts in an address book
- Keeping records of expenses
- Enhancing to-do lists with alarm reminders
- Playing simple games such as Sudoku
- Accessing information through the WWW

It is not intended to support multiple users at a time or to be a Web server. Accordingly, the real-time and multitasking characteristics of the OS are not exposed to the application programmer through the application programming interfaces (APIs).

Another unusual aspect of these systems is that in general there is no secondary storage—all of system memory is primary storage (electronic main memory). The limited memory and CPU performance in these handheld systems lead to special designs for memory management and some special treatment for basic input and output operations. Some of these devices come with plug-in capability. This allows various types of **cards** or **modules** to be attached to the device. These cards can be memory cards preloaded with specific applications, global positioning systems (GPS) navigational devices, digital cameras, or even hard disks. The basic hardware, however, has no secondary storage, so the design of the OS must reflect this. Support for secondary storage has been grafted onto the main system design, as we discuss in more detail later.

The Palm OS supports a GUI to display output to the user. There are special considerations for programming this interface because of its small screen size. In particular, there is usually only a single window (form) visible on the screen at any point. There may be smaller dialog or alert boxes that are displayed in front of that single window. Finally, these systems support several mechanisms for accepting

---

[3] In 2003 PalmSource, Inc. lost a suit over the use of the original Graffiti software. The software now used is known as Graffiti 2. We use the simpler term as a generic name for the function.

user text input but they try to hide the differences between these mechanisms from the applications.

4.2 THE PALM OS ENVIRONMENT AND SYSTEM LAYOUT

There are several characteristics of Palm devices that had to be taken into consideration when designing the Palm OS. These were:

- Basic memory is volatile RAM
- Typically no secondary storage
- Small screen size
- Keyboard is not standard
- CPU is slow to reduce battery drain

4.2.1 Basic memory is volatile RAM

There are several unusual characteristics about the handheld computers that the Palm OS is designed to support. First, the devices are battery powered, and the design of the hardware and the OS reflect this. If the system is unused for a few minutes it will put itself into a **sleep mode** that uses very little power. The CPU is still running so the OS can sense when the user presses buttons, but it is running very slowly and in a small loop where it is waiting for interrupts. Power to the memory is actually *never turned off*. Even when the CPU and the OS are shut down the memory is still powered on. The hardware has a small current flow to maintain the contents of memory. (It is also possible to add memory modules to the system that contain read-only memory [ROM] or programmable read-only memory [PROM], sometimes called flash memory, but the basic design assumes that all main memory is volatile.)

4.2.2 No secondary storage

The second unusual characteristic about these handheld systems is that in the original design they do not have any secondary storage—no disk, CD, DVD, or tape drives. All data and programs are kept in a single address space. Some of this memory is ROM on modules (cards) that can be removed from the computer. This allows programs and databases to be loaded onto these modules and inserted into the machines as desired. Whether on a removable card or built in to the machine, all of memory is visible all the time so that all programs and all databases are always directly accessible. Some vendors of Palm OS–compatible hardware have added a separate class of memory that is accessed through I/O commands just as a secondary storage device is. This memory is not part of the main address space and thus requires special OS commands to access it. This class of memory is removable and is intended to be used to move information from one system to another. It is designed to emulate a disk drive so that it is physically compatible with other hardware systems as well.

4.2.3 **Small screen size**

The next feature is the nature of the LCD that presents the GUI to the user. Its system function is similar to CRT (cathode ray tube) or LCD screens used in other current systems, such as PCs utilizing OSs with GUI implementations. The fundamental difference is the size of the screen. Since these devices are literally designed to fit in a user's hand, the screen display is limited. With most other GUIs there can be multiple windows open on the screen at the same time. Often these windows overlap such that parts of some windows are hidden by other windows that are "in front" of them. It is usually possible to "maximize" one window so that it fills (almost) the whole screen.

In contrast to other GUIs, an application window in the Palm OS will fill the whole screen. The application may still use pull-down menus and dialog boxes but there will usually be no other application windows partially hidden behind the window of the running application.

4.2.4 **No keyboard**

One final interesting aspect of PDA handheld systems is that they initially did not have a keyboard. There are some attachable keyboards available, and some later models do have an actual keyboard, but this is not the way the system is normally assumed to obtain user input. The usual mode of input is through Graffiti input, as discussed in Section 4.1. This is generally acceptable, as most applications for PDAs do not expect large amounts of input.

Figure 4.2 shows an overall layout of the Palm OS. Immediately above the hardware is a software layer known as the hardware abstraction layer (HAL). Its function

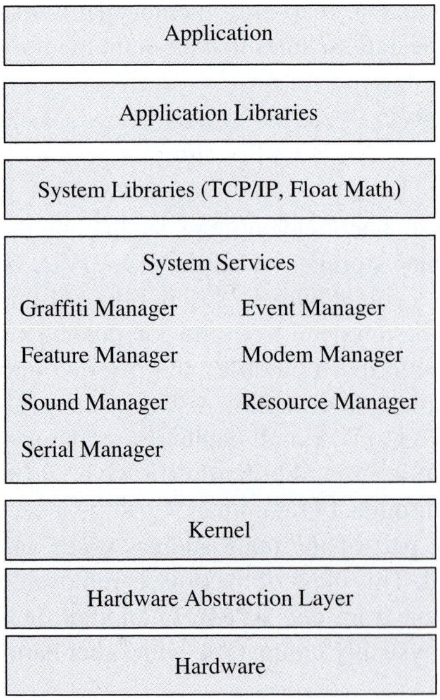

FIGURE 4.2
Palm OS
architecture.

Application

Application Libraries

System Libraries (TCP/IP, Float Math)

System Services
Graffiti Manager   Event Manager
Feature Manager   Modem Manager
Sound Manager   Resource Manager
Serial Manager

Kernel

Hardware Abstraction Layer

Hardware

is to isolate the rest of the software from the specifics of the hardware devices. This allows the developers of the OS kernel to build an OS that can easily be moved to another hardware platform. The kernel of the OS lies on top of the HAL. Many services provided by the OS are not part of the kernel, but lie above it. On top of the System Services area (which is always there) would come optional system library routines; on top of that would come application library routines, and, finally, the applications themselves.

4.3 PROCESS SCHEDULING

In the Palm OS multitasking environment, one needs to distinguish between OS processes and application processes. In this section, we discuss some processes of each type, and describe how the Palm OS handles and schedules these processes.

4.3.1 Processing Graffiti input—A real-time OS task

As was mentioned in the first chapter, there are many tasks that can best be done in the OS. There are several reasons for putting functions in the OS. Often it is because they are used by many applications. Putting the function in the OS simplifies development for the application programmers, guarantees that all applications will function similarly, and decreases the likelihood of having bugs in that part of the applications. The prime example of such a task in the Palm OS is the Graffiti input function. The display of the Palm OS systems is an LCD panel that is touch sensitive. Users generally input data into the Palm by drawing characters on this screen. This is such a specialized task that it is done by the OS. Two OS tasks are involved: **stylus tracking** and **character recognition.**

In order to track the path of a stylus across the face of the Graffiti area of the LCD screen, the CPU must rapidly and repeatedly check the current location of the stylus. This tracking is a real-time task because the system needs to be able to guarantee that it can check the position of the stylus frequently and quickly enough to track the movement of the stylus. This task is further complicated because the CPUs in these devices are running more slowly than those in PCs or workstations. The tracking task will recognize when the stylus changes direction and will divide the path into small vectors, which it will pass to the character recognition task. Once the position vectors of the stylus are analyzed and discovered, then the character can be recognized. Again, this is done by the OS. Every application developer does not want to have to write a handwriting recognizer. Indeed, this is one of the advances in PDA technology that the Palm OS brought to the market. This is a task that can be approached more leisurely than the tracking of the stylus. As the characters are recognized, the recognition task will give them to the application, which must display them back to the user in appropriate places on the LCD screen so that the user will get feedback about the characters input—just as with keyboard input on a PC.

4.3.2 Application processes—One focus at a time

In most systems a user can be running several applications at the same time. In the Palm OS only one user application will be visibly running at a time. Most Palm applications, however, do not have an "exit" function that the user can invoke. When the user selects a new application, any application that was running will be hidden from the user by the OS. So in the Palm OS, only one application will be running at a time that is in **focus**—that is, in control of the *screen window,* accepting and displaying input. However, other applications may run at times but do not have the focus. One example of such activity is a text search function. If the user does a text search, the Palm OS will sequentially call every application that has indicated to the OS that it will provide a text search function for its own database files. Each application will be asked to search its database for the search string that the user has input. These applications, however, will not gain control of the screen, and will only report their results to the OS.

Another example of a task that is running but does not have the focus of the screen is found in the **Sync application.** This application synchronizes database files on the handheld unit with those on a PC. The PC is running a corresponding synchronization program and the two systems communicate using some type of serial communication link. This connection might be an infrared or Bluetooth™ link or a USB cable. While this application will normally have the focus, there is no user input while the synchronization is running. However, the user might want to stop the synchronization before it finishes. One way to make this happen would be for the sync application to be in a loop, sending a block of data and then checking the screen for a stylus tap. However, this would slow the serial communication and would delay the response to the tap. Instead, the Palm Sync application uses two tasks: a real-time task to respond to screen taps via an interrupt and a synchronization application that can devote all its time to the communication task.

4.3.3 Typical user applications

Most Palm OS applications primarily involve a database and GUI interface and are designed for organizing information. Typical applications include to-do lists, address and contact information, appointment calendars, and various alarms. As such, they do not directly involve real-time tasks. As was previously described, the OS uses real-time tasks for stylus input. The applications themselves merely input and display information about things such as the user's appointments. Normal user applications, therefore, do not need to start extra tasks, as does the Sync system application. The main part of each application is a loop called the **event loop.** The OS "launches" the application. The application checks to see if this is the first time it has been run. If so, it will initialize any databases it maintains. It then enters the loop in which it waits for events. Most events are activities such as the recognition of a character by the Graffiti input or the selection of an item in a menu list.

There are a few unusual system events such as a notification to all applications that the system is about to enter sleep mode. Another frequent type of event is the "appStopEvent." As was mentioned before, when the user selects another application to run, that application will become the active application and the OS will force the currently running application to stop. In a different environment another OS would not want to stop an application merely because it did not have the focus. Too much I/O and CPU processing would be required to restart the application if the user switched back to it. On Palm handheld systems, however, there is no need to do such tasks as allocate memory to the program, read the executable module from a disk drive, and open its files, since both the program and the files are already in main memory at all times. If the user reselects an application that has been stopped, all the application does is realize that its files are already initialized and go into its loop of checking the queue of events that it needs to process. For a typical application that is merely waiting for the user to select some action from a menu or via the GUI, stopping may not mean much. But a game where a user is playing against the computer probably will pause its actions if the user switches to another application, for example.

4.3.4 Will the real scheduler please stand up?

As far as the actual process scheduler used by the Palm OS, it is a preemptive multitasking scheduler. This means that it is prepared to run many tasks, shifting among them as needed in order to service the needs of the system. Different types of tasks have various priorities and the OS scheduler will dynamically determine which task is the most important and will interrupt a less important task to run a more important one. Interrupting one task to run another is called **preemption.** The CPU is being taken away from the less important task so the more important task can run first. Various types of OS CPU schedulers will be discussed in more detail in Chapter 9.

4.4 MEMORY MANAGEMENT

Because there are many processes in a Palm system that are sharing the primary memory, the OS must provide lots of memory management functions. The first job is to see that the various processes don't access any locations outside their assigned memory. It must also keep track of memory that is not currently in use.

4.4.1 Memory fundamentals

Memory access in the Palm system uses 32-bit addresses, allowing for a 4 GB total address space. The actual physical memory is on one or more cards and the view of memory that the application sees reflects this. Each card has a minimum 256 MB portion of the logical address space. The cards are normally replaceable so the amount of memory in a system can be upgraded. While initial hardware designs supported only one memory card, newer systems allow for more. Memory cards may contain three different types of memory:

- **Read-only memory (ROM)**
- **Programmable read-only memory (PROM;** also called **flash memory**) or **nonvolatile RAM (NVRAM)**
- **Random access memory (RAM)**

All cards contain at least some RAM; the presence of the other two types of memory on a card depends on the card. The OS and the entire initial set of applications were initially contained in ROM but are now usually in PROM so that they can be upgraded. Additional applications can also be installed in the PROM or RAM.

Logically, the RAM is divided into two sections: (1) one section of the RAM is treated as being volatile and is called **dynamic RAM** and (2) the other section of RAM is treated as being *nonvolatile*[4] (**NVRAM**) and is called **storage RAM.**

If there is PROM on the card it is always considered to be storage RAM since it really is nonvolatile. The dynamic RAM is used like conventional RAM as it is in most computer systems. The contents of the entire RAM are preserved when the system is *turned off* (i.e., turned to low-power sleep mode). However, when the system is *turned on* (or **booted**) the contents of the dynamic part of the RAM are reset by the OS. The storage portion of the RAM is used in the same way a disk drive is used in most systems—to contain **persistent data** that is intended for retention for a long time (i.e., files or databases). Storage RAM can also contain extensions (and presumably fixes) to the OS as well as additional applications.

Since the cards are replaceable, there needs to be a mechanism for preserving the data contained in the storage RAM. The method is to use the Sync application to synchronize the contents of the storage RAM with a PC, replace the memory card, and then resynchronize the Palm with the PC. When used this way the PC is a backup device for the memory card contents. Alternatively, we can consider the Palm to be a **mobile device** that **caches** copies of part of the user's files and databases that normally reside on the PC.

4.4.2 Allocating memory

Memory is managed by the Palm OS as a **heap**[5]—that is to say that pieces of the memory are allocated and tracked by the OS and accessed within the heap as the application program runs and finally is released by the programs and returned to the available pool of memory by the OS. Those pieces are known in the Palm OS as memory **chunks.** There are a minimum of three heaps, one for each type of memory: ROM, dynamic RAM, and storage RAM. In newer versions of the Palm OS some of these blocks of memory may be broken into more than one heap. Within each heap, the OS allocates chunks of memory when an application makes a request. The chunks can be of any nonzero size up to slightly less than 64 KB in increments of 2 bytes. Memory chunks can be returned to the OS in any order and can be made smaller or larger through OS service calls.

Memory chunks are randomly allocated and freed and they may change size. If they are made larger then they may have to move to another place in the heap. Ultimately this process will lead to a condition known as **external fragmentation.** This term describes a condition where there are free chunks available for use and the total amount of free memory is sufficient to satisfy a new request but the largest free

---

[4] Nonvolatile memory does not lose its contents in case of power failure.

[5] A heap is a structure in which memory is allocated as needed in no particular sequence or order.

chunk is too small to satisfy the request, so the memory request cannot be directly satisfied. This is illustrated in Figure 4.3.

When this happens, the OS will attempt to move the currently used chunks so that the free space is contiguous. This kind of reorganization of fragmented space is known as **compaction.** There is a potential problem with this memory reorganization: an application has been allocated these chunks of memory and has pointers to them. If the OS is going to move the data then the application must still be able to access the data.

To allow for this moving of chunks in memory, the occupied chunks are accessed in a controlled manner. First, the data are accessed indirectly by the code rather than being accessed directly. That way the OS can move the data in the heap and the process will still be able to access it through the pointer. Each chunk in a heap is pointed to by an entry in a table called the **master pointer table** (**MPT**). The MPT is itself a chunk of RAM at the start of the heap. When a chunk is allocated, the application is not given a direct pointer to the chunk. Instead, it is returned a **master chunk pointer** (**MCP**). This pointer is actually the offset in the MPT of the pointer to that chunk, as illustrated in Figure 4.4.

The second aspect of the controlled access to memory is that an application must **lock** a chunk prior to using it. When the application wants to use the data in a chunk of memory it calls the OS to lock the MCP of that chunk. The OS will maintain a count of the locks for each chunk and will increase the lock count for that chunk by 1 (the maximum is 16) and return to the application the current physical address of the chunk. The application can now access the chunk as it needs to. The application unlocks the chunk when it is finished using it and the OS will decrement

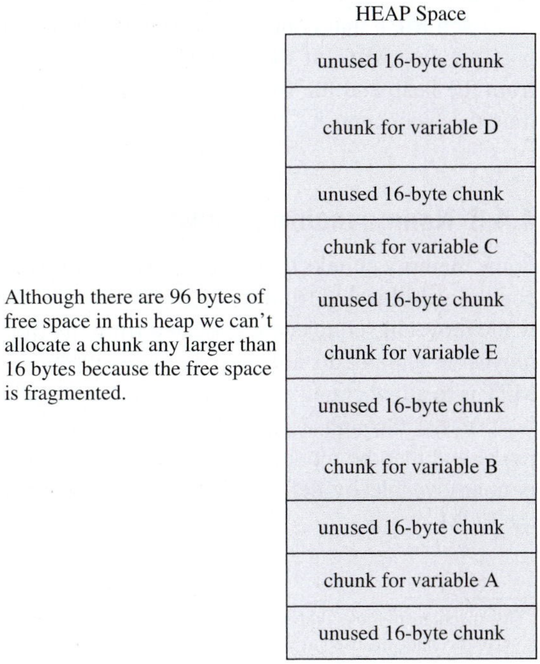

HEAP Space

FIGURE 4.3
External fragmentation.

Although there are 96 bytes of free space in this heap we can't allocate a chunk any larger than 16 bytes because the free space is fragmented.

HEAP Space
unused 16-byte chunk
chunk for variable D
unused 16-byte chunk
chunk for variable C
unused 16-byte chunk
chunk for variable E
unused 16-byte chunk
chunk for variable B
unused 16-byte chunk
chunk for variable A
unused 16-byte chunk

FIGURE 4.4
Master pointer table.

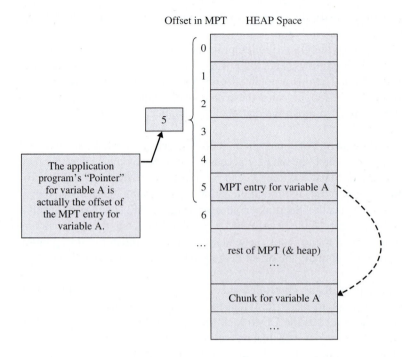

the lock count. When the OS needs to do compaction it will not move chunks that are locked by an application, as the lock means that the application is currently using the data.

Each MPT that controls one specific heap segment also contains a pointer to a possible next MPT. If the first MPT fills up, then a second MPT will be allocated from the heap and the first MPT will point to the second. Figures 4.5 and 4.6 illustrate these concepts.[6]

4.4.3 Nonmoveable chunks

Some memory chunks cannot be moved—for example, program code. Nonmoveable chunks are allocated from the high order end of the heap (higher memory addresses) while moveable chunks are allocated from the front (lower memory addresses). Nonmoveable chunks do not need an entry in the MPT since the only purpose of the MPT is to allow chunks to be moved during compaction. For consistency, even ROM is accessed through a chunk table. This allows an application to be debugged in RAM and then be moved to ROM without any changes. Since the code in the ROM is nonmoveable by definition, there will be no MCPs in the MPT for the heap in the ROM.

---

[6] This mechanism looks quite complex, and it *is* complex. However, it is typical of the memory access control mechanisms used in many OSs today, so it is worth looking at it in detail.

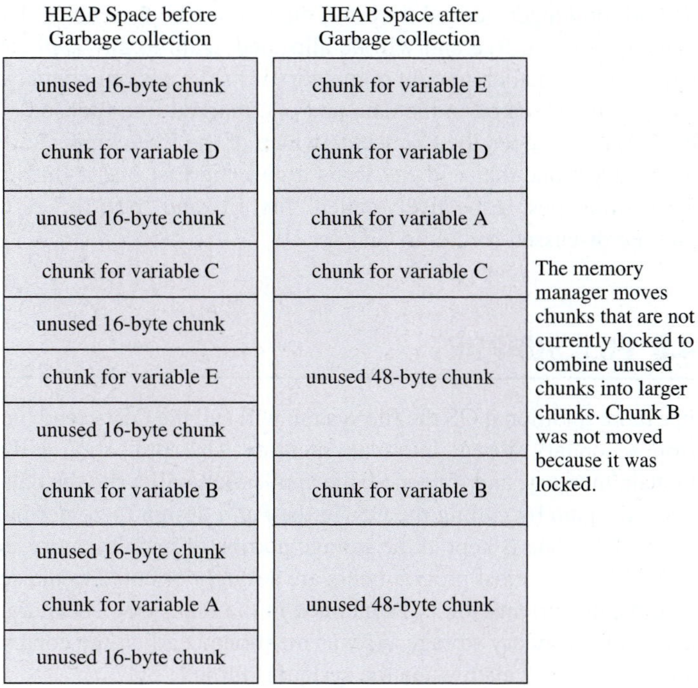

HEAP Space before
Garbage collection

unused 16-byte chunk
chunk for variable D
unused 16-byte chunk
chunk for variable C
unused 16-byte chunk
chunk for variable E
unused 16-byte chunk
chunk for variable B
unused 16-byte chunk
chunk for variable A
unused 16-byte chunk

HEAP Space after
Garbage collection

chunk for variable E
chunk for variable D
chunk for variable A
chunk for variable C
unused 48-byte chunk
chunk for variable B
unused 48-byte chunk

The memory manager moves chunks that are not currently locked to combine unused chunks into larger chunks. Chunk B was not moved because it was locked.

FIGURE 4.5
Garbage collection.

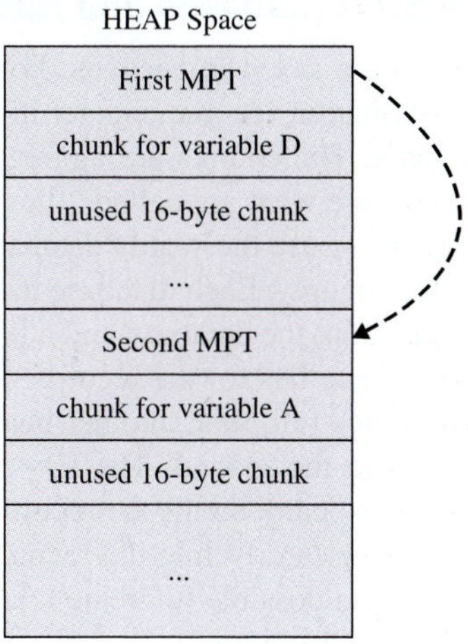

HEAP Space

First MPT
chunk for variable D
unused 16-byte chunk
...
Second MPT
chunk for variable A
unused 16-byte chunk
...

FIGURE 4.6
MPT chaining.

4.4.4 Free space tracking

When the heap is initially created by the OS, the storage management software will create the empty MPT. As was mentioned, moveable chunks are allocated from the front of the heap and nonmoveable chunks are allocated from the end. The area between the two is considered to be free memory. When applications have chunks that are no longer needed they call the OS to free the chunk. The freed chunks are marked as being free and will be allocated again to any application if needed. If a request for a smaller amount of memory is made, a larger chunk will be split into two pieces, one allocated to the data and one marked free (unused). This fragments the heap. But how does the OS decide which of the free chunks to divide? Does it pick the smallest one that will fit? Does it pick the first one it finds that is big enough? These strategies, respectively called "first fit" and "best fit," as well as other strategies are discussed further in Chapter 10.

4.5 FILE SUPPORT

In a more traditional OS the file system will call the OS to read individual file records from secondary storage into main memory. The application will operate on the data in main memory, and if needed, the application will write the data back to secondary storage, again by calling the OS. In the Palm design there normally is no secondary storage. All data is kept in the storage portion of main memory, either flash memory or RAM. Since most programmers are strongly oriented to the concepts of files and records, this orientation is maintained in the Palm OS. The storage RAM is used as a kind of secondary storage. As was mentioned earlier, the contents of storage RAM are never erased, even when the system is turned "off."

4.5.1 Databases and records

Data are saved in **records.** For example, a record might correspond to the contact information for one contact in an address book. Each record is saved in a memory chunk. The chunks are aggregated into collections called **databases.** (These databases are what are called "files" in most OSs. They are not what we normally mean when we use the word "database," a system that automatically indexes data, among other things.) Each database has a **header.** This header contains some basic information about the database and a list of records in the database. This list is actually a list of unique IDs for the records. If the initial chunk that contains the list of record IDs becomes full, then another header chunk will be allocated and the first header will point to the second. The IDs are only unique within the address space of a single memory card, so all the records for a given database have to reside within a single memory card. While the record ID is simply an integer with no relation to the data, it is also possible to create a key field in each database record that can be searched for by a program.

On some (non-Palm) systems with limited data storage the data can be compressed to save space. Because the CPU power in the Palm OS platforms is also modest, the information is not usually stored in compressed form. When secondary storage is on a rotating memory such as a disk there is a time lapse (latency) between the time when an application asks for a record and the time when the hardware can access the data. That time can normally be traded against the time required to do the compression and decompression. Since there normally is no rotating memory in the

Palm OS platform there is no time to be gained, so any time used for compression would be visible to the user. As a result, compression is not normally used with the Palm OS.

4.5.2 Resource objects

In a GUI there are elements that appear on the screen such as buttons, text boxes, slider controls, and so on. The Palm OS defines the various elements of a GUI interface as **objects** called **resources.** These resources are not objects in the traditional sense; instead, they are merely *data structures.* Each resource has a specific structure so that the OS can handle it in certain default ways. For example, if an application wants to display a confirmation alert for a record deletion it merely defines the alert and calls the OS to display it. Figure 4.7 shows such an alert box. When the alert is displayed, the OS does all the work of saving the window under which the alert will be displayed and updating the window on the form so that the user sees the alert. After the user confirms the alert the OS will restore the saved window to the form and tell the application which button on the alert box the user selected. The application can always override the default action and cause some special action to happen. The resources are saved in chunks just as with database records and are tagged by the OS so that it knows what kind of resource each object represents.

4.5.3 Secondary storage

We mentioned that there typically was no secondary storage on the Palm OS platform. From the standpoint of most applications that is true. However, other developments in the area of small handheld devices have led to a requirement for a more general storage mechanism. As of Palm OS release 4.0, support is included for a different category of memory device. These devices are assumed to have an organization that is more typical of common secondary storage devices. One popular model comes initialized with a file system that mimics that found on a DOS disk drive. The intended use of these modules is that they would be written to by another device, such as a PC, and then inserted into the Palm OS hardware device for later access. A user can store many files on a PC and load individual files onto memory modules that can later be inserted in a Palm system for access. In order that the PC need not have special software to access regular Palm memory modules, a file organization that is already supported by many OSs was used. Because of the ubiquitous nature of the Microsoft OSs, virtually all OSs today support those file formats for removable secondary storage devices.

FIGURE 4.7
An Alert box form.

4.6 BASIC INPUT AND OUTPUT

4.6.1 Hiding hardware details

The Palm OS was designed so that to a programmer the system looked like a conventional computer system as much as possible. A good example of this is in the handling of user input. It is normal for an OS to hide many of the details of user keyboard input. Generally there are at least two levels of abstraction:

1. Some programs want to see every keystroke. A good example would be a screen-oriented text editor like the UNIX text editor program vi. Such application programs interpret every keystroke so that they can implement very powerful editing commands with only a few keystrokes. This is known as a **raw interface.**
2. A second level of abstraction is available for applications that only want to read an entire line of input. The OS will provide various editing operations of the line as the user enters it. These might include character or string insertion or deletion, duplication of the previous line, backspace and strikeover, and so on. The program only sees completed input lines. This is known as a **cooked interface.**

Programmers used to writing in C will know the cooked keyboard interface is exposed as the function **stdin** (standard input). C libraries also usually provide a cooked style of interface for printer output called **stdout** (standard output) and a similar output interface for reporting errors called **stderr** (standard error). Originally, these output streams were designed to be directed to a hardcopy printer, but later implementations usually directed the stdout to the terminal screen instead of a real printer. The Palm OS is similar. It provides all three of these interfaces. The unusual thing about the handheld hardware, of course, is that it normally has no keyboard. This point serves to reinforce the utility of these abstractions. The user may be using the stylus to select character icons from a display on the handheld screen that looks like a keyboard or to write free form characters in the Graffiti area. The OS hides all those details and allows a program written in C to use stdin, ignore those hidden details, and accept an entire line of input without worrying about the details of how it was actually entered. When an actual keyboard is attached to a handheld unit it will allow the user to enter commands through the keys and the application program will never know the difference.

4.7 DISPLAY MANAGEMENT

4.7.1 The hardware

The standard display is a touch-sensitive LCD panel with a resolution of 160×160 **pixels** (picture elements or dots). A high-resolution display may have up to 480×320 pixels. The original models were only black on white but later models could display a four-level grayscale. Newer models are capable of displaying color with 2, 4, 64, 256, or 65 K colors. As with early PCs, the screen is refreshed directly from memory rather than being a device that must be written to with I/O instructions. As the actual displays vary, it is strongly recommended that applications access the display by using standard system calls and leave the hardware details to the OS. This is a typical abstraction that an OS makes so that applications do not have to deal with hardware details and are thus more portable.

4.7.2 Top-level GUI elements

The Palm OS has a GUI that is based on the concept of **forms.** These forms are similar to what is called a window in other GUI OSs, but they normally fill the entire screen. A form is typically a view of some portion of an application's data. For example, an address book application might have one form to view the list of addressees, another for editing a single address, and so on. The OS also supports an element called a window, but in this case the term **window** refers to an object that can be operated on by the system's drawing features. There may be windows that are not forms. These are used to create dialog boxes, for example. All forms are windows. In most cases the application will not draw directly on the windows. All manipulation will be done as a result of the definition of **GUI elements**—such as buttons or menus—or as a result of system calls made by the application. For example, the OS knows how to draw a button and how to handle a tap on the button by the user. The application only needs to define the label on the button, tell the OS where to place the button on the form, and what numeric code to provide the application when the user touches the screen over the button. This is presented to the application as an event. The application will only use the low-level drawing facilities if it wants to provide animation, for example, or if it wants to define its own additional GUI elements that the OS does not provide. These application-specific GUI elements are known in the Palm OS as **gadgets** or **objects.** (In other OSs they are often called widgets.) They are not "objects" as that term is used in programming. They are merely date structures that may have certain subroutines associated with events such as the completion of a field or the "tapping" of a button on a form on the screen.

4.7.3 Special form types

There are two special types of forms that do not fill the entire screen. The first of these is an **alert box.** A typical alert box might be a confirmation of a record deletion as was shown in Figure 4.7. The alert box is displayed by an application. The application requires that this box holds the focus until the user acknowledges the box. This is called a **modal form.** In some cases there is a single button the user must touch to acknowledge the box. In the case shown in Figure 4.7 there are two buttons and the user selects one of them by touching them with the stylus. Then the OS removes the box from the screen. The other special thing about this form is that the application does not have to create the form specifically—it merely fills in a structure that defines the text that appears in the box and on the buttons and asks the OS to create the box. The OS will handle all the events such as the taps on the buttons.

The second type of special form is a **progress dialog.** This form is similar to the alert box but is more dynamic. It is intended for use when an application is doing some lengthy processing such as a file transfer. There is a separate call that the application can make that will change the text that is currently being displayed. This is normally an indicator about the progress of the application. If the application is sending a 100 KB, file and has sent 50 KB, it might draw a bar that is 50% colored.

TABLE 4.2 **Palm OS Controls**

System-Defined Controls	
Control	**Details**
Button	Invokes a function (e.g., "Display")
Push button	"Radio buttons"
Selector trigger	Opens a specialized dialog box (e.g., for date input)
Increment arrow	Varies a value in an associated control
Checkbox	True/false–On/off
Pop-up list	Invoked by a pop-up trigger
Pop-up trigger	Opens pop-up list (downward pointing triangle ▼)
List	A pull-down list (e.g., in a menu)
Menu	Access less frequently used functions
Text box	Basic data entry box
Scroll bar	When the data overflows the display area of a form

This gives the user an indication of the time left to finish the operation. There is normally a button that the user can press, for example, to cancel the operation. Watching for a click on this button is one of the real-time tasks that the OS can do for an application without interrupting the application flow and still provide a timely response to the button. This relieves the application from having to check for the button click in its processing loop.

4.7.4 Lower-level GUI controls

The Palm OS GUI controls are not traditional objects. Having no methods or properties, they are merely data structures. For a given type of control there are various OS calls that can be made that will cause them to be displayed. When the user touches one of the controls on the screen there will be an **event** generated that will be passed to the application. The application will receive the event and execute the appropriate code.

Table 4.2 shows the controls that the Palm OS supports and some examples or other details about the control.

4.8 EVENT-DRIVEN PROGRAMS

Under the Palm OS, most applications are written to be interactive. They do not generally process batches of data like a payroll application on a mainframe or respond to complete individual requests like a server. Instead, they focus on the user's immediate interactive inputs. These applications are therefore organized in a special way. When a Palm application runs it first initializes its files (if any) and then goes into a loop in which it checks for events that are being given to it by the OS. An example is shown in Figure 4.8.

```
static void EventLoop(void)
{
  UInt16 error;
  EventType event;
  do
    {
    EvtGetEvent(&event, evtWaitForever);
    PreprocessEvent(&event);
    if(! SysHandleEvent (&event))
        if(! MenuHandleEvent(NULL,&event,&error))
           if(! ApplicationHandleEvent(&event))
              FrmDispatchEvent(&event);
    #ifEMULATION_LEVEL != EMULATION_NONE
        ECApptDBValidate (ApptDB);
    #endif
    }
  while (event.eType != appStopEvent);
}
```

FIGURE 4.8
An event-driven program main loop.

If there are no events for it to process then it tells the OS that it wants to WAIT for more events. When another event occurs the OS will pass the information to the application as a return from one of the calls to check for various classes of events. The user has started the application for some specific task—perhaps to look up a phone number in the contact file. Until the user gives the program a specific task the program does not have anything to do so it merely waits. The user will use the menus and other controls in the form to tell the application what to do. Perhaps a name is being keyed into a text box. As each character is keyed the application will get an event signal and will update the display to reflect the name that is being keyed.

For many of the controls defined in a form, the application is able to specify actions to be taken such that the OS can do much of the work without the involvement of the application. For example, the OS knows how to automatically increment a value in a control with an increment arrow. For other buttons the application may need to do special processing. Each control that the application defines may result in event codes being passed to the application when that control is touched. Consider, for example, the confirmation dialog shown in Figure 4.7. When this control is displayed and the user touches one of the buttons, the application will be sent an event. The value sent to the application will identify which control the event was from and which button was tapped.

Because the operation of the touch screen is asynchronous with the application (i.e., screen events can happen at any time while the program is running), several events can happen faster than the application can process them. The OS therefore has to maintain a queue of the events that have happened but that have not been given to the application yet. This queue is maintained in priority order so that more important events can be processed first by the application.

A few such events are system-related events. For example, events are sent to the application when the power is being turned off (i.e., the system is going into the low-power sleep mode). In this case the application will suspend any other operations such as communication to another system.

4.9 SUMMARY

In this chapter, we discussed the features and concepts of a simple modern OS—the Palm Operating System™ developed by Palm, Inc. This OS was developed for small handheld devices. Although this is a single-user system, it can concurrently run some OS processes and a small number of applications. Thus, it supports a limited number of concurrently executing tasks, making it a simple multitasking system.

We started this chapter with an overview of the Palm OS and discussed some of the unusual hardware characteristics of the handheld computers that use the Palm OS. These special characteristics force the choices of some of the decisions made in the Palm OS design. Then we discussed the nature of multitasking and how an OS works to schedule application processes and OS tasks. We then discussed memory management, and the different types of memory storage supported by the OS. Because the Palm platform does not normally have a hard disk, it uses a part of memory called storage RAM to keep persistent data. When power is turned off and the system is in sleep mode, storage RAM maintains its contents. We discussed how memory is divided into chunks, and how the OS locates different chunks in memory tables and uses compaction to manage the free memory.

Then came an overview of the organization of files in the Palm OS, followed by coverage of the basic I/O functions that the Palm OS provides. These include the Graffiti input system that allows users to input freehand text. We next described the display subsystem and simple GUI programming, followed by a brief discussion of event-oriented programming, a paradigm used in most Palm applications. Next, we described the design of a typical Palm OS application.

In the next chapter we move on to an OS more complex than the Palm OS. It generally handles multiple programs running concurrently at the application level. It is correspondingly more complex and contains more system overhead.

BIBLIOGRAPHY

AMX/FS File System User's Guide. Vancouver, BC, Canada: KADAK Products Ltd., 1995.

AMX User's Guide. Vancouver, BC, Canada: KADAK Products Ltd., 1996.

Exploring Palm OS: Palm OS File Formats, Document Number 3120-002. Sunnyvale, CA: PalmSource, Inc., 2004.

Exploring Palm OS: System Management, Document Number 3110-002. Sunnyvale, CA: PalmSource, Inc., 2004.

Palm OS® Programmer's API Reference, Document Number 3003-004. Sunnyvale, CA: Palm, Inc., 2001.

Palm OS Programmer's Companion, Volume 1, Document Number 3120-002. Sunnyvale, CA: Palm, Inc., 2001.

Palm OS Programmer's Companion, Volume 2, Communications, Document Number 3005-002. Sunnyvale, CA: Palm, Inc., 2001.

Rhodes, N., & J. McKeehan, *Palm Programming: The Developer's Guide,* 1st ed., Sebastopol, CA: O'Reilly & Associates, Inc., 2000.

SONY Clié, Personal Entertainment Organizer. Sony Corporation, 2001.

WEB RESOURCES

http://www.accessdevnet.com (ACCESS Linux Platform Development Suite)

http://www.freewarepalm.com (free Palm software)

http://oasis.palm.com/dev/palmos40-docs/memory%20architecture.html

http://www.palm.com (Palm home page)

http://www.pocketgear.com/en_US/html/index.jsp (software for mobile devices)

http://en.wikipedia.org/wiki/Graffiti_2 (article on Graffiti 2)

REVIEW QUESTIONS

4.1 Since the Palm processor can only have one program on the display at a time, why does the system need a multiprocessing OS?

4.2 Outside of a slow processor and fairly small memories compared to modern systems, what is the most unusual part of the basic hardware design that the OS is based on?

4.3 Is the Palm OS a microkernel or a monolithic kernel?

4.4 What does the Palm OS use a real-time kernel for?

4.5 What is the basic logic flow of most applications?

4.6 Why is memory allocated to a process accessed indirectly through the MPT?

4.7 How does the OS track free memory?

4.8 As is typical in much of information system technology, the developers of the Palm OS overloaded a perfectly good term with a different meaning. What does the Palm OS documentation mean when it refers to a "database?"

4.9 Considering that the Palm platforms do not have much memory, why do they typically not use compression on the databases?

4.10 The Palm OS gives the programmer several abstractions for I/O so that the application programmer did not have to worry about the hardware details. What were some of the abstractions that were mentioned?

4.11 True or false? The screens are memory mapped rather than handled by I/O instructions so most applications directly move data to the screen area in memory.

4.12 Briefly describe event-driven programming.

4.13 How does an application programmer draw the forms that he wants to display on the screen?

Chapter 5

A Single-User Multitasking/ Multithreading Operating System

In this chapter:

5.1 INTRODUCTION

The Mac OS represents an interesting level in our spiral evolution of OSs because it has gone through a series of evolutions itself. It was initially intended to be an OS for an affordable personal computer that had a GUI. At the time this was revolutionary. There had been other systems that used a GUI, but they were considerably more expensive. But other than the GUI, in most ways the first release of the Mac OS was less sophisticated than the Palm OS that was discussed in Chapter 4. However, as time went by, pressure from other systems caused an evolution in the Mac hardware and the Mac OS, and at the end of its line it was roughly as powerful as the multiuser

Linux OS that we will discuss in the next chapter. The difference was that Linux was designed from the outset to support multiple concurrent users, and this made some significant differences in its structure and design. So we discuss the Mac OS as an intermediate step between the Palm OS, which was intended for a very sparse environment with only a single user, multitasking but no user multithreading, limited screen space, and no secondary storage, and Linux, an OS intended for a multiuser, multitasking, multithreading environment with large secondary and tertiary storage and a GUI that supported large screens with overlapping windows.

Because the Mac OS went through several profound changes during its history we use a different approach in this chapter than we did in the other spiral chapters.

We start this chapter in Section 5.1 with an overview of the Mac OS and some background about the underpinnings of the original kernel. After this short introduction we follow the releases of the Mac OS in Sections 5.3 through 5.12 and describe the additional features in each release. This is because the Mac OS began with such humble origins, being little better than CP/M in most features, and ultimately evolving into a full-featured, modern OS capable of supporting multiple users and multiple processes as completely as the Linux system discussed in the next chapter. Following the evolution of the Mac OS is in itself a bit of a mini-spiral approach. We stop short of the Mac OS X release in favor of describing an alternate system in the next chapter, Linux. We will say only enough about it to position it with regard to the other major PC OSs on the market today. We conclude this chapter in Section 5.13 with a summary.

5.2 THE ORIGIN OF THE MACINTOSH COMPUTER

In 1973 a revolutionary computer system called the ALTO was designed at the Xerox Palo Alto Research Center—aka Xerox PARC. This computer was never sold, but over 200 were given to universities and other research institutions. They cost about $32,000[1] each to build, and included revolutionary technology such as a forerunner of the GUI interface we know today, a type of Ethernet and a mouse, among other things. A later system, the Xerox Star, contained many of the same features. It retailed for $16,600.[2] This was still too costly for a computer intended to be used by only one person and the system was not a commercial success. However, these systems were seen by some other visionary pioneers of the personal computer business, and they began a drive to produce affordable systems that incorporated these ideas. Among those pioneers was Steven Jobs, whose Apple Computer systems had been among the first commercially successful personal computers.

Apple first developed the Apple Lisa, which retailed for $10,000.[3] Like the Xerox Star, it was also a commercial failure. But Apple persevered, and eventually introduced the Macintosh personal computer in 1984,[4] which retailed for $2,500, in the

---

[1] $157,000 in 2007 dollars.

[2] $42,000 in 2007 dollars.

[3] Almost $21,000 in 2007 dollars.

[4] Over $5,000 in 2007 dollars.

same range as an IBM PC. The Mac seemed more affordable than the Lisa to average people, and the GUI interface made it a very usable system, so it was an immediate success. The Macintosh hardware used the Motorola 68000 family of CPUs.

5.3 THE MACINTOSH OS—SYSTEM 1

The initial release of the Mac OS was known as System 1. System 1 had several characteristics that were typical of OSs of the time. It also had a few unique features because of its GUI.

5.3.1 The GUI

System 1 had a desktop, windows, icons, a mouse, menus, and scrollbars. See Figure 5.1. The desktop had a trash can icon that could be used to delete items by dragging and dropping them on the icon. These are all metaphors and features we take for granted today, but they were fairly revolutionary for the time. Unlike the Palm OS, the OS design assumed that the screen was large enough to hold more than one window or to show the desktop with a window that did not take up the entire screen. The screens were only black and white and only had a resolution of 520×342 pixels, so the graphics were very limited. Nonetheless, it was a GUI and many users found it friendlier than a command-line interface, especially novice users. Compare this with the command-line prompt in CP/M, which merely said:

A>

And awaited input from the user with no hint of what to do.

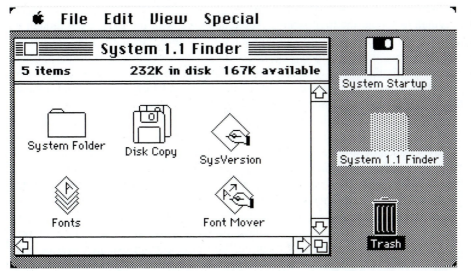

FIGURE 5.1
The Mac OS GUI.

Source: All of the MAC OS screen shots in this chapter were made with the Mini vMac emulator. It is available at http://minivmac.sourceforge.net/.

The GUI is probably the most significant thing about the Mac OS, not because it was so original or so well done, but because of what it *did not have to support.* In the rest of the world the OSs typically evolved from legacy systems that originally had command-line interfaces (as with DEC, UNIX, IBM, etc.). The applications were standalone programs invoked through entry of one-line commands on an interface called a command line. These interfaces simulated the way a typewriter attached to a computer worked. So they were designed around keyboard use and had little or no mouse support. Each application team was free to use whatever key they wished for any given function. So to invoke a spelling check, a word processor might use the F7 key while a spreadsheet program might use the F12 key. Even worse, there was no dominant package in most application areas, so the WordPerfect word processing program might use one key to print and a competitor program like WordStar might use a different key for the same function. For each individual application there were keyboard templates available that showed what every function key did, when used alone or when used with any combination of Shift, CTRL, and ALT keys!

With the Mac there were no legacy applications. From the outset there was a key sequence assigned to the Print function and a new application had no reason to deviate from that assignment. As a result, Apple was able to truthfully advertise the ease of learning to use software on a Mac. For example, suppose a user had mastered a word processing application on a MAC. If that user understood how a spreadsheet tool worked, then that user would be able to easily use a spreadsheet program on the MAC because all the standard functions would be invoked just as they were on the word processing program. Even today this problem persists in Windows and Linux applications. The point is that one should not underestimate the impact of a requirement for backward compatibility—something the Mac did not have.

5.3.2 Single Tasking

In order to deliver an affordable product, the early Macintosh had to run with very limited memory since it was still quite expensive. As a result, Apple's developers decided to forego the multitasking Apple had used with the Lisa. Even though an application window probably did not take up the entire screen, the Mac OS did not initially allow more than one program to run at the same time, even for background printing. To allow some parallel functionality, the OS included Desk Accessories, which included functions such as a Calculator, Alarm Clock, system Control Panel, and Notepad, but these were carefully limited so that they would not use too much RAM. They were implemented as "device drivers" rather than separate programs, and could open a single window. Figure 5.2 shows how primitive these were by today's standards. Figure 5.3 shows the **Control Panel,** which allowed the user to change many system settings. The system had an application called **finder** that was used to find files in the system. The finder window was the command processor that in most OSs was a command-line console. So it was also the mechanism for running other programs. The finder window is visible in Figure 5.1. The System 1 version of finder was referred to as a single application finder. Since only one application program was running at a time (not counting the Desk Accessories), there was no need for protecting one program from reading or changing another program in memory,

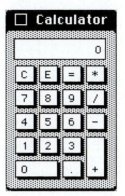

FIGURE 5.2
The Calculator
desktop accessory.

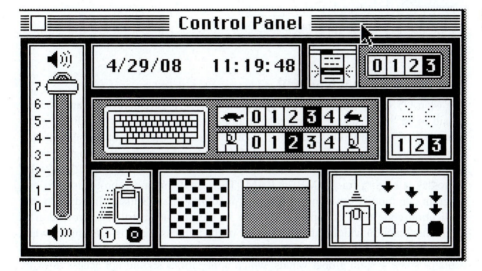

FIGURE 5.3
The Control Panel.

so the OS had no such scheme. System 1 also did not even protect the OS from the applications. This was also true of most other OSs available at the time.

5.3.3 Secondary storage

As with the CP/M system discussed in Chapter 3, programs were kept on a single floppy disk drive and loaded into RAM only when they were to be executed. The disk system that was available on the early Macs was only 400 Kbytes. This is a small enough space that it was fairly easy to find files, so all files were kept in a single directory. Still, the developers of the OS realized that the idea of grouping like files together was useful, so the system showed **folders** on the disk. As with CP/M, however, these folders were only a simulation. Each file directory entry could be marked with a folder name, and the system would allow the user to look inside the folder, essentially listing all the files marked with that folder name. As a result, it was also not possible to nest folders within folders.

FIGURE 5.4
System 1 memory
layout.

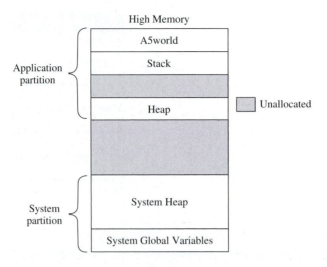

5.3.4 Memory management

The Mac OS has a single address space, as seen in Figure 5.4.[5] This architecture is said to be "flat," which means that at any time any instruction can directly reference all of memory. Other designs of the era used a more complex scheme that allowed large amounts of RAM but limited the addressing such that a program could only address segments of 64 KB with any instruction. The 68000 CPU has 24-bit addresses, allowing for 16 MB of RAM. There is no memory protection, so any program can modify anything in memory, including the OS itself. In addition, the application code runs in supervisor mode so there is no instruction protection to limit what the application can do. The size of the address space is determined when the OS boots. The lowest part of RAM is occupied by a **system partition.** This area contains some system global values, which applications should not access directly. Rather, they should use the OS APIs to read and manipulate any system data. But with no memory protection or instruction protection, there is nothing to prevent an application from taking a shortcut and accessing such information directly. In the early days of personal computers, application writers would often take such shortcuts and tried to justify their actions in the name of performance.

An **application partition** is allocated from the top of memory downward. The layout of an application partition is seen in Figure 5.5. At the top is a fixed size datablock called the **A5world,** which contains the application's static data and some metadata about the application. The name arose because the Mac OS loaded the A5 register of the CPU with a pointer to this area so that the application would know where it was located in memory and could access its global data by addressing relative to the A5 register. Below this is the stack, with the "top" of the stack growing downward. The heap grows from the bottom of the application partition upward and

---

[5] The initial releases of the Mac OS did not support multiple processes. That came later.

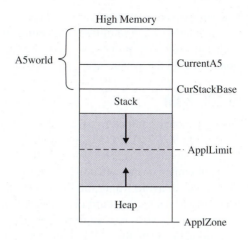

FIGURE 5.5
Application memory partition.

includes code segments. So one problem that the OS has to manage is to make sure that these two areas do not run into one another.

An upper limit on the size of the heap is set for an application when it starts. Growth of the heap is controlled by the memory allocation routines, so they always check to make sure that a requested allocation will not exceed the limit. But the stack is automatically maintained by the hardware. As subroutines and functions are called and return, data are pushed onto and popped off of the stack. Since many applications call multiple levels of subroutines, sometimes recursively, this stack tends to grow as the program runs. But there is no hardware protection against the stack's extending below the limit. Instead, a **stack sniffer** subsystem runs during the interval of the monitor vertical retrace (about 60 times a second) that checks the stack level against the limit.

A big problem for the designers of the Macintosh was how to make optimum use of the 128 KB of RAM. In some ways this was a large amount of memory. Other personal computers of the same era had 16 or 64 KB of RAM. But the Mac was intended to have a GUI, and such interfaces take a good deal of RAM. As was mentioned above, the developers decided to limit the Mac to run only one program at a time. Their main concern appears to have been memory fragmentation—repeated allocation and deallocation of memory leads to many small, isolated areas of memory, which cannot be used because they are too small, even though the total free memory may be enough to satisfy a particular request. In order to avoid fragmentation of heap memory the Mac OS supports relocatable memory blocks. These are accessed indirectly via a pointer into a nonrelocatable **master pointer block.** The Palm OS discussed in the last chapter uses a similar mechanism. The relocatable blocks are compacted from time to time in a garbage collection process. Relocatable blocks can also be marked purgeable, which means the system may free them during compaction if the free memory space falls below a predetermined limit. Pointers were initially only 24 bits long, but were stored in a 32-bit field for anticipated future growth in the processors. So the top 8 bits (of the 32) were often used for flags marking blocks as relocatable, temporary, purgeable, and so on.

The OS implemented two areas with this scheme: the **system heap** used by the OS, and the **application heap.** As long as only one program was run, the system worked well. Since the application heap was erased when the program quit, fragmentation was minimized. Unfortunately, as was mentioned above, the OS provided no memory protection, and crashes caused by application program errors manipulating the system heap were not uncommon.

5.3.5 ROM

Most personal computers used only a small amount of ROM to contain code for Power-On Self-Test (**POST**) and some Basic Input/Output System (**BIOS**) routines, typically about 8 KB. The Mac OS ROM was significantly bigger (roughly 64 KB) and held much of the actual OS itself. The initial purpose of having so much code in ROM was to avoid filling the limited storage available on a floppy disk, given that the early Macs had no hard disk. It also helped the system to boot faster since that code did not have to be read from the floppy drive. Only the 1991 Mac Classic model was bootable using the ROM alone. This architecture also helped to ensure that only Apple computers and licensed clones could run the Mac OS.

5.3.6 Incremental releases

As with most OSs, between major releases there are incremental releases. These releases are often given fractional numbers. They are released for various reasons: speedup of some specific function such as the loading of the OS, bug fixes, and occasionally some new feature or application that is scheduled for some later major release that is falling behind schedule. In the Mac OS System 1 there was one such release, 1.1, that did a bit of all of these.

5.4 SYSTEM 2

System 2 was theoretically a major release, but there were no features that were significant from a theoretical point of view. The Finder was somewhat faster. Certain icon/commands were eliminated, and icons for creating a New Folder and for Shutdown of the system were added. Floppy disks could now be ejected merely by dragging their icons to the Trash, instead of selecting the Eject Disk command and then dragging the icon to the Trash. A Choose Printer desk accessory was added, which allowed a user to select a default printer. This utility would later become the **Chooser,** a utility for accessing shared resources, such as printers, modems, and disk volumes hosted on other systems and made available through a network.

5.4.1 GUI

Users of the Mac liked the GUI and the ability to cut and paste information from one application to another. But this meant cutting the data from one program, stopping that program, starting the new program, and then pasting the data into it—an operation that usually took minutes. Each new Macintosh model included more RAM than the previous models, and the Macintosh 512K (aka the Fat Mac), contained four times the RAM of the original Mac. This was enough to support some form of multitasking. It was first implemented in the **Switcher** program. Switcher allowed a user to start several programs. The user could then switch between these applications by clicking an icon on the menu bar. The current application would horizontally slide out of view, and the next one would slide in. When a user switched to one of the running programs it was said to "**have the focus.**" The user could thus cut and paste between applications in seconds instead of minutes.

5.4.2 Multitasking

Switcher created a number of fixed slots in RAM into which applications were loaded. The Switcher program allocated a separate heap for each application that the user started, subject, obviously, to the availability of RAM. When the user toggled from one process to another the Switcher could perform a context switch and fix the OS memory management data so that the OS would begin working with the new application. Since there was no memory or instruction protection the Switcher could tweak the OS memory structures to affect a switch. However, this was very limited multitasking, somewhat like the Palm OS in that there was still only one process running at any one time. The user could switch from one process to another, but while a process did not have the focus, that process was not actually running. Despite its awkwardness, this approach worked with the existing system's memory management scheme, as programs did not need to be changed to work with Switcher. The changes were also transparent to the OS kernel. A typical memory layout with multiple processes in the system is shown in Figure 5.6.

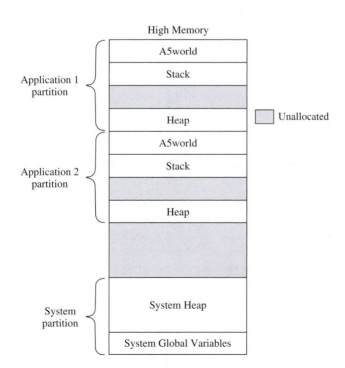

FIGURE 5.6

System 2 "Switcher" memory layout.

5.5 SYSTEM 3

5.5.1 Hierarchical File System

Disk drives were getting bigger and users tended to fill them up then as they do now, wanting to have quick access to all their information. This meant that the number of files was growing much larger, so it was getting hard for a user to keep track of files. So a new file system design was released known as the Hierarchical File System (HFS). It replaced the old Macintosh File System (MFS). Folders were now actual subdirectories instead of just tags in the directory entries, and folders could contain other folders. It was so much more useful that it came to be called the Mac OS Standard File System (to distinguish it from a later extended version). The directory entries contained timestamps showing when the file was created and when it was last modified, the file type and creator codes, a file name of up to 32 characters, and other file metadata. (The creator code told the OS what application had created the file.) The free space was tracked by a bitmap and the directories are stored as B-trees. These ideas will be further explained in Chapters 12 and 13.

There were a few bug fix releases until the next real advance in the OS capabilities.

5.5.2 Networks

Local area networks (LANs) were becoming extremely popular. They allowed shared access to expensive devices such as large disk drives, high-end laser printers, modem pools, and other exotic devices such as microfilm output. They also facilitated communication through shared files and directories on central servers. So with System 3.3 Apple added support for **AppleShare,** a proprietary file-sharing protocol. The protocol stack also included proprietary technology at other layers: **AppleTalk** at the network layer and **LocalTalk** at the data link and physical layers. Now the Chooser utility took on much more importance than just selecting the default printer. LaserWriter printers could be directly connected to the network and shared by several users. The Macintosh began to be viewed as a powerful desktop publishing system and these printers were a large factor in that view and in the general success of the Mac product line.

5.6 SYSTEM 4

System 4 was introduced with the Macintosh SE and Macintosh II. At this stage in the development of OS technology, new releases were often required just to support new models of a computer. System 4.1 added support for disk drives larger than 32 MB.

Different references disagree about when the Mac OS supported a version of finder that could launch multiple applications. Most likely this is because the naming of the releases was somewhat confusing. The main software had one number, the finder had another, and the MultiFinder (to be discussed shortly) had another. For example, one reference[6] lists System Software 5.0 (System 4.2, Finder 6.0, and

---

[6] http://en.wikipedia.org/wiki/Mac_OS_history

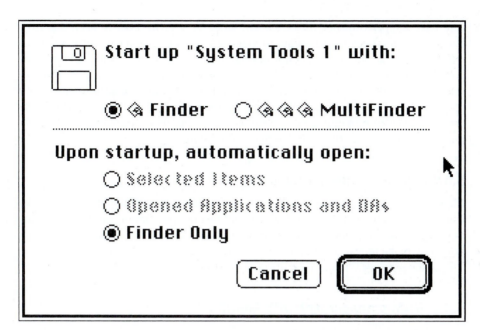

FIGURE 5.7
MultiFinder.

MultiFinder 1.0), while another reference[7] states that System 5 was never released. In addition, because MultiFinder was new and Apple was not certain that all existing programs could operate correctly under it, Finder continued to be distributed with the OS, compounding the release naming issue.

5.6.1 MultiFinder

The consensus seems to be, however, that System 4.2 implemented MultiFinder—users could switch between Finder, which supported only one program at a time, and MultiFinder, which could support multiple programs. See Figure 5.7. MultiFinder extended the OS significantly. Unlike Switcher, which merely switched the OS from running one application to running another, MultiFinder allowed each program to keep running, giving each application CPU time. Unlike OSs, which we will study later, the Mac OS did not set hard limits on how long a process could continue running without switching to another process. The technique used in the Mac OS is known as **cooperative multitasking.** With this technique a process can run as long as it wants to. If the process makes a call to the OS that the OS cannot service immediately, such as a disk read, then it will make the process wait—a mechanism known as **blocking.** When a process makes such a blocking call, then the OS will add the blocked process to a queue of processes that are waiting for something and will switch to running another process. If a process makes no blocking calls then it can run as long as it likes. In order for all processes to give a quick response to user requests, they all need some CPU time. So if one process runs for too long it

---

[7] http://www.macos.utah.edu/documentation/operating_systems/mac_os_x.html

can make the performance of the system seem uneven. In order to keep this from happening, all processes are supposed to make a special system call fairly often that tells the OS that the process is not through but that it is voluntarily relinquishing control and is ready to run again. This allows other processes to have a fair share of the CPU time. Of course, some vendors want their software to appear to be the best responding, so they don't call that routine often enough. In other cases a software error may cause a program to go into a loop and never yield control or make a blocking call. In these cases the system will essentially freeze.

5.6.2 The GUI under MultiFinder

MultiFinder provided a way for windows from different applications to coexist by using a layering model. Now that there could be multiple running applications, they might each have multiple windows open on the desktop at the same time. When a program got the focus, all of its windows were brought forward together in one layer. This was necessary for compatibility with existing windowing APIs.

5.6.3 RAM management with MultiFinder

MultiFinder also provided a way for applications to communicate their memory requirements to the OS, so that MultiFinder could allocate RAM to each program according to its need. Unfortunately, the amount specified would not be enough for some tasks, so the user was given an interface to override this number. This strongly went against the Apple theory that users should be kept away from such technical information. In this case their theory was correct, since users often had no idea how much memory a program might really need. One program was often given much more memory than it really needed and another program was given much too little. As a result, the starved application would perform poorly. When multiple applications are running, the management of RAM is usually much more complex than when a single application is running. But when MultiFinder was being developed, a key consideration was that programs that ran under the single Finder should work without change under MultiFinder. So the memory architecture is very similar, just slightly more complicated. With one application running the architecture looks like that in Figure 5.1. When several applications are running the architecture looks like that in Figure 5.3. As execution shifts from one application to another the OS will change the contents of certain system variables to reflect the sizes and locations of the application partition and its pieces for the new application. This change is known as a **context switch.** As we will see later, with modern OSs a context switch is often much more complicated than this.

5.7 SYSTEM 5

As was stated above, some references say that System 5 was never released and others say it was released only for a short time. In either case there is nothing significant about it for the purposes of studying OS evolution.

5.8 SYSTEM 6

In the eyes of many observers, System 6 was the first true upgrade of the Mac OS.[8] RAM was getting cheaper and larger and users always wanted more of it. So System 6 began the migration to supporting the Mac in the true 32-bit memory addressing modes that had appeared with the Motorola 68020 CPU. These 32-bit addresses allowed the Mac OS to address up to 4 GB of RAM. Earlier versions of the Mac OS had used the lower 24 bits for addressing, and the upper 8 bits for flags, which indicated, for example, that the block pointed to was marked as "locked," "purge-able," or as a "resource." This had been an effective solution for earlier hardware with limited RAM, but became a liability later. Apple referred to code that used the 24 + 8-bit addressing model as being not **32-bit clean,** and suggested that developers remove such code from their applications. As was noted before, much of the Mac OS was in ROM. Unfortunately, much of that ROM code was not 32-bit clean, and so older Macs could not be migrated to this new mode. The new mode required new versions of the hardware. The change to 32-bit addressing mode made for a lot of compatibility issues that linger even into today's versions of the Mac OS. The OS maintains the capability of running applications in a 24-bit mode, though it is much slower than the 32-bit mode. So Apple was now feeling the pinch of supporting legacy applications.

In the early part of the PC era, developers still saw the RAM in a system as a very tight resource and would go to great lengths to save a byte or two here and there. As time went by it was often found that such savings had a very negative impact later. Indeed, the **Y2K bug** (Year 2000)[9] was another example of this sort of problem caused by the desire save a few bytes of RAM by shortening the format of the year part of dates to the last two bytes. The end of the century was 20 years away and developers assumed that the systems they were developing would not still be in use by then anyway. When the last year of the century rolled around, systems that had stored dates as only two digits would make incorrect conclusions, calculating that a date in the year "00" (i.e., 2000) came before a date with the year "99" (i.e., 1999.) The Mac OS was apparently designed from the start to avoid the Y2K problem, though Apple never officially certified any system release before System 7 as being Y2K compliant.

5.9 SYSTEM 7

System 7 was the biggest change to the system software up to that time. It continued the migration of the Mac OS to full 32-bit addressing and improved its handling of color graphics, networking, and **multitasking,** and it introduced a form of **virtual memory.**

Many features that had been available as options in earlier versions of the Mac OS were integrated into System 7. This release dropped the single program version

---

[8] http://en.wikipedia.org/wiki/Mac_OS_history

[9] http://en.wikipedia.org/wiki/Y2k

of Finder, eliminating the Finder versus MultiFinder issue. Cooperative multitasking thus became the normal mode of operation of the system. Networking via Apple-Talk and file sharing via AppleShare were built into the operating system, instead of being optional.

5.9.1 The GUI

System 7 had several usability improvements, many in the area of the GUI. A menu was added to the right end of the menu bar called the Application menu. It showed a list of running programs and allowed users to switch among them. Next to the Application menu was the Help menu. Users could now drag and drop—a block of text could be dragged from one program to another with the mouse instead of having to copy and paste. System 7's Finder finally utilized color features and made some interface elements look more three-dimensional. Other usability features were also added to the OS in the System 7 releases. WorldScript provided system-level support for languages besides English. Technologies such as AppleScript, a macro language for task automation; ColorSync, color management utilities; QuickTime multimedia software; and TrueType font management were also released. Over time, many of the features that we associate with modern GUIs were added to the Mac OS. For the most part we will not detail these features in each release. We will only note that the GUI was evolving in a piecemeal fashion and was becoming more usable over time.

5.9.2 Virtual memory

Sometimes a user wanted to run more programs than would fit into RAM at the same time. Or perhaps the program was used with a data file that was very large. For example, a word processor might normally fit fine in a small space if it was just being used to write interoffice memos. But if it was used to edit a large report it might require a great deal more RAM. When performance is poor because more memory is required but a larger memory is not available or is too expensive, then one solution is called **virtual memory,** or **VM.** VM is a technique that uses some space on a hard disk drive to simulate a larger primary memory. It requires extra memory management hardware support to work. Briefly, memory is divided into blocks known as **pages.** When a program starts running, only the first page of the program is brought into RAM. When the running program references a part of the program that is not yet in memory the hardware will cause an interrupt called a **page fault,** and the OS will read the missing page into RAM from the disk drive. This technique is discussed in greater detail in Chapter 11.

As was mentioned, special hardware is required in a computer system for the OS to be able to support VM. The computer must have a special **memory management unit** (**MMU**), which is capable of translating the **logical addresses** that are generated by the program running in the CPU and translating them into a **physical address** so that the pages of the program can be located anywhere in RAM. Apple's 68040- and 68030-based machines have a VM-capable MMU built into the CPU and can thus support VM with no additional hardware. A Macintosh II (68020-based) could have a special MMU coprocessor on its main logic board in place of the standard address management unit (AMU).[10] This MMU would also support VM.

VM was first implemented in the Mac OS with System 7. However, the virtual memory support was very preliminary and performed very poorly in many circumstances. The design of the OS Memory Manager used RAM in such a way that it caused excessive page faults under VM.[11] VM features that are commonly found in VM implementations of other OSs today—such as protected address spaces, memory mapped files, page locking, shared memory, and so on—were not present. Many of these were provided in later releases of the Mac OS. As Apple gained better understanding of the workings of VM and modified the behavior of certain portions of the OS, the system performance when running VM also improved.

5.9.3 A new CPU

Sometime around 1990 Apple formed an alliance with IBM and Motorola to develop a new processor family based on a combination of the IBM RS6000 architecture, the Motorola 68000, and the Intel PC line. It would be known as the PowerPC family, and it would determine Apple's hardware direction until 2006. The initial Mac with the PowerPC CPU was the Power Macintosh 6100, or the Performa 6100 series. Support for this processor family came in System 7.1.2. It required changes in the design of the Mac OS. This architecture was a RISC design, unlike the CISC design used in the Motorola 68000 family, so it represented a radical change in the code used by the CPU. It would have taken far too long to completely port an OS based on the 68000 architecture to a RISC architecture, so the design of the PowerPC architecture allowed it to emulate the 68000 CPUs.

A small piece of code dubbed a **nanokernel** managed the PowerPC CPU. It executed in supervisor mode and supplied low-level interfaces for hardware management to the rest of the system. The API for this nanokernel was restricted to system software and debuggers. A 68000 emulator was started by the nanokernel at system startup time. It only emulated a 68000 user-mode instruction set without emulating the MMU. This allowed for more universal compatibility. The OS was thus able to begin to run on the PowerPC-based systems almost immediately. However, emulation of the execution of a 68000 CPU on a PowerPC is significantly slower than execution of native PowerPC code. Programs could be compiled and linked to produce executable modules that contained both native 68000 code and native PowerPC code. This allowed a single version of the program to run on both older machines and newer machines. Such dual-mode programs were known as **fat binaries.** Switching between the two modes was done by a set of library routines called the **Code Fragment Manager.** Over time, more and more of the OS was modified to include native PowerPC code as well as code that could still run on the 68000 family of systems.

The architecture of Apple computers was always proprietary. This had several side effects, some good and some bad. The main Apple system bus in the Macs was

---

[10] http://developer.apple.com/documentation/mac/Memory/Memory-152.html#HEADING152-0

[11] http://developer.apple.com/technotes/tn/tn1094.html

called NuBus. Since it was proprietary, Apple could exercise firm control over all hardware development. Thus, controllers were more likely to work on a Mac than on an ISA bus machine, and the drivers were more likely to work as well. On the other hand, it meant that there was less competition in this market, and users thus paid a higher price for hardware and software than they might have otherwise. Also, fewer vendors could afford to hire extra staff to develop hardware for additional buses. Around 1990 work began at Intel on a standardized bus called the Peripheral Component Interconnect bus or PCI. By 1993 the full specification was available, card vendors started creating I/O cards for this new bus, and system manufacturers began including them on the new motherboard designs. Apple found that this put them at a competitive disadvantage. Since the volumes vendors could sell in the PCI bus market were significantly greater than in the Apple NuBus market, the prices Apple had to pay for interface controllers was much higher, and this both cut into their hardware margins and made the price of their systems less competitive. Apple Computer therefore incorporated the PCI in the Power Macintosh computers it introduced in 1995. The System 7.5.2 release supported these new machines and thus had to incorporate new drivers and chip set support for the PCI bus and controllers.

5.9.4 Input/output enhancements

The Macs existed in a world that was being dominated by Intel-based PCs running Microsoft software. As a result, there was considerable pressure to provide bridges to that world. Certainly the networking support was evolving in that direction, and many Microsoft-oriented protocols were added to the Mac OS support. Another example was that System 7.1 introduced software called PC Exchange that could access MS-DOS formatted floppies. Earlier releases only supported Apple floppy disk formats. While floppies for the IBM PC and the Apple Mac were physically identical, they are used differently in two ways. First, the **low-level formatting** is different. New floppy disks in most cases do not have any predetermined number or size of sectors. A process called low-level formatting writes headers on the tracks that later will tell the hardware where each sector starts, what the track and sector numbers are for the sector, and how long it is. Different systems can use different numbers and sizes of sectors, and early on there were many competing formats, both with regard to the sizes of the media and the low-level formats. Today the sizes and formats have been fairly well standardized, but in the early 1990s there were still several competing standards. Once the low-level formatting is done the user can have the OS "format" the floppy at a higher level, creating an empty file system on the disk. In the case of the IBM and Apple systems the file systems were different as well as the low-level formatting. Adding to the Mac OS the ability to read and write MS-DOS floppies made Macs much more acceptable in the office world where easy exchange of files among users was a necessity.

By this time laptop systems were in frequent use, and they often included a **PC Card** slot. These were called **PCMCIA** slots at that time but were since renamed. PC Card slots allowed the insertion of a device that was not built in to the original laptop. Typical examples were network cards, controllers for external disk drives, disk drives themselves, and RAM cards. A RAM card could not be addressed as primary memory because the PCMCIA slot was on the I/O bus. So a common technique for dealing with such a card was to treat it as a special type of disk drive and create a file system on it. Because the floppy format was about the right size, these were often created with an MS-DOS-compatible file system since they could then also be used to move data from IBM-compatible PCs to Macs since the Mac OS could read these devices as well.

Because of general enhancements to the OS and the fat binaries for use with the PowerPC, the System 7 release was the first version of the Mac OS where a full installation was too large to fit on a 1.44 MB floppy disk. As a result, System 7.5 and later would not run from a floppy drive but required a hard disk on the computer.

5.10 SYSTEM 8

By this time Apple was adding Macs to their product line that were intended to be used as servers. In some cases these new systems had multiple CPUs. System 8 therefore added support for these new Mac multiple-CPU models. These machines would experience better performance in a server role. Support in modern OSs for such systems is called **symmetric multiprocessing,** or **SMP.** In such situations the OS runs on any CPU that is available.[12] This can pose special problems for the OS because it can literally be running on two or more CPUs at the same time. This means that it must take special precautions to prevent having two running instances manipulating any one data element at the same time. Since the Mac OS is primarily a single-user system, we will defer a more in-depth discussion of SMP to the next chapter on Linux, a system designed from the outset to support multiple users and run many other services.

Personal Web Sharing was also introduced in System 8. This facility allowed users to host Web pages on their computers.

5.10.1 Hierarchical File System Plus

As time went by, hard drives were getting larger and larger. Unfortunately, the file systems that were designed earlier for smaller drives used smaller pointers to save valuable space both on the disk and in RAM. These pointers could not address all the sectors on larger drives, so mechanisms were invented to extend the early file systems to larger drives. The first technique was to allocate multiple blocks instead of single sectors. For example, the Hierarchical File System that had been introduced with System 3 used a 16-bit pointer in its data structures. This meant that only 65,536 sectors could be directly addressed. With the standard sector size of

---

[12] In asymmetric multiprocessing the OS runs on only one of the CPUs while applications run on any CPU. While simpler than SMP, this technique is rarely used today since it limits the total system performance.

512 bytes, this meant that drives larger than 32 MB could not be supported. So HFS allowed allocation to be based on blocks of multiple sectors instead of single sectors. If the allocation was done on a basis of two sectors, then the same 16-bit pointer could address a 64 MB drive. This could be increased to any number of sectors that was a power of two. As with many techniques that Apple introduced into the Mac OS, this was not a new technique. It had been used in the earlier CP/M system. Allocation of larger blocks had some drawbacks. For example, on a 1 GB disk, even a 1-byte file would take up 16K of disk space. If many short files were used this became very inefficient, so a new file system had to be designed to address the larger drives efficiently. System 8.1 therefore included an improved version of the HFS called Hierarchical File System Plus, or HFS + . It used a 32-bit pointer and was capable of directly addressing a 4 GB drive. Using an allocation block of 32 sectors, it could support drives up to 128 GB. HFS + also allowed file names to be 255 bytes long.

5.10.2 Other hardware changes

Hardware continued to evolve in the computer field generally and in the Mac products specifically. System 8.1 was the last version to support 68K Macs since Motorola was putting all development efforts into the PowerPC line. System 8.6 added enhanced power management and improved support for new device classes such as USB and FireWire.

In order to allow a single application to use more than one CPU, System 8.6 introduced the idea of allowing an application to split itself into multiple independent threads (called tasks in the Mac OS), which the OS then schedules to run on multiple processors. We discuss this technique in-depth in Chapter 8. Apple modified the nanokernel to support this multithreading. It also added support for priorities to be associated with tasks. This allowed the application to designate some tasks as being more important than others. If a task had been waiting on some event that was finished and that task had a priority that was higher than the currently running task, the OS would preempt the CPU by stopping the running task and starting the higher priority task. We saw this feature in the Palm OS in the previous chapter. There was still no process preemption—the system still used cooperative multitasking between processes.

5.10.3 Unicode support

In System 8.5 Apple begain supporting an new mechanism for displaying other languages than English using a standard called **Unicode**—a worldwide character-encoding standard. Compared to older mechanisms for handling character and string data, Unicode simplifies making software work with other languages, a process called **localization.** By using Unicode to represent character and string data, a programmer can facilitate data exchange using a single binary file for every possible character code. Unicode supports numerous scripts used by languages around the world. It also covers many technical symbols and special characters.

Unicode can represent the vast majority of characters in computer use. It provides the following:

- Allows any combination of characters from any combination of languages in one document
- Standardizes script behavior
- Provides a standard algorithm for bidirectional text
- Defines mappings to legacy standards
- Defines semantics for each character
- Defines several different encodings of the character set, including UTF-7, UTF-8, UTF-16, and UTF-32

There are many different ways that Unicode can be used, and today most OSs support Unicode at one level or another. A more comprehensive discussion can be found at the website of the Unicode Consortium: http://www.unicode.org.

5.11 SYSTEM 9

By this point the development of the Mac OS had become very convoluted. Several major attempts at creating a new OS were started and either abandoned or sold off to companies that had partnered in their development. One major event was the acquisition of the NeXT Computer, and with it the NextStep OS. This OS would eventually evolve into the next release of the Mac OS, System X. In the meantime, releases of the Mac OS had to continue, so over the next several years some important features that were either invented or improved for one of the cancelled OS projects were added to the Mac OS. It was a steady progression from Mac OS 8. The version number was increased from 8 to 9 to pave the way for the transition to System X. It was felt that a gap in the numbers might have discouraged some users from migrating from the classic Mac OS to OS X. System 9 was released in 1999, and Apple called it the "best Internet operating system ever." The rise of the Internet began to impact the OS in several ways.

5.11.1 Multiple users

Originally it was assumed that a personal computer was used by a single person, and the Mac OS reflected that orientation. There was initially no such thing as a login. The design assumed that there was a single user of the system and that if security was an issue then physical access to the machine was limited to that one person. Many forces combined to gradually weaken that assumption. In the workplace it was common to have machines that were shared by users who only needed access for short intervals. At home the younger members of the family had always wanted to use the computer to play games, but now they began to value access to the Internet and needed to use software for various assignments, whether writing, researching, or using special applications. They also used it for access to social connections, ranging from multiplayer games to instant messaging to chatrooms. Whether at home or in the business world, each of these persons had distinct preferences in the setup of the system. These included many options on the GUI, a home page for the browser, and so on. They also frequently wanted to have files on the system that others did not have access to—a personal diary, perhaps. So support for multiple users was added in System 9. This required each user to login to the system before using it. This feature lets several people share a Mac while sheltering their private files and supporting separate system and application preferences. It is set up and maintained through a Multiple Users control panel, which lets one user create accounts for others, allowing them either normal or limited access to applications, printers, or the CD-ROM drive. The multiple users feature does not offer the same level of security found in more modern OSs or in Mac OS X. These OSs have file system-level security while System 9 does not. A knowledgeable user can access protected files by booting off a different volume, for example. Still, the multiple users feature solved a lot of the long-standing problems Mac users had when sharing a machine.

Being able to limit the rights of certain users is a sound practice. Unfortunately, many users are not very experienced with computers and allowing them unrestricted access can mean that they can easily cause problems with the system. In the minimum case they change things so that they do not work right. In the worse case they can wipe out an entire system, including much valuable data. Good practice says that even knowledgeable users should not normally run with unrestricted rights. Instead, they should use a special administrative login when they need to perform system maintenance.

Passwords are a perennial problem in computer system administration. Having many passwords and logins for different applications leads users to unsecure practices such as writing them on Post-it notes and leaving them on the monitor. System 9 implemented a mechanism known as **Keychain** Access. This feature managed users' multiple IDs and passwords and stored them securely. Once a user unlocked the Keychain by typing in the password, every application that was Keychain-aware could get the correct application username and password from the Keychain database without having to ask the user.

Since the file protection was not quite secure, System 9 also added a capability for file encryption. While the encryption scheme is very robust, it was proprietary to the Mac OS, so files encrypted in this way could only be decrypted by machines that were also running Mac OS 9. If recipients on Windows or UNIX machines needed to decrypt these files, then a cross-platform encryption program was still needed. But if file protection was not secure enough in a specific multiuser situation, the encryption added a measure of security.

5.11.2 Networking

By the late 1990s the Internet had become such a success that TCP/IP had become a requirement for all personal computers. Apple had provided support for TCP/IP since System 7, but only for certain functions. System administrators prefer to have a minimum number of different protocols to administer. Since AppleTalk did not provide any major features that were not also available in TCP/IP, there was considerable pressure on Apple to support TCP/IP for all networking functions. So, under System 9, file sharing was modified to support the TCP/IP protocol. Since

AppleTalk was not supported over the Internet, users previously could not easily access files at work on their Mac remotely through the Internet unless they resorted to complex, difficult techniques. Adding support for file sharing over TCP/IP meant that Mac users could work more easily from home over their standard Internet connection.

In addition, a new software update function allowed users to obtain Mac OS software updates over the Internet, and would notify users of updates as they became available. This greatly simplified the work of system administrators.

5.11.3 APIs

When System 9 was being developed, OS X was already well underway. As we will see shortly, OS X is essentially a different OS. However, Apple did not want it to be perceived that way. Accordingly, it was essential that many old applications be executable on the new OS. We have already discussed the emulation that was needed during the transition from the 68000 to the PowerPC. It was similarly possible to execute most older APIs under the new OS, but it was far preferable if an old application could be modified to support the APIs that would be available in OS X. So, Apple created a new API for System 9 that would be forward-compatible with OS X but still included support for most older API functions. This new API was known as the Carbon API. It included support for about 70% of the legacy Mac OS APIs.

5.11.4 Video

One of the driving forces behind the development of powerful advanced video features for personal computers is computer games. While other applications such as desktop publishing can also benefit from the features, there are many more people who play games than use systems to do desktop publishing. Naturally, the hardware vendors want to develop products for the larger markets. Apple computers are no exception, and there are many games available for Macs. One of the features for which support was added in System 9 was support for video cards that had built-in hardware support for accelerated rendering of 3D objects and for software APIs for technologies such as OpenGL, which allowed an improved video and gaming experience.

5.12 MAC OS X

OS X may be one of the most revolutionary changes in the history of OSs, and not just because Apple changed the release naming from System 10 to OS X. In OS X Apple completely discarded the System 9 kernel and replaced it with another one. Microsoft's Windows 3.x had been very successful since its release in 1990. They had followed that with the release of another successful OS in 1993, Windows NT. NT was an advanced OS designed for high-end applications and included features such as preemptive multitasking, the ability to run applications written for several legacy OSs, multiple CPU support, and a new file system. Apple needed an OS that would be competitive with these Microsoft products. As was mentioned before, they partnered with various firms in several OS projects, but none provided the OS they needed. They also considered building a new OS on top of a kernel from Solaris (Sun Microsystems), BeOS (Be), and reportedly even NT (Microsoft). They ultimately settled on a microkernel based on the Mach kernel and the FreeBSD implementation of UNIX, which were the basis for NextStep, an object-oriented operating system developed by NeXT Computer Inc. For performance reasons some of the FreeBSD code was merged with the Mach kernel so that the result is not a true microkernel. The exact evolution of OS X is hard to trace and not very relevant to this text. Much information is available on the WWW for those interested in the varying opinions.

Changes were made in OS 9 software to allow it to be booted in the **classic environment** within OS X. So the Classic Environment is an OS X application that provides a compatibility layer that can run a version of the System 9 OS, allowing applications that have not been ported to the new APIs to run on OS X. It is fairly seamless, but classic applications keep their original OS 8/9 appearance and do not look like OS X applications.

5.12.1 New features

So OS X is actually a different OS that supports the APIs formerly used in the Classic versions of Mac OS. Many of the capabilities of OS X came from the UNIX utility packages. In the next chapter we look at another UNIX variant in depth. For now we simply mention some of the features that OS X brought to the Mac world:

- A new memory management system allowed more programs to run at once and supported full memory protection that kept programs from crashing one another
- A command line (part of UNIX terminal emulation)
- Preemptive multitasking among processes instead of only among threads
- Support for UNIX file system formats
- The Apache Web server
- Full support for symmetric multiprocessing

5.12.2 A new CPU, again

Since the greater capabilities of OS X put higher demands on system resources, this release officially required at least a PowerPC G3 processor.

In June 2005 Apple computers announced that they would be converting the Mac product line from PowerPC processors to Intel products. In January 2006 Apple released the first Macintosh computers with Intel processors. The Classic (emulation) Environment does not work in the x86 version of OS X. Most well-written "classic" applications function properly under this environment, but compatibility is only assured if the software did not interact directly with the hardware at all and interfaced solely with the operating system APIs.

5.13 SUMMARY

In this chapter, we discussed the features and concepts of a more complex modern OS—the Mac OS developed by Apple Computer, Inc. This OS was developed to bring to market an inexpensive personal computer with a GUI. It is the Macintosh OS™ (or Mac OS) developed by Apple Computer, Inc. It generally supported only a single user. Later releases allowed many processes that execute at the same time and the ability for user applications to start multiple threads. We began this chapter with an overview of the Mac OS in Section 5.1. We used a different approach in this chapter and followed the releases of the Mac OS, describing the major new features in each release. This is because the Mac OS began as a quite simple system, offering no more functionality than CP/M except for the GUI, and even that was very primitive compared to what we think of today.

Ultimately the Mac OS evolved into a modern, full-featured OS that can supporting multiple users and multiple processes. We ended this saga with only brief mention of that Mac OS X release. Instead, in the next chapter we describe an alternate multiuser system, Linux.

BIBLIOGRAPHY

Apple Computer, *Inside Macintosh* series. Pearson Professional Education, 1992.

Danuloff, C., *The System 7 Book: Getting the Most from Your New Macintosh Operating System.* Chapel Hill, NC: Ventana Press, 1992.

Lewis, R., and B. Fishman, *Mac OS in a Nutshell,* 1st ed. Sebastopol, CA: O'Reilly Media, 2000.

WEB RESOURCES

http://applemuseum.bott.org (an outsider's view of Mac OS history)

http://developer.apple.com/documentation/ (contains links for all the *Inside Macintosh* series, downloadable in PDF format)

http://developer.apple.com/technotes/

http://www.apple-history.com (an outsider's view of Mac OS history)

http://www.macos.utah.edu/documentation/(operating_systems/mac_os_x.html

http://www.online-literature.com/orwell/1984/ (the book behind the 1984 TV ad)

http://rolli.ch/MacPlus (links to vMac, a Mac emulator)

http://en.wikipedia.org/wiki/Mac_OS_history (an outsider's view of Mac OS history)

http://en.wikipedia.org/wiki/NuBus (the original Mac bus)

http://en.wikipedia.org/wiki/Y2k (an explanation of the "Y2K bug")

http://www.parc.xerox.com/about/history/default.html

http://en.wikipedia.org/wiki/Mach_kernel (the kernel in Mac OS X)

REVIEW QUESTIONS

5.1 Which was the first system with a GUI?
   a. Xerox Star
   b. UNIX X Windows
   c. Xerox Alto
   d. Apple Lisa
   e. None of the above was the first system with a GUI.

5.2 True or false? The Apple Macintosh was introduced somewhat after the IBM PC and was slightly less expensive than the IBM system.

5.3 Which CPU did the Macintosh systems use?
 a. The Motorola 68000 family
 b. The Motorola PowerPC family
 c. The Intel 80x86 family
 d. None of the above
 e. All of the above

5.4 What was the great advantage that the Macintosh systems had over most other personal computer OSs?

5.5 The Apple Lisa was a precursor of the Mac and could run multiple applications at the same time. How many applications could the original Macintosh run at one time? Why was that?

5.6 True or false? The original Mac did not support memory protection, which would keep an application from corrupting the OS or its data.

5.7 How many folder (directory) levels did the original Mac OS support?

5.8 How large were the portions of the memory that the 68000 could address at one time?
 a. 16 KB
 b. 64 KB
 c. 128 KB
 d. 1 MB
 e. The 68000 could access all of memory at any time

5.9 True or false? In the Mac OS the kernel runs in supervisor mode and the applications run in user mode.

5.10 What was the difficulty with the way the application stack and heap were implemented in the Mac OS?

5.11 What did the Mac OS do to avoid the problem in the previous question?

5.12 What is the problem caused by the way that heap memory is managed? How did the Mac OS deal with it?

5.13 How does the Mac OS solution to the heap management problem differ from the Palm OS?

5.14 Unlike most other PC OSs, the Mac OS put much of the OS in ROM. Why was that?

5.15 With early releases of the Mac OS, a cut-and-paste operation typically took minutes instead of seconds. What new feature of the OS changed this?

5.16 Did the change mentioned in question 5.15 make the Mac OS a multitasking OS?

5.17 What major change was introduced with the Hierarchical File System?

5.18 What did MultiFinder do?
 a. It allowed the user to search a file for multiple strings.
 b. It allowed multiple users to log on to the system.
 c. It allowed the user to search the network for other users.
 d. It searched the Internet much like Google does today.
 e. None of the above describes MultiFinder.

5.19 What interesting new feature was made available with System 5?

5.20 System 6 supported new models of the Mac that used 32-bit addressing. What problem did that cause?

5.21 What was a "fat binary" for?

5.22 True or false? Virtual memory uses software to simulate missing blocks of memory.

5.23 What is the primary use of multithreading?

5.24 Quite a few enhancements made it into the various System 9 releases. Name three.

5.25 Why did we not say much about Mac OS X?

Chapter 6

A Multiple-User Operating System

In this chapter:

In this chapter, we discuss an operating system that is still more capable than the Mac OS discussed in the previous chapter, at least as far as the versions of the Mac OS prior to OS X. This is the Linux™ Operating System. The intent of this chapter is not to discuss the Linux OS in all aspects, but rather to focus on those points where the multiuser requirement of the OS lead to the inclusion of some additional features. We return to Linux in Chapter 19 in a more complete case study that examines the decisions made about the individual mechanisms for supporting the major system modules.

We start this chapter in Section 6.1 with an overview of Linux and some background about its history. In Section 6.2 we discuss the nature of a multiuser OS and how this design decision impacts the features of an OS. Next is Section 6.3 where we discuss the scheduling of processes and tasks in Linux. We have seen some of these features in other OSs, but Linux is the first OS we have studied that started out with a full implementation of all the concepts of both processes and threads. We conclude with a chapter summary in Section 6.4.

6.1 INTRODUCTION

The design of Linux is based on UNIX, an earlier OS that was originally developed primarily for supporting several users at remote terminals, usually display screens and keyboards with a serial data cable. These terminals were connected to a centralized computer system, perhaps even over a modem and phone line. UNIX was originally created to give a large computer development environment feeling to a much less expensive mini-computer. (It was also developed as something of a hobby for its two creators, who have won very prestigious computing awards for the concept of UNIX.) There are also versions of Linux that are intended for many other situations. Among these would be systems designed to:

- support a single user at the console of a personal computer
- act as servers for various remotely accessed functions such as file, print, and directory services
- serve as platforms for other higher-level services such as database management systems, Hypertext Transport Protocol (HTTP, or Web) servers, and File Transfer Protocol (ftp) servers
- act as routers in networks
- control real-time systems, and
- be embedded in equipment where there is no direct human user.

6.1.1 The history of a multiuser OS

Linux was inspired by UNIX™, so it makes sense to discuss briefly the origins of UNIX before addressing Linux. In 1969, Ken Thompson of Bell Laboratories began experimenting on creating a multiuser, multitasking operating system using a cast-off PDP-7 mini-computer. He teamed up with Dennis Ritchie and they and the other members of their small research group produced the first versions of UNIX, then called Unics as a dig at the Multics project on which they had both worked. (Multics was a giant project with over a hundred people working on it whereas a handful of programmers created UNIX.) Early versions of UNIX were written in assembly language, but the third version was written in a programming language called C, which was crafted by Ritchie expressly as a programming language for writing operating systems. C was designed as a fairly low-level, simple language that allows the programmer to ignore many hardware details in most cases, but still write programs in such a way that the compiler can take advantage of special hardware features. UNIX was a proprietary product of AT&T, the parent company of Bell Labs, where it was developed. AT&T made very reasonable charges for licenses to UNIX for academic use. UNIX version 6 (around 1976) was free for universities and version 7 cost $100. This included all the source code, freely modifiable. However, government labs and commercial entities had to pay $21,000. This was not an unreasonable price at the time for an operating system for a machine that cost hundreds of thousands or millions of dollars. And for universities the academic license was an irresistible deal since they had eager students who could port it to other machines or "improve" it as they saw fit. This was especially true of the utility programs that are typically distributed with an OS—such things as text editors, for example.

The allure of UNIX, a simple, consistent, small (it ran in a few kilobytes of memory and the source code was only several thousand lines of mostly C), and yet very flexible OS was compelling. Several companies and research groups wrote UNIX "work-a-likes," they worked like UNIX with the same OS system calls and OS utilities, but the source code was completely rewritten (to avoid AT&T property, and avoid needing to license anything from AT&T).

In 1991, Linus Torvalds, a University of Helsinki (Finland) computer science student, was familiar with UNIX from his classwork and was looking for a UNIX-like

OS to use at home. One of the few free options (it came with a textbook) was MINIX, a limited UNIX-like system written by Andrew Tanenbaum for educational purposes. There were other free OSs that were UNIX-like, but most weren't mature or stable yet, or required higher-end hardware than most users had at home. While Torvalds used MINIX, he felt that there were many features missing, so he decided to rewrite MINIX. He initially kept the file system design but later replaced it with his own. MINIX ran on a very basic 8088 CPU and floppy disks, allowing it to run on very inexpensive hardware systems. But it did not take advantage of the power of newer processors and hard disks. Torvalds used an Intel 386-based PC and started to add features and eventually wrote a new OS, initially using the C compiler on MINIX to do the development. Before long, Linux had become a "real" OS. The resulting Linux kernel contains no UNIX or MINIX code. Rather, it is a complete rewrite based on UNIX interfaces and utilities. Linux is actually only the kernel of an OS. It is built with, and uses a lot of, the GNU (GNU's Not UNIX™) software produced by members of the Free Software Foundation in Cambridge, Massachusetts, for the utilities and applications that must come with a complete OS. Indeed, the bulk of the OS outside the kernel is also part of the GNU project. So, one of the more interesting, important features of the Linux system is that it is not proprietary to a single company. All of the OSs that we have discussed to this point are (or were) owned by a company. They consider the source code to be a trade secret and generally do not release it to the public. Linux and the GNU software are "open source" projects.[1] The source code is available for free, and users are encouraged to correct bugs and to enhance the code. There is a wide-ranging debate as to whether the proprietary process produces better, more robust OSs than the open source process or vice versa.

Although it is accurate to say that Linux provides a free version of an OS that supports UNIX operations, this is not as clear or useful a statement as it might appear to be on the surface. For one thing, (in part because of the almost free price for the source code for UNIX to universities), the history of UNIX development has been replete with variants. Many programmers who were porting it to another environment could not resist the temptation to "improve" something or to add some favorite feature. Not until the late 1980s was a fairly standard UNIX API created by an independent IEEE committee. This standard is known as POSIX. Unfortunately the IEEE charged substantial fees for access to this standard, with the result that the developers of the free variants of UNIX-like OSs were usually not able to afford to have their products certified by the IEEE as being POSIX compliant. Later work has produced another specification that is more accessible to small companies or to unpaid developers, the **Single UNIX Specification (SUS)**.

When Linux was first made available, a would-be Linux user needed to be something of a UNIX expert, knowing what libraries and executables were needed to successfully get Linux to boot and run as well as the details concerning configuration and placement of some of the files in the system. Many potential users just wanted the system to use for their work, hobbies, or research and were not interested in working on the kernel or in becoming an expert on building the system from scratch. Linux source

---

[1] There are many variations on the concept of "open source" licenses. The adherents of the various versions are generally adamant about the variations. We are using the term in a loose, generic sense.

code is free, and at the same time, anyone can make a copy of the system and sell the copy. As a result, individuals, universities, and companies began creating **distributions** of Linux. A Linux distribution usually includes compiled versions of the Linux kernel and GNU system libraries and utility programs. Many distributions provide an install procedure like that provided with other OSs that will customize the OS for a given machine. The distributions were originally just a convenience, but today they have become the usual installation method even for UNIX or Linux gurus because of the savings in time and the decreased probability of overlooking some small but important detail in building the system from the source. Now, most distributions of Linux are certified as compliant with SUS. There are many different distributions of Linux designed for special purposes, such as booting from a device other than a hard drive, using Linux as a server, or supporting different languages as the default.

The management of a Linux system is an interesting topic in itself. One of the key features of Linux is the numbering of the various releases. The major **release number** is the first integer. The preliminary versions that Torvalds first released were release 0. The current release is 2. The next part of the number is odd for development releases (sometimes called "hacker" releases) and even for production releases (sometimes called "user" releases). So, for example, the current production release of Linux is 2.6 and the current development release is 2.7. Another integer is added to distinguish various patch levels.

Linux has really outgrown its very humble beginnings. It started as an OS kernel that was only available on single processor Intel 386 CPUs (or better) systems. Now it is available on almost every hardware platform available, including, in many cases, platforms where the hardware vendor also offers a proprietary OS, sometimes even a version of UNIX. (Naturally, some of the implementations are better than others.) For example, IBM has adopted Linux with considerable enthusiasm. They have ported it to all four of their E-series systems lines. This strategy takes advantage of the portability of applications using Linux. IBM now makes a greater portion of their income from writing, installing, and supporting applications than they do from selling hardware or OSs. They quite likely often found themselves in the position of creating an application on one of their four hardware product lines and then having to port the application to other platforms for other customers. With Linux and Java™ they can create applications one time and easily move them to other platforms, including all the installation and support procedures using Linux packages, scripts, and so on.

6.1.2 Basic organization of Linux

Linux uses a **monolithic** kernel. This means that the entire kernel is loaded into a single program that contains all the modules of the OS. Every module has direct access to any function, object, or data structure in the kernel. This means that monolithic OSs are often faster than microkernel OSs. The risks in this approach are several. First, all the OS code runs in supervisor mode so that any bug can theoretically cause more drastic problems. Also, porting to new architectures is harder because the machine-specific portions are not necessarily as well isolated. In addition, if the designers are not careful, the source code can quickly become very complex because it is not absolutely essential to have clean, well-defined interfaces between the various modules as it is with a microkernel.

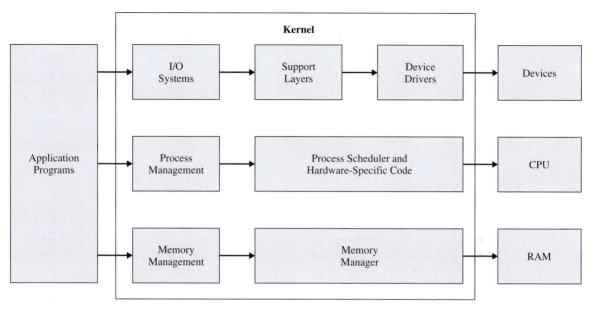

FIGURE 6.1 The Linux system architecture.

Also, adding support for new devices is more difficult with a monolithic kernel. Often it requires compiling the new driver and relinking and reloading the kernel. This obviously means that the OS has to be stopped and restarted—something not appreciated in a multiuser system or a server offering many network services or serving many users or both. But modern Linux versions have overcome many of these problems, as we will see shortly. The organization of the Linux kernel is shown in Figure 6.1.

As was discussed earlier, another type of organization for an OS is to be built on a **microkernel.** Such an organization is shown in Figure 6.2. Again, this means that the code in the kernel has been minimized to include only that part of the code that absolutely must be in the kernel in order to execute privileged instructions. These portions typically include process management, basic memory management, and interprocess communication. The remainder of the functions that we normally think of as being part of the resident OS may be run in user mode. This organization has some benefits and some costs. It is easier to produce a kernel that is robust, and it is easier to port it to a new platform. The major cost of this organization is that it often introduces more overhead—the interrupt handling and context switching often make the OS run slower than a monolithic kernel. MINIX was designed and created as a microkernel system.

6.1.3 Dynamically loadable modules

Linux was initially envisioned to be a small, simple project. For this reason it did not seem to be important to go to the trouble of creating a microkernel OS. At one time in the early development of Linux, Tanenbaum actually sent an email to Linus Torvalds that dismissed Linux as being "obsolete" because of the monolithic kernel approach. At that time, many in the computing science community viewed the microkernel

FIGURE 6.2

A microkernel system architecture.

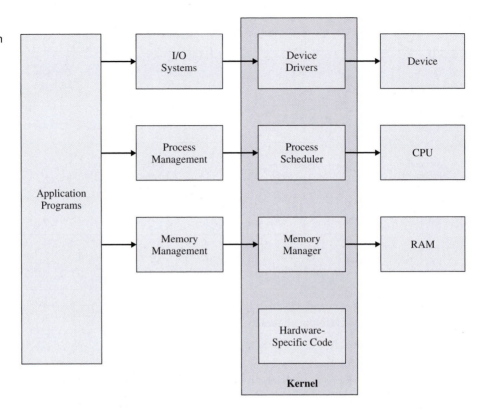

approach as a preferred approach for the reasons previously listed. As Linux became a viable OS alternative, Torvalds and the Linux community came up with an interesting approach to modify or augment a purely monolithic kernel. The key idea was introduced in version 2.0 of Linux. This version supports **dynamically loadable modules, or DLMs.** This concept allows the basic kernel to contain a minimum amount of functionality and be embellished by modules that can be loaded (and unloaded) after the system has started running. Many of the functions that are basic to Linux are developed as DLMs because they may not be needed in every installation. These include such functions as file systems, specific device drivers, SCSI high-level drivers (disk, tape, CD-ROM), network drivers, line printer drivers, and serial (tty) drivers.

In order to support DLMs, the core kernel has to have well-defined interfaces. This removes one of the significant objections to the monolithic approach. When a module is loaded it calls an OS function to "register" itself with the kernel. The exact function to be called depends on the type of module being loaded. An illustrative set of such calls is listed in Table 6.1.

One of the interesting effects about the DLM interface is that it allows software developers to create enhancements to the Linux system for which they do not want to provide the source code (which is necessary to be in accordance with the various open source licenses). This allows Linux to remain an open source project but still incorporate functions that are kept as proprietary by the developers.

TABLE 6.1   **Dynamic Module Registration Functions**

Purpose	Dynamic Registration Function
Modules	init-module
Symbol tables	register_symtab
Console drivers	tty_register_driver
Transport protocols	inet_add_protocol
Network protocols	dev_add_pack
Link protocols	register_netdev
Serial interfaces	register_serial
File systems	register_filesystem
Binary formats	register_binfmt
Block devices	register_blkdev
Character devices	register_chrdev

Another point about DLMs is that they need to be linked with the core kernel functions and data structures. (That is, they need to be findable by the kernel and they need to be able to access parts of the kernel in return.) This is accomplished by having a **symbol table** loaded as part of the kernel. This table is called **ksym.** Any function or data structure that is to be exposed in the kernel will need to have a definition in this symbol table. A module being loaded will call a function that will search the symbol table and resolve any references in the module being loaded. This may sound as if it would slow down the system, but modules are generally loaded once and then remain a part of the system. Even if they are added and removed repeatedly, such as for a removable USB device, perhaps it is usually at intervals that are long compared to the CPU speed.

It is also likely that a module that is being loaded by the kernel will want to expose its own functions and data structures. A simple function, EXPORT_SYMBOL, allows the loading module to add entries to the symbol table.

6.1.4 Interrupt handlers

As was previously mentioned, device management in Linux is interrupt driven. Hardware interrupts are a mechanism by which the hardware can notify the OS of asynchronous events. A primary example would be the arrival of a packet at a network adapter. When the adapter has received a packet it will generate an interrupt so that the OS can stop what it is doing and take care of this packet that has just arrived. Sometimes the amount of processing required to take care of the packet can be quite lengthy. In addition, the complete processing of the packet may be much less important than what else the system was doing at the time. However, there is a minimum amount of work that does need to be done by the kernel immediately. At the very least the OS will probably need to assign a new buffer for any additional packet that might arrive. While this work is being done it is typical that either all interrupt levels are disabled or that the current interrupt level and any lower priority level interrupts are disabled. Naturally it is not a good idea to leave the interrupts disabled for very long or some external events will be missed. Therefore, an interrupt handler in Linux followed a well-known, popular **top-half** and **bottom-half** organization. The top-half consisted of those things that needed to happen immediately and the bottom-half were those things that could be done at a more leisurely pace. The top-half would record sufficient information so that the bottom-half could finish the work later. In later releases of Linux the structure of a bottom-half was redesigned and given a new name—a **tasklet.** The primary reason for the redesign is that tasklets can run on more than one processor in an environment with multiple CPUs, whereas bottom-halves could only be run by one CPU at a time. Existing bottom-halves were mostly redesigned to conform to this change.

6.1.5 File system directory tree

Linux, like UNIX, has a strong orientation around the file system. Many things appear in the file system tree that are not files at all. This is shown in Figure 6.3. The root of the directory tree is shown at the top level. Neither the proc nor the dev directories are actually directories. Rather, they represent the running processes and the hardware (or virtual) devices on the system. References to these names will cause the Linux OS to invoke other functions that will return appropriate information about these elements when they are accessed. These are discussed further in Chapter 19. The other interesting directories that can be seen in Figure 6.3 are the subdirectories under the /home directory. These are directories for individual users. When a user logs on to the Linux system the OS will set the current working directory to be the home directory for that user.

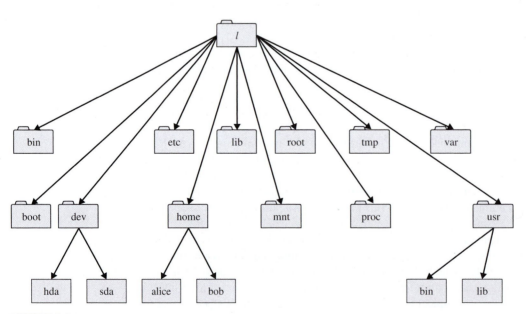

FIGURE 6.3 A partial Linux directory tree.

6.2 THE MULTIUSER OS ENVIRONMENT

Since Linux is modeled after UNIX and UNIX is a multiuser system, Linux is a multiuser system. Assuming that there are multiple users on the system introduces from the start a problem that we have not had to worry about too much until now—information security. When only one person can use a computer, the OS typically does not need to concern itself with the right of the user to access any files on the computer. It is assumed that any user of that computer can access any file and that file security is provided by limiting access to the machine or by using utility programs, external to the OS, to safeguard files by encrypting them. Multiple users on the system at the same time require that the OS provides a facility to protect each user's files from all other users. This will mean that the OS will need to know who the user is. This, of course, means that the user will need to log on to the computer with a user ID (identifier) and a password. Of course, sometimes users will want to share files, so the OS will need mechanisms to allow some files to be shared. All multiuser systems also function as servers and may have multiple users logged on remotely. These OSs therefore also have security features, which are discussed in a later chapter. Of course, as we saw with the Mac OS, as computers are added to a network, even single-user systems will need to provide mechanisms for protecting various assets, so user logon and such is now a common feature in most OSs if only for network access. The server version of the Linux OS allows multiple users to access files and other resources on the system remotely. This was not the main thrust of this OS, but the ability to run many services and many user applications at the same time meant that it also had to provide support for such advanced features as multiprogramming and multithreading. Supporting multiple users does not introduce any new requirements in this area, but Linux does take a different approach to this subject, especially considering its UNIX origins.

6.2.1 File permissions

Linux supports the same model of file protection and sharing that other UNIX-like systems support. With respect to any particular file, Linux regards all users as being a member of one of three sets. The first set has only one member. This set is the file owner. Initially when a file is created the owner is the person who created the file. The second set is one that is predefined by the system administrator, or **sysadmin** as that person is commonly called. This set is normally a bunch of users that share some common interest in a set of files. Perhaps it is a project team that is working to develop the documentation for a new product or is using the same source code and wishes to share it among the team members. The sysadmin designates a new group by name and assigns users to be members of the group. The third set is "everybody." In this case, it refers to every user who is not a member of one of the other two sets. For members of each set, three types of access can be allowed for a specific file: reading, writing, and executing.

The file owner can set the permissions on a file by using a utility called **chmod.** This typically obscure Linux command stands for "change mode." This utility takes two arguments, a file name and a "mode" that specifies the changes to be made to the file **mode.** Traditionally, this mode is a three-digit number. The digits of the number are limited to octal digits—that is, they can range from 0 to 7. Each octal digit can be considered to be three bits. These three bits are used to allow the various operations—read, write, and execute, respectively—and the three digits relate to one of the three sets—owner, group, and everybody, respectively. The ls command, which lists the contents of a directory, can list these mode settings for a file or directory. Consider the following entry printed by the ls command:

```
-rwxr-x--x gil develop spellcheck
```

This entry describes an executable file named "spellcheck." The first part of the line is the settings of the permissions. The leading "-" has other uses. The initial mode of "rwx" applies to the owner of the file, in this case "gil." The group for the file is "develop" and its mode is "r-x" and the mode for everyone else is "--x." This means that user gil has all rights to the file, even the right to modify or remove it. The other members of the group "develop" can read it and execute it (if it is an executable script or program) but not write it, and everyone else can only execute it. The chmod command to set these permissions would be:

```
chmod 751 spellcheck
```

The 7 corresponds to binary 111, all rights on, and the 5 corresponds to 101, or read and execute only.

If we wanted to allow the group "develop" to modify this file we would have used another command, chgrp, for "change group." We would enter:

```
chgrp develop spellcheck
```

The rather cryptic chmod command use has been enhanced in Linux and other current UNIX-like systems to support more symbolic arguments. For example, the command

```
chmod g+w spellcheck
```

would add the write permission to the permissions for the group assigned to the file.

6.2.2 File control blocks

Since there are multiple processes running for multiple users, two or more users might be working with some of the same files. But they might be processing in different parts of the file. As we see in Figure 6.4, the structures are in two pieces to support this use with a minimum duplication of information. As we can see, there is a **systemwide open file table.** It is in the kernel and it contains metadata about the file that is the same for all users—where is the first block, how long is it, and so on. Each process has a **per-process open file table** as well. Each entry contains an index into the systemwide open file table and information about the use of the file by this process such as the current pointer.

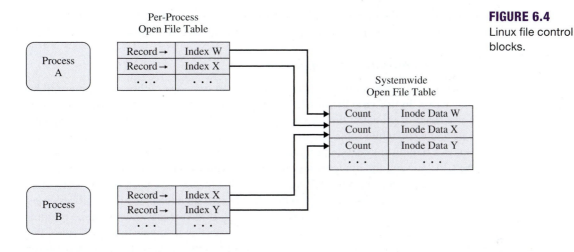

FIGURE 6.4
Linux file control blocks.

6.3 PROCESSES AND THREADS

6.3.1 Linux tasks

We have not yet fully discussed the idea of threads. This is just as well, since Linux does not distinguish between processes and threads, but it is common for writers to use those terms when writing about Linux because they are otherwise in common use. Linux documentation uses the term **tasks.** Under UNIX, when a process (called the parent process) wants to start another process (called the child process), it first issues the system call "fork." This will create the child process as a copy of the parent process. (We will see later that there are ways the system can make this happen without actually copying all of the program.) With Linux, however, the corresponding system call is **clone.** Like all OSs, Linux maintains several different segments of memory for every process. These will be described in more detail later. The clone system call specifies a set of flags that tells the OS which of these segments are to be shared between the parent process and the child process. The flags are shown in Table 6.2.

In order to support programs written for other UNIX systems, Linux must also support the standard UNIX calls for forking a process. Unfortunately, the clone function provided by Linux does not provide identical functionality. Several data structures used for supporting tasks are not automatically shared between the parent and

TABLE 6.2   **Linux Clone Call Flags**

CLONE_VM	Share memory
CLONE_FILES	Share file descriptors
CLONE_SIGHAND	Share signal handlers
CLONE_VFORK	Allow child to signal parent on exit
CLONE_PID	Share PID
CLONE_FS	Share the file system

child tasks by the clone system call, including access rights. Libraries that intend to support POSIX compliance must then provide this service themselves.

6.3.2 Preemptive multitasking

When a single user is running multiple programs, only one of those programs will be interactive. In this case there will be no problem if that application takes more than a fair share of the CPU time because the user will not care if other programs pause now and again while some lengthy processing takes place in the interactive program. But in a multiuser system a program running for one user should not be able to seize the CPU and run indefinitely. Accordingly, as with the later versions of the Mac OS, Linux is a preemptive multitasking system. This means that when the OS starts running a process it will set a timer so that the OS will be interrupted if the process runs too long without making a blocking system call. If the timer expires then the running process will be put back into the queue of processes that are ready to run (i.e., the CPU is preempted from that process). This prevents a single process from getting control of the CPU and keeping any other process from running. This may be due to a bug in the application that has caused it to go into an endless loop. Often, the process just has a lot of work to do. Note that the resources consumed by the preemption itself are not being used to do actually useful work—it is not something that is being done on behalf of any user process. However, it gives a smoother overall response to the user, and is generally perceived to be better, even though it is slightly less efficient than not preempting would be. In general, all modern OSs use preemption, except for some parts of hard real-time OSs. We discuss these questions more thoroughly in Chapter 8.

6.3.3 Symmetric multiprocessing

Multiprocessing systems are those that run multiple CPUs in a single system. This architecture has been common on systems where not enough CPU power was available to run the entire processing load. Given the alternative of adding a complete second system, which often had to be synchronized with the first system, multiprocessing is a capable and less expensive option. One reason it is less expensive is that a single system can share many expensive hardware components such as power supplies, primary and secondary storage, and the main system bus.

Figure 6.5 shows the architecture of a typical multiprocessor system. This is a simplified diagram—for example, modern systems have several different buses. Note that the main memory and I/O architecture are shared among all the CPUs. On a single CPU system we can only be executing one program at any given instant. On a system with multiple CPUs there can literally be two or more processes (or threads) running at the same time.

Beginning around 2004, integrated circuit design engineers decided that it would be more cost effective to embed multiple CPUs in one chip rather than to continue to make each individual CPU faster and faster. These circuits are known as tightly coupled multiprocessors, chip-level multiprocessors (CMP), or multicore processors (MCP). They are even more tightly coupled than the previously available MP systems, which incorporated multiple individual CPU chips. MCP circuits often share a single L2 cache, for example. This means that most systems as large as a personal

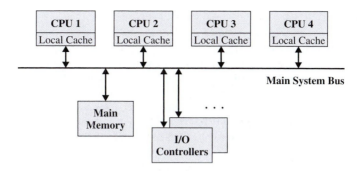

FIGURE 6.5
A simplified multiprocessor system architecture.

computer will be multiprocessor systems, though single CPU systems will still be common in embedded systems for the foreseeable future.

There are two different approaches that an OS can take to supporting multiple CPUs. The first approach is called **asymmetric multiprocessing.** In this approach the OS runs on only one designated CPU. The other CPUs run only applications. This design has the advantage that the OS itself can ignore some of the complications involved in having the same process run on two CPUs at the same time. Although simple, this approach is not commonly used because of performance bottlenecks due to running the OS only on one processor. Instead, most modern OSs support multiple CPUs with a different approach, **symmetric multiprocessing (SMP).** In this approach the OS is treated like every other process in that it can be running on any CPU. A running program obviously will be modifying its state (data). It is easy to see that having two (or more) CPUs running the same code that is modifying the same data has to be thought about very carefully. Multiple instances of the OS running on different CPUs must be prevented from changing the same data structure at the same time. We look at this topic more closely in Chapter 9. Because the individual CPUs may each be caching the same data, the hardware must do a lot of work to ensure that all the caches contain the same information. The techniques involved in this synchronization have so much overhead that most current systems will not scale up beyond a fairly small number of processors—say, 64 or so.

Since the 2.0 release Linux has supported SMP.

6.4 SUMMARY

In this chapter, we discussed the features and concepts of a multiuser OS, Linux. This chapter is fairly brief because it only addresses the additional features found in Linux because it is a multiuser OS. Chapter 19 is a more traditional case study of the Linux OS modules.

We started this chapter with an overview of Linux and a bit of the history of its evolution. We then moved to a brief discussion of the characteristics of a multiuser OS. Next, we discussed the support of files in Linux. We then gave an overview of the scheduling of processes and tasks in Linux.

In the next chapter of the book we discuss an example of distributed OSs—one that runs on multiple systems at the same time and attempts to make the many systems appear to the user as a single environment. The subsequent chapters begin an in-depth look at the various components of OSs.

BIBLIOGRAPHY

Beck, M., et al., *Linux Kernel Programming,* 3rd ed. Reading, MA: Addison-Wesley, 2002.

Bovet, D. P., and M. Cesate, *Understanding the Linux Kernel,* 2nd ed. Sebastopol, CA: O'Reilly & Associates, Inc., 2003.

Gorman, M., *Understanding the Linux Virtual Memory Manager.* Upper Saddle River, NJ: Prentice Hall, 2004.

Love, R. *Linux Kernel Development.* Indianapolis, IN: Sams Publishing, 2004.

Stevens, R., *Advanced Programming in the UNIX Environment.* Boston: Addison-Wesley, 1992.

Stevens, R., *Unix Network Programming.* Upper Saddle River, NJ: Prentice Hall, 1990.

Yaghmour, K., *Building Embedded Systems.* Sebastopol, CA: O'Reilly & Associates, Inc., 2003.

WEB RESOURCES

http://www.linux.org (the home of Linux kernel development)

http://www.kernel.org (a repository of historic kernel sources)

http://www.tldp.org (the Linux Documentation Project)

REVIEW QUESTIONS

6.1 Why is a "distribution" important in Linux?

6.2 Why is SUS important to Linux?

6.3 Why would a large organization probably not want to use release 2.7 as a standard installation for all of their Linux systems?

6.4 True or false? Linux is only the kernel of an OS and relies on other groups to provide the needed utility programs to make it a usable OS.

6.5 True or false? Linux is a microkernel OS.

6.6 Modern OSs are used in a wide variety of environments. There are an incredible variety of devices and controllers that have been interfaced to Linux and a wide assortment of different file systems, disk schedulers, and so on, most of which are not needed on any given installation. How does an OS like Linux avoid becoming overloaded with modules that are not needed in most situations?

6.7 Why are interrupt handlers in Linux divided into a top half and a bottom half?

6.8 Describe briefly how the Linux clone mechanism differs from traditional UNIX processes and threads.

6.9 True or false? Linux is a nonpreemptive multitasking OS.

Chapter 7

Parallel and Distributed Computing, Clusters, and Grids

In this chapter:

7.1 INTRODUCTION

So far we have been discussing the designs of Operating Systems that run on a single machine. But many systems are now designed for processing in situations where many processors are used together. In this chapter we discuss computing on more than one CPU and how we can manage such systems. There are several common configurations for multiple CPU systems, and many unusual ones.

We start by introducing a few key concepts encountered in distributed processing. Then, after covering these concepts, in Section 7.3 we introduce some theory about computation and programming in parallel environments. Next, Section 7.4 covers the common architectures found in distributed systems. OSs designed to run in such environments have special concerns that do not arise in uniprocessing situations, so in Section 7.5 we cover these OS issues. These topics include such questions as what needs to be managed, how does resource management differ from uniprocessor systems, and what interfaces are presented to programmers and users. In Section 7.6 we discuss some real systems that fit into this chapter and we close with a summary in Section 7.7.

7.2 KEY CONCEPTS

Moore's law recognized that computers will become more capable year after year. It predicts that CPUs double in transistor count every 18 to 24 months. Usually there has been a corresponding increase in CPU speed. Memory and disk capacities double at an even faster rate as well. Moore's law has been a fairly accurate rule-of-thumb for more than three decades. In the last few years CPU speed has increased by exploiting parallelism inside the CPU chip; such techniques as pipelining, multiple execution units in the CPU, and multicore integrated circuits have featured in the relentless pursuit of CPU speed. At the same time, they have all appeared transparent to the programmer.[1]

Unfortunately, there is a rapidly approaching limit—the speed of light, at $3 \cdot 10^8$ meters per second. This means that at a clock speed of 3 Gigahertz (GHz) a signal can travel only 10 centimeters in a vacuum between clock cycles, and significantly less distance in the silicon material that makes up an integrated circuit. Since CPUs are typically more than a centimeter across, this limits how much a CPU can do in one clock cycle. Yet CPUs have been getting faster clocks and faster processing every year. This forces computer architects to make CPUs do work in parallel (on the chip) yet hide those implementation details from programmers and users (who don't want to redesign and rewrite programs for each new CPU chip). We would like to exploit parallelism in our computing problems on a higher level (parallel computing or clusters) as well, but this requires some modifications to the programs and enhancements to the OSs and the middleware. We describe those issues and how one may take advantage of these hardware facilities through OSs and other (middleware) software.

7.3 PARALLEL AND DISTRIBUTED PROCESSING

It is common to use the term "parallel" to refer to work being done in multiple places simultaneously. We have used the term parallel for that meaning, so far. There are several possible ways that we can configure multiple processors to provide parallelism. In this section we briefly describe the differences. Later we discuss each one in greater detail.

More precisely, we now describe parallel processing (or parallel computing) to refer to multiple processors sharing one big pool of memory and other resources (disks and printers, for example). This type of computer architecture is usually called **multiprocessing (MP).** Today, most MP systems run under an OS that uses symmetric multiprocessing (SMP), as was discussed in Chapter 6 on Linux. While MP computers may have any number of CPUs sharing common memory, there are general guidelines to most MPs:

- CPUs share one common pool of memory, and any CPU may read or write any memory location (even if it is being used by another CPU).
- All CPUs are of the same type and speed.

---

[1] In this case "transparent" only means that a program that will run correctly without them will still run correctly with them. It does not mean that a skillful programmer might not want to take advantage of these features when extra performance is needed and the extra work is warranted.

- All other computer resources (disks, networking, and printers) are shared among all the CPUs.
- There is usually only one copy of the OS running, and it knows about all of the CPUs and shared resources. (It is much less common to have multiple OSs running or to have the OS running on only one CPU.)
- Programs must be specially written or modified to take advantage of running on multiple CPUs.
- MPs may have two, four, or more (usually a power of two), but currently two- or four-processor (CPU) MPs offer the best performance per dollar, even better than single-processor CPUs; and more than eight-processor MPs are expensive. Many rack-mounted systems are two- or four-processor MPs. For hardware reasons these rarely run over 64 CPUs in a single system.[2]

On the other hand, distributed computer systems:

- don't share memory;
- often have their own resources (such as disk drives);
- communicate with each other through a network;
- may not use the same hardware; and
- run a separate copy of the OS on each machine.

While sending a message (or sharing data) between computers in a distributed system may only take a few microseconds, it is usually at least a hundred times slower than sharing memory on an MP system. There are several different classes of distributed systems as well, and each class has unique performance characteristics.

Clusters are a special class of distributed system. A cluster is comprised of individual computing nodes. These nodes may be single processors or MP systems. They are managed and protected from each other by special software and are connected over a dedicated LAN that is separate from other LANs connecting the cluster to other resources. Usually the cluster shares a single connection outside the cluster, commonly to the Internet. Normally each cluster node has identical software and hardware to all other nodes in the cluster. It is possible, though less common, to build clusters from nonidentical nodes. Clusters are usually administered by a single group of people (or person) and all login user names and passwords are identical for each node in the cluster. This means that a user can run jobs on one or more nodes with a single user name and password. Nodes in clusters typically share storage resources utilizing **SAN (storage area network)** and **NAS (network attached storage)** systems. These are essentially marketing terms for a pool of disks operating as a single networked resource using protocols such as **NFS (network file system)**. Clusters typically have multinode job schedulers running through designated "head nodes," which allow jobs, queues, and workflows to be managed. One such scheduler, **PBS,** or **portable batch system,** is discussed later in Section 7.6.6.

Grids (grid computer systems) are comprised of multiple workstations or clusters with different administrators. As a result, they do not share resources directly, do not

---

[2] Some hardware configurations exist with a few thousand CPUs sharing memory. However the architecture is not a completely shared memory. These systems are referred to as Non-Uniform Memory Access (NUMA) systems, and not the sort we are discussing here.

share common logins, and may have totally different hardware and software configurations. But the administrators of the individual clusters have agreed to allow some jobs belonging to users of other clusters or computer systems to run on their clusters.

Other common shared, distributed configurations include **peer-to-peer** (**P2P**) systems, **clusters of workstations** (**COWS**), and volunteer computing systems (such as the BOINC system used for SETI@Home, physics, and biology processing, among many other projects). While such configurations are often more difficult for a developer to utilize, they may offer potentially hundreds of thousands of nodes, spread throughout the world.

In the following sections we discuss the utilization and potentials of these configurations for processing large computational work, sharing data and processing, gathering results, and monitoring progress of work being done.

7.3.1 Just to start, a little bit of theory

Work to be done may be described in **workflows.** These workflows specify the processing steps that need to be done, the inputs and outputs of these steps, and the dependencies between the elements. Often a directed acyclic graph (dag) describes this process, as is shown in Figure 7.1. The nodes A, B, C, and D are shown as boxes and represent units of processing work to be done. The edges are shown as arrows and represent the dependencies between the processing nodes. We have omitted describing inputs or outputs of the processing.

This workflow graph shows the flow of this job: first step A must process some data. After step A has completed, either step B or step C may run. Since there are no dependencies of steps B and C on each other, they may run at the same time. After both steps B and C have completed, then step D may run. For example, step A reads some data then passes a part of the data to step B and a part to step C. Then steps B and C each process their part and pass their results to step D, which processes their results. Let's say that step A takes 10 minutes to run, step B takes 60 minutes, step C takes 60 minutes, and step D takes 20 minutes. If these were done on a single computer they would take: 10 + 60 + 60 + 20 minutes = 150 minutes. On two computers (ignoring overhead such as communication) this flow should take 10 + 60 + 20 minutes (steps A + B + D side) on one processing node, and 60 minutes on the other node (step C). The total work done in either case is 150 minutes but the two-computer solution reduces the "wall-clock" time (observed time) to 90 minutes, an hour faster. Notice that running step D on the second computer would not help to

FIGURE 7.1
A workflow graph.

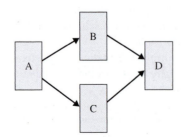

complete this work faster since we still have to wait on steps B and C. Nor would having three or four nodes improve performance because of our flow dependencies. Suppose we had special computers that can run steps B and C faster. How much benefit do we gain? If we could speed up the runtime of B and C by a factor of two, each taking only 30 minutes, we would complete the flow in $10 + 30 + 20 = 60$ minutes. This is often called Amdahl's law: the speed up of a portion of the work makes only that part faster, not the entire flow. Thus, even a 10 times faster processing in B and C only speeds up:

$$(10 + 60 + 20) \text{ minutes (old)}$$
$$(10 + 6 + 20) \text{ minutes (new)} \qquad = 2.5 \text{ times}$$

Not bad (2.5 times faster), but not 10 times faster (the speed increase of B and C). Amdahl's law will make it very difficult for a practical system to approach the ideal of parallel computing: linear speedup. Linear speedup would mean that work done on a 10-node system happens 10 times faster than on a one-node system, and on a 50-node system it would be 50-times faster. Sometimes there can be a superlinear speedup! On 10 nodes, processing is more than 10 times faster! This is very unusual, and is normally due to caching effects in memory. When 10 processors are running, then we also have 10 times as much cache memory involved and this can drastically speed up the processing.

Workflows are usually composed of two structures, as seen in Figure 7.2.

Pipeline flows indicate dependencies, but sweep flows may be done simultaneously in parallel. Most workflows are combinations of these patterns. One valuable insight is the condition where some part of a pipeline may actually allow partial processing, where a stage in the pipeline (a processing node) may process data one record at a time and then pass those results to the next stage, which may begin processing of that record immediately, while the previous stage of the pipeline processes the next record, in parallel.

In workflows there are several items that would be interesting to measure:

- Work time—total time spent on all nodes to process the work.
- Wall time (or clock time)—elapsed time, start to finish.

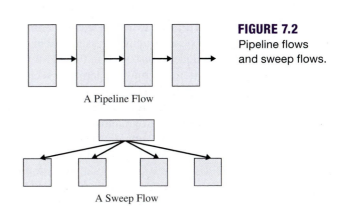

A Pipeline Flow

A Sweep Flow

FIGURE 7.2
Pipeline flows
and sweep flows.

- Utilization (resource utilization)—percentage of time each node (or the average of all nodes) is busy.
- Throughput—number of jobs or workflow processes run per hour (or day).

7.4 DISTRIBUTED SYSTEM ARCHITECTURES

7.4.1 Overview of execution environments

There are significant differences between the various distributed system architectures and single processor, multitasking systems. While each of the architectures allows us to run jobs in parallel, the effort that we must expend to utilize any one particular architecture, as compared to the others, varies quite a bit. So this section discusses each of these possible architectures in a bit more detail so that we can better understand some of the problems that can occur.

As we have seen in previous discussions, as we take advantage of more advanced features, we need to be a bit cautious about side effects and interactions between different features. For example, recall that the ability to run several processes concurrently allows more efficient use of computer resources. But it also introduces the difficulties of interprocess communication that arise because we build so much separation and protection between processes. Then we need locking and unlocking to avoid conflicts that arise when sharing resources, and then we need to worry about the deadlocks that can arise from the use of locks.

7.4.2 Symmetric multiprocessing systems

SMP systems share memory, and applications that process large amounts of data and pass data between stages or share tables can benefit substantially from being run on such architecture. There are parallel versions of many common programs (software tools). As you might recall, in SMP systems there is a single copy of the OS running and it may run on any CPU available. It must manage process scheduling for each CPU, memory allocation (there is only one shared physical memory space), and other resources (disks, terminals, and so forth). So, how does one utilize an SMP system to do work in parallel? Such a system is seen in Figure 7.3.

There are two main techniques that are used to take advantage of the power of an SMP system: multiprocessing and multithreading. (The distinction between these two techniques is discussed in Chapter 8.) If this seems familiar, these are the same facilities offered by most modern OSs such as with Linux and the Mac OS, as we discussed previously. The key concept to the use of an SMP system is that it is very similar to a traditional uniprocessor computer but with more main memory and more CPUs.

From a programmer's view, harnessing the power of multiple CPUs may be done by simply dividing the system into many separate programs, which run as separate processes. Usually this means running at least as many processes as there are CPUs in the system. Usually we run more processes than there are CPUs in order to allow some to run when others are blocked and waiting. A program or a workflow (a group of programs/processes) that has been written to create many processes that

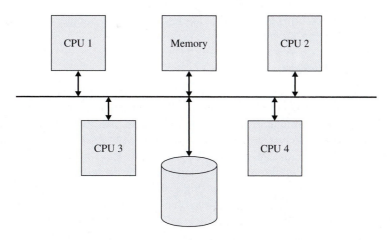

FIGURE 7.3
A multiprocessing system.

run simultaneously will run on a single processor computer. But they will also run just as well on an SMP system without any change, only faster. (In some unusual cases—such as a situation where almost all of the processes are blocked waiting for input—there won't be any speedup benefit.) While this method of parallelism is a common one, there are difficulties in having multiple processes share data such as the race conditions previously mentioned. Interprocess communication and synchronization work well, but incur overhead that may be avoidable by other methods. If work can be partitioned into sets that don't require much interprocess communication and synchronization (such as do several types of sweep workflows, described previously), multiple process models work very well.

So then what does the OS need to do to manage multiprocessing or multithreading on an SMP as opposed to what it had to do on a uniprocessor? It turns out that there is not a great deal of difference. Since memory is shared in one big pool, memory management is the same as on uniprocessor computers. CPU scheduling is more complex than with uniprocessor systems because the additional CPUs must be handled separately. Time-slicing scheduling is commonly used in SMP systems, just as in uniprocessor systems, so that part of the design is not much different. But the scheduler does have to consider where to schedule processes since work may be sent to different CPUs. This is not much more difficult than scheduling one CPU. However, one recent advancement in CPU architecture may complicate the scheduling. Recall that most CPUs have cache memory on the chip that contain copies of portions of main memory, but whose access is much faster. If the scheduler randomly assigns processes and threads to processors, the benefits of caching will be impaired. The system will still work correctly, but it will run much more slowly than if the data were in the cache for the correct CPU. Sophisticated SMP schedulers try to keep a process (or multiple threads from one process) running on the same CPU once they have started. This is called **CPU preference** or **processor affinity.** This technique also allows a programmer or administrator to provide a suggestion to the scheduler to run a process or thread on a specific CPU.

The other problem that SMP OSs face is that there may be multiple copies of the OS running at the same time. These copies may try to update the same data at the same time. Therefore, SMP OSs must make use of locking mechanisms to prevent different executing copies from interfering with one another. This issue is discussed more fully in Chapter 9.

7.4.3 Clusters

Cluster systems are more loosely coupled than SMP systems. They usually have essentially identical system software on each node as well as several options for sharing and communicating between processes. An example is seen in Figure 7.4, where there are two groups of two systems with close coupling between the odd-numbered systems and even-numbered systems and additional coupling between the two groups. In addition, each system has local memory and local storage. Clusters are normally administered by a single authority such as a corporation or university. They rely on **middleware,** software that facilitates interfaces between systems but is not part of the OS—it is in the "middle" between the OS and applications. Middleware attempts to provide abstractions that facilitate distributed processing in ways that are independent of the underlying OSs involved. They are said to be **platform agnostic.** This allows us to connect existing systems together, among other things, and let the middleware sort out the differences. But middleware can be used in clusters that are homogeneous as well.

Commonly found middleware packages include **MPI/PVM, CORBA, DCOM, .net remoting,** and Java/**RMI (remote method invocation)**. MPI/PVM (**message passing interface, parallel virtual machines**) offers a language-independent manner for a process to send or receive messages, data, and parameters to or from other processes on other nodes in the cluster, even if the processes are written in different programming languages. CORBA (**Common Object Request Broker Architecture**) is similar but allows one object to invoke methods on another

FIGURE 7.4
A clustered
multiprocessing
system.

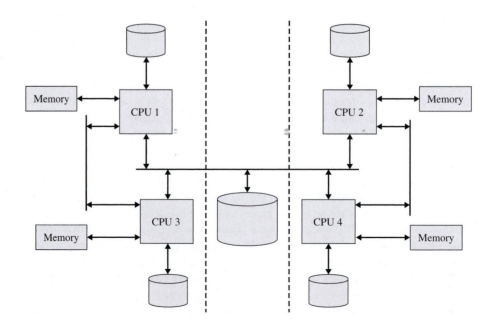

object that resides on a different computer. RMI is similar to CORBA but is specific to the Java language. DCOM (Distributed Component Object Model) is a method for invoking methods on remote objects that was created by Microsoft. It is considered to be a binary mechanism rather than a language-oriented mechanism like CORBA or RMI. This means that it finds its target interface via what amounts to a branch table on the remote object. Due to the widespread presence of the Microsoft OSs, DCOM has been implemented on most other OSs as well. It is an older mechanism that is not favored for new development but is still supported because it is in such widespread use. Newer development is directed to the .net remoting methods.

These middleware packages allow processes that do not directly share memory to pass information between themselves—ideal for a cluster. But these middleware mechanisms are actually better suited to general distributed computing than they are to cluster computing. When programs are designed to exploit the parallelism in computing clusters, they can make use of other specific cluster interfaces for the OS. These are discussed later, for example, the use of PBS cluster scheduling commands.

7.4.4 Computing grids

Grids are even more loosely coupled than clusters. They are loose aggregates of individual nodes or clusters administered by different institutions. The primary advantage of grid computing is that each node can be an inexpensive computer, and by combining them into a grid they can produce computing power similar to a multiprocessor supercomputer at lower cost due to the economy of producing commodity hardware compared to the higher cost of building a small number of single-purpose supercomputers. The greatest disadvantage is that the nodes do not have high-speed, low latency interconnections. So this arrangement is best for applications in which many parallel computations take place independently.

Nodes in a grid don't usually share user logins and passwords and the nodes typically have different configurations. They normally run the same OS, however. Neither multithreading nor MPI, RMI, or similar middleware mechanisms will be effective in distributing work, sharing data, or monitoring work progress in grid systems because the systems are so loosely connected. A consortium of industry, academic, and other interested parties have contributed to a freely available **Globus** Toolkit that is widely used to administer computing grids. This package is a set of utilities, interfaces, and protocols that allow cluster administrators to share some of their resources as a part of a grid.

Since the nodes are administered separately, security is a large concern with a grid system. For security reasons, rather than creating temporary user logins for jobs, "tickets" are issued by **ticket granting agencies.** Many different administrative authorities will be concerned with the administration of a given grid. Any source that the various administrators can agree to trust can be a ticket granting agency. Transferring data and programs among nodes in a grid, reserving local space, and retrieving results are done by Globus commands and interfaces. Coordinating between sites (clusters) is somewhat more difficult than on a single cluster, and very little software has been made grid-enabled. There are many other systems designed to facilitate grid computing besides Globus.

7.4.5 Volunteer computing

Individual people worldwide control millions of computers that sit idle for a large percentage of the time. Even when working at their assigned tasks most personal computers have many unused CPU cycles caused by the need to wait for I/O task completion. For many years, utilizing this otherwise wasted computation time on these computers has been a desire of several large projects. Many individual systems have been developed to take advantage of this otherwise wasted computer processing capacity. These systems needed to handle several problems, including allowing individuals to register their computers in the system, getting jobs to those computers, allowing those jobs to be suspended when other, more important work needs to be done on the computer, returning results to the originator, and keeping track of the "credit" each user or group of users has amassed. Eventually the Condor Project at the University of Wisconsin and BOINC at Berkeley developed common infrastructures to allow many different projects to be run in such a mode without the need for each project to develop the infrastructure from scratch. While both offer the possibility of aggregating many otherwise unused computer resources, they have important differences.

Most volunteer computing projects are based on parameter sweep flows in which large amounts of data are broken up into small sets and sent to volunteers' computers. These computers all run the same science program to analyze their particular set of data, then send the results back. The amount of work to be done in one sweep is usually a few hours and the data initially sent to the volunteer and results sent back to the server is usually not too large (several hundred kilobytes to several megabytes) so that volunteers are not overly burdened. Also, if a job is abnormally terminated for some reason, not too much work is lost.

BOINC

If the computing work of a project can be partitioned into reasonable-size chunks and the potential of using millions of volunteer computers will facilitate the project, then the BOINC infrastructure will be attractive. BOINC provides the common infrastructure and allows a project to submit its computing application to be run by millions of user computers, which have CPU cycles that are not currently being used.

Following on the success of early volunteer computing systems, BOINC (Berkeley Open Infrastructure for Network Computing) created an infrastructure for any software system to be distributed to millions of volunteer computers. BOINC is composed of a server system that sends out work and receives results. It may be configured to use any volunteer computer or to prefer computers where the software has already been installed and is running Linux or Windows. The BOINC client part is sent to volunteer client computers and it then downloads the actual science applications. When users register with BOINC they can select which science projects they want to participate in and what portion of the spare cycles should go to each project. The BOINC client software then takes care of the rest of the problems. It schedules when the science applications will run. This might be any time when the computer is idle for a certain time or it might run all the time in the background using idle CPU cycles. The BOINC client will keep the version of the science applications current, checking with the server, and handle communication with the server, sending results back. Most BOINC science applications have a screen saver graphic display that shows the work being done in graphs, charts, and animated graphics. Currently BOINC supports several particle physics experiments, climate prediction, protein structure, epidemiology and medical disease projects, cancer research, and SETI@home. In early 2008 BOINC had over 2.5 million active computers worldwide, providing a bit more than 800 TFLOPS. Of course these numbers will continue to increase.

Condor

The Condor system is a different approach that allows an administrator to create a local cluster of idle workstations to do distributed processing without the limitations or constraints of a cluster and without going to the trouble of setting up a cluster in hardware and software or organizing a grid. It provides an infrastructure similar to BOINC but each project administers its own single project and a private set of nodes. These nodes are probably owned by a single institution.

Condor is an ongoing project at the University of Wisconsin that allows users of computers to register them as being available and to describe a computer's capabilities: what type of processor(s) it has (Pentium, PowerPC, Athlon, etc.), how much memory and disk space, what software libraries are installed, and other characteristics. Someone who wants to run a program or a group of programs (a workflow) describes the requirements of those programs in a similar manner. These descriptions are called ClassAds (like classified advertisements) and are used by Condor to matchmake (i.e., to find the best matches between providers and requestors). Condor allows computers to describe preferences about when they should do this work. For example, a system might be allowed to do the work in the background, or when no one has pressed a keyboard key for a few minutes. After many years of development, Condor has become very popular and widespread and is a very stable system that requires only a simple procedure to install on computers wishing to provide service.

Common problems

Volunteer computing systems must cope with several problems of the computers used:

> They are heterogeneous, so the software must adapt readily.
>
> They join and leave the system unpredictably.
>
> Their availability is irregular.
>
> The systems should not interfere with normal system use.

In addition, volunteer computing systems must deal with a few problems concerning reliable results, stemming from the fact that volunteers are often anonymous and therefore unaccountable:

> Some volunteer computers may malfunction and return incorrect results.
>
> Volunteer computers may have their speed set too fast in order to gain extra credit and therefore more often malfunction.

Volunteers may intentionally return incorrect results.

Volunteers may claim excessive credit for results.

One common approach to all of these problems is to have each batch of data processed on at least two computers. The results and the credit are accepted only if they agree fairly closely. Another technique used is checksumming or performing a CRC (cyclic redundancy check) on the results. These are mathematical functions computed over the result data that detect transmission errors or tampering.

7.5 HOW OPERATING SYSTEM CONCEPTS DIFFER IN SMPs, CLUSTERS, AND GRIDS

In this section, we discuss several of the OS concepts that we have described in previous chapters and how they differ from the uniprocessor systems discussed there. In some cases, the concepts and implementations in parallel systems are almost identical to single CPU systems; in a few cases, the differences are noteworthy and important.

7.5.1 Process synchronization and communication

Recall that processes often share work with other processes. Sharing work usually also implies sharing data. This distribution of work and partitioning or sharing data requires coordination between processes. Even in simple cases where there is not very much interaction between these executable elements, one needs to exercise caution in those small parts of the program code where data (even a single number) may be shared between processes running on different systems. The problem we are trying to avoid is caused by two processes that are trying to change a single data item at the same time. This is called a **race condition.** Traditionally, interprocess communication is done using shared memory or message queues. Synchronizing concurrent access to data is done using semaphores or similar locking mechanisms in those **critical sections** of the processes involved where they actually manipulate the data. These mechanisms are based on shared memory and special CPU instructions. They will be elaborated on in Chapter 9. On some distributed architectures these mechanisms are not available and other mechanisms must be used. Perhaps a simple example best illustrates the question of how systems can accomplish synchronization and communication in distributed architectures.

7.5.2 An example

Suppose we have a very long list of information about many people. For example, it might include telephone numbers, names, email addresses, and some value such as the family income for the last year. We would like to sort this list into ascending order by phone number and calculate the average income at the same time. This is an ideal problem for the architectures discussed in this chapter. (In fact, this problem may be too ideal since it can be structured as a highly parallel application and thus yields a speedup factor that may be atypical for distributed computing.)

The obvious method to solve this problem is to partition the list into smaller, separate lists. If we had eight processors to divide the work among we could have each processor sort and calculate the average on one eighth of the data, and then we could merge the result. This is a sweep flow, as was described earlier. The merge step at the end is a pipeline, as is the partitioning of the data at the beginning of the work flow. While each processor is sorting and averaging its own part of the list there is no interaction between processes. But at the time of merging the resulting lists and calculating the average there will be data sharing.

It would be more efficient if we could start processing (merging) results before all the results have been calculated. But this might create a race condition where some of the processors started trying to merge the results before all the processors had produced their first output. Furthermore, even if all eight processors were the same type and speed it would be very unusual that they completed their work at the same time. We could try to balance this by giving more work—more numbers in their list—to faster processors. If a processor was twice as fast as the others we could give it twice as many numbers to work with. But, this doesn't work since it takes more than twice as long to sort this longer list, because sorting is not a linear time function. Predicting the running time of parallel processes is important, but usually difficult—and not very precise.

7.5.3 But it gets difficult

Now our simple example is getting complex—merging the results of sorted lists, as they become available, and calculating the average (a few adds, maybe scaled with multiplications, and a divide) shared data—and before we can use the result of a sweep process we need to know if it has finished. On a single CPU computer this is not difficult. We can communicate using shared memory and signal completion by setting flags in the data to indicate completion.

7.5.4 The SMP case

How would this be done on a SMP system? Fortunately, it can be done exactly the same way as on a single CPU computer. SMPs share memory among all the CPUs, so most of the common techniques used to communicate among processes work the same way as in a uniprocessor system. We discuss the issues involved in SMP OSs further in Chapter 9.

7.5.5 The cluster case

How are sharing and locking done on a cluster of computers? This architecture is somewhat more difficult than with a single CPU or an SMP system. Sharing memory is not possible (it may be simulated, but that is quite slow). Messages must be sent between processor nodes via a local area network. Work is partitioned and distributed. Since data is not shared in memory between processors, it must be sent to each processor node separately. If the data is originating in a file, there may be file sharing across nodes, minimizing the impact of this distribution.

It is common to try to partition the processing of problems for a cluster so that there is almost no interaction between processes until the end of each process because communication between systems in a cluster is much slower than in an SMP system. For this reason, usually the rewriting and restructuring of a work flow for a cluster requires more programming and design than for an SMP system or single CPU and it does not end up doing as much work in parallel. But, the tradeoff is that the per-processing node cost in a cluster is much lower.

7.5.6 The grid case

How are locking and sharing done on a system with a grid architecture? This is the most difficult case. Sharing memory is not physically possible between clusters in a grid and is very difficult to simulate. Messages must be sent between nodes or between clusters via a network that may be protected by firewalls. The nodes may be very far apart and thus have very high communication latency. The work is therefore partitioned and distributed. Since data is not shared in memory between processors it must be sent to each cluster through a network, primarily the Internet, which is often slow, but perhaps over the Internet2, which is usually a bit better performing. Results must similarly travel back over the same network. Even if the data is stored in a file, the files being shared must still be copied to another cluster, where they may be shared between nodes in that cluster.

Why is this effort worthwhile? Why do we use grids for computation? We use them because grids also share, but instead of only sharing memory, they share whole clusters of computers between users. Rather than being limited to using *only* the perhaps few hundred or so nodes available in a local cluster, a researcher may be able to use 50 clusters of computers, ranging from 10 to 400 nodes in each cluster. This high-level sharing may allow the use of many thousands of nodes for a short time. Since one is using someone else's cluster, then one may not be able to use it for *too* long, maybe only a few thousand hours. But one should also share one's own local cluster, so things should balance out in the long run. Users of grids therefore form **virtual organizations.** These organizations agree to pool and share resources such as their clusters. Such organizations are very dynamic. A virtual organization may form to computationally analyze one problem. It might be one task, such as a bioinformatics work flow that takes 100,000 compute hours in total, but is done by two dozen (24) clusters creating a small grid, and done over the weekend. Then the virtual organization disbands until the next big problem. This problem might take more than 10 years if done on a single computer similar to nodes on the cluster, or half a year on a typical local cluster such as that described later in this chapter.

For very large data sets, for example, the output of the LHC (Large Hadron Collider, a large-particle accelerator at CERN, in Europe) physics experiment, the analysis work will take many millions of compute hours, so the virtual organizations will be around for quite a while. These organizations depend on Moore's law, that computers and capacities will increase, year-by-year, so that in later years, processing will speed up, and possibly the researchers will discover new principles of science that would otherwise never be found.

7.5.7 File-sharing techniques

Large-scale computation users typically need lots of files. Files contain raw data values, parameters, intermediate and final results, and other information. It is not unusual that some of these files are very large, perhaps many gigabytes each. Clusters with many terabytes of storage (in a few cases, a hundred terabytes) are common, and the previously mentioned LHC will need petabytes of storage.

File sharing for SMPs is relatively easy since the processes also share the file system. Of course, the processes that share files may need to coordinate using locks or similar mechanisms. In most SMPs there is a primary file system (or a few) managed by the OS. Since the OS handles file operations it can coordinate among multiple processes that are creating, reading, writing, and performing other file operations.

In clusters, there are multiple instances of identical OSs running on the different processors and they manage the sharing of files. This may be done by creating special file-sharing nodes, which allow files that they control to be manipulated by any (or many) nodes in the cluster. These nodes support an interface that provides essentially the same functions as those provided by a local OS in a single node or SMP system. Since it is possible to have race conditions on files in a cluster, file sharing nodes usually also provide locking commands to lock all or part of a file to allow error-free data sharing.

Grids do not share parts of files, nor do they allow locking between clusters. They do allow entire files to be copied, and some grid tools may simulate cluster-like file sharing. Ensuring that all nodes in multiple clusters have a consistent, identical view of every shared file is very challenging and is an active area of grid research. Even more difficult is the management of files that are almost the same between clusters, but have been changed a little, and yet still have the same name.

7.5.8 Using remote services

Applications often need to access remote services. These may include remote subroutines or function, methods on objects, or separate processes. The topic of remote services has been a very popular topic in parallel and distributed computing for many decades. This refers to how remote services are started and invoked remotely, how parameters are passed, and how results are returned.

On SMP systems services outside a particular process are most typically invoked through remote procedure calls (RPCs) or remote method invocations (RMIs). This is the same mechanism as discussed previously for interprocess management. Systems running on clusters employ middleware that enhances RPC calls or RMI invocations to be similar to the same calls in SMP or multiprocessing uniprocessor systems. Grid systems present challenges due to the difficulty of sharing (particularly of sharing data) and the issues of security. Naturally, most cluster administrators are very wary of allowing direct contact with a node in the cluster they are allowing remote access to. Grid systems have potentially long network delays, so usually grid services are provided by batch-like, noninteractive servers. New grid service models, for example, the new Globus model discussed in Section 7.4.4, do provide Web services as a model and provide security through certificates.

With a long history and many opinions and implementations of remote servers and services, this area will be contentious and important for many years to come.

7.5.9 Handling failures

Lastly, we come to the somewhat unpleasant question of what happens *when* something goes wrong?

As more components, more computers, and more software are aggregated into a larger system, the chances that something will go wrong increases, maybe just something minor. This is why SMP systems, clusters, and grids must all recognize and deal with the eventuality of failure.

What can fail? The first thing that comes to mind is a hardware failure—a disk goes bad, maybe a chip fries, and a computer stops working. This will result in a node failing or not responding and losing the work it was doing. Network failures are probably more likely than node failures. A cable might come loose or a switch or router might fail. A network or server might suffer a denial of service (DOS) attack. (We discuss such attacks in Chapter 16.) Even more commonly a network or router will get very overloaded and drop traffic. In general, network failures will mimic node failures.

But software may also cause failures. For example, the wrong version of a program or the wrong version of a runtime library may be loaded on a system. This is a very common problem. Unfortunately, software bugs may cause failures that are not detected until long after the failure actually occurred.

Software must be written to account for failures. For example, middleware can use timeouts to check that a remote procedure call or other server request is responded to within a reasonable amount of time. And if the service does not respond within the time limit another call is made, perhaps to a different server. If the original request response shows up later, then the result is simply thrown away.

Monitoring systems can watch network traffic, trying to detect failures. They can also watch individual node or cluster performance for failures due to hardware or misconfigured software. There are tradeoffs to be made here. For example, too little monitoring will cause failures to be unnoticed and unmanaged for a long time but too much monitoring creates a substantial overhead in computing resources and network bandwidth.

7.6 EXAMPLES

7.6.1 Scientific computing on clusters and grids

In the last few years several significant, computationally intensive natural science projects have used large computational clusters and grids. In this section, we discuss a few such projects. The continually declining price of commodity computers, disk storage systems, high-speed networking equipment, and network bandwidth and software to control the distribution of work and data have very recently reached the point where such systems are affordable by most research communities. As a result, many new projects have only achieved results in the last year and others have not yet reached such milestones. The following projects are not the largest or perhaps the most significant; rather, they are a representative sample of different approaches and technologies employed to accomplish intense computational work.

7.6.2 The human genome DNA assembly

In the early 1990s, J. Craig Venter suggested using a whole genome shotgun assembly approach for large genomes. (It is not possible with current technology to simply read each nucleotide, one at a time, in very long pieces of DNA.) A genome assembly starts with ripping a DNA strand into many short pieces. These pieces are then "read" by sequencing machines in strings of up to 900 bases at a time. The four bases are adenine, guanine, cytosine, and thymine, normally shown as A, G, C, and T. A genome assembly algorithm works by taking all the pieces and aligning them to one another, and detecting all places where two of the short strings overlap. An example is shown in Figure 7.5, where several overlaps of short segments of the original string can be seen. This method has become very popular, due, in large part, to the availability of computer clusters to assemble the large number of overlapping fragments. While smaller genomes had already been sequenced by Venter using shotgun assembly, assembling the human genome needed much greater computing resources and very sophisticated software. This approach scans a slightly more than 3 billion base pair human genome that has been broken into more than 50 million overlapping pieces. Since the chemical process for breaking up and reading sequences is not perfect, the algorithmic looks for near matches to align ends.

The processing done in this work on the human genome assembly initially took about 20,000 CPU hours. But it was done on a cluster of 40 four-processor SMP systems in a few days. This system, which at the time cost $40 million, would now cost, for an equivalent amount of processing power, a few hundred thousand dollars.

The major alternative approach, used by the public Human Genome Project, was to assemble ever-longer sequences, growing pieces into longer, known sequences. This hierarchical approach also requires significant computational resources. A custom written program, GigAssembler, was developed that ran on a 100-node Linux cluster. In both approaches, the computational needs were large enough to require using computational clusters. These were cases where there really was no other reasonable choice.

Original string	XXX**ACGATCGTCGAGTCATCGTTAGCGTA**XXXX
1st sample–A	XXX**ACGATCGTCGAGTCATCGT**XXXXXXXXXXX
1st sample–B	XXXXXXXXXXXXXXXXXXXXXXX**TAGCGTA**XXXX
2nd sample–A	XXX**ACGATG**XXXXXXXXXXXXXXXXXXXXXXXX
2nd sample–B	XXXXXXXXX**CTCGAGTCATCGTTAGCGTA**XXXX

FIGURE 7.5
Genome assembly.

7.6.3 IBM Computational Biology Center and cluster computing

IBM has been active in parallel and distributed computing for many years, and has taken a leadership role in developing very large-scale computer clusters and software infrastructure and biological applications to use those systems. Blue Gene/L is a 131,000-processor cluster, with multiple network pathways to each node. This system, which was co-designed by Lawrence Livermore Labs, is used for science research. About half of the 500 largest computational clusters in the world are IBM computers. The Blue Gene series of computers, all very large clusters, use relatively modest-speed CPUs and employ a modified version of Linux as the OS.

The Computational Biology Center has several large projects of interest, including bioinformatics, medical informatics, and functional genomics research. One of these projects, a biomolecular simulator called Blue Matter, simulates modest-size systems (10,000–100,000 atoms) for long time scales (hundreds of nanoseconds to a few microseconds). Using 4,096 processors on Blue Gene/L, a 43,000 atom membrane protein system ran for a simulated time of one microsecond in a wall clock time of slightly less than two months.

7.6.4 Volunteer computing clusters

The goal of using processor cycles that would otherwise be wasted has appealed to many people for years. SETI@home, a project that searched for extraterrestrial intelligence, utilized years of data collected from radio telescopes that had been stored in repositories but for which no computing resources had been available to analyze this data. SETI@home has been remarkably successful from a computing view. More than 5 million participants have contributed over 2 million years of aggregate computing time over the years. In early 2008 it was estimated that at any given time all of the computers in the SETI@home system together provide 370 TFLOPS ($370 \cdot 10^{12}$ floating point operations per second). As a comparison, Blue Gene/L can reach the peak performance of 478.2 TFLOPS, with about one-sixth the number of processors as SETI. But note that the SETI computers are connected over home networks and phone lines, composed of a mixture of older and newer machines, and sometimes do other real work for their users. While no conclusive signs of extraterrestrial intelligence have been found, there have been several interesting findings that may warrant further investigation. One concern voiced in a recent astronomy publication is that the digital signals collected at radio telescopes and sent over the Internet might expose the earth's Internet to extraterrestrial viruses. While this would confirm extraterrestrial intelligence, no extraterrestrial viruses have yet been detected on earth. SETI@home is considered to be the largest grid/cluster computation in history.

Folding@home is an effort to simulate protein folding and misfolding; it was created by the Pande Group at Stanford. It has simulated folding in the 5- to 10-microsecond range, which is a time scale thousands of times longer than was previously thought possible. It is the second largest volunteer project (after SETI@home). On September 16, 2007, the Folding@home project officially attained a performance level higher than one petaflops. It has been used lately for analyzing protein misfolding, which is thought to be applicable to diseases such as bovine spongiform encephalopathy (BSE), or mad cow disease.

7.6.5 A typical computer cluster

Here we describe a typical computer cluster with 98 two-processor computers. It happens to exist, but it is intended merely as a typical example of such a cluster and some samples of commands one might use in such an environment. Each node has a local disk and two processors inside the computer, and each computer's two processors share two gigabytes of memory. The 98 computers communicate with each other and with the Internet via a one-gigabit per second switched Ethernet LAN. There are also several NAS disk arrays using **redundant array of independent disks (RAID)** technology. (This technology is explained in Chapter 14). Together they comprise 100 terabytes of storage. The cluster also has five "head" nodes connected to firewalls that allow an external user to connect to the cluster or to several dedicated database servers. It also has a few Web servers outside of the firewall for general status and information about the system.

Each computer node is running a separate but identical copy of Linux as the OS, and each node has common software installed such as OS utilities, high-level language compilers, libraries, and several science applications. Individual computational nodes and storage are isolated from the Internet. Access is granted through the aforementioned head nodes. The head nodes run clustering software that allows a user to log in to the head node and run multiple parallel jobs by using PBS (portable batch system—now called TORQUE, but almost always still referred to as PBS). Head nodes also do monitoring and some other accounting work, but are designed to be used primarily as portals for running an actual workflow on multiple compute nodes.

7.6.6 Utilizing a Globus cluster

The Linux OS on the cluster has good support of the two-processor nodes and for managing scheduling on the two CPUs. These OSs don't know that they are part of a cluster. Rather than modifying the OS, the cluster work management is done by middleware, running on top of the OS. The middleware scheduler called PBS is freeware, as is the Linux OS underneath it. While PBS is a sophisticated system with many interfaces, a user can make effective use of it while knowing only a few commands.

First, one has to tell PBS what kind of CPU resources are needed. One can specify individual parameters on separate lines, like this:

```
#PBS -M dave@mymailer.uta.edu
#PBS -l nodes=10:ppn=2
#PBS -l cput=02:00:00
#PBS -l mem=213mb
#PBS -l walltime=00:20:00
```

Or combine the last four lines, like this:

```
#PBS -l
nodes=10:ppn=2,cput=2:00:00,mem=213mb,walltime=00:20:00
```

This PBS command requests 10 nodes, two processors per node, and 213 MB of memory. It requests a total of two hours of CPU time to run in 20 minutes of wall clock time to run all of the workflow that users will submit. The M parameter tells the system who the user is.

In order to see the results of a program's execution a user will need to tell the system where the normal output and error output streams should go. Here they are redirected to files, so they can be retrieved later:

```
#PBS -o outputfile
#PBS -e errorfile
```

Since the job may take some time to finish (weeks or even months, in some cases, even on large grids), a user can ask for an email to be sent when the job begins to run, and another when it terminates or aborts.

```
#PBS -m bae
```

And finally, the OS needs to know where the program is that is to be run:

```
cd /temp/my_working_dir
echo "I am running on host 'hostname'"
execute my_program
rm ./junk
exit
```

Specifically a user asks the OS to run some programs, probably with different files as input data, clean up any leftover temporary files, and exit. Note that frequently the user will put all of these commands into a shell script file and then run it.

A user submitting jobs using PBS needs to keep in mind that it is a batch-oriented system. Most modern OSs are primarily interactive—when an icon is clicked to tell the OS to run a job, it tries to start it immediately. In a batch system the job may not be able to run immediately because the resources asked for are not available at the time. So the jobs may be placed in a queue for later execution. There are a number of commands that a user can use to manage the jobs and queues available. Here are a few of them:

```
#qalter       Alter a batch job
#qdel         Delete a batch job
#qhold        Hold a batch job
#qmove        Move a batch job to another queue
#qrls         Release held jobs
#qrerun       Rerun a batch job
#qselect      Select a specific subset of jobs
#qstat        Show status of batch jobs
```

For those users who are not comfortable with command-line interfaces there is also a GUI version of PBS called XPBS.

7.6.7 Portals and Web interfaces

After an application is working on a cluster, it might be desirable to make it available to others, either within a group or to a wider community. Or a user might simply want an easy-to-use interface to an application. In the past, creating a windowing interface was an option, and many applications still do this. But it is now possible to make a grid workflow or application Web-enabled.

Portals are server computers that allow users to access data, applications, information, and to share results. A local portal allows anyone to login, look at ongoing research, match interests to faculty researchers, and apply for an account. Account holders may access local applications, get datasets, chat with whoever is online, and share data and opinions.

7.7 SUMMARY

Prior to this chapter we discussed the designs of OSs that run on a single machine. Modern systems often are designed for applications where many processors are used together. In this chapter we discussed computing on more than one CPU and some of the difficulties that arise in constructing and using such systems. We covered several common designs for multiple CPU systems, and a few unusual designs as well. After an introduction and definitions of a few key concepts, we discussed a bit of the theory of parallel computing and the issues of computational models and programming. Then we discussed some common architectures for distributed systems. OSs

designed to run in such environments have special considerations that do not arise in uniprocessing situations, so we covered some extra issues OSs face in distributed systems. These topics included such questions as what facets need to be managed, how does multiprocessor system resource management differ from uniprocessor systems, and what interfaces are presented to programmers and users. Finally, we discussed some real applications that are implemented as distributed systems, including a look at a typical cluster installation in a grid.

In the next part of the book we begin looking at individual topics in Operating Systems in more depth.

BIBLIOGRAPHY

Dubois, M., and F. A. Briggs, "Synchronization, Coherence, and Event Ordering in Multiprocessors," *Computer,* Vol. 21, No. 2, February 1988, pp. 9–21.

Geer, D., "For Programmers, Multicore Chips Mean Multiple Challenges," *Computer,* Volume 40, Issue 9, September 2007, pp 17–19.

WEB RESOURCES

http://www.globus.org (Home page for the Globus Alliance)

http://www.globustoolkit.org (Open source software toolkit used for building grids)

http://boinc.berkeley.edu/ (BOINC home page - SETI project, among others)

REVIEW QUESTIONS

7.1 Moore's law says that computers are getting faster and faster all the time. Why do we then go to the trouble of building cluster systems and other exotic designs that require a programmer to work hard to exploit any possible parallelism in a design?

7.2 True or false? SMP systems and clusters (almost) always use the same CPU in every node but grid systems can use different CPUs in each node.

7.3 Which is true about the nodes in a cluster system?
  a. They share a single memory.
  b. They have no local peripherals.
  c. They communicate over a separate dedicated LAN.
  d. A dedicated node runs the OS.
  e. None of the above is true about the nodes in a cluster system.

7.4 True or false? A pipeline flow is an example of a workflow where there is parallelism that can be exploited.

7.5 What does Amdahl's law say about the speedup of a workflow?

7.6 What common technique used in uniprocessor systems allows a programmer to exploit parallelism on SMP systems?
  a. memory mapped files
  b. multithreading
  c. critical sections
  d. semaphores
  e. none of the above

7.7 What common hardware technique requires an SMP scheduler to make some special provisions for scheduling processes?

7.8 What is the term used to describe the mechanisms that are commonly used to exploit parallelism in distributed applications running on cluster systems?

7.9 Which of these techniques used in SMP systems or in clusters are also used to distribute processing in grid systems?
  a. multithreading
  b. RMI
  c. virtual systems
  d. CORBA
  e. none of the above

7.10 In uniprocessor systems we have to use critical sections to protect shared memory when it is being accessed by multiple processes. Why do we not usually need to use such mechanisms on clusters and grids?

7.11 What mechanism is suggested to mitigate most failures in distributed systems?

7.12 How does work get distributed on a multiprocessing computer system?

7.13 How does work get distributed on a cluster computing system?

7.14 How does work get distributed on a volunteer computing system?

7.15 How does work get distributed in a Globus system?

Part 3

CPU and Memory Management

In this part:

Parts 3–5 of this book are similar to the bulk of most OS textbooks. They provide in-depth treatment of individual aspects of OSs. In particular, Part 3 treats some of the more fundamental topics that all modern OSs have to deal with: process and thread management and memory management. Together these constitute two of the major portions of an OS.

There are four chapters in this part of the text. The first two deal with processes and threads and how they communicate and otherwise interact. Chapter 8 defines a process and discusses the algorithms and data structures that have evolved to manage and schedule processes. It also defines the concept of threads and how they are used and implemented.

When high performance systems are developed that place great demands on an OS, it is usually necessary to break them into separate parts and allow them to run separately. Chapter 9 discusses the reasons why we often end up with systems comprised of multiple process or threads. Multiple processes will need to communicate to coordinate their work. So this chapter discusses mechanisms for such communication. It then points out some of the pitfalls involved in such communication and introduces the notions of synchronization and the deadlocks that may result.

The last two chapters in this part of the book deal with issues of memory management. Chapter 10 deals with memory management in simple systems. In part this is historical, but today it is clear that miniaturization of computer hardware will mean that we will continue to find computers in environments where resources are scarce, and these simple techniques will continue to be applicable in the foreseeable future.

Chapter 11 deals with how memory is managed in larger systems. The two main techniques that have evolved are paging and segmentation. This chapter first explains how these work and then goes on to explain the notion of effective memory access time and the effect that paged or segmented memory would have. It then introduces the idea of a translation lookaside buffer and how it mitigates this problem. It next explains the notion of virtual memory and discusses some algorithms for the management of virtual memory.

Chapter 8

Process Management: Concepts, Threads, and Scheduling

In this chapter:

In this chapter we talk about processes and threads. A fundamental function of an OS is the execution of a program and an executing program is known as a process. A program is a static thing. In most OSs a program is stored in a file on secondary storage. Eventually an OS is instructed to run a program, usually by a user, but sometimes by another process, perhaps one running on another system. The OS brings that program into primary storage and begins to execute it. That running entity is known as a **process.** Note that we may run many copies of the same program at the same time on one system. For example, it is possible to start several copies of a program development environment running at the same time. Each running copy of the program would be a separate process. Other terms often used for a process are a **job** or a **task.**

In the first section we define a process and speak about the abstraction of a machine that the process runs on. An OS must keep track of much information about each running process, especially when that process is not actually executing on a CPU. In Section 8.2 we explain the main control structure that OSs use to store this data for a process, a process control block. As a process executes it will be in various states such as ready to run, running, waiting, and so on. Various events cause the process to transition from one such state to another. Section 8.3 discusses the various states that a process can be in and the events that can cause the transitions between the states. When systems are running multiple processes the OS must decide which process will run next. Section 8.4 addresses the various algorithms for scheduling the execution of processes. In order for a complex application to accomplish many things at once it is sometimes desirable for the process to start another process to do some of the work, so Section 8.5 explains how one process can start another process.

Switching between processes turns out to have substantial impact on the performance of an OS and the programs it is running. As a result, another mechanism was developed that will allow a single process to accomplish more things at the same time using the mechanism of threads. Section 8.6 covers this topic. In Section 8.7 we discuss some real implementations of threads in some different OSs. Threads are also available in some high-level languages and in a standard thread API available on many OSs, so we discuss those in this section as well. In Section 8.8 we close with a summarization of the chapter.

8.1 INTRODUCTION TO PROCESSES

As a process runs it will change its **state.** Most obviously it will be changing the program counter (or instruction address register) as it runs and as it calls subroutines or functions or invokes methods, loops, and so on. It will also be changing the contents of the CPU registers, the system status register, and the stack pointer, at least on most machines. These items (and more discussed later) are collectively known as the process state. If we were only running one process on a system then there would be nothing much more to say about the process state. But these days we are not normally running only one process. We are rapidly switching between many processes in an effort to keep the hardware very busy and responsive to the user(s).

While we want the system to be able to run many processes at the same time, we want this switching among processes to be transparent to the processes themselves (i.e., a process does not need to know whether or when it will be suspended and another process run). We are creating a "virtual CPU" in the sense that every process can act as if it were the only process running. Since we are doing all this switching between processes, when we stop one process to start another we will have to save the state of the process we are stopping and restore the previous state of the process we are starting. (This assumes that the process we are starting is not a new process.) We will create a structure in memory where we will save the information describing the state of the process we are stopping. We will call this structure a **process control block** (**PCB**). Some OSs call this structure a **process descriptor.**

8.2 PROCESS DESCRIPTOR—PROCESS CONTROL BLOCK

As was just described, when a process is stopped by the OS for any reason, the state of the CPU at that time is saved in the PCB. There are many other pieces of information in the PCB as well. A typical PCB is shown in Figure 8.1. Different OSs

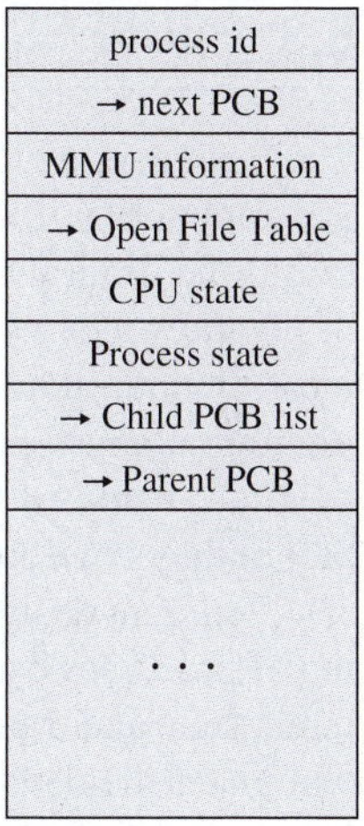

process id
→ next PCB
MMU information
→ Open File Table
CPU state
Process state
→ Child PCB list
→ Parent PCB
. . .

FIGURE 8.1
A process control block.

will keep different information in the PCB, but here are some things that are fairly common:

- Program name
- Process ID, a number assigned by the OS to identify the process
- Parent process ID or a pointer to the parent process PCB
- Pointer to a list of child PCBs
- Pointer to the "next" PCB, probably in a queue
- Accounting information
- Pointer to a table of open files
- CPU state information
  - Instruction counter
  - Stack pointer(s)
  - System status register
  - Other system registers
- Event descriptor, valid if the process is waiting for something
- Process state information (see next section)
- Process owner (user)
- Memory management information
- Pointer to a message queue
- Pointer to an event queue

It is important to understand that while a process is actually running, the *CPU state information* is not updated. It is saved only when the process is stopped for some reason. Note that the term "state" is overloaded. We have been talking about the "state" of the CPU and said that we saved that information in the part of the PCB called the "CPU state information" when we stopped a process. You may have noticed that the PCB also has another entry called "process state information." This is something different, and it is coming up next.

8.3 PROCESS STATES AND TRANSITIONS

The designers of OSs have to document the external view of their systems so that programmers will know how to write programs for them and users will know how to run the programs. Some of the things that need to be discussed can be described in several ways. An example is the concept of "states" that a process can be in. The most obvious state for a process is that it is running. But only one process can be running at any time on each CPU, so what are the other processes doing? Some of them are ready to run and some of them are waiting for something else to happen before they continue.

Different designers (and authors) will use different models to explain the managing of processes by an OS. In Chapter 2 we introduced this five-state model with different state and transition labels, but it is also common to see a **three-state model** that eliminates the new and exit states. The five-state model is shown again in Figure 8.2. It is convenient to describe these states with a state diagram. The states (or nodes) are indicated by the hexagons. The arrows (or transitions) are the events that cause the transition from one state to another state. The five states are seen as New, Ready, Run, Wait, and Exit. These states often have different names in other references.

The **New** state represents a process that the OS is currently preparing to run but that is not yet ready. When the user tells the command processor module to run a program it goes through the transition marked "0–Program Loaded" and is put in the New state. First, the OS has to create a new PCB, assign a process id, and fill in all

FIGURE 8.2

A five-state process model.

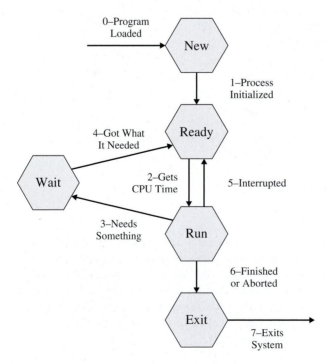

the other PCB parameters. Then it usually has to reserve memory, read the program in from secondary storage, and so forth. Especially on a multiple CPU system we don't want an instance of the OS running on another CPU trying to dispatch this process, so until it is actually ready to run it is marked as being in the New state.

When a process is ready to run it is put in the **Ready** state. This is seen as transition "1–Process Initialized." Eventually it will be selected by the OS as the next process to run. Then it will be **dispatched** (i.e., it will be put into the **Run** state). This transition is indicated by the arrow labeled "2–Gets CPU Time." As a process is running it may decide to wait for something else to happen before it continues. A very common cause is that the process has requested a synchronous I/O operation (like a normal high-level language Read operation) and wants to wait until the operation is complete and thus it is moved to the **Wait** state, sometimes known as the **Suspended** state. This transition is labeled "3–Needs Something." We will later see that there are many different kinds of events that a process can wait for. When a process is in the Wait state, sooner or later the event that the process is waiting for may occur. (Of course, that event might never occur, for example, a process that is waiting for possible errors or for an incoming request for a service that is rarely used.) As an example of this transition, perhaps the I/O that a process had requested has finished. This transition is labeled "4–Got What It Needed" and the OS puts the process into the Ready state. The next transition in this model is labeled "5–Interrupted." The OS may elect to interrupt a running process for several reasons, but not all OSs do so. The first instance is a time-slicing system where each process in turn is given a short amount of time to execute. If it has not done something in that time to cause it to go into wait state then the OS will take it out of Run state and put it into the Ready state and allow another process to run. A second instance would be where a process with a high priority has been waiting for an event and the event occurs. If the process that is running has a lower priority than the process that was waiting, then the OS may stop the lower priority process, put it back in the Ready state, and put the higher priority process into Run state. But not all OSs use priority scheduling.

The **Exit** state is reserved for processes that are being ended by the OS. There may be many reasons for a process to reach this state. This transition is labeled "6–Finished or Aborted." Finishing is obvious. Abort is fairly clear. Either the process or the OS has detected a problem and the process is being stopped before more damage occurs. But there are also other reasons why a process might leave the run state and go to the exit state. As one example: A parent process to this process may decide that this child process is no longer needed and ask the OS to kill it. For most purposes we don't want to clutter up this model so we leave these more rare transitions out of the figure.

The Exit state is rather peculiar in that processes don't stay in it very long, but these processes are not running, ready, or waiting, so we could reasonably talk about this state as being something distinct from those other states. The OS will need to do some housekeeping for this process such as freeing up resources that the process may have acquired and not yet returned, ensuring files are closed, and tearing down the PCB for the process. Until the resources are fully recovered we don't want this process being selected to run, so we leave it in this state as we work.

Other OS documentation includes even more complex models. In at least one case[1] the model used by the designers has nine states and many transitions. While the designers of this system may have felt it was necessary to explain to application programmers some special facets of the system, this level of complexity is not seen in most documentation.

Note that except for the Run state, there can normally be many processes in any given state. So, we should not be surprised to find that for most OSs there is an elaborate mechanism for tracking all the processes that are in any of the other states. The Ready state will consist of at least one structure. Often we speak of it as the **Ready queue,** but technically we often use it in other ways than a strict queue would operate. In fact, it might be several linked lists. We discuss this more in the next section. The Run state contains only one process unless we have a multiple CPU system. In that case the processes running on the various CPUs might be linked on a separate list, but it is probably sufficient that they merely be removed from the list(s) of the Ready state. For the Wait state there may be many queues. In this case they sometimes are operated in a FCFS manner so it is legitimate to call them queues. In other cases we will do more advanced scheduling of operations and the word "queue" might not actually apply. However, the term is well entrenched in OS literature, so we will stick with it, realizing that it might not always be technically correct.

8.4 PROCESS SCHEDULING

As was just discussed, a process may leave the Run state for several reasons. When it does, it may go immediately into the Ready state, for example, if it was interrupted for reaching the limit of its time quantum. If a process is waiting on some event, perhaps an I/O completion, and the event happens, then we will need to put the process into the Ready state so it can get to the Run state and handle the event. When we put a process into the Ready state, we need to decide when it should run in relation to the processes that are already in the Ready state. This decision is made by an OS module called the **short-term scheduler.** There are a number of ways the OS can make this decision. We might want to design our OS so that we can plug in various short-term scheduler modules to suit the needs of the system users and administrators. First, we describe the algorithms and then we discuss some of the pluses and minuses of them in various situations.

8.4.1 FCFS scheduling

The simplest method, and one historically used by many OSs, is simply to run a first-in, first-out schedule with an ordinary queue. This is called the **FCFS,** or first come, first served algorithm. It has several advantages. It is easy to implement. It is well understood by designers, users, administrators, and even teachers. Finally, it is by definition the **fairest** (i.e., it does not favor any one process over another in any

---

[1] UNIX SVR4. See Bach, M. J., The Design of the UNIX Operating System. Englewood Cliffs, NJ: Prentice Hall, 1986. No. 1, January 1988.

circumstance). FCFS is often enhanced by allowing a running process to make a system call that yields control to the next process in the Ready state. This is known as cooperative multitasking. It was typical of a generation of OSs that included the pre-X Mac OS, Microsoft Windows, and many others. Of course, the running process might have a bug or might be trying to make itself have better user response by using more CPU time that it ought, so it was not an ideal solution.

8.4.2 Priority scheduling

There are some circumstances when we might not want to use a FCFS algorithm. For one thing, we may have some processes that are much more important than others. In a modern OS we want to process keystrokes and mouse operations promptly so that the waiting time of the interactive user is minimized. We will want the process that is managing the window that has the focus of the OS to be fairly responsive—perhaps we are browsing a website. We are less interested in the performance of other processes that might be running but that don't currently have the focus—perhaps our email reader is checking our mail servers to see if we have any mail. We are even less interested in the performance of some other processes—perhaps the SPOOLING system is printing a document that we downloaded some time ago. In such cases we might use a **priority** scheduling algorithm. In a priority algorithm we will associate a priority with each process. Our keystroke and mouse handler might be the highest priority, the window with the focus the next higher priority, windows without the focus the next, and background processes like the SPOOLING system still lower. There normally is a process in most OSs called something like the **idle** process that runs in a loop when no other process is ready to run. (Note that the "highest priority" might be the lowest number, not the highest number. The choice might depend on the instruction set of the computer or might just be an arbitrary decision on the part of the developer. As long as the scheduler is consistent it is perfectly normal to have the lowest number represent the highest priority.)

Whenever we allow some jobs to have priority over other jobs there is a special problem that we have to worry about. It is possible that higher-priority processes keep postponing a low-priority process to the point that the lower-priority process never gets to run. This problem is known as **starvation.** There are several ways we can deal with this potential problem. Collectively these are known as **aging.** Generally we will monitor those processes that are being postponed, and whenever we postpone a process too many times we simply raise its priority temporarily. Eventually it will reach a high enough priority that it will run one time. Then we will let the priority drop back to where it was originally. Eventually even fairly low-priority processes will finish, but higher-priority jobs will still be given the majority of the time.

8.4.3 Guaranteed scheduling

FCFS scheduling gives each process a fair chance to run, but if a process does many blocking calls then it will not receive a fair amount of CPU time if other processes are running that do fewer blocking calls. It is possible to guarantee that if n processes are running then each process will get $1/n$th of the CPU time. In **guaranteed scheduling** the OS needs to track the total amount of CPU time per process and the total clock time. Then it calculates the ratio of the CPU time the process actually used to the amount of time each the process is entitled to and runs the process with the lowest ratio. This is sometimes called **fair-share scheduling.** In essence, this is a type of priority scheduling.

8.4.4 SRTF scheduling

Even large batch-oriented mainframes can have priorities among the jobs. Typically programmers developing new jobs will want fast job turnaround so that they can get their work done. Other jobs can run overnight. Nevertheless, some jobs are more important than others. Everyone wants the payroll to be on time! When timesharing is also incorporated in the system, typically the interactive window-based jobs all run at a higher priority than the batch jobs. One way to make this happen is to use an algorithm called **shortest runtime first** (sometimes called shortest remaining time first; **SRTF**) or **shortest job next** (**SJN**). This algorithm is fairly self describing. It merely selects the job to run next that will run for the shortest amount of time. Incidentally, this algorithm will produce the shortest possible turnaround times for all jobs.

Recall that when processes are running they will normally compute for a short time and then do an I/O operation. The interactive time-sharing jobs typically run for short amounts of time between I/O operations. Large batch jobs may run much longer before doing an I/O operation. So, one way we can give a higher priority to the interactive jobs is to base the priority on the amount of time that the process will run in its next CPU burst before doing an I/O operation. However, most computers don't come with the "mind reader" option installed, so we usually don't know how long the next CPU burst of a process will be. However, we can track the past performance of each process and guess that it will behave in the next CPU burst much as it has in the past few bursts. To make this guess we will use an exponentially decaying function. We will use the following variables:

T_i will be the actual time taken by this process in the i'th time interval.

E_i will be the time we estimated in the i'th time interval.

There is a parameter in this formula that will be used to tune the performance: θ. It is the percentage of the guess that we want to be based on the last actual CPU time taken by the process. Its value is therefore between 0 and 1. The rest of the guess will be based on the last guess we made. The formula will be:

$$E_i = (\theta * T_{i-1}) + ((1 - \theta) * E_{i-1})$$

θ is often initially set to .5, so that half of the guess for this time slot is based on the last actual time and half $(1 - \theta)$ is based on the last guess. Each time we make another guess, the effect of both the past guess and the time actually taken is reduced by half. This is why the function is described as **exponentially decaying.** If we raise the value of θ, then more of the next guess will be based on the actual CPU performance. This will make our estimate respond more quickly to changes in the CPU use, but we will tend to overcorrect for small fluctuations. If we lower the value of θ

then we will do the opposite—we will respond to changes more slowly but will not overreact to short fluctuations.

We will use this guess to select the processes to run next, choosing the process we guess will use the smallest amount of CPU time before it does an I/O operation. We will leave for later those processes that we think will take longer. In this way the SRTF algorithm is a variation on the Priority algorithm. We are merely setting the priority of the process based on our guess of the length of the next CPU burst.

8.4.5 Highest response ratio next

Highest response ratio next (HRRN) scheduling is similar to Shortest job next, in which the priority of each job is dependent on its estimated runtime. But HRRN also includes the amount of time the process has spent waiting. A process gets higher priority if it waits longer. This variation is used mainly because it lessens the likelihood of starvation.

$$Priority = (time\ waiting + estimated\ runtime)\ /\ estimated\ runtime.$$

8.4.6 Preemption

In each of these algorithms we have assumed that when a process has the CPU we will let it run as long as it wants to—typically it goes to Wait state for an I/O operation. However, what if we were running the priority algorithm and currently had a process running that was of fairly low priority? Assume another process with a higher priority has been waiting on an I/O event that finishes. Since we know that this process has higher priority than the one that is running we can stop the one that is running and start the higher-priority process. Taking a resource away from a process is called **preemption.** In this particular case the resource we are preempting is the CPU itself.

We can apply this idea of preemption in each of the algorithms we have studied so far. In most cases we will give a new name to the algorithm when we are allowing preemption. If we allow preemption in the FCFS algorithm it becomes the **round-robin** algorithm. In this case the preemption is not based on priority but on a time quantum. We allow each process a specific amount of time to run without doing any I/O. If it exceeds that time then we preempt the CPU and put that process at the back of the run queue.

If we apply preemption to the shortest runtime first algorithm then it becomes the **shortest remaining time first** algorithm. When we preempt a running process for a higher-priority process we note in the PCB the amount of time remaining in our guess of the runtime of that process. When we restart it later we don't make a new guess—we just use the time that was remaining when the process got preempted.

In the priority algorithm we can apply preemption when a higher-priority process enters the Ready state. We don't give this modified algorithm a special name. It is simply referred to as **priority with preemption.**

8.4.7 Multilevel queues

Modern OSs use a more complex scheduling algorithm called **multilevel queuing.** As the name implies, instead of a single queue we will use several queues. A new job will be placed in one of the queues. The individual queues can all use the same scheduling algorithm or they can use different algorithms. If the algorithms are all doing timeslicing then the queues may each have a different time quantum assigned. The queues will have different priorities, and the highest-priority queue is serviced first. A question that must be decided is the mechanism used to share the CPU between the queues. There are basically two approaches. First, we could make the mechanism a strict priority mechanism. That is to say that as long as there are processes in the higher-priority queues, those are run first. Of course, with this mechanism we would have to worry about starvation. An alternative approach is to share the CPU among the queues. For example, we might dedicate 50% to the first queue (as long as there were jobs in the queue to be run), 30% to the second, and 20% to the third. Since the lower-priority queues are always getting some service they will not starve.

Most modern OSs add a **feedback** mechanism to the multilevel queues. The initial assumption is that a new process is interactive so it is put in a high-priority queue. If the process runs for more than the allowed time quantum for this queue without doing any blocking OS call, then the OS assumes it is not really an interactive process, so it moves it to the next lower-priority queue. This queue may also have a longer time quantum. Remember that context switches are not productive work and they slow the execution of the processes down temporarily for hardware reasons that we will cover later. So if the process is not finishing its time quantum on the fast queue, we may want to give it more time at the lower queue. Typically there are at least three such queues. So if a process running in the second queue still does not do any blocking call in the time quantum for this queue it is moved to a lower queue, perhaps with a still larger time quantum.

Of course, all processes will have some intervals in which they are doing more computing than in others. So a process that is basically interactive may have short periods where it is doing a lot of computing and sinks to a lower queue. Thus, we will want to have some mechanism that will allow a process to rise back to a higher queue. This might be as simple as elevating a process to a higher queue anytime it does a blocking call without finishing the time quantum at the current level. This might be too reactive, however, and we might find it necessary to wait until a process does not finish its quantum several times in succession.

8.4.8 Selecting the best algorithm

With so many algorithms, how do we compare them? There are a number of measures of system performance that have been used to compare scheduling algorithms. A few of these include:

- throughput—jobs run per hour or per minute
- average turnaround time—time from start to end of the job
- average response time—time from submission to start of output

- CPU utilization—the percent of time the CPU is running real jobs (not switching between processes or doing other overhead; of more interest in big systems)
- average wait time—the time that processes spend in the ready queue

The first three depend on the job mix, so they are difficult to compare fairly and accurately. CPU utilization is interesting and is easy to measure, but in personal computer systems we really don't care about it. These CPUs are reasonably cheap and we are more concerned with optimizing perceived user performance. The average wait time is the measure that makes the most sense in most circumstances. We want to make sure that the most computing is getting done with the least amount of wasted time. Average waiting time seems to reflect that most accurately.

The easiest way to compare the average waiting time of the various algorithms is to use a method known as **discrete modeling.** We take a sample set of processes and their runtimes and we simulate by hand the execution of each process on that sample data. We then calculate the waiting time of the nonrunning processes and compare the values.

First, consider this set of processes:

Process ID	Arrival Time	Runtime
1	0	20
2	2	2
3	2	2

For our purposes, it does not matter what the time units are, so let's just say they are microseconds. Also, note that we show P2 and P3 both arrived at time 2. With only one CPU they can't really both arrive at time 2 since the computer can only do one thing at a time. But our clock isn't very fast, so for the purposes of this algorithm they both arrive at time 2. For each set of data we produce a timeline showing the processes running on the CPU. For this set of data, using the FCFS algorithm, we would see the following timeline:

```
0                                         20   22   24
|  P1                                     | P2 | P3 |
|_____|____|____|
```

Now let us compute the average waiting time. P1 arrives at T0, so it starts immediately. P2 arrives at T2, but does not start running until T20 when P1 finishes, so it waited for 18. P3 also arrived at T2 but did not start until P2 was over at T22, so it waited for 20. So the average waiting time was $(0 + 18 + 20) / 3 = 38/3 = 12.67$.

Now suppose that the same three processes arrived in a slightly different order:

Process ID	Arrival Time	Runtime
1	0	2
2	2	2
3	2	20

The timeline looks like this:

```
0   2   4                                         24
| P1 | P2 | P3
|____|____|_____|
```

This time the short processes came first. P1 and P2 had no wait and P3 only waited 2. Thus, the average waiting time was

$$(0 + 0 + 2) / 3 = 2 / 3 = 0.67.$$

This small difference in arrival times illustrates a major problem with the FCFS algorithm. It is called the **convoy effect** or "**head of line blocking**"—a short job arriving just after a long job will have to wait a long time before it gets to run. This will give a system running this algorithm a highly variable average wait time.

Let's look at the first set of data again, but this time we assign priorities to the arriving jobs − lowest number = highest priority:

Process ID	Arrival Time	Runtime	Priority
1	0	20	4
2	2	2	2
3	2	2	1

Now our timeline will look like this:

```
0   2   4   6                                     24
| P4 | P3 | P2 | P1
|____|____|____|_____|
```

Now P1 starts immediately, but at T2 it gets preempted by P3, which has the highest priority, so P3 starts immediately. P2 has to wait for 2, then P1 starts again at T6 after waiting 4. So now the average waiting time is:

$$(4 + 2 + 0) / 3 = 2.$$

This is not quite as good as FCFS, when the processes happened to arrive in the optimum order, but it certainly is better than what happened when they arrived in the wrong order. In this case the lower-priority job happened to be the longest job. When we are running SRTF, the process with the shortest estimated runtime gets the highest priority. This is just what happens in SRTF, so this simulation applies to that specific case of priority scheduling as well.

Next let us look at another example for SRTF. Suppose we had the following set of processes and that we were not allowing preemption:

Process ID	Arrival Time	Runtime
1	0	12
2	2	4
3	3	1
4	4	2

The timeline would look like this:

```
0                           12    13      15        19
| P1                        | P3  |  P4   | P2      |
|_____|_____|_____|_____|
```

and our average waiting time would be:

$$(0 + 13 + 9 + 9) / 4 = 7.75.$$

Now suppose that we allow preemption. Our timeline would look like this:

```
0    2   3   4    6       9                         19
| P1  |P2|P3| P4  |   P2   | P1                      |
|_____|__|__|_____|_____|_____|
```

Notice that the total execution time of the processes themselves was the same as without preemption. But now our average waiting time would be:

$$(7 + 3 + 0 + 0) / 4 = 2.5.$$

Clearly, we would prefer this result—but at what price? We know that everything has a price. Observe that in the case without preemption we only did three context switches and in the case with preemption we did five context switches. We should recall that the time taken to do a context switch is not time that the system is doing productive work. It is all overhead that we spend to make the average waiting time smaller so many things appear to happen faster, especially the high-priority things. Later we will see that context switches are even more expensive than just the time it takes to save and restore the CPU state of the processes and the time we spend running the chosen scheduling algorithm. Switching contexts also slows down the hardware for a short time—in some cases quite dramatically. As a result, we want to do as few context switches as possible. We have to take a hard look at the typical decrease in the average waiting time and balance that against the context switch overhead (hardware system dependent) and the resulting slowdown of the processes.

8.4.9 A long-term scheduler

Some OSs also have another scheduler module called a **long-term scheduler.** In a PC OS with a GUI there normally is not such a scheduler. When the user clicks on an icon, a process associated with that icon starts running. In large computer systems with batch-oriented job streams (perhaps in addition to interactive processing) the system does not automatically start all the jobs that are submitted. Instead, they are put in a queue for starting later. It is the job of the long-term scheduler to decide how many jobs to try to run at the same time and which jobs to run when. The first aspect of this decision is that there will be some minimum number of jobs that we want to have running at the same time. We will start executing at least this minimum number of jobs, assuming that there are more to run than we can run at one time. One aspect of this decision has to do with the level of CPU utilization. If all of the jobs that are running are primarily jobs heavily using I/O, the long-term scheduler will try to find some jobs that it thinks will raise the level of CPU utilization. To some extent this information may be conveyed by accounting information submitted with the job. In other cases the scheduler will just pick one, probably on a FCFS basis. In Chapter 11 we discuss a problem that this approach may cause when memory becomes too full. The long-term scheduler can use most any of the short-term scheduling algorithms instead of FCFS. Since the long-term scheduler runs only once for each process that is started, it does not need to be extremely fast and can spend more resources selecting the next job carefully.

8.4.10 Processor affinity

We have mentioned several times that there is considerable overhead involved when a CPU switches from one process to another. Because of memory caching that the hardware is doing, the execution of the new process will be slowed dramatically for some period of time until the cache buffers switch from the old process to the new process. We may have some processes in a system that we consider to be much more important than the other processes. Perhaps our system is being set up to be a dedicated database server, for example. We might want that database program to have the very highest priority. As a result, in a multiprocessor system it is often possible for the OS to maintain a **processor affinity** for a given process. This affinity is value that the OS will use to indicate a preference for this process to run on some particular CPU whenever possible. In some instances a system administrator may indicate that a particular process is to be closely coupled to a particular CPU. In other cases the OS will merely try to run a process on the same CPU it ran on the last time it ran. In some OSs it is possible to dedicate a CPU to a process so that only that process will run on that CPU.

8.5 ONE GOOD PROCESS DESERVES ANOTHER

When a user signals to the Command Interpreter to start a new process, there has to be a way for that Command Interpreter process to start the user's process. The Command Interpreter uses a normal supervisor call to start another process. This supervisor call is known as a **fork.** The process that makes the call is called a **parent** process and the process that is started as a result is called a **child** process. The entire mechanism is referred to as "forking a child," or sometimes as "spawning a child." So it is clear that the Command Interpreter needs to be able to start another process, but why would a user application need to do so? The first reason is for performance. If a process has many tasks to do that can be started at the same time, then it can start additional processes to perform some of those tasks and the OS can keep all the processes running at the same time. This is especially true if the system has multiple CPUs. There are other reasons why an application might be broken into several processes. In the next chapter we discuss these at some length.

But there are several complications that arise when we let one process start another. For one thing, if the parent process ends for any reason, do we let any child process continue running or do we end it as well? Most OSs will automatically end any child process if the parent process ends. Some do not. In most modern OSs we can have our choice. A child process who's parent process has ended is known as an **orphan** process.

Another question has to do with the ownership of resources. If a parent process has a file open, can the child process access the file? Yet another question has to do with the program that is running in the child process. In most cases of a fork call, the child process is an exact copy of the parent process in another block of memory. Note that both the parent process and the child process will next execute the instruction following the fork call. An interesting question is, How does each of the processes know which instance is the parent and which is the child? In general, the return code from the fork call is set to zero for the child process and a positive nonzero number (the child process ID) for the parent process. The following code is an example of a typical fork system call:

```
int main(void) {
    pid_t pid = fork();
    if (pid == 0) {/* If pid=0, we are in the child process.*/
    do_something(from_the_child);
    }
    exit(0);
    }
    else if (pid > 0){/* If pid is positive we are in the
        parent process and pid is the child process id.*/
    do_something_else(from_the_parent);
    }
    exit(0);
    }
    Else {/* If pid is negative then there was an error;
        E.g., the number of running processes reached
        the maximum. */
    fprintf(stderr, "Can't fork, error %d\n", errno);
    exit(1);
    }
}
```

Usually having another instance of the parent process run is not what we really want. This is obviously the case with the Command Interpreter. We don't want another copy of the Command Interpreter. We want it to run some other program. Generally, what we really want is another program running in a child process. So after the fork call, another call is made to load a new program into the memory space allocated for the child process. This is usually an **exec** system call.

Of course, if what we really want is for another program to run, then the initial step of copying the parent process into another block of memory is a waste of many resources. So some OSs provide a different call known as a **shell** command. This command creates a new process but never copies the parent process to the child space—it loads the desired program immediately. Some OSs offer both a fork/exec pair and a shell command and others only offer one or the other. In some systems a high-level language library will offer a shell command, but if the OS does not have a corresponding function call then the library may have to use a fork/exec sequence to do the work.

One last question has to do with the actions of the parent process while the child process runs. In a manner analogous to I/O, which can be either synchronous or asynchronous, when a parent process forks a child process it can elect to continue execution itself in parallel with the execution of the child process or it can elect to wait until the child process is finished. A parent process might initially elect to continue but later need to wait until a child process has finished its work. In such a case there is usually a separate **wait** system call that a process can make to put itself into a Wait state until the child process finishes.

8.6 THREADS

8.6.1 What is a thread?

Suppose that we picture the logical address space of a process as the vertical axis on a graph. As time goes by we keep moving to the right at intervals and making a mark everywhere the instruction counter has been in that interval. We might end up with something like Figure 8.3. We could instead imagine that we unwound a thread and placed it on the graph instead of marking the space with a pencil. This is an analogy that gave rise to the phrase "**thread of execution.**"

Now suppose that we stopped this process, and saved all the data that represented the CPU state in a table (we might call it a **thread control block,** or **TCB**). Then further suppose we started the process over from the beginning. Again we let it run for a time, then stopped it and saved the CPU state in another TCB. We could now go back and restore the saved CPU state of the first thread and resume its execution. How would this be different from running multiple processes? There are several ways that using multiple threads can be better than using multiple processes. For one thing, we only have one copy of the program and data in memory, so we have more memory to use for other things. For another thing, there is a much smaller overhead to switch between threads than to switch between processes since we are only saving the CPU state. Generally this means saving only a few registers (including the instruction pointer) and the pointer to the stack space. On some computers this can be done with a single instruction. We are not saving accounting data, OS scheduling information, execution statistics, etc. In addition, as we have previously discussed, there are hardware performance problems we will cause when we switch the CPU between one process and another. We want to avoid the heavy overhead of a process context switch whenever we can.

Finally, when multiple processes are being used to implement a system, they have a difficult time communicating. This is natural. The OS designers have gone to a great deal of trouble to isolate processes from one another so that one process can't change the contents of memory in another process, intentionally or not. Many different mechanisms have been invented to allow cooperating processes to communicate. We look at several of them in the next chapter. However, threads don't have this problem. By definition, all the threads created by a single process are running in the same address space and share both the code and the data. Therefore interthread communication is trivial—all threads simply access the same variables. The main difficulty is keeping the individual threads from manipulating the same data at the same time. This problem is discussed in depth in the next chapter.

Actually, when we start a second thread we don't really start it at the beginning of the process. Recall that we just said that the various threads share a single copy of the program code and the data that the process owns. Normally, one of the first things a process does is to initialize data tables. Since the first thread has already done this setup we don't want the second thread to redo it. More to the point, the startup of a second thread is not something that the OS does on its own. It is initiated by the running process in order to let the system do more work on behalf of the process without incurring that heavy overhead of a full process context switch. For this reason, a thread is sometimes called a **lightweight process.** As a process is running it will reach a point where there is some additional work that can be done in parallel with the work the main thread is doing, so the process (parent thread) will start a child thread to do that extra work. In Figure 8.4, we see an example of two threads in a single process. The first thread is shown as a solid line. At some point it calls the OS to start a second thread, shown here as a dotted line. Eventually, the OS switches back

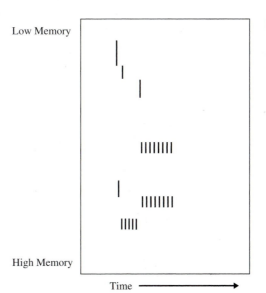

FIGURE 8.3
Tracing the instruction counter in a process.

Low Memory

High Memory

Time ⟶

to the first thread again. Both of these switches were done without the overhead of a context switch between processes. And if the system has multiple CPUs or a CPU that is capable of running multiple threads at the same time, then both of the threads can literally run at the same time.

One example of how threads work can be seen in a word processing program. As this is being written a check shows that the word processor has 18 threads running. Some are fairly obvious, but it is hard to come up with 18:

- foreground keystroke handling
- display updating
- spelling checker
- grammar checker
- repagination
- "smart tag" recognition
- periodic file save

Another example is commonly seen in server applications such as a Web server. One thread will wait for incoming HTTP requests. For each incoming request a new thread is started. The thread will do (at least these) several steps:

- Parse the incoming request
- Look up the requested file
- Read the page
- Format it for output
- Request the transmission of the page
- Exit

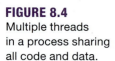

FIGURE 8.4
Multiple threads in a process sharing all code and data.

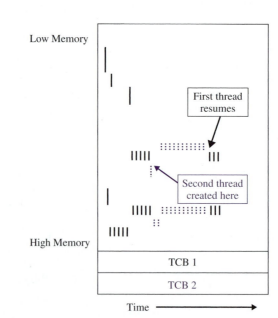

This sequence keeps the handling of each request in a separate thread of execution and makes the program logic much simpler than having a single process keep track of the state of hundreds or thousands of individual requests.

8.6.2 User-level threads versus kernel-level threads

Historically, the use of multiple processes came before the idea of threads. When programmers realized that switching between processes used so many resources and slowed things down so much they begin to develop the concept of threads. However, the OSs of the time did not have threads built in to them. So the original development of threads was done as a set of library subroutines. Of course, this meant that the entire thread package ran in user mode and the OS was unaware that an application was trying to keep multiple activities running in parallel. Accordingly, if any of the threads in a process made a system call that would block for some reason, the entire application, including all the threads of that application, would be blocked at the same time. Such a thread package is referred to as a **user-level thread** package because it runs entirely in user mode. Designing programs that utilize such user thread libraries must therefore be done very carefully so that one thread does not put the entire process to sleep.

Eventually, however, OS designers decided that threads were such a good idea that they would incorporate the thread functions into the kernel. Now the OS was aware that the application was using threads. In many circumstances the OS did not need to block an entire process if a single thread did a blocking call to the OS. Such thread packages are called **kernel-level threads.** Also, since the OS is aware of the individual threads, it is possible for the threads to execute on separate CPUs in a multi-CPU system. This is a major advantage for kernel-level threads, especially in an era when a multicore CPU system will soon be the normal case for average workstations rather than something found only in powerful servers.

In general, kernel threads are much easier to use than user threads because the programmer does not have to avoid blocking calls. This makes the programming model much easier. For example, consider writing a Web server using threads. The application sits in a loop, waiting for requests in HTTP commands to come in from the network. When a request comes in to return a page, the main application thread starts a separate thread to handle the request and goes back to waiting for more requests. Now the child thread has a very simple task, as we outlined before. It parses the HTTP request, looks up the page on the disk, reads the page in a series of reads, formats the page into HTTP messages, sends the answer back (assuming the page was found), and exits. This makes each thread very straightforward since it does not have to be designed to cope with multiple requests at the same time. The alternative would be for the main application to issue asynchronous calls for each of the I/O operations. While this is certainly possible, it is a much more complex model and it is difficult to take advantage of a multiprocessor system.

A later development is a user-level thread package that is designed to give some of the advantages of the simplicity of programming one gets with kernel-level threads without relying on kernel-level thread support. Such packages are called

green threads. Green thread libraries capture blocking system calls and turns them into nonblocking calls. They then handle scheduling of the various user threads. This model allows a program to run unmodified in either mode by loading with the kernel-level thread library or with the green user thread library. However, there are some disadvantages to this approach. First, if the system is a multi-CPU system, the individual threads will not take advantage of the multiple CPUs because the kernel is not aware of them. As we have mentioned, the trend in processors is that most systems already include multiple CPUs. Second, kernel-level threads can be scheduled preemptively, so a thread that takes too long to do its job cannot dominate the system. Green threads do not offer this level of control.

8.6.3 Thread support models

When OSs began to offer kernel thread packages, the application programmers were not anxious to rewrite their applications just to use kernel threads. So the OS designers would take the existing user thread libraries and rewrite them so that they would use the mechanisms provided by the kernel threads. There are three common methods for making the user library routines utilize kernel threads. The main question that distinguishes them is the method of mapping the user threads to kernel threads. The three methods are one-to-one, many-to-one, and many-to-many. **One-to-one** mapping is fairly simple. When the application calls the library routine to create a new thread, the library routine calls the kernel thread mechanism to create a new kernel thread. Figure 8.5 shows a schematic diagram of the one-to-one thread mapping model. This model has the advantages of being fast and very simple to develop and for the user to understand. Although other models appear to give the user more control, they are significantly more complex to use and therefore more prone to errors. Most OS vendors are moving away from the more complex models on the grounds that the advantages of finer control are outweighed by the disadvantages.

The second mapping model is called **many-to-one.** Recall that the user library that is being modified will block the entire process when any thread in the application makes a blocking call to the OS. In that case, this model will do exactly the same thing. Only one kernel thread is created and all the user threads will be mapped onto that same kernel thread. Figure 8.6 shows the many-to-one thread mapping model.

FIGURE 8.5
The one-to-one thread mapping model.

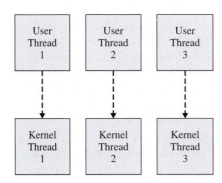

This model is less desirable than the one-to-one model because it does not offer the advantages of kernel threads. It is used only when an operating system has no kernel thread support. The single "kernel thread" in this case is the running process itself.

The last model is called **many-to-many.** In this model the programmer will tell the system something about how many user threads and kernel threads will be needed and how they should be mapped. The basic idea is to have a group of kernel threads available and dynamically assign user threads to them as they are needed. It may also be possible to have multiple groups of user and kernel threads and to specify that some user threads are bound to a single kernel thread. Figure 8.7 illustrates the many-to-many thread mapping model. As was mentioned before, this model theoretically gives the user finer control over the behavior of the entire system, but it is more difficult to use correctly and is losing favor since modern systems have such large memories and speedy processing that the performance gain perceived by the user is very slight and not worth the programming problems that come with using the more complex model.

Although threads are easier to create and destroy than processes, there is still some overhead involved in creating them. As a result, some thread packages will create a group of thread structures when the procedure first calls the thread package. This group is called a **thread pool.** When the parent thread calls for a new thread, one structure is taken from the pool, initialized for the specific thread, and used. When that thread exits the structure is returned to the pool.

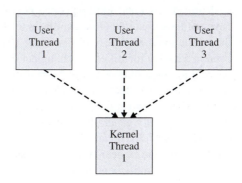

FIGURE 8.6
The many-to-one thread mapping model.

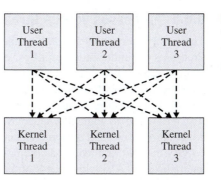

FIGURE 8.7
The many-to-many thread mapping model.

One problem with threads is that not all library subroutines are prepared to be called multiple times without completing one call before another call starts. (This is called "**reentrancy.**") This is specifically a problem when a process is running on a system with multiple CPUs. Suppose a library routine is called by a thread and it uses a static local variable during its work. Now another thread of the same process running on another CPU calls the same library routine and it tries to use the same static local variable. It is easy to see that there will be a problem here. The library routine should be able to handle this situation by always allocating local variables on the stack. Libraries that are coded in this way are called **thread-safe,** and most modern libraries are thread-safe.

8.6.4 Simultaneous multithreading

In simultaneous multithreading (SMT), instructions from more than one process can be executing in a single CPU at one time. The hardware essentially creates a second "logical" CPU. This CPU is not a completely distinct CPU since it shares many resources between two logical CPUs. The term "multithreading" is somewhat misleading since the executing threads can be from distinct processes. The largest gains come when one process tries to access data that is not in the cache. Without the SMT the CPU would be idle until the data are ready. Other small gains can come when parts of the CPU are not being used by one process and can be used by the other.

The main additions to the CPU are the ability to load instructions from more than one thread (or process) during a cycle and a duplicate set of registers to hold data from each thread. A second addition concerns some memory management hardware that we have not looked at yet. On most machines there is a memory addressing cache called the translation lookaside buffer, or TLB. The problem here is that each TLB entry must contain data that identifies which logical CPU each entry is for because the two logical address spaces could not otherwise be distinguished by the hardware. The greatest gain from the SMT architecture will come when both of the CPUs are running threads from a single process since they will be able to share the resources more effectively. Chip design complexity generally limits the number of logical CPUs to two. Measuring the effectiveness of SMT can be difficult. In some cases an increase of performance of 30% or more can be seen, but in a few cases the performance actually decreases. The most common implementation of SMT today is Intel's Hyper-Threading™.

8.6.5 Processes versus threads

Threads and processes are both methods of adding parallelization to an application. Processes are independent entities, each containing its own state information and address space. They only interact with one other via interprocess communication mechanisms through the OS. Applications are typically divided into processes during the design phase. A single controlling process invokes the other processes when it makes sense to logically separate significant application functionality. In other words, processes are a design concept.

By contrast, a thread is a coding technique that doesn't affect the architecture of an application. A single process often contains multiple threads. All the threads in a process share the same state and same memory space and they implicitly communicate with each other directly by manipulating the shared data.

Threads typically are created for a short-term use that is usually thought of as a serial task that does not have to be executed in sequence but rather can be run in parallel. They are then deconstructed when no longer required. The scope of a thread is within a specific code module so that we can introduce threading into a process without affecting the overall application design.

8.7 CASE STUDIES

We have discussed processes and threads using an ideal model that is intended to explain their various features. In the real OS world, no OS works exactly as we have described. In addition, although the model may be very close to reality, the terminology used by the OS documentation may differ from our model. In this section we cover a few modern systems and show how they differ from our idealized model and discuss their terminology a bit.

8.7.1 POSIX threads

We have previously explained about the POSIX standards that attempt to bring some uniformity to the UNIX APIs that had proliferated so wildly. One of these standards has to do with threads. This standard is so well known that it goes by the special name **Pthreads.** Beyond UNIX, however, POSIX libraries are available on many OSs because of the large number of programs that have been implemented with these API system calls. You may recall that even the Windows NT family has a library that supports some POSIX API system calls at the source level. Because of this wide availability POSIX threads have a real niche: They provide a very high level of portability for an application. The standard is so well known that there is even an implementation of them in an IBM Fortran compiler![2] It is important to remember, however, that POSIX is not a package, it is a standard. Each implementer is free to implement the services in any way seen fit.

Any implementation of POSIX threads can be written as purely a user thread package. But if the OS supports kernel threads, then the POSIX thread package is usually implemented using either the one-to-one or many-to-many models. This shows the downside of the POSIX thread standard when developing an application to run with the POSIX API. If the system is to be run on a package where the implementation will utilize user-level threads, then a single blocking call in any thread will block the entire process. But if the package will support kernel-level threads, then the OS can run multiple threads for a single process at the same time. Therefore, if an application programmer really wants to take full advantage of multithreading regardless of the particular package to be used, then the program must be written with asynchronous I/O operations to avoid blocking the entire process. As a result, if the program is running in an environment where the implementation is using kernel-level threads and will not block an entire process because one thread

---

[2] www-4.ibm.com/software/ad/fortran

issues a blocking call, the effort that was spent developing the program with the asynchronous calls has been wasted. This is the price that the developers had to pay to gain the portability of POSIX.

There are over 60 functions available in the Pthreads standard. Only 22 of these have to do with the basic functioning of the threads themselves. The other two-thirds are related to synchronization and interprocess communication. We address these additional topics in the next chapter.

8.7.2 Windows NT

None of the OSs that we are discussing implements threads and processes exactly according to the way we have been describing them. Windows NT is the first such example. NT does implement processes, but it does not schedule processes. Instead, it implements a thread for every process, even if the application never indicates that it wants to use threads. NT schedules the threads instead of the processes. In this way the kernel only has to worry about one sort of scheduled entity, a thread. Some information is kept in a process control block and some is kept in a thread control block. If the application never calls a thread package to create any more threads, then only the first thread is used.

The scheduling mechanism in NT is a multilevel feedback queue. It uses 32 queues. See Figure 8.8. The top 16 queues are considered to be "real-time" queues. Normal applications run in the bottom 16 queues. NT will always service all the threads that are in the ready state at a higher-level queue before it will service a thread in a lower-level queue. In addition, NT is preemptive. If a thread has been waiting for an event and the event happens, then if the thread that is currently running is of a lower priority than the thread that had just become ready, then the running thread will be preempted and the thread that just became ready will be run. As threads run, if they finish their time quantum without doing any blocking I/O operation, then they will be

FIGURE 8.8
NT thread priority relationships.

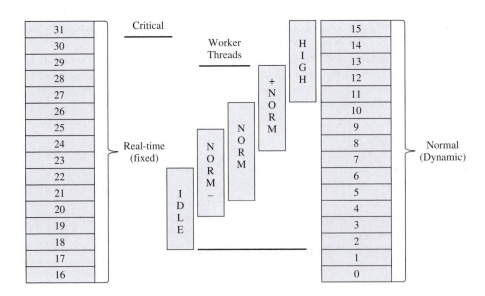

demoted to the next lower level. The assumption is that the thread is acting more like a background task than a foreground task—it is computationally intensive—so we will run it less often. Similarly, threads that do not complete their time quantum will eventually be promoted to a higher-level queue. When a thread is created it will have associated with it a maximum priority level and a minimum priority level. The thread will not be promoted or demoted past the associated priority limits.

Since the main intent of a personal computer with a GUI is to enable a user to get work done more efficiently, the threads associated with the GUI usually run at a higher priority than threads that are running the processing aspects of an application. In addition, one window will always be the window that has the focus. Any threads that are associated with the window that has the focus will be temporarily promoted several queue levels and will have their time quantum multiplied by three. This promotion will help to ensure that the user's actions are responded to quickly and that the threads are able to complete their task without being preempted.

The lowest priority is reserved for a job that is called the system idle task. This thread will run only when no other thread in the system is ready to run. In many cases on a personal workstation this thread will often consume about 98% of the available CPU time. Our personal computers are often much faster in this respect than we need them to be for many tasks that we do. This vast amount of available CPU cycles is beginning to be tapped in such applications as SETI[3] and GIMPS.[4] These programs use the idle CPU cycles on volunteer computers to processes batches of data for large-scale scientific experiments. The data are downloaded and updated over the Internet. These systems are similar to **grid computing,** a technique that attempts to tap these unused CPU cycles in the desktop computers in a campus environment to run some programs that are computationally intensive. This concept was discussed in Chapter 7 and is explained further in Chapter 17.

Windows NT can also be used as a server. In general, the code is the same for the server version of the software as it is for a personal workstation. The main differences are in the values assigned to the system tuning parameters. One example is that the time quanta for the various queues are six times longer than the same queues in the workstation version. You should recall that switching program contexts is considered overhead rather than useful work, so we want to avoid it when we don't need it. In a workstation the entire focus is on the user and there are many idle CPU cycles anyway, so we will pay the extra penalty to make the OS more responsive to those inputs. In a server environment we are more concerned with overall throughput to many service requests and we have less idle CPU time so we increase the time quantum and as a result we spend less time in the context switches.

8.7.3 Solaris

The Solaris OS threading support has been a staple for OS discussions for some time because the architecture was quite complex and offered the programmer a choice of models to use to achieve the best possible balance between a user-level thread

---

[3] http://setiathome.berkely.edu/

[4] http://www.mersenne.org/

implementation and a kernel-level thread implementation. The basic model used by Solaris has been a many-to-many model. Solaris created a structure called a "light-weight process," or **LWP.** A LWP was the unit that was set to run on a processor by the operating system. User-level threads were bound to LWPs. An application programmer had considerable flexibility on how the threads were bound to the LWPs. Threads could be created in groups. On the one hand, the program could ask for a single thread to be bound to a single LWP. Thus, the programmer could approximate the one-to-one model, although the library routines would be somewhat slower than a library created for a pure one-to-one model because it also supported more complex mappings. For example, the program could ask for M threads and N LWPs to be in one group. In a group, if a particular thread made a blocking call, then the LWP that was bound to that thread would be blocked. But other LWPs in that group would not automatically be blocked, and user threads in that group could be dynamically assigned to the LWPs whenever one was ready to run. Additionally, for really high performance applications, a "processor affinity" could be specified, as was mentioned earlier in this chapter. This mechanism allowed only the LWPs bound to that application to be run on that CPU (or CPUs).

However, beginning with Solaris release 8 this elaborate mechanism was being phased out. The OS designers at Sun determined that all this mechanism is not worth the trouble. Probably as a reflection of the continuing decrease in the cost of memory, this complex model is being gradually withdrawn. A new alternative thread library called the T2 library has been created. It supports only the one-to-one model. The older library was still supported in Solaris 8. However, as of Solaris release 9 the T2 model became the standard library and the older model is being phased out. Sun expects the increased simplicity of the library to result in faster operation in most cases and in fewer bugs and support issues. The model should be simpler for the programmers and system administrators as well.

8.7.4 Linux

The approach Linux takes to procedures and threads is also different from our basic model. Official Linux literature does not use either of those terms (though many writers do). Instead, they speak of **tasks.** A task is equivalent to what we have been calling a procedure. Linux supports the **fork** system call with the same effect as most UNIX systems, but it uses a memory management technique called copy-on-write to create the child task. This technique allows the child task to be created with very little overhead. Copy-on-write will be discussed further in Chapter 11. Differences arise in Linux when a primary task starts another task with the **clone** system call. Here is the syntax for the clone system call:

```
#include <sched.h>
int clone(int (*fn)(void *), void *child_stack, int flags,
    void *args);
```

The first difference is that with a fork system call both the parent task and the child task will continue execution with the next instruction after the call. In the clone system call, a function name (*fn*) is passed as an argument to the system call. The parent task returns and continues at the next instruction after the fork, but the child task will instead call the function that was passed as an argument. When that function exits the child task ends and the value of the function is returned to the parent task as a return code. This is similar to the way that thread calls work in other OSs.

The other major difference with the clone call has to do with the information shared between the parent and child tasks. Normally, all threads running in a single task (or process) share the code segment, data segment, and other resources such as open files, but each thread has its own thread control block to save the CPU state and its own stack (possibly two stacks, one for user mode and one for kernel mode). Under Linux, when a task clones a child task it provides a bit mask that specifies which elements the child task will share with the parent. Some of the flags available to the clone call are:

- CLONE_VM—share the entire memory space
- CLONE_FILES—share file descriptors
- CLONE_SIGHAND—share signal handlers
- CLONE_PID—share PID (Process ID)
- CLONE_FS—share file system

As an example of how these flags might make things different, if the child and parent task do not share the same file system, then if the child task executes a chdir call, changing the current working directory, the current directory for the parent task will not change. If the two tasks share the same file system then both tasks will see the change. The clone call can be used to create a new task such that the new task is equivalent to a new process in most OSs. This is done simply by sharing nothing between the parent task and the child task. Starting a task that is the equivalent to a thread in most OSs involves sharing everything except the process ID.

```
clone (CLONE_VM| CLONE_FS| CLONE_FILES| CLONE_SIGHAND, 0);
```

Before executing the clone system call, the parent process will allocate the stack space for the child task. It will pass to the clone call a pointer to the stack space that was set up for the child (*child_stack*). It will have to decide how much space is required for the operations the child process will perform. Typically this will be set the same as for the parent process. The last parameter to the clone call is a pointer to the arguments that will pass to the function that the child process will execute.

8.7.5 Java

The Java programming language and runtime environment is an interesting example of threads because Java is a language rather than an OS. Java supports threads at the language level rather than through subroutine calls, as is done with other programming languages. Java, of course, is implemented on many different OSs. Java threads originally had the same problem as do POSIX threads—there was no way of knowing whether the program would be executing with kernel-level threads or with user-level threads. So Sun has implemented two thread libraries for Java, including a "green" library that can be implemented without kernel-level thread support but still provides the same nonblocking model as is provided with kernel-level threads. Depending on the OS these libraries might be based on kernel-level threads or might be based on user-level threads.

8.8 SUMMARY

In this chapter, we defined the state of a process and how that state is captured in the contents of a process control block. We then defined various models for the states of a process in the system and the events that cause transitions from one state to another. We then covered the various algorithms that are used to schedule processes in OSs and discussed how to evaluate them using deterministic modeling. We wrapped up the discussion of processes with a brief discussion of process forking.

Next, we defined a thread and discussed the differences between processes and threads. Then we explained the difference between user-level threads and kernel-level threads. Next, we showed various ways that user-level threads could be mapped onto kernel-level threads. Finally, we covered the implementation of threads in modern OSs and discussed a couple of special cases of thread mechanisms.

In the next chapter of the book we discuss how processes can communicate and cooperate and some of the problems involved in these areas. They are not as simple as they might seem at first.

BIBLIOGRAPHY

Abbot, C., "Intervention Schedules for Real-Time Programming," *IEEE Transactions on Software Engineering,* Vol. SE-10, No. 3, May 1984, pp. 268–274.

Bach, M. J., *The Design of the UNIX Operating System.* Englewood Cliffs, NJ: Prentice Hall, 1986.

Brinch Hansen, P., "The Nucleus of a Multiprogramming System," *Communications of the ACM,* Vol. 13, No. 4, April 1970, pp. 238–241.

Henry, G. J., "The Fair Share Scheduler," *Bell Systems Technical Journal,* Vol. 63, No. 8, Part 2, October 1984, pp. 1845–1857.

Jensen, E. D., C. D. Locke, and H. Tokuda, "A Time-Driven Scheduling Model for Real-Time Operating Systems," *Proceedings of the IEEE Real-Time Systems Symposium,* December 3–6, 1985, pp. 112–122.

Kay, J., and P. Lauder, "A Fair Share Scheduler," *Communications of the ACM,* Vol. 31, No. 1, January 1988, pp. 44–55.

Liu, C. L., and J. W. Layland, "Scheduling Algorithms for Multiprogramming in a Hard-Real-Time Environment," *Journal of the ACM,* Vol. 20, No. 1, January 1973, pp. 46–61.

Woodside, C. M., "Controllability of Computer Performance Tradeoffs Obtained Using Controlled-Share Queue Schedulers," *IEEE Transactions on Software Engineering,* Vol. SE-12, No. 10, October 1986, pp. 1041–1048.

WEB RESOURCES

http://web.cs.mun.ca/~paul/cs3725/material/web/notes/ node19.html (Allocation of processes to a processor)

http://www-4.ibm.com/software/ad/fortran (IBM Fortran compilers)

REVIEW QUESTIONS

8.1 What is a PCB?
   a. A class of toxic chemical compounds
   b. A process control block
   c. A program counter boundary
   d. A partially completed buffer
   e. None of the above

8.2 In the context of processes, the word "state" is overloaded. Distinguish between the two meanings of this word with respect to processes.

8.3 How many unique OS states can a process be in?

8.4 How many queues are there in the ready state?

8.5 How many queues are there in the wait state?

8.6 Why do we care if a process scheduler is fair?

8.7 The SRTF process scheduling algorithm is optimum, so why do we not use it as it was described initially?

8.8 Since FCFS process scheduling is so fair, what is the problem with it?

8.9 Why do systems with GUIs generally not have a long-term scheduler?

8.10 What is the purpose of processor affinity?

8.11 What does a process do to start another process?

8.12 Distinguish between a process and a thread.

8.13 Why do we usually say that kernel-level threads are better than user-level threads?

8.14 User-level thread packages were developed before kernel-level thread packages. When kernel-level threads were made available, users did not want to throw out or rewrite their multithreaded applications. So the user-level thread packages were recoded to work with kernel-level threads. What were the three models we spoke of that were used to map user-level threads to kernel-level threads?

8.15 What do we mean when we say that a library is "thread safe"?

8.16 True or false? Simultaneous multithreading refers to having multiple processes create threads at the same time.

8.17 POSIX threads would appear to be ideal in the sense that they are ubiquitous. What is the major drawback to POSIX threads?

8.18 What is unique about Windows NT process scheduling?

8.19 What is unique about Linux process scheduling?

8.20 Solaris provided an elaborate mechanism for mapping user-level threads to "lightweight" processes. Why was this done?

8.21 What is unusual about Java threads?

Chapter 9

More Process Management: Interprocess Communication, Synchronization, and Deadlocks

In this chapter:

In this chapter we continue the in-depth discussion of processes and threads. We discuss techniques for designing applications that are divided into multiple parts in order to keep the system busier working on behalf of the application. When we break applications into multiple parts, the parts will need to cooperate, and to do that they will need to communicate with one another. Since we spent considerable time explaining how and why an OS isolated processes, we now need to explain the mechanisms that have evolved to allow them to communicate.

OSs devote a great deal of their resources to ensuring that processes are independent of one another. More formally, an **independent process** cannot affect or be affected by the execution of another process. On the other hand, we sometimes need for two or more processes to cooperate with one another. Again, formally, a **cooperating process** is one that can affect or be affected by the execution of another process. When we try to develop systems we may need to allow for the system to include multiple cooperating processes. Sometimes we will need for parts of the process to run on different machines, and sometimes they will run on the same machine.

In any case, the parts will need to do several things in order to cooperate successfully with one another to do the job. They will certainly need to **communicate** with one another. For example, one process might be taking in sales orders. It may then pass those orders to another process, which will enter a transaction to ship the merchandise. Processes may also need to **synchronize** their actions so that they do not interfere with one another by trying to update the same piece of information at the same time. As the processes run they may need to ask the OS to give them exclusive access to a resource for some time. It turns out that this can lead to a special kind of problem called a **deadlock** that the OS will need to worry about.

This chapter will talk mostly about separate processes, but much of the material also applies to multiple threads. In particular, threads share memory and will have many of the synchronization and deadlock issues addressed in this chapter. They will generally not use the message-passing mechanisms often used between processes.

In Section 9.1, we discuss the motivating factors behind this idea—why do we sometimes have to divide applications even though we might not necessarily desire to do so? Next, Section 9.2 describes various mechanisms used by cooperating processes to communicate among themselves. In Section 9.3, we explore the need for processes to synchronize their activities and discuss some mechanisms for doing so. In Section 9.4, we discuss a potential problem called a deadlock that can arise when processes seek to have exclusive access to resources. We conclude with a chapter summary in Section 9.5.

9.1 WHY HAVE COOPERATING PROCESSES?

Before we get into the details of how processes can communicate, it makes sense to ask why we might want to divide our system into multiple processes. There are a number of reasons why we may want to develop systems where the application runs in several pieces:

Performance. When we design a system we may have more work to be done than can be done on one inexpensive processor. It may be more economical to put in several inexpensive processors and run some portion of the process on each machine than it would be to buy a bigger system that could do the entire task itself. If the system will need to service a large number of users it might not be possible to service them all with a single system.

Scaling. When we first develop an application we do not necessarily know how big the system load will get. What we think of as a small service might become an overnight sensation and require that it serve many more users than we originally thought it would. A good example is the Google™ search engine. Whatever the dreams of the originators of this service, it is very doubtful that they ever imagined that by the year 2004 they would have 65,000 servers running the application. This reason is obviously closely related to the performance problem, but it is different.

Purchased components. We may want our system to include some function such as a Web server. It is unlikely that we would find it economical to develop our own Web server. We would most likely use an existing Web server program and fit it into our system somehow—perhaps by writing parts of the system that dynamically create pages that the purchased server displays.

Third-party service. Our system might make use of a service that is provided by another organization. A typical example is to enter a credit card charge. Again, it is unlikely that we could develop a system to do this function as cheaply as buying the service unless we have a very high volume of transactions to process.

Components in multiple systems. We might be building a number of different systems that do similar jobs. Rather than build similar parts of many systems and be required to maintain them separately, we can build the common components to run as a separate process and have the various systems feed transactions to the common components. For example, these days a company selling directly to the public will likely have a website that allows customers to place orders online. It might also have retail counters in the stores, a telemarketing group that takes orders over the telephone in response to infomercials run on TV, and a mail-order catalog group that enters orders as well. Each of these systems might accept orders in a different way and use the common services of other processes to first verify and later charge customer credit cards, to order shipping from the warehouse, to monitor inventory, and to place orders with suppliers when goods appear to be running low. These common components may be run as separate processes.

Reliability. When systems are built in one piece and are all on one computer, then a significant failure in that computer will terminate the entire system. If systems are built in a modular fashion then there can be multiple instances of each module. Returning to the Google design, if one system out of 10,000 fails, then the system will continue to run. There might be a few users whose searches were already allocated to the failing server. They may have to click the "reload" button, but will probably be totally unaware that a server at the host site has been lost. In the case of Google, they have even split the servers among several different sites, so that a physical disaster such as a fire or flood will not take out the entire system.

Physical location of information. Even a small company will sometimes end up with multiple facilities. Often this situation arises because one company buys another. Whatever the reason, we may end up with multiple warehouses, for example, and for most transactions we will want to have an inventory system at the site. For other purposes, we will want to have parts of the system at a central location. Due to volume discounts, for example, we will want a single centralized purchasing function. If we have designed the various warehouse inventory systems so that they feed inventory requests to the purchasing system, then we can view this as a single system, parts of which are at various physical locations.

Enable application. There are a very few applications that have such massive computational requirements that they literally could not be done on existing computer systems. Sometimes this is partly a question of economics—a big enough machine could be built but the organization wanting to solve the problem could not afford it. Sometimes we would only have to wait a few years. Roughly speaking, the power of available processors doubles every 18 months. With the continuous application of this law we might have a big enough machine soon. An example of such a system is that employed by SETI (Search for Extra-Terrestrial Intelligence). This is a system that takes large volumes of data recorded by a large radio telescope and searches it for patterns that might indicate an intelligent origin to the data. The amount of data is so massive that in order to get it processed by the machines available today they divide it up into smaller data sets and distribute those data sets to various interested users who have volunteered to let the idle time on their computer system be used to process this data via the mechanism of a screen saver. Regardless of your opinion of the scientific merits of this endeavor, it was certainly one of the first systems to employ this technique. When viewed as a single, loosely coupled system, it currently represents the world's single largest computer system. Without this "divide and conquer" approach, they literally could not have processed this data.

9.2 INTERPROCESS COMMUNICATION

For one or more of these reasons, people have been building systems of multiple cooperating processes for some time now, and the number of such systems is growing rapidly, both in absolute numbers and as a percentage of new applications. Obviously, if we are going to have a system that is comprised of multiple processes, those processes will have to communicate to get the work done. However, we have spent a great deal of time and effort making sure that two processes running on the same system can't interfere with one another. Therefore, we need to develop mechanisms to allow processes to communicate. As developers began to recognize this need, those of them in different environments saw the problem in different terms. They also had different tools to work with. IBM mainframe customers using SNA and SDLC saw things differently from PC users using Novell Netware, and they saw things differently from UNIX or VAX users with XNS or DECNet or TCP/IP. As a result, there are dozens of different mechanisms that exist for processes to communicate with one another. There are two fairly different types of mechanisms for IPC. On the one hand, there are message passing mechanisms. They operate much as the term specifies—one process sends a message to another process using some facility of the OS. Message passing is generally done between processes. On the other hand, is the use of shared memory. With such a mechanism two or more tasks share access to one block of memory. Sharing of memory space is implicit between threads of a single process, but it can also be done among processes. Before discussing these classes of mechanisms we will first abstract the common features of all the mechanisms so that when you are faced with a different mechanism you will have an organized structure with which to identify the important characteristics. Then we look at a few of the more common mechanisms.

9.2.1 Attributes of communication mechanisms

The services available for processes to use for communication can be characterized by several different attributes:

Number of processes that can use a single channel at one time
One-way or bidirectional connections
Buffering strategy (none, 1, N, infinite)
Connection oriented or connectionless
Naming strategy (name, one way or two way, mailbox, port)
Multicast, broadcast, unicast

Multiple or single connections possible

Streaming or message oriented

Heterogeneous or homogeneous only

Synchronous or asynchronous

Persistent or transient

Number of processes supported. In most cases there are only two processes involved in a specific interprocess communication. But in some cases there can be many processes involved in communicating among themselves at the same time. For example, many processes might be able to simultaneously share a connection to a single process that would write records to a log file.

One-way or bidirectional. While it might be somewhat unusual for cooperating processes to have communication that was only one way, it is not unusual to have communication channels that are one way. What normally happens with one-way channels is that two channels may be set up between two processes, but the channels are going in opposite directions. This type of mechanism is usually found where the communication is much heavier in one direction than in the other. For example, one process is sending transactions to a second process and the second process is only sending back acknowledgments. We might need many large buffers on the first channel but many fewer or much smaller buffers or lower bandwidth on the return channel.

Buffering strategy. There are four different cases of handling the buffers in a communication channel based on the number of buffers available: none, one, N, and infinite. The first case is where there is **no buffer** to which both processes have access. Both processes must be accessing the channel at the same time so that one process can send the message to the other process. The second case is that there is only **one buffer** with both processes having shared access to it. In this case, the sending process will put a message in the buffer and then tell the OS it is available. The OS will tell the receiving process that the message is there and it will take the message out of the buffer. It will then tell the OS that the sender can send another. The case of one buffer might appear to be just one possible instance of the case of N buffers, but in the case of one buffer we can use simple mechanisms to synchronize the processes. The processes always know which buffer to use, and the processes only need to coordinate whether the buffer is now available for the sender to insert a message into it or not. In the case of **N buffers** we have much more information to coordinate. The communication channel mechanism for each process must know where the buffers are and which ones contain messages and which do not. We discuss these problems further in Section 9.3.9. The last case is where the channel mechanism has some external memory that it can use to expand the buffer space by essentially an infinite amount. An example might be a spooling system that uses a disk file to hold a message stream until a printer is available on which to print it. For practical purposes the sending process can consider the buffer to be infinite.

Connection oriented or connectionless. A communication channel can be connection oriented or connectionless. Sometimes communicating processes need to establish a complex conversation. In this case they will be likely to establish a connection that they will use for the duration of their interaction. A good analogy is a telephone call where one person calls another. The terminology comes from a time when connections were made between devices using an actual physical connection. Today the connection is likely to be a logical or virtual connection. Sometimes, however, one process simply has information to send and does not care what other processes might be listening. An example might be an application where a server in a company is broadcasting stock purchase information so that clients can receive it if they want. An analogy might be to a radio broadcast. There might be millions of listeners or none.

Naming strategy. When two processes are going to communicate with one another, they will need some mechanism to identify one another. This is called the naming strategy. In the strictest case, both processes must explicitly name each other. The name is most often the name of the executable file used to run the program, but names can be associated with running processes in other ways—in some systems the process id number might be used as a name. This specific naming mechanism has the advantage of having the least margin for error, but also requires the most effort to maintain. It is generally only useful when the same developers are responsible for both processes and there is only one sender and one receiver. In a somewhat looser model, the message sender must specify the name of the receiving process, but the receiver is willing to accept transmissions from any sending process. The third model is that both processes agree on some other reference that they will both use. Examples include mailbox numbers and TCP/IP ports.

Another attribute of interprocess communication is whether the messages are sent as a **unicast,** a **multicast,** or a **broadcast.** Unicast messages are sent only to the receiver, so if many processes are cooperating, then many messages may need to be sent for all processes to receive the message. Unicast messages are private, however. Broadcast messages are sent so that every process (in a given environment) can hear them. An example might be a time server that periodically sends clock update messages so that any process can read them. Unfortunately, broadcast messages must be received and processed by all processes, whether the process is interested in the message or not, so it may waste resources. Some messages might need to be received by all processes—a system shutdown request, for example. Multicast messages are intended only for a group of receivers. Sometimes this is for security reasons, so that membership in the group might be restricted. Sometimes multicast groups are created only to save resources for those processes not interested in the messages—a stock ticker application might be a good example.

Multiple or single connections possible. Most of the time it is sufficient to allow only one connection between two processes. Sometimes it is desirable to have separate channels for data messages and control messages. FTP is an example of a standard that uses two connections in this manner. There can also be multiple parallel data connections. An example of multiple connections is the mechanism used in some Web browser/server connections using the HTTP version 1 protocol. In this protocol a single channel could retrieve only one object from the server and then the server would close the connection. In order to speed up the process, a browser could retrieve a main page and parse it to find the other elements needed to display the page. It then could open as many connections as there were objects to retrieve. (In practice the client usually opened only some limited number at one time in order to keep from bogging down the server.)

Streaming or message oriented. For some applications it is important that the communication link supports the idea of discrete **messages.** The sending application will send a block of data and that same block will be presented to the receiving application in the same manner—as a discrete message. The blocks may be of fixed or variable length, depending on the implementation. Other applications do not identify blocks in the data. Instead, the communication is viewed as a **stream** of data flowing from the sender to the receiver. As easy example is a telnet client. Each keystroke that the user types on the keyboard is sent from the client to the server without regard to the content. Certain keystrokes may take priority over others (e.g., CTL/C), and the protocol may bundle many keystrokes together for transmission in order to minimize transmission overhead, but generally the keystrokes are sent as a continuous flow of information.

Heterogeneous or homogeneous only. Some communication systems assume that the sender and receiver of the messages are operating on the same type of hardware and the same OS. The strongest case is when the assumption is that the two communicating processes are running on the same machine. Other communication systems do not make this assumption. In this case they may try to cope with a set of problems that have to do with the representation of information. Different systems store information in different formats. Often this is due to hardware considerations. One example is the storage of integers. On Intel 80 X 86 series hardware the most significant byte (MSB) of the number is stored in a higher memory address. On most other hardware the MSB is in a lower memory address. (This is known as the "little endian/big endian" problem, a reference to *Gulliver's Travels*.) If a system is sending messages between platforms that may implement integers in different formats then that system may want to solve that problem in a universal way. For example, a subroutine called with Remote Procedure Calls (RPCs) may need to perform arithmetic operations on the arguments, so the sender and receiver will need to solve this problem in a way that is transparent to the applications. On the other hand, the FTP protocol simply moves files. Any reformatting of the contents is not the concern of the communication mechanism. However, FTP may need to consider the differences in file naming conventions. The name of a file on a sending system might not be a legal name on the receiving system. Some examples of formatting questions concern not the hardware but the language of the implementation. For example, strings may be stored one way in C and another way in BASIC, so systems that have components written in different languages may have to convert data between these formats. (Of course, this can be true of a single program running on a single CPU as well as for multiple processes.) One other problem that might be encountered is that a parameter to a message might be a memory address—possibly a pointer to an error routine. Obviously, if such a parameter were passed directly to a process running on another platform it would be meaningless. If we are going to pass memory addresses as parameters we will have to invent some other mechanism for supporting them.

Synchronous or asynchronous. When a program reads a record from a file in most high-level languages the model that is normally used for this function is that when the next instruction is executed the read has been completed. This model of I/O is known as **synchronous** I/O or **blocking** I/O. If a process has other tasks to attend to while the reading is being done then it may choose to issue the read as an

asynchronous or **nonblocking** read. In this case the read instruction will return to the program immediately and the read will take place independently. Eventually the program will want to find out if the read has finished. The means to do that depend on the language and the OS. Communication channels are similar. A process might want to check a channel for messages but continue on if no messages are available. So with some communication mechanisms a receiving process can issue an asynchronous read of the channel, and if there is no information to read, the OS will return from the call with an indication that no data was transferred, and the process will not wait. Similarly, an asynchronous write might be rejected if there were no buffer space available to receive the message.

Persistent or transient. In the simplest case both the sending and receiving processes must be running at the same time for them to exchange messages. If one of the processes is unavailable then the system cannot function. This sort of mechanism is called **transient.** In other systems the OS will retain messages that are intended for a process that is not running now or deliver messages from processes that are no longer running. Such communication services are said to be **persistent.**

9.2.2 Examples of IPC systems

In the simplest case, a sending process may need to pass only a minimum amount of information, a single bit, to indicate that some event has occurred. In this case they can make use of the synchronization mechanisms described in the next section. Most of the time, however, processes need to send more information than a single bit, so they will use more elaborate schemes to send entire messages.

One widely used method of message exchange between processes is the use of **pipes.** A pipe is essentially a circular buffer (or queue) that one process will put data into and the other will take data out of. The two processes can make use of system calls to put and get the data. This mechanism lets the processes avoid having to worry about synchronization issues. (We will discuss the nature of this problem shortly.) The OS will watch for a full buffer or an empty buffer, but the calling routine needs to be aware that the call might not succeed. For example, if the buffer is full then a sending routine that tries to put data into the buffer will be blocked. Usually a receiving routine can call a nonblocking system routine to try to read data from the buffer. If data is available then it will be returned. If no data is in the buffer then the call will return immediately, but there will be a return code indication that no message was read. Usually there is also a blocking type read as well. A receiver might use a blocking read if it had nothing else to do except wait for incoming information. Pipes first appeared in UNIX, and in UNIX and Linux the pipes are byte streams rather than discrete messages and the pipes are one-way channels. In the Windows implementation the pipes can be byte streams, but they can alternatively be used to send messages, and the pipes are bidirectional.

Another issue with pipes is the question of how they are set up in the first place. In some cases the sending and receiving processes must name each other explicitly. This is generally undesirable because it is more difficult to maintain than other methods. Alternatively, the receiver might not care who is sending but the sender must name the receiver explicitly. An application that is writing messages to a log file might offer this service to many clients at the same time. It will receive an indication of which client sent the message and can log that information as well. A final method is for the sender to provide some other reference rather than the name of the receiving process. This is sometimes called a **mailbox.** In this case the sender is looking for a service that can be provided by many different processes. It does not care which process is providing the service. An example of such a mechanism is **named pipes.**

The mechanism of **sockets** has been in use for quite a while now, so one of the benefits of it is that it has many compatible implementations—they are available on every OS. Sockets are designed to run over a standard networking layer. Most often this layer is TCP or UDP over IP, but other implementations exist. The client (sending) host names the server (receiving) host and also names a specific socket (sometimes called a port) on the receiving host. These are only logical designations and not references to hardware ports. In many cases, this socket will be a **well-known** number. Well-known sockets (below 1024) are assigned by standards bodies for protocols that are also standardized. A higher range of socket numbers is reserved for applications that are not standardized. The client will be assigned a socket number for its use when it tries to connect to the server. Unlike the simpler one-way buffering mechanism used for pipes, sockets support a much more elaborate model. Once the client and server have connected, the protocol they use is determined by the application. Either the client or the server can send a message at any time. For some applications the application layer protocol is standardized, but new applications can design any sort of protocol that is needed. Applications can also use existing protocols for different purposes. For example, it is common for applications to support the HTTP protocol because many firewalls are set to pass this protocol. The server normally establishes a socket by making a series of OS calls and then waits for incoming connections to the socket. If the server is offering a complex service such as FTP, it is common for the server to start a separate thread to handle each client. If the service is very simple, such as a quote-of-the-day service, then the server may just send a message and break the connection.

Another advantage of the socket design is that the server and the client can be located on the same machine. This is especially handy when developing new applications. It also means that the same program can serve both local and remote clients without any changes in either program. It is a very clean model without some of the complications of other mechanisms. Of course, it does mean that for local clients a lot of work is being done that is not strictly necessary. If performance is an issue and the system will always run with the client and server on the same machine, then more efficient mechanisms should be used.

One kind of persistent communication system is called **message queuing.** Such systems create named queues of messages. A process wishing to write messages to the queue calls the OS with the message and the name of a queue to put the message in. A process wishing to read messages from the queue will call the OS with an empty buffer and the name of the queue. The processes may or may not be running at the same time. Other processes or system utilities are normally used to create and destroy the message queues. The queues are normally maintained in secondary storage is order to ensure this persistence, so there is a large amount of overhead to using them.

9.2.3 Examples of shared memory systems

In many OSs it is possible for two (or more) processes running on the same machine to ask the OS to allow them to share access to a block of memory, a technique known as **shared memory.** Usually this is done by having one process call the OS and asking for a segment of memory (of some specified length) to be allocated and given a name. Other processes wishing to share this memory will have to know the same name. They will then give the OS the name and ask for access to the segment. The memory address settings of both processes will be altered so that they can have access to the shared block of memory. The exact mechanism is discussed in Chapter 11. Some applications are very simple and will not need complex synchronization to make sure that the two processes do not interfere with one another. Other systems may require more elaborate synchronization mechanisms to control access to the data in the shared memory block. This topic will be elaborated upon in the next section. You should recall that while separate processes must use such an elaborate mechanism to share memory, threads within a single process always share their memory by definition.

A special case of shared memory is sometimes provided in the form of **memory mapped files.** This is a slight modification of the shared memory technique. In this case the initiating procedure calls the OS and gives it the name of a file on secondary storage. The OS will locate the file and will allocate space in the calling process to contain the entire file. However, the file will not immediately be loaded into memory. As parts of the shared file are accessed for the first time the hardware will signal the OS and it will load the appropriate portion of the file into the memory and then resume running the process. This mechanism is described more fully in Chapter 11.

9.3 SYNCHRONIZATION

9.3.1 The problem

Now that we have an understanding of why processes need to communicate and some of the mechanisms they can use to do so, we need to turn our attention to a problem that can occur when two processes want to share a piece of data in memory. Consider the following example where two processes, A and B, are using a buffer to communicate and are attempting to update a shared record counter, X, which initially has the value 8. Process A has put a record into a buffer and is trying to increment the counter by adding 1 to X. Process B has taken a record out of the buffer, so it is trying to decrement the counter by subtracting 1 from X. So process A has an instruction $X = X + 1$ and process B has an instruction $X = X - 1$. After these two instructions execute we would expect X to still contain the value 8. However, there is a small potential problem.

The high-level language instructions we have shown are normally broken into three separate machine instructions: a Load to a register, an Add or Subtract, and a Store back into memory. Consider the execution shown in Figure 9.1. Process A loads the value of X into register A, so register A contains an 8. Process A is now interrupted because its time slice has finished. The registers are saved in the PCB for process A. Now process B gets a time slice. It loads the value of X into register A,

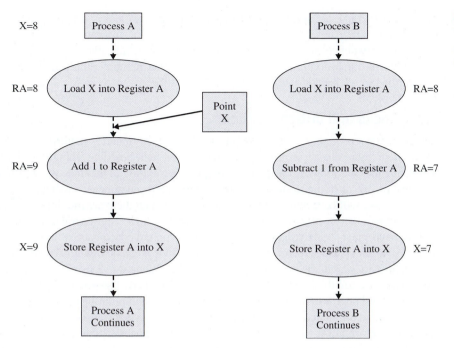

FIGURE 9.1
Two processes updating a shared variable.

so register A is not changed. Process B subtracts 1 from register A, yielding a 7, and stores it in the memory location for X, leaving X at a 7. It continues on. Eventually process A gets another time slice. The registers for process A are restored from its PCB, so register A now contains an 8 again. It adds 1 to Register A, giving a value of 9, which it stores in the memory location for X, leaving X at a 9. This result is not exactly what we were expecting. To make matters even worse, this problem is timing dependent. There is a very small window in which this problem will occur. Almost all the time these two processes will share this variable very nicely, assuming this was the only modification they were making to the variable. This kind of problem is quite hard to debug because it is intermittent. It is called a **race condition.** A race condition, or **race hazard,** is a defect in a design whereby the output of the system is dependent on the sequence or timing of other events. This problem can also occur in a multiprocessor system when process A is running on one CPU and process B is running on another CPU. Regardless of the cause of the problem, we need a solution. Although multiple CPU systems have been uncommon outside of high-end servers, the focus of the current generation of CPU chips is to have multiple CPUs within a single chip. As a result, this sort of problem will become more common.

9.3.2 Atomic operations

The trick we need is to make those operations **atomic.** This word means that the operation we are doing is indivisible—specifically, it cannot be interrupted by another process that wants to update the same information. One possible solution might be to compile that instruction into a single uninterruptible instruction. For example, some machines can add 1 to (or subtract 1 from) a variable in memory without loading the variable into a register. However, when we are writing our program in a higher-level language we want to not worry about such hardware details. We would like to be able to move our program to a different machine that perhaps didn't have such an instruction. So we have to use a more general solution.

9.3.3 Locks and critical sections

Sometimes our processes will be sharing a single variable and sometimes they will be sharing a more elaborate structure. Sometimes we will be doing a single operation and sometimes we will be doing more complex operations. Sometimes we will have only two processes trying to share a single resource and sometimes we will have many. Sometimes we will be trying to share a resource for which there are multiple instances and sometimes there will only be one instance of the resource. The general technique we will use is to use a special kind of variable called a **lock** to control access to the shared variable. A lock is also sometimes called a **mutex** since it can be used to provide mutually exclusive access to the item the lock is protecting. When we look at a process that is using a lock we can think of the program as having four parts, as seen in Figure 9.2.

A **critical section** is a part of the process that is manipulating information that may also be manipulated by another process. The **entry section** is code that locks the shared information—it first ensures that no other process is currently in its critical section and then locks the lock so that no other process sharing this information can now enter its critical section. The **exit section** is code that releases the lock after this process has finished with this critical section. The **remainder section** is the rest of the process. Note that this process can contain other critical sections and locks. This description is merely a structured way of looking at the parts of a single locking operation. The effect of this structure is that we have made the operations we are performing on the shared information atomic. No other process that wants to manipulate this shared information can interrupt this critical section. This structure does not keep process A from being interrupted. It does mean that if process A is interrupted, any other process that tries to enter its critical section (for this variable) will be made to wait until process A finishes its exit section.

9.3.4 Hardware locking instructions

There are many ways that the entry and exit section can be coded. In a very simple embedded OS or in the kernel of an OS we may use special machine instructions to lock and unlock the locks. These instructions are themselves atomic instructions. There are only a few common variants. One is a **Test and Set** instruction. This

FIGURE 9.2
The parts of a process manipulating shared memory.

```
Main() {
    entry section      /* make sure the lock is free */
    critical section   /* manipulate the shared data */
    exit section       /* show the lock is free */
    remainder section  /* everything else */
}
```

instruction will set a variable in memory to a nonzero value (i.e., lock it) and will also return a result that tells us whether the lock was already set before we executed this instruction. If the lock was already set then we did not gain access to the lock, so we just retry the operation:

```
while (TestAndSet(MyLock)) ;
```

Note that the scope of the while statement is null (the ;), so this loop does nothing but wait until the lock is not set when the instruction is executed. This type of coding is sometimes called a **spin-lock** or **busy-waiting.** Another common atomic instruction is a **Swap** instruction. It exchanges the values of two variables in a single step. This instruction is slightly more powerful than the Test and Set instruction in the sense that it can put any value into the lock variable. Other than that, the instructions are equivalent. Another similar instruction is called **fetch-and-add.** It fetches an integer used as a lock from memory and at the same time adds one to the value and writes it back to the same location. An XADD instruction that works this way has been used in the Intel processors since the 80486 CPUs. The choice of which of these atomic instructions to implement is a function of hardware design issues. With the first two of these instructions the exit section of our process is merely to set the lock variable to false (zero). Storing a zero into a memory location is normally an atomic instruction on any hardware.

9.3.5 Semaphores and waiting

If a process actually contained that while loop that we showed with the Test and Set instruction, it would be wasting CPU cycles while it was waiting. As a result, in most cases an application will not use these instructions to implement an entry section. Instead, it will issue OS system calls for both the entry and exit sections. Normally the variable used in these calls is declared to be a **semaphore.** Semaphores can be more complex than the simple locks we have been describing. A lock is always a binary condition but semaphores are often more general. So the simple semaphores are called **binary semaphores,** and only support locking.

While different OSs and languages use many different names for these routines, generally the system call for the entry section is simply:

```
wait (MySemaphore)
```

and the call for the exit section is:

```
signal (MySemaphore)
```

When we call the *wait* routine, if the locked resource is not available, then instead of putting our process into a loop the OS will take our task out of run state and put it into wait state. The process will be waiting for the lock to be released. This will happen when the task that currently has the lock falls through its exit section and executes a *signal* system call on the lock we are waiting for. The OS will take our task out of wait state and put it in ready state. At the same time, it will give our task the lock so that no other task can get it. As was mentioned earlier, there can be any number of tasks waiting on the same lock, so the OS may need to have a queue for all the tasks waiting for each semaphore.

9.3.6 Counting semaphores

But in the more general case a count is associated with each semaphore, which is a positive integer. Such semaphores are sometimes called **counting semaphores.** They are normally used to control access to a group of similar resources such as the records in a buffer. The count associated with a counting semaphore is initialized to the number of available resources. The code in the application for using counting semaphores is normally the same as for binary semaphores. When a process wants to access an instance of the resource it calls the *wait* routine as shown. If the count associated with the semaphore is zero then no instances of the resource are available and the requesting process is blocked. If the count is greater than zero then more instances of the resource are available. The count will be decremented to show that an instance is in use. When the process calls the *signal* routine the associated count will be incremented, and any waiting processes will be dispatched with the available resource.

Counting semaphores can also be used to synchronize access to files where processes will do many reads and only a few writes. Many readers can be allowed at the same time, but we may not want to allow readers to be active when a process is trying to write to the file. So we can allow multiple readers with a counting semaphore and only allow a writer to access when the count of readers reaches zero. Once a writer tries to access the lock we will not allow any more readers to get the lock until the writer has gotten the lock and finished its work.

9.3.7 Synchronization and pipeline architectures

When multiple CPUs are present in a single system and the CPUs have a pipeline architecture it is possible for a CPU to execute instructions out of order. This can cause timing problems with synchronization instructions such as the test and set. As a result, a mechanism is usually provided that allows an application (or the OS) to issue a command that forces the CPU to execute a particular sequence of instructions in the order they are in the program, thus avoiding the problem.

9.3.8 Synchronization in SMP systems

We mentioned in earlier chapters that the trend is for computer systems to include multiple CPUs, in particular multicore processors where multiple CPUs are incorporated into a single integrated circuit. Such systems require OSs that can manage the resources of the multiple CPUs. The preferred solution is known as **symmetric multiprocessing,** or **SMP.** In this architecture the OS is designed so that it can run on any of the CPUs. (An alternative architecture is known as asymmetric multiprocessing where one CPU runs the OS and the others only run applications. This architecture is seldom seen today.)

The multiple execution streams of the OS running on separate CPUs can attempt to reference the same data at the same time. In order to avoid this an SMP OS will use locks. We had said that user programs did not use spin locks since they would waste valuable CPU cycles for an unknown amount of time. Within an OS, however, we presumably know that we will hold a lock only for a very brief, predetermined amount of time. Also, we can't very reasonably make an OS call to a *wait* routine since we are already in the kernel! As a result, OS kernel code normally uses a hardware spin lock mechanism in spite of the waste of CPU cycles.

This brings up an interesting hardware problem though. Suppose that one of the several processors wishes to write a value into memory. To protect that critical section it uses a lock. The semaphores are in the shared memory, and each CPU may also have the value of the semaphore in its cache. You can see the problem—now there are many processors that are using those same atomic instructions, potentially at the same time. This requires that CPUs that share memory in SMPs be a little smarter about sharing. One common way to do this is for every CPU to watch for manipulation of shared memory by **snooping** the memory bus. This is more work for the CPU hardware, but it is worth the effort—the potential for speedup by using multiple CPUs is quite large. The cache hardware must also be smarter because each CPU might have a copy of the semaphore in its cache and if one CPU changes the value of the semaphore then all the other copies must be updated as well. These are very important problems for CPU architects, and are very widely argued about.

9.3.9 Priority inversion

Priority inversion describes a situation that can arise when a lower-priority task holds a shared resource that is required by a task running with a higher priority. This inversion causes blocking of the high-priority task until the resource is released. This effectively inverts the priorities of the two tasks. If some other medium priority task not using the shared resource tries to run it will take precedence over both the low- and high-priority tasks. Priority inversion often does not cause great harm. The delay of the high-priority task goes unnoticed and eventually the low-priority task releases the shared resource. However, priority inversion can cause serious problems. If the high-priority task is delayed long enough it might lead to triggering of a timer and the resetting of the OS. The Mars Pathfinder mission had a priority inversion problem that caused it to reset itself several times. At the very least priority inversion can make a system seem unreasonably slow. Low-priority tasks usually have a low priority because it is not important for them to finish in any particular time frame so long as their job gets done eventually. A high-priority task probably has strict time constraints. It might be working with the user interface or on a soft real-time task. Thus, priority inversion can lead to reduced system responsiveness.

9.3.10 A classical problem

There is a problem that occurs quite often in OSs called the **producer–consumer problem** or the **bounded-buffer problem.** It is an example of a multiprocess synchronization problem. It concerns at least two processes, one of which is a producer of data and another of which is a consumer of the data, and they all share a common, fixed-size buffer. The job of a producer process is to continuously generate blocks of data and put them into the buffer. At the same time, a consumer process is consuming the data by taking it from the buffer a block at a time. But a producer should not try and add data to the buffer if it's full and a consumer should not try to remove data from an empty buffer. One solution to this problem is shown in the following procedures. It works for multiple consumers and multiple producers but we will discuss it as though there were only one of each.

The solution for the producer is to block if the buffer is full. Each time the consumer removes an item from the buffer, it signals the producer who starts to fill the buffer again. In the same way, the consumer blocks if it finds the buffer is empty. Each time the producer puts data into the buffer, it signals the consumer. The counting semaphore *full* is the number of buffers that are currently full, the semaphore *empty* is the number of empty buffers, and *mutex* is for establishing mutual exclusion.

```
semaphore mutex = 1
semaphore full = 0
semaphore empty = BUFFER_SIZE

procedure producer() {
 while (true) {
  item = produceItem()
  wait(empty)
  wait(mutex)
  putItemIntoBuffer(item)
  signal(mutex)
  signal(full)
 }
}

procedure consumer() {
 while (true) {
  wait(full)
  wait(mutex)
  item = removeItemFromBuffer()
  signal(mutex)
  signal(empty)
  consumeItem(item)
 }
}
```

9.3.11 Monitors

Although it does not look that difficult on the surface, the use of locks and semaphores is a very error-prone part of programming. In order to make locking and unlocking more robust, some high-level languages have introduced a mechanism for expressing synchronization requirements. This mechanism is known as a **monitor.** Monitors are not OS constructs so much as they are a way to package OS constructs in a less error-prone way. A monitor is an item with built-in mutual exclusion and thread synchronization capabilities. These features are defined by programming languages so that the compiler can generate the correct code to implement the monitor. Though they take different forms in different languages, there are some general things we can say about monitors.

A monitor is associated with an item in the language such as a procedure or a class. A mutex will be associated with the procedure. Only one thread of an associated process can be executing with the monitor at any given time. A monitor procedure tries to access the lock before doing anything else, and holds it until it either finishes or waits for a condition. When a procedure finishes, it releases the lock so no deadlocks can take place.

Monitors may also have **condition variables.** These allow a thread to wait if conditions are not right for it to continue executing with the monitor. In this case the thread will be blocked and another thread will be given the lock and allowed to execute. The other thread may change the state of the monitor. If conditions are now right for the waiting thread to continue, the running thread can signal the waiting thread. This will move the waiting thread back to the ready queue so that it can resume execution with the monitor when it becomes free. The following code uses condition variables to use a communication channel that can store only one message at a time:

```
monitor channel {
 condition can_send
 condition can_receive
 char contents
 boolean full := false

 function send (char message) {
  while full then wait (can_receive)
  contents := message
  full := true
  signal (can_send)
 }

 function receive () {
  var char received
  while not full then wait (can_send)
  received := contents
  full := false
  signal (can_receive)
  return received
 }
}
```

9.4 DEADLOCKS

9.4.1 What is a deadlock?

A very simple case

Suppose that we have two processes, A and B, which are attempting to share two different resources, 1 and 2. Process A locks resource 1 and then locks resource 2. It does its work and then releases the resources. Process B locks resource 2 and then locks resource 1. It does its work and then releases the resources. These events are shown schematically in Figure 9.3.

Now consider what happens if process A gets interrupted at Point X—perhaps it has used up its time quantum and the operating system takes it out of the run state and puts it back in the ready queue. Process A has already locked resource 1. Now process B starts. It locks resource 2 and then tries to lock resource 1. Since process A is holding a lock on resource 1, the OS puts process B into the wait state and some other process is started. Eventually process A comes to the head of the ready queue and is restarted by the dispatcher. It runs briefly and tries to lock resource 2. Since process B is holding a lock on resource 2, process A is put into the wait state and these two processes are now in a deadlock. Neither process will ever finish because each is holding a resource that the other is waiting for.

This simple example easily shows two of the necessary conditions for a deadlock to occur. The first is that there must be resources involved that are not sharable. This is called **mutual exclusion.** In the case of locks, this is clear from the definition—only one process can hold a lock at any one time. In the case of some resources it is not as clear, as will be discussed later. The second condition necessary for a deadlock is that it must be possible for a process to hold one resource while it waits for another. This is called **hold-and-wait.** Again, in the case of locks we can see that normally a process can get as many locks as it needs without releasing any that it holds.

Some more elaborate examples

A favorite example in the computer science literature is the "Dining Philosophers" problem. In this problem, shown in Figure 9.4, there is a table at which there are three philosophers who alternatively eat or think. After thinking for a while, a philosopher will want to eat. The meal being served is rice, and it requires two chopsticks to eat. Between each two philosophers is a chopstick. When it is time to eat, a philosopher picks up one chopstick on the left and one chopstick on the right and begins to eat. It should be clear that this setting can easily lead to a deadlock. Suppose that more or less simultaneously, each philosopher decides to eat. Each reaches out to the left and picks up a chopstick. Each philosopher then gets interrupted and has to wait for a while (as in the simple example).

FIGURE 9.3
Two processes sharing two resources.

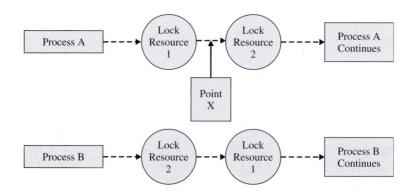

FIGURE 9.4
The "Dining Philosophers" problem.

When it resumes processing (trying to eat), it tries to pick up the chopstick to the right, but finds that chopstick already in use, so it waits on the right chopstick. Eventually we make it all around the table and each philosopher is holding one chopstick and waiting for another. The difference between this example and the first is that in this case there are more than two processes (philosophers) and more than two resources (chopsticks). Each process is holding one resource and is waiting for another resource. This condition is known as **circular wait.** It was present in the first example but the circle was harder to see because there were only two processes. Each process then had a resource that was needed by the other. As is seen in the dining philosophers problem, all that is needed is that there is some sequence of processes, each holding a resource wanted by another, and ultimately one process in this sequence that is holding a resource wanted by the first process. There is a simple method of avoiding this situation, which we discuss later in the chapter.

An often cited example of a deadlock in the real world is a gridlock in traffic on city streets. For example, Figure 9.5 shows a simple traffic gridlock. (To keep it simple we have shown one-way streets.) In this case you see a number of different processes (cars), each wanting to use a resource that the car in front of it is already using. In this case the resource is a position on the street. It is clear that there is mutual exclusion—no two cars can be in the same position at the same time. There is also circular wait—it is obvious from the picture. Consider, however, the car identified as A. Although this car is also waiting, it is not a part of the deadlock because no other car is waiting on the resource it holds.

In many analyses of deadlocks a fourth condition is stated—that preemption not be allowed. Preemption would mean that we could take away from a process some resource that it is currently holding, thus breaking the deadlock. In our analysis, preemption is a solution to a deadlock. Adding a "condition" of no preemption is merely a way of saying that one possible solution to the deadlock problem is not used. It is not really a necessary condition for a deadlock. We discuss this further later in the chapter.

FIGURE 9.5
A deadlock in city
traffic.

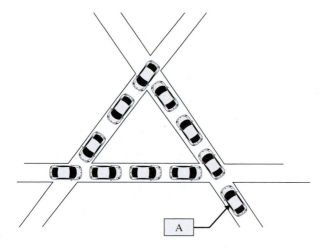

Resource-allocation graphs

A tool often used to explain deadlocks is called a **resource-allocation graph.** These graphs show processes and resources and which processes are waiting for or holding instances of each resource. An example is shown in Figure 9.6. Each node in the graph represents either a process (shown here as a triangle) or a resource (shown as an oval box). A directed edge is drawn from process B to resource 2 to show that B is waiting for 2, and from 1 to A to show that A holds 1. If there is a deadlock then there will be a loop in the graph and it will be obvious from the diagram. In a computer system there is usually more than one instance of a resource. In this case it is traditional to represent each instance of a resource in the graph as a single dot inside the resource node. In such a case a loop in the diagram does not necessarily mean that there is a deadlock because there may still be free instances of each resource available. Unfortunately, OSs don't understand pictures, so this technique is not as useful to them as it is to a human analyst. A programmer can simulate a graph, however, and write a program to do a search with a graph in mind, but that is not quite the same thing.

FIGURE 9.6
A resource allocation
graph.

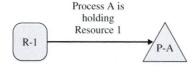

Process A is
holding
Resource 1

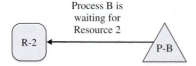

Process B is
waiting for
Resource 2

9.4.2 What can we do about deadlocks?

There are basically four approaches to solving the deadlock problem. First, we can **prevent** deadlocks from ever happening by making sure that one of the necessary conditions does not exist. Second, we can allow all three conditions to occur, but **avoid** deadlocks by making sure that we do not allocate resources in such a way that they will ever happen. Third, we can allow deadlocks to happen, **detect** that they have happened, and perhaps do something about them. Finally, we can ignore them.

9.4.3 Prevention

Preventing deadlocks would involve making sure that one or more of the three necessary conditions for deadlock cannot occur. We address these three conditions in turn.

Mutual Exclusion

In a computer system some resources are very clearly not sharable. If one process is printing the payroll checks on a printer it will not work well for another process to begin to print an email message on the same printer. (We can simulate simultaneous access to a printer by spooling the output. We discuss this further later in this section.) Similarly, if one process is writing records to a tape drive it will not be practical for another process to start using the same tape drive. Other resources are clearly sharable. For example, a network interface card is very likely to be shared by several applications at the same time. A server might be running several different services over the same network adapter—perhaps a Web server, a file server, and an FTP server. Requests can come in randomly from other hosts in the network and responses can be queued up by the server processes. One might argue that the messages are not going out together—that the line is not really being used "at the same time." However, the point is that no process will ever have to wait for the network to send data. Assuming enough memory space is available for buffers, no process will ever enter a deadlock because it is waiting to send data to the network. (It may have to wait for a response, but that is not the same thing.) Similarly, access to files on a disk drive is sharable at the software level. Two processes can have files open on a hard drive and can read from and write to those files on a single drive without waiting for the other process to completely finish with its file processing.

Some resources are less clear. Consider RAM, for example. One could argue that RAM is sharable since many processes can be using parts of it at the same time. However, processes generally are given exclusive access to blocks of RAM and are not allowed to access blocks allocated to other processes. So in that sense RAM is really not sharable. However, there are many instances where processes do share memory, so memory is very difficult to categorize in this regard. With most OSs access to a single file may be sharable. If we have a spelling dictionary on a timesharing system each user can be checking spelling on different documents at the same time. However, if the system is an inventory system and we have several processes trying to allocate inventory to customers at the same time, the applications need to lock the files (or at least parts of the files) so that we do not try to ship the last widget to three different customers. So files are not intrinsically either sharable or nonsharable. It depends on the use being made of them.

Even with nonsharable devices like printers we can use some mechanisms to make most uses of a printer a sharable event. The solution is to use spooling. Rather than write data directly to the printer, the OS will take the data from the application and temporarily store it in a disk file. Later, when it knows that the printer is available, has the right forms mounted, and so on, it can actually print the data on the printer. Since we have removed the mutual exclusion involving printers, we have removed them from the list of resources that can cause a deadlock. On the other hand, a deadlock of a sort can occur even with spooling. When an OS is spooling the printer output for several applications it is temporarily writing the output to disk. It is entirely possible that the disk space allocated to the spooling fills up. This can once again leave the system exposed to a possible deadlocked state.

But the bottom line is that since some resources are intrinsically nonsharable, removing mutual exclusion is not a generally applicable solution.

Hold and wait

There are two ways we can avoid the hold-and-wait condition necessary for a deadlock to occur. We can require that a process must request all resources it will ever need when it starts. For a few simple batch systems this might be possible, but for most modern applications it is not feasible. There are simply too many combinations of possible events to make prediction of all requirements practical. Furthermore, in many cases the 80/20 rule applies—in 80 percent of the cases we will only need a few resources. In only 20 percent of the cases will we need a big allotment of extra RAM. If we have to ask for the worst case in advance then most of the time we will be tying up resources that we will not need.

The second option is to require that any process that is asking for a resource must first release all resources it is holding before it asks for any other resources. So, in our first example, when process B wants to ask for resource 1 it must first release resource 2 and then ask for resources 1 and 2 at the same time. This set of resources can't be allocated because process A has resource 1, so process B will now wait, but it will no longer be holding resource 2. Process A will eventually get its next time slice and it will release resource 1 and attempt to allocate resources 1 and 2 at the same time. Since it currently has the CPU it will be allowed to lock both resources and will continue. When it is finished with these two resources and releases both of them, then process B will eventually be put into the ready state and will be granted both resources and continue. Thus we have prevented a deadlock. However, if an application was using a nonsharable resource, how could it release it? Furthermore, this constant releasing and relocking is just too inefficient to use except in the most trivial circumstances. So, as with mutual exclusion, eliminating hold and wait is generally not a useful solution to the problem of deadlocks.

Circular wait

The last condition of a deadlock is a circular wait. There is a very simple method of preventing deadlock by not allowing this condition. The solution is to establish an ordering of all the resources in a system. (There is no real significance to this ordering except that it works best if the ordering matches the order in which programs are most likely to lock the resource.) The next requirement is that all processes must lock resources in the same order. This will prevent the circular wait condition. Consider once again the first example. If process A and process B both try to lock resource 1 before they try to lock resource 2, then a deadlock between these two will never arise. When the second process tries to lock resource 1 it will be forced to wait. This works just as well if multiple processes and multiple resources are involved.

Unfortunately, as a general-purpose solution for deadlock avoidance in OSs, resource ordering is not a practical solution. OS utility programs, third-party software, and end user applications all would have to be written with some such standard in mind and no such standard exists. However, for a development team working on a large system with multiple concurrently running subsystems, ordering of locks on resources is a useful technique to avoid creating deadlocks within the application system itself. So this is an important technique to be aware of, even if it is not a general solution to the deadlock problem.

9.4.4 Avoidance

So far all our examples of resources have shown a single instance of each resource. A simple lock can only have one user at a time, a printer can only have one user, and so on. With other resources there can be many instances of the resource. The most obvious example is RAM—there are always many blocks of RAM to be allocated. Similarly, we might have multiple tape drives on which a tape can be mounted. On a large mainframe we may even have multiple identical printers and not really care which one we get to use. In studying the avoidance mechanisms, we consider the more general case where resources can have multiple instances.

There are two mechanisms for deadlock avoidance. Each of these mechanisms requires that before a process runs it must provide the OS with a maximum number of instances of each resource that it will ask for under any circumstances. It might say that it will only need 543 KB of RAM, one printer, and three tape drives. There are then two ways the OS can use this number. The first is to use the numbers to decide whether to run the job at all. When the OS is going to start a job it can look at the resources it has available right now and see if it can satisfy the maximum demand that the application might ask for. It might have the printer and three tape drives it can allocate to the program, but only 506 KB of RAM. If the OS can't ensure that it will be able to grant the maximum number of all the resources that the job might request, then it does not run the job. In this way the OS will **avoid** putting itself into a situation where a deadlock can occur. This is certainly safe but is not a very optimum solution since the job might often run without asking for the worst case of its resources. This is equivalent to requiring that the process ask for all resources in advance.

The second solution is harder, but more nearly optimum. In this case the OS will start the job without checking the maximum resource allocations, but when the program asks for any resource the OS will determine whether it knows it will be able to grant that request and still be able to finish all the other jobs it has running. If the system can't safely grant the request that the process has made then it will put that process into a wait state. A state where the OS knows it can finish running all the

FIGURE 9.7

Showing a safe state.

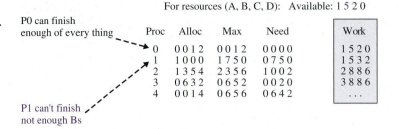

For resources (A, B, C, D):   Available: 1 5 2 0

P0 can finish
enough of every thing

Proc	Alloc	Max	Need	Work
0	0 0 1 2	0 0 1 2	0 0 0 0	1 5 2 0
1	1 0 0 0	1 7 5 0	0 7 5 0	1 5 3 2
2	1 3 5 4	2 3 5 6	1 0 0 2	2 8 8 6
3	0 6 3 2	0 6 5 2	0 0 2 0	3 8 8 6
4	0 0 1 4	0 6 5 6	0 6 4 2	. . .

P1 can't finish
not enough Bs

currently running jobs even if all the jobs request the maximum amount of all resources they have said they might use is known as a **safe state.**

In the example shown in Figure 9.7, the OS is monitoring four resources, A–D. For these resources it currently has unallocated (Available) 1, 5, 2, and 0 instances, respectively. We show these lists of resource counts without commas for simplicity. There are five processes, 0–4. When these processes started running they each gave a maximum number of instances of each of the four resources they might ask for. These are listed in the column titled Max. That is, process 1 said that at a maximum it would need 1 instance of resource A, 7 of B, 5 of C, and no Ds. Each process is currently holding some number of instances of each resource, as listed in the column titled Alloc. As we can see, process 2 currently has allocated 1 A, 3 Bs, 5 Cs, and 4 Ds. The OS can determine that process 1 could not ask for any more As because it is already allocated as many as it said it would ever need. If it asked for more we could terminate the job. It could ask for 7 Bs and 5 Cs but no Ds. These are shown in the column titled Need. The OS can check to see if it will be possible to finish this set of jobs without a deadlock occurring. We notice that process 1 will be not be able to finish because it can ask for 7 more Bs and we only have 5. But process 0 will be able to finish since it can't ask for anything more. When it finishes we will recover the resources allocated to the process—in this case 0 0 1 2. This will leave us with 1 5 3 2. This is shown in the column titled Work. Now process 1 still can't finish, but process 2 can finish because its need is less than our working resources. When it finishes we will recover its resources, giving us 2 8 8 6. Now process 1 can finish, giving us 3 8 8 6. Similarly, process 3 and 4 can also finish. Since we know that all the processes can finish we know that the system is in a safe state.

So in order to avoid deadlocks the OS must check each request by a process for a resource allocation to make sure that if it grants the request the system will still be in a safe state. Note that an unsafe state does not mean that we have a deadlock or that we will definitely have a deadlock. It only means that we *might* eventually have a deadlock. By never allowing the system to enter an unsafe state we will avoid deadlocks. However, we will once again be using the system in a suboptimum manner because we may be making processes wait when they could have successfully run without a deadlock. The algorithm we just informally described is known as the Banker's Algorithm. It was used in an OS known as THE Operating System. However, for many systems it is impossible to know in advance what every process will request, so deadlock avoidance is not used in current OSs.

9.4.5 Detection

Our next approach to the deadlock problem is simply to let deadlocks happen, when a deadlock happens, discover that it happened, and then try to recover from the deadlock. The main advantage of this approach is that it is optimum in the sense that it lets all processes try to run and never makes processes wait just to avoid a possible deadlock.

If we were actually concerned about detecting resource allocation conflicts with multiple instances of each resource we could utilize an algorithm similar to the Banker's Algorithm. Instead of maximum resources yet requested, we would be looking at the resources currently requested but not yet allocated. If we were not able to find a "safe state" then we would know that the processes that were unable to finish were involved in a deadlock. However, no real OS today incorporates such an algorithm. Instead, they leave it up to the applications to worry about deadlocks since these are the sorts of deadlocks that are actually encountered. The OS provides an API call that allows the application to examine the list of all waiting tasks. The application can then examine all the waits to see if there is a loop in them. This examination is actually done by a debugger program that is running a user application. If the debugger finds a loop then the programmers can examine the data and fix the problem.

9.4.6 Preemption and other real-world solutions

Some resources are used in such a way that once a process starts using them the process needs to finish what it is doing before we can use the resource. Good examples are writing a file to a tape drive or to a printer (without spooling). Other resources are different—RAM, for example. If two processes are running and each demands more RAM than the system can supply, we can temporarily suspend one of the processes, save all the information it currently has in RAM to secondary storage, and let the second process have all the RAM. When the second process finishes we restore the first process into RAM, give it the extra RAM it wanted, and let it continue. This technique is known as **preemption.** In Figure 9.5, we could apply preemption by having a police officer ask the driver of the car in the lower left corner of the figure to back it up, preempting its position on the street.

The next question is then which job(s) should be preempted. The best choice is usually the one that has the minimum cost—the one with the smallest current RAM use that is large enough to satisfy the current request, for example. If preempting the largest process does not free enough resources for the remaining jobs to finish, then the preemption may need to be repeated with the next smaller process.

If all the processes involved in a deadlock are waiting on resources that cannot be preempted, we may have no choice but to abort some or all of the processes. As unusual as it may seem, the normal choice is to abort all the processes in the deadlock. Deadlocks are usually a rare event—so rare that it is probably not worth spending the time to develop more complex algorithms. Plus, the available data on which to develop such algorithms is sparse. A better choice would be to successively abort the lowest cost processes until the deadlock disappears. The deadlock detection algorithm should be run after each attempt.

As was mentioned, the most often used solution is to ignore the problem. Unfortunately, the deadlocked processes may consume some large amount of resources. Probably other processes will eventually begin to stop and wait because of the deadlocks held by the originally deadlocked processes. Eventually, the system may stop running any processes. Hopefully, the system operator will notice this problem and will begin to solve it, probably by aborting jobs until the system resumes operation.

In the future it seems likely that OSs will incorporate more mechanisms for coping with deadlocks. Although the algorithms for detection do require some CPU and memory resources, deadlocks are very mysterious to users—the system they are using just appears to hang and they have no idea what to do to fix it or to avoid it in the future. Computer hardware continues to get more powerful and RAM less expensive. Deadlock detection is being implemented for debuggers and we surmise that they will find their way into the kernel as a background function in the future.

9.5 SUMMARY

In this chapter, we discussed the nature of systems that are comprised of multiple cooperating processes. We started this chapter with an examination of the reasons why systems are often built this way, a trend that seems to be increasing. We looked at the mechanisms that processes use to communicate with one another. We then studied the problems that arise when each of two processes is trying to access data that the other process is (or may be) accessing at the same time. We described some tools that have been developed to allow processes to synchronize their activities so that these issues can be avoided. Finally, we discussed another class of problems called deadlocks that can arise when multiple processes use the synchronization mechanisms to lock resources. We described four theoretical mechanisms for keeping deadlocks from bringing our systems to a halt.

In the next chapter we cover management of primary system memory.

BIBLIOGRAPHY

Ben-Ari, M., *Principles of Concurrent Programming.* Englewood Cliffs, NJ: Prentice Hall, 1982.

Bernstein, A. J., "Output Guards and Nondeterminism in Communicating Sequential Processes," *ACM Transactions on Programming Languages and Systems,* Vol. 2, No. 2, 1980, pp. 234–238.

Brinch Hansen, P., "Structured Multiprogramming," *Communications of the ACM,* Vol. 15, No. 7, July 1972, pp. 574–578.

Brinch Hansen, P., *Operating Systems Principles.* Englewood Cliffs, NJ: Prentice Hall, 1973.

Coffman, E. G., Jr., M. J. Elphick, and A. Shoshani, "System Deadlocks," *Computing Surveys,* Vol. 3, No. 2, June 1971, pp. 67–78.

Courtois, P. J., F. Heymans, and D. L. Parnas, "Concurrent Control with Readers and Writers," *Communications of the ACM,* Vol. 14, No. 10, October 1971, pp. 667–668.

Dijkstra, E. W., "Co-operating Sequential Processes," in F. Genuys (Ed.), *Programming Languages.* London: Academic Press, 1965, pp. 43–112.

Dijkstra, E. W. *EWD 126: The Multiprogramming System for the EL X8 THE* (manuscript), 14 June 1965.

Dijkstra, E. W., "Solution of a Problem in Concurrent Programming Control," *Communications of the ACM,* Vol. 8, No. 5, September 1965, p. 569.

Dijkstra, E. W., "Hierarchical Ordering of Sequential Processes," *Acta Informatica,* Vol. 1, 1971, pp. 115–138.

Eisenberg, M. A., and M. R. McGuire, "Further Comments on Dijkstra's Concurrent Programming Control Problem," *Communications of the ACM,* Vol. 15, No. 11, November 1972, p. 999.

Habermann, A. N., "Prevention of System Deadlocks," *Communications of the ACM,* Vol. 12, No. 7, July 1969, pp. 373–377, 385.

Havender, J. W., "Avoiding Deadlock in Multitasking Systems," *IBM Systems Journal,* Vol. 7, No. 2, 1968, pp. 74–84.

Hoare, C. A. R., "Towards a Theory of Parallel Programming," in C. A. R. Hoare (Ed.), *Operating Systems Techniques.* New York: Academic Press, 1972, pp. 61–71.

Holt, R. C., "Some Deadlock Properties of Computer Systems," *ACM Computing Surveys,* Vol. 4, No. 3, September 1972, pp. 179–196.

Howard, J. H., "Mixed Solutions for the Deadlock Problem," *Communications of the ACM,* Vol. 16, No. 7, July 1973, pp. 427–430.

Isloor, S. S., and T. A. Marsland, "The Deadlock Problem: An Overview," *IEEE Computer,* Vol. 13, No. 9, September 1980, pp. 58–78.

Kessels, J. L. W., "An Alternative to Event Queues for Synchronization in Monitors," *Communications of the ACM,* Vol. 20, No. 7, July 1977, pp. 500–503.

Knuth, D., "Additional Comments on a Problem in Concurrent Programming Control," *Communications of the ACM,* Vol. 9, No. 5, May 1966, pp. 321–322.

Lamport, L., "A New Solution to Dijkstra's Concurrent Programming Problem," *Communications of the ACM,* Vol. 17, No. 8, August 1974, pp. 453–455.

Lamport, L., "Synchronization of Independent Processes," *Acta Informatica,* Vol. 7, No. 1, 1976, pp. 15–34.

Lamport, L., "Concurrent Reading and Writing," *Communications of the ACM,* Vol. 20, No. 11, November 1977, pp. 806–811.

Lamport, L., "The Mutual Exclusion Problem: Part I—A Theory of Interprocess Communication," *Journal of the ACM,* Vol. 33, No. 2, 1986, pp. 313–326.

Lamport, L., "The Mutual Exclusion Problem: Part II—Statement and Solutions," *Journal of the ACM,* Vol. 33, No. 2, 1986, pp. 327–348.

Lampson, B. W., and D. D. Redell, "Experience with Processes and Monitors in MESA," *Communications of the ACM,* Vol. 23, No. 2, February 1980, pp. 105–117.

Levine, G. N., "Defining Deadlock," *Operating Systems Review,* Vol. 37, No. 1, pp. 54–64.

Newton, G., "Deadlock Prevention, Detection, and Resolution: An Annotated Bibliography," *ACM Operating Systems Review,* Vol. 13, No. 2, April 1979, pp. 33–44.

Patil, S. S., "Limitations and Capabilities of Dijkstra's Semaphore Primitives for Coordination among Processes," M.I.T. Project MAC Computation Structures Group Memo 57, February 1971.

Peterson, G. L., "Myths About the Mutual Exclusion Problem," *Information Processing Letters,* Vol. 12, No. 3, June 1981, pp. 115–116.

Raynal, M., *Algorithms for Mutual Exclusion.* Cambridge, MA: MIT Press, 1986.

Zobel, D., "The Deadlock Problem: A Classifying Bibliography," *Operating Systems Review,* Vol. 17, No. 4, October 1983, pp. 6–16.

WEB RESOURCES

http://boinc.berkeley.edu (SETI and BOINC)

http://research.microsoft.com/~mbj/Mars_Pathfinder/Mars_Pathfinder.html

http://www.softpedia.com/get/Others/Home-Education/Deadlock-Avoidance-Simulation.shtml

http://webscripts.softpedia.com/script/Development-Scripts-js/Complete-applications/Banker-s-Algorithm-Demonstration-15119.html

REVIEW QUESTIONS

9.1 We listed eight reasons why it is sometimes desirable to have a system separated into different processes, sometimes running on different machines. For each of these reasons, give a different example than was given in the text.
  a. Performance -
  b. Scaling -
  c. Purchased components -
  d. Third-party service -
  e. Components of multiple systems -
  f. Reliability -
  g. Physical location of information -
  h. Enable application -

9.2 For each attribute of interprocess communication mechanisms there were various alternatives for that attribute. Discuss some good and bad points for the alternatives for the following attributes:
  a. Multiple or single connections possible -
  b. Naming strategy -
  c. Connection oriented or connectionless -
  d. Persistent or transient -
  e. Number of processes -

9.3 True or false? Pipes are an example of a blocking communication mechanism.

9.4 True or false? Sockets are an example of a persistent communication mechanism.

9.5 What is the big problem with shared memory IPC mechanisms?

9.6 Why are synchronization problems so difficult to debug?

9.7 What is the special feature of all the hardware locking instructions that we discussed for synchronization?

9.8 Why do applications not use spin-locks? What do they do instead?

9.9 What are the normal names of the locking and unlocking system calls?
  a. Lock and unlock
  b. Set and clear
  c. Wait and signal
  d. Enter and exit
  e. None of the above

9.10 There are special semaphores called counting semaphores. What kinds of things are they used for?

9.11 True or false? When running on SMP systems, applications must take special precautions to make sure that the values of any locks are seen by all CPUs.

9.12 Briefly describe the concept of priority inversion.

9.13 What caused the development of monitors in high-level languages?

9.14 There are three conditions for a deadlock. What are they?

9.15 We said that for a deadlock to happen there had to be a sequence of processes, each holding a resource and waiting on another resource that was held by another process, with the last process waiting on a resource held by the first process. How many processes does it take to create a deadlock?

9.16 Some devices are not sharable, but we have found a way to make a virtual device that allows us to pretend that we are sharing them. What is that mechanism?

9.17 Ordering of locks on resources can eliminate circular waits and thus eliminate deadlocks. When is this technique applicable and when is it not?

9.18 We discussed two different types of avoidance. In general, what's wrong with avoidance?

9.19 The algorithms for deadlock detection are well known and not too hard to write. So why do we not use them more often?

9.20 What is the case where preemption is easy to do and works well?

Problems possibly requiring further reading:

9.21 Modern OSs use several different kinds of semaphores for different purposes. Pick a modern OS and name some of the different types of semaphores they support with a brief explanation of each.

9.22 There are several classic problems involved in synchronization. We described two. What were they and what other classic problems can you find?

Chapter 10

Basic Memory Management

In this chapter

10.1 INTRODUCTION: WHY MANAGE PRIMARY MEMORY?

In the last two chapters we discussed one of the main jobs that an OS has to do: managing processes running on the CPU. In this chapter we discuss the second main job of the OS: managing primary memory. As with all system resources, the OS attempts to manage the primary memory of the system. Usually primary memory is random access memory (RAM) made of electronic circuits.[1] The basic goal of memory management is to allow as many processes to be running as possible. The OS provides API functions to allow us to allocate, access, and return memory. When memory is allocated to processes, the OS must keep track of which parts of the memory are free, which parts are allocated, and to which processes they are allocated. The OS sometimes may also preempt memory from processes. In this case it must be prepared to save the current contents of the primary memory on secondary memory, to track where the contents are stored for each part of each process, and to restore the contents of primary memory when the preempted process is resumed.

---

[1] Systems have been built with other types of primary memory. Early systems used acoustic waves in tanks of mercury or rotating drums, for example. For some years almost all computer systems used the polarity of magnetization in iron oxide cores to store bits. The phrase "core dump"—a printout of the contents of the memory allocated to a program that had crashed—comes from this era. This memory had the property that it retained its contents even when the power was turned off. This strikes us as a peculiar property today since we normally presume that primary memories are volatile.

In most situations the OS will try to manage memory in ways that are transparent to the application. However, we note later in the next chapter that in some cases the transparency is not complete. Naive use of memory services can sometimes cause problems for a large system that is trying to optimize performance. Indeed, one of the main reasons we study OSs is to gain the information and understanding necessary to get past such problems.

Having discussed why we want to manage memory, in Section 10.2 we show the traditional model of the cycle of developing and running a process and the steps in the binding of a reference to an item in a program to the physical memory location where that item is stored. We later use these steps to explain the various memory management mechanisms. We then discuss memory management in progressively more complex situations, starting with a single process in Section 10.3 and discussing such aspects as relocation and overlays. We then move to situations where multiple processes are involved, again discussing gradually more complex mechanisms, including operating with a fixed number of processes in Section 10.4 and with a variable number of processes in Section 10.5. We end with a summary of the chapter.

10.2 BINDING MODEL: STEPS IN THE DEVELOPMENT CYCLE

First, let us describe the standard model of the steps of building an application, loading it into memory, and running it. In the later sections of the chapter we use this model to explain the common features of how an OS manages the way a process uses memory.

There are really five steps in the sequence of events that result in a process in execution in memory. First, we write (or **code**) the program. Usually this is done with some symbolic language, either a lower-level assembly language or a higher-level problem-oriented language. Second, we use a translator program (usually an assembler or a compiler but occasionally an interpreter) to **translate** this symbolic program into a sequence of instructions for the target machine, creating an "object module." Normally this object module is not ready to run yet. In the third step, we **link** that module with similar modules that were created separately. Those modules might be other modules we created. They may also be library modules that we purchased or that came with the OS. Fourth, we **load** the program into memory, and fifth we actually **run** the program.

A word of caution about the names of these steps: Historically there have been many different software packages designed to assist a programmer in implementing a program. Because different systems were used to solve different problems in different environments, the capabilities of some of these steps have sometimes been combined into a single model. The function we described as combining the modules together is most often called **linking** and the function of bringing the process into memory is usually called **loading.** Sometimes, however, these functions have been done in one step. In other literature you may see either word used to describe either step or to a combination of both of these steps at one time.

Let us suppose that we are creating a process that consists of two modules. We have a main procedure that we call a subroutine named XYZ that we have written earlier. As we go through progressively more complex models, the idea we focus on is a question of **binding.** Binding is the process of determining where in the physical memory the subroutine should go and making the reference in the main routine point to the subroutine. However, binding occurs with all references to items that are not a part of our main program, not just with subroutines, but including data items as well.

10.3 A SINGLE PROCESS

10.3.1 Binding at coding time

In a very simple environment like an embedded system with a very tiny BIOS, we might manually decide where each piece of the program was going to go. We might put the main module at location 100 and the subroutine XYZ at location 500. If we coded the main module in assembly language we might include assembler directive like **ORG 100** and in the subroutine we might include an **ORG 500.** These directives cause the assembler to generate code that absolutely references these memory addresses. In our main module we would know that the subroutine XYZ was going to be at address 500, so instead of issuing a call to XYZ we could actually issue the call to location 500. In this case we have made the binding decision during the coding step and have told the assembler of this through the ORG directives. As unlikely as this might seem to us today, it is by no means an extreme example of early binding. Here are three extreme examples:

> When computers were first developed, and again when minicomputers and personal computers were first developed, the first systems had very little software and few peripherals. Programmers not only assigned the addresses manually, they wrote the programs in machine language and even entered them into the memory manually by manipulating switches and buttons on the front panel of the machines. In some machines there were peripheral devices that used a fixed memory address as a buffer so that the programmer did not even have a choice. Needless to say, having programmers allocate memory manually was error-prone and time-consuming. It was a phase that didn't last long.
>
> The IBM 650 had a primary memory that was a rotating drum. The instructions took a variable amount of time to execute. While the instruction was executing, of course, the drum continued to rotate. As a result, each instruction included a field that gave the address of the next instruction. The programmer had to try to optimize the program by placing the next instruction in the location that would be coming up next under the drum's read head when the current instruction finished. Obviously that phase didn't last long either. An assembler called SOAP, Symbolic Optimizing Assembler Program, was developed at Columbia University. Its main job was the optimum placement of the instructions on the drum.
>
> When programs were routinely punched into cards and no magnetic tapes or rotating memories were available, it was a fairly complex process to load the assembler program into memory, feed in the source program, obtain an object module punched into cards, load the linker program into memory, feed that object module to the linker, punch out an executable program, and finally load the object program into the computer and run it. As a result, it was common to **patch** executable programs that had been punched into cards. The assembler listings included the machine language that was output for each instruction. This allowed the programmer to find the

card containing an incorrect instruction, load it into a keypunch, and fix the program by changing the machine language. Unfortunately, that practice did continue for some time, and it was also error-prone. Programmers would insert multiple patches in a card deck. Eventually the number of patches would become unwieldy, so the programmer would go back to the source deck, make all the changes to the source program, and do the reassembly. Unfortunately, it was all too easy to miss one of the changes to the source, so it was not uncommon to find oneself fixing bugs in the source code that one had already fixed with a patch.

10.3.2 Binding at linking time

In the environment of CP/M, all programs were supposed to start at location 100, so we might include the ORG 100 statement in the main module. However, we probably did not care where subroutine XYZ ended up, so in our main routine we use the symbolic name XYZ. When the assembler outputs our object module, it includes all of our instructions and data, but it also includes information that will tell the linker program that we have some references that it needs to fix up, or link. After the linker processes our main routine it will have a list of names that it needs to resolve. It will then begin to process other modules we told it to include. As it includes these modules in the load step, it will find in those modules the names that were defined in them. In this case, "XYZ" will be defined in one of the modules that we tell the linker to process. When the linker figures out where the module XYZ will reside in our address space, it will go back and link (or bind) the references in the main module to the addresses in the subroutine module. Now we have made the binding decision at link time rather than at coding time. Notice that when we put off the binding until a later step we gain somewhat in flexibility. If we decided at coding time to put module XYZ at location 500 and we later found that we needed to move it to some other location, we have to go to a lot of trouble to change all the references to that address. Letting the linker decide where to put the module makes it easier. However, we pay a little for the increased flexibility. In this case we are carrying around extra information in the object modules that define the names and the references to the names, and we spend a little extra time in the link step while it does the binding. As computers have gotten bigger and faster, however, this extra time and space has become such a small price to pay that we most likely don't even give it a thought.

10.3.3 A single process

In the CP/M environment, the OS resided at the top of memory. Application programs started at location 100 to avoid the interrupt vector in low memory, and grew upward. Unfortunately, as the operating system grew (and it always does) it might eventually get so big that an upgraded OS might be using the memory that was needed by a program that had been running fine before the upgrade. It would now crash and it was probably not obvious what the problem was. MS-DOS, therefore, took a different tack: The OS was loaded into low RAM and the program was loaded above it. When the application tried to load, if there was enough memory left over, then the program would load and run. If not, then at least the failure was clearly defined. Initially, when one created an application program under MS-DOS, one linked the program to run on a specific release of the OS. This step defined the address of the service routines in the OS and the address at which the application should begin loading. Unfortunately, this meant that when a release of MS-DOS came out that changed the absolute size of the resident OS, all applications had to be relinked to run on the new release.

Many mainframe OSs had similar architecture, but they employed additional hardware to protect themselves. In Figure 10.1 we see a typical early OS architecture for a mainframe that ran only a single process. The executable program would be created to reside at a particular address that was above the OS kernel. In addition, a **base register** would be loaded with an address below which the executable program could not address. If the program did reference memory below this address, an interrupt would be generated and the program would be terminated. Such systems still had the problem that if the OS grew then the programs had to be linked with new addresses. The solution to this problem was to change the function of the base register somewhat.

10.3.4 Dynamic relocation

This change in function also resulted in a change in name. What had been called a base register was now called a **relocation register,** as shown in Figure 10.2. The value loaded into the register was no longer a limit. Instead, the executable program was created to act as though it were located at address 0, and the value in the relocation register was added to every memory reference made by the program. Now the program did not have to be relinked every time the OS changed since every memory reference is automatically relocated as the program runs.

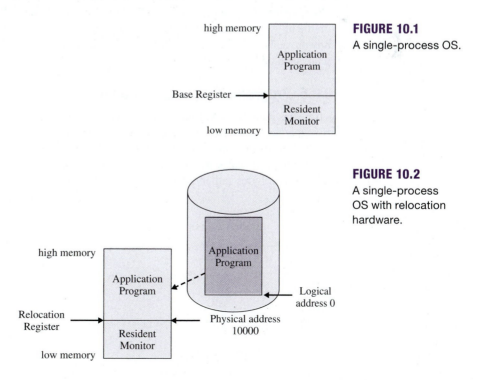

FIGURE 10.1
A single-process OS.

FIGURE 10.2
A single-process OS with relocation hardware.

10.3.5 Physical RAM space versus logical RAM space

This new relocation function introduces an important concept: the difference between the logical address space and the physical address space. Originally when we compiled a program we created a program that was to be loaded into RAM at the address that was assigned to it either in the translation step or the linking step. The executable program was compiled to reference a range of addresses that corresponded one to one with the actual physical memory addresses. Though it was not clear at this point in the evolution of the hardware, there were actually two different address spaces in use. The first address space is the set of addresses that the CPU would generate as the program executed. This address space is called a **logical address** space. We loaded the executable program into the primary memory. The set of addresses used to access this memory is known as the **physical address** space. When we introduced the relocation register it became clear that the program's logical address space and its physical address space were different. We see this illustrated in Figure 10.2. The executable program on the disk was created so that it generated addresses with a low address of zero. But when it was located into memory it was actually loaded into physical memory address 10000. The memory address hardware dynamically relocated the logical addresses generated by the program as it ran, and by adding the value in the relocation register it mapped the logical address space into the physical address space. Figure 10.3 shows a more specific example of the process. The application as it is running in the CPU generates a memory reference. This might be the address of the next instruction in the program, a subroutine call, a reference to a data item, or many other things. In this case the reference is to address 456 in the logical address space of the program. The OS, however, has loaded the relocation register with the physical address of the start of the program, in this case 10000. The memory hardware adds the value in the relocation register to the logical address and generates the physical address of 10456.

10.3.6 Programs larger than memory

As time has gone by, RAM has gotten much cheaper. But at one point primary memory was a very large part of the total price of a system. As a result, most early systems had fairly small primary memories. It was quite common to have a mainframe, minicomputer, or early microprocessor with a primary memory measured in Kilowords or Kilobytes rather than Gigabytes. Programmers spent a lot of time trying

FIGURE 10.3

The memory address hardware dynamically maps the logical address space into the physical address space.

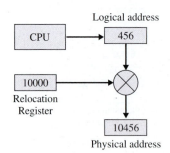

to squeeze more function or more information into very small memories. It was this pressure that lead to the Y2K problem, for example. Since it was going to be 30 years or so before years started with anything but "19," why waste memory on storing those two extra digits in every date? Today we may still have to deal with embedded systems that have limited primary memory. But typically this is now done for reasons of space or power requirements, not because of the price of the memory.

10.3.7 Overlays

Programmers often needed to add functions to programs that ran in these small memories. It was (and still is) fairly common to have a program that has three parts: an initialization phase, a main computation loop, and some final reporting phase. Programmers realized that these parts of a program didn't need to be in memory at the same time, so they decided to let these parts of the program **overlay** one another in memory. Figure 10.4 shows such a program. The main portion of the program is just a series of calls to subroutines that implement the three phases, perhaps "init," "main-loop," and "wrap-up." OS function calls would be added to the program to load the appropriate subroutine before the call was made. The main portion was always in memory and the other phases were brought in before they were called. In elaborate interactive systems this could get to be a bit tricky. A simple program like an assembler or compiler might easily fit into memory without using overlays, but having it broken into phases allowed the translator to process larger source programs in a given memory space.

10.3.8 Swapping

As the price of main memory began to fall relative to the rest of the machine, the administrators of the machine looked at what was going on and realized that with only one program running they were not getting very good utilization of their very expensive system. Some programs would do a little I/O and compute for a long time and others would mainly do I/O with very little CPU execution because the program

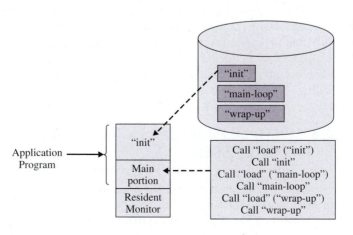

FIGURE 10.4
A program with overlays.

FIGURE 10.5
An OS with
swapping.

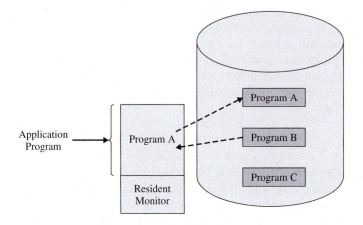

was always waiting on the I/O to complete. Some techniques like SPOOLing grew out of this situation. In a single-process batch system the OS could read in the cards that contained the next programs to be run and the associated data and store them on the disk. This reading would be overlapped with the execution of the current job. As the job tried to print its output the print lines would be stored in a disk file and the actual printing would be overlapped with the processing of the following jobs.

But in the long run it was realized that even SPOOLing was not enough—there was still much waste in lost CPU cycles and lost I/O time. It began to look like the solution was to run several programs at the same time. Hopefully, some would be computing while others were doing I/O and the whole machine would stay busier. This was quite desirable when the machines cost a million dollars. By this point in the history of computing most systems had a secondary memory comprised of magnetic disks or drums. The first technique was to keep several programs running by **swapping** them out. This worked as shown in Figure 10.5. The figure shows program A running in the main memory. This program calls for a line to be printed on the printer, an operation that will take hundredths of a second at least. In this time we can do a lot of disk I/O and a lot of computing, so we would swap program A out by writing the contents of the primary memory to the disk and swap in program B. We would let it run until it issued an I/O to a slow device and then we would swap it back out and bring back in program A. Swapping is sometimes called **roll-out/roll-in.** Obviously the time to wait on the I/O operation must be greater than the time for the swap, but with direct memory access hardware swapping a contiguous block of memory can be very fast and places little overhead on the CPU.

10.4 MULTIPLE PROCESSES WITH A FIXED NUMBER OF PROCESSES

Even the technique of swapping was not enough however, and the owners of these expensive machines wanted to get more work done for the money they were spending. So the OS designers began to search for better ways to organize the processing.

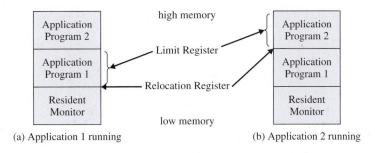

FIGURE 10.6
A multiple-process OS with a fixed number of processes.

(a) Application 1 running   (b) Application 2 running

Primary memory was continuing to get cheaper, so they began thinking about ways to keep multiple programs in primary memory and run more than one by alternating between them without swapping them out—swapping being an operation that requires lots of resources. Eventually they realized that the relocation register could run a program anywhere, not only at the top of the resident OS. So they moved to an OS memory organization like that shown in Figure 10.6a. At first the base register had been used to keep applications from harming the OS. Then the use of this register was changed to a relocation register, primarily to solve the problem of the growth of the OS. Now when the OS is running multiple programs and one program does an I/O operation to some slow device, the OS simply puts the memory address of the second program in the relocation register and starts to run the second program. This situation is shown in Figure 10.6b. (It does more than that, but here we are focused just on the memory aspects.)

At this point we progressed to where there were other applications running in the primary memory, so it was necessary to fix things so that the applications couldn't harm one another. The solution was to add a limit register that would establish an upper bound beyond which a program could not address, just as it couldn't address below the relocation register setting. One might expect that this would be simply another register that contained the high address, but for reasons we address later it is almost universally true that this register instead contains the size of the program rather than the high address. The hardware adds this address to the relocation address on the fly to establish the upper bound. As with the lower bound, if the program tries to access memory beyond the limit set by the limit register, the hardware will generate an addressing error interrupt and the OS will abort the application. So when the OS shifts from running one program to another it must now set both the relocation register and the limit register.

10.4.1   Internal fragmentation

When this type of OS is installed the administrator will decide how much memory to set aside for each program area, or **partition.** The OS will not change the size of these partitions as the system runs. With the earlier OS models a program might not use all of the memory. If it didn't use it all then we didn't worry about it. Now the OS is trying to put more programs into the same memory. If we have set aside 100 KB for each partition and we want to run a program that only needs 6 KB, then we are wasting the rest of the space in that partition. This unused space is called internal fragmentation

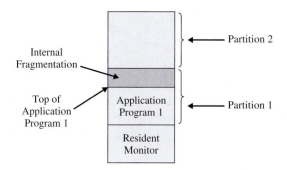

FIGURE 10.7
Internal
fragmentation.

and is shown in Figure 10.7. We might set up a small partition or two to run small quick jobs and a larger partition or two for our big applications. This would tend to minimize the space wasted due to internal fragmentation. If the administrator is clever about setting up the partition sizes, then the programs that are running will come close to filling primary memory and we will have a better chance of keeping that expensive hardware fully utilized.

10.4.2 Time Sharing

Another case where swapping is utilized is in systems that are designed to support many users at terminals in a mode called **time sharing.** When users are interactively editing programs and testing them, the vast majority of the time that process is waiting on the user at the terminal. In this case the system can swap out the process while the user is thinking or keying. In the case that was described in Section 10.3 there was only one partition and thus only one process actually executing. Any other processes could be swapped out to secondary storage. In the case of time sharing it is more likely that we will have several partitions, perhaps even many partitions. We might keep in memory only the ones that are not waiting for the user to finish entering a line and are either running, ready to run, or waiting on something other than terminal I/O. The fixed size of the partitions wastes memory, of course. Recall the internal fragmentation that we just discussed. In that case we only had fragmentation of a single partition. Now we have internal fragmentation in every partition. We would like to be able to use those fragments. If we saved enough memory then maybe we could run another program and keep the CPU busier. Although these techniques worked well enough for the time, modern time-sharing systems generally use techniques described in the next chapter.

10.5 MULTIPLE PROCESSES WITH A VARIABLE NUMBER OF PROCESSES

A partial solution to that internal fragmentation is to not make the partitions fixed in size or in number. Instead, we use as much memory as we need to run a program. We require that a programmer estimate in advance of running the program the maximum amount of primary memory that the program will need. When we start the program we allocate that much memory to the program. If the program tries to use more memory than the programmer said it would, then the OS will end it with an error. When a program ends the OS will again make that memory available to run another program. This space is normally referred to as a **hole,** or sometimes an **external fragment**—a block of memory that we are currently not using at all. In Figure 10.8a we see a situation where the system is currently running four applications. In Figure 10.8b we see that applications two and four have ended, so the holes where they were running are now available for use in running other programs. The OS usually keeps a list of the holes available. In Figure 10.8c we see that the OS has started application 5 in a part of the hole left where application 2 was running. There is now a smaller hole left over.

Now suppose that the OS has another program to run and there are many holes available to choose from. Which hole should the OS choose? As with most of the algorithm classes we study in this book, the first algorithm is simply to scan through the list of holes and use the first one we find that is big enough to run the program. This algorithm is called **first fit.** It has the advantage of being simple. But this may not be the best choice. Another algorithm is to use the hole that is the smallest that will fit the program we want to run. This algorithm is called **best fit.** It has an intuitive appeal—we waste the smallest amount of primary memory. Unfortunately, this algorithm requires that we either scan the entire list or keep the list in order by size. Either requires extra processing.

But what if our average program needs 10 MB, we have a program to run that needs 8 MB, and we have holes of 12 MB and 18 MB? If we use the 12 MB hole then we will have a leftover hole of 4 MB and on average we will not be able to use it. If we use a part of the 18 MB hole then we will have a 10 MB hole left and we will be able to use it, on average. So the next algorithm says that we should use the hole that is the **worst fit** on the grounds that it leaves the biggest (and therefore most useful) hole. Again, this algorithm requires that we either scan the entire list or keep it in order by size.

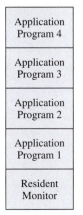  

(a) 4 jobs running   (b) Jobs 2 and 4 ended   (c) Jobs 5 goes in a hole

FIGURE 10.8
A multiple-process OS with a variable number of processes.

A slight variation on the first fit algorithm is called **next fit.** In this variation we do not start each search from the front of the list. We do not keep the list sorted, and we always start the next search from where the last one left off. The first fit algorithm will tend to break up the holes at the front of the list the most, so we will end up with a bunch of small holes that we keep looking through but can seldom use. The next fit variation will tend to distribute this fragmentation through the list. In practice, worst fit turns out to be worst. Either best fit or next fit are better, and next fit is very easy to implement.

Now suppose that we have two holes that are each 5 MB and we have a process to run that says it may need 8 MB. We have 10 MB of free memory blocks in the two holes, enough free memory in total to run this process. But the free memory is not in one piece so we can't run the program. This situation is known as **external frag-mentation.** Recall that our processes are relocatable—they can run anywhere in the physical memory because the memory hardware relocates their logical addressing space dynamically as they run. So, it is possible to move a program in memory even after it has started running. Normally, the process is suspended, moved to another location and restarted. The OS only has to change the value that is placed in the relocation register to point to the start of the new location of the application in physical memory. For example, in Figure 10.9a, if the two holes (marked "unused") were together big enough to run application 6, the OS could stop application 3, move it to the space just above application 5, and put that address in the relocation register whenever application 3 was restarted, It could then start application 6 running in the resulting larger hole. This result is shown in Figure 10.9b This process is called **compaction.** Naturally, the situation is usually much more complex than this simple case, and often several programs have to be relocated to find a hole large enough to run the program we want to run. One can appreciate that when the OS is moving programs around in memory, no work is being done on behalf of the applications. The OS is choosing to spend the CPU and memory bandwidth for the purpose of running more jobs in parallel.

FIGURE 10.9
Compaction.

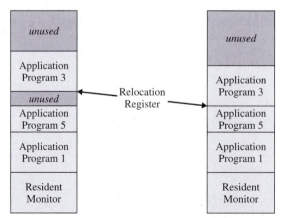

(a) There is enough RAM for Application 6
but the holes are not contiguous

(b) Application 3 is relocated to
bring the two holes together

Now we can appreciate why the relocation hardware uses a length for an upper bound instead of using the upper end of the program. If it used the upper address then when we relocated a program we would also have to recompute the upper bound. This is not an overwhelmingly complicated calculation, and it does not need to be done all that often, but if the hardware can work just as well the other way then we are lucky not to have to do it.

One complication in this process can be that the I/O hardware may not utilize the relocation hardware. In other words, I/O is done using physical addresses rather than logical addresses. This means that if a process has I/O pending, then we cannot move it in memory. So processes that start I/O may have to be marked temporarily as unmovable.

We also may still suffer from internal fragmentation. This comes about because our holes can keep getting smaller and smaller. It is not efficient for the OS to keep track of very small chunks of memory, so there is some minimum amount of memory that the OS will try to manage. It is common for this minimum to be in the range of 256 bytes to 4 KB. When the program starts it will be allocated a block of memory that is an integral multiple of this minimum piece. On the average, any program will not need half of its last piece, so it will go to waste—internal fragmentation.

10.5.1 Dynamic loading

With overlays we do not load the entire program into primary memory at one time. Instead, the programmer explicitly decides when to load the overlays and when to call the routines that are in the overlay. It is also possible for the system to do something similar. When the OS loads a program into main memory it might load into memory only the main body of the program. To access various subroutines it might make use of a table that shows which routines are already loaded into memory and which are not. Many programs follow roughly the "80-20" rule—80% of the code of a program is for situations that only happen 20% of the time. So if we don't load the subroutines when the program first starts we might never need to load them at all. Therefore, the program starts somewhat faster. If the program later calls the routine then we can load it at that time and we will have paid very little penalty for waiting—a small bit of RAM for the table and a few extra instructions executed whenever we first call the routine.

10.5.2 Dynamic link libraries

We can, however, postpone the binding even a step further. We can put off even linking the subroutine with the main module. In this case the library routine itself does not become a part of the executable program. Instead, we leave intact the symbolic reference to the library routine that was produced by the compiler. As with dynamic loading, if the routine is never referenced, then not only did we not bother to load it into memory, we didn't even bind the symbol to a logical address. We leave the subroutines in special libraries that are usually called dynamic link libraries, or DLLs. In Linux and most other UNIX variants such libraries are referred to as shared object libraries or dynamic libraries and normally have ".so" as a part of their name. When a subroutine in such a library is referenced, then the OS will load the routine into memory and bind the link at program execution time.

Notice that we get several other benefits from this mechanism at the same time:

- Since the subroutines are not a part of the executable program, the program is smaller so it take up less space on the disk drive and loads faster into RAM.
- Normally, we will have many programs that use the same library modules. Some library modules are so commonly used that they will be referred to by literally thousands of programs on the hard drive. Having only one copy of the code can save us a lot of disk space.
- If a bug is fixed in one of the library modules it is only necessary to fix the one library routing and load it onto the system. This will automatically fix that bug in every program that references that DLL.

This last feature is a great boon to application software developers because it means that if a fix is made to a system library by the OS manufacturer, the application developer does not have to reload their application with the new libraries and redistribute the executable programs to every customer who is running that platform. If the customer calls with a complaint related to a DLL provided by another vendor, the application developer merely explains that the problem is in the system libraries and that a fix is available in release x.y.z.1.5 of the library module, which is downloadable from the library vendor's website at . . . If the application vendor is really lucky, the customer finds the problem in some other application first and the fixed library is downloaded before the customer ever has a problem with their application.

Unfortunately, there is a problem with dynamic libraries. When the developer of a software package is using a particular set of functions in a DLL, their code may also depend on bug fixes in a particular version of the library. They will want to make sure that the set of functions and bug fixes they are using is in the version of the library that is available on any system the package is installed on. So the package installation can include a version that is at least as late as the one the vendor developed with. Unfortunately, the target system may already include a later version that was installed by another package that depends on functions or bug fixes in that version. Installing an older version would cause the already installed package to fail. The vendor of the package that suddenly quits working may be quite surprised to get the resulting request for support and will be understandably annoyed when the problem is finally resolved and time has been wasted solving a problem that is not related to anything their company did. Of course, the installation software is supposed to check to see that any DLL being installed is a newer version than the one already installed. Unfortunately, this is not always done or may be done incorrectly. This problem is colloquially called **DLL Hell.** Newer OS releases allow an application to specify a version number for a dynamic link library, so this problem is being minimized by allowing a system to carry multiple versions of a single library. This takes up some additional space, but nowhere near as much as was consumed by having the library as a part of every application that used it.

10.6 SUMMARY

In this chapter we discussed many ways that primary memory can be managed by the OS. We began with a discussion of why an OS manages memory, that purpose being to run programs that are larger than the primary memory of the machine and to allow as many programs to be running as possible. We then discussed the software development cycle as an aid to understanding the various possible times for address binding. Next, we looked at progressively more complex memory models, beginning with a single process and covering fixed and variable multiprocessing contiguous memory organizations. Through this discussion we also focused on the hardware required to support these OS techniques. We ended with a section that covered the advantages and disadvantages of dynamic loading of routines.

In the next chapter we discuss some modern approaches to solving the problems of memory management through paging and segmentation.

BIBLIOGRAPHY

Daley, R. C., and J. B. Dennis, "Virtual Memory, Processes and Sharing in Multics," *CACM*, Vol. 11, No. 5, May 1968, pp. 306–312.

Dennis, J. B., "Segmentation and the Design of Multiprogrammed Computer Systems," *Journal of the ACM*, Vol. 12, No. 4, October 1965, pp. 589–602.

Kilburn, T., D. J. Howarth, R. B. Payne, and F. H. Sumner, "The Manchester University Atlas Operating System, Part I: Internal Organization," *Computer Journal*, Vol. 4, No. 3, October 1961, pp. 222–225.

Knuth, D. E., *The Art of Computer Programming: Fundamental Algorithms*, Vol. 1, 2nd ed. Reading, MA: Addison-Wesley, 1973.

Organick, E. I., *The Multics System: An Examination of Its Structure*. Cambridge, MA: MIT Press, 1972.

The bibliography for this chapter overlaps considerably with the next chapter.

REVIEW QUESTIONS

10.1 What is the fundamental reason an OS has to be concerned with managing primary memory?

10.2 What are the five steps leading from the creation of a program to its execution in memory?

10.3 What is meant by the term "binding"?

10.4 In which of the five steps listed in Question 10.2 can binding be done?

10.5 What is the difference between a logical addressing space and a physical addressing space?

10.6 Attempting to run several jobs at the same time we created a few fixed partitions. We ran into a problem of internal fragmentation. Describe this problem.

10.7 An alternative to fixed partitions was to allow variable partitions. This minimized the internal fragmentation but created a new problem—that of external fragmentation. Describe this problem.

10.8 What did we do about that external fragmentation?

10.9 When running variable partitions we might have several holes that were big enough to run the next job we wanted to run. We listed four algorithms for selecting the hole to use from among those large enough to run the process. Name and briefly describe those algorithms.

10.10 Describe the difference between dynamic loading and dynamic linking.

10.11 Dynamic linking has one huge advantage and a number of smaller ones. Name the huge one and a couple of the little ones.

Chapter 11

Advanced Memory Management

In this chapter:

This chapter continues the discussion of memory management techniques. In particular, it covers the more advanced techniques used in modern systems. The first section discusses the issues that arise from the mechanisms covered in the last chapter and why the newer techniques were developed.

Section 11.2 describes the action of paging hardware and how it further separates the logical and physical addressing spaces. Section 11.3 discusses an alternative hardware mechanism known as segmentation and Section 11.4 shows how paging and segmentation can be used together. In Section 11.5 we move on to the subject of demand paging—bringing pages into memory only when they are to be accessed—and some of the problems that arise with this technique. Section 11.6 then covers a few special advanced memory techniques and Section 11.7 summarizes the chapter.

11.1 WHY DO WE NEED HARDWARE HELP?

Multiprocessing with contiguous memory allocation causes external fragmentation, wasting memory and CPU resources when we are not able to run programs even though sufficient RAM is available to run them. In the last chapter we saw that we can mitigate this problem somewhat, but the solution requires running compaction routines, an unproductive use of the CPU and memory. In order to do away with this problem we need to further separate the memory address space that a program sees (the logical address) from the address space used by the hardware (the physical address) in such a way that all the parts of a program do not have to be in contiguous memory. Making this separation requires hardware assistance. There are several different approaches to this problem and these approaches are covered in the following sections.

11.2 PAGING

Earlier we discussed the idea of the separation of the logical addressing space from the physical addressing space. We changed the memory management unit (MMU) to make this work. Instead of using the base register to check an address we used it to relocate an address. This allowed us to put any program anywhere in memory—dynamic relocation. However, we found that allowing variable-sized programs to come and go in memory caused us to have external fragmentation of the memory and to spend valuable CPU time doing compaction. Unfortunately, compaction is not "useful work" in the sense that it is not anything the user is trying to do. It is merely a task that the OS does to make things work better in an overall sense. Eventually another solution was developed—we divide the memory into fixed-size blocks and instead of allocating to an application the entire space it needs in one large segment, we allocate enough of the smaller blocks to give the program what it needs. However, the blocks we allocate do not need to be contiguous—they can be anywhere in memory because we ask the MMU to dynamically relocate each block separately. This technique is known as **paging.** This means that we have to make our memory management unit a lot more complex.

We will divide our physical address space into blocks of uniform size, which we call **frames.** We will conceptually divide the logical addressing space into blocks called **pages,** which are the same size as the frames. Commonly these blocks are 512 bytes to 8 KB long. For byte addressable machines the number of bytes in a block is always a power of 2. Today a common page size is 4 KB, but the increasing size of RAM and hard drives means that in the future we are more likely to see larger page sizes. Figure 11.1 shows the process of relocating each address reference.

We see that the CPU generates a memory address. In general, the program ignores the fact that the memory is handled in separate pages, so these addresses are regarded as just a binary number in the range of the logical address space. This address might be the address of the next sequential instruction, a jump to a subroutine, a reference to a data item or to the stack. The purpose of the reference does not matter. As before, we call this the logical address. However, the MMU will regard the address as being composed of two parts, shown here as the **page number, p** and the **displacement, d.** The displacement is the address of the specific byte within the frame. If our frame size is 4 KB then our displacement field is the exact size needed to address every byte in a frame, or 12 bits. When we relocate a logical address to a physical address we will still be addressing the same displacement in the frame as we were in the page. So we will not change the displacement part of the logical address. The rest of the

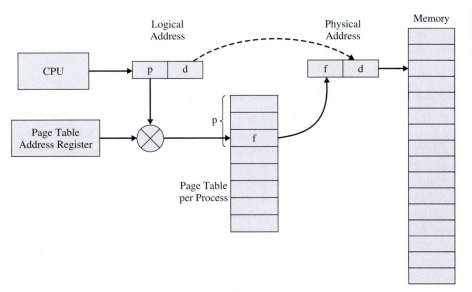

FIGURE 11.1
Paged memory access.

logical address is the page number. What we need to relocate is the page, so we will look in a **page table** of relocation addresses for the frames. We will have a register that holds the memory address of the page table for the running process. This register is called the **page table address register.** The memory control unit will add the page number from the logical address generated by the process running in the CPU to the value in the page table address register. The value stored in that location of the page table will be the relocation address of the particular **frame** we are trying to access. In this case it is shown as the value **f.** The value of **f** is combined with the displacement we already had to address the particular byte in physical memory.

Figure 11.2 shows a more complete page table. We are ignoring the displacement portion of the address and considering only how the pages map to the frames. Here we see the logical address space for a process that is running. It is divided into pages that are labeled A–H. The third page is labeled C, for example. If the CPU generates a reference to this page, then the memory management unit will translate this address by looking in the third entry in the page table for the process. Here we see

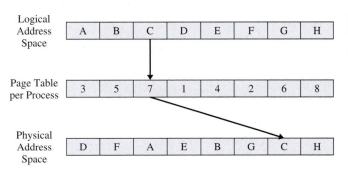

FIGURE 11.2
Mapping logical addresses to physical addresses.

that this entry contains the number of frame 7. So the memory management unit will look into frame 7 to find the information we are accessing. Of course, in a real system the frames would be spread out and mixed in with frames from other processes.

11.2.1 Dual memory accesses required

As we have described this mechanism, however, we have a problem. For each reference to memory we have to make a second reference to memory to find the page table entry to use as the relocation factor for this page. This will make our process run at half speed when accessing memory, an obviously unacceptable penalty. As with many other things in computer systems, our solution is for the memory management unit to cache the last few relocation factors so we can use them again without having to look them up in memory. This caching is done with a special kind of hardware device called a **translation lookaside buffer,** or TLB. The TLB is a type of circuit that goes by several names. It is sometimes called a content addressable memory (CAM) or associative memory. The essence of this circuitry is that when it tries to check to see if it has a page number in it, all the entries are searched in parallel. This means that the entries in the TLB do not have to be kept in any order since they are all compared at the same time. If the page we are trying to access has been accessed lately then it will be in the TLB and it will be returned very quickly—maybe 100 times faster than if we had to access the page table in main memory. The TLB is obviously a complex circuit. As a result, they are typically rather small. On current machines they are rarely over about 1,000 entries and usually much fewer. However, that is normally enough for most processes to find the information in the cache most of the time. The use of a TLB is shown in Figure 11.3.

FIGURE 11.3
The translation lookaside buffer.

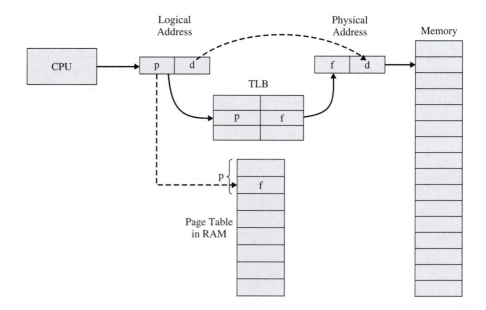

11.2.2 **Effective memory access times**

There is a formula by which we can estimate the impact of the TLB on the execution speed of the computer. We will calculate the **effective access time,** or EAT. The formulas use the speed of a TLB lookup, which we will call **E** and the speed of a main memory reference, which we will call **M.** Some percent of the time we will find the page number we are referencing in the TLB. We will call this percentage **A.** This percentage is often called the **hit ratio.** Obviously, the percentage that we will not find the referenced page in the TLB (a **TLB miss**) will be 1-A. For example, if we get a hit 80% of the time then we are going to get a miss 20% of the time. When we find the page number in the TLB, then the memory reference will take E + M time − E to search the TLB and M to make the normal memory reference. When we do not find the page number in the TLB, then the total memory reference will take 2* M—two memory references, one to get the frame number out of the page table and one for the normal memory reference. The EAT will then be:

$$EAT = A(E + M) + (1 - A)(2 * M).$$

For example, suppose our TLB lookup time (E) was 5 nanoseconds, our memory access time (M) was 100 nanoseconds, and our hit ratio (A) was 80%. Then the effective memory access time would be .8(100 + 5) + (1 − .8) * (2 * 100), or 124 nanoseconds. This is a slowdown of 25%.

Depending on the hardware design, the TLB lookup may take place while the first memory reference is being started. If the TLB lookup is not successful, then the main memory reference will continue. In this case, the formula just given applies. But other hardware may not start the main memory reference until the TLB lookup has failed. In this case, the equation for EAT becomes:

$$EAT = A(E + M) + (1 - A)(E + 2 * M).$$

The larger we make the TLB the higher the hit ratio will be. For example, using the same numbers as before but with a hit ratio of 90%, the EAT will be .9(100 + 5) + (1 − .9) * (2 * 100), or 114.5 nanoseconds. This is a slowdown of less than 15%. Unfortunately, this is a hardware design decision, not a software question or even a decision the purchaser of the system can make. Unlike RAM, for example, TLBs are generally not upgradeable, being an integral part of the memory management unit itself and normally embedded in the CPU chip.

Note that each process has the same logical addressing space—it starts at 0 and goes up to the size of the program. On most systems the TLB hardware does not concern itself with which process is running. As a process runs, the TLB will fill up with frame numbers that correspond to the page numbers of the running process. When we switch to another process the OS must tell the hardware to forget all the current frame numbers since the new process will have different frame numbers that will need to be mapped to the same page numbers that the previous process had used. Therefore, after we do a context switch to the new process, for the first few memory references we will not get any TLB hits, so our process will run at half speed on memory reference instructions. This is one reason why we don't want to switch processes any more often than we have to and why switching threads is faster than switching processes. A few hardware designs do have **address space identifiers,** or **ASIDs,** stored in the cache with the frame numbers. These designs do not require that the TLB be flushed. They will still get many TLB misses and will therefore run more slowly for a short time until the TLB is repopulated. This sort of TLB is very useful with CPUs that are running multiple processes in parallel.

11.2.3 Memory access control

When we were accessing main memory with one relocation register for the entire program we also had a limit register that prohibited a process from accessing outside the memory area assigned to it. With paging hardware we will need a similar mechanism. There is no problem with the individual pages themselves since they are normally of a fixed size. However, we will need some mechanism for limiting the access to the page table. There are basically two approaches to this problem. Both depend on the hardware, so the decision is not up to the OS designer, but we will discuss them so that you will be aware of them. The first approach is to use a fixed page table size. In this case, we will need a **valid** bit in each page table word to indicate whether a page table address is valid. So, for example, if we had a fixed page table size of 10 entries and the process only took three pages in the logical address space, we would fill in the first three entries with the addresses of the corresponding memory page numbers and set the valid bit "on" for those three entries. For the rest of the entries in that page table we would set the valid bit to "off" because they do not hold a reference to a valid page. When the memory management unit accessed any entry in the page table it would generate a memory addressing error if the entry had a valid bit that was set to off.

The other approach to memory address control is to use a page table with a variable size. In this case, we will have a **page table length register.** With a single relocation register we had a length register that specified the length of the process in main memory. A page table length register will work just as it sounds like it would. It holds the address of the largest valid page number for a process. If an address generated by the CPU when the process is running contains a page number bigger than the number in the page table length register, then the hardware will generate an addressing error interrupt because the process has generated a reference to a page that is not in the logical address space of the process. These days most systems use a valid bit for reasons that we will see later.

Page access protection

In addition to limiting memory addressing, paging allows the OS to restrict the kinds of access that may be made to the various pages. The hardware can be set up to allow only read access to a page, for example, or only execute access. In order to make effective use of this the compilers (and assemblers) must be able to force the linker to place portions of the executable file on a page boundary. In this way, the data portions of the module can be marked as read–write but not execute. Similarly, the program code can be marked as execute only. There are some problems with this sort of mechanism that need to be addressed. For example, it might appear that the stack should not allow execution of items on the stack. But it is common for Java virtual machines to compile Java program byte codes into instructions on the stack and execute them there.

11.2.4 Large page tables

In modern machines with modern OSs and modern compilers the programs are getting very large. This means that the page tables are also very large. Also, it turns out that in many cases the page tables are sparse, meaning that they may have large parts of the table that are in the logical address space but do not point to a valid frame. Later, we discuss some of the reasons why this happens. In any case, it became increasingly difficult to manage the memory allocated to the page tables themselves. Several different approaches were taken to deal with these large, sparse tables.

The first technique was to make a **multilevel page table.** Figure 11.4 shows a two-level page table—essentially we page the page table. As with the single-level tables we have been discussing, the MMU will consider the logical address generated by the CPU as being made up of several parts—in this case, three. As before, we have the page displacement, which will be carried over and used as the frame displacement. Now we view the page number as being made up of two parts, here shown as p1 and p2. P1 will be used by the hardware to access into the top-level page table, just as before. However, the number stored in this entry will not be a frame number, but another memory address, that of a second-level page table. The remaining bits of the page number, here shown as p2, will be used to access within the selected second-level page table. This entry will be the frame number for the page number represented in the original address by p1 and p2 together. This frame number

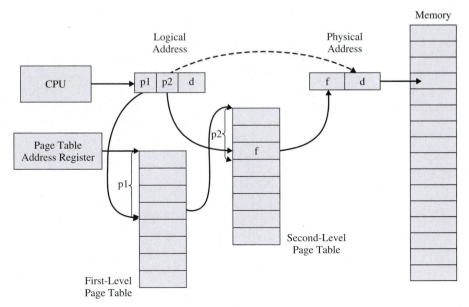

FIGURE 11.4
A two-level page table.

will be used with the original displacement to access the desired memory location in physical memory. The DEC VAX systems used a two-level paging architecture.

Two-level page tables turned out to be such a useful technique that the process has been extended. Modern processors normally have three- or four-level page table architectures. Note that this could potentially really cause problems with our EAT. In the worst case, with a four-level page table we can take five memory accesses to reach a single byte in memory because each of the page table references may not be in the TLB. Thus our equation for the EAT becomes something like:

$$EAT = A(E + M) + (1 - A)(5 * M).$$

Fortunately, most of the time our TLB will hold those final physical memory references and on the average we will pay a performance penalty only slightly greater than with a single-level page table.

It is worth noting that this technique has the effect of creating a **virtual page table.** Since the address spaces are so large, the page table is generally very sparse—there are large parts of it that are not really used. In such cases those portions of the lower-level page tables do not need to be allocated and filled in until they are actually needed. This can save considerable table space and the resources necessary to access it.

11.2.5 Inverted page table

A slightly different approach to the problem of external memory was to turn the problem around. The idea was to map the physical frames into the logical pages. Figure 11.5 shows an inverted page table approach to process page mapping. The table is kept in order by the physical frame number. The table itself is searched to find a reference. Since there is only one table, the page numbers from the various processes

FIGURE 11.5
Inverted page table.

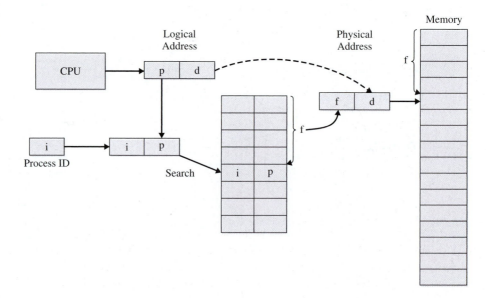

are not sufficient to specify the mapping. For instance, every process will have a page number 0. A process identifier must therefore be stored with the page number. The time to search an inverted page table will often be slower than for a normal page table. The OS can speed up this search by using a hash function to access the table. This method will require a chaining scheme to resolve collisions since some processes may have page number/process ID combinations that hash to the same value. So even more than with a normal page table, we rely heavily on the TLB lookup to resolve most of our lookups. Inverted page tables take much less RAM than normal page tables.

11.2.6 Page tables with multiple page sizes

In later systems it has become common to have more than one page table size. In the Intel Pentium architecture, for example, the normal page size is 4096 bytes, but there is another possible page size of 4 MB. The reason for this is so that the kernel of the OS can be mapped in the page table with the process without taking up so much RAM in the page table. Most of the kernel pages will be the same in every process; they will never move around and cause fragmentation and they will always be there, so there is no need to divide them into small pages as there is with processes that are of unknown size and duration. In addition, as we will see shortly, in the application part of the logical space of a process the pages will sometimes not even be in memory. This is usually not the case with the kernel, though some OSs page portions of the kernel. Therefore, having only one or a few pages to map the kernel through is a big advantage since it can be set up and manipulated more easily and only takes one TLB entry to map the entire kernel.

In some of the later UltraSPARC® processors the software can select multiple page sizes for different parts of the application. We will see in the section on segmentation with paging how this works.

11.2.7 A historical footnote

While modern systems normally use these techniques in the context of running multiple processes concurrently, historically there were a few systems that used paging while only running a single process. Programs could refer to portions of the program that were not yet in memory much as if they were calling overlays, as discussed in the last chapter. This had the advantage of allowing the running process to be much larger than the physical memory. In the era of smaller memories this was a big advantage, but it is not utilized much in current systems. Modern OSs use demand paging, discussed in a later section.

11.3 SEGMENTATION

At about the same time that paging was being devised, a different track of development evolved that was designed mostly to help solve the same problems that paging addressed, but a few others besides. This technique is called **segmentation.** It arose out of the observation that we can consider a program as being made up of several distinct parts. We usually have a main routine and we often have subroutines and functions that are recognized by the compiler as being separate items. Sometimes we even compile the subroutines and functions separately and put them into libraries. We have areas where we keep the stack, static data items, constant information, file buffers, communication buffers, and so on. Each of these areas can be created and controlled separately. Figure 11.6 shows a collection of segments of a program that make up a process after being loaded into primary memory.

Each of these parts can be considered to be separate from the other parts and can have a separate logical addressing space. For example, since there is a separate addressing space for the data, we would consider that the first data item was at address 0 in the data segment address space. We now need for the hardware to relocate all references to addresses in each segment in the same way it relocated references to the entire process with a relocation register. So we will use a mechanism that is much like a page table, with a couple of small differences. Figure 11.7 shows a sample segment table. We will still consider the logical address to be broken into two parts, but they will be a **segment number** (**s**) and a **displacement** (**d**). With paging we had quite a few pages of a fairly small size so the displacement was a small number of bits and the page number was much larger. With segmentation we have a relatively small number of segments, each of which can be fairly large by itself, so the segment number will usually be a smaller number of bits and the displacement within the segment will be a larger size. In addition, while the entries in a page table contained a frame number, the entries in the segment table will contain memory addresses. The programmer does not normally exert any overt control over the segmentation. The compilers will generate separate segments for the major portions of the module being compiled—the program code, the stack, the heap, global variables, and so on—and place symbolic references to them in the object modules. The linker will assign actual segment numbers to be used when combining the object modules into the executable binary program and for the OS to use when dynamically loading library modules.

FIGURE 11.6
Segmenting
a process.

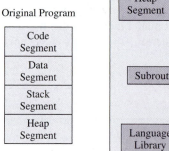

Original Program

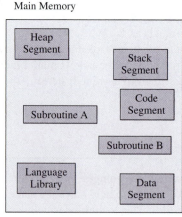

Main Memory

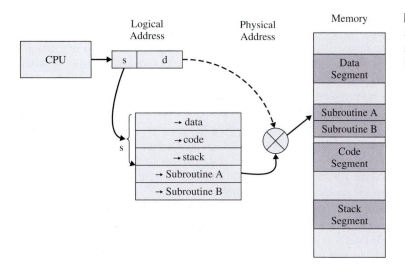

FIGURE 11.7
Segment table and segments in main memory.

In Figure 11.7 we see a memory reference to the segment containing Subroutine A. The hardware will use the segment table entry specified by the number in the segment part of the address. It will take the segment table address pointer found in that entry of the segment table and it will add it to the displacement part of the logical address. The paging hardware simply replaced the page number with a frame number. This worked because frames and pages were always the same size so they were also always located on block boundaries. Since segments are of variable size they can also be located anywhere, so we will use the segment table pointer **plus** the displacement to get the physical memory address. Note that use of segmentation causes an extra memory reference for each access, just as it did with paging. So systems with segmentation will also use a TLB to speed up access.

Since segments can be anywhere and are not all the same size, this is not an optimum solution to avoid external fragmentation. We will still have to keep track of memory holes. We will still not allocate tiny pieces of memory. Instead, we will have some minimum granularity—perhaps 1024 bytes. We will therefore have some internal fragmentation. But now the range of sizes of the holes will be smaller than the range we had to consider when keeping track of entire processes because we are breaking each process up into (potentially many) segments. Therefore, we will have less of a problem with external fragmentation than we did with memory management for entire processes.

Since the segments are of variable size, we must provide a way for the system to check the addresses so that we can make sure the process is not addressing outside the limits of the segment. The limit for each segment is stored in the segment table along with the pointer to the segment. Since the segments have different purposes we can also increase the protection we are providing to the system by limiting the kinds of accesses we make to the various segments, much as we discussed with paging. It is common to have a set of bit flags with each segment that controls the kinds of access we can make. For example, a segment of data constants can be marked as read only. The program pages can be marked as execute only. Stacks and data pages will allow read and write but not execute.

In some OSs it is possible for processes to share segments. For example, we might have several users running a program editor at the same time. We could create a process per user and map the code segments in their respective segment tables so that they all pointed to the same parts of physical memory. If we had common runtime libraries for standard languages, we could also map segments to point to the same physical memory segments, even for different programs. Managing the segment numbers across multiple processes can be quite a chore for the OS.

Programmers who are writing in high-level languages will not normally be aware that segmentation is being used by an OS until their program generates a segmentation fault, most often by overflowing the segment used for the stack. The compilers and the linker will generally take care of assigning the segment numbers for the various pieces by calling OS routines that manage the segment numbers. Programmers working in fairly low-level languages will need to be aware of segmentation and how the OS is using it and they can control the segmentation if need be. The Windows NT family does not use segmentation because it is not needed on many hardware designs and not available on others and using it would make the software less portable. Linux uses segmentation only in a limited way, which we discuss in the next section. Most UNIX-derivative OSs use segmentation with paging, also discussed in the next section.

11.4 SEGMENTATION WITH PAGING

There is a fundamental difference between paging and segmentation. Paging is transparent to the running process. An application program that was created to run in an OS where the process is mapped into a single large partition could run unchanged on a system that used a paged memory architecture. Segmentation, on the other hand, requires that programs somehow be structured so that they are divided into logical parts with different address spaces. An interesting aspect of this is that with the proper hardware design we can run a segmented program architecture in combination with a paged memory architecture. In the documentation for various OSs the segments may be known as **regions** or **memory areas.** The segmentation works as we have described it, but the address that is generated is not used as a physical memory address. Instead, it is now treated as a logical address and run through a paging mechanism. This allows us to have both the fine control over the types of references as with segmentation and the fixed page sizes of paging, which result in no external fragmentation.

There are two generally different ways that segmentation and paging can be combined. The first design originated with the Multics project.[1] In this design we will have a page table for each segment of a process rather than a single page table for the process. This design is shown in Figure 11.8. First, the segment portion of the address is looked up in a segment table. This lookup returns a pointer to a page table that maps the page numbers within the segment to frame numbers in physical memory.

---

[1] http://www.multicians.org/fjcc1.html

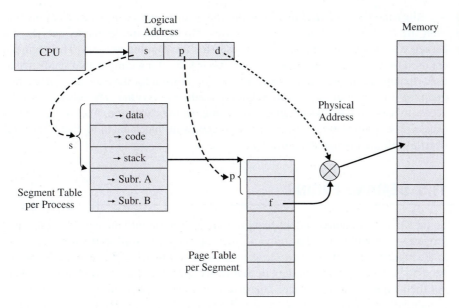

FIGURE 11.8
Segmentation with paging.

The second design is used in more modern systems. In this design there is still a segment table, but instead of pointing to separate page tables for each segment, the addresses in the segment table lie within a linear address space, which is then mapped into the physical memory in the same manner that a paged system works. This design is seen in Figure 11.9. In this case a segment table entry describes a portion of the linear address space, which can be viewed as the page table for the segment. But as far as the hardware is concerned, it is just a part of a single-page table.

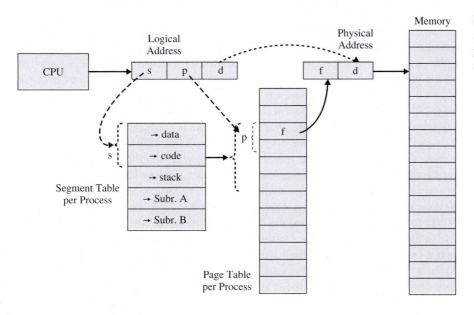

FIGURE 11.9
Segmentation with linear addressing.

Most modern OSs use this latter mechanism in one form or another, but they limit the use of the segments. Linux, for example, uses the segments only for the kernel, except for one segment that it uses for the running process. The segments are used to restrict addressing and control access. So, for example, two segments are used to map the same kernel address space. One is used for the execution of the program, so it is set to allow execution but not reading or writing. The other is used for access to data, so it allows reading and writing but not execution. Another is used for accessing a runtime stack. This allows the hardware mechanism to check for stack overflow efficiently and dynamically.

11.5 DEMAND PAGING

So far we have assumed that when a program is brought into memory that the entire program is brought in and a frame of physical memory is allocated for every page in the logical addressing space. However, it was eventually realized that this was not necessary. As programs run they do not really access addresses randomly throughout their logical address space. The instructions in the code segment are accessed sequentially to a large extent, so for about a thousand instructions we might be accessing a single page in the code portion of the logical address space. Or the program may go into a loop, sometimes for quite a while, and stay in a single code page. To be sure, we will frequently call library routines, which may in turn call other library routines. The program steps through an array or scans through a string or searches through an incoming message. When we divide the execution of a program into small time slots and look at the pages accessed by the memory references in that time slot we will normally find that only a few pages are accessed by the process in any given time slot. This phenomenon is quite important in OS design. It is called **locality of reference.** We use the same idea in caching and in many of our other OS algorithms.

The trick that was developed to take advantage of this phenomenon is called **demand paging.** The idea is that we slightly modify the meaning of the valid bit in the page table. The hardware associated with the use of the bit will not change. All the bit indicates is that there is no frame allocated for this page. In our previous design this meant that this page was outside the logical address space for the program. Now it may still indicate that, but it may only indicate that no physical frame is currently mapped to this page. When we load the first page we will set its valid bit to true to indicate that it is in memory. We will mark the valid bit of every other page to show that that page is not in memory. Then we will start the program running. In theory, we could begin the execution of a program without bringing in to physical memory *any* pages. The OS could simply branch to the process in memory and let the page fault mechanism bring in even the first page of the program. This is known as **lazy loading.** Even if we load the first page of the program, it will soon reference data in another page that is not yet in memory. Figure 11.10 shows an example of such a page table. This reference will fetch the page table entry and the setting of the valid bit will cause a "memory addressing error" interrupt. The memory management subsystem will look at the reference to see if the reference is to a page that

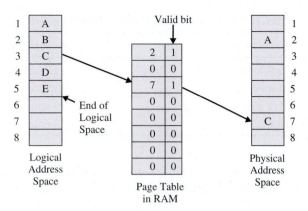

FIGURE 11.10
A page table showing pages not in physical memory.

really is in the logical address space of the program, but that has not been brought into memory yet. If the reference is to a page that is not really in the logical address space of the process, then the program has made an error and an addressing exception is raised, most likely aborting the process.

If the address that caused a fault is in the logical address space of the process, then the page simply is not currently mapped into physical memory, either because it has never been brought in or because it has been taken out. This condition is known as a **page fault.** The memory management subsystem will now request a read of the page from secondary storage and the OS will put the program into wait state until it has finished. Once the block has been read in, the OS will update the page table to point to the new frame, mark the entry valid, and restart the process that generated the page fault at the instruction that caused the fault. Note that this mechanism is still transparent to the application. In other words, the application programmer does not normally need to be aware that this process is going on, much less do anything about it.

In some cases this would allow us to run programs that were so large they would not fit into memory at all. The "80/20 rule" usually holds—80% of a program is written to take care of things that only happen 20% of the time. In many cases, therefore, much of that 80% of the program will never be loaded into memory. As an extra benefit, this will allow our programs to start faster, because if a page is never referenced we never load it into memory at all. As well, in an environment where we are trying to run many programs, perhaps for many users, with a given amount of physical memory, on the average we will be able to run more programs at the same time.

11.5.1 EAT with demand paging

You may recall that when we first looked at the paging mechanism we saw how the use of a page table by itself would double the effective access time of memory. This necessitated the introduction of the TLB to cache the frame numbers for the page references in the working set. Now consider what happens when we access a page that is not in memory. Our effective access time will have four components, as shown in Table 11.1. (The speeds shown are simply approximate relative speeds, not specific expected values.)

TABLE 11.1 Demand Paging Effective Address Time

Component	Relative Speed
TLB lookup	1 nanosecond
Memory access	100 nanoseconds
Disk write (dirty page)	20 milliseconds
Disk read	20 milliseconds

As the table shows, the disk I/O vastly overwhelms the memory speeds. This domination will lead to several mechanisms that may seem at first to be overly complex that are developed merely to avoid doing a single-disk I/O for demand paging.

11.5.2 The working set and page replacement

So far we have assumed that there are enough pages free in memory to bring in any page we need when a process references it. Unfortunately, we normally will soon run out of free pages. At that point we need to get rid of some pages that are in memory. Frequently this will not cause us any problem at all. As a program runs it will be referencing some set of pages—a page in the main process, perhaps a few pages of library routines, buffers for the input and the output, doubtless a few pages of data. This group of pages that a process is referencing in a short period is called the **working set.** We typically measure the working set over some fixed interval known as a **sliding window.**

For example, suppose a process had a logical address space containing seven pages identified as 1 through 7, and had the sequence of references to those pages as follows:

```
1 2 1 5 7 1 6 3 7 1 6 4 2 7
```

We will track the working set by looking at the last four references. As this sequence of references unfolds the working set will change, as seen in Table 11.2. As the process runs, the working set typically changes from time to time. It is normal to find that a process will have in memory several pages that it is no longer referencing. In the table we can see that page 5 is no longer referenced after step 4, so we could get rid of it. What we would like to be able to do is to identify those pages and remove them from memory when we no longer need them. (Removing pages that we think may not be needed anymore is called **page replacement.**) Unfortunately, we can't really do that. Just because we have not referenced a page in a while does not mean that the very next instruction won't reference that page. In the table we saw that page 2 was not referenced between steps 2 and 13, so we no longer saw it as being in the working set since we were only looking at a four-step window. Fortunately, removing a page from memory that is needed later doesn't break anything. It is just not quite as efficient. The next reference to the page will cause a page fault and the page will be fetched again.

TABLE 11.2   **Tracking a Working Set**

Event Number	Working Set
1	1
2	1 2
3	1 2
4	1 2 5
5	1 2 5 7
6	1 2 5 7
7	1 5 6 7
8	1 3 6 7
9	1 3 6 7
10	1 3 6 7
11	1 3 6 7
12	1 4 6 7
13	1 2 4 6
14	2 4 6 7

There is a very simple page replacement strategy, **first in, first out,** or **FIFO.** The OS keeps a queue of the page numbers as they are brought in for each process and simply ejects the oldest one. This algorithm is a low-overhead algorithm, which requires little overhead from the OS. While FIFO is cheap and easy to understand and implement, it performs poorly and erratically so it is rarely used today. This algorithm experiences Belady's anomaly. It was used in the VAX/VMS OS.

Theoretically, there is a **optimal page replacement** algorithm (also known as OPT). It would work as follows: when a page needs to be replaced, the OS replaces the page whose next use will be the furthest in the future. For example, a page that is not going to be used until 200 milliseconds from now will be chosen over a page that is going to be used in 10 milliseconds. This algorithm can't be used in general because it is impossible to know how long it will be before a page is going to be used except in very limited circumstances. If it were implementable it would be the best we could do, so it is worth discussing. Assuming that we had only three free frames to work with, if we used this algorithm with the reference string shown previously, we would generate nine page faults, including the page faults required to bring in the first three pages.

There are several other mechanisms we can use to select a page to replace. One possibility is to try to figure out which page has not been referenced for the longest time. As is commonly said, this page is the **least recently used (LRU)** page. We will make the assumption that this page is the most likely not to be used again, and we will take it out of memory. If we tried to actually save the time of the last reference to every page, we would end up making at least one extra memory reference for every real memory reference. So real OSs do not implement an LRU algorithm. However, with the help of some hardware features we can identify pages that have not been used for some time. The simplest of the algorithms that use this feature is

FIGURE 11.11

The page reference and valid bits.

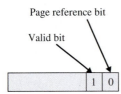

Page reference bit

Valid bit

known as the **clock algorithm.**[2] At a fairly low cost (in terms of additional memory references) the hardware can ensure that a bit in a page table entry is set when a page is referenced. This bit is often called a **page reference bit,** or sometimes an **access bit** or **use bit.** (See Figure 11.11.) When a page is referenced (via the page table), the hardware will check this bit. If it is already set, then nothing needs to happen. If it is not yet set, it will be turned on, perhaps costing one extra memory cycle. Occasionally, the OS can clear these bits for the pages that are currently in memory. We clear the bits for all the pages in a page table and we let the process run for a while. The hardware will set the bits on for all the pages that are referenced. When we need to find a page to take out of RAM we will search through the table and find a page with a valid bit set on and a reference bit that is cleared. This page will be a good candidate for replacement.

We can also enhance this mechanism a little bit. For each page we can keep a byte or more of information about the past history of the setting of this bit, called (somewhat misleadingly) a **reference count.** This mechanism is sometimes known as **aging.** When we periodically clear the reference bits, we first shift the reference count right one bit and shift the latest value of the page reference bit into the high-order position of the reference count. If a page was referenced in the last cycle, this count will therefore have a high value. As refresh cycles go by in which this page is not referenced, the shift operation will effectively keep dividing the count by two each time, so the number will get smaller and smaller. Figure 11.12 shows a reference count for a page. In the last two refresh cycles the bit shifted into the high-order position was a zero, so this number is getting smaller each time. When we need to replace a page we pick the page with the smallest reference count. This gives us a much better idea of the recent history of the usage of a page than a single bit that shows only that it has or has not been referenced in the last time interval.

11.5.3 Dirty pages

When part of a program is loaded into a page and we replace it with something else, we don't need to save it anywhere because we can go back to the original program and get the page if it is referenced again. This is one of many reasons why programs are not supposed to ever modify themselves while they are running. However, if a page contains data and some of the contents of the page have been changed since the page was brought into memory, then we can't just replace the page—we must save

---

[2] This unfortunate term has no reference to the system clock. It refers to the idea that when the OS reaches the end of the page reference list it simply starts over, much as a clock sweeps past 12 and goes back to 1.

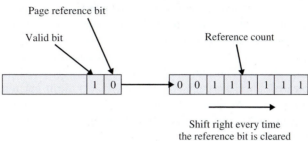

FIGURE 11.12
A page table entry
and associated
reference count.

the data currently in the page in case it is referenced again. We refer to pages that have been modified as **dirty** pages. We will write those dirty pages out to secondary storage in a special place. This place is variously called a **swap file** or a **backing store.** This swap file therefore acts as an extension of the primary memory of the system. This is the origin of the term **virtual memory.** The swap file can be many times larger than the primary memory. In some OSs this file is literally a file in the normal file space and in others it is in a special block of disk space that lies outside the regular file system. In either case it is accessed in such a special way by the OS that accesses to it do not go through the normal file system interface, but use raw mode I/O routines. With some OSs there is only one such file. With others it is possible to place separate swap files on separate drives to increase performance.

11.5.4 More page replacement algorithms

Modern OSs use a variety of algorithms to try to optimize page replacement. One such algorithm is called the **second chance algorithm.** It is a modification of the clock algorithm, which looks through the page table in the manner that we first described, looking for a page that has not been referenced. However, as it checks each page, if it finds the reference bit set, then it clears it. In this way it updates the reference bits to reflect a later time than the latest reference refresh cycle. As it moves through the page table, if it does not find any pages that are free on the first pass, then it will find some on the second pass. In some OSs this searching for pages is done by a background process rather than by the page replacement process. If the free memory space in the system is very low, then the OS will run the background process more often and for a longer time than if there is plenty of memory available. It will run less often and for a shorter time if the free memory is not an immediate cause for concern. **Background** operations are chores that are done when there are no high-priority processes in the ready state. Instructions that are executed in a background task are thus not executed at the expense of any user process, so they are more or less free.

It is worth noting that replacing a dirty page is twice as expensive as replacing a read-only page or a clean page. This is because the OS must make two accesses to the disk and the disk is roughly 1–10,000 times slower than the primary memory. Therefore, we can afford to burn lots of CPU cycles trying to figure out which is the "best" page to replace given what is known at the time. One way we can see such an expenditure of processing resources to save I/O is to enhance the second chance algorithm by using the dirty bit in conjunction with the reference bit. This algorithm is sometimes known as the **enhanced second chance algorithm** and sometimes as the **not recently used (NRU)** or **not used recently (NUR) algorithm.** In this case we will divide the pages into four classes according to the settings of these two bits: (1) clean and unreferenced, (2) dirty but unreferenced (the referenced bit has been cleared since the page was modified), (3) clean but referenced, and (4) dirty and referenced. We first look through the page table for entries in the first class to find a page that is unreferenced and clean. We can use this page immediately. If we do not find a page in this class then we look through the table again for class two, and so forth. By the fourth pass we are assured to find a page, but we usually will have found a better one before then.

One question that arises in demand paging systems is how to choose the process the OS should take a replacement page from. There are two possibilities. Either the OS can select the page only from the process that caused the fault (**local replacement**) or it can select the page from any process (**global replacement**). We would like for programmers to write programs that use the fewest resources. If a programmer writes a program that generates fewer page faults, then his programs should run faster. With local replacement a poorly performing program will hurt itself the most. With global replacement a poorly written program can hurt other processes by having too large a working space and therefore generating too many page faults. As a result, a program that is well designed and generates fewer page faults can be penalized by another, less well designed program that generates many page faults. Having a background process that runs the second chance algorithm to identify suspect pages works well with global replacement. UNIX and related systems generally use global replacement and the Windows NT family uses local replacement.

Page replacement algorithms are an area where much research is ongoing because of the very dynamic nature of both RAM and hard disks. As the sizes, speeds, and costs are changing, the tradeoffs change and different algorithms become useful.

11.5.5 How many pages for each process?

When an OS is being designed with demand paging, we are not going to let programs grow indefinitely in RAM. For one thing, as we saw in the discussion on the working set concept, eventually there will be pages in memory that the program will not reference again. There will be others that it will not need for some time, but that we could profitably let another process use for now, reloading them again when we need them. So the question arises of how many pages each process should be allowed to use. Different schemes are commonly used to set this limit. To begin with, there is some minimum set below which we don't want a program to fall. For example, a common type of instruction on some machines is a memory-to-memory operation. In this case, the instruction itself may span across a page boundary so that we need two pages just to access the instruction. Both the source and the target operands may also span a page boundary, so that on this type of machine there is an absolute lower limit of six pages for a single process. Even in this situation a program will likely have a working set that is larger than that. But what is a reasonable upper limit?

We could study running programs on a prototype system and set some arbitrary limit. But, if there are not enough processes running to fill up all of the available memory with pages, then we will produce page faults when we don't need to. So setting an arbitrary limit is not a good idea. We can make the system a little more dynamic by simply dividing the number of available pages by the number of processes that are running. This mechanism is known as **equal allocation.** But this is not usually reasonable either. If one of the processes was a GUI calculator and the other was a Web server, then we would probably reasonably infer that the Web server would use extra pages to more benefit. One simple method of guessing which programs could use more pages is to compare the sizes of the programs. The Web server program on the disk might be 100 times larger than the calculator program, so it would be reasonable to allocate 100 times as many pages to the Web server as to the calculator. This mechanism is known as **proportional allocation.** But it is still not a perfect solution. Consider a word processor that can open either a small memo file or an entire book. Clearly, opening an entire book would probably effectively utilize more pages than opening a small memo file. What we would like to do is have a mechanism that allocates pages to a process in proportion to its use of the pages.

11.5.6 Automatic page limit balancing

Most modern operating systems use just such a mechanism. Most of these mechanisms are variations on the **page fault frequency (PFF) algorithm.** They depend on the idea that the page fault rate of a process is a good indicator of whether it has the right number of pages. If it has too few pages, then the page fault rate will go up rapidly. If a process is not generating any page faults, then it may also have pages in RAM that it doesn't need. This mechanism sets an upper and lower limit on the page fault rate. Figure 11.13 shows this mechanism at work. If the page fault rate of a process falls below the lower limit, then the OS will subtract one from the maximum frame count for that process. If the page fault rate exceeds the upper limit, then the OS will add one to the count. This mechanism will tend to keep all the processes in the system running at a similar page fault rate and will allocate only as many frames to a process as it needs to stay in this range.

11.5.7 Thrashing

Assume for a moment that we have set a hard upper limit on how many pages a process can use—let's call that limit N. Suppose further that the design of this process is such that it has reached a phase in its execution where its working set is more than the N page limit. Finally, assume that we are using only local page replacement so that when the process creates a page fault we will replace one of the pages that this process already has mapped. This process will constantly be creating new page faults and will spend most of its time waiting on the disk I/O. As a consequence it is going to get little real work done and the system will see an excessive amount of disk I/O. This phenomenon is called **thrashing.** In this case a single process is thrashing. Thrashing does not depend on those restrictions we imagined here. If the sum of the working sets of all the running processes is greater than the real main memory, then the whole system is going to spend

FIGURE 11.13
Automatic page limit
balancing.

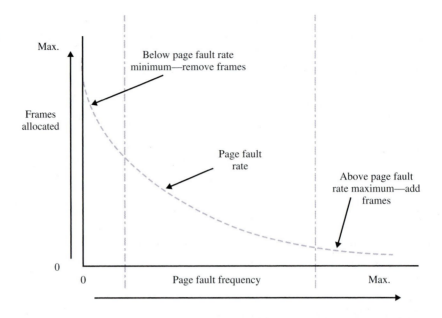

more time replacing pages than it will spend running processes and we will say that the system is thrashing. When it happens it can be difficult to stop because the very act of executing operations to stop some processes that might not be essential will itself cause more code to be brought into memory and may actually make the situation worse.

11.5.8 Page locking

Primary memory is commonly used as a buffer for input and output operations. If a buffer page has an I/O operation pending, then it is probably not currently being changed by the application, so it might end up being selected by the paging mechanism for reuse—clearly with disastrous results. In order to prevent such an unfortunate event, an OS that is doing demand paging must allow an application (usually a device driver) to **lock** a page so that the paging mechanism will not select it. The following calls from the POSIX specification are typical for these functions:

```
int mlock (const void *addr, size_t len)
```

This routine asks the OS to lock a range of pages from the logical address space of the calling process. The range of pages to be locked starts at address *addr* and is *len* bytes long. Only whole pages can be locked, so the range actually includes any pages that contain any part of the specified address range. If the function returns successfully then each of the pages is bound to a physical frame and is marked to stay that way. This means that a call to this function may cause page-ins if some of the pages in the range are not currently resident and the function will block to wait for them. If the function succeeds, the return value is zero. Otherwise, it is −1 and the global *errno* variable is set accordingly.

```
int munlock (const void *addr, size_t len)
```

The munlock routine asks the OS to unlock a range of pages of the calling process. It is the inverse of mlock.

11.5.9 Clean page mechanisms

As was mentioned, it is important to use a page for replacement that is clean rather than a dirty page so that the dirty page does not have to be written to the swap file. In addition, because the disk is 1–10,000 times slower than main memory, we can spend many instructions trying to avoid one disk I/O operation. Alternatively, we can try to do some of the disk operations in the background rather than when we are waiting for a page to be loaded.

We can lessen the impact of the use of a dirty page by keeping available for use a pool of free frames that are clean. When the page replacement algorithm selects a dirty page as the victim for replacement, the OS can use one of the clean frames from the pool. Then in the background the contents of the dirty page can be written out to the disk. When it is clean then the frame can be placed in the pool.

Another task that can be done in the background is to clean pages that are dirty. A background task can look for pages that have not been referenced lately (and thus are likely candidates for replacement) but that are dirty. A background write operation can be started for those pages so that when they are selected for replacement they will be clean. Of course, the page may become dirty again while the process runs, but we are doing this work in the background at the lowest priority so we are not wasting I/O or CPU cycles that could be spent doing something else.

11.5.10 Program design and page fault rates

In general, we say that virtual memory and demand paging are transparent to an application program, However, there are a few observations about how program design can affect the rate of page faults. Consider, for example, searching a large table. Assume that the table is large enough that it covers many pages and that it is to be searched many times for different items. With a binary search we will hit the middle page every time we start a search. Then we will likely hit one of two other pages, either in the first half or the second half. These three pages at least will probably stay in memory most of the time so we will rarely get a page fault on these pages. With a hash table search, however, almost every lookup will cause a different page to be read in since the basic intent of hash tables is to randomly address the entire table in hopes of hitting the desired entry with the first reference. So very large hash tables do not work well with virtual memory systems.

Next, consider a portion of a program that does a matrix multiplication:[3]

```
for(i=0;i<500;i++)
      for(j=0;j<500;j++)
            for(k=0;k<500;k++)
                  x[i][j]=x[i][j]+y[i][k]*z[k][j];
```

---

[3] Patterson, David A. and John L. Hennessy, *Computer Organization and Design: The Hardware/ Software Interface,* Morgan Kaufmann, 2004, p. 617.

When this code was run with arrays of double precision floating point numbers on a Silicon Graphics system with a MIPS R4000 processor and a 1 MB cache, the running time was 77.2 seconds.

We can make a small change to vary the order of the loops so that the innermost loop is stepping through the memory in the same page like this:

```
for(k=0;k<500;k++)
        for(j=0;j<500;j++)
                for(i=0;i<500;i++)
                        x[i][j]=x[i][j]+y[i][k]*z[k][j];
```

The problem with the first example is that the array is stored in memory so that adjacent row elements (the first subscript) are contiguous. Since the variable that is controlling the innermost loop is not the row subscript, then each reference will be to a different page. When we change the loops as in the second example, then each iteration is referencing the same page and the runtime decreases to 44.2 seconds due to the lower number of page faults.

So it is true that in general the action of virtual memory and demand paging are transparent to applications in the sense that the programmer does not have to pay a great deal of attention to the mechanism—this code will work correctly in either format. But as we have just seen, this doesn't mean that they have no effect in every case.

11.6 SPECIAL MEMORY MANAGEMENT TOPICS

11.6.1 Sharing memory among processes

Both segmentation and paging allow for portions of memory to be shared between processes. This can result in large savings in memory. For example, on a mainframe supporting many users it might be common for many users to be running a word processing program at the same time. With paging the page tables for many processes can both point to the same frames in memory so that only one copy of the program code is actually resident. Similarly, with segmentation the segment tables for many processes can point to the same physical memory segment. While this can be handy, it can also cause problems. If the portions of memory that are being shared are data segments, then the individual processes will be changing some of the pages. This may or may not be desired. Several processes might be using shared memory to communicate among themselves. In this case, we would want each process to see all the changes to the pages, so they should be looking at the same frames in physical memory. But consider the case where one process forks itself. Initially, it would be ideal to share the entire physical address space between the two processes. But as they run, changes made by one process should not be seen by the other process. In order to allow this to happen, an OS can use a mechanism known as **copy on write.** Initially, the two processes will be mapped to the same physical frames. But the page (or segment) tables will be set as read only. If either process tries to write to a shared portion of the memory, then an interrupt will occur. When this happens the memory management subsystem will make a separate copy of the shared portion for each process and remove the write protection flag from the table, allowing each process to see only its own version of the data.

Solaris supports access to a shared memory block (Solaris calls it a segment) using the shmget() routine. One process creates a shared block with the first call. The block is described by a control structure with a unique ID that points to an area of physical memory. The identifier of the block is called the shmid.

Here is the call used to access a shared memory block in Solaris:

```
int shmget (key_t key, size_t size, int shmflg);
```

The key argument is either of type key_t or is IPC_PRIVATE. It is the numeric key to be assigned to the returned shared memory block. The size argument is the size in bytes of the requested block. The shmflg argument specifies the starting access permissions and creation control flags.

If the call succeeds, it returns an ID to identify the shared memory block. This call can also be used to get the ID of an existing shared block by another process.

The following code illustrates shmget():

```
key_t key;          /* key to be passed to shmget()    */
int shmflg;         /* shmflg to be passed to shmget()  */
int shmid;          /* return value from shmget()       */
int size;           /* size to be passed to shmget()    */
shm_id = shmget(IPC_PRIVATE, size, shmflg);
if (shm_id<0) {
     printf("shmget error\n");
     exit(1);
}
```

Server and clients can be created with a fork call or can be unrelated. For a child process, if a shared memory block is requested and attached prior to forking the child, then the server may want to use IPC_PRIVATE since the child has a copy of the server's address space, which includes the attached shared block. However, if the server and clients are separate processes, using IPC_PRIVATE is not a good idea since the clients will not know the key.

11.6.2 Memory mapped files

Most modern OSs allow a special mode of memory sharing referred to as **memory mapped files.** In this mode a process will ask the OS to open a file and associate all or part of the data in the file with a region of the logical address space of the process. Then the process can refer to the information in that space as an array or through memory pointers. There are two main advantages of such a system. The first is that the process does not have to use I/O statements to access the data—the demand paging system takes care of accessing the right data from the file. The second advantage is that two or more processes can ask the OS for access to the same file at the same time. The same memory frames will be mapped into the logical address spaces of both processes, allowing them to share access to the memory. This mechanism therefore provides a simple mechanism for sharing data between two processes. Of course, the processes may need to use synchronization techniques to avoid interfering with one another. In addition, if the real purpose of the "shared file" is to provide a shared memory region between two or more processes, the shared file does not actually need to reside on the file system as a file.

As an example, here is how memory mapped objects (including files) can be created under the Windows Win32 libraries:

```
HANDLE WINAPI CreateFileMapping(
  _in  HANDLE hFile,
  _in_opt LPSECURITY_ATTRIBUTES lpAttributes,
  __in  DWORD flProtect,
  __in  DWORD dwMaximumSizeHigh,
  __in  DWORD dwMaximumSizeLow,
  _in_opt LPCTSTR lpName
);
```

The meanings of some of the parameters are:

- hFile—A handle to the file from which to create a mapping object. If hFile is −1, the call must also give a size for the object in the dwMaximumSizeHigh and dwMaximumSizeLow parameters and a temporary file is created in the system paging file instead of mapping to a file system file.
- A pointer to a security descriptor structure for the object that contains access control lists (ACL) and other security information.
- flProtect—Protection to be applied to the object
    - PAGE_READONLY
    - PAGE_READWRITE
    - PAGE_WRITECOPY (copy on write)
    - PAGE_EXECUTE_READ
    - PAGE_EXECUTE_READWRITE
    - PAGE_EXECUTE_WRITECOPY
    - Etc.
- dwMaximumSizeHigh—High-order DWORD of max size of the object.
- dwMaximumSizeLow—Low-order DWORD of max size of the object.
- lpName—The name of the file to be mapped.

11.6.3 Windows XP prefetch files

Various OSs have developed some interesting tricks to optimize the use of demand paging. One interesting technique used in Windows XP is designed to speed up the loading and initialization of programs. The idea is that when a program is loading it will go through the same sequence of instructions each time. Therefore, it will generate the same sequence of page faults. Furthermore, it will tend to generate these faults in clusters. For example, as the code executes it will pass through a contiguous sequence of pages in the code. As it does so it will be generating other page faults as it calls subroutines and references data in other pages. As a result, the disk drive gets a workout seeking back and forth to fetch these pages in random order. XP (and sometimes other OSs as well) uses a better technique. The first time a program starts, the OS will keep track of all the page faults it makes in the first few minutes. It will record those page faults in a file called a **prefetch** file. Later, in the background it will sort that file so that subsequently when the program is launched the OS can fetch all the code pages that will be used as the program initializes. It can fetch all the needed pages of the main program in a few large read operations. Then it will move to another place on the disk to fetch all the subroutine code, then move to another place to fetch those data pages that will be used, and so forth. This technique will save a lot of page fault interrupts. It will also save a lot of disk head movement and rotational delays as larger chunks of disk storage are read in single operations.

11.6.4 Symbian memory management

The Symbian OS was created for use in cell phones. This OS has a unique way of utilizing the paging hardware found in modern CPUs. The problem they faced was this: In a cell phone it is presumed that there is no secondary storage—no disk drive. As was discussed in Chapter 4 on the Palm OS, all the programs that are stored in the phone are always in primary memory. Therefore, primary memory is even more scarce than in most systems, especially given the need to maintain a low power budget in cell phones. But the processor architecture used in the phone includes paging hardware since most system environments do include secondary storage. In most OSs there are three functions that the memory management hardware is supposed to perform: (1) dynamic relocation of the program, (2) restriction of addressing to the space reserved for a given program, and (3) allowing for random dynamic loading of any page from secondary storage into primary storage. In the Symbian OS the dynamic loading function is not needed. In addition, storing a page table for each program would take up valuable RAM. So the problem faced by the Symbian developers was how to use the hardware most efficiently to do the two jobs that remained. The solution adopted by the Symbian OS developers was to use a single-page table for all the processes in the system.

The single-page table is modified when a context change is needed and a program is about to be put into run state. Figure 11.14 shows how this change is made. In Figure 11.14a we see the page table when process B is running. The page table has a normal mapping for the frames of both process A and process B and for their respective thread data pages. But there is also a reserved section of the page table that always points to the frames for the process that is currently executing. When it is time to make a context switch and start executing process A, the OS will copy the page table entries for process A into the page table entries reserved for the running process. This is shown in Figure 11.14b where we see that the page table has been changed to run process A. The result is that pointers to the frames of the running process always appear in two places in the page table, once where it actually resides and once where the running process appears. This allows the paging hardware to support

FIGURE 11.14
Symbian memory
page table.

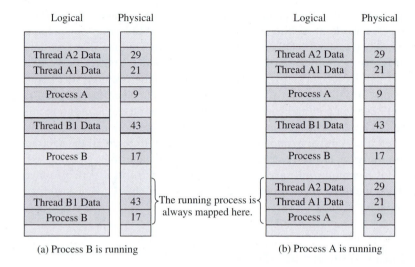

(a) Process B is running   (b) Process A is running

the dynamic relocation function needed to simplify code generation and still restrict program access to its own memory areas without consuming extra RAM for a page table per process.

11.7 SUMMARY

In this chapter we discussed the designs of memory management through paging and segmentation systems and their hardware requirements as well as a combination of segmentation and paging. We then discussed demand paging memory management. We examined the effect of demand paging and some problems that arose in its implementation. Throughout this discussion we also focused on the hardware required to support these OS techniques. We ended with a section that covered some subtopics related to advanced memory management.

BIBLIOGRAPHY

Belady, L. A., "A Study of Replacement Algorithms for Virtual Storage Computers," *IBM Systems Journal,* Vol. 5, No. 2, 1966, pp. 78–101.

Belady, L. A., and C. J. Kuehner, "Dynamic Space Sharing in Computer Systems," *Communications of the ACM,* Vol. 12, No. 5, May 1969, pp. 282–288.

Carr, R. W., and J. L. Hennessy, "WSClock—A Simple and Effective Algorithm for Virtual Memory Management," *Proceedings of the Eighth Symposium on Operating Systems Principles,* Vol. 15, No. 5, December 1981, pp. 87–95.

Denning, P. J., "The Working Set Model for Program Behavior," *Communications of the ACM,* Vol. 11, No. 5, May 1968, pp. 323–333.

Denning, P. J., "Virtual Memory," *ACM Computing Surveys,* Vol. 2, No. 3, September 1970, pp. 153–189.

Denning, P. J., "Working Sets Past and Present," *IEEE Transactions on Software Engineering,* Vol. SE-6, No. 1, January 1980, pp. 64–84.

Mattson, R. L., J. Gecsie, D. R. Slutz, and I. L. Traiger, "Evaluation Techniques for Storage Hierarchies," *IBM Systems Journal,* Vol. 9, No. 2, 1970, pp. 78–117.

Prieve, B. G., and R. S. Fabry, "VMIN—An Optimal Variable Space Page Replacement Algorithm," *Communications of the ACM,* Vol. 19, No. 5, May 1976, pp. 295–297.

Stephenson, C. J., "Fast Fits: New Methods for Dynamic Storage Allocation," *Proceedings of the Ninth Symposium on Operating Systems Principles,* ACM, Vol. 17, No. 5, October 1983, pp. 30–32.

The bibliography for this chapter overlaps considerably with the previous chapter.

WEB RESOURCE

http://www.symbian.com (Symbian OS)

REVIEW QUESTIONS

11.1 What hardware development solved the problem of external fragmentation?

11.2 While the paging hardware is translating a logical page address to a physical frame address, what happens to the displacement part of the address?

11.3 When we first looked at translating memory references through a table that was also in memory, what was the effect on the effective access time of memory? What did we do about it?

11.4 Using page tables, we need some way to know where the end of the logical address space is in the table. We discussed two different techniques for doing this. What mechanisms did the two techniques use? Under what circumstance is one technique preferred over another?

11.5 Eventually, page tables started to grow very big and sparse. What technique was employed to solve this problem?

11.6 An alternative to paging is segmentation. Briefly describe this technique.

11.7 What is the basic idea behind demand paging?

11.8 When running demand paging, how does the OS know a page is needed by a process?

11.9 What is the "working set" of a process?

11.10 Why do we worry about page replacement algorithms so much?

11.11 Why do we prefer not to replace dirty pages when a page fault occurs?

11.12 When an OS is selecting a page to replace in a demand paging system, what is the difference between local replacement and global replacement?

11.13 What is the minimum number of pages that a process needs to run?

11.14 If a process frequently starts thrashing, what should the architect of the process do to improve the situation?

11.15 What kind of background operations can an OS do to improve demand paging performance?

11.16 Hash tables are very poor performing structures as far as demand paging goes. We mentioned that binary lookups were probably pretty good. What other basic system structure gives very good demand paging performance?

11.17 What is the purpose of a prefetch file in Windows XP?

11.18 How are memory mapped files used by multiple processes?

11.19 The Symbian OS uses the paging memory hardware in a very special way. Why is that?

Part 4

A Depth-Oriented Presentation of OS Concepts: File Systems and Input/Output

In this part:

Not all operating systems have file systems, but any of those devices we would normally think of as a computer certainly would have one. Indeed, many of the devices that we might not think of as a computer may have file systems as well, including many gaming systems, cell phones, music players, and personal digital assistants. This part of the text covers those aspects of an OS that are concerned with the management of secondary storage and the file systems found thereon.

Chapter 12 discusses the layout of typical hard drives and explains the basic concerns that a file system has. The topics covered here start with the concepts of directories and how they are laid out in modern file systems. Then the chapter discusses the concept of file access methods, including sequential, random, and indexed access. Next, it covers the tracking of free space within a file system and the layout (allocation) of the files themselves.

Chapter 13 first covers several modern file systems as case studies to show how the individual mechanisms discussed in Chapter 12 are used in real OSs. It then covers advanced file system features often found in modern OSs but not so fundamental to the normal application. These topics include virtual file systems/redirection, memory mapped files, file system utilities, and log-based file systems.

Chapter 14 moves to a lower level that is normally isolated from the file system. It discusses the entire input/output management subsection present in any OS. It discusses various classes of I/O devices, including those used for secondary storage. This chapter is included in this part of the text since secondary storage management is such a dominant use of the I/O subsystem. Other aspects of I/O are treated separately in the chapters on networking, for example.

Chapter 12

File Systems—Basics

In this chapter:

Files are one of the most important abstractions an OS can provide. The concept of files predates computers, so they are a metaphor that everyone understands. Programmers do not want to think about disk drives, tapes, or any other media. They want to think about the data they are processing, and they think of the data as a collection. In a computer, that collection is abstracted as a file. Programs need data to work on. We usually keep that data on secondary storage devices because primary storage is too expensive to keep all the data we need to have access to. Today, these devices are almost always rotating magnetic disk drives. As application programmers we do not want to be concerned with the details of operation of the thousands of different types of disk drives. We want to think of our data in terms of some abstraction. Usually, we think in terms of a file as being a collection of records or bytes. Therefore, a major function of most OSs is to provide for the abstraction of a file on secondary storage. The contents of a file are usually meaningful only to application programs. By this we mean that the OS is typically not aware of the internal structure of the files. There are a few exceptions such as the executable (binary) programs that the OS can run and the object modules that are used to make those files. Such files have structures that are defined by the OS itself. These structures will be known by all the linker or loader utilities that are used to make the executable files and the compilers and assemblers that are used to produce the object modules from source program files.

In Section 12.1 we introduce the concept of file systems and how they fit in an OS. Modern computers typically contain hundreds of thousands of files. It must be possible to organize the files so that things can be found. Next, we discuss the mechanisms used for supporting directories in file systems. Different applications have different needs in terms of how they access the data in files. Sometimes the data can be processed sequentially. Sometimes the transactions are random. Sometimes a special key number makes it easy to find a record. Other times we need to access records based on their content. Section 12.3 describes various methods that applications can use for accessing the data in files. File systems on random-access media need to keep track of what parts of the media contain data and what parts are free to use. So next we explore the need for tracking the space in a file system that is not currently allocated to a file, and the different structures used to track that space. In Section 12.5 we present the topic of the structure of the files themselves and discuss the tradeoffs of the various methods. We conclude with a chapter summary in Section 12.6.

12.1   INTRODUCTION

File systems generally have layered designs, with each layer providing services to the layer above it. Every OS has a unique partitioning of the functions across these layers. Two things are true about all file systems: the top layer API is an abstraction of the concept of files and the bottom layer interacts directly with the hardware. As an example, a Linux file system organization is shown in Figure 12.1 with the layers flowing left to right. We discuss file abstraction in this chapter and the bottom layers in the next chapter.

FIGURE 12.1
Linux file and I/O systems.

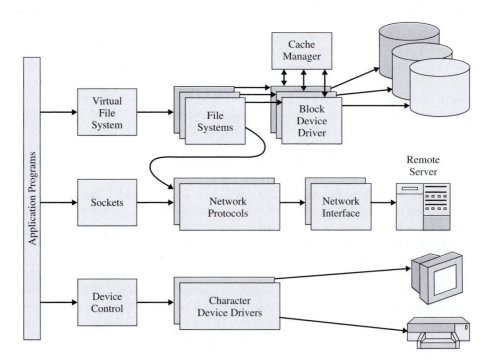

TABLE 12.1   **Some Possible Directory Information Items**

File Name	Archived?
→ Starting Block	Protection (can be very complex)
Maximum File Size	Encryption Information
Current File Size	Compression Information
→ Last Block	Owner ID
Date & Time Created	File Allocation Type
Date & Time Last Written	Date & Time Last Accessed

12.2 DIRECTORIES

Before a program can use a file, it will need to find the file. The OS will need to provide some sort of an index to the files that the program can search. We call these indexes **directories.** (Since more people have begun using computers who are not very knowledgeable about them, another term has also come into common usage for these structures: **folders.**) Directories will obviously have to store the name of the file, but they will also store other data about the file as well. In some OSs there may be a lot of other information kept for each file, but in others there is only a small amount. This other information about a file that is not part of the file data is referred to as **file metadata.** Some of these other items are almost universal and others are found only rarely. Clearly, we will need a disk address that points to the start of the file data. Usually, we also want to know the size of the file. Table 12.1 shows some examples of metadata we might find for a file on various operating systems. It is unlikely that any OS will have all of these items—in some cases they represent different ways of accomplishing the same ends. In some OSs this information is stored in the directory entry for a file. In other OSs it is stored in a separate structure—most notably, UNIX-derivative OSs use an external table called an inode.

12.2.1 Logical structure

There are many different logical structures that can be used to store a directory structure for a file system. We look at several common structures in this section.

Single level

How we logically organize the directory on a disk depends to some extent on the size of the disk. As was discussed in Chapter 4, early disk drives were fairly small (a few hundred thousand bytes) and the number of files was therefore small. In order to make maximum use of the limited space, the names were kept short (6–8 characters was fairly common) and the pointers to the blocks on the disk were kept small. There was normally only a single directory for the entire disk. In Figure 12.2, we show such a single-level directory structure. As we mentioned in earlier chapters, some OSs with a single-level directory structure attempted to give the appearance of

FIGURE 12.2
A single-level
directory.

Filename	Length	Start
MSDOS.SYS	14	0000404
IO.SYS	12	0000303
AUTOEXEC.BAT	2	0000505
CONFIG.SYS	1	0000506
COMMAND.COM	50	0000600

a two-level structure by associating a group name with files so that a user could look at the directory and see only the files for a specific group.

Tree structure

Disk storage capacities have grown dramatically over time. Current disk drive technology is such that drives with the capacity of several hundred billion bytes (**GB**) are standard equipment on a typical new personal computer. It is normal for such a disk to have hundreds of thousands of files on it. An average user would have no specific knowledge about many of them. A single directory would not work on such large drives. So a key development in the organization of the logical structure of disk directories was to allow for multiple directories. The main trick is simply to allow directories to refer to other directories in addition to referring to files. If we limit such references to link only to directories with no other link to them (including the starting directory), the resulting structure is a tree structure with the starting directory as the root of the tree. See Figure 12.3.

With such a hierarchical directory organization we can divide the files up into different categories. On machines that are used by more than one user, we can

FIGURE 12.3
A tree directory
structure.

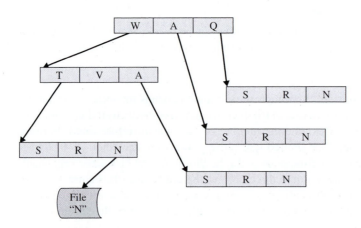

give each user a "home" directory, which will contain all their data files in sub-directories. The various subdirectories can also be dedicated to different types of files—perhaps one for utility programs, one for games, one for email, and so on. This process can be continued to arbitrary depths. Email, for example, could be further divided into directories related to work, school, family, friends, and technology. The school directory could be further divided into directories for each class, and so forth.

A side effect of this organization is that we can have many files with the same file name just by keeping them in separate directories. This would allow a group of people working in different home directories to use identical file names. Figure 12.3 shows the unlikely but perfectly legal case that many subdirectories contain the same set of file names. However, there was a price to pay for this feature—the names of files can no longer be uniquely specified by a single name. In order to unambiguously refer to a file we will have to give the entire **path** of the directories leading to the file. It is common to separate the subdirectory names with some delimiter that cannot be used as part of a file name. The characters / and \ are the most often used characters. So in Figure 12.3, in order to unambiguously name the one file shown, we would have to give the name "\W\T\N."

Acyclic graph directories

Unfortunately, the real world can't be accurately modeled by a tree structure. For example, a canary is a bird. If we had a digital picture of a canary and we were studying biology, then we might put it in a directory with cats and other animals. It also flies, so if we were studying engineering we might put it in a directory with airplanes and other things that fly. It also is yellow, so if we were artists we might put it in a directory with butter and lemons and other things that are yellow. But if we were studying biomedical engineering and working on color vision systems, we might be at a loss as to how to classify this file. With only a tree structured directory we are often in a quandary as to how we should classify some file. Furthermore, sometimes we later can't remember which folder we decided to put the canary picture in. A solution that is sometimes employed to help with this dilemma is to allow directories to form **directed acyclic graphs** (**DAG**s). The way to accomplish this is to use a special kind of directory entry called an **alias.** An alias is an entry that does not point directly to a file, but rather points to another directory entry. (The alias could actually point to the file, but there are some problems that arise with this mechanism, which we discuss later. The distinction between the two mechanisms is not relevant here.)

Unfortunately, moving from a tree structure to a DAG introduces some problems that must be considered. The simplest example is a one that would occur when a program tries to sum up all the space in all the files on a system. If the aliases are not considered, then the program might come up with the wrong total if some files are referenced more than once. Another large problem is how the system should decide that a file can actually be deleted. Consider the case in Figure 12.4. Here we see three directories. The top directory has two entries pointing to subdirectories, **W** and **Q.** It also has a directory entry pointing to a file, **A.** The subdirectory **W** contains an entry that also points to file **A.** Suppose the user deletes file **A** while

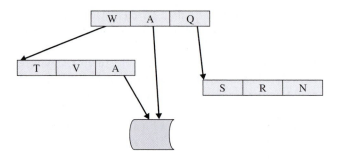

in subdirectory **W.** The OS shouldn't actually remove the file because of the other reference to it in the top directory.

There are two mechanisms that are sometimes used to resolve this issue. The first is to distinguish between the primary reference to a file and any aliases to a file. The OS will also include a reference count in the primary directory entry. When an alias is added for a file, the reference count is incremented. Then if an alias is deleted, the primary reference count is decremented, and if the count goes to zero then the file can actually be deleted. There remains the issue of what happens when the primary reference is deleted but aliases remain. The second technique is to make all aliases **symbolic references,** including any path information. This is what we meant earlier when we said that the alias should point to the directory entry for the file instead of to the file itself. In this case, if the lower reference in the figure was the primary reference, then the second directory entry would actually contain "\W\A" rather than a pointer to the file on the disk.

12.2.2 Physical structure

In older systems there was considerable attention given to the speed of searching directories. As a result, older systems sometimes used techniques such as hashing to speed up directory searches. However, over the last 20 years or so CPU and memory speeds have speeded up by a factor of at least 10 faster than disk drives have speeded up. Therefore, most modern OSs don't worry about such matters, and directories are not sorted in any particular order. The search is simply sequential. In most cases people tend to keep directories fairly small—under 100 entries or so.

12.2.3 Operations on directories

The OS must support several different operations on directories. One might think that these would only be the operations that are supported on files, since directories are essentially files. However, there are a few differences. For one thing, because of the potentially catastrophic consequences of having an error in the file system, most OSs do not allow an application program to write into a directory. Instead, the application must call special routines to create a new file or directory or do any other such operations on directories. Table 12.2 shows a number of operations that an OS might support on directories.

TABLE 12.2   **Operations OSs Must Support on Directories**

Change Working Directory
Create Directory
Delete Directory
List Directory
Create File
Delete File
Search for a File
Rename a File
Completely Walk the Directory Tree

The first operation listed is to change the working directory. As was mentioned, each subdirectory can contain files with the same local name as other subdirectories, so that a path name is required to unambiguously name a file. When we are entering names into a command line to run a program, we don't want to have to keep typing path names all the time, so OSs use the concept of a working directory. The idea is that the user will take some action that specifies a specific directory to be the **current working directory,** or sometimes just the working directory. One way the working directory can be determined is to log in to the system. Systems supporting such logins will usually assign the user's home directory to be the current working directory at login time. A reference to a file name that does not include any path information is called an **unqualified name.** Any commands that make reference to an unqualified name will imply that the file is in the current working directory. So, in Figure 12.5, if directory **W** were the current working directory, then a reference to file **S** would be assumed to be a reference to the file in that directory. In order to refer to the file **S** in the subdirectory **T** of directory **W,** the program would have to specify a path to that directory as a part of the name. In this case it could say either "**\W\T\S**" or "**.\T\S.**" The first reference is an **absolute pathname.** It begins with the delimiter that separates directory names in the path so it is interpreted as starting at the root of the tree. The second reference is called a **relative pathname.** The "**.**" is a special name that specifies the current working directory. So this pathname says that

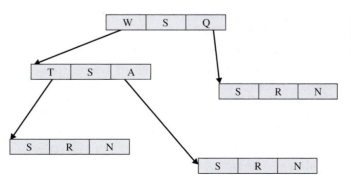

FIGURE 12.5
Paths in a directory structure.

the path starts in the current working directory and goes to the subdirectory **T,** where it will then find the file name **S.**

The other common mechanism for changing the current working directory is a Change Directory command—usually something like **cd** or **chdir.** This command can specify an absolute path or a relative path. Often, shorthand notation can be used, for example, so that **cd ..** will change the working directory to the parent directory of the current directory. On Linux and other UNIX-like systems the cd command with no arguments will place the current working directory at the user's home directory.

The commands to create and remove directories are fairly straightforward. Again, these functions exist since we don't usually let applications write in directories. Rather, we demand that they use special OS calls to do these functions. Special utility programs **mkdir** and **rmdir** exist to allow the user to request these operations through the command interpreter. Normally, the OS might not provide a built-in function to list the contents of a file, but directories are very special files, so the OS must provide a function to list the contents of a directory for an application. Again, utility programs (**dir** or **ls**) are provided to make this function accessible to a user through the command-line interface. However, when an application program needs to create a new file, it must have a way to ask the OS to do that. Similarly, a program may want to delete a file that is no longer needed. There is generally no simple utility to create a new file because such a file would be empty. Usually a file is created as a byproduct of some other action. The closest thing to a utility would be a file copy command (**cp** or **copy**). Under Linux one can copy the special pseudo file /dev/zero to a file name to create a file of binary zeros. Of course, files are often created with text editor utilities like **vi** or **notepad.** Other applications create their own files such as .doc files or .xls files under Microsoft Office. File deletion is usually exposed to the user with a utility that will delete files like **del** or **rm.** Deleting directories is also a special utility with a name like **rmdir.** Searching a directory for a file is often something an application needs to do. This is not for the purpose of opening the file for input. The OS (or the language library modules) will do that. Rather, it is for when the application wants to create a new file. It will first need to check to make sure that such a name is not already in use in the current directory. (Some language libraries might do that as well.)

12.2.4 File system metadata

We mentioned before that directory entries contain information about files that is not a part of the file itself and that this information was called file metadata. There is also other information in the file system that is not about specific files and thus is not part of the directory entries. For example, where is the first directory located in the file system? We will see later that there will be other structures that will tell us things such as how to find free disk blocks. The details will vary with the particular file system, but there are always these other structures, and they are very important to the integrity of the file system. They are collectively known as **file system metadata.**

12.3 ACCESS METHODS

An OS presents an application program with an API that represents the abstraction of a file. The API has to include semantics on how the application tells the OS which portion of the file it wants to access. Different applications need different modes of access.

12.3.1 Sequential access

Initially, computer applications were designed to process information in batches that were sequenced by some key information such as a part number or customer number. Such applications needed to process files sequentially. At one time these files were literally sorted decks of punched cards and later were sorted blocks of data on a magnetic tape. The system might have an input file of transactions such as time cards and a master file such as the payroll records, both of which might be in order by the employee number. The application would start reading at the front of each file and would incrementally read each file, keeping them synchronized by the key field, in this case the employee number. For decks of cards the records were a fixed size. For magnetic tape they could be any convenient size up to some maximum that the hardware or the OS would dictate. For sequential processing on disk storage the OS (or a software library) has to have some definition of what the record size is for each file and it then has to keep track of the **current position** (or **current record pointer**) for each application that has the file open. This is seen in Figure 12.6. (Note that different processes accessing the same file probably would have different current record pointers.) For normal sequential processing the OS will increment the current record pointer for each read or write. There is usually a command in the API to reset the current record pointer to the start of the file. This operation would be analogous

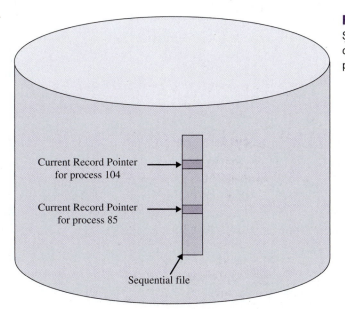

FIGURE 12.6
Sequential file with current record pointer.

Current Record Pointer for process 104

Current Record Pointer for process 85

Sequential file

to rewinding a tape to the starting position. Since the disk blocks are a fixed size and may not exactly match the record length requirements of the application, it is fairly common for the OS to combine more than one logical record into a physical data block. Blocking is covered more fully in the next chapter.

12.3.2 Random access

As disk drives got much cheaper, secondary storage migrated from being stored on magnetic tapes to being stored on disk drives. Once the data was mostly kept online it became possible to process each transaction as it occurred rather than accumulating them to be processed in sequential batches. Transaction processing is generally preferable to batch processing because it allows management to track the status of an enterprise more nearly in real time. However, this meant that the application had to access the master file data in random order rather than purely sequential order. So the file APIs were extended to include another model: random access. In this model the application will tell the OS which record in the file it needs and the OS will move directly to that record and access it for reading or writing. Usually this will require some simple mapping of a key value to the record number. For example, a small company might simply assign the employee numbers sequentially and use the employee number as the record number. In some OSs this addressing is expressed as a record number and in others it is expressed as a byte offset from the start of the file.

Note that sequential access is still possible on random access files. When the application accesses a record randomly this will leave the current record pointer positioned at the next record. The application can now issue a **read next** operation and the OS will return the next record and increment the current record pointer. We can see this in Figure 12.7, where the employee number for employee 34 is used to

FIGURE 12.7
A random access method file.

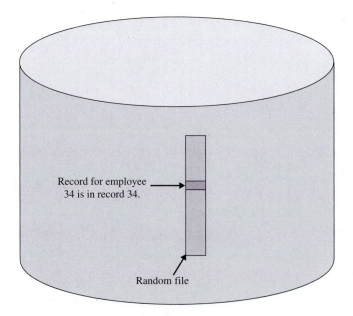

Record for employee 34 is in record 34.

Random file

access that record in the file. If the application does a read next operation it will get the next record.

In order to start accessing at any point in a random access file, the OS usually provides a **seek** command, which will position the current record pointer at the first record that has a key value greater than or equal to a given key value. When OSs only ran one process at a time this command would actually position the disk head to this position in the file (i.e., it would seek the physical location of the data). Now it is a logical positioning only.

12.3.3 Higher-level access methods

Most OSs provide at least these two different access methods. A few OSs provide one or more higher-level access methods. We describe two such mechanisms in the rest of this section. Most of these higher-level access methods are also subsumed in database systems and are sometimes provided as library modules as support for high-level languages. Having the access methods provided by the OS means that less development work needs to be done to support many high-level languages as long as the semantics of the APIs are similar enough for the OS access method to support them.

Indexed access

Random access often will not work as well for a larger company employee file as it did for a smaller company. After a while many employees will retire, leave the company, get fired, and so on. The result would be that there would be many records in the master file that would not represent a current employee. For such situations the OS might provide an access method called an indexed access method. A fairly common term for such access methods is **ISAM,** or **indexed sequential access method.**

How such access methods work can be seen in Figure 12.8. The figure shows a data file for a retail store. It has three areas: the **primary data** area where the data records are kept; the **primary key** area, which is an index to the main key field in the record; and a **secondary key** area, which is an index to a different variable. As records are added to the file they are written sequentially to the primary data area. However, for each record written to the primary data area an additional record is written to the primary key area and another record is written to the secondary key area. (Note that

Index	SKU No.	MFG No.	Other Info.	SKU No.	Index No.	MFG No.	Index No.
0	ABC	CBA		ABC	0	ABQ	3
1	XYZ	JKL		ABQ	3	CBA	0
2	MNO	CBA		MNO	2	CBA	2
3	ABQ	ABQ		RST	4	JKL	1
4	RST	UVW		XYZ	1	UVW	4
5		Unused		Unused		Unused	
6		. . .		. . .		. . .	
7							

Primary Data Area   Primary Key Area   Secondary Key Area

FIGURE 12.8

An indexed access method file.

there might not be a secondary key area or there might be several of them.) Each record in any of the key areas is stored in order by the value of the associated key field. In the figure there are two key fields that have been used to index the data: the SKU number (the stocking number of the retail store) and the manufacturer's item number. So when record 0 was written into the primary data area a record was written to the primary key area that showed that SKU number ABC was found in data record 0 and another record was written to the secondary key area showing that manufacturer's number CBA was in data record 0. When the second record was written into the primary data area, then similar records were written into the key areas. However, when the third data record was added, the record that was added to the primary key area caused a problem since it was not in order, so we had to sort this area by the value of the key. There are a number of techniques for building the key areas that avoid actual sorting of the entire file, including **binary trees** (or **B-trees**), hashing, and multilevel indexing.

Notice that the keys do not have to be a single field. An index might be created that concatenated a last name and a first name, for example. Also notice that the key fields may or may not allow duplicate keys. We see in Figure 12.8 that a single manufacturer's part number is stocked in the store with two different SKU numbers. In a more likely scenario, in our employee file we might have two Bill Smiths, but we should not have two employees with the same Social Security number. Such an access method is close to being a database system but is somewhat simpler.

The three "areas" that we discussed in Figure 12.8 could be portions of a single file or they could be stored as separate files. Having them as separate files might make it simpler to add an index on another key after the file was initially created. The risk of having separate files is that it becomes very easy when backing up and restoring files to end up with files that did not go together. Of course, we would likely have a utility program that verified and possibly rebuilt the secondary index files, but on a large file this could take some time, and we might not realize immediately that there was a problem such that we should run that utility.

Hashed access

Another higher-level access method sometimes provided by OSs is a hashed access method. Hashing a key field can be used to create a random key value for use in accessing a random access file when the key values are not all used. Of course, generating hash keys probably will create record numbers that collide for different values of the source key, so a mechanism must be provided to resolve these collisions. While not as common as indexed sequential access methods, a hashed file access method is still a useful tool for an OS to provide.

12.3.4 Raw access

For some applications the services provided by the file system would be counterproductive. This can happen when an application has high performance requirements and the patterns of accessing the files it uses are well known to the developers of the application. The services designed for most applications are provided for an "average" or "typical" application where the file processing demands are not unusual. In such cases the OS will sometimes provide a **raw access method.** In this case the OS does not provide any file structure, but reserves an area of the disk wherein the application can provide its own structure. Examples of applications where such raw access are useful include the paging store for the OS itself and database systems.

12.4 FREE SPACE TRACKING

The OS will be storing files and directories in blocks on the disk. In order to do that it will have to keep track of which blocks have not been used yet. There are generally two ways to keep track of this **free space:** linked lists and bitmaps. Initially, file systems kept track of the smallest chunk of space that could be accessed on a disk drive—a sector. As disk drives got larger, the size of the pointers to the sectors on the disk got larger. For example, modern disk drives are now extending into the terabyte range. Anything larger than a 2 terabyte drive would require a pointer greater than 4 bytes. Naturally, the file systems initially designed for floppy disks did not use pointers that big. So when the disk drives outgrew the pointers in the file systems, one easy solution was to allocate more than one sector at a time. Simply allocating two sectors together would double the reach of the pointer. The process was extended, and in some cases file systems have allocated up to 64 sectors at a time, though sizes of 4 KB are more typical. The resulting structure is referred to as a **block,** or sometimes as a cluster. This seemed good, but one problem with the mechanism was that it wasted space if the data stored on the disk included many small files. Most script (or batch) files, for example, are just a few lines of text. Few would fill a single sector, much less 64 sectors! Since this technique of allocating multiple sectors at a time is still very common, we will generally speak of allocating a block in this chapter rather than allocating a sector.

12.4.1 Linked list free space tracking

One way to keep track of the free space is to put all the free blocks in a list. Figure 12.9 shows blocks on a disk drive. The OS must keep track of the first block on the list. Each free block will then contain a pointer to the next free block. Notice that the list is not in any order. We might initially start with an ordered list, but when an application frees up a block we will want to be able to put it in the list at the front so that we do not have to change any other sector on the disk to point to this newly freed block. We will take the pointer to the block currently at the head of the list and put it in the newly freed block. We will write the sector of the block that actually contains the next free block pointer to disk and we will record the newly freed block as the first block in the list.

   One good aspect of this mechanism is that the only "extra" space it requires to keep track of the free space is the single pointer to the head of the list. All the rest of the pointers are kept in the free space itself. A bad aspect of this mechanism is that it is normally very difficult to allocate contiguous blocks of space. So if applications might want to have contiguous blocks of data on the disk drive, this is not

FIGURE 12.9

A free space chain.

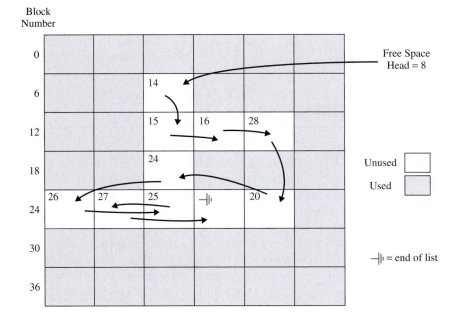

a good mechanism to use. Another problem with this mechanism is that to get the address of the next free block, the OS has to read the free block because it contains the pointer to the next one. In the next section we discuss some ways to get around this problem.

12.4.2 Improved linked lists

What linked lists need in order to work better is to have some way for us to not have to read each sector before we use it in order to find the next available free sector. There are several ways to do this. Two common ways include grouping and indexing. With indexing we merely store a bunch of free space pointers in a single block. Suppose a block was only a sector, 512 bytes, and our pointers were 32 bits, or 4 bytes. Then one block could store 128 pointers. So the block at the head of the chain, instead of just pointing to the next free block, would point at the next 128 free blocks. This first block would be called an **index block.** An example is shown in Figure 12.10. We could use all the blocks pointed to by the first index block and then use the index block itself. The last block pointed to should be another index block. As we use each data block we need to write the index block back to the disk so it will stay current, but a slight optimization there would be to take out several block pointers at the same time and rewrite the block, temporarily holding those block pointers in RAM. This is called **preallocation.** It is a technique that can be used with many of the free space tracking mechanisms in order to minimize the updating of the data on the disk. Of course, there is some possibility that the system might go down and the information on the disk would show that those blocks were in use when they were not. Having the system go down is a fairly low-probability event. If it does go down,

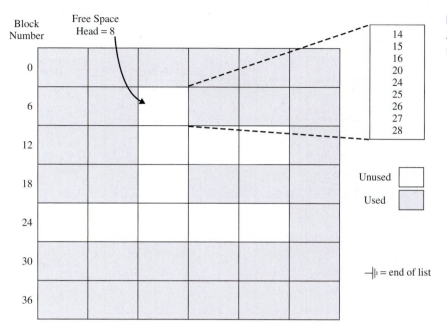

FIGURE 12.10

An indexed free
space chain.

the few blocks we lose track of is normally a small part of the available space. There will be no loss of data in the files or metadata. Also, we will have file system checking utilities that will recover the lost blocks at the cost of scanning the file system. Therefore, we will not worry about the possible loss of consistency in the metadata.

Another mechanism that can improve linked list free space tracking is **grouping.** In this technique the OS will take every opportunity to determine that two or more blocks in the chain are adjacent. This can easily happen if blocks can be allocated to files in multiples rather than only one at a time. In this case, the first block in that group will contain not only a pointer to the next free block, but also an indication of how many of the following blocks in the list are adjacent to one another. Such a mechanism is shown in Figure 12.11. This will allow the allocation mechanism to sometimes allocate contiguous blocks more easily. But also, this first block can be read and then the rest of the blocks of the group handed out without having to read the disk again.

12.4.3 Bitmap free space tracking

Another approach to free space tracking is to have a bitmap in which each block in the file system is represented by a single bit in a long string. If the bit is set one way, then the block is free. If it is set the other way, then it is in use. Whether the "1" bit indicates that the block is free or it indicates that the block is in use depends mostly on the instruction set of the computer. We will clarify this shortly. Recall that one problem with the linked list mechanism is the difficulty in allocating multiple contiguous blocks. With a bitmap this is much simpler than it was with the linked list mechanisms. It is merely necessary to find a string of contiguous bits of the required size. It is this

FIGURE 12.11

A grouped free space chain.

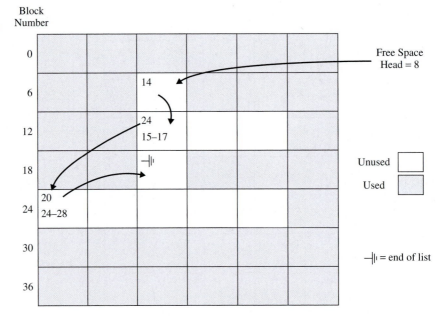

scan for a contiguous block that we will want to execute efficiently. The instruction set of the computer may be such that it is much more efficient to find a string of 0's than a string of 1's. Or it may be the other way around. These would be the only considerations that would make it important whether a "1" bit meant a free block or a block in use. An example of a bitmap used for free space tracking is seen in Figure 12.12.

Notice that using a bitmap to keep track of the available free space costs us more memory than does the linked list mechanism. We need to keep in memory a portion of the bitmap. Most likely we will keep an entire block because it will be easier to read it that way. With the linked list we only kept one pointer—maybe a few more if we were preallocating the blocks. However, the cost of memory is already very low now and is continually declining so this is probably not a significant factor. We do need to update the disk copy of the bitmap as we allocate the blocks. But we can still use the preallocation technique discussed with the linked list tracking mechanism. It is very important that we update the map before we actually begin to use the space. If we don't then we run the risk of having a block allocated to more than one file. This does not work well.

Not only does the bitmap take more RAM space, it also takes more disk space. The bitmap has to be in a dedicated spot on the disk. That location cannot be used for data storage. In the linked list mechanism the pointers were stored in the free blocks themselves. Once again, however, disk space is relatively inexpensive and the price is constantly declining, so this is also probably not a significant factor today, though it certainly was at one time.

There is one more common mechanism for tracking free space, but it is a byproduct of the mechanism used to link the blocks of the file together in the FAT structure, so we will discuss it under that heading.

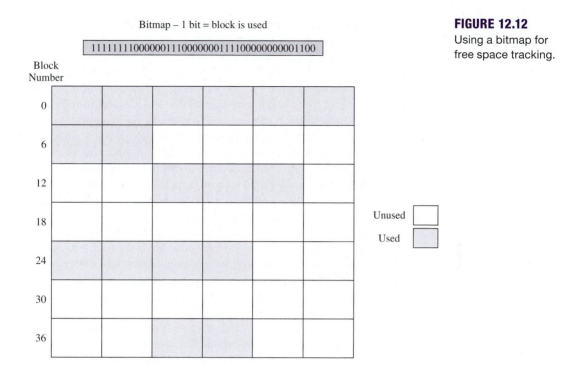

Bitmap – 1 bit = block is used

1111111100000011100000001111000000000001100

Block Number

FIGURE 12.12
Using a bitmap for free space tracking.

Unused

Used

12.5 FILE ALLOCATION

The other major design decision about file systems is how the files themselves should be organized on the disk drive. The abstraction(s) that the OS presents to the user through the API will partly determine the types of organization that the OS can use. There are basically three mechanisms for allocating the space to a file. These are contiguous, linked, and indexed mechanisms. Note that it is not necessary that an OS use only one of these mechanisms. Some OSs support multiple types of file allocation. All that is necessary are to have APIs that support both types of allocation requests and to keep track of the free space correctly.

12.5.1 Contiguous allocation

Contiguous allocation means that the blocks allocated to a file have numbers in a sequence strictly increasing by 1. For example, in Figure 12.13, we see File B occupying contiguous blocks 1000–1799. Such blocks do not necessarily start on a track boundary. They are merely adjacent in the numbering scheme. This method of file space allocation has some distinct advantages. For one thing, very little information is needed to find all of the data. All that is required are the sector address of the first block and the length of the file in blocks. This allocation method makes random access to the data very simple. The exact mechanism varies depending on the OS API and the block size being allocated. With some OSs, for example, the API requires that the application pass a byte number of an offset in the file at which the read is to start and a length of data to read—normally a multiple of the sector size. In this case the access method merely divides the byte offset by the block size and adds it to the starting sector address of the first block in the file. Sequential access is trivial, of course. As was mentioned above, if the space tracking mechanism is a bitmap, then allocating contiguous space is fairly trivial. All that is necessary is to find a contiguous string of bits in the bitmap that indicate free blocks. With a linked list free space tracking mechanism it would be highly impractical, though not technically impossible. The grouping mechanism we described might help somewhat in this regard.

One problem with contiguous allocation is that once a file has been allocated it can be difficult to make it any larger because it is likely that some other file will be allocated right after the file we want to make larger. For example, in Figure 12.13, File A could not be made larger without moving File B. In order to avoid this problem, programmers will tend to allocate more storage for the file than is currently required by the data. That way, the file can grow for some time before it needs to be made larger. For example, the programmer might know that the system now has 100 records and typically will add another two records per month. The file is then allocated with space for 130 records and can operate for somewhat more than 2 years without filling up and needing to be reallocated. We call this **programmer fragmentation.** Unfortunately, this is wasteful of storage. If there is sufficient free space on the disk drive to allocate another copy of the file, then the operation is fairly simple, but it can be time-consuming if the file is large. If there is not sufficient space for the new copy, then the file must be unloaded to a tertiary storage device, the old file deleted, other files moved around to make enough contiguous space for the new file, the new file allocated, and the data loaded into the new file.

The awkwardness of this procedure led to a variation on the contiguous allocation mechanism—the use of **extents.** In this scheme a file is not limited to a single contiguous allocation. The initial allocation is a contiguous block, but if it fills up, instead of making a new copy, a secondary allocation is made, not necessarily contiguous to the initial allocation. This secondary extent is also contiguous, but is typically smaller than the initial (primary) allocation. Additional secondary extents can be allocated, usually

FIGURE 12.13

Contiguous file allocation.

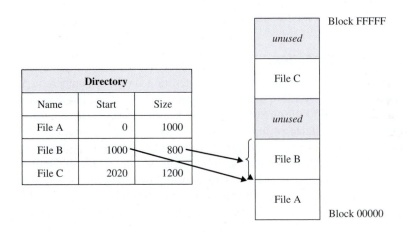

up to some small limit—16 or so. The calculation of random file addresses is now a bit more complicated. With a single contiguous file we took the record or byte offset and calculated a displacement from the front of the file. Now we need to have a table of starting logical and physical addresses and sizes for the various extents. We calculate the offset and then we look at the table. We find the extent that contains the offset and then we calculate the offset from the start of that extent. This is still fairly trivial compared to the speed of a hard drive. Extents are not a particularly new scheme, having been used, for example, at least as far back as OS/360 by IBM in the late 1960s.

There are several instances of waste in the contiguous allocation scheme. The first instance is caused by the fact that the smallest portion of the space that we can access is a sector. We usually compound that problem by tracking the allocation in blocks rather than in sectors. So, we might be allocating blocks of four sectors, but in most cases we will not need all of that allocation. Sometimes we will fill up the last block exactly, but sometimes we will only need one byte of the last block. On average we will use only half of it. This unused space caused by the allocation granularity is called **internal fragmentation.** We had exactly the same problem in Chapter 10 in which we discussed primary memory allocation. Unless we have very many files that are very short, internal fragmentation on disk drives is not usually of much consequence given the size and cost of disk drives today.

Of greater consequence is the problem of **external fragmentation.** Again, this problem was discussed in Chapter 10 on primary memory management. The problem arises when we come near to filling up the disk. As we allocate and free contiguous files we will tend to chop up the free space because we keep taking a contiguous free space out of bigger free spaces. Eventually, the leftover holes become too small for the next allocation we want to make, even though there is sufficient free space for the allocation. In Figure 12.13, for example, based on the sizes shown, we probably have space for about 2,000 blocks, but the space is broken into two pieces, so we could not allocate a file that big, even though we have enough free space to do it. The solution to the problem is somewhat ugly. It is known as **defragmentation.** The basic idea is to move some of the files into holes where they will fit, leaving larger holes for the files we want to allocate. The technique was described more fully in Chapter 10, so we will not rehash it here. The third sort of "fragmentation" is the **programmer fragmentation** we discussed where the programmer allocates more space to the file than is really needed. This, however, is more of a social problem than a technical problem, but it comes about because of the difficulty of making a contiguous file bigger, so it needs to be mentioned.

12.5.2 Linked allocation

The second common file allocation mechanism is a linked list. This mechanism is just like a linked list structure in primary memory, but here the linked elements are always the same size—one disk block. Each block will contain the starting sector address of the next block in the file. So, one downside of the linked mechanism is that a part of each block is spent on this link. In the worst case we have a single sector of probably 512 bytes with a pointer of probably 4 bytes, so the waste is less than 1%. If the blocks are bigger than one sector, then the overhead is even less. Figure 12.14 shows such a structure.

Block
Number

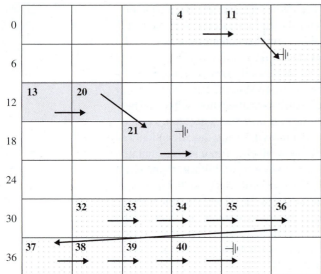

Directory			
Name	**Start**	**Size**	**End**
File A	12	4	21
File B	3	3	11
File C	31	10	40

FIGURE 12.14 A linked list file allocation method.

There is another downside to the linked list allocation mechanism: it is somewhat difficult to do random access methods on such files. It is not impossible, however. Consider the files shown in Figure 12.13. All that would be necessary to provide random access to this file is to enlarge on the idea of the extents discussed in the section on contiguous allocation. We merely need a table in RAM that contains a pointer to the start of each disk block allocated to the file. Though this table might be large in the case of a very long file, and it could take some time to follow the entire chain to build the table, it is probably a practical mechanism in most cases. If the file is not going to be open for very long, then the space and time required to build and store the table might be too expensive. If there is going to be a good deal of random access on the file and the file is not too big, then it would be practical. In addition, we would not necessarily need to follow the entire chain when the file was first opened. We might follow the chain and fill in the table only as references to records caused us to need to access a part of the file where we had not yet read the pointers.

In Figure 12.14, we see a directory entry that describes a linked file. It contains a pointer to the first block of the file and the length of the file in blocks. It also contains a pointer to the last block of the list. On first examination it might not seem necessary to store the pointer to the end of the file, and actually it isn't, because we could always follow the pointers in the list to find the end, but it is there for two practical reasons. The first is that sometimes we want to open the file in an "append" mode—we just want to add to the end of the file. Log files are a good example of such action. It will always be faster to be able to go directly to the end of the list. The second reason has to do with redundancy. It is always good to have some redundancy in the file system metadata. Then *when* problems arise, the utility programs that we will run to repair the file system have a better indication of what might be the correct course of action.

On the good side, with linked files we will have no programmer fragmentation. Since it is trivial to extend a linked file, there is no pressure to overallocate the initial file space.

In the section on contiguous file allocation we discussed the need for space compression when there was sufficient free space available to satisfy an allocation request but the available space was not contiguous. We mentioned that **defragmentation** was a name sometimes used for this process. Perhaps somewhat surprisingly, linked files also suffer from a related structural problem, and the defragmentation term is probably better applied to this problem. A linked file structure can be viewed as an extreme case of a structure using contiguous extents, where the extents are a single block long. The problem that happens with linked files is that as the file grows, the "next available" block can be anywhere on the disk. As a result, the linked list can tend to bounce back and forth on the disk, depending on which block was available when the file was lengthened. An example of such extreme allocation is shown in Figure 12.15. Processing such a file with a program that is doing much I/O and very little processing can be very costly. Rearranging all the files so that the blocks allocated to each file are in order and are contiguous is known as defragmentation. It can significantly speed up the processing of the files. As was mentioned earlier, some systems support both contiguous file allocation and linked allocation. Many modern OSs support

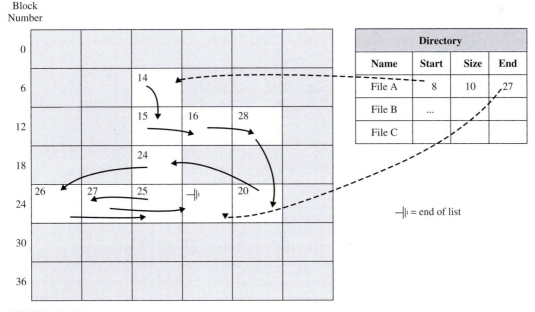

FIGURE 12.15 A fragmented file.

both types, and the result is that they have both the external fragmentation problem and the random chain problem. In such systems defragmentation can assist with both problems.

12.5.3 Indexed allocation

Just as there is an indexed method for keeping track of the free space, there is a similar mechanism for keeping track of the structure of a file. In the simplest terms, the indexed file structure is somewhat like a linked list except that we allocate a separate index block to hold the pointers rather than placing the pointers in each data block. Figure 12.16 shows a number of blocks in a file that are pointed to by an index block rather than being individually chained. As with the indexed free space tracking mechanism, in the simplest implementation we are limited to a single index block. This restriction will limit the file size, since the blocks are a fixed size and therefore the index can only hold pointers to a maximum number of blocks. There are two ways we can expand this mechanism to remove this limit. We can use multiple levels of indexes, similar to the way we did with RAM page tables, or we can link the index blocks themselves into a list.

Multilevel indexes

With multilevel indexes we will again use one block to contain pointers, much as with the simple index structure. But in this case the first index block will not contain pointers to data blocks. Instead, it will contain pointers to second-level index blocks.

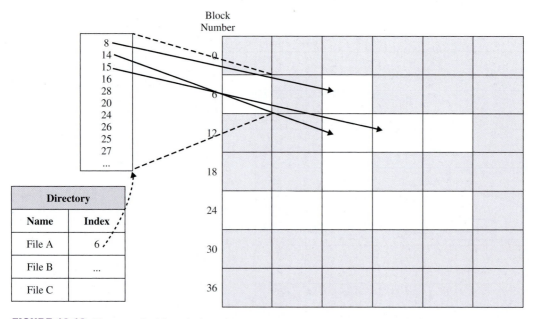

FIGURE 12.16 File stored with an indexed structure.

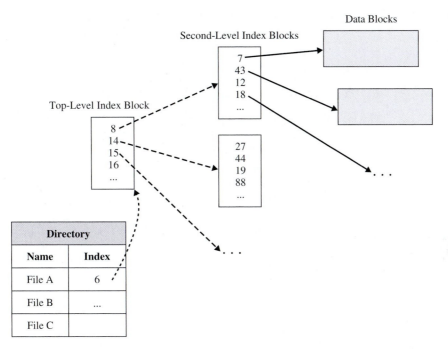

FIGURE 12.17
A multilevel indexed file.

With a two-layer index structure those index blocks will contain pointers to data blocks. If an index block contained 100 pointers, then when we introduced a two-layer structure we would multiply that by 100. We would then be able to address a file containing 10,000 blocks. If this was not sufficient we could introduce another layer of indexes, each time multiplying the original space by 100. The next level would allow for 1 million blocks. Notice that we do not necessarily need to read the entire set of index blocks into memory when the file is first opened. We can wait until the application tries to access the portion of the file covered by an index to read it. This is especially useful for very large files opened and read briefly—for example, looking up a word in a dictionary. Figure 12.17 shows a multilevel indexed file organization.

Linked index block lists

As with free space linked lists, we can simply link index blocks together in a chain. Each index block will thus contain one fewer pointers to data blocks because we need one pointer to access the next index block, but this is unlikely to be a significant factor for most block and disk sizes. Figure 12.18 shows a file organized with a linked index structure. If a file is being accessed randomly, then this mechanism will require that we follow the linked chain when the file is opened and read the index blocks into main memory. Of course, we can postpone reading all the blocks until we need them. If the file is being accessed sequentially we can just read each index block when we are nearing the last pointer in the previous block.

FIGURE 12.18

A linked indexed file.

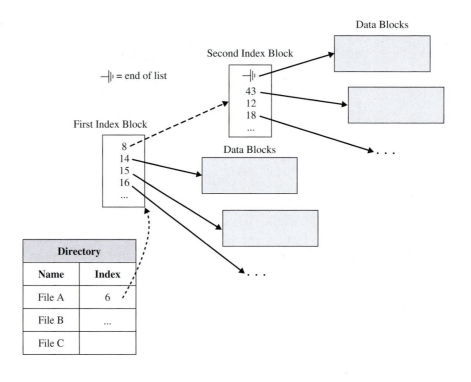

12.6 SUMMARY

Files are an important abstraction for an OS to provide. Files were in use long before there were computers, so they are something everyone knows about. Programmers do not want to think about hardware; they want to think about a collection of data. In a computer system that collection is a file. In this chapter we discussed the nature of file systems. We then introduced the idea of OS file systems. Modern computer systems have many files. It needs to be possible to organize the files so that we can find things. We discussed directories in file systems. Different applications need different methods of accessing data, so we described various methods that applications can be offered for accessing the data in files. File systems need to keep track of what parts of the total space is currently free. We explored different structures used to track that space. We then presented the topic of the structure of the files themselves and discussed the tradeoffs of the various methods.

In the next chapter we are covering a few case studies of file systems in well-known OSs and a few other miscellaneous topics about OS file systems.

BIBLIOGRAPHY

Beck, M., et al., *Linux Kernel Programming,* 3rd ed., Reading, MA: Addison-Wesley, 2002.

Bovet, D. P., and M. Cesate, *Understanding the Linux Kernel,* 2nd ed., Sebastopol, CA: O'Reilly & Associates, Inc., 2003.

Golden, D., and M. Pechura, "The Structure of Microcomputer File Systems," *Communications of the ACM,* Vol. 29, No. 3, March 1986, pp. 222–230.

Koch, P. D. L., "Disk File Allocation Based on the Buddy System," *ACM Transactions on Computer Systems,* Vol. 5, No. 4, November 1987, pp. 352–370.

Larson, P., and A. Kajla, "File Organization: Implementation of a Method Guaranteeing Retrieval in One Access," *Communications of the ACM,* Vol. 27, No. 7, July 1984, pp. 670–677.

Livadas, P. E., *File Structures, Theory and Practice.* Englewood Cliffs, NJ: Prentice Hall, 1990.

McKusick, M. K., W. N. Joy, S. J. Leffler, and R. S. Fabry, "A Fast File System for UNIX," *ACM Transactions on Computer Systems,* Vol. 2, No. 3, August 1984, pp. 181–197.

Nelson, M. N., B. B. Welch, and J. K. Ousterhout, "Caching in the Sprite Network File System," *ACM Transactions on Computer Systems,* Vol. 6, No. 1, February 1988, pp. 134–154.

Organick, E. I., *The Multics System: An Examination of Its Structure.* Cambridge, MA: MIT Press, 1972.

Rosenblum, M., and J. K. Ousterhout, "The Design and Implementation of a Log-Structured File System," *ACM Transactions on Computer Systems,* Vol. 10, No. 1, 1992, pp. 26–52.

Russinovich, M. E., and D. A. Solomon, *Microsoft Windows Internals,* 4th ed., Redmond, WA: Microsoft Press, 2005.

WEB RESOURCE

http://developer.apple.com/documentation/Performance/Conceptual/FileSystem/Articles/MacOSXAndFiles.html

http://labs.google.com/papers/gfs.html (the Google File System)

http://www.linux.org

http://pages.prodigy.net/michaln/history/ (OS/2 history)

http://technet.microsoft.com/en-us/sysinternals/default.aspx (Sysinternals originally an outside technical reference, later bought by Microsoft)

http://en.wikipedia.org/wiki/File_system

http://en.wikipedia.org/wiki/CP/M

REVIEW QUESTIONS

12.1 We mentioned several items that might be in a file directory. Some are fairly rare. What few items are most likely in every OS directory structure?

12.2 What is the main problem with single-level directory structures for today's systems?

12.3 Since hierarchical directory structures allow for the existence of multiple files with the same name, how do we have to refer to them to uniquely specify them?

12.4 What kind of problem motivates the use of aliases?

12.5 How are directories organized internally to optimize searching time?

12.6 Why does an OS typically provide special calls for accessing directory entries?

12.7 What is the effect of the working directory on a command such as erase <filename>?

12.8 If a file is being processed via a sequential access method, what happens to the current record pointer on a read?

12.9 True or false? An application using random access can't just ask the OS for the next record. It must always specify the record number.

12.10 True or false? For indexed sequential access, the primary key field must contain unique key values for each record.

12.11 What services does raw access provide?

12.12 What are the two BASIC mechanisms for free space tracking in file systems?

12.13 There are two broad "improvements" to one of our free space tracking mechanisms, and one of those improvements had a variant as well. These improvements were aimed at mitigating a significant performance issue associated with one of those tracking mechanisms. Which mechanism was this and what was the issue that we were concerned about?

12.14 The variant mentioned in the previous question was a technique that could also be applied in other free space mechanisms and their improvements. What was that technique?

12.15 What are the three basic mechanisms for file space allocation in file systems?

12.16 One of the file space allocation mechanisms is the most convenient for random access files. Which mechanism is that?

12.17 That same allocation mechanism makes it difficult to increase the size of files. This problem caused a secondary problem. What was the secondary problem?

12.18 That same allocation mechanism makes it difficult to increase the size of files. We described a variation on that basic mechanism that would allow the size to be increased. What was the variation?

12.19 What is internal fragmentation and why is it no longer much of a problem in most cases?

12.20 What is external fragmentation and why is it a bigger problem than internal fragmentation for some systems?

12.21 We referred to a problem of "programmer fragmentation" and said that one of the file allocation mechanisms did not have this problem. Which mechanism and why not?

12.22 That same mechanism has a serious drawback. What is it?

12.23 Briefly describe what defragmentation does for linked files.

12.24 The simplest indexed file allocation method limits the size of files because of the limited number of pointers that can be stored in a single index block. What two mechanisms were discussed for extending this limit?

12.25 Which of those mechanisms would probably work better for random file access?

Chapter 13

File Systems—Examples and More Features

In this chapter:

13.1 INTRODUCTION

In Chapter 12 we introduced the concept of file systems and how they fit in an OS. We covered many possible alternative mechanisms for storing the files and tracking free space. Designers of real file systems have to make choices about the mechanisms they will include. We will see that modern OSs use all of the techniques we have described, but none of them uses these techniques in exactly the ways we have described.

In Section 13.2 we take a look at several case studies of how modern OS file systems have been designed. We then discuss several other topics related to file systems and file processing. This begins in Section 13.3, where we address the concept of mounting a file system and making the information therein available to the applications. We continue with special topics in Section 13.4 on the reasons behind virtual file systems and related concepts and in Section 13.5 on the purpose of memory mapped files. OSs typically provide a number of utility programs to make standard manipulations of file system information. Section 13.6 addresses some of these utility programs. Section 13.7 discusses the important concept of transactional or log-based file system techniques, which make for more reliable file systems. We conclude with a chapter summary in Section 13.8.

13.2 CASE STUDIES

Often, real OSs use some combination of the basic techniques described in Chapter 12. We have already mentioned, for example, that some OSs allow both contiguous file allocation and chained file allocation. In the following sections we look a little more closely at some modern file systems and how they are implemented.

13.2.1 FAT

The first file system we look at more closely is a modification of a linked system. Instead of having each data block contain the pointer to the next data block, those pointers will be stored in a separate table. This system was used in the original Microsoft DOS and is known by the name given to the area used to store this table, the **file allocation table,** or **FAT.** In this case the FAT is not kept in the area that would be used for data storage. It is in a separate area of the disk just after the boot block. This table will contain space for one disk pointer for each block in the data area. If a block is not allocated to a file, then this pointer will be zero. If this block is a part of a file, then this pointer will normally contain the pointer to the next block in the file. If this block is the last one in the file, then it will contain a special pointer value that indicates that it is the end of the list. Figure 13.1 shows how a FAT might look with two files in it. We have indicated the end of file mark as FFFFFFFF.

There are some very interesting things to notice about the FAT mechanism. First, there is no separate mechanism to keep track of free space. The free space blocks have a zero pointer in the FAT. Second, it is very easy to allocate contiguous space for a file. Just as with a bitmap free space mechanism, all that is necessary to find a contiguous group of free blocks is to scan the FAT and find a contiguous string of zero pointers. It is also easy to allocate single sectors to support allocation of single blocks for chained file access.

The original FAT file system design was created for floppy disk drives, so the pointers were quite small. It later came to be called the FAT12 file system. It was used on early small hard disks, but the disks quickly grew so large that even allocating large blocks instead of individual sectors could not cover the entire space. So a new file system was designed that was much like FAT12 but used bigger pointers. This system was called the FAT16 file system. This was a fairly reasonable size to base a file system design around because the computers of that era had a 16-bit word size. This size was still fairly limiting and the FAT16 design was later replaced by the FAT32 system. A summary of these three file systems is given in Table 13.1.

13.2.2 NTFS

NTFS is the native file system for the Windows NT family. It is a variation on a two-level indexed structure. NTFS uses a **master file table** (**MFT**) to store all the metadata about files and directories. In the MFT it creates a **file record** for each file and a **folder record** for each folder, even for the MFT itself. These records are 1 KB

Directory		
Name	Start	End
File A	8	27
File M	0	3
File C	...	...

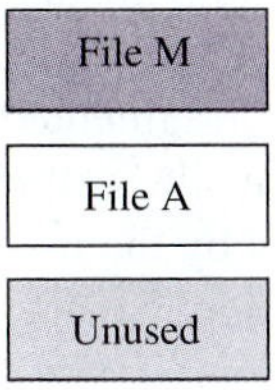

0	1
1	2
2	3
3	FFFFFFFF
4	0
5	0
6	0
7	0
8	14
9	0
10	0
11	0
12	0
13	0
14	15
15	16
16	28
17	0
18	0
19	0
20	24
21	0
22	0
23	0
24	26
25	27
26	25
27	FFFFFFFF
28	20
29	0

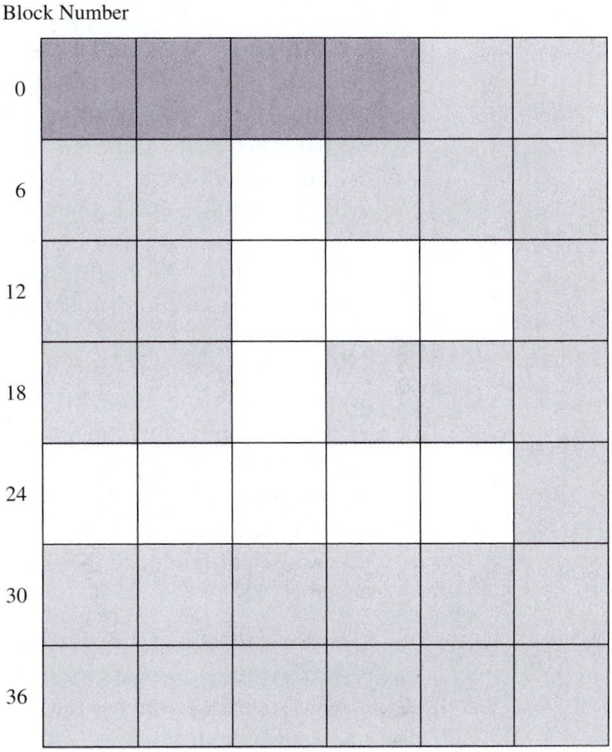

File M

File A

Unused

Block Number

FIGURE 13.1 A file in a FAT file system.

TABLE 13.1   Comparison of Various FAT File Systems

Attribute	FAT12	FAT16	FAT32
Used for	Floppies and very small hard drives	Small to midsize hard drives	Medium to very large hard drives
Size of each FAT entry	12 bits	16 bits	28 bits
Maximum number of clusters	4,096	65,526	> 260,000,000
Block size used	0.5 KB to 4 KB	2 KB to 32 KB	4 KB to 32 KB
Maximum volume size in bytes	16,736,256	2,147,133,200	About 2^{41}

FIGURE 13.2

NTFS MFT record for
small file or directory.

Standard Information	File or Directory Name	Data or Index	Unused Space

each[1] and they include all the attributes of the file. NT considers the data in a file or a directory to be one of the attributes for the file. If all of the attributes fit in the MFT record, then no separate space is allocated. This means that a small file or directory (about 900 bytes) will be stored entirely within the MFT record. Figure 13.2 shows an MFT record for a small file or folder. If the data attribute does not fit into the MFT record, then one or more blocks will be allocated to hold the data and an index to the blocks will be built in the MFT record. Each file typically has only one MFT file record. However, if a file has many attributes or is very fragmented it might need more than one record. In this case the first record for the file, called the base file record, stores the location of the other file records required by the file.

Folder (or directory) records contain index information. Small folder records reside entirely within the MFT structure, while large directories are organized into B-tree structures with pointers to external clusters that contain directory entries that cannot be contained within the MFT structure. The benefit of B-tree structures is evident when NTFS holds files in a very large folder. The B-tree structure groups similar file names into a block so that it need search only the group that contains the file. This will minimize the disk accesses needed to find a file. Some other points about NTFS:

- It uses a bitmap to track free space.
- It supports variable block (cluster) sizes in the later releases.
- It supports compression of the entire file system, directories, subtrees, or individual files.
- It supports file encryption of the entire file system, directories, subtrees, or individual files.
- It supports software RAID 1 and RAID 5 (see Chapter 14, Section 14.6).
- It maintains a separate map of bad clusters that it will not use.
- It will not write to disk (large) portions of a file that contain only binary zeroes (nulls).
- It is a transactional (log-based) file system (see Section 13.7).

13.2.3 UNIX and Linux

UNIX and many UNIX derivatives such as Linux support many different file systems, but the ext file system is fairly standard. It uses a version of a multilevel index scheme to hold the metadata about a file. This data is stored in a table on the disk called an **inode.** Each entry in a UNIX directory contains only the name of the item, and a numerical reference to the location of the item. The reference is called an **i-number** or **inode number,** and is an index to a table known as the **i-list.** Details

---

[1]The details of the NTFS system are actually proprietary. The figures used here are generally accepted, but might not always be exactly right.

of the i-list location and format and the contents of the inodes depend somewhat on the specific variant and version of UNIX, but typical inode information is shown in Table 13.2. Of interest here is what is and what is not in the inode. One thing that is not in the inode is the file name. UNIX allows files to have aliases, meaning that more than one directory entry can point to the same file. Among other things, there is no requirement that different references to the file use the same name. Therefore, the file name is stored in the directory and the directory entry points to the inode for all other metadata about the file. One of the entries in the inode is the number of directory entries that point to this file. When a directory entry is deleted for a file, the count of the references will be decremented, but the file itself will not be deleted until the reference count goes to zero.

The UNIX file system inode structure is a hybrid variation of an indexed structure. There are a number of pointers that point directly to data blocks. That number varies, but is typically 10–13. The inode is brought into primary memory when the file is opened, so if the file is fairly small, then the pointers to the first few blocks are already available. If the file is large enough that it requires more blocks than can be pointed to by these direct pointers, then the next pointer is a pointer to a single index block. If the system is using 4 KB blocks, then this block might contain 1,024 pointers to additional blocks. If all of this space is used up, then the next entry is to a double index block. This index block will contain pointers not to data blocks, but to other index blocks. So this index block will address 1,024 index blocks, which will altogether address over 1 million data blocks. If that is not enough, the next entry in the inode is a pointer to a triple index block structure. Using the 4 KB blocks described, this structure can address over 4 Terabytes of file space.

TABLE 13.2   Typical UNIX inode Contents

File type
Access permissions—read, write, etc.
Count of directories that reference the file
Owner
Group (owner)
Date and time created
Date and time last accessed
Date and time last modified
Size
Data block pointer 1
Data block pointer 2
. . .
Data block pointer 10 (sometimes 13)
Single index block pointer
Double index block pointer
Triple index block pointer

When a UNIX file system is initialized, the i-list is built to be a size appropriate for the size of the disk partition and the block size used. A number of empty inodes will be created and distributed evenly across the partition. As blocks are allocated to a file they will be selected from those available that are close to the inode. This process helps to keep all the blocks allocated to a file near each other. As long as other processes are not accessing too many other files on other parts of the drive, this will have the effect of minimizing the seek time required to access the file.

13.3 MOUNTING

Sometimes we have to deal with computer science terms that have multiple meanings, known as overloading. One such term is **mounting.** Actually, the two meanings for this term are related, but at first glance they appear to refer to different operations. The first meaning concerns what must be done when a disk drive partition containing a file system is going to be accessed by the OS. The second meaning refers to a process used to give a user a means of specifying files on a remote directory.

13.3.1 Local file system mounting

Before an OS can allow a user to access a particular file system, it will need to do certain things. The metadata that describes the partition must be read, some part of the free space mechanism must be read into RAM—perhaps some blocks preallocated, the directory that represents the root of the directory tree must be read in, and so on. This process is called mounting. When the OS is installed there will be some partitions that it is told to access, and normally those partitions will be mounted whenever the OS is booted. These partitions are normally the ones that are on local hard drives. There are differences between OSs, however, with respect to removable media, OSs treat them in one of three ways: (1) implicit mount when the media is inserted in the drive, (2) implicit mount when the media is first accessed, or (3) explicit mount command must be given.

UNIX and most of its variants have traditionally used the last mechanism. Until the user gives a specific mount command the removable medium cannot be accessed. Since floppy disks formatted for MS-DOS were so pervasive, this actually had a good side effect since it allowed the user to specify which file system format a floppy disk contained: UNIX, MS-DOS, or Mac. Later versions of Linux and UNIX have begun experimenting with implicit mounting when the media is inserted. The term used for this is **automounting.** MS-DOS and the Windows products have always used implicit mounting when an attempt is first made to access the media. Historically the Mac OS automatically mounted a removable media whenever it was inserted into the drive. Since Mac OS X is based on UNIX, it now mounts as UNIX does.

A different situation exists in the area of CDs. Fairly early in the days of CD development a large number of vendors convened and decided on a common format for data and audio CDs. This format ultimately was designated an international standard, ISO-9660. This common format means that there is no reason to postpone the mounting as was done with UNIX, so CDs are normally mounted immediately on insertion. This allows the OS to detect the format of the CD (i.e., audio, data, or mixed) and to have a default option to execute when such a CD is inserted. This means that if a user so chooses, inserting an audio CD will launch a CD audio player application of the user's choice to play the CD. Similarly, a data CD can contain instructions on what is to be done with the CD on common OSs. Many will automatically run a script file that depends on the OS to start the software on the CD.

13.3.2 Mounting remote file systems

A similar process must also take place when an OS is requested to provide access to a file system on a remote computer, but the details are vastly different. The remote file system might be an entire file system that is made available to users, but more likely it is some portion of a file system rather than the whole thing. A large difficulty that must be overcome is that the platform that the remote file system is running on may be entirely different from the local file system. Data representation may be different, file naming conventions may be different, directory structures may be different, and so forth. In order to overcome these differences we have to have well-established rules about how the information is to be presented and the protocols to be used for exchanging the information. In most cases the rules and protocols are de facto rules that are established by one platform vendor to allow their systems to interoperate. Other vendors will create packages to access these systems from other platforms. Sometimes these rules become open standards, as with **network file system** (**NFS;** see Section 13.4.2), and sometimes they are reverse engineered by other vendors. Whatever the case, the remote system will do the accessing of the directories but the information must be mapped into the context of the client OS. For example, if the client is a Windows system, then the metaphor of the remote file system is that of a "drive letter." Initially, these letters were used in DOS to indicate real drives on a system. Remote file systems use the same convention, assigning any drive letter that is not used for a local resource. In contrast, UNIX sees all file systems as a tree structure, including pseudo-directories like proc and dev. So mapping a remote file system in UNIX-like systems simply involves adding (or replacing) a directory node in the file system tree structure with a node that identifies itself as pointing to a remote resource.

From a programmer's point of view, remote mounting of file systems is a powerful tool. Generally speaking, the program is not aware of any difference between a local file and a remote file. Without making any modifications to programs at all they are capable of operating over a network. Unfortunately, this is not always a wise thing to do. Consider the case of a database software program accessing a database file that is remotely mounted across a network. When searching the indexes for data, the database program will end up reading and writing large amounts of data across the network. In a fast LAN with light traffic the performance might be acceptable, but if the connection is a WAN or there is considerable network traffic, then it might not be a good idea. In this case it would be far better to run the database program on the remote machine and send SQL commands across the network, getting back only the final answers. Even better would be to use commands previously stored on the remote server. Of course, it is not always possible to anticipate all queries so they can be stored in advance on the server. Sometimes ad hoc queries are necessary.

Letting a node in a file system become a reference to a remote file system causes a slight problem. Path names now become more difficult to parse. Without these remote reference nodes in the file system tree, parsing a path name was fairly simple. Given a path like /fred/work/expenses, as the OS parsed down the string, each "/" represented a move to another directory in the local file system. But with nodes possibly representing remote file systems in the tree, the file system must check at each level to see whether the node was a local directory or a remote file system and perform the appropriate lookup.

Another problem with remote mounting is that two different clients may mount a given remote directory at different points in their local file system. In Windows systems two users might assign the same remote file system to a different drive letter. In UNIX-like systems they might mount the same remote file system at a different logical node in their local file system. Then if a process on one user's machine passed a path name to a process on the other user's machine the second machine would not be able to find the file because the path is different. Administrators can mitigate this problem by defining standardized mounting scripts that run at user login time and provide more consistent path naming for all users for commonly accessed resources.

13.4 MULTIPLE FILE SYSTEMS AND REDIRECTION

As in many other instances, an OS will present to the API an abstraction of a file. The program should not be aware of what the file system is like. There are likely to be performance differences if the wrong file system is used for an application, but the coding of the application should not be affected. That is really a system engineering issue. If the application is designed for accessing a file randomly and the file system supports random access, then the application should be unaware of any other differences. In most systems it will be necessary for the OS to support several different file systems. If for no other reason, it is necessary because different file systems are best suited for different media. For CDs there is normally only ISO-9660 to consider, although a few very early CDs were created in proprietary formats. For floppy disks it is almost a given that the OS will need to be able to read and write FAT12 floppy formatted disks derived from MS-DOS. But Mac and UNIX formats are widely used as well. Even with hard drives it will sometimes be desirable to support a format other than the native format of the OS. This often happens when a system is upgraded to a new OS or a new version of the same OS. Even if the OS is the same, the new version may have a new wonderful file system that comes with it. When the upgrade is first performed, however, the file system will still be the old format. Usually a separate step is then needed to convert the old file system format to the new format. Not infrequently a system needs to contain two different OSs and be booted into different ones depending on the current need. Today it is even becoming common to see a virtual OS running two different client OSs at the same time and supporting different file systems on different drives. It may still be desirable to access all of the file systems on the disc drives regardless of the OS currently in use. For all of these reasons OSs will need to support a number of different file system formats.

13.4.1 Virtual file systems

UNIX developers created a mechanism exactly for the purpose of transparently supporting multiple file systems on the same system at the same time. It is called the **virtual file system, or VFS.** VFS was a separate layer added to UNIX on top of the file system module. Actually, it was loaded in a system with multiple file system modules supporting different file systems. VFS supported the same API as the existing file systems so that applications would not have to change. Figure 13.3 shows the interface between applications and the file system both before (a) and after (b) VFS was introduced. When a request was passed to the VFS layer it would examine the request by looking at the nodes in the file system tree and determine which file system module was the correct module for this file system. It would then pass the request to that module. When the file system module was finished with the request it would return control to the VFS module, which would then return control to the application that had called it.

13.4.2 Network file system

VFS was also used to redirect file system requests to remotely mounted drives using the NFS protocol developed by Sun Microsystems. This process was alluded to under the topic of remote mounting earlier. Figure 13.4 shows how this mechanism works. The client system is shown on the top of the figure. The application makes file requests through the standard file API. The VFS system realizes that this is a request for access to an NFS file that is being served on another system. That system is the NFS server shown at the bottom of the figure. The VFS layer on the client machine therefore sends the request to the NFS client system. It uses a remote procedure call mechanism to solve the problems of heterogeneous OS environments. This is discussed further in Chapter 17. The client system sends the request across the network to the NFS daemon that is running in the NFS server system. The NFS daemon takes the request and sends it to the VFS layer on the server system. The file

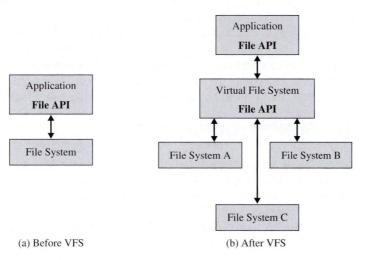

FIGURE 13.3
Introducing the VFS layer.

(a) Before VFS   (b) After VFS

FIGURE 13.4
NFS through VFS.

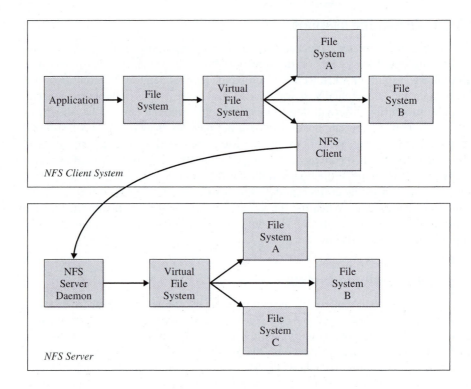

is accessed as requested as though the client were local, and the data are sent back to the application running on the client system.

The requests made by the application are redirected by the NFS client software to the system running the NFS server, so we say that the model being used is a **redirector.** This is a common technique, being used in other OSs as well. NFS is nearly completely transparent to a client application. But before the files can be accessed by the client application, the directories on the NFS server must be mounted so that the application can find the file. This step is not transparent, because the user (or the application) must designate the server. In UNIX-derivative OSs this is done with a mount command. The mount command will specify the name of the remote system and a directory on that system as well as a local directory. The remote directory will thereafter appear to be a part of the directory tree in the local file system and to all operations of any applications it will be transparent that these files are actually remote.

13.5 MEMORY MAPPED FILES

An alternative file access mechanism is found in many OSs, memory mapped files, discussed earlier in Chapter 11 on advanced memory techniques. This mechanism is very different from the standard metaphor of a file. Because it is so different it has some characteristics that make it very useful in certain situations. When an application process uses a memory mapped file it tells the OS the name of a file to map and the OS creates a byte-by-byte mapping of the addressing space for the file into the logical addressing space of the process. So the first interesting characteristic of a memory mapped file is that all of the mechanisms of the file system are not used to address the space. Instead, the application treats the memory mapped file as a large array and uses subscripting or pointer arithmetic to address the file. The virtual memory manager then keeps track of which portions of the file space are needed in physical memory, tracks changed pages, and writes them to the disk as required. These mechanisms use hardware support and are therefore much more efficient than the mechanisms of a file system. As you may recall, because of potential interactions with paging, normal file processing either locks pages into RAM and thereby inhibits the performance of the paging system or copies the I/O buffers into the kernel space before doing the I/O. Mapping the file onto the paging mechanism avoids these problems. Applications are also freed from having to do any memory allocation.

The second interesting characteristic of a memory mapped file is that multiple processes are allowed to memory map the same file at the same time. (Interestingly, because of the virtual memory hardware they do not have to map the file into the same logical memory address.) This creates a very efficient method for interprocess communication. In fact, the "file" does not actually have to exist. Both processes can name a temporary file purely for the purpose of interprocess communication. However, the memory mapped mechanism does not do any synchronization. If there is a possibility of conflicting operations being performed by multiple processes, then some external synchronization mechanism must be used to protect the critical sections of the processes. Another limit of the memory mapped file mechanism is that the mapped files cannot easily grow in size. It is sometimes possible, but requires careful remapping of the area. A third limitation is that there is no provision for doing asynchronous I/O. Since the paging hardware is doing the reading and writing transparently to the application, the I/O is blocking. When a page fault occurs the process will be blocked and will not be aware of it. One final precaution is that if the file is larger than the available logical addressing space, then the mapping must be carefully positioned over the file address space.

13.6 FILE SYSTEM UTILITIES

All OSs come with a handful of utility programs and included among these are always a group of programs for working with the file system. Some are designed to use while the OS is running. They include mundane things like making a new directory and deleting a file. These programs are often run from a command-line interface. Table 13.3 lists some common file system utility programs for DOS/Windows and UNIX-like systems. Later versions of most OSs use mostly a GUI interface and the commands do not have a name that most users are aware of. Note that some of the commands do not exist in all versions of DOS/Windows or in UNIX/Linux.

Those utilities are primarily things that a user decides to do. Other utilities are necessary as well that do things that may be important to the users but are not done to satisfy any real need of the user. Rather, they do things to the file system to confirm their integrity or improve the performance. Under DOS and Windows there were two verification utilities known as scandisk and checkdisk. UNIX-like systems

TABLE 13.3 **Some File Commands**

Purpose of Utility	DOS/Windows	UNIX/Linux
Change file permissions	attrib	chmod
Combine files	backup	tar
List files in a directory	dir	ls
Copy a file	copy	cp
Delete a file	del	rm
Delete a file system subtree	deltree	rm –R; rmdir
Edit a text file	edit	vi
Format	format	fdformat/ mkfs
Move or Rename a file	move/rename	mv
List a file	type	less
Change the working directory	cd	cd; chdir
View a file one page at a time	more	more
Create or edit disk partitions	Fdisk	cfdisk, parted, etc.
Make a new directory	md, mkdir	mkdir

have a similar utility known as fsck. Besides verifying the consistency and integrity of the file system, these utilities will optionally attempt to repair faults that they find. Windows also has a utility known as defrag, which reorganizes the files in a file system to improve the performance of the system. This problem was discussed earlier in the section on linked file allocation. The backers of UNIX-like systems claim that the designs of their file system preclude the need for defragmentation utilities. The fact that such utilities are not being marketed suggests that this claim is at least fairly accurate.

Some things that look like utilities are actually built-in commands in the OS command interface. For example, under DOS or Windows there are no executable files that execute the commands dir, del, time, type, and so on. These functions map very closely to supervisor calls in the OS API, so that the command interpreter (command .com in the DOS case) has these functions built-in and no external module is needed. This saves both disk space and time to load an external program into memory.

13.7 LOG-BASED FILE SYSTEMS

System failures are fairly rare, but they do happen. That is why those file system verification utilities were created. When an OS closes normally it will record an indication of a normal shutdown to the file system. When the OS boots it will check to see if the system was shut down normally or if it crashed. Traditionally, if the system had crashed, then before mounting the file system the OS will run the file system integrity checker. If a system that crashes is being used by only one individual, then the likelihood that anything was actually happening at the time of the failure will be low. Even in a fairly busy server there is not a high risk of loss. Any server failure is likely to cause problems for more people than a crash on a single-user system. Still, the single user would rather not lose anything in any circumstances. OS developers searched for a way to make file systems more resistant to failures.

When a block has been added to a file and the file is closed, then several things may have to happen. We will certainly have to write out records containing the data block. We may have to find the next free block, update the free space information to show this block was used, update any directory entry for the file to show the last time the file was written, and so on. We want all this information to be updated in an atomic fashion—either all of it should reach the hard disk or none of it should. In applications we call this **transaction processing.** OS file systems that operate in such a manner are called **log-based, log-structured, transactional,** or **journaling file systems.** In such systems, anytime metadata is to be updated, the system will first write a record to a log file that describes all the updates that are going to be made. Whenever the system starts it will check the log file to see if there was a transaction pending. If so, the system checks to see if all the steps of the transaction were successfully applied. If not, then the system will attempt to finish the transaction. If it can, then all is fine and we have dodged a bullet. If the transaction can't be finished for some reason, then the transaction will be aborted. We will have lost that last block of data that was to be written to the file, but the file system is safe from further corruption. Running with a file system with corrupt metadata would be disastrous.

Of course, nothing is free, and the price we pay for the security of a log-based file system is a performance hit. Since we take the time to write the transaction log every time before we write the metadata, we will see decreased performance in the system. Also, the transaction that is logged does not necessarily include the actual user data, though some OSs do include application data in the transactions. On the other hand, if a system has many files, then when it crashes we would have to do a complete file system scan to verify the integrity of the metadata before resuming system operation, and on a large server this could literally take hours. So it is normally preferable to slow the system response a bit in order to maintain integrity continuously. This is especially true in a single-user system where there is often lots of spare CPU and disk time for this task while the user is typing or thinking. As a result, most file systems developed in the last few years are transaction based. This includes JFS for OS/2, HFS Plus for the Mac OS, NTFS for the Windows NT family, and many systems for Linux, including Ext3, ReiserFS, XFS, and JFS.

13.8 SUMMARY

In Chapter 12 we covered the concepts of file systems and how they fit in an OS, including many possible alternative designs. Real-file systems reflect design choices about mechanisms included in them. We looked at several case studies of modern OS file systems. These brief overviews showed how some contemporary OSs use the mechanisms discussed in the earlier chapter. We then discussed other issues related to file systems, beginning with mounting a file system. We continued with special topics like the reasons behind virtual file systems and related concepts and the purpose of memory mapped files. We addressed some of the utility programs an OS must provide to manage file system information. We then covered the ideas behind transactional or log-based file techniques, which make more reliable file systems.

In the next chapter we cover the lower levels of the I/O system, primarily disk operation scheduling.

BIBLIOGRAPHY

Larson, P., and A. Kajla, "File Organization: Implementation of a Method Guaranteeing Retrieval in One Access," *Communications of the ACM,* Vol. 27, No. 7, July 1984, pp. 670–677.

McKusick, M. K., W. N. Joy, S. J. Leffler, and R. S. Fabry, "A Fast File System for UNIX," *ACM Transactions on Computer Systems,* Vol. 2, No. 3, August 1984, pp. 181–197.

Nelson, M. N., B. B. Welch, and J. K. Ousterhout, "Caching in the Sprite Network File System," *ACM Transactions on Computer Systems,* Vol. 6, No. 1, February 1988, pp. 134–154.

Organick, E. I., *The Multics System: An Examination of Its Structure.* Cambridge, MA: MIT Press, 1972.

Sandberg, R., et al., "Design and Implementation of the Sun Network File System," *Proceedings of the USENIX 1985 Summer Conference,* June 1985, pp. 119–130.

Sandberg, R., *The Sun Network File System: Design, Implementation and Experience.* Mountain View, CA: Sun Microsystems, Inc., 1987.

WEB RESOURCE

http://www.linux.org

http://technet.microsoft.com/en-us/sysinternals/default .aspx (Sysinternals, originally an outside technical reference, later bought by Microsoft)

http://en.wikipedia.org/wiki/CP/M

http://en.wikipedia.org/wiki/Virtual_file_system

http://www.yolinux.com/TUTORIALS/unix_for_dos_ users.html (A comprehensive comparison between DOS/Windows and UNIX/Linux commands)

REVIEW QUESTIONS

13.1 Why was the FAT12 system designed with such small pointers?

13.2 The FAT organizations do not require any separate mechanism for tracking free space. Why not?

13.3 In the Windows NTFS, the directory entry for a file might not contain a pointer to the data blocks for the file. Why not?

13.4 Why do UNIX/Linux i-nodes not contain a file name?

13.5 When does an OS mount the file system on a removable disk drive?

13.6 Why are CDs mounted differently than removable disk drives?

13.7 When a remote file system has been mounted by an OS, how does the remote file system appear to the user and to application programs?

13.8 The virtual file system layer was used to allow access to remote file systems. It had a more general purpose, however. What was the purpose?

13.9 Briefly describe why memory mapped files are more efficient than normal I/O.

13.10 Under the heading of File System Utilities we discussed some utility commands that do not exist as utilities on the system. Why do they not exist?

13.11 Briefly explain what it means to say that a file system is transactional or log based.

Chapter 14

Disk Scheduling and Input/Output Management

In this chapter:

14.1 INTRODUCTION

In the last chapter we looked at input and output from the way a user or an application programmer would look at it—what are the capabilities and services that the OS provides to the upper layers, what are the data structures needed to perform these services, and how are these functions performed? In this chapter we look in the lower layers to see how these things are done. In particular, the lowest layer of any file system is a collection of device drivers and interrupt handlers. In earlier chapters we discussed how I/O capabilities started with simple devices and structures and have progressed to more complex systems and services. We take a closer look at modern hardware and the OS organization necessary to manage these devices effectively and economically.

In Section 14.1 we introduce the topic of lower-level input and output management, with a special focus on secondary storage and disk drives. Next, in Section 14.2 we discuss some broad classes of I/O devices and how they differ. Section 14.3 describes some general techniques used in support of I/O devices. In Section 14.4, we then explore the physical structure of disk drives, and in Section 14.5 we discuss the logical organization of the information stored thereon. Section 14.6 covers the topic of

RAID, wherein assemblies of disks are used in special configurations to achieve greater throughput and/or reliability. The very important topic of scheduling disk operations for optimum performance is covered in Section 14.7. Section 14.8 is about a special type of device controller called a DMA controller that can significantly decrease the CPU load of I/O operations. This section also discusses some disk drive features that affect OS behavior. In Section 14.9 we conclude with a chapter summary.

14.2 DEVICE CHARACTERISTICS

There are some categories of input/output that broadly divide them into groups that are treated differently by OSs. We discuss a few of those categories.

14.2.1 Random access versus sequential access

In this chapter we are focused almost exclusively on secondary storage devices, specifically disk drives. At one time magnetic tapes were used for secondary storage on large mainframe computers. When personal computers were first developed they also often had tape drives as the only secondary storage devices—in this case it was a quarter-inch cassette tape drive that was originally developed for audio use. But tapes have the unfortunate characteristic that they can't be read randomly. To get to any particular piece of data on the tape you have to pass over all the other data between where the head is now and where it needs to be. Even on very fast tape drives this could take several minutes. Fortunately, disk drives don't have that characteristic. Because of this difference we speak of disk drives as being "random access" devices. However, as we will see when we later look at disk drives in more detail, this does not mean that the time to access the data is independent of the location of the data. This term is merely a reflection of the contrast with using a tape drive as the main secondary storage device.

14.2.2 Device classes

Most OSs broadly divide devices into three classes: block, character, and network. Each of those classes has substantially different characteristics and each class can be abstracted in a meaningful way. Table 14.1 gives some information about these classes.

TABLE 14.1   **Characteristics of Linux Device Classes**

	Block	**Character**	**Network**
Random access	Yes	No	No
Seek backward	Yes	No	No
Transfer unit	Block ($\times$ 512)	Character	Packet
Software	File System/Raw	Device	Protocol

Block devices

A block device is read or written one block (a group of bytes, usually a multiple of 512) at a time. Such devices include all sorts of disk drives and tape drives, for example. The size of a block is determined partly by the hardware, since disk controllers can only read or write whole disk sectors, but also by the system administrator when the file system is set up. Normally, the block size will be some small multiple of the physical sector size—typically 4 or 8 KB. These devices often support random access directly to any block on the device, that is to say that blocks may be read or written in any order. File systems typically reside on block devices and are the normal mechanism for accessing these devices. There are caching mechanisms in place for random access block structured devices. Sequential access block devices use double buffering, as explained later. Occasionally, some software needs to access these block devices directly rather than by using the file system. This is called **raw I/O.** Examples of such software include utilities for maintaining or examining the file system itself (e.g., **fsck** for Linux and UNIX) and software that places extraordinary demands on the secondary storage and is sophisticated enough to include a preferred mechanism for caching or for scheduling disk operations (e.g., very demanding database servers).

Character devices

Character mode devices transfer data a single byte at a time. They include printers, keyboards, mice (and other pointing devices), and so on. They support most of the same basic kinds of operations as a block mode file: open, close, read, and write. To perform an operation that doesn't fit the semantics of the file system model (e.g., reading the status of a printer), a program can use the **ioctl** system call. Character mode devices obviously cannot support seeking backward. For example, one cannot read the character typed on the keyboard 20 characters previously, or a character printed on the previous page. Some character devices will allow skipping characters in a forward direction. Character mode devices are never cached, though they may have a buffer.

Network devices

Network devices do not fit at all well with the traditional semantics of file operations. The problem is that applications waiting for input from a network never know when or even if the data might be available. A company might create a website with high hopes for selling widgets but never receive a single hit on the site. For this reason, network devices have an entirely different set of interfaces than do block and character devices with their read and write operations.

14.3 I/O TECHNOLOGY

In general, there are two ways that an I/O system can go about its work. Most large systems have many functions going on more or less at the same time, and the only way to cope with them all is to use an interrupt system such as was described in

Chapter 2. However, an alternative approach is often used in smaller systems with low-power CPUs, that of **polling.** In a polling system the control of the OS is written in a single large loop in which the OS will check the status of each device in turn to see if it needs attention. This technique is often used in imbedded devices or simple handheld games where only a few devices are available and checking them in turn is simpler than setting up an interrupt architecture and undergoing the overhead of context switching involved in servicing interrupts.

General Techniques Used in I/O Systems

There are several general techniques that are used in I/O systems. Before delving into other I/O system details we cover some of those general techniques.

14.3.1 Buffering

When we are inputting data into a computer system we typically are reading from one device and writing to another. For example, a user is writing a document by keying it on a keyboard and the computer writes it to disk. At another extreme we might be backing up our hard drive to a tape drive. In each case we will use a technique called **buffering.** A buffer is a portion of memory where we store a record that will be used in an I/O operation. There are several reasons why we might use a buffer. The first might be the size of the transfer. The user writing a document is producing a single character at a time. However, we can't write a single character to a disk. The smallest unit of access is a sector. Block devices like disk and tape drives can only transfer data in large blocks. So we use a buffer to hold the characters that the user is keying until we have enough to fill a sector. Then we write the sector to the disk and start a new sector.

In this particular situation the disk is probably fast enough that we can write the buffer and empty it to receive the next keystroke before that keystroke could possibly arrive. However, suppose that the difference in speeds between the devices were much smaller—say a factor of three or four. In this case we might resort to a slightly different technique, **double buffering.** We will assign two buffers to the process. We will first fill one buffer and then start the operation to write it to the output device. As we start the write we will begin using the second buffer for the incoming data. By the time the second buffer is full the write of the first buffer should be finished and we can start to write the second one while we start to fill the first one again. Figure 14.1 shows this process. In Figure 14.1a we see that Process A is filling Buffer 1 and Buffer 2 is waiting. In Figure 14.1b Process A has filled Buffer 1, so it is now filling Buffer 2 and Buffer 1 is being written to the disk drive.

Another reason we would use buffers might be that we are dealing with two devices that are both block access devices, but the devices have a different block size. For example, Ethernet network adapters typically transfer a maximum block size of about 1,500 bytes. Token Ring adapters would allow a maximum transfer size of about 18,000 bytes. If a packet was being transferred from a Token Ring connection to an Ethernet connection we would have to use a buffer to hold the Token Ring packet while we were breaking it up into multiple Ethernet packets to send out. (There are other complications to this activity as well, but they are beyond the scope of this text.)

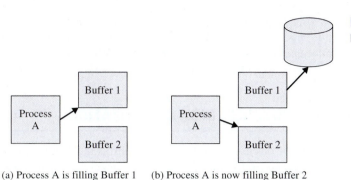

FIGURE 14.1
Double buffering.

(a) Process A is filling Buffer 1
and Buffer 2 is waiting.

(b) Process A is now filling Buffer 2
and Buffer 1 is being written
to the output device.

14.3.2 Caching

One of the most profound techniques in computer systems is caching. It is used both in the hardware and in the software. Its purpose is to make a larger, slower, but cheaper memory appear to perform at the same speed as a smaller, faster, and therefore more expensive memory. As was discussed in Chapter 2 and again in Chapter 11, caches work because processes do not actually access memory randomly. Instead, they operate according to the principle of locality of reference. This principle says that a process is more likely to reference memory addresses that are near to those it has already referenced than it is to reference addresses that are not. For example, most of the time a process runs instructions sequentially rather than branching around randomly. Subroutines are often called, but many instructions are typically needed to set up the next subroutine call. Also, processes perform linear searches through sectors, arrays, strings, packets, and so on. The other aspect of the locality principle says that once a process has referenced a memory location it is more likely to reference it again than to reference another random location. Again, typically a process might work for some time to initialize a table, accessing many of the fields in the table.

14.3.3 Blocking of small records

One final general technique used in an I/O system is that of blocking. Blocking is packing several logical records into one physical block to write to a device. It is somewhat similar to buffering between devices with different block sizes. Consider a system that was originally designed to use punched cards but was converted to run on magnetic tape. The record layouts are probably all very near to the 80-character size of the punched cards. It is certainly possible to write 80-byte records to a tape drive, but it is not very efficient. There is a gap between each tape record to allow for the time it takes the drive to get the tape moving to the right speed and then to stop the tape between records. This gap would hold many 80-character records and would thus waste much of the tape. By simply packing 10 records into a block and writing it to the tape in one operation, we save considerable space. A similar use of the term "blocking" is used on a disk file system where we will often allocate several sectors as a single block. This technique is used only because our file system pointers were not large enough to address all the sectors on some new large disk drive, so we allocated multiple sectors at a time. We will still normally read and write single sectors to the disk drive, however.

14.4 PHYSICAL DISK ORGANIZATION

Before we discuss the software that controls the disk drives we will review the hardware design so that we can see how the nature of the hardware dictates some of the software design.

14.4.1 Sectors, Tracks, Cylinders, and Heads

In Chapter 3 we showed a floppy disk in Figure 3.2. Hard disks are similar. In Figure 14.2 we show some additional concepts. Here we see two platters stacked on a spindle so that they rotate together. Four arms reach out over the platters, each containing a magnetic read–write head. The arms can move in and out. With the arms stationary in any given position the platters will rotate so that a ring of a disk surface will pass under the head. This ring is called a **track.** The four arms are connected together so that they move in and out as a unit. This means that there will be four tracks that the drive can read without moving the arms, one for each head and surface. This group of tracks is called a **cylinder.** Of course, if there are more platters

FIGURE 14.2
A hard disk.

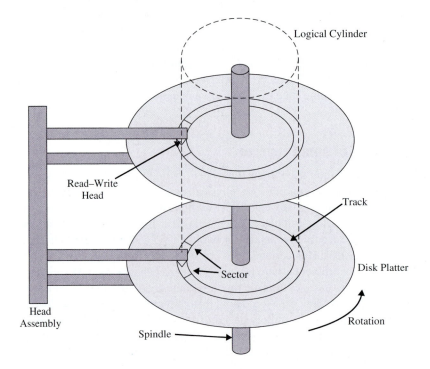

and more heads there can be any number of tracks in a cylinder. A stack of 16 platters is about the maximum one will find in modern drives.

A track is logically divided into **sectors.** As we mentioned before, disk drives are block devices and will only transfer a complete unit of data rather than individual characters. The sectors are the smallest unit of data that a disk drive will transfer. In almost all cases, for a given disk drive all the sectors on the drive will be the same size. On most modern hard disk drives these sectors contain 512 bytes of data plus some additional information. Other sector sizes are available, however, notably 256, 1,024, or 2,048 bytes. Almost always the size is an even power of 2. CDs using the ISO 9660 standard use 2,048-byte blocks.

This arrangement of disk drive hardware leads to the concept of a disk address which could be specified by the cylinder, head and sector numbers, or **CHS addressing.** A disk with C cylinders, H heads, and S sectors per track has $C \times H \times S$ sectors in all, and can normally store $C \times H \times S \times 512$ bytes. For example, if the disk label says C/H/S = 4,092/16/63, then the disk has $4,092 \times 16 \times 63 = 4,124,736$ sectors, and can hold $4,124,736 \times 512 = 2,111,864,832$ bytes (2.11 GB).

14.4.2 Sector count zones and sector addressing

The number of bits that can be stored on a magnetic track is directly proportional to the linear distance that passes under the head. A hard disk drive rotates at a constant speed. The circumference of the outer tracks is longer than that of the inner tracks, so more information can be stored on the outer tracks than on the inner tracks. Older disk drives used the same timing on all the tracks, so the bits on the outer tracks were longer than those on the inner tracks. This was a waste of potential bits. The electronics in the disk drives has gotten more sophisticated, and drives now include a separate computer. As a result, most drives produced since the mid-1990s have used a different technique for the timing called **zone bit recording (ZBR)**. They divide the disk tracks into zones of tracks with a similar size and change the timing for the tracks in each zone. As a result, they place more sectors in the tracks in the outer zones and fewer sectors on the tracks in the inner zones.

Since the number of sectors on a track was no longer constant for the whole drive, the idea of addressing a sector with a CHS format no longer worked, so something had to change. But since some software was heavily oriented to the CHS concept, it was desirable to try to keep as close to that format as possible. A CHS disk address was 24 bits, divided as follows:

cylinder number	0–1023	(10 bit)
head number	0–254	(8 bit)
sector number	1–63	(6 bit)

So the largest disk address that could be expressed with CHS addressing was 8 GiB. In order to conform to the interface pattern of the older drives, newer drives continued to use the pattern of CHS addressing, and the OS was told that the drive had some very large number of cylinders, heads, and sectors. The drive would take those parameters and compute a **logical block address, or LBA.** This simply means the sectors of a disk are sequentially numbered starting with zero and every sector is identified by its LBA number. The drive would then recompute the actual physical address of the block desired based on the varying number of sectors in each zone. BIOS routines and drives were developed that allowed the OS to ignore the artificial CHS format and pass an LBA address directly.

Eventually the drives got so large that the maximum LBA address that could be specified was not large enough to address the entire disk drive. In order to accommodate these larger drives new address formats were specified that allowed either 28- or 48-bit addresses to be used. This results in a disk size limit of 128 GiB or 128 PiB, respectively, assuming the standard 512 bytes per sector.

14.4.3 Low-level formatting

When disk drives are originally manufactured they contain no information whatsoever. The sectors that we want to access do not yet exist. A special writing mode must be invoked to have the disk actually write the bytes on the disk that define the location of the sectors. This mode is called **low-level formatting.** Each sector will contain a header that identifies the cylinder, head, and sector numbers of that sector. The sector will be blank and a checksum will be appended to the sector. (More information about checksums in Section 14.5.3.) With older drive technologies the user was expected to do this low-level formatting. Thankfully this is now done by the manufacturers.

14.4.4 Speeds: Seek, transfer, and buffering

One of the most important factors in OS performance is the hard drive **seek time.** It is the time it takes the drive to move the head assembly from one track (or cylinder) to another. In most modern systems the CPU is idle much of the time, waiting on the disk drive to transfer needed information. The biggest factor in the time taken to access the information is physically getting the read–write head to the location of the sector. There are several possible ways to measure seek time. The measure we are interested in is the average seek time, but for simplicity we will just refer to it as seek time since it has become an industry standard for specifying disk drive performance. Leaving aside some early developments in the field, the seek time of disk drives has changed very little. The rate of change is about -8% per year. This works out to a drop of 50% over 10 years. For about the last 30 years this has been quite accurate. Today the average consumer drive has an average seek time of about 6–12 milliseconds. The highest performance drives are about half that, ranging down to about 3 ms.

A related factor is the rotational latency. Assume that we are looking for a particular sector and we seek to the right track. When the head assembly arrives at the right track it will stop. There are several sectors on a track and we are looking for a particular one. (We might be going to transfer several sectors, but we will have specified that the transfer starts at some particular sector number.) Most of the time the next sector that will pass under the head will not be the one we are looking for. On the average we will be in the wrong place by one-half the rotation time. This delay is referred to as **rotational latency.** The rotational latency varies inversely with the

TABLE 14.2 Rotational Latency as a Function of Drive Rotation Speed

Spindle Speed (RPM)	Average Rotational Latency (ms)
3,600	8.3
4,200	7.1
4,500	6.7
4,900	6.1
5,200	5.8
5,400	5.6
7,200	4.2
10,000	3.0
12,000	2.5
15,000	2.0

rotation speed. Table 14.2 shows the most common rotation speeds for disk drives and the associated average rotational latency.

Until fairly recently the rotational delay was largely ignored since it was not very easy for the OS to monitor the rotational position, and the seek time was so large that the rotational latency was not a big factor. Notice, however, that this delay is now about the same magnitude as the seek time. As a result, the rotational latency is beginning to be considered in disk scheduling algorithms. We have more to say about this later in the chapter.

14.5 LOGICAL DISK ORGANIZATION

An application program typically views secondary storage as a set of files filled with records. At the lowest level the I/O system sees disk drives as masses of sectors. There needs to be some basic organization of the information on a disk drive so that the I/O system can find the information it needs. Because personal computers are so widely available we describe the organization of a disk drive for a personal computer. Other platforms will use different organizations, but they will have similar elements.

14.5.1 Partitions

When IBM released their first PC it did not even have an option for a hard disk—floppy disks were the only disk media. When the first hard disks were available they only contained 10 MB or so. They used a file system organization called FAT12, which was discussed in the last chapter. In a fairly short time it was clear that this file system would not support the newer drives that were rapidly becoming available. We previously discussed the idea of allocating multiple sectors at a time as one solution to this problem. Another simple solution was to allow a single disk drive to be divided into multiple pieces and have each piece treated as a separate drive. Then the old file

FIGURE 14.3
A disk drive
containing several
OSs in different
partitions.

system could still be used. This solution is called **partitioning.**[1] A utility program called **FDISK** was provided with DOS that could be used to divide the disk into separate partitions. The original version of FDISK allowed a drive to be divided into only four partitions and only one could contain a bootable OS. With Windows NT a new version of FDISK was released that allows more partitions to be defined on a single drive and allows multiple bootable (a.k.a. primary) partitions. This is a good step forward, but of course it is incompatible with older OSs that were created before this change in format. Most modern OSs support this format of extended partition tables. For some time most other OSs simply used the same utility program because it was not used often and there was not much of a way to enhance the features. Today, most OSs provide their own partitioning utility program and many have a GUI interface.

As it turns out, creating partitions is a useful technique for other things as well. For one thing, it is a simple way of allowing a machine to contain two different operating systems and still allow each OS to assume it has sole control over the disk drive. In Figure 14.3, we see a disk drive divided into four partitions containing three different OSs. In normal situations each partition will contain a file system. But another use for partitions is for applications that are so specialized that they want to manage their own I/O rather than utilize the default file–oriented I/O that the OS provides. An example might be a database management system. Such systems are heavily optimized for the specific access patterns they expect to see and would not be nearly as efficient if they could only use the standard OS file I/O support. This API is known as raw I/O and it allows the application to treat the partition as an array of blocks that can be accessed randomly rather than through the normal metaphor of a file.

Eventually, new file systems were developed with larger pointers that could support very large hard drives. Some applications required a larger file space than could be covered with a single hard drive of the sizes that were available at the time. As a result, the mechanisms of partitioning can be reversed, allowing two or more hard drives to be combined with the partitioning mechanism and to appear to the upper layers of the OS as a single drive. Figure 14.4 shows a single partition spanning parts of two disk drives.

FIGURE 14.4
A single partition
spanning parts
of two disk drives.

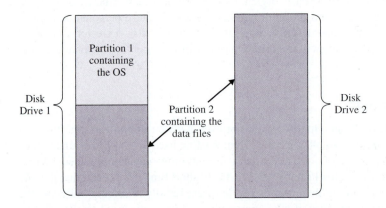

---

[1]This technique did not originate with PC systems. It was earlier used on some mainframe systems for some of the same reasons alluded to here.

14.5.2 Boot block

In Chapter 3 we discussed the concept of booting the system from a disk drive. When a computer is reset it will normally try to bootstrap an OS from one or more of the devices on the system. Most PCs contain a special memory that is powered by a battery. It is commonly referred to as the **CMOS memory,** or sometimes as the BIOS. Settings in this memory may specify a set of several different devices that the system is allowed to boot from, among other things. The system will try to boot from them in the order specified. A given device may not work when the system tries to boot from that device. For example, a floppy drive or a CD-ROM drive might not contain a disk. A hard drive might not have an OS installed on it yet. If the OS cannot boot from one device, then the next device is tried. If they all fail then a diagnostic error that no normal user would understand is displayed on the video screen. If the OS finds a drive that it can boot from, the bootstrap program in the hardware ROM will load the first sector from the device and begin executing the code that is contained there.

The information about the partitioning of a hard disk is stored in a part of the first physical sector on the disk, regardless of how the partitioning is set up. This sector is called the **master boot record (MBR)** or **boot block** of the disk and it contains the **partition table.** It also contains a short program that looks in the partition table, checks which partition is currently the **active partition,** and reads the first sector of that partition. That partition's boot sector contains another small program that reads the first part of the OS stored on that partition and starts executing it. The remainder of the bootstrap program will read in parts of the kernel and mount the root of the directory structure that is found in that partition.

After the OS bootstraps itself into memory it will mount the file system that it finds on the boot volume. The details of mounting the file system depend on the OS and the format of the partition that the OS was booted from. It may mount other partitions as well.

14.5.3 Error detection and correction

When information is written to a hard disk unit, extra information is written with it. This information is used for detecting errors and often for correcting them as well. There are various schemes for creating and using this information. The schemes used depend on the type of errors expected in the drive, the amount of reliability desired, and the intended relative price of the drive. The more elaborate techniques produce a more reliable drive. At the same time, they require more complex calculations and therefore they require a faster and more powerful processor in the disk drive. In addition, the more complex techniques store more redundant information on the disk, so they will hold less user data. Thus, for a given amount of user storage they will require a larger drive. But error correction allows manufacturers to make faster, higher-capacity drives that appear to the user to be error-free. The more the technology for storing data is pushed, the more sophisticated the error correction mechanisms need to be to reach the same level of reliability.

A large body of research and development has been done on the calculation of this redundant information, called **error detection codes (EDC)** or **error correction**

codes (ECC). The techniques all compute a small number that is a function of the contents of the data block. The computation is made when the data is written to the disk and the computed value is written along with the data. When the data is read back from the disk, the function is computed again and compared with the value stored during the write operation. If the two values do not agree, then an error was made either on the read or on the write. (Errors on the read may reflect that the data has been damaged since it was written.)

The simplest error detection codes include a **cyclic redundancy check,** or **CRC,** also sometimes called a **longitudinal redundancy check,** or **LRC.** In this case the function calculated is expressed as a polynomial. For example, the polynomial $X^4 + X^2 + 1$ would be 10101. The binary digits represent the multiplier of the exponents of the values of the polynomial. We could write $X^4 + X^2 + 1$ more exactly like this: $(1 \times X^4) + (0 \times X^3) + (1 \times X^2) + (0 \times X^1) + (1 \times X^0)$. The calculation can be thought of as dividing the data in the block by the binary number expressed by the polynomial. After this division the remainder is the CRC. This type of calculation is in widespread use in computing, especially in networking. Because the types of errors expected in networks are somewhat different than those expected in a disk drive, the polynomials used are usually different. Several different commonly used polynomials are shown in Table 14.3. Sometimes errors are likely to occur in a number of bits in a row. Such situations are called **burst errors.** A polynomial code can detect any error burst of a length less than or equal to the length of that polynomial. This type of calculation has been used for some time because a simple, fast hardware implementation using shift registers was developed.

CRC-12 is used for serial communication lines of 6-bit characters and generates a 12-bit CRC. Both CRC-16 and CRC-CCITT are used for 8-bit serial communication and result in a 16-bit CRC. The last two are widely used in the United States and Europe, respectively, and give adequate protection for most applications. CRC-CCITT is used in disk drives. CRC-32 generates a 32-bit CRC. The CRC-32 polynomial is used in IEEE-802 networks such as Ethernet, Token Ring, and wireless LANs.

More complex calculations are used in more modern drives. These functions include Hamming and Reed-Solomon codes. They produce more redundant information than the various CRC functions. A typical drive might store 12 bytes of redundancy code with a 512-byte data block and be able to correct burst errors as long as 22 bits. In particular, Reed-Solomon codes are used in CD-ROM drives where they store 24 data bytes and 8 error correction bytes in a frame for error correction purposes. This higher level of redundancy is required since the media is easily damaged and the drives are often used when a system is in motion, such as a car CD player.

TABLE 14.3 Several Commonly Used CRC Polynomials

CRC-12:	$X^{12} + X^{11} + X^3 + X^2 + X + 1$
CRC-16:	$X^{16} + X^{15} + X^2 + 1$
CRC-CCITT:	$X^{16} + X^{12} + X^5 + 1$
CRC-32:	$X^{32} + X^{26} + X^{23} + X^{22} + X^{16} + X^{12} + X^{11} +$
	$X^{10} + X^8 + X^7 + X^5 + X^4 + X^2 + X + 1$

14.6 RAID

Modern hard drives are very reliable. We measure the reliability in terms of the **mean time between failures,** or **MTBF.** However, we can improve on this reliability to give even longer lifetimes by using multiple drives in special ways. The techniques we describe in this section are called **redundant arrays of inexpensive disks** or **RAID.** Some writers replace the term "inexpensive" with "independent," but the former term is the one that was used when the term "RAID" was first coined by the researchers who systematically investigated the use of multiple-drive arrays. The original purpose was to show that by combining inexpensive drives in clever ways the reliability of much more expensive drives could be achieved with less money. But these days even inexpensive drives are very reliable. However, an important point in these techniques is that in order for them to work well, the failure modes of the drives must be independent. This means that the drives must be operating on separate I/O channels and I/O controllers as well to achieve optimum reliability and performance. If not, the techniques will still keep data from being lost, but the data might be unavailable while a shared component is replaced.

Support for RAID configurations is often done in the disc controllers. However, RAID does not have to be done in a special controller. For some of the RAID configurations it is possible to control the RAID process with a software module in the OS. Today, RAID 0 and 5 are commonly offered in software in most OSs. These configurations are explained in the next section.

The original RAID specifications included six configurations. They are called RAID 0 through RAID 5. Most of these configurations will be more reliable than using individual drives. Some of them also yield improved performance in some areas and worse performance in others. RAID 0 is the exception since it yields only improved performance on reads.

14.6.1 RAID configurations

The following figures show several RAID configurations. Each is intended to represent a storage system that holds the same amount of user data. In each case the drives are all of the same size and we are showing how many drives it takes to yield four drives' worth of storage with that configuration. The higher levels of the OS will see each configuration as a single drive with four times the storage as the individual drives of which it is made. There are three main techniques used in RAID. These are mirroring (copying data to more than one drive), striping (breaking files across more than one drive), and error correction (redundant data is stored, allowing detection and possibly fixing of errors). Different RAID configurations use one or more of these techniques.

RAID 0—Striped disk array without parity. This configuration utilizes **data striping,** spreading out blocks of each file across multiple disk drives, but no redundancy. The developers of the RAID technology used the term **strip** rather than the term **block,** but in practice the implementations are always based on blocks. It improves performance because multiple reads and multiple writes can be carried out in parallel. But it does not increase fault tolerance. In fact, this configuration actually decreases reliability, since if one drive fails then all data in the array is lost because the OS is treating the array of drives as a single drive. Having *N* drives spinning means that the configuration is *N* times as likely to fail. If the RAID support is being provided by the disk controllers, then the OS has no access to the remaining drives at all. If the support is being done by the OS device driver software, then the remaining drives would theoretically still be accessible, but it is unlikely that any files would reside completely on the remaining drives. See Figure 14.5. The numbers in the drives show the logical block numbers (seen by the file system) as they are written to the drives.

RAID 1—Mirroring (a.k.a. **duplexing**). In RAID 1 there is a duplicate set of disk drives. When any data is written to one drive it is also written to the duplicate (mirror) of that drive. See Figure 14.6. The shaded set of drives is the mirror set. Assuming that a primary drive and its mirror can be read at the same time, this configuration provides twice the read transaction rate of single disks. It has no effect on the write transaction rate because each individual block must be written to both the primary and the secondary so the effect of any parallelism is lost. If one drive fails, the data will be safe but the performance will be reduced when accessing that mirror pair because only one drive will be available to service that request. This is the most expensive RAID configuration.

RAID 2—Error-correcting coding and **RAID 3—Bit-interleaved parity.** These two techniques turned out to be prohibitively expensive and inferior to other techniques so we will not describe them here. For high performance they also required that the spinning of the drives needed to be synchronized. They are not in use today.

RAID 4—Dedicated parity drive. This configuration provides block-level striping (like Level 0) with a parity disk. The parity block that is written to this drive

FIGURE 14.5
RAID 0—Striped disk array.

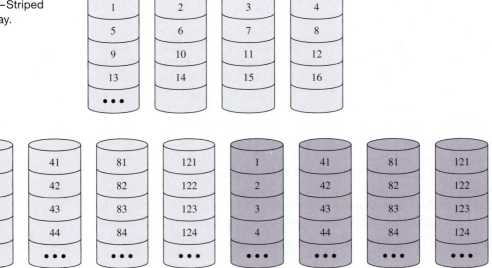

FIGURE 14.6 RAID 1—Disk mirroring.

covers the other blocks in the stripe, in this case, blocks 1–4. See Figure 14.7. If a data disk fails, the parity data is used to create a replacement disk. A disadvantage to RAID 4 is that every time a block is written the parity block must also be read, recalculated, and rewritten. The parity disk therefore becomes an I/O bottleneck. It provides almost the same reliability as RAID 1, but if a drive fails the performance hit will be much worse. However, the cost is a single extra drive, so it is much superior in price if the configuration has several drives in it.

RAID 5—Block interleaved distributed parity. RAID 5 is very much like RAID 4, except that rather than keeping the parity block always on the same drive the parity block is assigned to the drives in a round-robin fashion. See Figure 14.8. This technique removes the problem of excessive use of the parity drive that we saw with RAID 4. Level 5 is one of the most popular configurations of RAID.

The following RAID configurations were not part of the original RAID specification. These have been fairly widely accepted and can generally be regarded as standard.

RAID 6—Independent data disks with double parity. Provides block-level striping with parity data distributed across all disks as in RAID 5, but instead of a simple parity scheme it computes parity using two different algorithms at the same time. Several methods of calculations, including dual check data computations (parity and Reed-Solomon), orthogonal dual parity check data, and diagonal parity have

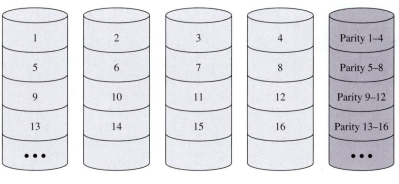

FIGURE 14.7
RAID 4—Dedicated parity drive.

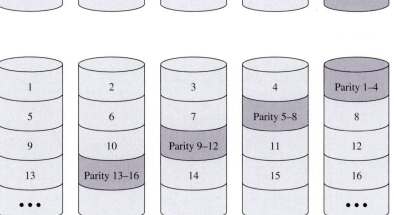

FIGURE 14.8
RAID 5—Block interleaved distributed parity.

been used to implement RAID 6 configurations. See Figure 14.9. The two different parity blocks are shown as P&Q functions of the blocks (or strips) in the stripe and are shown in contrasting shades. RAID 6 requires an extra disk drive (over RAID 5) but it will tolerate the loss of two drives at the same time.

RAID 0+1—Mirror of stripes. In this configuration two RAID 0 stripes are created, and a RAID 1 mirror is created over them. This is shown in Figure 14.10. The striping provides improved performance and the mirroring provides reliability. Generally, it will perform better than RAID 5.

RAID 1+0 (a.k.a. **RAID 10)—Stripe of mirrors.** Multiple RAID 1 mirrored drive pairs are created, and a RAID 0 stripe is created over these. See Figure 14.11. This configuration has performance and reliability characteristics similar to RAID 0+1. However, the performance and reliability is slightly better when a drive is lost. With RAID 0+1 the loss of a drive means that the entire stripe set is lost, so the other stripe set will have to take on all the work. With RAID 1+0 only the drive that loses

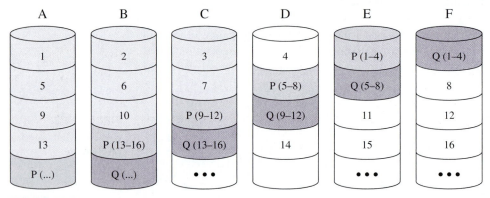

FIGURE 14.9 RAID 6—Independent data disks with double parity.

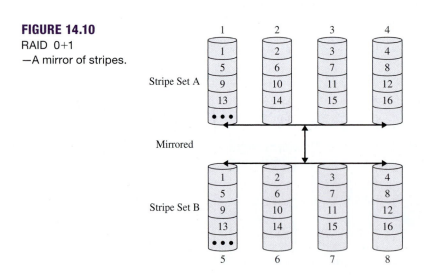

FIGURE 14.10
RAID 0+1
—A mirror of stripes.

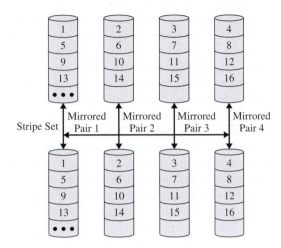

FIGURE 14.11
RAID 1+0
—A stripe of mirrors.

its mirror pair will have to do all the work for that pair. The work on the other pairs can be distributed across both drives as before.

14.6.2 RAID failures

We could build a RAID 0+1 configuration by using two controllers to build the stripe sets and using software at the device driver level to mirror the two stripe sets. In this case the failure of a single drive would result in the loss of the entire stripe set, as described earlier. However, if the controllers running RAID 0+1 were aware of the entire configuration, then when drive 3 failed it would continue striping to the other four drives in "stripe set A," and if drive 6 later failed it would use drive 2 in its stead, since it should have the same data. This would theoretically make RAID 0+1 just as fault-tolerant as RAID 1+0. Unfortunately, most controllers aren't designed this way.

When a failed drive is replaced the system will have to rebuild the information that was on the lost drive. In RAID 0+1, if drive 2 fails, the data on five hard disks will need to be rebuilt, because the whole "stripe set A" will be wiped out. In RAID 1+0, only drive 2 has to be rebuilt. Again here, the advantage is to RAID 1+0.

There is also a plethora of other RAID configurations that are proprietary. They include many trademarked terms. They may or may not be of some benefit in a particular situation. Analysis of test configurations and especially their behavior in a variety of failure scenarios is a nontrivial matter but might be warranted in special situations.

When a single drive fails in RAID configurations more advanced than RAID 0, the array can continue to run. Sometimes the performance is lower and sometimes we simply have more exposure to risk. For example, loss of a drive in a RAID 1 configuration mostly means that we are now at some increased risk since failure of the other drive in that pair would mean that we had lost all of that information. We can continue to run with only one loss. We will notice some drop in performance in some reads since we only have one drive to do the reads where we had two to share it before the loss of the drive. At other times we will probably have to shut the system down because the performance of the system would be unacceptable. For example, in RAID 6, if we lose a drive, the performance of a write will be very bad because we will have to read all the other drives to be able to calculate the parity for the missing drive. This would probably be only marginally acceptable. However, as soon as the broken drive has been replaced we can begin the processes of rebuilding the information that was on the bad drive.

This brings up a point that for RAID configurations we will want to use drives that are "hot swappable." This means that the failed drive can be unplugged from the system and a new drive plugged in without turning off the power on the system. While this technology is well understood, it does require special hardware that is more expensive than normal drives. The decision will probably hinge on whether the running system is critical to some operation or whether it is only the existence of the data that is critical. In the latter case we might prefer to take some system downtime rather than pay extra for the drives.

In some cases the running system is a requirement. Systems in hospitals, for example, may be critical to patient care and the loss of the system might mean the loss of life. In such cases we might choose to go a step further and have a spare drive on the shelf ready to plug in if one of the drives fails. In extreme cases we may have the drive in a **warm standby** situation—already plugged in to the drive rack but not powered on or at least not spinning. When the OS detects a failure it can turn on the power to the drive, spin it up, and begin the rebuild process. Of course, disk mirroring is the extreme form of **hot standby.**

14.7 DISK OPERATION SCHEDULING

We mentioned earlier that seek time was one of the most critical measurements of a disk drive as far as performance of the system is concerned. If we have a large number of disk operations to do, it turns out that the order in which we handle the requests can have a significant impact on overall system performance. The performance of CPUs has been increasing by a rate of roughly 50% per year for at least the last couple of decades. The performance of disk drives has only increased at a rate of about 10% per year during the same time. It is reasonable to assume that we can spend some of that CPU speed to improve the performance of the disk systems. To illustrate the point, let us assume that we have a series of disk requests to service. A seek operation on the disk drive moves all the heads together to some track or cylinder. So we will just look at track numbers, and realize that we are actually positioning (potentially) many heads at the same time—certainly at least two. Accordingly, we will take a list of track numbers that have come to the I/O system from various processes that are running on the system. We will look at the seek time necessary to perform those requests and then see if we can improve on that. In all these cases we assume that the disk drive has 80 tracks, that the head is presently resting at track 28 and we have the following set of requests in a queue:

17, 30, 24, 37, 15, 27, 11, 75, 20, 5

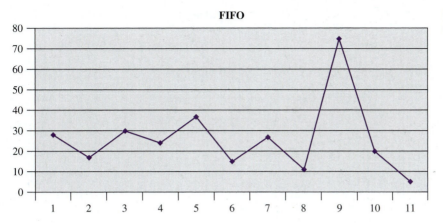

FIGURE 14.12
FIFO.

14.7.1 FCFS

The simplest way to handle these requests would be to take them as they are in the queue, **first in, first out,** or **FIFO.** (This is also often known as **first come, first served,** or **FCFS.**) This algorithm is appealing because it is simple to implement. It also has the advantage that it is **fair.** It is fair in the sense that the process that asked first gets served first. However, this does not necessarily give the best overall system performance. Moreover, it might not even give the best performance to a single application, as we will see later. In the case of the FCFS algorithm, the OS will move the head from track to track in the order that the requests are in the queue. So it will move from 28 to 17, then to 30, then to 24, and so on. In processing this queue in this order the system will seek over 227 tracks. This is shown in Figure 14.12. Since we have no idea about the rotational latency involved, we will use the number of tracks that the system has to seek over to service the requests as our measure of how efficient the algorithm is.

14.7.2 Pickup

A variation on FCFS that is mentioned by some authorities is called **pickup.** In this algorithm the requests are generally taken in order as with FCFS, but as the system is moving the head it will stop for any tracks that are being passed over that have a request in the queue. (In Linux this is called the **Noop** scheduler.) For example, given the requests in our sample, it would start at track 28 and begin moving toward 17, the first request in the queue. But on the way it would pick up tracks 27, 24, and 20. The total sequence would be:

27, 24, 20, 17, 30, 37, 15, 11, 75, 5

This sequence would result in a total seek time of 191 tracks, a considerable improvement over FCFS. Figure 14.13 charts the Pickup algorithm.

FIGURE 14.13
Pickup.

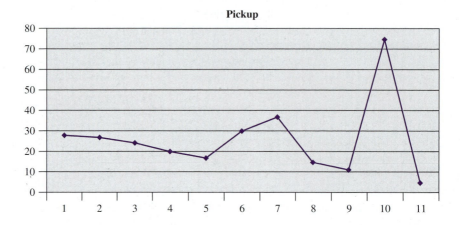

14.7.3 SSTF

Next, we will look at an algorithm called **shortest seek time first,** or **SSTF.** (It is also sometimes known as **shortest positioning time first,** or **SPTF.**) When we used similar algorithms in other parts of an OS such as virtual memory page replacement or process scheduling we usually said that they were optimum, but that we could not really use them because we could not predict the future. In the case of disk scheduling, however, we can use this algorithm because all the requests we are concerned with are there in the queue for us to look at. Again, we start with the head at track 28. The nearest entry on the queue is 27, so we next move the head to that track. Now the next nearest is back at 30, so we move there. As is shown in Figure 14.14, the sequence is

28, 27, 30, 24, 20, 37, 17, 15, 11, 5, 75

for a total of 133 tracks. This is almost twice the performance of FCFS. However, it is not very fair. The first request in the queue, the one that has been waiting the longest, is not serviced until the queue is about half empty. Also notice that the head

FIGURE 14.14
SSTF.

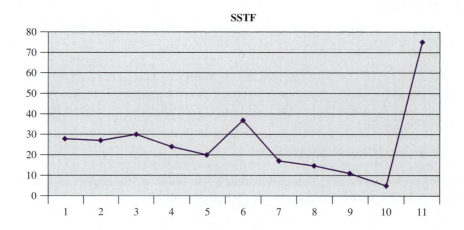

kept passing back and forth across the middle of the disk. As a result, a process that was accessing blocks that were located in the middle of the disk would tend to get better service than one that was accessing blocks located at either extreme on the drive. Also, notice that while this algorithm is running, more requests will probably be made of the OS and will get placed in the queue with the rest. Since processes in the middle are getting favored, they will also get more opportunities to place additional requests, compounding their advantage. This algorithm can be looked at as giving priority to some requests—notably those closest to the current head position. As with any prioritization mechanism, we have to be concerned about starvation of the lower priority requests. The outlying blocks can be gradually raised in priority so that they will be serviced sooner. This variant of SSTF is sometimes called **aged shortest seek time first,** or **ASSTF.** The algorithm simply adjusts the actual seek time by subtracting a weighting factor times the time that the request has been in the queue. If T_{eff} is the effective (or weighted) seek time for a request, T_{pos} is the actual time the seek would require, W is a weighting factor we want to assign to old requests, and T_{wait} is the time the request has been in the queue, the aging formula would be:

$$T_{eff} = T_{pos} - W \times T_{wait}$$

14.7.4 LOOK

The next algorithm we will study is commonly called **LOOK.** Another popular name for it is the "**elevator algorithm.**" In this algorithm, once the OS starts seeking in one direction it will not reverse the direction it is seeking until there are no other tracks to access in that direction. In other words, the system "looks" ahead to decide when to reverse the seek direction. This is analogous to the way an elevator works. Once it starts going up it will only go in that direction until it has no more requests in that direction. It will then reverse itself. (As with many analogies it is a bit weak, because an elevator also considers whether the request from a floor is to go up or down and will not stop for users wanting to go up if it is going down. But an OS only needs to position the head to the track. The seek request contains no notion of direction of the seek.) Let us again look at our reference string. Let us also assume that the OS starts seeking in the direction of the lower numbered tracks. In this case the order of the seeks would be

28, 27, 24, 20, 17, 15, 11, 5, 30, 37, 75

for a total of 93 tracks. This is shown in Figure 14.15.

If the OS had started in the direction of the higher numbered tracks the sequence would be

28, 30, 37, 75, 27, 24, 20, 17, 15, 11, 5

for a total of 117. This is shown in Figure 14.16. In either case it would be better than FIFO or SSTF. However, for every time it moves toward either end it will pass over the middle of the disk both coming and going; it still tends to favor blocks in the middle of the disk, so it is less fair than FIFO but not as bad as SSTF.

FIGURE 14.15
LOOK starting down.

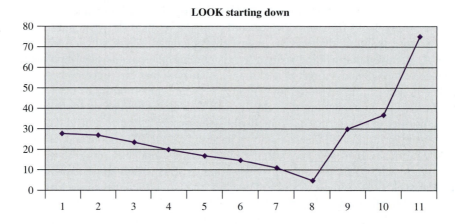

FIGURE 14.16
LOOK starting up.

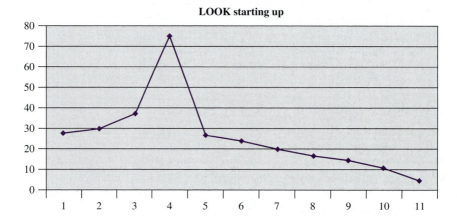

Some authorities also discuss a separate algorithm called **SCAN.** This algorithm is the same as LOOK, but instead of reversing direction when no more requests are in the queue in the direction that is currently being traveled, this algorithm would have to move all the way to the end of the disk in the direction of the travel. Since nobody would actually implement this algorithm we will ignore it, mentioning it only for completeness, since some of the other algorithms are called something related to SCAN.

14.7.5 C-LOOK

In an effort to make a fairer algorithm, a variation on the LOOK algorithm was devised. When the disk head has moved to the last track in one direction, instead of reversing direction and seeking to the nearest track, the OS will seek to the track that is the furthest in the queue in the opposite direction. It will then begin to perform the seeks moving back in the direction it was originally traveling before. The objective is to remove the unfair advantage given to files in the middle of the drive since on one pass over the middle the disk is not servicing any requests. The name of this algorithm is **C-LOOK,** short for **circular-LOOK** (some authorities call this method **cylindrical-LOOK** or **cyclic elevator**). The thought behind the name is to consider the address space (track numbers) of the disk as being wrapped around a cylinder, so that after seeking to track 0, say, the next track to be considered is track 80. Unfortunately, this algorithm results in a very long seek in the middle of servicing the queue. But this long seek is not quite as bad as it might seem. Normally, we quote the average seek time when we talk about the seek performance of a disk drive. However, seek times do not increase linearly with the distance of the seek. Just as with a moving object, the arm on a disk that holds the heads will start slowly and gradually get faster and faster. As a result, a seek across the entire disk will not be double the average seek. It will be somewhat quicker than that. Since it is not possible to predict this exactly, we will ignore it and simply make the same sort of calculation that we have made before, stipulating that things will not really be quite this bad. Again, the exact sum will depend on whether we start in the direction of the lower numbered tracks or the higher numbered tracks. Because of the long seek in the middle of the sequence, the difference between the two directions will not be as large a percentage as it was with LOOK. As seen in Figure 14.17, the sequence is

28, 27, 24, 20, 17, 15, 11, 5, 75, 37, 30

for a total of 138. In Figure 14.18, we see a sequence of

28, 30, 37, 75, 5, 11, 15, 17, 20, 24, 27

for a total of 139. The attraction of C-LOOK is that it offers lower **service variability**—the performance of any given disk request is more predictable in general and less dependent on file placement on the disk. C-LOOK is better than LOOK only when the disk access level is a very high load since it reduces the starvation problem. As with the SCAN algorithm mentioned above, some authors discuss a C-SCAN that also travels to the extremes of the disk before reversing directions.

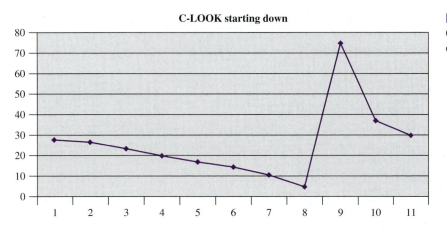

C-LOOK starting down

FIGURE 14.17
C-LOOK starting down.

FIGURE 14.18

C-LOOK starting up.

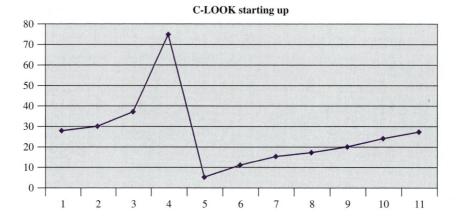

14.7.6 F-SCAN

Another disk scheduling algorithm is commonly called **F-SCAN.** Despite the name, it is a variant on the LOOK algorithm. This mechanism uses two queues, say X and Y. Queue X is started first and the system freezes request queue X when a scan is started. Any requests that come in while this scan is under way are put into queue Y. After the scan with queue X is finished, queue Y is frozen and another scan is started with it, any incoming requests now going into queue X. This mechanism is a compromise between the fairness of FCFS and the efficiency of LOOK without the expensive long seek of C-LOOK. It thus avoids long periods of starvation.

14.7.7 N-step SCAN

One last variation of the LOOK algorithm batches requests in groups of *N* requests. One batch is scanned before the next batch is processed. Like F-SCAN, N-Step SCAN prevents indefinite postponement (starvation). The other purpose of N-Step SCAN is to set an upper bound on how long a request can go without being serviced. It is thus useful for very heavily loaded systems, and for systems with a large number of soft real-time applications. Note that the effect of N-Step SCAN is heavily dependent on the size of *N*. If *N* equals 1, then N-Step SCAN is effectively FCFS, and if *N* is large enough that almost all requests are serviced in the first scan, then N-Step SCAN is equivalent to LOOK.

14.7.8 Linux schedulers

Linux has more scheduler variations available than most OSs. We look at three that it currently supports. They are variants of the sorts of algorithms we have been looking at.

Anticipatory scheduler

The **anticipatory scheduler** was for a time the default scheduler in Linux. It merges requests like the Pickup algorithm and uses a one-way elevator sequence like the LOOK algorithm. A unique feature is that it tries to anticipate reads by holding off a bit after a synchronous read command if it thinks a process might ask for more data nearby. If a new request comes in from the last process it may reverse the seek direction if the distance is not too great.

Deadline scheduler

The **deadline scheduler** also merges requests like the Pickup algorithm and uses a one-way elevator sequence like the LOOK algorithm. It also imposes a deadline on all operations to prevent resource starvation. Linux returns immediately from a write request and holds the data to write in the cache. So the deadline scheduler will give priority to read requests as long as the deadline for a write request hasn't passed. This is the preferred scheduler for database systems, especially if the disks are high-performance drives.

Complete fair queuing scheduler ("cfq scheduler")

The **complete fair queuing scheduler** also merges requests like the Pickup algorithm and uses a one-way elevator sequence like the LOOK algorithm. In addition, it tries to give all processes using a particular device the same number of synchronous IO requests over a measured time interval. It is likely to be more efficient for multiuser systems than are the other schedulers. It is currently the default scheduler for most Linux distributions.

14.7.9 Sending commands to the controller

Tagged queuing is a technique initially developed in the realm of SCSI disk drives. It is sometimes called **command queuing** or **native command queuing** (**NCQ.**) It basically delegates all or part of the task of disk operation scheduling to the disk controller. The device drivers for such drives pass all I/O requests directly to the drive controller and the controller does all the scheduling of the I/O operations. The theory is that the disk controller has a different level of information about the disk geometry and the current status of the disk mechanism and can therefore do a better job of scheduling multiple disk requests. Such migration of functions closer to the hardware is a phenomenon we often see in the OS world. Once a technique proves useful in the OS we start thinking about putting the function into the hardware where it can often be done more cheaply and sometimes better and frees up valuable CPU and memory resources. In this case, the controller can do a better job because it is able to also consider rotational latency. When much of the work was initially done on these disk scheduling algorithms the seek time was much greater than the rotational latency. Improvements in the seek mechanism over the last couple of decades have meant that the seek time is now about the same as the rotational latency. (See Table 14.2.) In general, the OS does not have that much information about the rotational position of a drive. In addition, because of sector zoning and LBA addressing the disk driver may not even understand the real geometry of the drive. The controller, however, has all that information and can therefore use an algorithm that includes both rotational and seek time to arrive at an optimum schedule. In many situations a performance increase of 30% has been reported, but this depends highly on the details of the situation. Tagged queuing is implemented in most modern OSs. The technique is also now finding its way into the latest high-performance ATA disk drives.

14.7.10 Which algorithm is best?

After all this discussion of disk scheduling algorithms it would seem reasonable to ask which algorithm is the best. Unfortunately, the answer to that question is one frequently heard in the computer business—"that depends." In fact, there is no one algorithm that is the best in all situations. FCFS is the simplest and consumes the least resources. If a system is usually so lightly loaded that there are not multiple disk requests in the queue, then all algorithms behave the same—like FCFS. In this case no other algorithm would be justified.

However, many systems are moderately to heavily loaded, so we can't get away with such an easy answer. In such cases FCFS will give high service variability and is thus generally the worst choice. The next question that needs to be asked, then, is what parameter are we trying to optimize? In most cases we are trying to optimize disk throughput. However, we saw earlier that the optimum throughput came at the expense of some unfairness to processes that were accessing files that were not in optimum places. These requests would suffer either significantly delayed response time or a variance in response time that was unpredictable and therefore unacceptable. Users can stand a long response if the program can warn them, but high variance in the response time makes it impossible for the program to adequately warn the user. In most cases, then, some variation on the LOOK algorithm is probably the best. This assumes that your system does not contain new equipment that can handle the scheduling itself. If such hardware is available, then it can almost certainly do a better job than the OS can.

14.8 DMA AND DISK HARDWARE FEATURES

There are several special hardware features of disk controllers that need to be discussed as they will impact the design of OS device handlers.

14.8.1 DMA Controllers

Originally I/O controllers were designed to transfer one byte or one word of data at a time. The CPU would load control information into the proper registers. This information would include the type of operation (read, write, or control), a memory address, and possibly a device address. The CPU would then issue an I/O instruction. When the I/O operation was complete the controller would issue an interrupt and the CPU would set up for the next word or byte. This was acceptable for devices like keyboards, modems, and even for the early text-only CRTs that were on very early PCs, because very many instructions could be executed by the CPU before the next interrupt would occur. However, when devices began getting faster, the number and timing of interrupts began to overwhelm the CPU.

As a result, an innovation was made in the design of the I/O section of computers—a **direct memory access** controller, or **DMA.** The main CPU will give the DMA controller the same information it would have put into the registers before, plus it will add a length of the data to be transferred (in the case of a read or write). The DMA controller will take on the job that the CPU was doing before, except that when the device controller has finished transferring one word it will notify the DMA controller rather than interrupt the CPU. As each byte (or word) is transferred to or from the memory the DMA controller will decrement the count of the data to be transferred and increment the memory address to be used. When the count reaches zero the DMA controller knows it is finished and it will then interrupt the CPU. This technique greatly reduces the overhead of I/O on the CPU. Many modern controllers will have a DMA circuit built-in to the controller rather than sharing one with other controllers.

14.8.2 Other disk drive features

There are several other common features of modern disk drives that will have an effect on operating systems. The first is buffering in the disk drive. A common specification for the small disk drive of today is that it contains 8 MiB of RAM. This ram is used as a cache memory. In this case it can also be called a **track buffer.** The main limiting factors on disk drive performance today is the combination of the seek time and the rotational latency. In our discussions of caching we always mention spatial locality—the idea that when a program references a piece of data it is highly likely that it will soon reference data that is located near to the first data. If we were reading a file sequentially and processing the blocks fairly quickly, then we might ask for sector 5 and begin processing it. We soon finish that sector and ask for sector 6. In the meantime, however, sector 6 has already begun to pass under the head, and we will have to wait for an entire rotation of the disk before we can read sector 6. Then the same thing will happen on sector 7, and so on.

So when we give a command to a modern disk drive to read a specific sector on a track it will most often read the entire track into memory once the head is over the track. If sector 10 comes up next it will begin reading and will read the entire track until it wraps around and reads up to sector 9. It will then return the sector we had asked for and hold those others in the cache buffer as long as it can, knowing that it is probable we will ask for some of them soon.

14.8.3 Sector sparing and sector relocation

Over time disk drives will start to fail. The process starts slowly, however, and may be very gradual at first. Occasionally, a brand new disk drive will have a few bad sectors at the outset. In order to cope with these failures, disk drives are typically formatted with a few "spare" sectors scattered around—perhaps one per track. These sectors are not originally part of the numbering scheme. Instead, they are held in reserve so that when a failure is detected the system can reassign them—that is, data from the old sector will be copied to the spare sector, and its number will be changed to match the failed sector. The failed sector will get a number that will not be used.

In some cases the drive hardware may perform this function. In other cases it is up to the device driver software to do the recovery and relocation.

14.8.4 S.M.A.R.T.

Sector sparing is a reactive technology. It addresses how we cope with failure when we find it. **Self-monitoring and reporting technology, or S.M.A.R.T.,** is a predictive technology. It addresses how we might project a future failure and avoid it or mitigate it. It is a standard interface through which a hard disk drive can report its status to the host OS, and provide an estimation of a future failure date. With sufficient notice, a system or user can back up data prior to a drive's failure. S.M.A.R.T. is defined for both ATA and SCSI environments. Originated by Compaq, it is under continuing development by disk drive manufacturers.

S.M.A.R.T. technology includes a set of parameters specific for each model of disk drives because drive architectures vary from model to model. Attributes and thresholds that detect failure for one model may not be useful for another model. A disk drive must be able to monitor many elements in order to have a thorough reliability management plan. One of the most crucial factors in such a plan is understanding failure modes. Failures can be divided into two classes: predictable and unpredictable.

Unpredictable failures occur quickly, like electronic and mechanical problems, such as a power surge that can cause chip or circuit failure. Improvements in quality, design, process, and manufacturing can reduce the incidence of unpredictable failures. For example, the development of steel-belted radial tires reduced the number of blowouts common among older tire designs.

Predictable failures are characterized by degradation of an attribute over time, before the disk drive fails. This creates a situation where attributes can be monitored, making it possible for predictive failure analysis. Many mechanical failures are typically considered predictable, such as the degradation of head flying height, which would indicate a potential head crash. Certain electronic failures may show degradation before failing, but more commonly, mechanical problems are gradual and predictable. For instance, oil level is a function, or attribute, of most cars that can be monitored. When a car's diagnostic system senses that the oil is low, an oil light comes on. The driver can stop the car and save the engine. In the same manner, S.M.A.R.T. gives the system administrators sufficient notice to start backup procedures and save the system data. Mechanical failures, which are generally predictable, account for 60 percent of drive failures. This number shows a large opportunity for reliability prediction technology. With the S.M.A.R.T. system many future failures can be predicted, and data loss avoided.

14.8.5 A look into the future

Over the last two decades the performance of CPUs as measured in operations per second per dollar has increased by a factor of 100% per year. The cost of storing a megabyte of data has dropped from $70 to $1 over the same span. In addition, the transfer rate of disk drives has increased from one megabyte per second to over

300 megabytes per second. However, the limiting factor in our utilization of disk drives for secondary storage is the average seek time and the rotational latency. Each of these factors has only dropped about a factor of 10 in that same time frame. Furthermore, the rotational latency is limited by the speed of sound at the outer tracks and this will not change. This means that these two factors now totally dominate the time it takes to randomly access any particular information on a hard drive. Having drives that are still very slow in relation to CPUs has pushed the performance of computer systems way out of balance.

On the OS side we have thrown large blocks of cache RAM at the disk drive in order to make the speed seem more like RAM. We also developed elaborate scheduling algorithms to optimize the performance of the head positioning mechanism. We are spending large amounts of our resources to manage these devices that are increasingly out of synch with the processors.

Tape drives were once the normal secondary storage device on mainframe computers. By the 1970s they had vanished in that role and had been replaced by the disk drive. Tapes were relegated to tertiary storage because of the low cost of the media. It is becoming increasingly clear that the same thing needs to happen to the disk drive. It is not yet clear what that new class of devices will be, but we make a strong prediction that within the next 5–10 years we will see a new class of storage devices available that will essentially have near random latency and costs below the disk drives of today. Two likely candidates are pure electronic memories and microelectromechanical systems (**MEMSs**). **Hybrid hard drives** (**HHDs**) are already available that incorporate flash memory as well as rotating media. Windows Vista can already utilize extra flash memory as a high-speed extension to the cache memory. Much of the technology of this chapter will become obsolete and we will have to rethink how we use secondary storage. Perhaps we will do something more like the Palm OS does.

14.9 SUMMARY

In this chapter, we introduced the topic of lower-level input and output management, with a special focus on secondary storage and disk drives. Next, we discussed some broad classes of I/O devices and how they differ. We described some general techniques used in support of I/O devices. We then explored the physical structure of disk drives, and we discussed the logical organization of the information stored thereon. We covered the topic of RAID, wherein assemblies of disks are used in special configurations to achieve greater throughput and/or reliability. The very important topic of scheduling disk operations for optimum performance was covered. We addressed a special type of device controller called a DMA controller that can significantly decrease the CPU load of I/O operations. We also discussed some disk drive features that affect OS behavior, drive reliability, and so on.

BIBLIOGRAPHY

Hofri, M., "Disk Scheduling: FCFS vs. SSTF Revisited," *Communications of the ACM,* Vol. 23, No. 11, pp. 645–653.

Iyer S., and P. Druschel, "Anticipatory Scheduling: A Disk Scheduling Framework to Overcome Deceptive Idleness in Synchronous I/O,"

Symposium on Operating Systems Principle, 2001, pp. 117–130.

Love, R., *Linux Kernel Development.* Indianapolis, IN: Sams Publishing, 2004.

Patterson, D., G.A. Gibson, and R. Katz, "A Case for Redundant Arrays of Inexpensive Disks (RAID)," *SIGMOD Conference,* 1988, pp. 109–116.

Russinovich, M. E., and D. A. Solomon, *Microsoft Windows Internals,* 4th ed., Redmond WA: Microsoft Press, 2005.

Teorey, T. J., and T. B. Pinkerton, "A Comparative Analysis of Disk Scheduling Policies," *SIGOPS Operating Systems Review,* Vol. 6, No. 1/2, 1972, pp. 114–121.

WEB RESOURCES

http://www.osdata.com (Operating System technical comparison)

http://www.pcworld.com/article/18693/how_it_works_hard_drives.html (hard disk characteristics and architecture)

http://www.littletechshoppe.com/ns1625/winchest.html (disk drive price per megabyte)

http://www.answers.com/topic/hard-disk (disk transfer rates)

http://en.wikipedia.org/wiki/RAID

REVIEW QUESTIONS

14.1 Distinguish between double buffering and caching as applied to disk systems.

14.2 True or false? The reason that disk scheduling algorithms traditionally ignore rotational latency is that it is so small compared to the seek time.

14.3 Briefly define a cylinder.

14.4 Which of these disk drive organizations provides increased performance but no redundancy?
  a. RAID 0
  b. RAID 1
  c. RAID 5
  d. RAID 6
  e. All of the above require the same number of drives.

14.5 Which of these disk drive organizations provided redundancy but at the highest cost in extra drives?
  a. RAID 0
  b. RAID 1
  c. RAID 5
  d. RAID 6
  e. All of the above require the same number of drives.

14.6 What is the advantage of RAID 6 over RAID 5?
  a. It is faster on a multiblock read.
  b. It is faster on a multiblock write.
  c. It can stand the loss of two drives at the same time.
  d. It requires fewer extra drives.
  e. None of the above is an advantage of RAID 6 over RAID 5.

14.7 True or false? The C-LOOK disk scheduling algorithm gives about the same number of tracks seeked over regardless of whether the first direction selected is up or down.

14.8 At the end of Chapter 14 we discussed several mechanisms that had been introduced to increase the abilities of disk systems. Several were for performance and some were for reliability. Which of the following was **NOT** for increased performance?
  a. Tagged queuing (native command queuing)
  b. Disk (controller) hardware buffering
  c. Dynamic memory access
  d. Sector sparing
  e. All of the above were for increased performance.

14.9 What does the acronym CHS refer to?

14.10 What does the first sector on a PC hard disk contain?

14.11 If the FIFO algorithm is the fairest (by definition), why don't we just use that?

14.12 Briefly describe the "pickup" disk scheduling algorithm.

14.13 Why was the concept of partitioning drives introduced?

14.14 What is the function of a CRC or LRC on a disk drive?

14.15 What is the function of a ECC on a disk drive?

14.16 How is the C-LOOK scheduling algorithm an improvement over LOOK?

14.17 What is the main advantage of a DMA controller?

14.18 Some new disk drives support native command queuing or tagged queuing. What is that and why is it an improvement?

14.19 Some new disk drives support so-called S.M.A.R.T. What is that about?

Part 5

Networks, Distributed Systems, and Security

In this part:

This part of the text deals with topics that are not found in all operating systems. One infamous computer hardware system officer noted that "the network is the computer." This is a strange statement, but it does point to the importance that we today place on the connection of most of our computers to other computers in general and to the Internet in particular. So this part of the book deals with those aspects of operating systems that deal with networking, distributed systems, and the issues of security and protection that arise in such instances.

Chapter 15 deals with the basics of computer networking. This topic by itself is the subject of many computer science textbooks and a very active research area, so this treatment is very brief. It takes a top-down approach and deals mostly with only the hardware and protocols in use today. The Internet features heavily, of course. The topics covered include why we want to network computers, application layer protocols, TCP/IP, the Data Link layer, WANs, the Physical layer, and network management, including remote monitoring.

Simple single-user systems that were not connected to one another by networks often did not need protection and security mechanisms. As a result, early OSs did not provide many features in this area, if any. However, today we find that many machines have multiple users, especially in homes, and most machines are connected to local area networks or the Internet or both. So security is today an important consideration, and Chapter 16 deals with it accordingly. The topics include authentication, authorization, and encryption.

After computers were networked we soon began to develop systems that include portions that ran on different computers, distributed systems. So this is the topic of Chapter 17. Again, this is topic that fills many books and courses, and much current research is being done in this area, so the treatment is also brief, as in Chapter 16. Subtopics include communication, processes, naming, alternative distributed system paradigms, synchronization, and fault tolerance.

Introduction
to Computer Networks

In this chapter:

We study operating systems because we cannot write large high-performance applications without a sound understanding of the functions and mechanisms of an operating system. It is fair to say that today we study networks for the same reason—it is rare that a large application is written today that does not make some use of networking technology. What was true of operating systems in general is also true of networks. If we do not have a sound understanding of the basics of networking we cannot build and deploy large distributed application systems.

This chapter starts with a brief introduction to explain some of the many reasons why we want to have computers connected in a network. In Section 15.2 we present a layered model of network functionality, which is traditionally used in discussing computer networking. Section 15.3 describes some typical protocols used in the application layer. Then in Section 15.4, we discuss the TCP/IP protocols as examples of the transport and network layers. In Section 15.5 we present the topic of the Data Link layer in LANs as typified by Ethernet. We give an overview of WAN data link technology in Section 15.6. Section 15.7 covers the technologies used in the Physical layer. Section 15.8 is a brief introduction to the topic of network management. We conclude with a chapter summary in Section 15.9.

15.1 WHY DO WE WANT TO NETWORK COMPUTERS?

At a more detailed level there are several reasons why we might want to build an application that was distributed across a network. As computer systems were maturing the initial reason we wanted to use networks had to do with sharing access to expensive resources. At first, that resource was a mainframe computer and we accessed the computer with simple terminals rather than through a personal computer. We were accessing data that was on the mainframe and programs that ran there. Later, as local area networks began to become common, we started using them to access other shared devices—a departmental file server, an expensive laser printer, a pool of modems, and attached communication lines. These resources were too expensive to provide to each user, and were typically not used full time. Therefore, making them accessible through a network spread the cost over many users. A shared resource might not be as easy to use as a local one, but the price more than made up for that. Another specific instance of sharing an expensive device is backing up individual systems to a single machine that had a tertiary storage device attached—probably a tape drive.

As networks became more common it became apparent that there were some special things that could be done with them. One of these special things was building a system by combining several smaller machines in a redundant configuration so that if one of the machines was lost, the system would continue to function, even if in a degraded manner.

Sometimes we will distribute the computation of a process across multiple machines to speed up the computation. We divide the processing into smaller parts that can be handled by individual machines. In a similar way, it is possible to configure multiple smaller machines into a system in such a way that additional machines can be added as the scale of the application grows. For example, this allows a company to start a website with a single machine and if the site is successful to add additional systems as the demand grows. Related to aggregating systems for speed improvement is the factor of cost. In some cases there are applications that simply could not be done at all with a single large system because of the mass of data and processing involved. Or in some cases a single large computer could do the job, but is not usable because of the cost. But systems can be designed using many smaller processors. Probably the first example of such a system is the SETI project. This project collects large amounts of radio telescope data and sends it out through the Internet to users who voluntarily process the data with a "screen saver" application that normally runs only in the background. The application is looking for signals that might represent intelligent life on another planet. Today, there are millions of registered users of the SETI screen saver. Viewed as a single, loosely coupled system operating in parallel on multiple streams of data, this is the fastest supercomputer in the world. There is no way that a nonprofit organization could afford to buy a single system that would have that much processing power, so without this technique they literally would not ever get the job done. SETI was the first such system, but today there are many other systems processing data doing research in cryptography, DNA, mathematics, gravity waves, and other scientific projects. We will visit this topic again in the next chapter on distributed systems.

After the great growth of the Internet in the last few years it has become clear that the most profound impact of networking lies in increased access to information. The relatively quick response time of the Internet has made practical the exchange of information in ways that were not economical before. An example is the idea of "telecommuting"—working from home. Many jobs require frequent, ongoing interaction between employees. To some extent this interaction can be closely approximated by email. Even closer interaction is available with instant messaging software—an interactive "chat" facility. In other cases this interaction might require voice communication, a "shared whiteboard," or even videoconferencing. All of these can be done today through the Internet, provided enough bandwidth is available at a low price, and may enable more of us to work from a home office rather than commute to a central office, at least on a part-time basis. Thus, networking may contribute to the solution of some societal problems by lessening the consumption of resources (and the resultant pollution) necessary for commuting.

Other instances of sharing information over the Internet also exist. It may be possible for us to collaborate on a project with other persons who live in distant parts of the world. For example, consider those people who work together to create the libraries of utilities that make the Linux OS a complete system rather than just an interesting example of a kernel. It is probable that most of those people have never met in person. Most of them work together only through the Internet.

On a less intense scale, think about the average user of the Internet. Most of us now use email daily and frequently employ the resources of the Web to answer questions, find people, buy products, download software updates, do our personal banking and other financial transactions, and so on. Such uses would not be possible without the Internet. It initially existed largely for other reasons, but information sharing was always a primary feature. We suggest that in the future it will be likely that the majority of the applications you might work on will be running in multiple parts on multiple hosts, and you will not be able to design sound applications without some understanding of networks and how they are used by operating systems.

15.2 THE BASICS

15.2.1 Models

In order to study and implement networks, models have traditionally been created that divided the subject into smaller topics by considering them as layers of software. In these models each lower layer provides some set of services to the next higher layers. While there is generally pretty good agreement about what functions are performed in what layers, the models are not perfect and they are not always followed exactly. As a result, functions are sometimes found in more than one layer. For example, we can find security functions available in almost every layer. In addition, in some cases it is useful to take a lower-level layer network protocol and run it as a layer on top of another higher-level protocol. In these cases the layer models can become quite confusing. These models are still quite useful in organizing our thinking and a large part of the literature about networking is structured around them, so

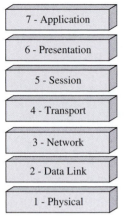

FIGURE 15.1
The OSI network
layer model.

we discuss them briefly. Furthermore, OS software is often modularized along the lines of these layers.

The most widely known network layer model is called the **OSI model,** shown in Figure 15.1. It was developed by the International Standards Organization, or ISO. It was an abstract design that did not reflect any existing protocol, though a set of protocols was later designed around this model. At one point the U.S. Government even mandated the implementation of the protocol on all computer systems purchased by the government under the umbrella term "GOSSIP." However, that effort never was very successful and was eventually abandoned. As an abstract model the OSI model has some problems, the most notable being that it has two layers that are almost never implemented as such, the Session layer and the Presentation layer.

In response to the OSI model, another model was constructed as a description of the TCP/IP protocol suite, which already existed. This model focused heavily on the upper layers (TCP and IP, for the most part) and pretty much ignored the lower layers, apparently assuming that the hardware and drivers were merely commodities and that one just ordered them from a vendor.

In this chapter we use a common hybrid model that is roughly the bottom two layers of the OSI model and the top three layers of the TCP/IP model. This model is shown in Figure 15.2. The **Physical** layer defines the actual medium used for communicating and the techniques for getting the information on and off of the medium. The medium might be a metal wire or cable, an optical fiber or an electromagnetic signal. The **Data Link** layer is responsible for accessing the shared medium. It is concerned with packaging information in discrete packets and arbitrating access to the network media. Today, Data Link layer devices called bridges (or switches) are used for connecting devices as though each pair of devices were directly connected, so the function of media access arbitration is largely unused and growing more so. The **Network** layer is responsible for routing the information through a complex internet composed of multiple networks, often of differing Physical layer technologies. The **Transport** layer is responsible for creating a reliable connection between two network entities, though not all applications require either a connection or a guarantee of reliability. Finally, the **Application** layer consists of a process in one host exchanging data with a process in (usually) a different host.

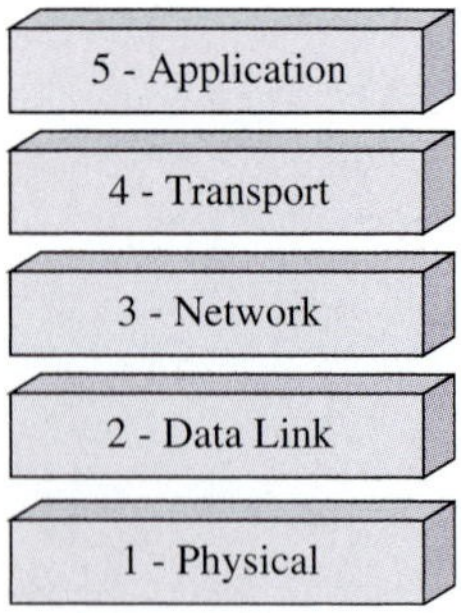

In a device attached to the network there will be an entity at each layer that is responsible for the functions of that layer in that device. At the Physical layer this entity will be in hardware. Some functions at the Data Link layer may be in hardware as well. For most devices, the entities at the other layers are all software. Each entity relies on the entity in the layer below it to provide services to it through an API. In turn, each entity provides services to the layer above it. As a packet in a sending device travels down the layers from one entity to the next, each entity will add a small block of information to the front of the packet. This block is called a header. For example, a data packet might have an application header, a TCP header, an IP header, an Ethernet header, and a Physical layer header. As the packet flows up the stack in a receiving device each entity strips off the header for its layer and hands the packet to the next higher layer. These headers carry a dialog between the corresponding entities in the sending and receiving devices.

FIGURE 15.2
A practical network
layer model.

This division of networking technology into layers has both good and bad aspects. On the good side, small modules are easier to understand, develop, and debug. They can be replaced with newer equivalent modules if improved versions are developed. Different organizations can specialize in different layers and develop better algorithms and implementations. On the other hand, it is extremely important that we have very good definitions of the interfaces between the layers and the dialog between the entities in the sending and receiving hosts. As a result, there are many different sources of standards. In some cases we have **de facto** standards where one vendor comes up with a good idea and other vendors follow the lead or some organization of vendors and users comes together and agree upon a standard. In other cases we have **de jure** standards, which technically have the force of law behind them. These standards are set by professional, national, or international organizations such as the IEEE, ANSI, and the ISO. In the networking arena many standards were created by members of the **Internet Engineering Task Force** (**IETF**). Each of these standards is known as a **Request for Comments** (**RFC**). There is a website that contains these documents at http://www.ietf.org/rfc.html. From time to time we refer to an RFC that defines some aspect of the Internet protocols.

15.2.2 LANs and WANs

There are several different ways to view the variety of possible network technologies. Each different view will shed some light on the differences among networks and their performance characteristics. The first major characteristic we want to consider is topology—what is the pattern of connections between the individual machines? Part of the difficulty in understanding networks arises from the fact that the physical topology of a network might be different from the logical topology of the network. The first broad division of network topologies is between **local area networks** (**LANs**) and **wide area networks** (**WANs**).[1,2] Generally speaking, in WANs the network connections are point-to-point. That is to say that when two systems are connected, the communication goes only between the two hosts and is not seen by any other host. The packets therefore do not need an address in them since there is only one device to read them. Since there are no addresses, there is no way to send a **broadcast** packet (one intended for all devices attached to the network) or a **multicast** packet (one intended for devices interested in one specific transmission stream). Frequently WAN links are **full duplex,** meaning that both of the hosts can transmit at the same time. In addition, since the link can be used in both directions at

---

[1] Some networking texts also describe metropolitan area networks (MANs) as a different class, but the distinction is not useful in this context.

[2] Some authorities specify that the difference between LANs and WANs is a matter of geography— LANs being small in area and WANs being spread over a wide area. Actually, geography makes very little difference in the characteristics of connections. FDDI LANs can cover distances of over a hundred kilometers. Historically it was very common to find two modems sitting on top of one another connecting two hosts through a WAN mechanism with a wire that was only a foot or two long because it was the only interface that two systems had in common. This was technically a WAN connection but was certainly not distributed geographically.

the same time there is no need to arbitrate access to the media—a host that is ready to transmit just does so.

On the other hand, LANs traditionally are broadcast connections. When two hosts are communicating with one another on a LAN their communication is across some medium that is shared among many devices. Devices communicating on a LAN therefore have to share access to the medium with all other devices connected to it. Since the packets must have addresses, it is possible to use special addresses like a **broadcast** or a **multicast.** And finally, since many hosts share a single link, it is necessary for the hardware to control access to the media.

Switching is a fairly new technology that has blurred the distinction between LANs and WANs. Individual devices are connected directly to ports on a network switch using technologies such as Ethernet, which was originally used to connect those devices to LANs. However, the switch reads the addresses in the packets and forwards them only to the port connecting to the correct device. Thus, the devices connected to the switch do not share a medium as with previous shared access technologies, so the connection can be full duplex and any device can transmit at the full speed of the network as long as the switch can handle the traffic, and most of them can handle all that can be sent their way. However, the packets still have to have addresses and both broadcasts and multicasts are still supported.

15.2.3 Topologies

With both WAN and LAN networks there are multiple topologies by which many devices can be connected. In WANs we can have hosts connected in pairs in any of the following topologies:

- Linear (Figure 15.3)
- Hierarchical (Figure 15.4, the top node is the focus point)
- Star (Figure 15.5, the central node is the focus point)
- Ring (Figure 15.6)
- Partly connected mesh (Figure 15.7)
- Fully connected mesh (Figure 15.8)

FIGURE 15.3
A linear topology.

FIGURE 15.4
A hierarchical or tree topology.

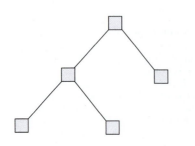

Each of these possible topologies has some distinct characteristics. First, let us consider these topologies when used in a WAN. Each WAN connection between two devices is relatively expensive, so the linear, star, and hierarchical topologies have the lowest cost because they have the fewest connections. The linear topology has the longest path to get information to all nodes, so communication to all devices in the network can be somewhat slow. The hierarchical topology is used when all the network devices are attempting to reach some centralized service. It was very typical in the era of large mainframes. The ring and mesh topologies are progressively more reliable (assuming that communication can go both ways on a ring) because there is often a redundant path for communication. In particular, the loss of a single link will not result in a loss of communication with any host in a ring topology. The fully connected mesh topology is the most expensive because it has so many links. It is also the fastest because every node is only one link away from every other node and the most reliable because the loss of a link only means that the two nodes on the opposite sides of the broken link have to use one intermediate node to communicate. The partially connected mesh is a compromise and is fairly typical. It is the topology used in the Internet. Networks with redundant pathways require more complex routing decisions for the packets at the Data Link or Network layers.

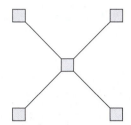

FIGURE 15.5
A star topology.

In LANs the two most common forms are a linear bus and a ring. A linear bus looks somewhat like the bus shown in Figure 15.3, but is actually connected as shown in Figure 15.9. In Figure 15.3 each node had a connection to the next node, and for a node on one end to communicate to a node on the other end the message had to be relayed through each intermediate node. In a LAN that is a linear bus topology, the bus is a separate medium and every node is connected to it. In order for the two end nodes to communicate, they merely have to gain access to the medium and then they can exchange their message directly. In a technical sense, a LAN in a ring topology does actually pass the message from host to host, but most of the hosts never process the message. Such LANs act as though each node were connected to the ring much like a linear bus, and when a device wants to send a message to another host it just waits its turn and transmits the message on the ring. The receiving host will read the message and hosts that are not addressed by the message will merely pass it along.

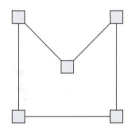

FIGURE 15.6
A ring topology.

A sort of blending of these two technologies is also possible—a physical linear bus in which the access to the medium is controlled by passing around a logical token as though the LAN were a ring. This is called a token passing bus. There were two instances of such protocols. One, ARCNET™, was once widely used for small networks but today is mostly confined to special applications such as inside of automobiles. The other, 802.4, was primarily confined to a single industry, automobile manufacturing, and is not under further development today.

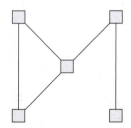

FIGURE 15.7
A partially connected mesh topology.

A bit of confusion can arise in determining the topology of LANs. A ring may be physically connected to resemble a star, as shown in Figure 15.10. The box in the center of the figure is a central connection point. The media appear to run from each node to a central point, but the central point is not a node and the signal actually passes from node to node in the manner of a ring.[3] Similarly, a linear bus can be

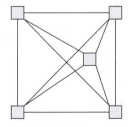

FIGURE 15.8
A fully connected mesh topology.

---

[3] The central hub may contain a node for purposes of management and data collection, but the node is not a part of the hub function.

FIGURE 15.9
A linear bus topology.

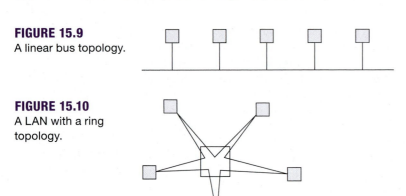

FIGURE 15.10
A LAN with a ring topology.

collapsed into a single concentrator, or hub, and appear to be a physical star or a physical hierarchical network, but the signals are broadcast throughout the network all at one time, so the electrical connectivity is that of a bus, not a tree or a star, in the sense that all the nodes will see the signal but will not have to relay it to another node.

Today, most LANs are actually switched networks. Again, the network might look like a star topology, but the central box is a high-speed switch that reads the packets sent by connected devices and sends them only to the device addressed. Switches can typically forward all the traffic that can be sent to them on all ports at one time. This is known as **wire speed.** If the switch has many ports or the ports are high-speed ports, then this requires considerable bandwidth in the switch. We discuss LANs and switches further in the section on the Data Link layer.

15.3 APPLICATION LAYER PROTOCOLS

15.3.1 The Application layer

At each of the layers of the protocol stack, every network attached device will have some entity that is interacting with a corresponding entity in another network device. In the Application layer there is an entity in one end system that is interacting with another application in another end application on a server system across a network. For example, one might use a Telnet client on a PC to talk to a Telnet server on a shared UNIX system. Each application will use a specific protocol, often one designed specifically for that application. Sometimes they will use a generic protocol designed to serve a wide variety of custom applications. In this section we briefly look at several Application layer protocols. Many of these Application layer protocols are widely used and have been assigned a **port number** for the server to use. This port number is used by the next lower layer, the Transport layer, to determine which application should receive an incoming message. Consider that a system running an FTP server may also be running other services such as Telnet, www, and so on. Messages arrive from the network at random, so each layer needs some information in the header that the sending entity applies to the packet to determine which entity at the next higher layer should be given the incoming packet. For a given application the port number to be used may be a **well-known port** number, that is, one that was reserved by the IETF to be used only for that application. If it is not a well-known number it may use a port number of 1024 or greater and less than 49151. Numbers greater than 49151 are used for dynamic assignment to clients by the OS software.

Today most networking uses the TCP/IP protocol suite. Figure 15.11 shows the format of the header used by IP layer. It shows the source and destination port numbers as well as other fields discussed in this chapter.

15.3.2 HTTP

HTTP, or **HyperText Transfer Protocol** is the protocol used to exchange messages between World Wide Web servers and browsers. The well-known port for Web servers is port 80. HTTP messages are sent in ASCII and as a result they can be easily read by a human, though they usually are not. Each message sent by a browser starts with one of only a few commands, such as GET, PUT, POST, or OPTIONS. The server sends back a response message. This message contains a code that gives the result of the browser's input and returns a requested page element when it is applicable. When a browser requests a page it makes a connection to the server and requests the page with a **uniform resource locator (URL)**. The page referenced by the URL is returned by the server in its response message. Most pages contain much more than a few lines of text, however. Usually, there will also be references to other items such as pictures to include with the page. Each of these contained elements must be separately requested from the server. In early versions of HTTP the server would break the connection after each request for a single element, so the browsers would optionally open several connections at the same time if there were multiple elements to fetch to complete the page. Later versions of HTTP optionally do not break the connection immediately, so that after the initial page is returned the browser can issue additional requests for many elements at the same time.

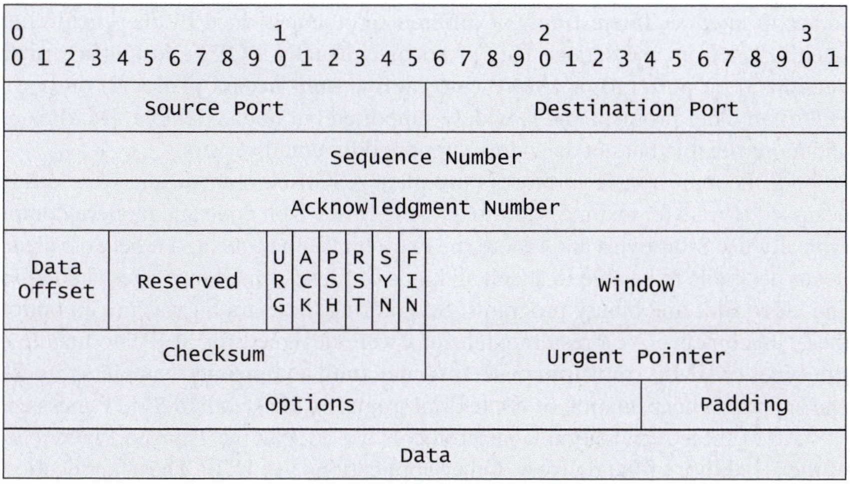

FIGURE 15.11
TCP header format.

While HTTP was designed specifically for fetching Web pages from servers, it has found other uses as well. Since access to the Web is so desirable, most institutions that have implemented firewalls to protect their networks from harm allow HTTP messages to pass through the firewall and freely admit connections to port 80. As a result, HTTP is often used in custom-distributed applications to minimize support problems.

15.3.3 FTP

Another common Application layer protocol is **file transfer protocol,** or **FTP.** FTP is unusual in that it uses two ports instead of one. The main port, 20, is used for transferring data. Port 21 is also used by the FTP protocol, but only for sending control messages. This design allows a large transfer to be interrupted, for example, by a user who suddenly realizes that the very large file that is now being downloaded is not the file that is needed after all. Another unusual aspect of FTP is that it is not only the name of the protocol, it is also the name of a program that uses the protocol. This program is a command-line utility and is somewhat difficult to learn to use well. One solution is to use stored scripts to run the program, but another common solution is to embed the protocol in a more user-friendly application. Many GUI utility programs are available for transferring files that incorporate the FTP protocol. Even most browsers are capable of using the FTP protocol when the URL starts with ftp:// instead of http://.

While the commands used by FTP are strictly ASCII messages, the files being transferred might be programs, for example, and often contain binary data. They might, therefore, contain strings that looked like FTP commands by accident. This is another reason why the data transfer uses a channel separate from the command channel. FTP includes a BINARY setting so that it can transfer programs and other files containing arbitrary binary data.

15.3.4 SMTP/ POP/ IMAP

SMTP is the **simple mail transfer protocol.** It is used in email applications to send email from a user's email client program and also to forward email from one email server to another. Interestingly, a different protocol is used by the email client to fetch email from the server. This protocol is usually **POP3 (post office protocol version 3)** on port 110 or **IMAP (interactive mail access protocol)** on port 143. POP is an older protocol and is widely supported but not as flexible. IMAP is newer and more flexible but not as widely supported by email servers.

All the mail transfer protocols use plain ASCII commands and were originally designed to transfer text messages only. ASCII is a 7-bit code and modern computers typically use 8-bit bytes and ignore the extra bit. Some time ago it became clear that it was desirable to be able to attach all kinds of files to email messages such as sound and video files and binary programs. So ignoring the extra bit was not an option for these attachments. As a result, extensions were designed for SMPT to handle other file types. **MIME (multipurpose Internet mail extensions)** supplements SMTP and supports encapsulation of nontext messages inside standard SMTP messages.

All of these Application layer protocols use TCP at the Transport layer because of the reliability of the delivery. Other applications use UDP. These applications do not need the extra reliability of TCP. In particular, multimedia applications often use UDP. Unlike data applications, streaming multimedia applications do not normally require 100% accurate data delivery. A missed packet in a sound stream will often not be noticed at all if the stream is not highly compressed. At the Application layer these programs mostly use proprietary protocols rather than IETF standards.

15.4 TCP/IP

Application layer protocols are supported by entities that implement a Transport layer protocol. Only a few years ago there were a number of different sets of networking protocols (called "suites") at this layer. The phenomenal success of the Internet, however, has changed this situation. With few exceptions all computer installations large enough to want a network also want to connect to the Internet. In order to access the Internet they must use the TCP/IP protocol suite. Within their own network they can also use other protocol suites. For example, it was a simple matter to load the IPX protocol on a computer in addition to TCP if one wanted to use IPX to access Novell Netware servers. Each additional protocol suite adds complexity, however, and the people managing the systems want to avoid that complexity whenever they can since it is expensive to support multiple options. Accordingly, they have put increasing pressure on system vendors to support TCP. As a result, almost all vendors now support the TCP/IP protocol suite. Since the other protocol suites do not provide significant services that TCP/IP does not provide, then most network managers have dropped the other protocols. Thus, TCP/IP has come to dominate the networking landscape.

15.4.1 The Transport layer

In the TCP/IP protocol suite, **IP** is the major Network layer protocol. **TCP,** or **transmission control protocol,** is one of two principle Transport layer protocols, with **UDP,** or **user datagram protocol,** being the other. Given an IP Network layer address, the IP protocols will try to deliver a packet of data to that address. UDP merely extends that function to the Application layer. This limited functionality is called an "**unreliable datagram.**" In this case the word "unreliable" does not mean that it is likely to fail—only that the protocol doesn't make any guarantees about the delivery. In many cases this "**best efforts**" functionality is all that is needed or desired. If the application is exchanging messages with a corresponding application on the other end of a connection, the two application parts can usually tell if something has gone awry. For example, most network management tools use UDP to send requests and responses. If the manager does not get a particular response when it is expected, then it will simply retry the operation.

In contrast, the TCP protocol provides "**connection-oriented, reliable**" communication. Given an IP address and a port number the TCP layer will attempt to contact an entity running at that port address on the addressed system and establish a connection. It will then transmit data to the entity at the other end and receive responses, relaying them to the calling application until one of the Application layer entities breaks the connection. This protocol uses various mechanisms such as message numbers and acknowledgments to ensure that the data are delivered once and only once to the other end and are delivered in the order they were sent. It also uses other mechanisms to cope with senders that are too fast for the receivers and for congestion in the network.

15.4.2 IP addressing and routing

As was mentioned, connection to another host requires that the calling host knows the **IP address** of the destination host. IP addresses are 32 bits long. When they are displayed for humans they are normally written in a specific style known as **dotted decimal notation.** This style breaks the 32 bits into 4 bytes and displays each byte as a decimal number separated from the other bytes with a period. Thus an address of all 1 bits would be written as 255.255.255.255. Each IP network that is connected to the Internet has a distinct network number. Within that network number the administrator of the network would assign individual addresses to each host system. At one time IP addresses were divided into **classes** depending on what portion of the address was to be used as the network number and what portion was the host address. These classes were known as A, B, and C. (There were also classes D & E for special purposes.) In 1993 this mechanism was replaced with a new mechanism called **CIDR,** or **classless interdomain routing,** and the technical distinction between the classes of address has mostly gone away, though people often still refer to a particular address as belonging to one of these classes.

A class of devices called **routers** are responsible for delivering IP packets from the source device to the destination device. Each router will look at the IP address in the packet and try to determine the best path to the destination network. It is therefore making decisions about where to send each input packet based on information at the Network layer. We therefore sometimes say that they are making forwarding decisions at layer three. IP network addresses are not assigned geographically (for the most part), so the routers that connect IP networks together need to learn how to find any other network in the world. They learn this information mostly by talking among themselves. They use a variety of protocols for this exchange of information. The protocol that two routers will use between themselves depends on their administrative relationship, among other things. There are several such protocols. They can be divided into groups depending on the underlying algorithm. The larger group is the **distance vector** algorithm group, including **RIP (routing information protocol), RIP2 (routing information protocol version 2), IGRP (interior gateway routing protocol), EIGRP (enhanced interior gateway routing protocol), and BGP (border gateway protocol.)** The **link state** algorithm group currently has one major representative, **OSPF (open shortest path first).**

Routers in the Internet will be connected in a partial mesh topology with many redundant links so that loss of one link will not normally **partition** the network into pieces that cannot communicate. Loss of a link may still cause some degradation of the service since some portions of the network will have to carry a heavier load. In the early days of networking, the term **gateway** was used to refer to the class of device we now call a router. You may still see the term used when configuring the IP protocol on any device, especially as part of the phrase **default gateway.** This name refers to the local router that a host is to use when it has no idea of the best path to use to access a host that it wants to communicate with. The phrase **default router** should be used these days. The term gateway is now more correctly applied to a service that connects two agents running at the Application layer. A good example would be an email gateway connecting a mainframe-oriented email system such as IBM's OfficeVision and a TCP/IP email system running SMTP and POP3 protocols.

It is possible for each network device to be specifically configured with a predetermined, **static** IP address, but this is difficult to administer. Servers that are known by name throughout the Internet will usually have a permanently assigned address. In other cases it is far easier to let the address be assigned dynamically. Computers are often moved as people change departments, for example. Laptops make the situation even worse as they are moved from the office to home to a neighborhood hot spot. So a protocol was designed to facilitate this moving around: **DHCP,** or **dynamic host configuration protocol.** Each network administrator will set up a DHCP server, which will be configured with a range of IP addresses that the network has been assigned. A host that is just turned on will send out broadcast messages looking for the DHCP server. The DHCP server will reply to the host and will tell it which IP address to use, among other things it will need to know. This address is **leased** to the workstation for some period of time after which it must be renewed. The DHCP server can also be configured to deliver the same IP address each time to a specific machine. This is normally only done for servers, printers, and such systems that normally do not change often.

15.4.3 Name resolution

Humans find that remembering IP addresses is not easy, so the TCP/IP protocol suite includes mechanisms for translating from a user-friendly name to an IP address. The protocol that is used to make this translation is called **DNS,** the **domain name service.** DNS relies on a hierarchy of servers to make these translations. A host might use a DNS server, for example, to translate the name "webserv" on the local network to an IP address. The DNS server might return an IP address like 223.1.2.1 if the user were in the domain where the name was located. Outside of that domain, a user trying to find this same server would have to use a different form of the name, called a **fully qualified name** such as webserv.example.com. In such a name, each of the parts between the periods is called a domain. The domains are organized into a tree structure. Various higher domains are owned and managed by different authorities, with the **top level domain,** or **TLD** (.com in this case) being administered under the authority of the IETF. If a host wants to look up such a fully qualified name, it begins by asking its default DNS server. The IP address of this server is either learned through DHCP or is configured manually into the host when the IP protocol is configured. If the local DNS server does not know the IP address of webserv.example.com, then it will ask the server at the next level in the DNS hierarchy. Eventually, the address will be found and returned to the host that started the request.

15.4.4 IP Version 6

By the early 1990s it began to look as though the world was going to quickly run out of IP addresses. As a result, there was a big push to define a new format for the TCP/IP protocol and IP addresses. This new format is known as IP version 6, or **IPv6.** Among other things, IPv6 would allow much bigger IP addresses, to the point that it is very unlikely that we would run out of IP addresses while we were still using TCP/IP. Several things happened that lessened this exploding demand. First, CIDR allowed the reuse of many IP addresses that had previously been allocated to institutions that would never need them. Second, DHCP allowed the dynamic reuse of IP addresses when hosts were frequently turned off for long periods or regularly came and went from the network so that institutions could get by with fewer IP addresses. And finally, **network address translation** (**NAT**) was developed. NAT is a technique for using one set of addresses inside a network and translating those addresses to a different (and much smaller) set of addresses that are seen outside the local network on the Internet. Together, these techniques meant that the pressure for going to IPv6 was largely removed. This migration will probably still happen in the long run because of other features of IPv6. Fortunately, IPv6 was designed to allow for a graceful migration. Most router vendors are already supporting IPv6 and new versions of most OSs include support for it, but not many users appear to be migrating to IPv6 yet. There is a research network parallel to the Internet known as the Internet 2 that uses IPv6 exclusively.

15.4.5 Common utility programs

There are a number of utility programs that are commonly distributed with TCP/IP protocol stacks. A few are designed for accessing common services such as:

> browsers for HTTP (Web) servers
>
> **ftp** clients for FTP servers (sometimes also done by a browser)
>
> **telnet** for a remote command shell
>
> pine for SMTP POP3, and IMAP for email

Other commonly distributed utilities are designed for network management. Knowledge of these tools will help any system designer understand the operation of the local network and how it affects the system design. These tools are discussed more in Section 15.8.

15.4.6 Other protocols

Although the other protocols running at the Network layer have largely gone by the wayside, there is still a significant install base of systems running the IBM protocols in the SNA/APPC family. Some of these protocols predate the TCP/IP stack. Some devices running these protocols are not programmable and cannot easily be upgraded. Furthermore, these protocols have special features that make them more useful in high-demand situations, so they are likely to remain in use for some time to come. Another very common protocol from the past is IPX, popularized by Novell for use with their Netware™ servers. IPX had one feature that made it very popular. The MAC layer address was used as a part of the Network layer address and a client system could automatically learn the remaining part of the address. This meant that the IPX protocol drivers in a client workstation did not have to be configured with an address, even when a system was moved to another physical network. This greatly simplified network administration and was probably a significant factor in the popularity of this operating system. But the popularity of the Internet eventually overwhelmed this factor and lead to the ultimate withdrawal of the protocol by Novell. However, IPX has found a niche in online multiplayer gaming, so it will also probably be with us for some time to come. Various other protocols were also used, mostly related to specific OSs. Examples include DECNet and LAT used with Digital Equipment hardware and Vines used with Banyan systems. The NetBIOS protocol was developed originally for IBM for small LANs. It was eventually adopted by Microsoft and has only begun to disappear with the later releases of Windows NT. Other vendors have been bought out, merged, or vanished. In some cases there are remnants of the NetBIOS protocol developed by IBM and used extensively by Microsoft. In particular these include the **server message block** (**SMB**) protocol and the Open Source Samba package used with UNIX/Linux to access Microsoft servers. However, the latest releases of the Windows NT family have made it clear that TCP/IP is their preferred direction.

15.4.7 Firewalls

Unfortunately, the world contains people who are ignorant, incompetent, or malevolent. Bad things can come into a network that is exposed to the world through the Internet (or any similar network). As a result, devices have been developed that are designed to protect networks from such traffic. In general, these devices are routers. The routers are placed at the ingress to the network from the Internet and accept the packets from the Internet as usual. Before they forward the packets to LANs inside the network, they perform an extra function of looking inside the packets and checking for things that the network administrators decide they do not want to pass through the router. These checks can include many things. Here are a few representative examples. (We discuss many of these in Chapter 16.)

- PINGs
- SPAM email
- Viruses
- Known denial of service (DOS) attacks
- Access to undesirable websites (e.g., parental control)
- Access to ports that are not in use

15.5 THE DATA LINK LAYER

The types of networks called LANs originally had a special characteristic: the data are transmitted in such a way that all the hosts connected to the same link will actually "see" every transmission. Each host will normally be configured so that it will only "read" information that is actually addressed to it. Another phrase often applied to such LANs is "multiaccess networks." Since many such hosts connected to one physical medium there had to be a mechanism devised to allow them to share access to the medium. These mechanisms are known as **media access control,** or MAC. Another term derived from this name is a **MAC address.** Every host is connected to the LAN with a **network interface card,** or **NIC,** sometimes called a network adapter. Every NIC has a 6-byte address assigned by the manufacturer. The first 3 bytes identify the manufacturer and the last 3 identify that specific adapter. For the most part one can safely assume that these addresses are globally unique, though there have been reports of unscrupulous vendors manufacturing cards under another vendor's identification number.

There have been many different contending mechanisms for the MAC function. Only four were very successful: **Ethernet™**, **ARCNET™**, **Token Ring,** and **FDDI** (**fiber distributed data interface**). ARCNET was one of the first LAN technologies but had substantial limitations. These same limitations turn into advantages in embedded systems, and ARCNET survives today in such environments but has virtually disappeared as a general LAN technology. Ethernet and Token Ring were eventually standardized by the IEEE as 802.3 and 802.5, respectively. FDDI was an ANSI standard. Although it is not precisely correct, we will simply refer to "Ethernet" since that is fairly common usage. Ethernet had a distinct advantage in that it is a simpler technology than either Token Ring or FDDI. It was therefore generally easier to install correctly and it was cheaper. There was, however, a serious set of drawbacks to Ethernet.

15.5.1 Ethernet

Ethernet relied on the probability that most of the time the network was not busy. If it was busy then the sender would wait until the network was free and then transmit. If two stations started transmitting at the same time, their transmissions would interfere with one another, causing a **collision.** The Ethernet MAC mechanism was known as **carrier sense multiple access/collision detection,** or **CSMA/CD.** It led to two major problems. First, the bandwidth was not fully usable. In heavily loaded networks the throughput would reach a maximum at 40–50% utilization in most situations. Second, if the network was pushed past this point it would eventually reach a state where collisions were happening all the time and the network would stop transmitting data at all. Token Ring and FDDI did not suffer from these problems. They were not stochastic, as was Ethernet, but rather were deterministic. When a device was added to the LAN the average response time for a single host would drop by a predictable amount. Each station always got equal access and it was fairly easy to run the LAN at very nearly 100% utilization. Installations such as banks, hospitals, and police stations that could not tolerate failures and needed to be able to predict the response times would often spend the extra money for Token Ring or FDDI.

15.5.2 Bridging and switching

Eventually, a solution was developed that allowed Ethernet to overcome these difficulties. The shared wiring concentrator (or **hub**) was replaced with a switch. A hub was a simple Physical layer device that merely repeated an input signal from any port out to all the other ports. A **switch** is a multiport device that only sends a packet of data out the port that leads to the device it is addressed to. The address used at this level is the Ethernet address of the NIC. So this forwarding decision is being made at the Data Link layer (or Media Access Control layer). This is sometimes knows as **layer two switching.** Furthermore, such switches are able to accept and forward input on all ports at the same time (subject to limitations of the switch backplane). In addition, changes were made that allowed the attached devices to run in full duplex — sending and receiving at the same time—and to run at either 10 or 100 Mbps. Newer equipment can automatically sense the best mode of operation of the switch and the attached device so that installation is really as simple as a hub. Inexpensive switches now can commonly run the ports at Gigabit Ethernet speeds as well. This series of developments took Ethernet from a system where the top throughput was roughly 5 Mbps to a system where a fairly modest switch can deliver one Gbps of throughput at 100 Mbps. Larger, more expensive switches can deliver even higher performance.

Before multiport switches became common, smaller switches (known then as **bridges**) were used to divide large LANs into small sections. Dividing networks into smaller sections allowed better throughput and response time for the devices on each segment. Bridges were initially devices with only two ports. By reading all the traffic on the LANs they were connected to they would learn that MAC addresses could be reached through each port. When they saw a packet on one port that was addressed to a device that they had learned to be reachable through the other port, they would forward the packet out that other port. This was called a **transparent bridge** or a **learning bridge.** A problem with transparent bridges would arise if two bridges were connected in parallel between two LANs. (This is a desirable thing to do since it provides a redundant link in case of the failure of one bridge.) The bridges would form a loop and the packets would be continuously transmitted around the loop. A feature was developed for transparent bridges that allowed them to be connected in parallel (or in more complex mesh networks) without actually making a loop. The bridges would coordinate among themselves, and by not forwarding traffic on selected paths would form a **spanning tree** that would forward data everywhere but would contain no loops. If a bridge (or a port) failed, then the bridges would sense this and form a new spanning tree. The biggest problem with this solution arose when some of the connections were not LAN connections but WAN connections. The WAN lines are fairly expensive (relative to the other network costs) and having a bridge that shut a WAN path off to keep from forming a loop was a luxury that few could afford.

When multiport switches were introduced to the market they could usually forward traffic from all the input ports to output ports as rapidly as it could be sent by the attached hosts. This was known as **wire speed** forwarding. The marketing staff wanted to distinguish this behavior from the earlier bridges, so they adopted the word **switch.** The performance of multiport switches began to cut into the market for routers. By redesigning routers and using **application-specific integrated circuits (ASICs)**, engineers were able to build devices that could make the forwarding decisions at the Network layer but could do this at wire speed as did the layer two switches. So the marketing people once again got involved and they called these new high-speed routers **layer three switches.**

15.5.3 Token Ring

Token Ring hardware had a MAC mechanism that was entirely different from Ethernet. The hardware used a special empty packet known as a token that was passed from host to host until it reached a host that needed to transmit a frame. At that point the host changed the token into a data frame and sent it on its way. Although this sounds inefficient, it actually worked very well. As was mentioned before, Token Ring hardware could easily reach 98% utilization of the bandwidth. Shared Ethernet, on the other hand, rarely reached 60% utilization and usually not even that.

Token Ring bridges could operate in the same manner as Ethernet bridges, but they also had a more complex mode known as source route bridging. In this mode the attached hosts would learn a path through the bridges and each packet would contain this routing information. Several advantages arose from this alternative:

- Bridges did not have to learn addresses and were simpler and cheaper.
- Bridges could be connected in a mesh and still utilize all links.
- Load across redundant links tended to self-balance itself.

Unfortunately, the source routing feature required some configuration (relative to the transparent bridge, which required essentially none). They also used broadcasts to find the preferred route and were often accused of causing **broadcast storms.** When Ethernet overcame its problems by utilizing fast switching, the Token Ring option lost out, along with source route bridging.

15.5.4 Other data link methods

FDDI is a technology that was initially developed for use over optical fibers rather than over copper wire. It was thus intrinsically more expensive to build and to install. It ran at 100 Mbps, long before Fast Ethernet did. FDDI rings could be over 200 km in circumference. Because of its cost it is normally not used for attachment of individual hosts but rather for a **backbone** LAN that connects bridges, switches, or routers between buildings on a campus. FDDI was later modified to also run over copper wires at shorter distances.

There have been many other technologies that have contended for the LAN. One that has enjoyed limited success has been **asynchronous transfer mode** (**ATM**). As was Token Ring, ATM is a rather complex technology. However, ATM offers features that make it attractive in situations where it is desirable to mix data transmission with voice and video transmissions over a single network and guarantee the most appropriate **quality of service** (**QoS**) to all users. ATM has been a clear winner in the WAN arena. In the LAN arena the goal of delivering services that require different QoS has been achieved by overbuilding the network so that any application can have any service it wants. This has been possible because bandwidth cost is currently so low. The best overall performance would be achieved if communication were done using ATM end-to-end. Where it has been used the success rate is high. At this point it is doubtful if ATM will be a major factor in the LAN arena.

ARCNET was also once very popular. It was an ANSI standard rather than an IEEE standard, and lost out mostly because it did not support bridging and it had a Network layer address that was only one byte and was configured with hardware switches—an error-prone process.

15.5.5 Mapping IP addresses to MAC addresses

We mentioned before that humans usually refer to human-friendly names like webserv.example.com, and that the Network layer used DNS to translate the name to an IP address. We also said that on the LAN the information is actually addressed to the MAC address of the NIC. The obvious question, then, is how does the software map from the IP address to the MAC address? The answer is that it uses a special protocol called **address resolution protocol,** or **ARP.** A host looking for a server will make an ARP packet that contains the IP addresses of both the host and the server. In the MAC header it will include its own MAC address, but it does not yet know the MAC address of the server, so it will send the packet to all hosts by using a broadcast MAC address (of all 1 bits). Every host will read the packet and pass it to the IP software. The IP module will pass the packet on to the ARP module. The ARP module in the correct server will recognize that it is being addressed by the ARP and will prepare an ARP response packet. This packet will be sent directly back to the inquiring host and that host will then continue the conversation using the new MAC address. The IP software in all the other hosts except the one addressed will merely ignore the packet. The OS will typically cache the MAC addresses in an **arp table.**

15.5.6 Functional migration into hardware

As networking has become more established, some of the functions that were initially done in software by the device drivers have migrated into the hardware. This evolutionary step takes some time, because a function should not be migrated to hardware until it is very well understood. Mistakes in hardware are quite expensive to fix. Two examples of functional migration to hardware have occurred in NICs. First is the calculation of **cyclic redundancy checks** (**CRCs**). CRCs are a class of functions that are computed on blocks that are transmitted over a network. They were discussed at some length in Chapter 14. The CRC is transmitted with the block and the receiver makes the same calculation as the sender. If the calculated CRC does not match the CRC sent with the packet, then the receiver knows that an error was made. Originally this function was computed by the software driver for the NIC. It was fairly expensive to compute in terms of CPU cycles. However, hardware engineers discovered a fairly trivial way to do the same computation as the packet was being transmitted. This was an inexpensive way to take a considerable load off the CPU. This function might not make much difference in modern machines, but at the time it was developed machines were much slower so it was a bigger deal.

Another function that has migrated into the NIC hardware is the recognition of **multicast addresses.** Multicast packets are sent out over the network and every NIC will see them. Several multicast streams might be in use on a given LAN at any one time. A specific system might or might not be interested in a particular stream. A good example of a multicast would be a stock ticker application that might run in a stock brokerage. Not all systems would need to see that stream, but many of the brokers might want to watch the ticker, so they would run a specific application that would look for the particular multicast address that was assigned to that stream. At one time all multicasts were received by all adapters and passed up to the Network layer where they might be dropped if the system were not interested in that stream. This was especially unproductive in systems that were not interested in any streams. They still got interrupted by every multicast packet and the software had to examine the address. Eventually, this function was also migrated to the NICs. The protocol stack would notify the NIC of any multicast addresses it had applications interested in. Packets to those addresses would be passed to the protocol stack and any other multicast packets would be dropped by the NIC and the CPU would not be interrupted.

15.6 WANS

In contrast with LANs where the hosts are usually in the same building or at least the same campus, wide area networks, or WANs, are connections between devices where the data must pass over a serial point-to-point connection. Often these connections are between two bridges or routers but sometimes a host will link to a bridge or router, especially if the connection is a dial-up link. For dial-up links through **plain old telephone service** (**POTS**), the highest speed available is 56 Kbps. When a WAN link is connected permanently, the link is known as a leased line. These lines are usually digital (as opposed to the dial-up link, which is analog). Typically the slowest leased line speed is 56 Kbps, though 64 Kbps is also common. The next speed line available is a **T1** line, which runs at 1.544 Mbps. Speeds between 64 Kbps and T1 are sometimes available as well. These lines are called **fractional T1** lines, or **Frac-T1.** Higher speed lines are also available that are multiples of T1 speeds. T1 lines were originally designed to carry voice traffic. These calls were analog signals that had been digitized to a 64 Kbps stream. Up to 24 such slow digital streams could be combined by synchronous **time division multiplexing** (**TDM**) onto one T1 line that ran between phone company switching centers.

15.6.1 Frame relay

When a large network is built with WAN lines, a big factor in the total line cost is that portion of the circuit that goes from the customer premise to the local phone company office—called the **last mile.** If the customer has a number of leased 56 Kbps lines connecting different sites from the home office, they can usually multiplex them in groups of 24 onto a single T1 line. This can result in tremendous line cost savings since that T1 line can usually be run over one standard twisted-pair copper line. Another technology was also developed that goes even further in this direction. Rather than use synchronous time division multiplexing as was described above, the line is used to send packets instead of streams of data and each packet is addressed and switched through the network separately. This technology is known as **frame relay.** It makes good sense because often the capacity of some of the individual 56 Kbps circuit is underutilized. A network using synchronous TDM circuits is designed for something near the peak load traffic rates. Since the worst case does not often arise, there is usually unused bandwidth. Thus, a T1 line might actually be able to carry all the packets for 40–50 lines running 56 Kbps when using frame relay instead of TDM. Alternatively, a single 56 Kbps frame relay circuit to the carrier's office might carry all the frames from three to five 56 Kbps circuits that were not heavily used all the time. Thus, frame relay networks can save their users a lot of money.

15.6.2 Other WAN technologies

One LAN protocol that enjoyed a brief period of popularity was **integrated services for digital networks,** or **ISDN.** A single copper circuit could be brought to a home or small office, which could carry two 64 Kbps channels.[4] This type of service was called **basic rate interface (BRI).** These channels could each carry a single digitized voice call or a data channel. The two data channels could also be logically combined and used as a single 128 Kbps channel. This was substantially better than a POTS line. A large attraction for ISDN came at the core of the network where the interface was a **primary rate interface (PRI),** which carried 23 channels of 64 Kbps each plus one 64 Kbps channel for signaling. The main advantage to PRI was that the calls could be either digital calls originating from an ISDN BRI device or analog calls originating at a regular modem. The analog calls would be digitized by the carrier at their office and delivered digitally. ISDN PRI services are also still used today in telephone support offices for pure voice traffic.

As was mentioned earlier, another technology was developed specifically for WANs: ATM. ATM is frame relay carried to an extreme. The essence of ATM is that all traffic is broken into small pieces—48-byte cells. These cells can be switched rapidly and cheaply and can give each user exactly the types of traffic service needed. This is highly desirable for the carriers since they have contracts to offer all kinds of different services, from Teletype traffic to ultra high-speed data circuits. With ATM they actually deploy only one network and use different equipment at the entrance and exit points to the network that make it look like the service the user contracted for. The carrier only has to train operators and technicians to maintain one network; they only need one kind of management software; and so on. It is not hard to see why ATM has captured many of the WAN backbones.

For homes and small businesses there are two other competing technologies for high-speed WAN services: **cable modems** and **digital subscriber lines (DSL).** These two services use ATM and similar technology to provide permanent connections to the Internet at the same time as they provide some other service. In the case of cable modems, that other service was originally cable TV. In the case of DSL, that other service is POTS. Since ATM technology is employed, cable modems can also be used to deliver POTS service, but that is a later add-on to the original concept. As fiber optic cables are extended further into the local community, the available bandwidth to each customer is going up and eventually should reach directly into the home or office. Such technology goes by many different names, mostly like **fiber to the Curb,** or **FTTC.**

---

[4] Technically there was also a 16 Kbps channel that was used for network signaling or low-speed applications such as credit card authorizations.

15.7 THE PHYSICAL LAYER

For information to flow from one device to another there must be some medium that connects the two devices. That medium must be capable of being changed in some way such that the change can be sensed by the other device. Historically, for computer data this has meant that a metal wire of some type has connected the two devices and conducted a flow of electricity. In the last few years the copper wire has often been replaced by glass or plastic, which conducts light. Wireless transmission via electromagnetic transmission is also frequently used for sending information. For decades it was used only for analog audio and video transmission and telegraph transmission of text. In the last few years wireless has become more common for data transmission. Originally this was for digital transmission of analog data, but is now being used for data transmission, especially for laptop and handheld computers.

15.7.1 Copper wire specifications

The metal in communication wiring is most often copper and there are usually two wires for each line. Sometimes there are two wires that are identical and are twisted together. This is known as **twisted pair.** Wires that are twisted together are less likely to pick up radiated signals from other wires and to radiate signals that can be picked up externally. There may also be a layer of foil wrapped around a pair of wires or around several pair of wires that are grouped together as a single cable. This is known as **shielded twisted pair** wiring, or **STP.** Without the shield it is called **unshielded twisted pair,** or **UTP.** STP is less susceptible to outside interference and to having the signal be picked up outside the network than is UTP. The wire that was historically used to install telephone wires in homes and businesses is one type of twisted pair. The UTP wire used for data needs to be higher quality than standard telephone wire. Quality in UTP wiring is standardized in terms of **Category** or **Cat** by the **Telecommunications Industry Association (TIA).** The lowest category currently approved for new data installations is Cat 5, rated at about 100 Mbps. The newest standard is for Cat 6 at 250 Mbps. The next step is for a Cat 7 standard that will run 10 gigabit Ethernet over 100 m of copper cabling.

There is another configuration of copper wiring called **coax,** shorthand for **coaxial cable.** In this case there is a single center conductor wrapped with an insulation material. Then a layer of very thin wires are braided around this insulating layer. (Occasionally the outer layer is solid, like a tube.) This layer becomes the second "wire" in the pair. The center wire is at the center (or axis) of the outer layer, so the two wires are coaxial. Coax is even less likely to radiate its signal or to pick up external signals than is STP. However, it is more expensive so it is limited to special uses. Coaxial cable is the type of wire used for cable TV. The cable TV coax used inside a building is about the size of a pencil and is somewhat inflexible compared to UTP wire.

15.7.2 Fiber optic specifications

Fiber is almost totally free from problems with radiated signals. It is also somewhat expensive, roughly twice the cost of copper cabling, but it is widely used because it is almost totally free from errors. In addition, it can send data over rather long distances. Indeed, in 2001 a vendor demonstrated transmission across the continental United States over a single fiber without a repeater. It has very high bandwidth capability, so the price per bit transmitted can be very low where large volumes of data need to be handled. The vast majority of new WAN circuits are fiber and it is very common in the backbone LAN in a building or campus.

When the telephone carriers first put in fiber optic links they worked very well. They have very low error rates, for one thing. Each fiber was limited by the physics of the receiver circuits to about 5 Gbps of data. After they had been in use for a while, however, engineers realized that there was a simple, inexpensive, and reliable optical way to combine several signals over the same fiber by using a prism at each end. This technology is called **wavelength division multiplexing,** or **WDM** (or sometimes **DWDM** for **dense WDM**). As a result, each fiber that was installed can now carry 64 to 128 times as much data as was first thought. Since the cost of the right-of-way and of installing the fiber itself is a major factor, this has meant a precipitous drop in the cost of wide area bandwidth. This drop has manifested itself in a rapid drop in long-distance telephone rates over the last few years. Indeed, in many cases the local phone companies can afford to give their customers access to long-distance lines for free if they will agree to buy the local service.

15.7.3 Wireless networking

As was mentioned earlier, a relative newcomer to the transmission of digital data is communication over wireless media—essentially digital radio.[5] This technology is obviously applicable in laptop and handheld computers, but it is also applicable where hosts must be moved frequently or where physical limits preclude direct cabling. Another promising area is in mobile systems—robots, if you will. There is an IEEE standard for wireless communication, 802.11, known by its marketing term **Wi-Fi.** Devices are readily available to connect to wireless LANs— PC Card NICs, bridges, routers, PCI NICs, and so on. These devices will probably continue to fill these niches. Another wireless protocol, Bluetooth, facilitates exchange of information between wireless devices such as personal digital assistants (PDAs), mobile phones, laptops, computers, printers, and digital cameras via a secure, low-cost wireless link. Bluetooth is being standardized by the IEEE as 802.15. The protocol variants in this family are designed for very short range and are sometimes referred to as **personal area networks** (**PAN**s) or **body area networks** (**BAN**s.)

Wireless is very susceptible to picking up interference from external sources and to being picked up by other devices, either accidentally or intentionally. Its chief virtue is that it does not require a physical connection between the two communicating devices. Because of the problems with noise, wireless communication has resulted in more robust error detection and correction and security mechanisms. Development of these mechanisms had been allowed to lag somewhat because cable and fiber were so free from errors.

---

[5] There have been wireless networks used before. They traditionally have been used in military application or locations such as the Hawaiian Islands where it was prohibitively expensive to lay cable.

15.7.4 A note on network troubleshooting

As a practical aside, when troubleshooting network problems one should always begin the study by checking the Physical layer. Physical layer problems, especially intermittent problems, can cause all manner of problems to manifest at other layers. Therefore, one should always begin network troubleshooting by verifying that there is an error-free connection between the two devices at the Physical layer.

15.8 NETWORK MANAGEMENT

15.8.1 Simple management tools

Two special protocols are used with TCP/IP for network management: **ICMP (internet control message protocol)** and **SNMP (simple network management protocol).** ICMP serves several functions, but the most visible to the network manager is that it provides the basis for the **ping** and **tracert** (sometimes traceroute) utilities. The ping utility is a very simple tool primarily used to verify connectivity between two devices. It sends an ICMP echo command to a destination host. That host will normally reply to the echo command with an ICMP echo reply. Options on the ping utility allow sending a large block of data, retrying the ping operation in a loop, and so on. Measuring the response time and its variability can also help a network operator identify performance problems in the network. Tracert uses a succession of pings to discover the series of routers connecting two network hosts. It gives reports for each hop on the route and this can further assist in locating network performance problems.

15.8.2 SNMP and network device management

SNMP has historically been the protocol that network management software used to communicate with network devices to monitor, configure, and troubleshoot them. Most network devices that were manageable would have a set of parameters that they would furnish information about or allow to be changed. These parameters would be described by a **MIB,** or **management information base.** From the outside it is easy to believe that the device actually stores the MIB itself. Actually, the MIB is just a convenient, structured way to describe the data and its semantics and the format used to transfer the data. The device stores the data values in whatever fashion is convenient for it. The IETF has standardized quite a number of MIBs, including ones for specific hardware classes such as Ethernet ports and for protocols such as TCP and UDP, but vendors have also added many proprietary extensions.

Managers rarely see SNMP directly. Rather, the MIB for a networking device like a router was used to develop a software tool that would allow remote management of network devices using SNMP but with a GUI interface. Some of these tools were quite elaborate, showing images of devices with blinking lights and maps with colors indicating network status. Unfortunately, they were all proprietary, so many large **network operation centers** (**NOCs**) were filled with dozens of workstations all running different software packages. This required extensive cross-training of operators who knew the vagaries of each software package.

The trend today is to put a dedicated specific HTML server entity in the device and manipulate it with a Web browser using the HTTP Application layer protocol. This means that proprietary management software is less often required, and that the cross-training demand has lessened. It is still necessary to know the specific characteristics of the network devices, but much less training is demanded since the browser is standard to all such devices.

15.8.3 Packet capture

When Ethernet networks were built with hubs, every NIC on the network would see every packet that was sent over a LAN. Normally, an adapter would only read packets with a broadcast address, a multicast address, or the address of the adapter itself. However, some adapters could be placed into a **promiscuous** mode, in which case they would read every packet on the network. This became a useful tool for troubleshooting network protocols. Very elaborate tools were developed. The best known was the Sniffer™ line made by Network General Corporation. Such tools had many options. For example, they could be set up to capture only traffic meeting certain criteria, start capturing only after some trigger event was seen, save captured packets to a hard drive, and create a decoded display of the packets using only the layers of interest. Unfortunately, such tools had a dark side as well, as unscrupulous users could use capture programs to see privileged information and capture passwords if they were not encrypted.

The development of switched Ethernet has largely solved this latter problem, for these switches only forward traffic addressed to a specific device out the port where that device is attached. Thus, a packet capture device will see only broadcasts, multicasts, and traffic intended for the capture device itself. Of course, this means that the capture technique cannot be used for the purpose for which it was originally intended. For this reason, switches that are intended for use in a large environment will often have a feature called **port mirroring.** This feature will allow a manager to tell the switch to take all packets to and from a specific port and copy it to another port. The packet capture device can then be plugged into that mirror port and can capture the session as before, but only the network management folks will be able to turn on this feature.

15.8.4 Remote monitoring

One of the MIBs that is defined by the IETF covers **remote monitoring** (**RMON**) of networks. Traveling to remote network sites for troubleshooting and maintenance can be very costly, so it is much preferable to be able to diagnose network problems remotely through the network. Routers are in a unique position to perform this function since they are already examining every packet they forward. The RMON MIBs define counters that an RMON agent in a router can maintain that go far beyond those in the basic router MIBs. They can include full trace facilities, statistics based on Application layer protocols, and other useful information.

15.9 SUMMARY

In this chapter, we gave an overview of the basic components of networked systems. We started with some motivational material about why the study of networks is important to the understanding of computer systems in general and operating systems in particular. We laid the groundwork for a discussion of networking by discussing some of the fundamental concepts and describing a model of networking that would be used for the remainder of the chapter. We discussed a few Application layer protocols and the most well-known protocol used at the Transmission and Network layers, TCP/IP. We also discussed the continuing significant role of IBM and SNA. We discussed the Data Link layer, with special emphasis on Ethernet and we also discussed Token Ring and FDDI and compared them with Ethernet. We discussed the shortcomings of shared Ethernet and showed why switched Ethernet at all speeds has come to dominate LAN architecture. We covered WANs and a few unusual WAN protocols and why they are sometimes used. The topic of the next section was the Physical layer and some of the options therein. Finally, we covered network management, including simple utilities, SNMP and normal network management operations and the migration to HTTP and browsers. RMON was also profiled.

BIBLIOGRAPHY

Abramson, N., "The ALOHA System—Another Alternative for Computer Communications," *Proceedings, Fall Joint Computer Conference,* 1970.

ANSI/IEEE Standard, *Carrier Sense Multiple Access with Collision Detection (CSMA/CD) Access Method and Physical Layer Specifications,* Std. 802.3-1985, May 1988.

ANSI/IEEE Standard, *Token Ring Access Method and Physical Layer Specification,* Std. 802.5-1985, December 1987.

ANSI/IEEE Standard, *Token-Passing Bus Access Method and Physical Layer Specification,* Std. 802.4-1985, March 1986.

ATM Forum, *LAN Emulation Over ATM LNNI Specification Version 2.0* (AF-LANE-0112.000), February 1999.

Beck, M., et al., *Linux Kernel Programming,* 3rd ed., Reading, MA: Addison-Wesley, 2002.

Bertsekas, D., and R. Gallager, *Data Networks.* Englewood Cliffs, NJ: Prentice Hall, 1987.

Comer, D., *Internetworking with TCP/IP Principles, Protocols, and Architecture.* Englewood Cliffs, NJ: Prentice Hall, 1988.

Martin, J., and K. K. Chapman, *SNA: IBM's Networking Solution.* Englewood Cliffs, NJ: Prentice Hall, 1987.

Martin, J., and K. K. Chapman, *Local Area Networks Architectures and Implementations.* Englewood Cliffs, NJ: Prentice Hall, 1989.

McQuillan, J. M., I. Richer, and E. Rosen, "The New Routing Algorithm for the ARPANET," *IEEE Transactions on Communications,* Vol. COM-28, May 1980, pp. 711–719.

Metcalfe, R., and D. Boggs, "Ethernet: Distributed Packet Switching for Local Computer Networks," *CACM,* Vol. 19, No. 7, July 1976.

Perlman, R., *Interconnections: Bridges, Routers, Switches, and Internetworking Protocols,* 2nd ed., Reading, MA: Addison-Wesley, 1999.

Postel, J. B., C. A. Sunshine, and D. Cihen, "The ARPA Internet Protocol," *Computer Networks,* 1981.

Stallings, W., *ISDN: An Introduction.* New York: Macmillan, 1989.

Voydock, V. L., and S. T. Kent, "Security Mechanisms in High-Level Network Protocols," *Computing Surveys,* Vol. 15, No. 2, June 1983, pp. 135–171.

Zimmerman, H., "OSI Reference Model—The ISO Model of Architecture for Open Systems Interconnection," *IEEE Transactions on Communications,* Vol. COM-28, No. 4, April 1980, pp. 425–432.

WEB RESOURCES

http://www.bluetooth.com/bluetooth/ (commercial products)

https://www.bluetooth.org (standards organization)

http://www.ietf.org (Internet Engineering Task Force; defines all RFCs, including IP, TCP, UDP, NAT, RIP, RIP2, PPP, IPv6, CIDR, SLIP)

http://www.ipmplsforum.org (Internet Protocol Multi-Protocol Label Switching forum—succeeded the ATM forum)

http://www.w3.org/Protocols (mostly about HTTP)

REVIEW QUESTIONS

15.1 What was one of the main initial motivations for networking computers?

15.2 Ultimately what became the most significant benefits of networking computers?

15.3 In the networking models we discussed, each layer is represented by an entity in each computer. Each such entity has a conversation with another entity for each connection. What other entity is it talking to?
 a. The next higher layer
 b. The next lower layer
 c. The peer entity in the other system
 d. None of the above

15.4 In a WAN, which topology is the most efficient in terms of speed of reaching all nodes from a central site?
 a. Linear
 b. Tree
 c. Star
 d. Ring
 e. All of the above are the same in terms of communication speed

15.5 Which WAN topology is the most expensive in terms of line costs?
 a. Star
 b. Ring
 c. Partially connected mesh
 d. Fully connected mesh
 e. All of the above have equal line costs

15.6 Some shared LAN topologies were not very efficient—notably, shared Ethernet rarely ran over 60% efficiency. What major development allowed such LANs to operate at much higher throughput?

15.7 What is the DHCP protocol used for?
 a. To translate IP addresses to MAC addresses
 b. To translate names to IP addresses

 c. To obtain an IP address and other information
 d. To update pages on a Web server host
 e. None of the above describes the use of DHCP

15.8 What was the main thing that saved us from a precipitous migration to IPv6?
 a. DHCP
 b. NAT
 c. CIDR
 d. DNS
 e. None of the above helped us delay using IPv6

15.9 Each protocol layer must have some information in its header to tell the receiving entity what entity to pass an incoming PDU to. What information in the Transport layer header tells TCP or UDP which application to give the packet to?

15.10 What protocol is used to translate IP addresses to MAC addresses?
 a. ARP
 b. NAT
 c. DHCP
 d. IGRP
 e. None of the above protocols involve mapping IP addresses to MAC addresses

15.11 Which physical medium has the best immunity against interference?
 a. Coax
 b. STP
 c. Wi-Fi
 d. Fiber
 e. All of the above have equal immunity against noise

15.12 We mentioned that a LAN and a WAN were different in what significant way?

15.13 We mentioned that the FTP protocol had some unusual things about it compared to the other two protocols we discussed. Name one.

15.14 What is the mechanism by which most network devices are coming to be managed, especially the cheaper ones?

15.15 When troubleshooting networks, which layer should you check first?

15.16 We say that UDP is an "unreliable" protocol. Why did we not design a "reliable" protocol?

15.17 True or false? Ethernet is the only LAN media access control protocol in use today.

15.18 What does Cat 5 refer to?

15.19 What is a SNIFFER?
   a. A bomb detection device
   b. A proprietary device for analyzing network protocols
   c. A person addicted to inhaling volatile chemicals
   d. A software program for stealing passwords
   e. None of the above describes a sniffer.

15.20 When we use a PING command and get a response from a host we learn quite a few things all at one time. Assuming that we did not already know anything at all about the situation, what are some of the things we might have just learned?

15.21 What is the DNS used for?
   a. To translate IP addresses to MAC addresses
   b. To translate names to IP addresses
   c. To obtain an IP address and other information
   d. To update pages on a Web server host
   e. None of the above

15.22 An IP address typically would be shown like this: 129.107.56.23. Such an address has two parts. 129.107 is one part and 56.23 is the other part. How are these parts used?

15.23 A router that is routing IP traffic also might use a protocol called RIP. What is that protocol used for?

15.24 Email uses two distinct kinds of protocols, SMTP and POP3, for example. What is the difference between these two protocols?

Chapter 16

Protection and Security

In this chapter:

At one time there were few thoughts given to problems of security in computer operating systems. In most cases security was provided by controlling physical access. Computers were huge things locked away in a room with lots of air-conditioning. A user who could access a system was allowed to access any file and any program that was running. As time has gone by the situation has changed. Time sharing began the biggest change since there would commonly be many programs running at the same time on behalf of many users who might have competing interests. Today it is quite common to share access to systems, especially in our homes. Even when systems are not shared, they are more often than not connected to a network. In many cases, even at home, they are on a LAN. At the least, many machines can connect to the Internet via a dial-up connection. However, intermittent that connection might be, while the connection is made our system is exposed to the entire Internet world—a place where threats reside as well as wonders.

In Section 16.1 we discuss the origins of some of the security problems. We then break them down into several different categories and describe the mechanisms an OS needs to deal with them. Some of these mechanisms need to reside outside the OS itself. We then move on in Section 16.2 to a general discussion of the nature of the protection services that OSs need to offer to users, primarily to provide privacy to files. We describe how these services are designed in general. Beyond the services the OS must provide for users, a different level of services is needed for processes. We have built significant barriers between running processes and the OS in order to protect them all. In Section 16.3 we continue with a look at some of the services that are needed by processes that are trying to communicate and cooperate with one another. Section 16.4 covers security as it pertains to networks in general and the Internet in particular. It includes discussions of encryption, authentication, and digests. It also discusses the related topics of network security and protection found outside of individual OSs. Section 16.5 covers the problems that arise in the administration of security in a network and an OS. The chapter concludes with a summary in Section 16.6.

16.1 INTRODUCTION: PROBLEMS AND THREATS

There are many reasons why we should not blindly trust all programs. Programmers can be bored, exhausted, lazy, careless, ignorant, unintelligent, malicious, or thoroughly evil. Any of these, or all of them together in some cases, can produce a program that can damage our work or even our systems. There are generally two classes of people we need to worry about. Hackers are very dangerous for home users because they attack system weaknesses that most home users are not knowledgeable enough to even recognize, much less fix. Hackers are also the most notorious, but they are only one portion of the problem. A problem that is less well known is unauthorized use by persons who have legitimate access to the system. Such internal problems are wide ranging. They include sending abusive or threatening emails, stealing money from accounts or goods from inventory, wasting time visiting websites not relevant to work or playing games on the computer, snooping on personal information of other employees, copying projects or papers from fellow students, bribery, extortion, taking company secrets to sell to the competition, and so on. Most of these problems are hard to spot and control because the person engaging in these activities has legitimate access to the system. We generally have to identify them through some means other than the OS controls. We rely on physical inventories, audits, and so on. In some ways the hackers are easier to control because they are forced to use a small set of illegitimate mechanisms to gain access. If we are diligent enough we may eventually be able to identify and secure most of those mechanisms. Until this happens, securing large systems is very difficult (some say impossible) because of the complexity of the systems.

Hackers are generally exploiting some problem in the OS that allows them to execute an operation that they are not supposed to be able to execute. Often this allows them to gain access to a system with the permissions that a supervisor or administrator must have—permissions that basically allow them to do anything they want. Most often these mechanisms exploit a bug in the OS. Usually the OS vendors will quickly learn about these bugs and will release fixes for the OS that will shut off the hacker's ability to exploit that bug. Unfortunately, these fixes are not as well tested as a full release of the OS, so not all users are willing to install all these fixes, leaving the bugs exposed. This is especially true for corporate administrators who must manage many diverse systems doing many different tasks. Whereas an individual might be able to determine fairly quickly that a bug fix was causing a problem, a corporate administrator might be responsible for many systems and therefore might be less willing to risk such exposure.

The hacker threats that we might see can be grouped so that we can assess how to deal with them. First is the general category that we call today **malware.** Malware is a fairly new word that groups together several subcategories including virus programs, worms, Trojans, and spyware.

16.1.1 Computer viruses

Computer viruses are portions of programs that insert themselves into other programs in a manner analogous to the way that biological viruses insert themselves into living cells. When a program containing a virus is run on a computer system the virus will insert itself into other programs on secondary storage. The hardest part for the virus writer is getting a user to run the program containing the virus. Today, this is accomplished most commonly by attaching the virus program to an email in such a way that a user will execute it. When most software was distributed on floppy disks a common technique was to infect the program found in the boot sector of the floppy. If the system was rebooted after a software installation (as was often required) and the last floppy disk was not removed from the drive, the floppy would usually be booted and the virus propagated to the hard drive. From there it would infect every other floppy that was inserted into the system. Once such a virus got loose in a corporate environment it was almost impossible to eradicate completely because of the many floppy disks that were stored in various desk drawers, inside briefcases, at home on top of the dresser, and so on.

Today, we have protective programs known as virus scanners that reside in memory and watch for signs that a program containing a virus is about to be copied or run and prevent the copying or execution. These scanners work by matching known patterns of instructions or unusual behavior such as a series of system calls or attempts to modify certain system files or portions of the registry. Unfortunately, the databases of patterns of data and behaviors have to be maintained since new viruses are constantly being created. While the programs themselves have often been free, after some trial period the maintenance of the database has not been. As a result, many people do not bother to run the scanners or don't pay for the updates, so viruses continue to circulate that should have been eliminated long ago. Just as in the biological world, some viruses are only annoying but some cause catastrophic harm. The ones that crash systems are less likely to spread as far as the ones that are less damaging. Crashing a system gets the attention of the user and will probably result in the eradication of the virus on that machine. But a small slowdown might not be noticed or might be tolerated because the cure is too expensive or would take too much time.

16.1.2 Trojans

Trojans are programs that are not what they appear to be. The term comes from a technique allegedly employed during the Trojan war, when one side appeared to withdraw from the battlefield but left behind a large wooden statue of a horse. Hidden inside the horse was a team of soldiers. The army of the city dragged the horse inside the city and had a great celebration of the supposed victory. During the night the hidden soldiers came out of the horse and opened the city gates to admit the returning army who then sacked the city. Trojan programs appear to be one thing but either do something else entirely, or do what they appear to do, but do something else as well—something unnoticed by the user. For example, the program might appear to work as a screen saver but also installs a process that would log all passwords and send them to some website in another country. Generally, the same techniques that work against virus programs will also work against Trojans.

16.1.3 Worms

Worms are programs that are similar to viruses and Trojans, but slightly different. They do not infect other programs and do not pretend to do something. When a worm program is run for the first time it simply tries to send itself to other machines and trick the OSs into running it. From there it will try to send itself to other machines, and so on. In 1988 a doctoral student at Cornell University launched a small program that was destined to be known as The Internet Worm. His intention was that the program would do nothing visible. It was designed to spread itself to as many computers as possible without giving away its existence. If the code had worked correctly it would have been only a single process running on many Internet-connected computers. Unfortunately, the code didn't work as intended. The worm propagated itself too aggressively, and an infected machine often sent the worm back to the same machine that it had come from. The result was that these small processes, which didn't take up much CPU time individually, began to swamp the systems as more and more infected processes were started on each machine. In most cases in less than 90 minutes the worm had made the infected system unusable. Nobody is actually sure how many machines were infected by this worm, but it is estimated that it involved about 6,000 machines. It essentially shut down the Internet for about a day. Fortunately, it only attacked VAX and Sun machines running a specific version of BSD UNIX. Worms can also be detected and eradicated by virus scanners.

Worms are not necessarily destructive. The initial development of worms was at the Xerox PARC installation in the early 1980s. These worms were used for such activities as distributed processing, broadcast communication, and software distribution that took place during the off hours on the network.

16.1.4 Spyware

Spyware is a special class of Trojans. Such programs are relatively benign in the sense that they do not damage the computer they are running on or any of the user data. What they typically do is report local activity to some unrelated website. In the most benign case this information merely identifies which websites are being accessed and helps the system place ads on the websites that might be of more interest to the user. There is a gray area in which this activity could be viewed as being actually helpful. Unsophisticated users are misled by unscrupulous advertisers to install "screen savers" and "browser toolbars" that are actually Trojans containing such spyware. At the very least, the user is not usually notified that these additional functions are being installed. In the worst case vendors of music CDs and tax software installed spyware packages when one of their DVDs was played on the computer or their software was installed in misguided attempts to enforce **digital rights management,** or **DRM.** These installations were done without any notice to the user of this software. In both cases the performance of the system was degraded and new security flaws were exposed to the Internet. In more malicious instances spyware can be used to steal passwords to websites and even credit card numbers. Fortunately, special scanners exist that can recognize and remove most spyware. The degradation caused by one spyware program is not usually too substantial. But when running scanner software for the first time on machines owned by naive users it is not unusual to find hundreds of instances of spyware, and these systems are often essentially useless under the load. As of this writing the spyware detectors are beginning to merge with virus scanners into a more general category of malware scanners.

16.1.5 DoS attacks

The Internet Worm just described was intended to be benign. Unfortunately, as a side effect of its operation it is also an example of another class of attacks, **denial of service, or DoS.** The effect of this worm was that authorized users could not access the machines or that operating systems failed because they had seldom been tested at the limits of stress they were being put to. This effect is called denial of service. Usually a DoS attack is an intended consequence rather than a side effect. There are many such attacks—we describe two. The first is called the **Ping of Death.** A ping is a special message used by network administrators to test network connections. A ping command received by a server is echoed back to the sender, so the sender will know that the target machine is reachable. To make the program more useful the sender can send a large packet and send it several times to see what the average response time is. There is supposed to be a maximum of 64 KB on the attached packet, but it is possible to maliciously create a ping packet that contains more than 64 KB. Unfortunately, more than a few OSs had a ping utility that would try to receive this packet into a buffer that could be up to 64 KB, but no larger. If a larger packet were received, then the data would overwrite something unintended, often with fatal consequences. This would not cause any benefit to the sender—only harm to the target.

Another DoS attack is called a **SYN Flood.** TCP network connections start with a "three-way" handshake. The initiator of the connection sends a packet that contains a SYN flag, which tells TCP that it is starting a connection and that the receiver should allocate some buffers and reset some data fields regarding that connection. The receiver replies and the sender sends another packet that completes the connection. In a SYN flood attack the sender sends many initial SYN packets starting new connections but never responds to the receiver's reply, thereby tying up memory resources. After a sufficient number of unfinished connections are opened, the receiving system may either crash or simply be unable to accept further connections, thus denying service to authorized users.

Both of these problems have been fixed in all current OS protocol stacks, but they may persist in older network equipment that cannot be easily upgraded. Other such problems are discovered often and eventually get repaired. If we were not continually developing new protocols these problems would eventually all be solved. But other kinds of attacks are not so simple to prevent. An example is a coordinated attack using **zombies.** A zombie is a machine where security has been compromised to the extent that a remote user can run an unauthorized program at will. Given a large set of zombie computers a malicious user can synchronize them to all run a specific program at the same time. Networks of tens of thousands of zombie systems are not unusual because so many users are naive about the security on their machines and a zombie machine might not exhibit symptoms that are easy to detect. (Zombie machines are sometimes called **robots** or **bots** and a large set of such machines is called a **botnet.**) The program could consist of legitimate requests—perhaps to ask a Web server to deliver a specific page. Or the requests might be bogus, but legal from a protocol standpoint, and therefore difficult to detect or prevent. For example, we might send a page to a Web server. This is usually only used for maintenance, so most users are unauthorized, but the request itself looks legitimate. If several thousand zombie computers can be used at the same time they can overload a server to the point that legitimate users are denied access. Even if the server is not overloaded, the entire communication connection to the server may be filled, again denying service. No single zombie will appear to be under any load, so the systems' owners may not even be aware that anything is happening.

16.1.6 Buffer overflows

In order to do much damage, a virus or worm needs to somehow fool the system into running its code in supervisor mode. One of the most common ways that a virus or worm manages this feat is to exploit a type of program coding error called a buffer overflow, or buffer overrun. The ping of death we mentioned was one example. A buffer overflow occurs when a process stores data beyond the end of a buffer. What happens is that the extra data overwrites nearby memory locations. Buffer overflows can cause a process to crash or output wrong information. They can be triggered by inputs intended either to run malicious code or only to make the program operate in an unintended way by changing the data. Buffer overflows are the cause of many software vulnerabilities and the basis of many exploits. Bounds checking can prevent buffer overflows. Programmers often don't think about the problem, naively assuming that the input data will be valid. Compilers can generate code that always does bounds checking, but programmers typically turn such options off for the sake of efficiency.

In the following example, X is data that was in memory when the program began executing. Y is right next to it. Both are currently 0.

X	X	X	X	X	X	X	Y	Y
00	00	00	00	00	00	00	00	00

If the program tried to store the string "too much" in X, then it would overflow the buffer (X) and wipe out the value in variable Y.

X	X	X	X	X	X	X	Y	Y
't'	'o'	'o'	' '	'm'	'u'	'c'	'h'	00

Although the programmer did not intend to change Y at all, Y's value has now been replaced by a number formed from part of the character string. In this example, on a big-endian system that uses ASCII, "h" followed by a zero byte would become the number 26624. Writing a very long string could cause an error such as a segmentation fault, crashing the process.

The methods used to exploit a buffer overflow vary by the architecture, operating system, and memory area. Besides changing values of unrelated variables, buffer overflows can often be used by attackers to trick the program into executing arbitrary code that came from the malicious input. The techniques used by an attacker to gain control depend on the part of memory where the buffer resides. For example, it might be in the stack area, where data is pushed onto the stack and later popped off. But there are also heap overflow exploits as well.

Typically, when a function begins executing, local variables are pushed onto the stack, and are accessible only during the execution of that function. This is a problem because on most systems the stack also holds the return address—the location in the program that was executing before the current function was called. When the function ends, execution jumps back to the return address. If the return address has been overwritten by a buffer overflow it will now point to some other location. In the case of an accidental buffer overflow as in the first example, this will almost certainly be an invalid location, not containing any program instructions, and the process will crash. But by carefully examining the code in a system an attacker can cleverly arrange things so that the system will begin executing code supplied by the attack. Modern OSs are now starting to locate code and data randomly in the logical address space to make such exploits more difficult to create.

16.1.7 Scripts and applets

Another variety of malware is sometimes found on malicious websites. Several mechanisms have evolved that allow a website to send programs to client systems. These include scripting languages such as **JavaScript** and **VBScript** and **applets** intended to run on software virtual machines such as the **Java virtual machine** (**JVM**) from Sun Microsystems and the **Common Language Runtime** (**CLR**) from Microsoft. Both of these mechanisms normally execute programs inside the browser in a manner known as a **sandbox.** See Figure 16.1. This means that the actions of the program are restricted so that it cannot cause harm. For example, normally programs running in a browser are not allowed to access the local disk drives. Most browsers allow a user to override these limits so that a trusted program can do things we might

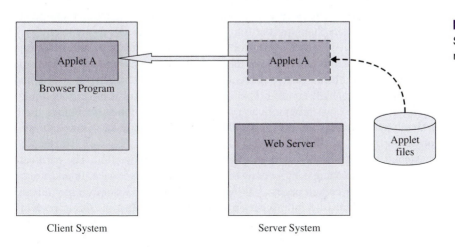

FIGURE 16.1
Sandbox execution model.

not want a program we are unsure about to do. If we got the applet from our company website we would probably trust it. If it came from another source we might not.

One additional mechanism that is widely believed to cause security problems is that of **cookies.** By design, Web servers are stateless—they do not keep any information about individual clients. (Applications that run in Web servers can do so, but it is not a feature of the server itself.) This stateless nature limits what servers can do. In order to expand on these capabilities, browsers were enhanced to allow a server to record information about a website on the browser system. These are fairly short strings of text. The server can read the cookie when a browser requests a page. These can help the server appear to be stateful. They can store a customer number, a last question asked, a last page visited, shopping cart information, and so on. They can be used to temporarily tell a website that you have logged in as you move from page to page on the site. It is a common misconception that cookies can contain viruses or other malware. Cookies called **tracking cookies** can be constructed to share information across multiple websites for advertising purposes, but there is no way that a cookie can harm a computer or other information or programs on the computer.

16.2 OS PROTECTION

16.2.1 OS protection

In earlier chapters we discussed several different aspects of OS protection, but they are worth mentioning again in this context. One example is the separation of Supervisor Mode for running the OS and User Mode for running application programs. This separation allows the OS to monitor various operations in an attempt to make sure that they do not do anything disastrous. It is possible for the OS to make sure, for example, that an I/O request does not overwrite part of the file system metadata. However, in many cases it can't prevent some abuses, such as deleting a file that a user might want. Some of this sort of abuse can be mitigated by file system protections, which we discuss a bit further on.

Similarly, the OS protects the use of the CPU by starting a timer and preventing user programs from changing the timer. This allows the OS to abort any program that goes into a loop, intentionally or not. In batch systems a runtime estimate is given when a program is started and the program will be terminated if it exceeds that estimate by more than a certain percentage. In interactive systems it is assumed that eventually the user will abort an operation and either retry it or do something else. In either case, a rogue program can't completely tie up the system since the OS is probably multitasking and the user will still be able to interact with the OS to kill a looping program.

One final aspect of the OS protection is memory protection. The hardware can usually check the addressing bounds of the logical address space. In addition, many systems can mark certain pages as allowing read-only access or execute-only access, giving an added measure of protection. These features allow the OS to protect itself from any user program and also keeps programs from interfering with each other.

16.2.2 Authentication

When users remotely access computer systems we may be concerned that they only access resources we want them to access, though sometimes we don't care what they access. Most Web servers, for example, will allow any user to access any page. However, an online banking system accessed by a Web interface certainly does not want any user to access all of the information on the server. We want users to access only accounts they are authorized to access. Controlling what a user can access on a system actually has two parts to it: authentication and authorization. **Authentication** is verifying the identity of a party to a communication. In the case of a user accessing a bank account we need to authenticate both parties. Obviously the bank wants to authenticate the user. Until recently it was not so obvious that when using an online banking system we want to authenticate the bank as well. A new class of computer fraud has arisen that is known as **phishing.** A phishing fraud is most often sent in an email. It directs a user to a website that pretends to be something it is not—your bank, for example. It asks that you enter some confidential information such as your credit card number or bank account number and ID and password. It uses some plausible-sounding reason for requesting the information, usually saying that it is needed to authenticate you, and often stating that the system needs this information because the system security has been compromised in some way. As a result, we now understand that it is important to authenticate the host system to the client as well as authenticate the client to the host system.

Authentication usually takes one of three forms: something you **have,** something you **know,** or something you **are.** Examples of something you have include your ATM card or your house key. Cards and keys can be stolen, however. Something you know might be your login ID and password or your account number. Any such information can be captured if a third party sees you enter it or reads the message from the communication line. Something you are might be a voiceprint, thumbprint, or a retinal scan. Such systems are just now coming into use and in theory should be harder to fool once they are further developed. Using two different methods of authentication at the same time is called **two-factor authentication.** This is seen when one uses an ATM card and must also supply a PIN.

Passwords are problematic because of social factors. The very worst password is the default password that sometimes comes with software or hardware. Surprisingly often these passwords are never changed. If passwords are not chosen carefully they can be easily guessed. Such passwords are considered weak. The Internet Worm mentioned earlier used several mechanisms for guessing passwords and was remarkably successful. So the use of **strong passwords** is recommended. Passwords are generally considered strong if they contain a combination of upper- and lowercase letters, symbols, and numbers and do not contain any names or words, repeated symbols, or sequences such as 123 or tuv. Passwords that are names or words can often be broken be guessing common words or names associated with the account. This is known as a **dictionary attack.** But the problem with strong passwords is that they are difficult to remember. This is especially true since it is normally recommended that you do not use the same password on different systems. As a result, strong passwords are often found on notes attached to computer monitors, seriously compromising their effectiveness. A good technique is to make up a sentence and use the first letter of each word in an acronym. For example, "World War 2 began in 1939!" could yield a password of WW2bi1939! That is a nice strong password. When you try to use it and you can't remember the year, just go to Google and enter "year wwii started." Now your note can contain some cryptic hint like "W2" that will be meaningful only to you.

16.2.3 Authorization

Once an OS knows who a user is, the next task is to decide what operations that user is allowed to do. More specifically, the allowed operations depend on the object being accessed—we normally do not have the same rights to all files on a computer. We have been discussing a user as a person, but in the context of an OS, a process can be a user as well. Deciding what operations a user can perform on an object such as a file is called **authorization.** Abstractly the OS could have a data table called an **access control matrix,** or **ACM.** One dimension of the matrix would be the user and the other would be the object to be operated on. The entries in the matrix cells would be the operations that would be allowed for that user on that object. Figure 16.2 shows a hypothetical ACM. In it we see that the rows are labeled with user names and the columns are labeled with objects. In this case we see three file objects and one printer object. Wendy is a designer in the art department and is authorized to use the laser printer but not the C compiler. Ann and Fred can read and write their own resumés, but nobody else can. Ann and Fred can both execute the C compiler, but neither can read it as data or write to it. Note that the set of possible operations for one object are likely not the same as the set of possible operations for another object of a different type. A file would not have a Stop Queue operation like a printer might.

One thing is clear even from this small piece of an ACM—most of the cells are empty. Trying to store an entire ACM would waste a tremendous amount of memory.

FIGURE 16.2

An access control matrix.

	Ann's Resumé File	Fred's Resumé File	gcc		Laser Printer
Ann	Read Write	nil	Execute		nil
Fred	nil	Read Write	Execute	. . .	nil
		. . .			
Wendy	nil	nil	nil		Write Stop Queue Start Queue

A large machine might have tens of thousands of users and hundreds of thousands of files and most users would be allowed to access only a small set of the files. For this reason, OSs do not use an ACM. Instead, they either use an access control list or a capability list. An **access control list,** or **ACL,** is attached to an object and would contain only the users who were authorized to perform some operation on an object. The list elements would list each specified user who could access the object and the operations they could perform on the object. Figure 16.3 shows some ACLs that correspond to the ACM in Figure 16.2.

Alternatively, an OS can use a **capability list,** or **CL.** A CL is shown in Figure 16.4 that also matches the ACM in Figure 16.2. The elements of the list show the objects that a user is authorized to operate on and lists the operations the user is authorized to perform.

Creating the entries in these lists the way that we have shown them, however, still creates many more references than we might like. Consider the problem of setting up rights for students at a large university to access the general system utilities on a computer. Not only are there thousands or tens of thousands of students, they change every semester—some enroll and some move on, one way or another. Setting up all the necessary rights for each individual student would be a significant administrative problem. Instead, we utilize **groups** or **roles.** We create a group called "student" and we assign the rights to the necessary objects to the group. Then, as students arrive and leave all the administrators have to do is to add the new

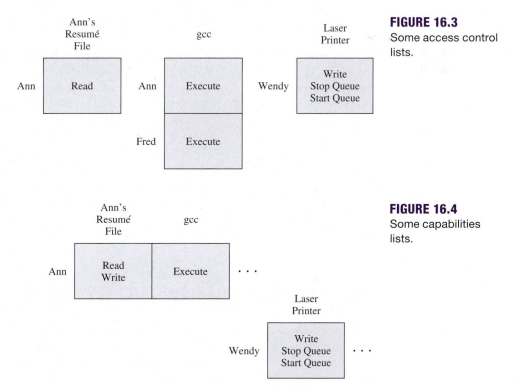

FIGURE 16.3
Some access control lists.

FIGURE 16.4
Some capabilities lists.

students to the group and remove them when they no longer have access privileges. The rights that are given to the group are inherited by the students. Roles are similar in that they allow for us to have a user in the system and have that user be assigned to a role. A role might correspond to being a member of a specific project team. All users who are members of that team inherit a set of rights in a set of objects shared by the team. When members leave the team and go to another, then all that the administrator has to do is change their roles and all their rights will be changed as well.

A question that must be answered is when the authorization should be checked. One option is to check the authorization when an object is first accessed—a file is opened, a socket connection is made, spooling to a specific printer is requested. After that, a set of operations implied by the initial access is allowed without further checking. If we opened a file for input, for example, reads to that file would be allowed, but not writes. Depending on the level of security desired in the OS we may feel that this is not enough. We may require that every separate option will be specifically checked against the lists—perhaps the user's privileges have been revoked since the initial access was made. For example, the user is going to be fired, finds out about it, and begins writing over files on the OS trying to remove evidence of malfeasance. The administrator revokes the user's passwords, but the operations are already ongoing. We discuss this more under the topic of security levels. Note that this is a case where the OS designer must decide whether to provide the mechanism in the OS to support a feature and the system administrator must then decide whether to invoke it. In a department store such security might not be worth the system and administrative cost to maintain; in a bank it might be a different story altogether.

Yet another question is at what level the authorization is to be made. Normally, the objects in a system are organized in one or more tree structures—as an example, the file system on a hard drive. We often will grant a user access to a specific home directory. By implication the rights to a directory will extend to a subdirectory unless they are overridden. Typically we can also override the rights to any file in a directory. In some systems we can also assign rights to individual portions of a database—sometimes a set of fields. Thus, a clerical worker in the HR department might be able to see the home contact information of all employees, but not the payroll information. Sometimes the restriction might be to a set of values—a set of records, for example. So a payroll clerk might be able to access the payroll records of most employees, but not those above a certain management level. Again, the OS designer must decide whether to supply those mechanisms and the administrators must set policies about their use.

16.3 POLICIES, MECHANISMS, AND TECHNIQUES

There are a number of types of security mechanisms that are commonly found in most larger OSs. In this section we look at a few of these common mechanisms. But before we worry about mechanisms it is important to establish policies that unequivocally establish what users can and cannot do and what they must do.

16.3.1 Security and protection policies

Any network that is to be secure must have a set of policies that clearly spell out several things:

- what users are allowed to do,
- what users are not allowed to do,
- what users are required to do, and
- what the punishments are if the procedures are not followed.

Even in a home environment, if parents wish to restrict access to certain types of websites they should clearly spell out what the restrictions are. Firewall mechanisms are not perfect and it is likely that the children in the family will end up being more computer literate than their parents and able to thwart many security mechanisms. The punishments for doing the things that are prohibited should be established beforehand. Firing an employee for sending a threatening email is difficult if the restriction was not spelled out clearly beforehand.

Similarly, employees must be clearly told what their responsibilities are with respect to backing up information, using encryption in certain environments, securing their computers, and so on. If they are supposed to run a virus checker and a firewall and to keep the software updated, then they should be told so in advance of any problems that might occur if they do not and what the penalties are for failing to adhere to the policies.

16.3.2 Crash protection: Backups

Crashes will happen. OSs must provide mechanisms to deal with them. First, the running system may crash. OSs are much better than they used to be, but no nontrivial program is ever truly debugged. When they crash we must be able to recover from these crashes. We have already discussed some mechanisms for dealing with these crashes. First is the mechanism of transactions. Often we have a series of file or database updates that work together to define a transaction. Perhaps we are moving a piece of expensive equipment from one warehouse location to another. If these are separate files or databases, then one update needs to reflect that the item left one warehouse and the other update needs to reflect that it is now in the other warehouse. If the system crashes before one of these updates is done, then we will either lose track of the item or we will think we have one more of them than we really do. By coupling the updates together as a single transaction the system can ensure that either both updates are done or neither is. We discussed the implementation of transactions through logging, checkpoints, and rollbacks.

Another possible source of data loss is the physical crash of a disk drive. Sometimes the read–write heads literally crash into the platters and scrape the coating off. Other times we have a failure of a bearing or the electronics. Recovering some or all of the data off a dead disk drive is sometimes possible but is certainly expensive. It is also time-consuming. A far better method to cope with this possibility is to back up the data to a removable medium. Historically, this copying was done to magnetic tape because of the low cost of the media. For small systems, floppy disks or their slightly higher capacity relatives were utilized. Today, personal computer backups are most often done via CDs or DVDs. Not only do disk drives crash, users sometimes "crash" too. Every system administrator gets used to hearing that a user has deleted a file that they really need accompanied by a fervent request to please recover it. So backups are also desirable because files can be deleted or corrupted by human error or software problems.

There are many approaches we can take to backing up a system, but there is one that works best. It involves the fact that most OSs have an indication in the file directories that shows whether a file has been changed since it was last backed up. It is often called an **archive bit.** The details of the best procedure can vary, but for the sake of illustration we will assume that we want to keep the system backups fairly easy to use, so every weekend we will create a backup copy of the entire system. This backup will clear the archive bit on all the files, showing that we have a backup copy. As the system runs during each day, it will set the archive bit on any file that is changed. At the end of the day we can run a different backup procedure that will copy only the files that have been changed that day. We will label this backup with the date. We will do that each day. Then when a user requests a file that was deleted, we can search all the daily backups in reverse order until we find it. In a large centralized operation the backup mechanism can keep track of which files are on which daily backups so that it is not necessary to search them all. There are a couple of other key features of such a system. First, the backups should not be in the same room as the computer. In case of a fire, backups in the same room would likely also be destroyed. Even more important, the backup media from the week before should not even be kept in the same building for the same reason. A flood might make the entire building inaccessible for some time. If an off-site backup is available, then the data can be restored to systems in another facility and operations resumed more quickly.

An alternative mechanism can be considered in environments where the data represent a great deal of money. Such data might include engineering or artistic designs where the value can be hard to even estimate because of the creative effort that went into them. They might literally be irreplaceable. In such situations we can employ a dynamic backup system that will write each file to a remote backup mechanism as it is changed. Such a solution is obviously more expensive, mostly because of the administration involved. But in such situations it can be well worth it, even if just for the peace of mind of knowing that the files are safe. It is still important to take the media to an off-site storage location.

If files are on laptops or the media used for backups are often physically taken outside the facility, then using encryption on the files or the media is a sound idea so that if the computer or the backup is stolen, the data will not be compromised.

An alternative to constant backups is the use of RAID disk organizations, as discussed in Chapter 14. Some of the RAID configurations provide substantially improved reliability at fairly low cost and mitigate the problems of losing data due to drive failures. They will not solve problems of file loss due to human or software errors, however.

16.3.3 Concurrency protection

We have mentioned that we build OSs with a great deal of protection between running processes. We also said that we want to build high-level systems out of multiple processes. Building systems out of multiple processes requires the ability to communicate among the processes. We therefore need mechanisms to facilitate that communication. One of those mechanisms that an OS can provide for such applications is the ability to share memory. In this case we provide a means for processes to stipulate that they want to cooperate and share access to some portion of memory. In Chapter 9 we discussed some potential problems that can arise with the use of shared memory and said that we could solve this problem with the use of locking mechanisms, which the OS also must provide. This opened up yet another potential problem involving a deadlock. In this instance, the processes can avoid deadlocks by the consistent ordering of setting and releasing the locks.

16.3.4 File protection

With multiuser systems the OS must also provide a mechanism to make files private. Privacy does not necessarily mean that only a single user can access a given file. It must be possible for multiple users to share a file. In Chapter 6 we discussed the mechanism used in older versions of UNIX and Linux for specifying the access rights of the file owner, a group whose membership is defined by the system administrator and all other users. These rights are set with the chmod utility. In Chapter 18 we cover the mechanism for specifying access rights to files in the Windows NT OS family and in Chapter 19 we mention the newer mechanisms available in Linux systems.

Sometimes communication between concurrent processes involves sharing information at a file level. Most OSs allow concurrent accesses to files by separate processes as a default. In order to avoid problems when one or more of the processes is writing in a file, the processes must use the same locking mechanisms and proper ordering of locking and unlocking to synchronize the use of the files just as we do to synchronize the use of shared memory. We discuss file protection further in the encryption section below.

16.4 COMMUNICATION SECURITY

Often a process running on one system will need to communicate with a process running on a different system. When we send information across a communication link from one computer to another there are three potential classes of problems that can occur at the level of sending the message. These can be seen in Figure 16.5. Communication in security systems is normally shown as being between two parties, known as Alice (A) and Bob (B). First, an outside party can **read** (or intercept) the message. Second, an outside party can **send** (or insert) a bogus message. And finally, an outside party can **change** a message that an authorized user sends. We are concerned with protecting a system against all of these problems.

One class of mechanisms that we will commonly use consists of elaborate protocols for specific functions such as authentication. As an example, a protocol known as Kerberos has been developed for authentication. It is widely used, having become almost a de facto standard. For example, as of Windows 2000, Kerberos is the default authentication protocol. Designing such protocols so they are secure is a very complex matter and a specialty in its own right. Using such secure protocols allows us to be certain that we are communicating with the other party we think we are communicating with. This mitigates most problems of having a third party insert messages into the communication stream undetected.

FIGURE 16.5
Communication
threats.

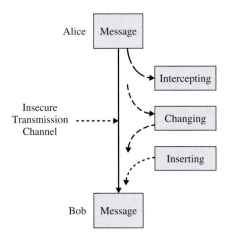

16.4.1 Encryption

Another class of algorithms has been developed for making sure that messages are not subject to any of the three problems outlined above. These algorithms are used to encrypt the messages between the systems in such a way that they cannot be easily read by a third party. If they can't be read, then they can't be changed. Thus, **encryption** can eliminate or at least mitigate two of these three problems. Encryption takes a message (often referred to as the **plaintext**) and uses a known algorithm to scramble the message. A special number called a key is used with these algorithms. Unscrambling the received message will reveal the original message and is called **decryption.** A schematic of this procedure is seen in Figure 16.6. These algorithms rely on the fact that when a third party captures an encrypted message it will be **computationally infeasible** to decrypt the message without knowing the key. An interceptor could theoretically try every possible key value in what is called a **brute force** attack. The phrase "computationally infeasible" therefore means that it would take so long to run the algorithm with all possible keys that the information would no longer be of value once it is discovered. Unfortunately, the meaning of computationally infeasible constantly changes. We know that the speed of processors doubles roughly every 18 months, so what was computationally infeasible 5 years ago may be easy now.

We have been discussing encryption mainly in the context of message transmission. But encryption also can be used in file systems. It can be very useful in protecting information that is very sensitive in case the computer is stolen or lost. As systems are becoming more and more portable, this can be a very useful feature. It is

FIGURE 16.6
Encryption.

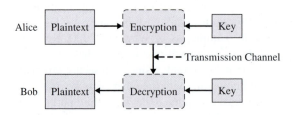

true for PDAs and cell phones as well as laptop computers. They have files stored in RAM instead of in secondary storage, but they can often still be encrypted.

Symmetric key encryption

Sometimes the decryption uses the same key as the encryption. In this case the key must be known only to the sender and the receiver (though there may be many receivers of a given encrypted message, and they must all know the key). Algorithms that use such keys are referred to as **symmetric,** or sometimes as **shared key** or **secret key** algorithms. Figure 16.7 shows how a shared key system works. The secret key shared between Alice and Bob is shown as $K_{A,B}$.

There are several different algorithms for using symmetric keys. For many years the standard algorithm used was **DES,** or **data encryption standard,** but it is no longer considered secure. In 2001 a new algorithm known as **AES,** or **advanced encryption standard,** was established. DES used a 56-bit key and AES uses a key that is either 128, 192, or 256 bits long, depending on the needs of the user. When AES was released, DES could be broken in a few hours by brute force with a specialized hardware system costing under $10,000. Breaking AES with a similar but much faster machine would take 149 trillion years. One problem with using shared secret keys arises when Alice and Bob do not know each other so they are reluctant to exchange secret keys. An older method of solving this problem was to use a **trusted third party** (**TTP**) to generate a key and send it to both of them. This solution requires that both users really trust the TTP and also that the TTP always be online and available. Today there are new protocols like Diffie-Hellman and RSA that allow two users to dynamically generate a pair of keys like those discussed in the next paragraph and exchange them over a nonsecure network.

Asymmetric key encryption

Other algorithms use a pair of keys that are generated together. One of the keys is used for the encryption and the other is used for the decryption, so these algorithms are called **asymmetric,** or **public key** algorithms. There are two interesting facts about these algorithms. The first is that one of the pair of keys can be known to the entire world. This key will be called the **public key.** The other key will not be public and is therefore called the **private key.** In fact, this usually is the case. How this works is seen in Figure 16.8. Bob's public key is shown as $K_B{}^+$ and his private key is shown as $K_B{}^-$.

If Alice wants to send an encrypted message to Bob, she can use Bob's public key to encrypt the message. Only Bob knows the matching private key, so only Bob will be able to read the message. Interestingly enough, it does not matter which key is used

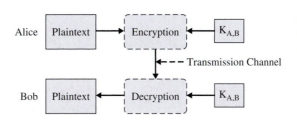

FIGURE 16.7
Symmetric key encryption.

FIGURE 16.8
Asymmetric key
encryption.

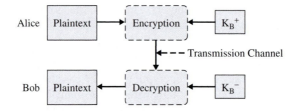

for the encryption as long as the other is used for the decryption. Bob could encrypt a message with his private key and send it to Alice. If Alice is confident that the public key she has for Bob really does belong to Bob, then she knows the message really came from Bob. (This assumes that the message can otherwise be validated by the protocol.) Another interesting fact about the use of public key encryption is that different key pairs can be applied in any order. So Alice can encrypt a message with Bob's public key and then with her private key. Bob can decrypt the keys in the reverse order or the same order. This property is used in some electronic commerce systems. There are several algorithms for public key encryption, just as there were for secret key encryption. The standard for many years has been **RSA,** or **Rivest, Shamir, Adleman** after the names of the developers of the algorithm. It is based on prime numbers and relies on the fact that there are efficient algorithms for testing whether or not a number is prime but no efficient algorithm is known for finding the prime factors of a number.

16.4.2 Message digests

In some circumstances we don't necessarily want to hide the contents of the message. We only want to make sure that it didn't get changed. In such cases we can compute a simpler, faster function known as a **message digest** or a **hash.** This function is seen in Figure 16.9. These functions chop a long message into short pieces (typically about 512 bits) and combine them with a one-way function—one that cannot be easily reversed. The result is a message digest of a fixed length—usually about 128 bits. Two algorithms are presently in use, **MD5,** which produces a 128-bit hash,

FIGURE 16.9
Message signing.

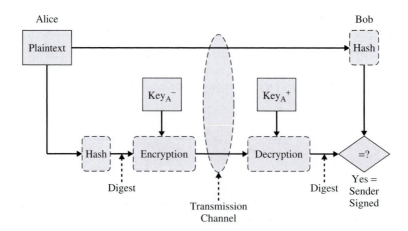

and **secure hash standard,** or **SHA,** which outputs a 160-bit hash. MD5 is commonly used to validate files downloaded from the Internet via HTTP or FTP, especially for programs. The file is downloaded along with a message digest of the file, commonly with an extension of .md5. Then a publicly available utility is run against the downloaded file and a new digest is computed. If the new one matches the downloaded one, then one can be assured that the file was not changed after it was uploaded to the server and that the download also did not change it. Unfortunately, MD5 is now known to be breakable with only modest amounts of computing power, so it is mainly useful to ensure that a file was downloaded correctly.

16.4.3 Message signing and certificates

By combining a message digest with public key encryption Alice can effectively sign a message electronically. Alice will take a message M and create a digest of the message. She will encrypt the digest with her private key and send both the message and the encrypted digest to Bob. Bob knows her public key, so he can decrypt the digest. He can then run the publicly available digest algorithm on the message and compare that computed digest to the decrypted one. If they are equal, then he knows (and can prove) that Alice sent the message. This ensures that Alice cannot later **repudiate** the message. Note that in order to prove this at a later date Bob must keep the message, the signed digest, and Alice's public key, since Alice might later change her public key. Note also that Bob cannot change the message and still claim that Alice sent it, so it also protects Alice against having Bob change the message.

A special use of signing of messages is used to authenticate either clients or servers. This process produces a **certificate** that verifies identity. A special program is run that produces a preliminary certificate. A bank would do this on their server. The preliminary certificate is sent to a **certificate authority,** and the CA encrypts the certificate with its private key and returns it to the requesting entity as a finished certificate. The bank now installs this certificate on their server. The bank can now send this certificate to clients to prove its identity. So when a browser tries to make a secure connection to the bank's server, the server will send back the certificate to the browser. The browser can decrypt the certificate by using the public key of the certificate authority to verify the identity of the bank. The public key of popular certificate authorities are built-in to most browsers. So the browser decrypts the bank's certificate with the public key of the CA and the user now knows that the browser has really connected to the bank.

We mentioned before that Alice can send Bob a message by encrypting it with his public key. The problem there is that Alice must be sure that the key really is Bob's public key. The way that she can ensure that is for Bob to use a certificate authority to sign his public key with their own private key. Alice can use the public key of the certificate authority to open the key and verify that it is Bob's key inside. Messages signed electronically in such a way are legally admissible in court.

16.4.4 Security protocols

As we saw in the last chapter, network support is divided into several layers. Each layer provides certain capabilities. An interesting question is, what layer in the protocol stack provides security? As it happens, security functions have been specified at several different layers. In the TCP/IP protocol used in the Internet, security has been specified for both the Transport layer and the Network layer. If we are using 802.11 wireless networking, then there may also be encryption at the Data Link layer. In the Transport layer security features are defined in a protocol called **SSL,** or **secure socket layer** (also called **TLS,** or **transport layer security**). This protocol is commonly used between Web servers and browsers for secure communication in combination with an application layer protocol called **HTTPS** or secure HTTP. The server is authenticated, as discussed in the last section, with a certificate assuring the client process that it is talking to the correct server. The two entities will initially use their own public and private keys for asymmetric encryption. They will then decide on a temporary secure **session key** and continue the session with symmetric encryption. Symmetric keys are more efficient to use than asymmetric keys but repeated reuse of them is risky, so they are commonly generated for a single connection and then discarded.

Security is also available at the Network layer with a protocol known as **IPsec,** or **IP security.** IPsec is a set of protocols developed by the IETF to support secure exchange of packets at the IP layer. It supports two encryption modes: transport and tunnel. Transport mode encrypts only the data inside the messages but ignores the header. Tunnel mode is more secure since it encrypts both the header and the message. IPsec uses shared public keys for both the sender and receiver. These are exchanged by a protocol known as **Internet Security Association and Key Management Protocol/Oakley** (**ISAKMP/Oakley**) which allows the receiver to obtain a public key and authenticate the sender using digital certificates. IPsec is more flexible than TLS since it can be used with all the Internet Transport layer protocols, including TCP, UDP, and ICMP, but is more complex and has processing overhead because it cannot use Transport layer functions that increase security.

Security is also available at the Application layer with a protocol known as **PGP,** or **pretty good privacy.** PGP uses a public key system in which each user has a public–private key pair. For creating digital signatures, PGP generates a hash from the user's name and other signature data. This hash code is then encrypted with the sender's private key. The receiver uses the sender's public key to decrypt the hash code. If it matches the hash code sent as the digital signature for the message, then the receiver is sure that the message was sent by the stated sender and was not changed, either accidentally or intentionally. PGP has two versions, one using RSA to exchange session keys and the other using a Diffie-Hellman protocol. The RSA version uses the MD5 algorithm to generate the hash code while the Diffie-Hellman uses the SHA-1 algorithm.

16.4.5 Network protection

There are several facilities that can be used in a network to improve security that are not actually inside an OS, but we will discuss them briefly because they impact the security features inside an OS. Actually, most of these facilities are applications that run inside a dedicated computer.

Most homes and organizations that run a local area network are connected to the Internet at only one point (though some businesses have dual connections if they can justify the cost of the extra reliability). This one connection is an ideal point to inspect communication messages for various problems. The facility that provides this function is called a **firewall.** Normally, this function is embedded in the router that connects to the Internet since the router is looking at the packets anyway. A typical firewall configuration is shown in Figure 16.10. There are several functions that a firewall can do. First, it can block certain types of connections altogether by looking at the port numbers used by the connection requests. It can also inspect the insides of the packets and disallow certain types of traffic—pings, for example. Some firewalls also are configured to disallow traffic from IP addresses that are considered to be unsafe or unsavory. Firewalls can be supplied with **signatures,** data patterns known to be associated with specific attacks. They can also include a **traffic monitor** that watches for patterns that indicate a significant deviation from normal traffic patterns. This monitoring is also known as **anomaly detection.** Network protection systems using signatures or anomaly detection are usually called **intrusion detection systems (IDSs)** and **intrusion prevention systems (IPSs).** The firewall in the figure also shows a **demilitarized zone,** or **DMZ.** This military term in this case refers to a separate network that can be accessed either from the outside network or the inside network. This allows local staff to maintain the contents of servers located there and still have those servers accessed from the Internet.

One problem with firewalls at the network connection point is that not all machines in the network need the same types of connections. While a large university with a big UNIX server would likely want to allow Telnet sessions to be set up through the firewall, it is not likely that a Telnet session is needed to a personal computer. Therefore, it is common to also provide a firewall function in a personal computer that will disallow such sessions. Interestingly, it often will be configured to disallow many outbound connections as well as inbound connections since a common technique of many viruses is to connect to rogue hosts to report purloined information. A local firewall will be an application program rather than a part of the OS, but in order to inspect the connections that are being requested and the traffic coming and going, they will need to be able to insert their functionality in the protocol stack. This is an unusual requirement for an application to make of a protocol stack, but OS designers have learned of the necessity to provide it for this special class of applications. Thus these programs are not only able to watch for text patterns in the messages but can

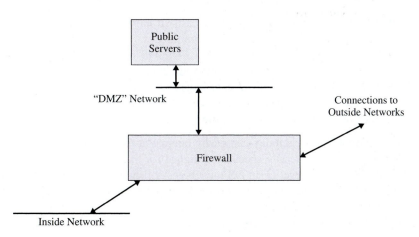

FIGURE 16.10
A modern firewall.

also monitor other system activity to detect behavior that is characteristic of viruses such as accesses to certain system files not normally accessed by applications.

16.5 SECURITY ADMINISTRATION

There are several things that a system administrator must do to ensure the security of the systems connected to a network. We have already discussed the need for a regular backup system, firewalls, and traffic monitoring. In addition, several actions should be logged and the logs reviewed regularly. First would be the log of failed login attempts. A small number of failed logins will be normal—passwords should expire from time to time, users will accidentally type something wrong or use a password from another system, and so on. Any spike in the number of failed logins should give cause for alarm as a likely indication of attempts at penetrating a system. Other failures should also be logged and analyzed, such as a failure to find a requested Web page on a Web server. Such errors may only show bad links, but close examination might expose attempts at hacking the server.

Some systems have substantially higher security requirements than do others. A home personal computer probably needs little security beyond keeping out viruses and hackers. A bank needs a higher level of security because of the money involved. A hospital system charged with patient care probably needs still higher security because problems with the system can literally be a matter of life or death for a patient. A military system might need still higher security because a failure could put millions of lives at risk. As a result, the National Computer Security Center (NCSC), an agency of the U.S. government, has published a definition of four major levels of security with some minor variants. With each higher level the OS must provide extra features, many in the area of logging of activities. Needless to say, we don't want to load down the OS of a personal computer in a home with all the features necessary for security on that military system. The lowest level is D, which has minimal security. A system with this level of security might be used by any user in an office or in a home. As an example of the increasing levels, the additional requirements (over those required for C1) for a C2 rating are:

- Access control works on per user basis. It must be possible to permit access to any selected subset of the user community.
- Memory must be cleared after use. The OS must ensure that disk space and memory allocated to a process does not contain data from previous operations.
- The OS must be capable of recording security-relevant events, including authentication and object access. The audit log must be protected from tampering and must record the date, time, user, object, and event.

Most commercial OSs today can easily operate at the C2 level. OSs that operate at higher levels are generally specially designed for that purpose. For government purposes, the security level of an OS must be established by an independent third-party auditing firm. Furthermore, the certification applies only to a specific release of the OS and a specific hardware configuration so generic certification by the manufacturers is not often done at these levels.

16.6 SUMMARY

Since computer systems are now accessible by many users and are more often connected to the Internet, it is necessary that the systems, the files therein, the running processes, and the communications between users and between processes be protected from harm, either accidental or intentional. In this chapter we discussed several facets of protection and security as they pertain to OSs. First, we gave an overview of system security problems. We classified some of the security problems we see as a result of being connected to the Internet and described how an OS needs to deal with them, including mechanisms outside the OS. Then we moved on to discuss the protection services OSs offer to users, primarily in the area of privacy of files. We described the general designs of such services. The OS must also provide services for processes. Significant barriers are erected between running processes and the OS. We looked at some of the services provided to processes that are communicating with one another. Section 16.4 covered security about networks, most specifically the Internet. It discussed encryption, authentication protocol, and message digests, and the related topics of network security outside of the OSs. We covered problems of administration of network and OS security.

In the next chapter we take a look at special considerations we must use when using OSs to create systems that are distributed across multiple systems.

BIBLIOGRAPHY

Akl, S. G., "Digital Signatures: A Tutorial Survey," *Computer,* Vol. 16, No. 2, February 1983, pp. 15–24.

Denning, D. E., "Protecting Public Keys and Signature Keys," *IEEE Computer,* Vol. 16, No. 2, February 1983, pp. 27–35.

Denning, D. E., "Digital Signatures with RSA and Other Public-Key Cryptosystems," *Communications of the ACM,* Vol. 27, No. 4, April 1984, pp. 388–392.

Dennis, J. B., and E. C. Van Horn, "Programming Semantics for Multiprogrammed Computations," *Communications of the ACM,* Vol. 9, No. 3, March 1966, pp. 143–155.

Farrow, R., "Security Issues and Strategies for Users," *UNIX World,* April 1986, pp. 65–71.

Farrow, R., "Security for Superusers, or How to Break the UNIX System," *UNIX World,* May 1986, pp. 65–70.

Filipski, A., and J. Hanko, "Making Unix Secure," *Byte,* April 1986, pp. 113–128.

Grampp, F. T., and R. H. Morris, "UNIX Operating System Security," *AT&T Bell Laboratories Technical Journal,* Vol. 63, No. 8, October 1984, pp. 1649–1672.

Hecht, M. S., A. Johri, R. Aditham, and T. J. Wei, "Experience Adding C2 Security Features to UNIX," *USENIX Conference Proceedings,* San Francisco, June 20–24, 1988, pp. 133–146.

Kramer, S. M., "Retaining SUID Programs in a Secure UNIX," *USENIX Conference Proceedings,* San Francisco, June 20–24, 1988, pp. 107–118.

Lamport, L., "Password Authentication with Insecure Communication," *Communications of the ACM,* Vol. 24, No. 11, November 1981, pp. 770–772.

Lehmann, F., "Computer Break-Ins," *Communications of the ACM,* Vol. 30, No. 7, July 1987, pp. 584–585.

National Bureau of Standards, "Data Encryption Standard DES," NTIS *NBS-FIPS PUB 46,* January 1977.

Needham, R. M., and M. D. Schoeder, "Using Encryption for Authentication in Large Networks of Computers, *Communications of the ACM,* Vol. 21, No. 12, 1978, pp. 993–999.

Organick, E. I., *The Multics System: An Examination of Its Structure.* Cambridge, MA: MIT Press, 1972.

Reid, B., "Reflections on Some Recent Widespread Computer Break-Ins," *Communications of the ACM,* Vol. 30, No. 2, February 1987, pp. 103–105.

Rivest, R., and A. Shamir, "How to Expose an Eavesdropper," *Communications of the ACM,* Vol. 27, No. 4, April 1984, pp. 393–394.

Rivest, R., A. Shamir, and L. Adleman, "On Digital Signatures and Public Key Cryptosystems," *Communications of the ACM,* Vol. 21, No. 2, February 1978, pp. 120–126.

Rushby, J. M., "Design and Verification of Secure Systems," *Proceedings of the 8th Symposium on Operating Systems Principles,* Vol. 15, No. 5, December 1981, pp. 12–21.

Rushby, J., and B. Randell, "A Distributed Secure System," *Computer,* Vol. 16, No. 7, July 1983, pp. 55–67.

Schell, R. R., "A Security Kernel for a Multiprocessor Microcomputer," *Computer,* Vol. 16, No. 7, July 1983, pp. 47–53.

Silverman, J. M., "Reflections on the Verification of the Security of an Operating System Kernel,"

Proceedings of the 9th Symposium on Operating Systems Principles, ACM, Vol. 17, No. 5, October 1983, pp. 143–154.

Simmons, G. J., "Symmetric and Asymmetric Encryption," *ACM Computing Surveys,* Vol. 11, No. 4, December 1979, pp. 305–330.

Spafford, E. H., "The Internet Worm Program: An Analysis," *Purdue Technical Report CSD-TR-823,* November 28, 1988.

Wood, P., and S. Kochan, *UNIX System Security.* Carmel, IN: Hayden Book Co., 1985.

WEB RESOURCES

http://ciac.llnl.gov/ciac/index.html (U.S. Department of Energy, Office of the Chief Information Officer—computer incident advisory capability)

http://www.cert.org (Carnegie Mellon University's Computer Emergency Response Team)

http://freshmeat.net (Web's largest index of UNIX and cross-platform software)

http://www.ietf.org (Internet Engineering Task Force, including all RFCs)

http://www.linuxsecurity.com

http://www.netfilter.org (packet filtering framework for Linux)

http://www.networkcomputing.com (networking magazine with online edition)

http://packetstormsecurity.org (nonprofit organization of security professionals dedicated to securing networks)

http://www.redbooks.ibm.com (IBM publications archive)

http://www.tasklist.org (software to list all processes running on a Windows system)

http://tldp.org (Linux Documentation Project [LDP])

http://www.usenix.org/publications/ (USENIX, the Advanced Computing Systems Association)

http://en.wikipedia.org/wiki/Identd (daemon program for providing the ident service)

http://www.windowsecurity.com

REVIEW QUESTIONS

16.1 Which is the larger problem, hackers or insiders? Justify your answer.

16.2 What characteristics of malware distinguish a virus program?

16.3 What characteristics of malware distinguish a Trojan program?

16.4 What characteristics of malware distinguish a worm program?

16.5 Briefly describe a buffer overflow.

16.6 What is the purpose of the sandbox model?

16.7 Authentication makes use of some special mechanism to verify the identity of an entity. Most often we are concerned with verifying the identity of a user. Which of the following did we *not* say was

something that could be used to verify the identity of a user?

a. Something you have

b. Something you see

c. Something you know

d. Something you are

e. All of the above can be used to verify a user's identity.

16.8 Once a user (or other entity) is authenticated, the actions allowed by the user must be authorized. We discussed two different mechanisms that are often used to support authorization. The first was an access control list. Briefly describe what an ACL is.

16.9 What is a capability list?

16.10 Where should backup copies of data be stored?

16.11 What is meant by the phrase "brute force attack"?

16.12 How many key values are used in a symmetric key encryption system?

16.13 True or false? In a asymmetric key encryption key system it is crucial for both of the key values to be kept secret.

16.14 If we are not particularly concerned about confidentiality but we want to ensure that a message that is sent is not altered by any party, what sort of mechanism would we use?

16.15 A certificate authority signs a user's public key with its own private key. How does a browser use that to verify the user's public key?

16.16 What secure protocol is used on the Web for HTTPS connections?

16.17 What is a common mechanism for protecting a network from an outside attack?

Chapter 17

Distributed Operating Systems

In this chapter:

D istributed systems are becoming very prevalent. We discuss Operating Systems because they stand between our application programs and the hardware. When we are developing a casual application there is no need to worry much about the OS. But when we are developing high-performance applications we need to have a better understanding of what is going on inside of the OS so that we are working with the OS and not against it. So it goes with distributed processing. As we will we see shortly, when we are developing systems designed to support a large number of users we will often be compelled to develop distributed systems— systems that have multiple parts running on different machines. Of course, we may build an application that is distributed for reasons other than performance or scaling, and in such cases we may still not need to know much about the details of the OS as it pertains to distributed systems. But if our system is a high-performance or high-volume application, we may still profit from knowing how the underlying services work so that we can better utilize them and not do something that forces them to do extra work for no purpose.

This chapter starts with an introduction where we discuss a number of reasons why this is so. It also introduces the notion of distribution transparency and why it is important. Lastly, it introduces the concept of middleware and explains why it evolved as it did. We then present a number of different models that are found in distributed systems, including both the client server model and more complex models as well. Section 17.3 reviews the topics of processes and threads and discusses how threads can be used in clients and servers to make distributed systems perform better.

When processes in distributed systems communicate they need to refer to other entities, so in Section 17.4, we discuss the concept of naming and name spaces. In Section 17.5 we present some different paradigms for distributed systems, including remote procedure calls, distributed objects, and distributed documents. We discuss synchronization in Section 17.6 because distributed systems have special issues concerning synchronization that make them different from monolithic systems. Then in Section 17.7 we present the topic of fault tolerance and the special problems distributed systems have regarding failure of one component in a system that otherwise continues to run. We conclude with a chapter summary in Section 17.8.

17.1 INTRODUCTION

There are many reasons why we may need to develop systems that are distributed. We discussed many of them at some length in Chapter 9 with regard to cooperating processes, so we recap them briefly here:

- Performance. Systems running on multiple machines have more CPU time and other resources to apply to the problems. Some processes need a lot of power just for a single processing run—simulating weather systems, for example.
- Scaling. Multiple systems means more transactions can be processed in a given amount of time.
- Purchased components. Many times it is much cheaper to buy a system component than it is to develop it in-house. Sometimes it is developed in such a way that it is essentially only available as a standalone process and may really need a separate system to run on.
- Third-party service. Sometimes an application component requires access to special databases that are not themselves for sale, so the component is only available as an online service (e.g., credit verification).
- Components of multiple systems. Often a component is developed in one system but later is needed as a component in other related systems. In such a case it may be better to isolate that component on a dedicated machine.
- Reliability. When a system has only a single instance of some component, failure of that component can cause the entire system to stop. Having multiple instances of each component allows the larger system to keep running, though perhaps with degraded performance.
- Physical location of information. If a system is supporting multiple physical facilities it may be desirable for parts of the system to be collocated with the facilities. Consider a warehouse inventory system supporting multiple warehouses where the bulk of the transactions are applied to a local database but connectivity is needed for a few transactions that have to be serviced out of another warehouse.
- Enable application. Some applications require so many resources that they literally could not be executed without a highly distributed system. SETI (Search for Extra-Terrestrial Intelligence) takes vast amounts of radio telescope and searches for patterns that might indicate an intelligent origin. They divide it into small data sets to distribute them to volunteers who process them via a screen saver. Otherwise, they literally could not process this data.

There are several goals that we ideally would like for distributed systems to have. First, they should connect users and resources. (Note that in this context a "user" may be another process.) Second, the systems should exhibit **distribution transparency.** Ideally, a user should not be able to tell that the system is distributed. There are several different ways that a user might notice a lack of transparency. These include transparency of:

- Heterogeneity. Different system parts may be running on different hardware systems or different OSs or both
- Access. Differences in data representation and access (floating point number formats vary from machine to machine)
- Location. Where a resource is located (Web pages can be anywhere)
- Migration. Whether a resource can move (scripts sent to your browser by a server)
- Relocation. Whether a resource moves while it is in use (your cell phone)
- Replication. Resource is replicated (Google data servers)
- Concurrency. Resource may be shared by many users (websites)
- Persistence. Whether a resource is maintained on disk or in RAM
- Failure. Whether a resource fails while in use (the Internet routes around failed links)

A key aspect of distributed systems is that they depend heavily on **open standards** to achieve most of the desired transparency. Many standards exist in the computer science industry. Some are proprietary and some are open. Proprietary standards are usually not as useful in distributed systems because it is too difficult for different vendors to test the components for interoperability. Thus, many OS facilities developed for distributed systems by a single vendor are often eventually placed in an open status so that other vendors can test their systems for interoperability. Examples include NFS (Network File System) by Sun Microsystems and CLR (Common Language Runtime) by Microsoft.

Most OSs have not traditionally supported many of the services that distributed applications need. As a result, these services have developed in a category called **middleware.** As seen in Figure 17.1, middleware modules are placed functionally between the OS network services and the application programs. Thus, the OS and

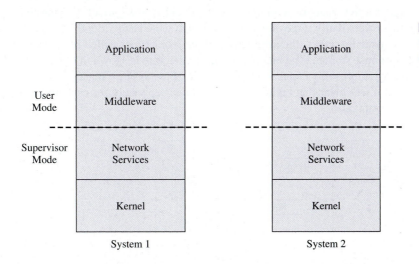

FIGURE 17.1
Middleware service layer.

the network modules provide services to the middleware but are otherwise ignorant of any distinction between the middleware and the application. The network services may be quite independent from one another, communicating via open network standards. The middleware modules also communicate via open standards, but by definition they cooperate to provide services that cross system boundaries.

17.2 DISTRIBUTED APPLICATION MODELS

Systems comprised of processes running on separate machines obviously need to communicate. There are several models that have been developed to describe the interactions between these components. We are describing the following models: a client–server model, a three-layer model, a multilayer model, horizontal distribution, and vertical distribution.

17.2.1 The Client-Server Model

The client–server model is shown in Figure 17.2. It is so well known that it almost needs no explanation. A client system needs a well-defined service so it contacts a server, which will provide that service. The main question we might need to answer in designing a client–server model is how much of the function of an application should be in the client and how much in the server. At one extreme the application will run on a central system and the client will be little more than a terminal. This model is sometimes referred to as a **thin client.** In other cases the application will run mostly at the client station and the server will provide only a very limited service such as a database to hold the information used by the application. There are many hybrid models that can be used as well. We elaborate more on this in the next section, since the principle is the same there, only operating in more layers.

17.2.2 The three-layer model

After a few years of working with the client–server model it began to be clear that there were really three major functions that were easily identifiable in most systems: the **user interface,** the **application logic** (sometimes called business rules), and the **database** storage. The model for this architecture is shown in Figure 17.3. This extra division probably came about because database systems began to evolve themselves, and it was clear that building such facilities separately for each application was not economical.

FIGURE 17.2
Client–server
architecture.

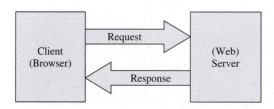

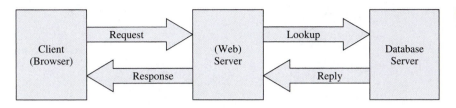

FIGURE 17.3
Three-layer model.

As with the client–server model, there are many variations that we can have in the three-tier architecture. The user interface can be very simple, perhaps only an X-Terminal in the UNIX environment. In other environments a Web browser on a personal computer may provide a simple way to have a GUI presentation for an application. In such an environment we can send a page from a Web server that contains a form for the user to fill in for the application. The user fills in the form and clicks a button on the form. This click will cause the browser to submit to the server the data the user input into the form. The server will check the data, and if all is OK the server will process the request and return some result. But we can improve the performance of such a design by moving some of the processing to the client side. When a user is inputting data into a form to record some business event, if a detectable error is input, the sooner we catch it and get the user to fix it, the better. For example, if we are expecting a field to contain a date and the user enters some alphabetic information (other than a month name), then the system should reject it. If we wait until the user has submitted the form and sent it to the server and we send an error message back to the user, we have separated the feedback from the input by quite a few steps, and this will render it less effective. It also disrupts the thought process of the user, who has mentally moved on from this transaction, thinking it to be already complete. It would be much better for the application to check the format of the data at the time the user moves the focus from the date field. Considerable design effort usually goes into deciding what checking can be done on the client side and what should be done on the server side.

Other features can also be moved to the client side. For example, because communication costs can be high or the network connectivity unreliable, it may be useful to allow the client side to do a considerable amount of data collection in an offline configuration and submit the transactions to the server later when the server or the connection is again available.

The third tier, data storage, is usually provided by a packaged database management system. Often these systems do little more than provide a higher-level file system that supports very reliable storage and retrieval of data in normalized tables. In other cases the database systems are used to run part of the system logic by executing procedures stored in the database, improve data validity by verifying referential integrity, summarizing data for reports, and so on.

17.2.3 N-tier applications

The three-tier model is often extended to **N-tiers.** This is sometimes called **vertical distribution** and is done when an application can conveniently be broken into several parts. An illustrative example is the architecture of the Google search engine, as shown

FIGURE 17.4
Google system
architecture.

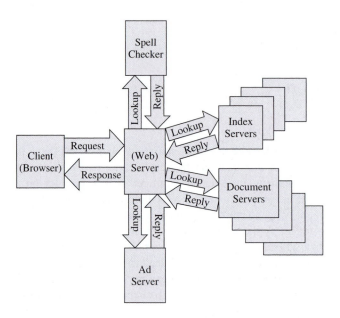

in Figure 17.4. It is broken into several portions. Although there is no detailed description of the architecture available, enough has been published to illustrate the point.

There is a front-end process that receives the request and parses it into separate words. Another server may be queried for spelling corrections. The front-end server then takes those words and passes them on to other servers, each of which is responsible for a database of indexes of Web pages that contain a given word. These servers pass a set of those pointers on to another server, which merges the sets of pointers to create a set of pointers to pages that satisfy the entire search. Usually such searches contain all the words in the query, but other forms of query are possible. Another server is queried that pulls advertising from a database, selecting ads that are related to the search terms or to other searches that this user has made in the past. The pages are ranked to determine their probable relevance to the user, and the pointers are used to fetch the cached pages from other servers so that short snippets of the referenced page can be merged into a Web page that is then returned to the client's browser. Thus, we see at least five different tiers in this application. Though they may not be tiers in a strictly vertical sense, they are interacting components, which are separate servers serving many clients.

17.2.4 Horizontal distribution

We also see another paradigm being used in the Google setup in two different ways—**horizontal distribution.** We mentioned that the database is distributed across a group of servers, each of which is responsible only for pages that contain a given individual word (or set of words). This arrangement is a type of **distributed database,** where part of the information is contained on one server and part on another. In addition, the servers that Google uses are inexpensive PCs, not high-performance machines. Exact figures are unknown, and estimates vary, but a research organization estimated that they had one million servers in mid-2007 and were adding more at a rate of 100,000 per quarter. Google expects that servers are going to fail. Accordingly, each of those servers that handles documents containing a specific word is actually several servers—at least three in a given Google network node. Furthermore, the word databases are replicated in at least three geographically distributed nodes in order to limit failures due to a disaster in a center containing a node. This is known as a **replicated database.** The Google databases are therefore both distributed and replicated.

But it is also the case that each of those other servers that we mentioned before is not a single server. No server in the world could possibly keep up with the number of search requests that Google gets per hour. Instead, the network is designed such that the requests are passed out among a group of essentially identical search engines. There are many instances of the advertising and spelling check servers as well. The entire system is designed to route around any failed node and use another instance of the data. Thus, all the various server functions are replicated, just as the database servers are.

17.3 ABSTRACTIONS: PROCESSES, THREADS, AND MACHINES

Processes are an abstraction that an OS uses to virtualize the CPU so that a running program does not need to be aware that it does not actually control the CPU. In order to have a system do more work on a single application we can have a process create other processes that will also run and thus get additional turns at the CPU. However, switching from one process to another requires a context switch on a uniprocessor system, and context switches cause a serious dip in performance of the system. All the caches must either be flushed, most specifically the TLB, which is caching page table entries, or will not find any cached entries until the new process has run long enough to reload the cache from the new process. This will also cause slowdowns because of the TLB misses, which must be handled until the TLB is reloaded to represent the full working set of the process that is being started.

As a result, threads were developed. They arose from the recognition that the state information held in a process control block really had two parts. One part represented the many resources currently being held by the process. The other part held the actual CPU state regarding the current point of execution of the CPU (for any process that was not actually running). Storage for the latter part could be duplicated, and the second block could then track a different point of execution of the CPU within the same process. So a program could effectively ask the OS to allow several parts of the process to continue to run while other portions were also running, so long as those parts could communicate and synchronize their operations. This allowed one program to have several parallel points of execution without incurring the penalty of context switching.

17.3.1 Threads

There are several ways threads can be used beneficially in distributed systems. In client systems threads can be used to allow processing to overlap with asynchronous communication. A primary example is in a Web browser that is running the HTTP protocol version 1.0. In this earlier version of the protocol a browser first fetched the base page of a document. It scanned the document for embedded elements and then had to make a separate connection to the server to fetch *each* of the other elements, one after the other. So a browser using this protocol could start separate threads for the retrieval of each element rather than fetching them one by one. This sped up the process considerably. Similarly, a client that was making a long set of remote procedure calls (RPCs) could make each call in a separate thread so long as the result of one call was not required in another call.

Servers can also make good use of threads. The primary use here is to process each incoming request in a separate thread. Initially, the system starts a primary or **dispatcher thread,** which listens for incoming requests. When a request comes, the primary thread will start a **worker thread** to process the request. This design has the added benefit of program simplicity. Assuming that we are using kernel-level threads, if the worker thread makes a blocking kernel call, for a disk read, perhaps, then that thread can simply block and the rest of the server can continue. Each thread proceeds through a series of (usually) simple steps to process the request, return the result, and terminate. See Figure 17.5.

17.3.2 Virtual machines

Virtual machines are another level of abstraction—virtualizing an entire machine rather than only the CPU. There are two different sorts of **virtual machines,** or **VMs.** This is an unfortunate overloading of the acronym VM since it is also used to refer to virtual memory, but the distinction is normally clear from the context.

Physical virtual machines

First, there is the concept of a virtual physical machine. A small OS kernel is loaded that will in turn execute other OSs on top of itself. The OS that is loaded first is the **host OS.** These other OSs will be known as **guest OSs.** The basic trick is that when a host OS loads the guest OSs it runs them in user mode. Whenever a guest OS tries to execute any operation that would normally require supervisor mode, the hardware will cause an interrupt that the host OS will receive. Then the host OS will do the operation, and when the results are ready will return them to the guest OS.

FIGURE 17.5
Multithreaded server.

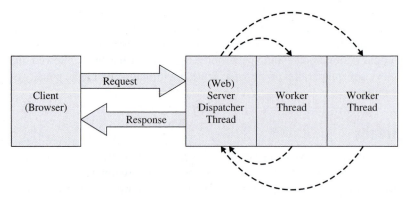

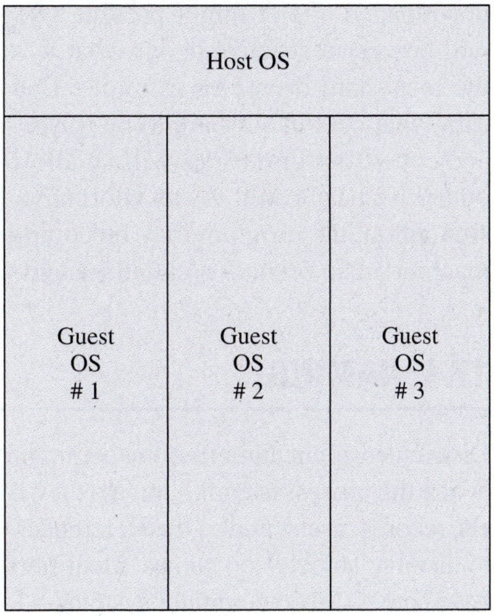

FIGURE 17.6
Physical virtual machine.

See Figure 17.6. There are several reasons why it can be useful to run multiple OSs on the same machine at the same time. As far as distributed processing goes, the main reason is to consolidate several servers onto one system. Building a server that is very reliable and high performance and placing it in a secure location is quite expensive. Often a server purchased today will be much more powerful than is actually required to run the service. Using VM allows several servers to be consolidated. This can save money on hardware since one larger server can replace several smaller ones, using less power and air conditioning. It is especially useful if the servers were running on different OS platforms, but even if they were running on the same OS, the VM can run multiple copies of any guest OS. This would seem strange, but it helps isolate the server functions since a crash of one guest cannot impact any other guest.

Abstract virtual machines

The other sort of virtual machine is an abstract virtual machine that is a software simulation of a machine designed to run some intermediate language. The primary examples are the **Java virtual machine,** or **JVM,** developed by Sun Microsystems and the **Common Language Runtime,** or **CLR,** developed by Microsoft as part of the .NET system. These are used widely in distributed processing, primarily for three reasons: code mobility, code portability, and security. Mobility allows a compiled program to be downloaded from a server to the client to be run locally. This happens when a Java applet is downloaded from a server to run in a client browser. The client browser contains an implementation of a Java virtual machine, so the Java program could be copied from the server and run at the client. This could be for any of the reasons we mentioned earlier. Code is more portable when run in a virtual machine because the virtual machine can be ported to any hardware and platform. This assures a software vendor a wide market because the target machine is virtual. Since the JVM may be running in a browser in the client we have some risk that the downloaded applet might present a security problem. So, as a default the browser will be very restrictive about what it will let the applet do—inhibiting accessing of the local hard drive, for example. Usually the client browser can be configured to show that certain sites are to be trusted—the client company headquarters, perhaps, and code from these sites will be allowed to do some of these things that would not otherwise be allowed. As an alternative to execution in the browser's virtual machine simulation, the program may be compiled into the native machine code of the target machine in an operation called **just-in-time** (or **JIT**) compilation.

17.4 NAMING

Distributed applications require communication between the various processes involved. When the processes communicate they need to refer to other entities such as files, sockets, records, users, and so on. References to entities can take several forms. We will need to distinguish between names, identifiers, and addresses. **Names** denote entities. Users have names. So do computer systems—for example, webserv.example.com. Names can be reused, so it would be possible for the example domain to replace the system currently called webserv with another system and call the new one webserv. This is especially likely with servers of any kind. Many other entities we might wish to access also have names. Names are not necessarily unique. Therefore, we create **true identifiers.** An identifier is generally issued by some authority. Identifiers are never reused and are never duplicated so they always refer to the same entity. Examples include a Social Security Number for a user or a burned-in MAC address for a network interface card (NIC). Finally, **addresses** denote access points for entities. Examples include a phone number, an IP address, and a socket (or port), which addresses a specific process or thread within a computer system.

Passing references within a single system is usually simple because the systems share a common frame of reference. Thus, for most platforms a simple file name without any other surrounding context will first be assumed to be in the current working directory. Failing that, a series of alternative directories is used. This set is usually specified in some global set of values defined for the system or for a given user. On Microsoft OSs these are called **environment variables.** One of them is known as the **path.** The path is the series of directories that the OS will search to find a file with no path name. Together these alternatives make up a common frame of reference in which a file name will have meaning. All the processes on the system share this reference frame.

Passing references to entities within a single system is usually not difficult because of that common frame of reference. However, distributed systems are much more complex. This is one of the problems caused by the heterogeneous nature of distributed systems—they do not share a common frame of reference. In order to provide common frames of reference the industry has established some global reference frames, often called a **name space.** Name spaces are organized collections of information in which a name can be located. The primary example is the **domain name system,** or **DNS.** The DNS is a hierarchical name space defined by the **Internet naming authority,** or **INA.** It is very simple for a process that has been passed a DNS name to look it up and find an IP address that corresponds to the name. Usually the process will have a socket number to use with the IP address and that concatenated pair of numbers identifies a particular software entity in the addressed system.

17.4.1 Discovery services and Jini

Jini™ (pronounced like genie) is a middleware design for dynamically creating distributed systems. It is an open specification that enables developers to create network services, either hardware or software, that are highly adaptive to change. This design specifies a means for clients to find services on the network and then to use the services to accomplish a task. Providers of services send to clients Java objects that furnish the client access to the service. This interaction can use any middleware technology because the client only sees the object and all network communication is confined to that object and the service it accesses.

When a service joins a Jini-enabled network it advertises itself by publishing an object that implements a well-known service API. A client finds services by looking for an object that supports the API it wants to use. When it finds the service's published object, it can download the code it needs to talk to the service.

17.4.2 Directory services, X.500 and LDAP

Directory access protocol (DAP) is a network standard specified by the ITU-T and ISO for use with an **X.500** directory service. It was intended to be used by client computers but was not successful because there were few implementations of the OSI protocol suite for personal computers. The basic operations of DAP were incorporated in **Novell Directory Service** (**NDS**) and later in the **lightweight directory access protocol** (**LDAP**).

LDAP was intended to be a lightweight alternative for accessing X.500 directory services and can run over TCP/IP. The intent of LDAP was that a client could access X.500 services through an LDAP-to-DAP gateway. But instead LDAP directory servers quickly sprang up. LDAP has become extremely popular in enterprises. It is the default directory services for Windows XP and is also usable with most other OSs today. It includes an authentication protocol that is quite robust so that accessing distributed services is quite secure.

17.4.3 Locating mobile IP entities

Devices that are communicating over the Internet using IP have a special problem if they are mobile. The problem arises because part of the IP address of a node specifies the network where the node is connected. If the node moves to a different network, then the IP address should change. But the TCP connectivity model and most other protocols are not designed to allow for a change in the IP address during a session. So tracking a mobile IP entity is quite difficult. Mobile IP is most often found in wireless environments where users move their mobile devices across multiple networks as they move from home to school to work.

A protocol suite for Mobile IP is defined by RFC 3344. A node that is going to use mobile IP will have an IP address called its **home address.** It will register with a server on its home network called a mobile IP **home agent.** When the node moves to another network it will be given an IP address on the new network. This will be called the **care-of address.** It will then search for a server called a mobile IP **foreign agent.** It will tell the foreign agent where its home agent is. The foreign agent will connect to the home agent and the home agent will store the temporary new IP address in a database and will register itself locally with that IP address. A host that needs to communicate with the mobile node initially connects to the home address of the node. The packets are received by the home agent and it forwards the packets to the mobile node's care-of address with a new IP header. The original IP packet is left inside the new packet. The mobile IP software in the node will strip off the outer packet header and deliver the inner packet to the application software in the node. This process is known as **tunneling.** The application software does not need to be aware that it is running in a mobile environment (i.e., the middleware provides mobility transparency).

17.5 OTHER DISTRIBUTED MODELS

We discussed the client–server model and several variations on that model. But there are other models that are also useful in distributed systems.

17.5.1 Remote procedure call

Often an existing monolithic system needs to be modified to become a distributed system. One model for dividing an existing process is to remove subroutines from the existing application and run them on a separate server. This is called **remote procedure call** (**RPC**). It is a useful technique because it involves a component model that programmers are already familiar with. In principle the idea is simple— take a subroutine out of a running system and put it on a server. Replace the removed routine with a new subroutine called a **client stub** that knows the subroutine is somewhere else and invokes the RPC middleware to find it and call it. The model for this process is shown in Figure 17.7. But this process is complicated by the possible heterogeneous nature of distributed systems. RFC 1831 that defines RPC assumes that the systems are heterogeneous. This means that the parameters being passed to the subroutine must be converted to the format of the server that is running the subroutine, and the answers must be converted the opposite way on the return. This process is called **marshalling** and unmarshalling. On the server system there will be another stub. This server stub takes the place of the original program in that it calls the subroutine. It receives the message from the client system, unmarshals the arguments into the formats required by the server platform, calls the subroutine, marshals the returned arguments, and packs them into a message to send back to the client stub.

Since the client system does not know what platform the server system is running on, the client stub converts the arguments into an intermediate form called

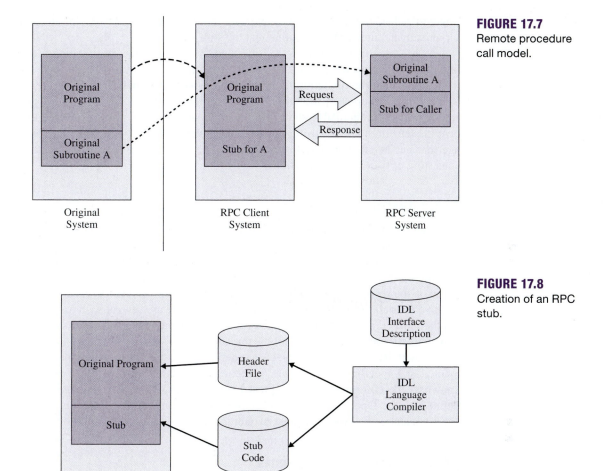

FIGURE 17.7
Remote procedure call model.

FIGURE 17.8
Creation of an RPC stub.

eXternal Data Representation (XDR), which was defined in RFC 1832. This intermediate format is platform neutral and allows us to represent any data in a standardized, platform-independent format. An implementation of RPC for a given platform must define the mapping from the XDR formats to native platform formats.

When a subroutine is removed from a program, the client stub must be substituted for it. Creation of the stub starts with a language called an **interface description language,** or **IDL.** Most IDLs are similar to C. The stub is used to declare the nature of the arguments to the removed routine. Once the interface is described in IDL, an IDL compiler that is specific to the client platform and source language is run against the description. It will produce two things—a header file that will be inserted into the original program to describe the missing routine arguments and a separate source program that should be compiled, which will become the client stub routine. This process is shown in Figure 17.8. The object form of this routine will be linked with the original application to produce the modified application. The IDL is standardized, so the same IDL file can be used on the server platform to produce the server stub and the modified routine that the stub will call.

As was mentioned earlier, RPC is defined by an RFC. This specification is then implemented in specific packages. In this case there is a fairly standardized implementation called the **distributed computing environment** (**DCE**) that was created by the Open Group (i.e., the **Object Management Group**, or **OMG**) as an open source project. Individual system manufacturers are certainly able to produce their own implementations, but using this source has the advantage of producing a package that has been rigorously tested already. The Open Group is an ad hoc group consisting of over 800 organizations.

17.5.2 Distributed objects

A model that is very similar to RPC is that of distributed objects. The techniques are very similar, but objects are more complex than subroutines. The naming of the components is a bit different. The stub on the client system is known as a **proxy** and the stub on the server side is called a **skeleton.** One additional component usually found on the server side is an **object adapter.** Its function is to enforce some administrative restrictions on how the object is invoked. There are several such restrictions, but the most common one is a serializer that restricts the object to one invocation at a time unless the object is known to be thread safe.

As with RPC, distributed objects are defined by a specification and then implemented in a specific package. One of the main standards for distributed objects is known as the **common object request broker,** or **CORBA.** This standard is also defined by the Open Group. In this architecture the middleware layer itself has a specific name—the **object request broker,** or **ORB**—pronounced "orb."

17.5.3 Distributed documents

Another model that is used in distributed processing is that of **distributed documents.** The most well-known instance of this model is certainly the **World Wide Web** (**WWW**). Originally the WWW was created as a mechanism for providing easy access to research papers related to atomic energy. It included a technique for referencing other papers called hyperlinks, though this was a concept that was not in itself new. Links could also be imbedded in the text document to reference graphics files that contained figures from the paper. Of course, today that model has grown wildly and is much more complex than that of a document. In fact, we normally speak of Web "pages" rather than documents. The idea today is that a Web page should only include a few thousand words at the most, and should link to other pages as needed. Web pages now include links to other multimedia elements such as sound and movies and forms that can allow a user to input information and interact with an application running on the server. More importantly, pages can now include programmable elements such as scripts and applets. It is possible to develop very sophisticated applications using the tools that were designed to create Web pages. The big advantage of such an interface is that the client only needs a browser to access the functions of the application. In theory this means that application Web pages can be accessed not only with a personal computer, but also with PDAs and cell phones. There are difficulties in such use, primarily based on the speed of the access and the smaller screen sizes. Most websites today are designed with an assumption of a fairly large user screen and a fairly fast connection.

Another less well-known system that uses a document model is **Lotus Notes.** It is a highly sophisticated application that exposes libraries of notes on various topics. Some topics are automatically pushed to all users as with email. Others are only accessed as the user requests them. There are not a great many institutions that are users of Lotus Notes, but they tend to be large organizations with many users, so the system merits at least a mention in any discussion of distributed systems using a document model.

Other systems that also use a document model include Internet E-mail and Network News. Each works in a different manner to distribute information to clients in specific ways using both push and pull protocols.

17.5.4 Distributed file systems

File are a concept that all programmers and most users understand, so naturally many systems have been developed that allow distribution of services by connecting the machines through the file system somehow. In Chapter 7 we mentioned the NFS model and we examined it more closely in Chapter 13, so we will not repeat that discussion here. NFS allows directories on a remote machine to appear to the local system as though they were local, providing location transparency. It was developed by Sun Microsystems in the UNIX arena, so it is also now available in the Mac OS X and Linux OSs. Microsoft also provides optional NFS client and server support with higher-level versions of its NT OS family.

Microsoft offers a similar service known under various names—**common Internet file system** (**CIFS**) and **server message block** (**SMB**). These are similar to NFS. Compatible clients and servers have been developed through reverse engineering for non-Microsoft OSs. These are known as Samba.

Both NFS and CIFS require that a nontransparent connection be made from the client to the server. Other systems have been developed that intend to make this part of the process more transparent. For example, Microsoft has a system called **distributed file system** (**DFS**). It is used to build a hierarchical view of file servers and shared directories that can be given a unique name. Instead of having to link to a bunch of different names a user will only have to remember one name. DFS supports replication of servers and routing a client to the closest available file server. It can also be installed on a cluster for even better performance and reliability.

Other distributed file systems exist that are less widely used. In particular these include the **Andrew File System** (**AFS**) and **CODA,** both developed at Carnegie Mellon University. AFS was designed to give each client workstation a homogeneous, location-transparent file name space. CODA is a newer product with an emphasis on fault recovery and disconnected operation (mobile computing). These systems are supported only in UNIX and derivative OSs.

The design of the Google search engine is also heavily dependent on a distributed file system architecture. They rely on triple redundancy in all systems.

Unfortunately for us the design is proprietary and not much detailed information is available.

17.6 SYNCHRONIZATION

Systems divided into multiple parts need to synchronize their actions, as we saw in Chapter 9. Distributed systems need to work even harder to enable synchronization. We will discuss several mechanisms for distributed clocks, synchronization, mutual exclusion, coordinator election, and concurrency control.

17.6.1 Clocks

In many distributed algorithms it is necessary to know the order of events. If two people make a withdrawal from a bank account at the "same time," we want to honor the first one before the second. Unfortunately, the speed of light limits the transmission time from one system to another. So even if two events do happen at the same time it is impossible to know this until sometime later. Among other things, it makes it virtually impossible to be sure that the clocks on two systems are synchronized. Fortunately, we often don't really care about the actual time that two events took place. We merely care about the order of the events. This makes the problem somewhat simpler. What we really need are **logical clocks.** The idea behind logical clocks is that there is some set of events for which we are worried about the order in which they happened. So in each system, whenever one of these events happens we increment a counter. We associate the value of the counter at that time with that event, calling it a **timestamp.** This becomes the logical clock by which we will order the events. For two events, if the timestamp of one event is less than the timestamp of the other, then we say that the first **happened before** the other.

There is one other step that we must take in a distributed system. We must also be concerned about messages between processes. We will want to assert that the event of sending the message happened before the event of receiving the message. We associate a timestamp with the sending of a message to another process, and we send that logical clock value with the message. Then when the message is received the receiving system will check the clock value that came in with the message. If that clock value of the incoming message is greater than the logical clock at the receiving process, then the receiving process will set its own clock to the value of the clock in the incoming message plus one, accounting for the event of the message arrival. Otherwise, it will simply add one to its own clock to account for the arrival. This mechanism is called **Lamport timestamps.**

Unfortunately, what we need is sometimes a bit more complex than this. Often we need to know what events at other systems might have had an effect on the event being described by an incoming message. The mechanism for keeping track of the timestamps of all processes in a distributed system is to attach to each event a **vector** of **timestamps.** The index of the vector is a number assigned by the distributed system to each process, and the value of the i'th item in the vector is the latest time stamp we know about from that process. When messages are sent, rather than sending the value of the local event counter as a timestamp, the entire vector of timestamps known by that process is sent with them. The receiving system updates the information in its own vector with the corresponding elements of the vector with the incoming message when they are greater than its own.

17.6.2 Mutual exclusion

When two processes are cooperating they often need to synchronize access to shared data in order to avoid conflicting updates. This part of synchronization is called mutual exclusion, and in each process it involves a section of code called the critical region in which it is updating the shared information. As we discussed in Chapter 9, this usually is implemented through semaphores, which are locked and unlocked. This works fine in a system running on a single processor, since the OS can coordinate the locking and unlocking, as we saw. But when the processes are running on separate systems, there is no single OS to do the locking and unlocking. Two different approaches have been developed for locking and locking in distributed systems: using a centralized **lock server** and using a distributed algorithm. Using a central server is fairly straightforward. A central server is created and all lock and unlock requests are sent to the server, as is shown in Figure 17.9. It operates on a first-come, first-served basis.

But a centralized server is a single point of failure and a potential performance bottleneck, so a distributed algorithm is sometimes used instead, as shown in Figure 17.10. In this algorithm a process desiring to enter a critical section will ask permission of all the other processes, including a logical clock timestamp in the requests. If a process receiving a request does not currently want access to its related critical section, then it will grant permission immediately. If that process does wish to access the critical section, then it will compare its own timestamp with that of the incoming request. It will grant the request if the timestamp of the request is earlier. Otherwise, it will not grant the request until it has finished its own use of the critical section. In Figure 17.10 all three clients want to access a related critical section in their processes. Client 3 sends a message to all the other clients with a logical clock

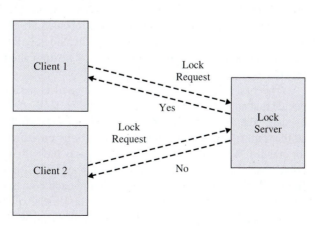

FIGURE 17.9
A centralized lock server.

FIGURE 17.10
Distributed locking.

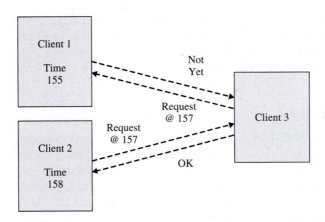

value of 157. Client 1 has a logical clock value of 155, so it will delay giving lock permission to client 3 until it has completed its own access. Client 2 gives client 3 permission since the request from client 3 had a lower clock value than its own. (The requests from clients 1 and 2 are not shown.)

17.6.3 Election

If a distributed system is using a centralized server function such as the lock server that was mentioned in the last section, then one design decision that needs to be made concerns the question of how it was determined that this server would perform that function, assuming that any of them could do so. Similarly, in some algorithms we will have one process that will be the **coordinator** of the algorithm. In most cases a server (or coordinator) is selected by the system administrator and the function runs there. However, the coordinator is a single point of failure—if we are interested in a more reliable overall system, then we need to be able to have that function run in more than one place in case the primary site is down or unreachable. In the most general and most reliable case we will allow the function to run anywhere. In this case we need to dynamically determine which process should run this function. Dynamically determining the server or coordinator process is called an **election.** There are two algorithms that are commonly used for such an election—the bully algorithm and a token ring algorithm. In each case the nodes will each have some preassigned priority for being the coordinator and the algorithm should elect the highest priority process as the coordinator.

The first question that must be addressed is a simple one. How does a node decide that an election is needed? There are basically three times an election might be needed: when a node joins the group, when a network failure partitions the network so that part of the group cannot connect to the coordinator, and when the coordinator crashes. When a node joins a group it may have the highest priority for being the coordinator, so in this situation it will always start running the election algorithm. In the other two cases the processes should each be using a timer to detect a lack of communication with the coordinator. If the timer expires without a message from the coordinator, then the process will start the election. This may necessitate that the coordinator send **keep-alive** notices to the group if there are no other messages so that the other participants do not start an unnecessary election.

In the **bully algorithm** each process is assigned a priority and a process that needs to start an election sends messages to all the other processes in the group, giving its own priority and declaring itself to be the coordinator. Any process, P, receiving this message will compare the priority given in the incoming message with its own priority.

- If the incoming message priority is higher than its own, then the receiving process merely quits the algorithm.
- If its own priority is higher than that in the incoming message, then it replies with its own message stating its superiority and the process that sent the original message retires from the algorithm.
- Eventually, the winning process will send a broadcast to the group announcing its coordinator status.

In Figure 17.11, we see three processes sending bully algorithm messages. If Priority 1 is assumed to be high, then that process will win the algorithm and become the coordinator.

An alternative algorithm is the **token ring** algorithm. In this algorithm each process is given a number that establishes an order in a logical ring. Each process will need to know the order of the entire ring. The process starting an election sends an election message containing its own process number and its priority to the process, which it believes is the next in the ring. If it receives no reply, then it sends the message to the next higher process. Eventually, some process will respond to the message. It will append its own process number and priority to the message and pass it on around the ring, bypassing any failed processes. When the message gets back to the process that started the election, it will contain an ordered list of all the current processes and their priorities. This final message will be sent around the ring again. As a result, each process will know the process number that is the coordinator and the complete order of the ring. This process is shown in Figure 17.12. Client A

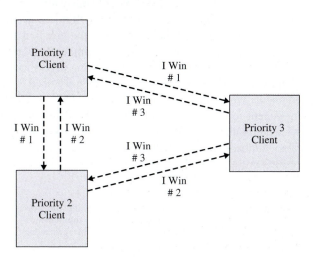

FIGURE 17.11
The bully algorithm.

FIGURE 17.12

A token ring election.

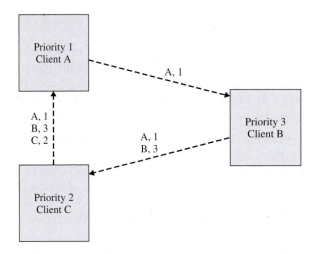

starts the message and Client B and C each add their ID and priority to the message as it goes around the ring. When the message gets back to A, A will know that it is the coordinator. The message will be sent around the ring one more time so that all processes will know the total group membership and the order of the ring.

17.6.4 Reliable multicast communication

Cooperating groups of processes frequently need to reliably communicate with every member of the group. Sending a message to all the members of a group and not to any other entities is called a **multicast.**[1] Unfortunately, TCP/IP does not support multicasting except within a single IP network, and MAC layer multicasting is restricted to a single LAN. UDP supports multicasting, but it is unreliable. So we have to figure out how to do reliable multicasting at the Application layer. The only mechanism that will work in all cases is for each member of the group to have a point-to-point connection to each of the other members. This is fairly easy to do over the Internet, though in a large group it will not scale well. So when a process wants to send a message to all the members of the group, it simply sends it to each of them over a point-to-point connection. That cumbersome process is unavoidable given the facilities available in the lower networking layers today. If we want to be sure that all the processes see all the messages, then we need to use some method of acknowledgment. We could use TCP, which has such assurance built-in. But TCP is very inefficient for this and would not scale very well to large numbers of processes. So we would rather use UDP and do the acknowledgments ourselves. This still entails a large number of **acknowledgment** messages (**ACKs**) coming back to the sender. As a result, several methods of minimizing these acknowledgments have been developed.

---

[1]Theoretically multicasting includes the idea of sending the message only once into the network and having the network deliver it to all the destinations simultaneously, delivering the messages over each link of the network only once and only creating copies when links to the destinations split. We are ignoring that optimization here.

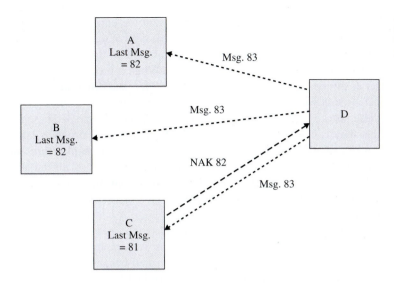

FIGURE 17.13
Reliable multicasting
with NACKs.

The first is to rely on the high reliability of today's networks and only have the receivers send a **negative acknowledgment** (**NACK**) if they infer from the incoming message sequence numbers that they have missed a message. This is seen in Figure 17.13, where process D has sent message 83 to the other processes. Process C shows that the last message it received was 81, so it knows it missed message 82. In this case process D will retransmit the missing message to all receivers who missed it. Other refinements have also been developed but are neither as significant nor as widely deployed.

17.6.5 Distributed transactions

In interactive systems we often are processing transactions that involve several updates to a database. A typical example would be an inventory transaction that moved an item from one warehouse (A) to another (B). This would normally require several steps:

1. Read the count for the item in warehouse A.
2. Subtract 1 from the count and update that item count in the database.
3. Read the count for the item in warehouse B.
4. Add 1 to the count and update that item count in the database.

If the system happens to crash after step 2 is completed and before the write of step 4 is completed, then the database will show an **inconsistent state**—we will have lost track of one item in the inventory. We could avoid losing track of anything by doing the two updates in the opposite order, but then we would run the risk of thinking that we had an extra item. This problem can be avoided with a mechanism known as a **transaction.** This looks like an overloaded term because we use that word to indicate something a user might want to do with a system. But that closely parallels the steps we are looking at here. Most user transactions involve updates to several files or database tables and we want the entire system to accurately reflect the event we are recording. We say that this type of update is **atomic,** meaning that it should result in all steps being recorded or none of them, even if one of the systems crashes during the sequence of updates. When a process is going to record such a series of updates, it issues an API call for a **transaction start.** As each update to the database is written, it may succeed or it may fail. The database system will make these updates in a temporary fashion, putting them in the database in such a manner that they can be recognized as something that was in progress but not finished. If any of the updates is rejected, the process will issue a **transaction abort** system call and the database will erase all the temporary updates. If all the steps are successful, then the process will issue a **transaction commit** system call and the database system will commit the updates, making them permanent and deleting any previous records.

In a system with a distributed database the operation is very similar, but since there are several different database servers working together on a single transaction, the commit process is a bit more complicated because a failure of one of the processes might have happened since the original update call was issued. One of the processes that is managing one of the elements of the distributed database may have crashed or the network may have failed and we may not be able to communicate with that process. In either case, the operation can't continue. With a nondistributed database the system is unlikely to fail in such a divided manner. In order to allow for such conditions, distributed transaction processing relies on a protocol known as a **two-phase commit.** We discuss this protocol in the next section.

One other problem with distributed database transactions is that in order to improve performance a database may try to interleave updates from different processes on the same data tables. As long as no two processes try to update the same data, then there will be no conflict so the operations can proceed in an interleaved fashion. If two processes attempt to update the same data at the same time, then one of the operations will be rejected. Note that at this point the best choice for the application that was rejected is to simply retry the operation. This is not something that would arise in a uniprocessing system, so it violates distribution transparency.

17.7 FAULT TOLERANCE

In our discussion of transparency we said that one goal was to make failures transparent to the user. There are many mechanisms that can be used to increase the fault tolerance of a distributed application, but they mostly center on redundancy.

17.7.1 Introduction

Failure is a more complex topic in distributed systems than in monolithic systems. When a monolithic system fails, all of it stops. When a distributed system fails, only a part of it may stop. Since the parts are not necessarily communicating constantly, the first problem is for the various components to figure out that another part has stopped. This can be very tricky to do. Usually we start with the idea of using timeouts. When a client asks a server to do something it starts a timer. If there is no reply within some certain time limit the client may infer that the server is down. But the server may not be down. It may be that there is a network problem and the server is not currently reachable. There may be a sudden burst of traffic at some point in the network such that an intermediate router was forced to drop either the request or the response. It may be that the server is currently overloaded and that the action has been executed already but the reply either has not been yet sent or it is still in transit. If we retry the operation, that might cause problems. If the operation was to subtract an item from an inventory count, we don't want the operation repeated. On the other hand, if we just counted the inventory and we are setting the count to the value we know is in the warehouse bin, then it would be OK to repeat the request as long as no other change to the inventory was processed in the interval. We say that the second operation is **idempotent,** meaning that it is recorded in such a way that it can be repeated without altering the result. It is worth noting that if we recorded the subtraction as a read of an old value and the write of a new value, it would be idempotent as well.

17.7.2 Process resilience

We can make functions more robust by distributing them across several processes running on different systems—if one fails the others can still run. We speak of such systems as having **process groups.** Process groups can be organized in either a **hierarchical group,** as seen in Figure 17.14, or a **flat group,** as seen in Figure 17.15. In a hierarchical group there is one process that is the coordinator. The other processes all report to the coordinator process with point-to-point links. Having a single coordinator means that the group has a single point of failure, though we can elect a new coordinator, as we saw in the last section. During that election time (and the timeout required to recognize the failure), the group is basically nonfunctional, so the system will appear unstable. Such systems are easy to implement and have a low communication overhead.

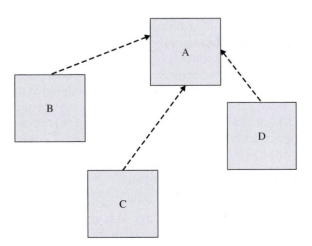

FIGURE 17.14
A hierarchical process group.

FIGURE 17.15
A flat process group.

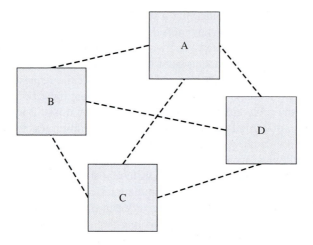

In a flat group the control is distributed throughout the group. Each process communicates directly with each other process. Thus, the communication overhead is much greater than with a hierarchical group. The group is more robust since a single failure will not shut the group down, but such systems are more complex to implement than hierarchical groups.

17.7.3 Reliable client–server communication

We already mentioned that a client has some special considerations to make if a server fails to respond. We may not want to resend the request because we do not want the operation to be redone. Similarly, if a server crashes we are in a quandary because we do not know if the server got the request and processed it and crashed before it could send the reply. However, sometimes it is very important that the request be acted upon. Perhaps we are sending in a fire alarm. Sending it more than once is not a big problem. This situation is known as **at least once** semantics. Sometimes it is highly undesirable to send the request more than once. Imagine a request to pay a bill out of our bank account! We would not want that to happen more than once. This is known as **at most once** semantics. Other times we are more or less indifferent—perhaps with a stock ticker that is only listing the latest transactions for a stock. This is known as **no guarantee** semantics. Finally, we would like for the middleware to guarantee that a transaction will be processed **exactly once.** It is possible for middleware to achieve this level of guarantee, but it requires extensive logging and double-checking and is thus relatively expensive to implement. In general, we must analyze each type of transaction separately and see what level of semantics guarantee is warranted.

17.7.4 Distributed commit

When discussing distributed transactions in a previous section we introduced a notion of a distributed commit. This algorithm is discussed here separately because it is relevant to failure transparency. It is known as a two-phase commit. One process will be the coordinator of the algorithm. It will send a message to each other process asking if it can commit the updates it was requested to do. If all the processes are still running and the network is working, then they will all reply affirmatively and the coordinator will then tell them all to commit the updates. If any of the processes has failed or the network is not working, then the coordinator will not receive an affirmation from at least one process, so eventually it will timeout the operation and will send an abort request to each of the other processes. There are complications if a process crashes. When a failed process restarts, it can learn from examining log files that it was in the midst of a commit operation. What it needs to do then will depend on the state it was in when it crashed. If it was in an abort state, then it should simply abort the operation. Similarly, if it was in a commit state, then it should continue with the commit. Each of these states could only be reached if the coordinator had instructed it accordingly. If the recovering process was in the ready state, waiting to hear from the coordinator, then it can simply ask the coordinator to repeat its instruction.

The big problem occurs when the coordinator crashes. In this case the other participants will timeout the coordinator. If the participant is in either the abort or commit state, then it acts accordingly. If it is in the ready state then it cannot tell what to do by itself. It will ask all of the other processes what state they are in. If any of the other processes is in an abort or commit state, then all of them can act accordingly, since that will mean that the coordinator had reached a decision and had started sending out instructions before it failed.

There is a small possibility that the algorithm can hang because the coordinator crashed before sending a commit message. For this purpose a three-phase commit variant of this algorithm was developed. In practice this situation is so rare that the three-phase commit is almost never used.

17.8 SUMMARY

If they are not already, distributed systems will soon be the norm rather than the exception. This chapter reviewed a number of reasons why we find distributed systems more common each day. It also explained the notion of distribution transparency and introduced the idea of middleware and explained why it takes the forms it does. We then presented several different models often used with distributed systems, including the client server model, three-tier and N-tier models, and horizontal distribution. Section 17.3 went over the principles of processes and threads and explained how threads can be used in distributed systems to make clients and servers perform better, or at least appear to do so. Processes in distributed systems need to communicate, and to do so they need to refer to other entities. Accordingly, Section 17.4 introduced the concept of naming and name spaces. In Section 17.5 we covered some different paradigms for distributed systems, including remote procedure calls, distributed objects, distributed documents, and distributed file systems. We then discussed synchronization because distributed systems have special problems with synchronization that are different from unified systems. Section 17.7 was about fault tolerance because distributed systems have special problems since failure of one component can allow the rest of the system to continue to run.

In the next part of the book we take a look at a few important modern OSs and see how they implement some of the features we have described in these in-depth topic chapters. Some of these OSs were covered in Part 2, but there we only discussed the kinds of features that such OSs needed to have to support a given level of features. We revisit some of those OSs in Part 6 of the text to look at them in greater detail and see how they use the mechanisms we have been discussing.

BIBLIOGRAPHY

Barroso, L., J. Dean, and U. Hoelzle, "Web Search for a Planet: The Google Cluster Architecture," Research Paper, Google, Inc., 2005.

Chandy, K. M., and J. Misra, "Distributed Deadlock Detection," *ACM Transactions on Computer Systems,* Vol. 1, No. 2, May 1983, pp. 144–156.

Knapp, E., "Deadlock Detection in Distributed Databases," *ACM Computing Surveys,* Vol. 19, No. 4, December 1987, pp. 303–328.

Lamport, L., "Time, Clocks, and the Ordering of Events in a Distributed System," *Communications of the ACM,* Vol. 21, No. 7, July 1978, pp. 558–565.

Obermarck, R., "Distributed Deadlock Detection Algorithm," *ACM Transactions on Database Systems,* Vol. 7, No. 2, June 1982, pp. 187–208.

Ricart, G., and A. K. Agrawala, "An Optimal Algorithm for Mutual Exclusion in Computer Networks," *Communications of the ACM,* Vol. 24, No. 1, January 1981, pp. 9–17.

Rivest, R., A. Shamir, and L. Adleman, "On Digital Signatures and Public Key Cryptosystems," *Communications of the ACM,* Vol. 21, No. 2, February 1978, pp. 120–126.

Sandberg, R., et al., "Design and Implementation of the Sun Network File System," *Proceedings of the USENIX 1985 Summer Conference,* June 1985, pp. 119–130.

WEB RESOURCES

http://www.opengroup.org/dce/ (the OSF Distributed Computing Environment [DCE], an RPC implementation)

http://www.w3.org (World Wide Web Consortium [W3C])

http://www-306.ibm.com/software/lotus/ (Lotus Notes and Symphony, among other distributed products)

http://en.wikipedia.org/wiki/Two-phase_commit

REVIEW QUESTIONS

17.1 We listed eight reasons why distributed systems are being found more and more often. Name four of the eight.

17.2 We listed nine facets of distributed systems that should ideally be transparent to users. List five.

17.3 Briefly define middleware.

17.4 We gave four models for building distributed systems. What is the model that underlies the World Wide Web?

17.5 What was the layer that was added to the WWW model to derive the three-tier model?

17.6 A further generalization of a distributed systems model as seen in Google was called what?

17.7 A different sort of model was described that was called horizontal distribution. Give an example of the type of system described by this model.

17.8 Early Web browsers using the HTTP 1.0 protocol had to open a separate connection to retrieve each component referenced by a Web page. What technique was used to make this more efficient.

17.9 Describe two ways that servers typically use threads.

17.10 When a physical virtual machine host OS loads a guest OS, what does it do to ensure that the host OS maintains control of the system?

17.11 Briefly describe the operation of an abstract virtual machine.

17.12 True or false? The Jini design allows applications to access services without any prior knowledge of the network mechanisms that will be used by the service.

17.13 What is the basic reason why mobile entities using IP are such a problem?

17.14 One of the middleware applications we looked at allows us to take an existing program and move part of it to another system. What was the non-object-oriented design for doing this?

17.15 What do we call the main standard for developing systems of distributed objects?

17.16 What does the Lamport timestamp mechanism do when receiving a message to ensure that the local logical clock reflects correct information about the order of occurrence of events in a distributed system?

17.17 How does a centralized mechanism for supporting mutual exclusion in a distributed system work?

17.18 What were the two different distributed algorithms for election a coordinator process for a system?

17.19 True or false? TCP supports reliable multicasting over the Internet.

17.20 Why are database transactions more difficult in distributed systems?

Part 6

Case Studies

In this part:

The first two parts of the book gave us some initial background and introduced a series of more complex operating systems in what we dubbed a "spiral approach." This approach was used in order to motivate the features being introduced and to give some perspective to the material. The next three parts treated various technical OS aspects in depth. In this part we once again turn to real OSs, now in the form of case studies. We describe in more depth how several modern OSs incorporate and implement the features described in Parts 3–5.

Chapter 18 covers the Windows NT family starting with the first release and through the existing release known as Vista. Some historical material is included to give perspective to the student. Other subtopics in this chapter include a discussion of the single-user OS environment, process scheduling, memory management, file support, basic I/O, GUI programming, networking, symmetric multiprocessing, a note about the significance of the startup speed of the later releases, and a few words about the new features in the Vista release.

Chapter 19 on Linux covers additional topics that were not covered in the second part of the text and how it implements some of the standard features that we expect to see in any modern OS. After a brief review of Linux we discuss the memory management features of Linux, and the organization of file systems. This chapter also cover basic I/O functions, support for GUI programming, networking support, and symmetric multiprocessing. We then introduce some interesting variants of Linux, primarily hard real-time systems.

Chapter 20 covers additional topics on the Palm OS. Subtopics include other interesting functions of the OS that were not necessary to the spiral approach section, the programming environments that are required when dealing with such systems, and similar developments in the cell phone market and how they contrast with the PDA market. Finally, the chapter discusses new applications that are being developed for these OSs because they are mobile, and how this impacts OS features.

Chapter 18

Windows NT™ through Vista™

In this chapter, we discuss an operating system family that is clearly the dominant personal computer OS in terms of numbers of installations, the Windows NT Operating System family developed by Microsoft. It may appear to a casual observer that it only supports a single user at one time using the console of a personal computer. It actually supports multiple users at remote terminals. It also supports many concurrent users by running services for various remotely accessed functions such as file, print, and directory services, and serves as a platform for other higher-level services such as databases, HyperText Transport Protocol servers (HTTP or Web), File Transfer Protocol servers (FTP), Web services, and many others as well. In the later versions it also supports a function known as fast user switching. This function allows one user to log off the system while any applications that were running stay in memory. A second user can then log in and start other applications. The second user can log off, again leaving all applications running and the first user log back in and resume work where it was left off without having to restart those applications.

Although the title of this chapter refers to Vista, we are using the term Windows NT to refer to the entire product release series. Formally, this term only applies to the NT Version 3.1, 3.5, 3.51, and 4.0 releases. However, the product family naming is not uniform and for the most part the differences between the releases are not significant for our purposes. Also, the term NT is often used casually to refer to the entire series of versions, and we will also use it that way. If we are referring to some feature that was dropped or added in a specific release, then we may mention the specific version's product name.

We start this chapter with an overview of NT and some background about the history of the various Windows OSs in order to give some perspective about the various features and design decisions. In Section 18.2 we discuss the nature of a typical environment for the NT OS. There is also a discussion of the main goals of NT—multiple hardware platform support and legacy OS application support.

NT supports many simultaneously operating user processes as well as concurrent server functions, so in Section 18.3 we discuss the scheduling of processes and tasks in NT. NT uses secondary storage as an extension to primary storage, so complex memory handling mechanisms are needed. These are discussed in Section 18.4. OSs that support multiple server functions and multiple users require complex file systems that provide for security of files as seen in the Linux OS. Section 18.5 thus covers the organization and structure of files and file system metadata in the NT OS and Section 18.6 covers basic I/O functions that NT provides to support those higher-level functions.

The NT GUI allows for multiple overlapping windows, just as do the Mac OS and Linux, and thus requires an elaborate API for the GUI, so Section 18.7 describes some aspects of GUI programming with NT. PDAs running OSs like the Palm have elaborate communication options, but for the most part they are used one at a time. In NT the user may be running many communication activities at the same time—checking email, playing a game over the Internet, synchronizing the database with a PDA, and so on. Section 18.8 is a discussion of the many kinds of networking support in Windows NT. NT often runs on systems with multiple CPUs, especially when being used primarily as a server rather than only as a workstation. Section 18.9 deals with the way NT supports such systems. In Section 18.10 we describe the goal of the startup speed of the XP release of NT and why it was important. We conclude with a chapter summary in Section 18.11.

18.1 INTRODUCTION: WINDOWS NT FAMILY HISTORY

First some history: As was mentioned, the Windows OSs were initially developed for supporting a single user on a personal computer. This support goes back to the 8088/8086 processors. Microsoft began development of an OS that supported a graphical user interface (GUI) in 1981. It was then called the Interface Manager (IM). The CPUs in use lacked the features necessary for protecting one process from another. Because of this hardware limitation, most personal computer OSs prior to this time were not multiprocessing systems, and neither was the IM. Multiple applications could be open at the same time, but only one would actually be running. The windows could not overlap but could only be tiled. Tiled windows do not partly cover one another, so the management of the windows is much simpler for the OS. By the time IM was formally announced in 1983 the name had been changed to Windows. As often happens in areas of technical development, the idea of a GUI was evolving at several places at the same time. The idea arose at the Xerox Palo Alto Research Center (PARC). So Windows was not the first OS for the Intel CPU family with a GUI. Personal Software (which later changed their name to VisiCorp) had released VisiOn before Windows was released. This was actually an environment that ran on top of the OS in a manner similar to X-Windows in UNIX. IBM was also working on a multiprocessing 8x86 environment called TopView, though it did not have a GUI.

The first release of the Windows OS was only marginally successful, primarily because of the hardware architecture limitations and the processor speed. Later releases took advantage of the more advanced features available in the 80286 processor to provide better support for memory management, but the performance of PCs of this era were still marginal when displaying graphics. In addition, these versions of Windows were actually shells that ran on top of the original 16-bit DOS. Also they were mostly or entirely written in assembly language and were increasingly harder to enhance, or even to maintain. When the 80386 processor became available, Microsoft released a version of Windows known as Windows 3.0. This version was extremely successful. Being built on portions of DOS, however, it still had substantial problems. There were various iterations of this product, including Windows 3.1 and Windows for Workgroups. Among other drawbacks, the instruction set and addressing space of the hardware allowed only for a design with a 16-bit memory addressing space. Later, substantial development went into a modified version of this Windows family, including use of a 32-bit instruction set and memory model. This OS series included Windows 95, Windows 98, Windows 98 SE (Second Edition), and Windows ME (Millennium Edition).

In parallel with the development of the early versions of Windows, Microsoft was also involved in the development of a similar OS with IBM called **OS/2.** OS/2 was originally viewed as a means of running several text-based programs at the same time. Subsequently other versions of OS/2 were released that had a GUI interface and ran on the 80286 and 80386 processors. At some point they decided that writing operating systems in assembly language (as was DOS) was not a good idea, so OS/2 was written mostly in C. OS/2 initially had an API that was an extension of the DOS API. Version 3 of OS/2 was started by Microsoft as a complete rewrite of the OS using the OS/2 API, but the enormous success of Windows 3.x caused Microsoft to reevaluate their initial direction. As a result, the primary native API was changed to be the 32-bit **Win32** interface developed for Windows 95 and later versions. Partly as a result of this change, IBM and Microsoft parted company on OS/2 and IBM was left to develop OS/2 by itself. Microsoft changed the name of this release to NT.

Besides the Win32 API, NT was also supposed to support the 16-bit applications developed for DOS and the Windows 3.x products. In addition, a UNIX-style API was required for many U.S. government and corporate procurements. As a result, NT also includes support for applications written to the POSIX.1 API standardized for UNIX systems. (The POSIX interface is actually OS independent, but it was driven by the splintered UNIX community and is based largely on that API.)

At the time the Intel x86 processor did not have quite the dominant position in personal computers (PCs) that it has today. If one processor family came to dominate the PC, Microsoft needed to ensure that their OSs would be able to run on that platform. If no processor dominated, then they needed to run on most or all of them. They thus determined that portability was a primary goal for their main OS product. This meant that they had to move away from the DOS-based Windows products and write a new OS. In order to ensure portability they decided to write this new operating system in a high-level language. There are also many other reasons to use a high-level language, of course. To create this new OS they hired a crew of experienced OS designers. They originally aimed to write it in C++ and to initially target the Intel i860 processor, among others. The i860 was a Reduced Instruction Set Computer (RISC) processor. The version of the processor chip that this team was using was called the N10, and Microsoft was using an i860 emulator called the N10 (N-Ten). This lead to the name NT, also referred to as New Technology. The hardware turned out to be too underpowered for supporting object-oriented programming, so the core of NT ended up being almost entirely written in standard C.

The biggest difference between the various Windows products and Microsoft's earlier systems was the graphical user interface. Today, GUIs are very common, of course—perhaps requiring little more explanation, but they were new to Microsoft OSs when Windows was first created. Such interfaces greatly enhance the user experience, extending the ways that a user interacts with the system well beyond what is available with text-oriented terminals and the ability to run more than one task at a time. This combination of multiple programs running in separate but possibly overlapping graphics-based task windows and controlled with a pointing device such as a mouse or a touch pad that moves an indicator on the screen has been wildly successful. Today, there are few OSs that do not contain such an interface other than systems embedded in appliances and other machines. In some OSs such as UNIX, Linux, and the Mac OS X the GUI interface is a separate layer on top of the OS. In the Microsoft Windows products the GUI interface is an integral portion of the OS design and has been a part of the kernel since at least the Windows 2000 release.

Early work for NT was sometimes done on MIPS systems. Afterward, Microsoft decided that they would like to replace all existing DOS and Windows systems with NT systems, so additional support was added for the 80x86 series of processors and the i860 was eventually dropped due to issues with the chip regarding general OS use. Support for other processors was also added, such as the DEC Alpha 64 bit processor, the MIPS RISC processor, and the PowerPC. (The MIPS chip is used in several families of machines, including Silicon Graphics workstations.) The market eventually decided against these three processors for use in PCs, so they are not supported by later versions of NT. In the XP release of NT, however, support has been added for the Intel Itanium 64-bit RISC processor and the Intel and AMD 64 bit x64 processor families. So the idea of hardware platform independence has remained as an important feature of the NT family.

The NT family included Windows NT 3.1, 3.5, 3.51, and 4.0, Windows 2000 (kernel version NT 5.0), Windows XP (kernel version NT 5.1) and Windows Server 2003, Windows XP x64 Edition, and now Windows Vista (kernel version 6.0). This OS product line includes support for a GUI interface, virtual memory, journaling file systems, preemptive multitasking, and a full suite of networking protocols. Basically it is a very high-end OS. Although there have been some significant enhancements to the product family during this time, much of the system architecture we are describing in this chapter is essentially unchanged from the first release.

18.1.1 Windows Vista

The latest version of NT is **Windows Vista.** Microsoft's primary objective with Vista was to improve the security in the NT OS, but there are many other enhancements as well. We briefly discuss a few of the features in this release as an illustration of the sorts of activity that are being undertaken in current OS development. Many of these features are also found in other contemporary OSs. Other features of Vista that are related strictly to NTFS are discussed in Section 18.5.5. Several of the new features are related to security or reliability:

> Code Integrity Verification. The OS loader and the kernel now perform load-time checks on all kernel mode binaries to verify that the modules have not been changed on the disk. This helps prevent malicious programs from taking control of a machine by modifying the OS.

> Service Security Improvements. Services can now specify which privileges they require (e.g., shutdown, audit, write-restricted, etc.), which limits the power of these services. Privileges not explicitly specified are removed, thus limiting the damage a damaged service can do to the OS.

> User Account Control. UAC improves security by limiting applications to standard user privileges until an administrator authorizes an increase in privilege level. A user may have administrator privileges, but an application the user runs has only standard user privileges unless it is approved beforehand or the user explicitly authorizes it to have higher privileges. UAC will prompt the user for additional privileges automatically or the user can right-click a program icon and select "Run as administrator."

> Address Space Layout Randomization. ASLR is a security technique for randomly assigning parts of the address space of a process. This usually includes the base of the executable program, libraries, and heap and stack space. This mechanism thwarts some security attacks by preventing an attacker from predicting the addresses of the components that are the target of the attack.

> User-Mode Driver Framework (UMDF). Most drivers run in kernel mode with complete access to the physical address space and system data structures. Such access allows a malicious or badly coded driver to cause problems that affect other drivers or the system itself and eventually crash the machine. Drivers that run in user mode have access only to the user address space and are a much less risk. Vista has added support for such user-mode drivers. UMDF is designed for devices like cameras and portable music players.

Some other new features are related to reliability:

> Windows Error Reporting. This feature captures application software crash and hang data from end users who agree to report it. Software developers can access data related to their applications online, monitor error trends, and download debug information.

Reliable Sleep State. Before now an application or driver could prevent the system from entering sleep or hibernate mode (a sleep state). The problem with this was that a laptop user often did not realize the system had not entered the state and would end up with an overheated laptop in the bag, a dead battery, and eventually lost data. Vista does not ask processes before entering sleep states and has reduced the timeout for user-mode notifications from twenty seconds to two.

Clean Service Shutdown. Before Vista services had no way to extend the time allowed for shutdown. After a fixed timeout the system halted with those services still running. This could cause problems for services that needed to flush data to disk. With Vista, services that request notification of a pending shutdown can take as long as they need to shut down. The notification service notifies these services first and waits for them to stop. After they all stop the system continues with a normal shutdown.

Service Shutdown Ordering. Vista allows services to specify a shutdown order where service dependencies need to be followed by the shutdown.

A few features are added to Vista, primarily to speed up the general performance or the time needed to shut down or restart the system:

Delayed Auto-Start Services. Services running in NT are often set to auto-start because they will probably be needed later. However, they have been multiplying and are thereby increasing the time it takes to boot the system. However, many auto-start services do not have to be part of the boot sequence; they just need an unattended start so that they are ready fairly soon after the system starts. Vista provides a new option called delayed auto-start. Services that are designated as delayed auto-start are started shortly after the system has booted. This improves boot and login performance for the user.

SuperFetch analyzes the regular use of applications and tries to keep the frequently used applications in main memory so they can launch more quickly. It will also notice when any prefetched data is moved out to the page file and will monitor the application that caused the prefetched data to be moved out to the page file. As soon as that application is done it will pull the prefetched data back into memory. When the user again accesses the application, the prefetched data will already be in main memory again.

ReadyBoost can create a cache memory on a flash memory device. Although the data transfer speed of such devices is less than current hard drives, flash memory devices have neither seek nor rotational latency so they can boost the apparent speed of the hard disk substantially. Note that this is consistent with our prediction in Chapter 14 about the future replacement of rotating memories.

Hybrid Hard Drives. These new drives incorporate a large flash buffer. They reduce drive power consumption significantly since the drive can be powered down most of the time while data moves between main memory and the flash RAM in the drive. Also, such drives will have increased reliability since the parts are moving less often. Finally, the system will have faster boot time since reading from the flash memory is much faster than waiting for the platters to spin up and then looking for the data. ReadyDrive is the name for the Vista features that support these hybrid hard drives.

18.2 THE USER OS ENVIRONMENT

Because the NT environment is primarily a GUI, the user can easily open up many windows on the screen and start multiple applications. It is not at all unusual for an NT user to have a dozen or more applications running at any one time. Often there will be an email reader checking for incoming mail from time to time; an appointment scheduler open; a Web browser, perhaps open to a portal page that updates the latest news and statistics on the user's stock portfolio; an office-type application such as a spreadsheet the user is working on; a window showing a dictionary that the user has just looked up a word in; and an "instant messenger" application. This does not include numerous other utilities that may be running such as local firewalls, clipboard editors, battery status indicators, sound volume adjustment panels, and so forth. There may also be server functions running such as shared printing, personal Web services, and so on. So while NT is viewed by many users as a single-user system, that by no means implies that the OS has only a few things running.

18.2.1 Goals: Multiple Hardware and OS Platform Emulation

Two of the main goals of the developers of NT were being portable across multiple hardware platforms and supporting applications from legacy OSs. To achieve the first goal, Microsoft used two methods. First, to a substantial extent, certain low-level hardware-dependent portions of the OS kernel are isolated in a single module called the **Hardware Abstraction Layer, or HAL.** Other modules also have portions of the code that have hardware dependencies; for example, the memory manager must know what the physical memory page size is. But having the HAL simplified the process of porting the system to a new hardware platform by partially isolating the hardware-dependent portions of the OS in a single module. The HAL varies with such factors as the support chips used with the CPU (the interrupt controllers, for example), whether the system is a uniprocessor or a multiprocessor system, and what power management features the BIOS supports. These chips connect the buses and other devices to the CPU and they sometimes require specific instructions, just as does the CPU. The second technique was to write all the rest of the OS in a higher-level language that was machine independent. The language initially chosen was C++ with the original intent of having the system be completely object oriented. Later, this strategy was relaxed and much of NT was built with C for reasons of efficiency. The fact that NT has been able to support several different CPUs without major rewrites shows that in this goal it succeeded well.

The second goal of running legacy applications correctly and efficiently has also largely been achieved. Since NT strongly enforces the restriction that only the OS is allowed to directly control the hardware, there are many DOS and a few Windows 3.x applications that will not run under NT because they use the hardware directly. Most applications that do not directly manipulate the hardware will run correctly under NT. The key concept for supporting legacy applications was to add another layer on top of the kernel. This layer supported legacy APIs by translating legacy API calls into native NT API calls. In the NT family these extra layers are called "environments" or "subsystems." In fact, even the 32-bit Windows API that is considered the standard for the NT family is not the native API for the NT kernel itself. These subsystems are shown in Figure 18.1. By the time XP was released, the world had essentially moved on from OS/2 and support for this subsystem was dropped in the XP release of NT. The POSIX support that was originally included with NT was only a minimal implementation of the IEEE 1003.1/ ISO 9945-1 standard. It was withdrawn in the XP release and subsequently replaced with a more complete implementation.

To be sure, originally there were many other goals of the NT OS family such as performance and reliability and a high-level goal of building a first-class operating system, unlike the earlier versions of Windows that were hobbled by limited resources. However, the goals of portability and compatibility were the ones that probably had the most impact on the system design.

These subsystems are not always straightforward, and running older applications can sometimes cause problems. For example, DOS was a single-user system so applications would typically start an I/O operation and then do a spin lock to wait for it to

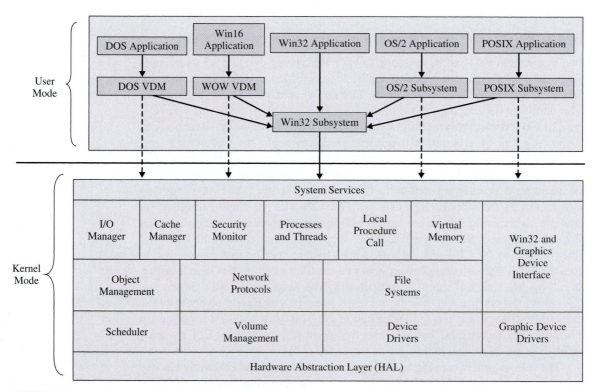

FIGURE 18.1 Original Windows NT family architecture.

complete. NT will virtualize the CPU, so other applications will not get locked out, but in the meantime the DOS application can be burning lots of CPU cycles. Similarly, by default all 16-bit Windows applications run as threads in the **Windows on Windows Virtual DOS Machine (WOW VDM).** The way the threads are dispatched, if one Windows application stops taking input, all those applications will hang.

18.3 PROCESS SCHEDULING

NT uses a complex mechanism to control scheduling of the running processes. It runs multiple processes and creates at least one thread for every process. Then it schedules the threads for execution, not the processes. The mechanism it uses is a multilevel feedback queue. Each thread in NT will have a priority ranging from 0 to 31 that tells the OS how important it is that the process be run as promptly as possible. The thread priority is derived from the **base priority** (defined below) of the process. For each of the 32 priority levels there is a separate queue of threads that are ready to run. When a thread starts running it is given a limited time quantum to run. When this limit is reached the thread is suspended and put at the back of the run queue for its priority level and the next thread at that priority level will be run. For each priority level the scheduler will move to the next lower level only when all the threads that are ready to run at that level have been exhausted. If an event occurs that a thread was waiting on, such as waiting for the disk to read some data, then the OS will check to see if the thread that was waiting on the event has a higher priority than the one that is currently running. If it does, then the current thread will be suspended and the higher priority waiting thread will be run. Interrupting threads for time-slice expiration and for higher priority events are both examples of preemptive multitasking, as was discussed in Chapter 8.

When a process is started, an initial **base priority class** for that process is determined. See Figure 18.2. This class is used to determine the base priority of all the threads in the process. As threads in the process execute, their priorities may change in response to the operations they perform. This is known as a dynamic priority. There are limits below which the thread priority cannot fall and above which it cannot rise. This changing of priorities as the thread runs is the "feedback" referred to in the phrase "multilevel feedback queuing." The intent of raising and lowering the priority like this is to give higher priority to the interactive processes that are closely focused on the user interface and lower to the background those processes that appear to be less involved with the user interface.

The NT scheduler therefore gives high priority to threads that are involved in such interactive tasks as typing on the keyboard. In order to do so it uses a mechanism that is slightly different from that discussed in Chapter 8. There are several cases when NT will raise the priority of a thread:

- When a thread has made a blocking call and that request is finished, its dynamic priority is raised so that it can make good use of the completed operation.
- When a window associated with a process that uses the NORMAL priority class gains the focus, the scheduler boosts the priority of the process so that it is greater than or equal to that of all background processes. The priority class

FIGURE 18.2

NT thread priority relationships.

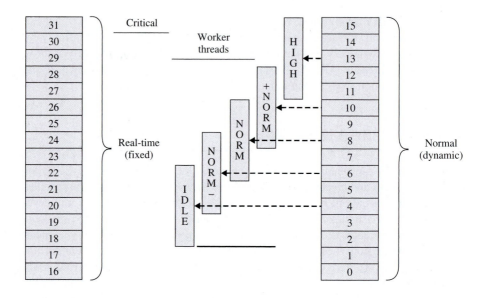

returns to its previous setting when the window associated with the process no longer has the focus.

- When a window receives input such as mouse events, timer events, or keyboard input, the scheduler boosts the dynamic priority of the thread that owns the window.

After raising a thread's dynamic priority, the scheduler decreases the priority by one each time the thread completes a time slice, until the thread drops back to its base priority. A thread's dynamic priority is never lowered below its base priority.

NT has some threads that it runs that it considers "real-time" threads. These include handling time-critical devices like moving a mouse. All of the priorities from 16 to 31 are considered to be real-time priorities. A normal user-created process runs threads that take on only priorities from 0–15. Most of the real-time threads are OS threads, but it is possible for a user process to also use real-time threads. NT is not a hard real-time system, so these processes are soft real-time processes. That is to say that the OS makes an effort to ensure that they get run as often and as soon as desired. However, it does not make any attempt to guarantee that any timing criteria will be met. The system does not boost the priority of real-time threads.

When no other thread is ready to run, NT runs a special thread called the idle thread. If the power circuitry supports it, this thread puts the CPU into a lower power state in which it runs more slowly, and then it goes into a tight loop. Having this special thread also allows the OS to determine how much of the system resources are being used for real work and how much is not being used because the system is waiting for something to happen—perhaps a direction from the user as to which other program to run. When a volunteer computing package such as BOINC is being run, the idle thread will be replaced by the volunteer application. Volunteer computing projects were discussed in Chapter 7.

18.4 MEMORY MANAGEMENT

NT supports a **virtual memory** system with **demand paging,** as was described in Chapter 11. When the CPU is running a process, it generates logical memory addresses for the memory hardware to use to fetch or store instructions or data. The memory management unit (MMU) hardware translates each of these generated addresses to a physical address that the memory system then uses to access the information. The memory is divided into pages of a fixed size. This size is determined by the hardware, so the OS must work with whatever page size the hardware uses. For the Intel x86 family, the size of these pages is normally 4 KB. For other systems, the page size may be different. Because NT is designed to be platform neutral, it must not depend on the actual size of these sections. Since NT was designed to run on many hardware platforms, it must be coded in such a way as to be flexible in the page size.

18.4.1 The address space

In NT the logical address space is divided into two parts, one for the OS and one for the user application. See Figure 18.3. The figure shows the address space to be evenly divided between the user space and the kernel space, but this can be overridden. This override might be used, for example, by an application like a database server that needed a very large memory space. Two other areas of the logical addressing space are set aside to aid in error detection. They are called the guard area and the null pointer catcher. If a program accidentally references an address in either of these spaces, then the hardware will signal an error and the program will be aborted. (This mechanism is a convention used by the language support generally used with the OS and is not actually enforced by the OS itself.) Recall that this address is a part of the logical address space, which is 4 GB. The purpose of these reserved blocks is to generate an interrupt via the hardware when these addresses are used accidentally.

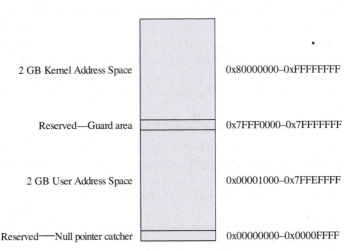

2 GB Kernel Address Space	0x80000000–0xFFFFFFFF
Reserved—Guard area	0x7FFF0000–0x7FFFFFFF
2 GB User Address Space	0x00001000–0x7FFEFFFF
Reserved——Null pointer catcher	0x00000000–0x0000FFFF

FIGURE 18.3
The default Windows NT family x86 memory map.

FIGURE 18.4
A multilevel page
table.

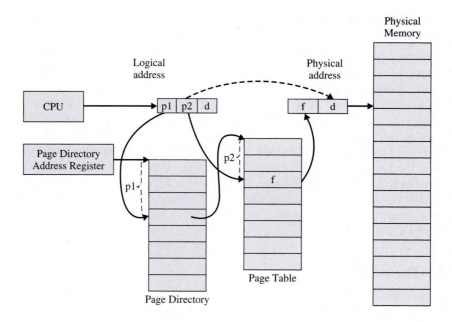

This means that there is no physical memory assigned to these addresses, so we are not wasting real memory for these functions.

There is a special hardware feature in newer CPUs that are compatible with the Intel architecture that lets the kernel use a page size of 4 MB for itself so that a smaller page table is kept and the tables only need a few entries to point to the static parts of the kernel and some additional pages for the parts of the kernel that can be paged.

18.4.2 Page mapping

The NT system running on Intel 8x86–compatible CPUs use a two-level table structure and special hardware to make this translation, as was described in Chapter 11.[1] Figure 18.4 is similar to a figure from that chapter but shows the specific terminology used in NT. The two tables that are used are called a **page directory** and a **page table.** The use of a two-level table allows the logical address space to be very large and very sparse and for the page table itself to be divided into pages. So if no page table entries are made in a given block of the logical address space, then that page table will not be created. The entries in the page table point to the actual frames in physical memory.

18.4.3 Page sharing and copy on write

We have seen that designers go to great lengths to build walls between the OS and the running processes and between the processes as well. However, sometimes it is advantageous for processes to be able to share access to the same locations in memory. This technique must be used carefully when the processes are intentionally sharing pages.

---

[1] Other hardware platforms may use a more complex design. Intel-compatible CPUs must be at least an 80386 architecture.

However, sometimes the OS can allow processes to share pages without the processes being aware of it. One simple case is where a process does a **fork**—that is, the process asks the OS to create another copy of the process and to run both the new and original copies. In this case, NT will create the second process, but will not create an actual copy of all the pages. Instead, it will create a new set of page tables and point the tables to the same physical pages. In both sets of page tables it will mark the pages as read only. Later, if one of the processes writes to a memory location in a given page, the CPU will generate an interrupt and the OS will make a separate copy of that page for each process and remove the read-only flag. This technique is called **copy on write,** discussed in Chapter 11. It will save a lot of time and memory in the case of large objects, especially shared libraries that should never modify themselves anyway.

18.4.4 Page replacement

In Chapter 11 we discussed the problem that occurs when a page needs to be brought into memory and no free frame exists. A currently used page must be selected to be replaced. There are a number of algorithms that we discussed for choosing the page to be replaced. Many of them use hardware features to assist the OS in choosing a page to be replaced. Since NT is designed to be relatively independent of the hardware, the designers chose not to depend on the most advanced features available for paging hardware. Instead, they use a (relatively) simple FIFO algorithm that is a variant of the clock algorithm. When a page is brought into memory for the first time a timestamp is recorded for the page. When a page is needed, the page table will be searched and the oldest page will be discarded. Unfortunately, this sometimes turns out to be a page that is needed frequently. But as soon as it is reloaded it will get a new timestamp, and it will likely not be chosen again soon. NT chooses the pages only from the faulting process, known as local replacement. Linux and most other UNIX variants use a global replacement policy, choosing from all pages in memory.

18.4.5 Prefetch profiles

A clever optimization is used by NT and other OSs to speed up the loading of applications. As was mentioned, when a program starts in a virtual memory system, the entire program is not loaded at once. Instead, when a process makes reference to a part of its logical address space that is not yet loaded, a page fault occurs and the desired page is loaded into physical memory. As a result, when a large program is loading, say a Web browser, it will tend to load pages from different parts of the program, almost in random order, as the initialization code for various data structures is run. As a result, there is considerable disk activity and head movement as the various pieces of program code are fetched. NT will keep track of the page faults generated for 10 seconds after a program starts. Later, when the system is not busy, it will sort this list of the page faults and save this list in a **page fault profile** for that program. When the program is run again later, the OS will prefetch all the pages that it knows will normally be fetched in those first 10 seconds. This can result in substantial time savings in moving disk heads, waiting for rotational delays and in doing I/O in larger blocks and therefore results in faster program startup times.

18.5 FILE SUPPORT

During the past 20 years or so, computing devices have dropped rapidly in price. At the same time, the capacity of disk memory has risen as rapidly. When disk capacities were small, the file system structures were designed to match them. Early DOS file system pointers were restricted to 12 bits because that was enough to point to all the sectors on the floppy disk drives then in use and the designers did not want to "waste" space on larger pointers. As drive sizes have grown, however, the file system designs had to change to support the larger hard drives. As a part of the goal of upgrading existing PC systems to the NT series of OSs, a migration path was needed for the various file systems that users might have. Most OSs have their own preferred file system. NT does as well. It is called **NTFS (NT file system)**. However, NT also supports other file systems, specifically those that Microsoft had developed earlier. These are the **FAT12, FAT16,** and **FAT32** file systems, which were inherited from DOS and Windows. XP also supports the **ISO 9660 CD-ROM** standard format for CDs (**CDFS** in NT), UDF, **ISO 13346** standard format for writable CDs and DVDs, the **HPFS (high performance file system)** that came from OS/2, and quite a few other standard file systems. The HPFS support was eventually dropped because the number of machines that had never been converted from OS/2 was too small to be concerned with. When NT was developed, there was not a large install base of any single version of UNIX on 80x86 machines, so Microsoft apparently did not feel it necessary to support any particular UNIX file systems.

18.5.1 NTFS

We discuss a few general characteristics of NTFS, and then the major goals for NTFS and how they were reached. Finally, we discuss a few advanced features of NTFS. A schematic of an NTFS volume is shown in Figure 18.5.

Master file table

The boot sector of an NTFS volume contains a pointer to the **master file table,** or **MFT.** File systems have to record a lot of metadata *about* files (as opposed to the data that the files themselves contain). Key metadata for an NTFS volume itself are stored as special system files in the MFT. Every file or directory in an NTFS volume has a record in the MFT that is from 1,024 to 4,096 bytes long.[2] The metadata about files and directories are stored in MFT records as **attributes.** The attributes are what we would normally think of as the fields in a file system directory record. Since the attributes needed for a given file can vary greatly depending on the type of the file, most of the attributes are stored as a pair, an identifier, and a value. A few attributes are always present and are stored at the front of the MFT entry for the file, but most of the attributes are in a variable sequence. Since the size of each MFT record is limited, there are different ways that NTFS can store a file's attributes: as either **resident**

---

[2] NTFS is technically proprietary, so some of the details are subject to dispute, having been inferred from observation.

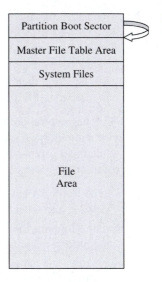

FIGURE 18.5
NTFS volume layout.

attributes that are stored within the MFT record, or **nonresident attributes,** stored either in other MFT records or in extents in non-MFT clusters of the file system:

Resident Attributes. Attributes that require only a little space are kept in the file's MFT record. Most common file attributes are resident. Some are required to be resident, for example, the file name and date/timestamps for file creation, modification, and access are always resident. Figure 18.6 shows an MFT record with resident attributes.

Nonresident Attributes (AKA external attributes). If an attribute will not fit in the MFT record, it is put in a separate place. A pointer in the MFT gives the location of the attribute. Nonresident storage is of two kinds: If the pointers to the value of an attribute will fit in the file's MFT record, then the value is placed in a data run outside the MFT record called an extent, and a pointer to the run is placed in the MFT record. (This is most commonly true of the

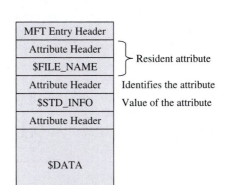

FIGURE 18.6
MFT record with resident attributes.

data attribute, but theoretically it can apply to any attribute.) Figure 18.7 shows an MFT record with nonresident attributes. An attribute may be stored in many different runs, each with a separate pointer. If the attribute value has so many extents that even the pointers to them won't fit in the MFT record, then the entire attribute may be moved to an external attribute in a separate MFT record, or even multiple external records.

NTFS has several predefined attributes. Some are associated only with a file or only with a directory or only with some other structure in the metadata for the volume, while others are associated with more than one structure. Here are some of the most common NTFS system-defined attributes:

Volume Name, Volume Information, and Volume Version. The key name, version, and other metadata for the volume itself.

Bitmap. Contains the cluster allocation bitmap. This attribute is only used by the bitmap metadata MFT record.

File Name. The name of a file or directory. A file or directory can have multiple file name attributes to allow an MS-DOS short filename or for POSIX support for hard links from multiple directories.

Standard Information. Data needed by all files and directories—date/ timestamps for file creation, modification and access, read-only, hidden, etc.

Index Root. An index of the files in a directory. If the directory is small, the entire index may fit in the MFT. Otherwise, some of the information will be in nonresident attributes.

Security Descriptor. Information controlling access to a file or directory (e.g., ownership, access control lists, and auditing information).

FIGURE 18.7
MFT record with nonresident data attributes.

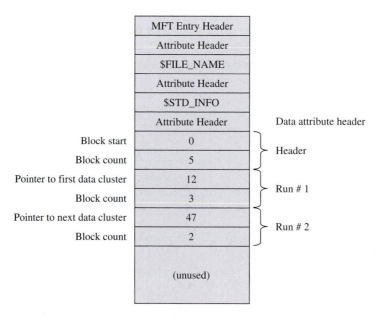

Attribute List. This is a meta-attribute—it describes other attributes. If an attribute is nonresident, then that attribute's identifier is placed in the MFT record with a pointer to the nonresident attribute.

Data. The data in a file is the value of the "data" attribute. If all of the attributes of a file (including the data) will fit in the MFT record, then the data attribute will be resident in the MFT record itself. Such files require no other storage space on the volume, and more importantly they do not require an extra disk access to read the data, improving performance.

Larger files are more complicated. If all of the attributes for a file do not fit into the MFT record, the attributes will be made nonresident. So most files will have their data stored outside the MFT record. The attributes for a file obviously include pointers to the data. Very large files may be so large that the attributes pointing to the data will not fit in the MFT record and thus become external attributes themselves.

Keeping the MFT contiguous on the disk improves performance, so when an NTFS volume is initialized, about 13% of the disk space immediately following the MFT is reserved as the "MFT zone." It is still usable, but normal files and directories will not use this space until the rest of the space is used. Eventually, the MFT may use up the "MFT zone." If this happens, NTFS will allocate more space for the MFT. This fragmentation of the MFT may reduce performance by increasing the number of reads required for some files, and the MFT cannot generally be defragmented.

Space tracking

NTFS allocates disk space in blocks of sectors called clusters. It uses a bitmap to track whether or not each cluster has been allocated to a file. The bitmap itself is stored in the master file table as a special system file.

Pointers to the clusters that have been allocated to a file are kept together in a block. In Chapter 12 we described these as "index blocks" to conform to the standard terminology in OS literature. (This term should not be confused with NTFS $INDEX attributes, which apply to directories.) The index block pointers give the cluster number of the start of a **data run,** which is a contiguous group of clusters that are all allocated to this file. The index block has a starting cluster number and a run length, or count of the contiguous clusters. An MFT record using such runs was shown in Figure 18.7.

Major NTFS goals

NTFS had two major goals: high reliability and security. High reliability was approached from two different directions, recoverability after a crash and software data redundancy and fault tolerance (i.e., RAID). Beyond these three main goals NTFS provides many other advanced features.

Recoverability   Probably the primary goal of the NTFS design was to increase the reliability of the file systems in the face of a crash. With previous file system designs, if the data that controlled the file system was corrupted due to an abnormal system shutdown, there was a strong possibility that whole files or large portions could be irretrievably lost. The mechanism that has evolved for the purpose of increasing file system recoverability is a **log-based file system** or **journaling file system,** as was discussed in Chapter 13. Whenever any update is to be done to the file system metadata, NT first writes out a record to a log file, which lists the steps of the update that are to be made. This set of steps is referred to as a **transaction.** Then the individual steps of the update are made. Finally, any file I/O for which the metadata updates were being done is executed. Once the entire series of steps is finished, the record listing those steps will be removed from the log file. If the system goes down, then when it comes back up it checks to see if an update transaction was in process. If a record in the log file shows an update was in process, then the OS can recognize what part of the operation was not completed successfully, and it can either finish the transaction if it is able or it can back out those portions that were already done if it cannot finish. In this way the file system will always be brought into a valid state. Some application data might have been lost, but at least the file system can continue to be used without fear that additional data will be lost in the future because the file system has been left in a corrupted state. The Vista release includes optional features called Volume Shadow Copy and Transaction Support, which can provide protection for data files. These features are discussed in Section 18.5.5.

Naturally, these extra steps take extra time and increase the load on the disk drive. Since NT is designed primarily for a personal computer, the extra load is tolerable because the system is probably not being overworked in most cases. Other NTFS design elements also allowed some performance gains over the other file systems that NT supports, so the performance of NTFS overall is acceptable because of the increased reliability over other Microsoft file systems. Also, if a system crashes and the file system is not a log-based system, then it is prudent to run a utility function to check the integrity of the file system. On a system with very many files this might take several hours to run. On a system that is being used as a server, such a long delay is unacceptable. In such cases it makes more sense to distribute this performance impact so that guaranteeing the integrity is spread over the normal day-to-day operation rather than incurred at one time after a system crash.

Data redundancy and fault tolerance   Another disk reliability feature of NT is support for three different software **RAID (redundant array of independent disks)** organizations. RAID was discussed in more detail in Chapter 14. The RAID forms supported by NT are RAID-0, RAID-1, and RAID-5. RAID-0 is strictly for performance enhancement and offers no increased reliability. RAID-1 is full mirroring— everything written to one drive is automatically written to another drive. It offers good reliability but at a higher hardware cost. For RAID-5 a parity block is written that corresponds to a group of data blocks. It offers good reliability at a lower hardware cost but with increased software overhead. Of course hardware RAID systems can be used with NT rather than using software solutions.

Security   In NT the fundamental building block of all OS data structures is an object. Included in this group are files and directories. Each object has an owner, originally the entity that created the object. Security can be applied to any object using an access control list. You may recall that an ACL for an entity lists the entities (including groups and roles) that are allowed to operate on an object and the list of operations that the entity is allowed to perform. The owner can do several things to the ACL, including changing it directly, allowing other entities to change it, and allowing other entities to become the owner. In NTFS the ACL for a file or directory is stored as an attribute of the object. The permissions used in NTFS are these:

* `R — read`

* `W — write`

* `X — execute`

* `D — delete`

* `P — modify the ACL`

* `O — make current account the new owner ("take ownership")`

18.5.2 Advanced features of NTFS

NTFS includes many advanced features for supporting applications. Some features are available to application programs as API calls and others are only used internally:

Read-only support. Before the XP release NTFS required that volumes be on writeable media so that it could write the transaction log files. XP introduced drivers that can mount volumes on read-only media. This feature is needed by embedded systems that have read-only volumes in NTFS format.

Defragmentation. NTFS makes no special efforts to keep files contiguous. It provides a defragmentation API that applications can use to move file data so that files occupy contiguous clusters. NT includes a defragmentation tool but it has several limitations. Third-party products usually offer more features.

Volume mount points. These are similar to UNIX mount points. In NTFS, this allows additional file systems to be visible without requiring a separate drive letter for each. This includes remote volumes as well.

POSIX support. One of the goals for NT was to support the POSIX standard. For file systems this requires support for case-sensitive file and directory names, a different method of determining access permissions when parsing path names, and a different set of timestamp semantics. None of these features is compatible with NT itself. NTFS includes these optional features in support for POSIX.

Encryption. Data stored on laptops can be exposed when a laptop is lost or stolen. File system protection is not perfect in this case because volumes can be read by software that doesn't require NT to be running. Furthermore, NTFS file permissions are worthless when another user can use an account with administrator privileges. So NTFS includes a function called encrypting file system (EFS) to encrypt the data stored in the data attribute. EFS is completely transparent to applications. Encrypted files can be accessed only by using the private key of an account's EFS private/public key pair, and private keys are locked using an account's password so the files can't be read without the password of an authorized account.

Volume shadow copy. This service keeps historical versions of files and folders on NTFS volumes by copying overwritten data to a hidden shadow backup. The user can later request a switch back to an earlier version. This feature allows backup programs to archive files currently in use.

Link tracking. Shortcuts allow users to place files on their desktop. Similarly, object linking and embedding (OLE) allow documents from one application to be linked to documents of other applications. Such links provide an easy way to connect files with one another but they have been hard to manage, since if the user moves the target of a link, the link will be broken. NTFS supports distributed link-tracking, which maintains the integrity of shell and OLE links when link targets move. With NTFS link-tracking support, if a link target located on an NTFS volume moves to another NTFS volume in the same domain, the link-tracking service can update the link to reflect the move.

Single instance storage (SIS). Sometimes several directories have files with identical content. Single instance storage allows identical files to be reduced to one physical file and many SIS references to the merged file. SIS is a file system filter that manages changes to files and a service that searches for files that are identical and need merging. Unlike hard links that point to only one file, each SIS file remains distinct as far as the externals to the file system are concerned, and changes to one copy of a file will not change the others. A distinct copy will be created for the one SIS file that is changed.

Per-user disk space quotas. Administrators often need to track or limit user disk space usage, especially on servers, so NTFS includes quota-management support, which allows for per-user specification of disk space quotas.

Change logging. Applications sometimes need to monitor volumes for file and directory changes. For example, an automatic backup program might make incremental backups when files change. One way for this to happen is for the application to scan the volume and record the state of files and directories. Then on a later scan it can check for differences. This process can significantly slow the system, however, especially when computers commonly have hundreds of thousands of files. NTFS allows an application to ask NTFS to record information about file and directory changes to a special file called the change journal. The application can then read the change journal instead of scanning the entire directory tree.

Transaction support. With Vista, applications can use transactions to group changes to files together into a transaction. The transaction guarantees that all changes happen, or none of them do, and it will guarantee that applications outside the transaction will not see the changes until they are committed. Transactions have been commonly supported in database systems and in the NTFS metadata. This feature brings the reliability of transaction-based systems to normal files.

Compression and sparse files. NTFS supports compression of file data. Compression and decompression are transparent, so applications don't have to be modified to take advantage of this feature. Directories can also be compressed, and any files in compressed directories are automatically compressed. NTFS has a related mechanism known as sparse files. If a file is marked as sparse, NTFS doesn't allocate space on a volume for portions of the file that are empty. NTFS returns 0-filled buffers when an application reads from empty areas of a sparse file. As with compressed files, sparse files are generally transparent to the application, though applications can be aware of sparse files and possibly save considerable CPU and memory resources when processing portions of files that are actually null.

Aliases. NTFS supports both hard and symbolic links. A hard link allows multiple paths to refer to the same file. They are implemented much as was discussed in Chapter 12. NTFS prevents loops by the simple expedient of not allowing a hard link to refer to a directory. NTFS calls symbolic links **junctions.** They are based on a more general mechanism called a **reparse point.** A reparse point is an extra attribute about the file or directory, such as its current location, that can be read by the I/O manager. When NTFS hits a reparse point during a file or directory lookup, it tells the I/O manager to check the reparse data. The I/O manager can alter the pathname specified in the original operation and let it restart with the changed path. Reparse points can also be used by tape archival software to show that a file has been moved to an archive system. It moves a file to a tape, leaving reparse points in their directory entries that tell the software where the file is now located. When a process tries to access a file that has been archived, the driver removes the reparse point attribute from the directory, reads the file data from the archival media back to the original media, and reissues the access. Thus, the retrieval of the offline data is transparent to a process accessing an archived file. Of course, opening the file probably takes a little longer than normal.

Dynamic bad-cluster handling. If a data read accesses a bad disk sector, the read fails and the data is no longer available. If the disk is a fault-tolerant (RAID) volume, however, the driver fetches a good copy of the data and also tells NTFS that the sector is bad. NTFS allocates a new cluster on the failed drive to replace the bad cluster and copies the data there. It marks the bad cluster and thereafter ignores it.

Indexing. NTFS allows **indexing** of any of the file attributes on a disk volume. Indexing sorts the attributes. This lets the file system quickly find files that match any criteria, such as all the files in one directory.

Complex file names. NTFS uses Unicode characters to store names of files, directories, and volumes. Unicode is a 16-bit character-coding scheme that allows each character in each of the world's major languages to be uniquely represented. Each element in a path name can be up to 255 characters long and can contain Unicode characters, spaces, and multiple periods.

Multiple data streams. In NTFS a file's data is considered to be an attribute of the file called the data stream. New attributes can be added by applications, including additional data streams, so files (and directories) can contain multiple data streams. NT uses an alternate stream to associate user "properties" with the file, such as a title, subject, author, and keywords. It stores the date in an alternate stream called Summary Information.

18.6 BASIC INPUT AND OUTPUT

The architecture of the total NT file system can be seen more closely in Figure 18.8. Unfortunately, as often happens with OS documentation, the names that we have been using in this text conflict with the names used by the NT system designers. For example, they call the top layer of the I/O system the "I/O Manager," while we have used that term for the lower-level I/O functions of an OS. In this chapter we use the terms as they are used by Microsoft. So the functions we were describing in the previous section actually reside in the Partition/Volume Storage Manager and the Disk Class Manager.

18.6.1 Partitions

Because hard drive support in PCs derived from the designs used in MS/DOS, there are certain things that any OS on a PC is going to support. For one thing, the design allows the system administrator to divide the disk drive into separate areas called **partitions.** The administrator will then use OS utility programs to establish a separate file system in each partition. These file systems may even be file systems native to other OSs. The I/O system will see each partition as a separate drive. As with the

FIGURE 18.8
NT I/O architecture.

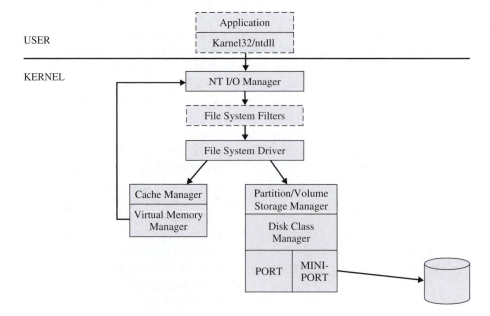

file systems themselves, the design of the partitioning structure has had to evolve to cope with the increasing size of hard disks. The partitioning mechanism creates a small table in the first sector of the hard disk called the **master boot block** (**MBB**) or **master boot record** (**MBR**). The original mechanism could create only four partitions on a single disk. Later extensions allowed one partition to be designated as an extended partition. This would allow up to 24 logical partitions to be created on one disk.

18.6.2 I/O system layering

The separation of the layers in the I/O system allows additional extra layers to be easily inserted into the OS architecture. In many cases the NT I/O drivers expose the same calls at their API as they use to invoke the drivers at the next lower level, and each alternative module at any given layer implements the same interfaces. Among other things, this layering allows a logical device to be defined on a system that is not really a local disk partition but is instead located on another machine across a network. In this case the system performs a **redirection** so that to the user and to programs, network devices appear to be no different from local devices. It also allows a device to appear to be a disk drive when it actually is something else—a USB flash drive, for example.

The layers also allow extra features to be inserted between layers. They are loaded as the system boots in the form of device drivers of a special class called **filters.** In the simple case where the average user might not want any extra features, the basic I/O functions can be supported with very little overhead. When a user does want some more exotic function, the extra features can be inserted between two layers in a manner that is transparent to both the higher and lower layers. One example of such extra functionality is that of virus scanners. By providing this interface between the layers, NT can allow third-party software to extend the features of the I/O system without violating the integrity of the OS code. Also, if any future unanticipated functionality is developed it will be easy to add it to the I/O system because of this well-defined standard layered interface.

18.6.3 Plug and play

When an OS is written it is a generic entity, capable of running on a wide variety of hardware configurations. When we install an OS on a specific machine it must be configured to match the hardware installed. If new hardware is later added or old hardware replaced or removed, then the OS must be adjusted to match the new configuration. We need drivers for new hardware and we also don't want to waste space on drivers that are no longer needed.

In the early generations of the large mainframes it was common for the systems programming staff to have to perform a **sysgen (system generation)** when installing or upgrading an OS. Briefly, this amounted to describing the hardware configuration with a file of specification records, which were then used to generate an executable version of the OS specifically tailored to match the hardware. For a moderate-sized configuration this took days and sometimes several tries to work correctly.

The original IBM PC was typical of hardware systems of that era, and configuration of DOS to fit the hardware was very difficult. There were two to four different pieces of information required to configure most controllers, including an interrupt request level (IRQ), a memory address, an I/O port (address), and a direct memory access (DMA) channel number. These were set manually using small switches or jumpers on the controller board. These addresses had to be selected so that they did not conflict with one another. Installing a new controller in a machine could be quite challenging because it was often difficult to find out the settings on the existing cards. In addition, the hardware then had to be described to the OS using a file called **config.sys.** Hardware vendors usually supplied a utility program that would attempt to adapt the config.sys file for the new hardware, but they often would cause more problems than they would fix.

Beginning with the IBM MicroChannel™ and EISA buses, the controllers were able to identify themselves to the OS and respond to configuration changes by the software. This activity is known as **plug and play,** or sometimes **PnP.** This trend continued with the PCI bus and today most OSs are capable of recognizing most new hardware, setting the parameters for the cards dynamically, selecting configurations, that will work with the existing hardware configuration, and customizing the OS by dynamically loading the correct device drivers for the hardware. The OS is still being adapted to fit the hardware, but the process is normally done dynamically by the OS and is much more transparent to the user.

18.6.4 Device drivers

All of the hardware characteristics of the I/O devices are isolated in the lowest level of the kernel, the device drivers. This means, for example, that all higher-level modules should not concern themselves with how many sectors are on a disk track or how many read/write heads a disk drive has. Nor should they be concerned with which bits in the status register indicate an error has occurred. Instead, they should focus on the things that are common to all disk drives, and confine the details of any specific device (or controller) to the device driver for that particular device or controller.

Since NT uses such device drivers to hide the details of the hardware, it is easy to change the hardware configuration of an NT system. Indeed, the drivers can be installed in or removed from the system dynamically. This means that when a device is added to the system it is not necessary to reboot the OS. Prior to this development such rebooting had been necessary when the hardware was changed. This was time-consuming and in the case of very important systems such as servers it was highly undesirable. With device controllers that are physically inserted into the bus—for example, a new graphics card—the system power has to be turned off anyway, so having to reboot the system is not a problem. However, several of the new methods for connecting peripheral devices to the computer assume the device is external, like a VCR or a camcorder, so powering it off is not necessary. Examples of such interfaces include **USB** (Universal Serial Bus), **IEEE 1394,** and **PC Card** or **Card Bus** (formerly called **PCMCIA**) devices. Furthermore, protocols are defined for these interfaces such that the device identifies itself to the computer in a manner similar to the plug and play features of a PCI bus. This dynamic identification means that the

OS can automatically load the drivers for any newly installed device without rebooting the OS and generally without any assistance from the user other than possibly providing a CD-ROM containing drivers for the device. Most users will also connect devices to serial or parallel ports without shutting off the power, though manufacturers of such devices do not generally recommend it. But devices connected through these ports may not be able to identify themselves automatically like those with the newer interfaces do.

18.6.5 Disk class, port, and miniport drivers

The File System module calls on **storage driver** functions at lower layers that move progressively closer to the hardware. These layers are called the **storage class, storage port,** and **miniport** drivers. At the top layer NT provides storage class drivers, which implement features common to all storage devices of a particular type such as disks or tapes. At the next layer are storage port drivers, which have features common to a particular bus such as SCSI or ATA. Disk drive vendors supply miniport drivers that support a particular device or family of compatible devices. The class drivers have the same API as the device driver interfaces. Miniport drivers use a port driver interface instead of the device driver interface. This approach simplifies the role of miniport developers because they have APIs that are compatible with previous Microsoft OSs. Storage class drivers can often handle many devices in the class without having a storage port or miniport driver. The prime example of this is the generic USB storage class driver, which can access many USB storage devices without any other drivers.

18.7 GUI PROGRAMMING

For the user, arguably the defining feature of Windows is the GUI. The programmer accesses the OS functions that manipulate the objects on the desktop through Windows' APIs. These interfaces provide functions that allow the programmer to draw windows, make menus and dialog boxes, and so forth. The OS itself takes care of common functions like making sure that when one window is closed that the appropriate parts of any windows that were behind the closed window are updated. Some facilities are provided for the programmer such as the common dialog box. See Figure 18.9. This is a standard window-based dialog that the program can use to find a file (or files) to open, specify a name to save a file under, select a font or a color, and several other common features that any program might want to allow. An application programmer can use this interface, but is not required to do so. Using this interface provides a similar look-and-feel to different applications. As programmers have developed more sophisticated interfaces, they have often tended to use them in the place of the standard interfaces. One can argue that these new interfaces are more user-friendly or more appropriate to a given task, but having a different interface for every application may make the overall system more difficult for a novice to learn, so it is not clear that the tradeoff is always worth it.

FIGURE 18.9
A File Open dialog
box.

18.8 NETWORKING

Another aspect of NT where the creators desired bringing compatibility with other OSs was in the networking protocols it supported. When NT was being developed the Internet was already fairly popular in academic circles, but the TCP/IP protocols used in the Internet were not the overwhelmingly dominant network protocols that they are today. The Novell Netware OS was the dominant personal computer file server platform and it had its own protocols in the form of IPX/SPX. There were many UNIX systems in operation, and in addition, many of the larger enterprises had IBM mainframes and midrange systems that used IBM protocols. Systems from Apple, Inc. ran a protocol known as AppleTalk over various hardware topologies. In order to gain a place in the networks of customers who used these other systems, Microsoft had to be able to install systems that could communicate easily with those systems by supporting the protocols they used. Of course, NT also had to provide compatibility with the protocols that earlier versions of Windows and DOS used. It therefore incorporated all the standard protocols used by these other systems. (These protocols were sometimes common to multiple systems—VAX systems often used TCP/IP, for example.) Typically these protocols included:

- IPX/SPX for Novell Netware
- TCP/IP for UNIX
- DECNet for Digital Equipment VAX systems
- SNA and NetBEUI for IBM systems
- LAN Manager for Windows legacy systems

Similar to most of the other major components of NT, the networking functions are layered. For example, the lowest layer of the networking stack uses an interface called **NDIS** (**network driver interface specification**) that was defined by Microsoft and

3Com. This interface is specifically designed to allow a single hardware device driver to support multiple Network layer protocols. This allowed the **network interface card (NIC)** vendors to write a single driver for each combination of NIC and hardware platform without regard for the operating system or the Network layer software. Indeed, it allowed the driver to support multiple Network layer protocols at the same time. As with the I/O system, this layered architecture allows the transparent insertion of extra functionality that is not needed by most users. One example is a layer to provide **SNMP (Simple Network Management Protocol)** functions in a PC so that it can be remotely monitored with an SNMP-based network management console. This protocol was discussed in Chapter 15. When such monitoring is not needed it does not have to be installed and waste resources.

An interesting feature of NT networking support is that it includes an interface for asynchronous transfer mode (ATM) hardware. ATM has several interesting characteristics that most people have overlooked in their rush to join the Ethernet bandwagon. For one thing, the maximum ATM frame size of 64 KB fits better with the maximum IP frame size of 64 KB than does Ethernet with a maximum frame size of 1,500 bytes. When the hardware can directly support the much larger blocks, it is a waste of resources to break them into smaller pieces. For another, ATM supports quality of service (QoS) features in the hardware without resorting to software contortions and extra software layers. As multimedia applications have become more important, some people have found that these applications work much better over ATM than they do over Ethernet, and that NT already includes support for those features.

18.9 SYMMETRIC MULTIPROCESSING

The hardware platforms that support the NT OS family can scale up to fairly large systems. One feature that is often found in systems that are designed for supporting high-volume servers is that they may have more than one CPU. Multiple CPU technology is now moving down into average desktop systems with CPUs that can run multiple processes concurrently and with multiple CPUs in a single chip. NT supports symmetric multiprocessing (SMP), as was discussed in Chapters 6 and 9. The maximum number of CPUs supported by the NT family varies with the CPU word size; 32-bit CPUs will support up to 32 CPUs and the 64-bit CPUs will support up to 64 CPUs. These limits are simply because masks about the individual CPUs are stored in a single data word.

18.10 STARTUP SPEED OF XP

One of the interesting design goals of the XP release was to speed up the time required to boot the operating system. The goal depended on the way in which the system was started. From a cold start the goal was considerably longer than from a standby mode or a hibernate mode. For a restart from a standby state a five second boot time was the goal. Note that this requires a hardware option called advanced configuration power interface (ACPI). The time interval of this goal is interesting because it is roughly the timeout of a human's short-term memory. If you begin to do some task and the actions required to start that task take more than about seven seconds, you will frequently find that your attention has wandered—you will have forgotten that phone number you just looked up, for example. So if your PC is turned off and you decide to turn it on to look up something interesting, if it takes more than seven seconds to boot up you may find that the hot idea you had has just slipped away. So this was an important feature that was probably not fully appreciated by many users but affected them nonetheless.

18.11   SUMMARY

In this chapter, we discussed the features and concepts of a more advanced OS—the Windows NT Operating System developed by Microsoft, Inc. We started this chapter with an overview of the NT OS and a bit of the history of the evolution of Microsoft OSs. We then moved to a brief discussion of the nature of a high-end single-user OS and the main goals of the NT family—support for applications from legacy OSs and support for multiple hardware platforms. Next, we discussed the complexity caused by running multiple-user applications and server applications at the same time. This additional complexity shows in both the scheduling of processes and threads and in the additional memory management functions supported by the NT OS family.

Then we gave an overview of the support of files in the NT OS and the higher functions required by having multiple users and possibly multiple servers configured on the system, followed by coverage of the I/O functions that the OS provides. We then briefly discussed some new aspects of the GUI functionality caused by having multiple windows open at the same time and we also touched on the subject of multiprocessor support under NT. Finally, we addressed the speed of the startup of XP.

In the next section of the book we provide a case study of the Linux OS by covering some features that were not covered in the spiral chapter where the focus was primarily on those features that were required when supporting multiple users.

BIBLIOGRAPHY

IEEE: Information Technology—Portable Operating Systems Interface (POSIX). New York: IEEE, 1990.

Ricadela, A., "Gates Says Security Is Job One For Vista." *InformationWeek News,* February 14, 2006.

Russinovich, M. E., and D. A. Solomon, *Microsoft Windows Internals,* 4th ed., Redmond WA: Microsoft Press, 2005.

WEB RESOURCES

http://www.activewin.com/awin/default.asp (outsider information on Microsoft)

http://book.itzero.com/read/microsoft/0507/Microsoft.Press. Microsoft.Windows.Internals.Fourth.Edition.Dec.2004 .internal.Fixed.eBook%2DDDDU%5Fhtml/ (Microsoft® Windows® Internals, 4th ed. Microsoft Windows Server™ 2003, Windows XP, and Windows 2000, by Russinovich, M. E., and D. A. Solomon)

http://msdn.microsoft.com/en-us/default.aspx (Microsoft Developer News)

http://www.osnews.com (news site on all OSs)

http://technet.microsoft.com/en-us/library/bb878161.aspx (Windows XP resource kit)

http://technet.microsoft.com/en-us/sysinternals/default .aspx (Sysinternals, originally an outside technical reference, later bought by Microsoft)

http://pages.prodigy.net/michaln/history/ (OS/2 history)

http://www.tasklist.org (software to list all processes running on a system)

http://www.windowsitlibrary.com (magazine site)

http://www.winsupersite.com (outsider information on Microsoft)

REVIEW QUESTIONS

18.1 What was the major change when Windows NT was being developed that made it different from most of the previous OS products from Microsoft?

18.2 What were some of the major goals for the XP family that were mentioned in the chapter?

18.3 When a process does a fork call, XP does not really create a second copy of the program. What does it do instead?

18.4 How was the goal of hardware independence addressed?

18.5 What sorts of objects does NT use to schedule the CPU?

18.6 Describe the difference between the normal priority class and the real-time class.

18.7 What is so unusual about how the NTFS supports the data in a file? Specifically, what happens if the data is rather short?

18.8 True or false? Windows XP supports the OS/2 HPFS file system.

18.9 Which RAID configurations does NT support in software?

18.10 Why is it important to have such a specific division between the IOS and the file system?

18.11 True or false? NT supports compression of files or entire portions of a file system.

18.12 What is the impact of a "log-based" file system?

18.13 What is the advantage of dynamically installable device drivers?

18.14 What is unusual about the command-line interface to Windows XP?

18.15 One school of thought says that it is better for applications to stick to standard elements in the GUI interface. Another argues that improved elements can make applications better. Justify your choice.

18.16 Why does XP support an ATM protocol stack?

18.17 What does the NDIS specification do?

18.18 Which multiprocessing mechanism does XP support?

Chapter 19

Linux: A Case Study

In this chapter:

I n Part 2 of the book we discussed some basic features of the Linux operating system and how a multiuser design placed some different requirements on an OS. In that chapter we also presented an overview of Linux and some background about its history and we discussed the general nature of a multiuser OS, the scheduling of processes and processes in Linux, and the nature of user logons and file protection mechanisms.

In this chapter, we present further information about Linux in a case study of OS and how it implements some of the standard features that we expect to see in any modern OS. This chapter is intended to be studied with Chapter 6 so that material is not repeated unnecessarily. We start this chapter with a brief review of Linux and its history. Section 19.2 discusses the scheduling of processes in Linux and Section 19.3 continues, discussing the memory management features necessitated by supporting many users who are working at many different processes. Section 19.4 covers the organization of files in the Linux OS. Linux supports many different file systems because of its unique evolutionary history. Section 19.5 covers the basic I/O functions that Linux provides and Section 19.6 describes support for GUI programming, which was derived from the design used in UNIX. In Section 19.7 is a discussion of the networking support in Linux, which, like the file systems, is complex because of the history of Linux and the environments it must coexist in. Section 19.8 deals with some special security aspects of Linux and Section 19.9 discusses a problem that arose with Linux support for multiple CPUs. Section 19.10 covers hard real-time and embedded variants of the Linux OS. We conclude with a chapter summary in Section 19.11.

19.1 INTRODUCTION

19.1.1 Linux history

The Linux OS is largely oriented around UNIX, an older OS that supported multiple users using terminals connected to a large computer. Today, there are versions of Linux that are used as the OS on a personal computer for a single user. These versions still maintain the internal structure of a multiuser facility. Indeed, a single user can run multiple virtual terminals and can switch between them as though there were several users on the system and can support concurrent sessions from users with remote connections. Other versions of Linux are intended to be used purely remotely as servers for various functions, to act as routers in networks, to control real-time systems, and to be embedded in equipment with no human interface. As was pointed out in Chapter 6, Linux is released in production versions and development versions. The features described in this chapter mostly relate to version 2.6.

The history of Linux is shorter than many other OSs. Here is a short summary of the more significant releases and features:

- V. 1.0, March 1994 supported only single-processor i386 machines
- V. 1.2, March 1995 added support for Alpha, SPARC, and MIPS CPUs
- V. 2.0, June 1996 added support for more processors and SMP
- V. 2.2, January 1999
- V. 2.4.0, January 2001
    - Hewlett-Packard's PA-RISC processor
    - Axis Communications' ETRAX CRIS
    - ISA Plug-and-Play, USB, PC Card, and Bluetooth
    - RAID devices

- V. 2.6, December 17, 2003
    - uClinux (for machines with no paged MMU)
    - Hitachi's H8/300 series, NEC v850, Motorola's embedded m68k processors
    - Intel's hyperthreading and physical address extension (PAE)
    - Maximum number of users and groups (each) now 4,294,967,296
    - Maximum number of process ids now 1,073,741,824
    - File systems of up to 16 terabytes
    - Infiniband support

19.1.2 Kernel architecture

The structure of the Linux kernel is monolithic. It is quite modular, however, allowing individual subsystems to be replaced with experimental versions quite easily. The relationships among the individual modules are complex. Indeed, there are few

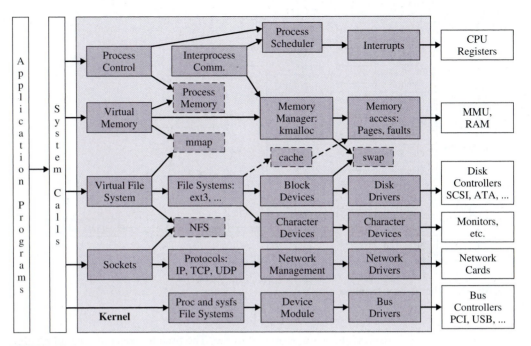

FIGURE 19.1 The Linux system architecture.

modules that do not interact with most of the other major modules in some way. Figure 19.1 shows some of the major components and the most significant relationships among the modules. In the remaining sections of this chapter we discuss the operation of some of the major system modules.

19.2 PROCESS SCHEDULING

The process scheduler module was redesigned in Linux 2.6. The motivation was to create a scheduler that used an algorithm that ran in O(1) time. The scheduler used in prior kernel releases was O(n) and performed poorly when the load was too high. The Process Scheduler module (SCHED) is responsible for selecting which process should have access to the CPU. Linux documentation often uses the term "task" instead of the term "process," but for most purposes we can consider these to be the same thing. Linux uses a priority-based scheduling algorithm to choose from among the runnable processes in the system. (A runnable process is one that is waiting for a CPU to run on.)

There is a **runqueue** made up of 140 lists, one for each priority. An example is shown in Figure 19.2. (In a multi-CPU system there will be similar structures for each CPU but we will ignore that for now.) The individual lists are each scanned in FIFO order. Processes that are scheduled to execute are added to the end of their respective runqueue's priority list. Most processes have a time slice, or **quantum,** that limits

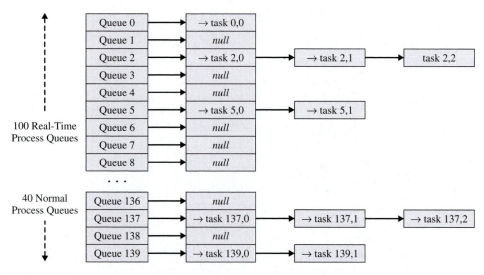

FIGURE 19.2 The active runqueue.

the time they are permitted to run. The time it takes the scheduling algorithm to find a process to run thus depends not on the number of active processes but rather on the number of priority lists.

The runqueue we have been discussing is properly called the **active runqueue.** In addition to this queue there is also an **expired runqueue.** When a process on the active runqueue uses all of its time slice, it is moved to the expired runqueue. At the same time its next time slice and its priority are recalculated. If there are no processes on the active runqueue, the pointers for the active and expired runqueues are swapped, and the expired runqueue becomes the active one. At this point all the processes will effectively have a fresh time quantum. A scheduling **epoch** is the time between when all runnable processes begin with a fresh time quantum and when all runnable processes have used up their time and the queues need to be swapped.

The scheduler always schedules the highest priority process on a system. If there are multiple processes at the same priority they are scheduled in round-robin fashion. The runqueue structure not only makes finding the highest priority process a constant-time operation, it also makes round-robin behavior within priority levels possible in constant-time. As well, having two runqueues makes transitions between time slice epochs a constant-time operation.

19.2.1 Real-time processes

The standard Linux scheduler provides soft real-time scheduling support, meaning that while it does a good job of meeting scheduling deadlines, it does not guarantee that deadlines will be met. This scheduler uses two different scheduling classes to ensure that all processes will have fair access to the CPU, but still ensure that necessary hardware actions are performed by the kernel on time. Linux thus separates processes into two classes: normal and real time. The first 100 priority lists of the runqueue are reserved for real-time processes, and the last 40 are used for user processes. Since real-time processes have lower priorities than non-real-time processes, they will always run before non-real-time processes. (This might be somewhat confusing because a "lower" priority number has a "higher" priority in the sense that it will be run first, but that is the way Linux documentation describes it.) As long as real-time processes are runnable, no normal processes will run. Real-time processes are scheduled with two scheduling schemes, namely **FIFO** (or SCHED_FIFO) and **round robin** (or SCHED_RR.) A process that needs to run as a real-time process will make a system call to tell the OS which of these schedulers to use. If it does not make such a call, then it is a **normal** process, as discussed in the next section.

FIFO processes are scheduled in a first-in first-out manner. If there is a FIFO process ready to run on a system it will preempt any other higher priority processes and run for as long as it needs to run since FIFO processes do not have time limits. Multiple FIFO processes are scheduled by priority and lower priority FIFO processes will preempt higher priority processes. RR processes are identical to FIFO processes except that they have time quantum limits and are always preempted by a FIFO process. Within a given priority level, SCHED_RR processes are scheduled in a round-robin fashion. Each SCHED_RR process runs for its allotted time quantum and then goes to the end of the list in its runqueue.

19.2.2 Normal processes

Non-real-time processes are marked SCHED_NORMAL (previously known as SCHED_OTHER)—the default scheduling behavior. To prevent a process from holding the CPU and starving other processes that also need CPU access, the scheduler can dynamically alter a process's priority. It does so by raising the priority number (and thus lowering the priority) of processes that are CPU-bound and lowering the number of processes that are I/O-bound. I/O-bound processes commonly use the CPU to set up an I/O and then wait for the completion of the I/O. While a process waits on I/O, other processes get access to the CPU. Processes that communicate with the user are generally doing lots of I/O and therefore are given preference over noninteractive processes, resulting in better interactive responsiveness.

The priority of I/O-bound processes is decreased by a maximum of five priority levels. CPU-bound processes have their priority increased by up to five levels. Processes are determined to be I/O-bound or CPU-bound based on an interactivity heuristic. The **interactiveness** of a process is calculated based on how much time the process executes compared to how much time it sleeps. Computing is much faster than typical I/O operations. Since I/O-bound processes call for an I/O operation and then wait for it to complete, an I/O-bound process spends more time waiting than computing, increasing its interactiveness.

19.2.3 Nice

Sometimes it is desirable to run a program with a priority other than the normal default. For example, a program might be providing a background function that is a lower priority than an interactive user function. Conversely, a process might be running that needs a higher priority than normal. There are two ways that a program priority can be changed. First, a user can run a program with a priority other than normal using the **nice** command, and second, a program can issue a system call to change its priority while it is running. The original concept of the nice command was that a user could voluntarily run a command with a higher priority number (and thus a lower priority). Such a command would look like this:

```
nice [-n increment]... [Command [Arg]...]
```

-n increment   increment must be in the range 1–19. If not specified, an increment
                of 10 is assumed. An increment greater than 19 is set to 19. A user
                with administrative privileges may run commands with priority
                higher than normal by using a negative increment such as −10.

command   The name of a command that is to be invoked.

argument   A string to be used as an argument when invoking the command.

Alternatively, a process can alter its own priority by calling an OS function such as **sched_setparam.** This is a POSIX function. There are other OS calls that may also be used. In the following example, sched_setparam sets the scheduling parameters associated with the scheduling policy for the process identified by *pid*. The interpretation of the parameter *p* depends on the selected policy. As discussed above, the following three scheduling policies are supported under Linux: *SCHED_FIFO*, *SCHED_RR*, and *SCHED_NORMAL*.

```
#include <sched.h>
int sched_setparam (pid_t pid, const struct sched_param *p);

struct sched_param {
    ...
    int
    ...
};
```

19.2.4 SMP load balancing

Since release 2.0 Linux has supported symmetric multiprocessing (**SMP**). We mentioned that when a system has multiple CPUs there will be multiple active runqueues—one per CPU. When processes are created in an SMP system, they're placed on the runqueue for some CPU. Some processes will be short and others might run for a long time and the OS has no way in advance to know which is which. Therefore, it is impossible to initially allocate processes across multiple CPUs in a balanced fashion. To maintain a balanced workload across CPUs, work can be moved from an overloaded CPU to a less loaded one. The Linux scheduler does such load balancing. Every 200 milliseconds, the OS checks to see whether the CPU loads are unbalanced. If so, it tries to balance the loads. One negative aspect of moving a process to another CPU is that the caches in the new CPU do not hold any information for the process. This makes the effective memory access time go way up temporarily, but lightening the load on the busier CPUs makes up for the problem.

19.3 MEMORY MANAGEMENT

The **memory manager** (MM) permits multiple processes to share securely the machine's main memory system. In addition, the memory manager supports virtual memory that allows Linux to support processes that use more memory than is available in the system. Unused memory is swapped out to persistent storage using the file system and swapped back in if it is needed again later.

Linux was designed from the outset to be independent of the hardware it is running on. This brings up several interesting points about the sizes of various internal data structures in the OS. The first problem that Linux must cope with is the fact that the basic word size of the machine may be different on different CPUs that Linux might be running on. Other details may also vary—the memory page size, how the memory management hardware works, and so on. Linux deals with these problems by being very modular and very configurable. Although Linux is a monolithic kernel OS rather than a micro-kernel OS, it is still very modular, and it is reasonably straightforward to replace one module, such as the memory manager, with a different one. Such module replacement may happen, for example, in an effort to use a new mechanism that is developed when research has shown that a mechanism that is currently used is not using the most efficient methods. It can also happen when the implementation of that replacement turns out to have been rushed and actually leads to worse performance than the previous release. In Linux 2.2, for example, the page replacement algorithm that had replaced the algorithms used earlier turned out to be flawed. While it worked in the general cases, there were some situations where the performance was very bad. So in release 2.4, parts of the earlier mechanism were reintroduced. The 2.6 version introduced the O(1) scheduler described earlier.

The memory manager in the modern Linux kernels is a full virtual memory manager with demand paging. We discussed this technique thoroughly in Chapter 11 so we will not repeat that here. Linux uses a two-level page table on x86 processors and a three-level table on 64-bit processors. In theory, paging eliminates the need for contiguous memory allocation, but some operations like DMA ignore paging circuitry and access the address bus directly while transferring data. To allow for this problem Linux implements a mechanism for allocating contiguous page frames called the **buddy system** algorithm. Pages are kept in one of 10 lists of blocks that contain 1, 2, 4, 8, 16, 32, 64, 128, 256, or 512 contiguous frames, respectively. When asked for a contiguous block the memory manager looks in the list for the right size or larger, dividing the block if necessary. When a block is released, the manager iteratively tries to merge together pairs of free blocks into larger blocks. Linux keeps a separate set of buddy lists for addresses that are in low memory and thus suitable for DMA operations.

Linux has a separate mechanism for dealing with requests for small memory areas called the **slab allocator.** Rather than allocate all storage requests randomly from a single heap, it views memory as collections of similar objects such as process descriptors. The slab allocator allocates similar objects from a block called a slab, which holds only objects of a single type. Initializing many of these objects takes more time than reallocating one, so when an object is released it is cached for later reuse as the same type of object. The slab mechanism is not limited to system-defined objects. Applications can create their own slab lists and have the memory manager manage them in the same way.

The modular design of Linux allows for using different memory managers in different versions or distributions. So, for example, a distribution intended for only a real-time version of Linux would probably have to avoid a virtual memory architecture because it would not have deterministic performance. Similarly, a Linux-based system embedded in a PDA or a microwave that did not have secondary storage could use a memory manager more appropriate for those environments. In Chapter 20 we describe a very clever use of paging hardware in the Symbian OS that shows such a memory manager.

19.4   FILE SUPPORT

One decision every OS designer must make is the physical and logical layout of the file system on secondary storage—usually disks. Several alternative file system layouts may be used and the differences can have dramatic effects on the performance of the OS. The modular nature of Linux shows again in the area of file support.

19.4.1   Standard file systems

As was previously mentioned, the original version of Linux was developed on a MINIX system. Not surprisingly, the file system that was used in that initial Linux version was designed around the physical and logical layout of the MINIX file system. Even today, the MINIX file system layout is still supported by Linux. Because various developers of Linux have had different uses as goals for their version of Linux OS, many other file system layouts, including MS-DOS, OS/2, CDs, and DVDs, as well as other (non-Linux) UNIX versions, are supported. Something of a standard file system does exist for Linux for hard disks, however, **ext2fs.** Much Linux system documentation discusses the "Linux file system" as though it were the only one currently used. One of the complications caused by open source projects is that developers are free to create whatever variations they like to the operating system. This is often good in that it encourages experimentation and creativity. It can, however, be a problem in that it can complicate choices for beginners. Some argue that from the viewpoint of the larger Linux user community, scarce resources might be more profitably spent if they were focused on only a few file systems. Table 19.1 shows some of the other Linux file systems that have been created.

19.4.2   The virtual file system

The idea of having many different, yet coexisting, file systems is not new with Linux. UNIX was developed in a fashion similar to Linux, in the sense that many universities took the source and "improved" it to fit some specific local need. One common change was to design a new file system for UNIX to work with an existing file system from some legacy OS. For example, see the HPFS in Table 19.1. In order to cope with this multiplicity of file systems, UNIX introduced the concept of the **virtual file system,** or **VFS.** The virtual file system was an additional layer in the OS between the kernel system calls and the file systems, and it is invisible to application programs. See Figure 19.3. The API for this layer is identical to the API for standard UNIX file systems. When a file is opened through the VFS layer, it looks to see what file system was on the device being referenced and passes the request to the appropriate file system driver for that device.

TABLE 19.1   Other Linux File Systems

EXT	Extended File System (replaced MINIX)
EXT2	Second Extended File System
EXT3	Third Extended File System
XFS	Silicon Graphics [IRIX] Journaling File System
HFS	Macintosh Hierarchical File System
EFS	Silicon Graphics [IRIX] Extent File System
VxFS	Veritas File System
UFS	Early BSD UNIX File System
BSD FFS	BSD UNIX File System
AIX	IBM RS/6000 UNIX
JFS	IBM's Journaling File System
HPFS	OS/2 High-Performance File System
BeFS	BeOS File System
QNX4 FS	QNX4 [OS] File System
AFFS	Amiga Fast File System
FAT16	MS-DOS File System
FAT32	Windows File System
ReiserFS	Balanced Trees (under development)
Xia	New MINIX File System

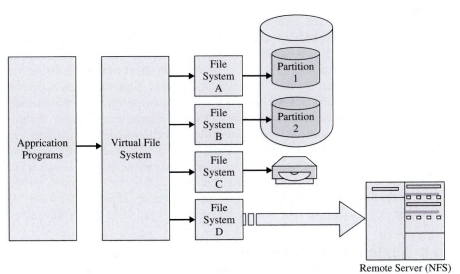

FIGURE 19.3
The Linux virtual file system (VFS).

Neither the driver nor the application program is aware of the additional layer. In other operating systems this concept is sometimes called a file **redirector.**

This simple mechanism has fostered many developments that might have been otherwise difficult. For example, when CD-ROM devices were introduced, the industry was able to standardize on a single data file format (music CDs follow a different, older format). In part, this was because UNIX (and other OSs as well) were able to support a different file system format on these devices than on hard disks or floppies. This has been a great benefit to the industry and to the user community. Imagine if every OS had its own format for CDs! You don't really have to think very hard to imagine it—it would be much like the floppy disk industry used to be. You had to buy floppy disks formatted for the OS you were going to use, disks could be hard or soft sectored, with various densities (number of sectors that would fit on a track). At least in the floppy disk case, when MS-DOS became popular, it's format was so ubiquitous that every OS was obliged to somehow cope with that format, so the situation was not as bad as it might have otherwise been. Sun Microsystems was able to use this mechanism to introduce a "file system" that was actually a network protocol that accessed files that were not on a local disk; rather, they were resident across a network. The remote nature of this mechanism was totally transparent to application programs, but naive use of this feature sometimes could seriously impact performance. This file system is called the **network file system,** or **NFS.**

19.4.3 The /proc file system

Linux (and some variations of UNIX) also makes use of the file system interface in a very creative way. The **proc** file system is not really a physical file system in that it doesn't refer to files on a disk. It is sometimes called a virtual or **pseudo file system** and is referred to as being nonpersistent. It responds to most of the same system calls that any other file system does, but instead of accessing a storage device it returns information about variables in the OS kernel. The root file system is accessed with standard I/O calls, so that one merely opens a proc entry (in the proc subdirectory) and reads its contents. The information that is returned does not actually exist, in that format, in the kernel (though some parts might), but is instead created on-the-fly when the read operation is performed. These records include information about the processes running on the system as well as information about other modules such as networking, memory management, and so forth. The proc file system even appears to users to have directories in it. For example, there is a /proc/net directory that includes all information about the network modules. Other directories correspond to the processes running on the system. These directories sometimes contain subdirectories corresponding to subfunctions of a particular module. For example, the /proc/net directory contains subdirectories for the arp table and for parameters and counters for the TCP and IP networking protocols. Note that the proc file system supports writing as well as reading, so that data in the kernel can be carefully changed. Normally this means that only a user with **root** (supervisor) privileges can write to this file system.

19.5 BASIC INPUT AND OUTPUT

19.5.1 The /dev table

Observable in a Linux system is a separate "file system" similar to the /proc file system called the /dev "file system." Most devices on a Linux system have a corresponding "file" in /dev, network devices being the exception. The files in /dev each have a major and minor device number associated with them. The kernel uses these numbers to map references from a device file to the appropriate driver.

The major device number identifies the driver with which the file is associated (in other words, the type of device). These numbers are assigned by the Linux Assigned Names And Numbers Authority (LANANA). The minor device number usually identifies which particular instance of a given device type is to be addressed. For example, with hard disks there may be different types of hard disks, SCSI and SATA, and there may be two SATA disks, differentiated by minor device number. The minor device number is sometimes called the unit number.

You can see the major and minor number of a device file by entering the following command in a Linux shell:

```
ls -l /dev/sda
brw-rw---- 1 root   disk    8,   0 Mar 3 2007 /dev/sda
```

This example shows the first SCSI disk on a Linux system. It has a major number of 8 and a minor number of 0. The minor device number is sometimes used by the driver to select the particular characteristic of a device. For example, one tape drive can have several different files in /dev representing various configurations of recording density and rewind characteristics. In essence, the driver can use the minor device number in any way that it wants.

Note that here the "ls" command, which normally is used to list files in a directory, is being used to show device characteristics just the same as if it were an actual, physical file.

19.5.2 Device classes

As do most OSs, Linux broadly divides devices into three classes—block, character, and networking—and treats each of those classes differently. Figure 19.4 shows a diagram of some of the kernel I/O modules and the relationships between them.

Block devices

For Linux the access to block mode devices is usually through the file system, even for tape storage. Linux also supports raw I/O directly to devices.

Character devices

Character mode devices transfer data a single byte at a time and include printers, keyboards, mice (and other pointing devices), and so on. A program can use the **ioctl** system call to access most character mode devices.

Network devices

Network devices do not fit the semantics of files since applications waiting for input never know when they might arrive. As a result, network devices have an entirely different set of interfaces than do other devices.

Network devices do not show up in the /dev table since their operations are so different. Instead, they have a generic network interface that conforms, most often, to the

FIGURE 19.4
The Linux I/O
systems.

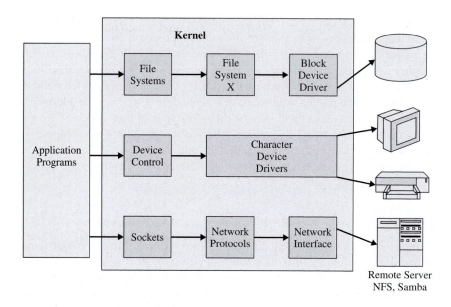

TCP/IP (or UDP) protocol stack model, and are most frequently accessed with a programming model called a **socket.** This model is an API that lets an application make a network connection to another application, presumably but not necessarily on a different system, and to send and receive either a stream of data or a series of blocks of data between the two applications. This model has layers for the data link, network, and transport control services. Most classes of device drivers keep various usage statistics about their operation (including errors) so that the system administrator can optimize performance of the system. Network drivers are more aggressive than most other drivers, and typically keep many different types of statistics, including error counters and number of packets sent and received. The network modules have a generic network interface with common operations for connecting, sending, receiving, timeout handling, statistic collection, and routing. Since the origins of UNIX are tightly connected to utilization of TCP/IP, it is not surprising to learn that the Linux drivers are optimized for TCP/IP support. Once again, however, the open nature of Linux and the diverse needs of Linux supporters have resulted in the adaptation of many other network protocols for Linux. Here are some of the many other protocols available for Linux:

- Network protocols (software protocols)
    - IP version 6 - the Internet and Internet 2
    - IPX/SPX - Novell
    - AppleTalk Protocol Suite - Apple
    - NetBEUI - IBM and Microsoft
    - NetBIOS - IBM and Microsoft
    - CIFS - Microsoft
    - SNA - IBM
    - APPC - IBM
    - DECNet - Digital Equipment Corporation

- Physical protocols (hardware protocols or router and switch interfaces)
    - ISDN - Integrated Services Digital Network
    - PPP - Point-to-Point Protocol
    - SLIP - Serial Line Interface Protocol
    - PLIP - Parallel Line Internet Protocol
    - Amateur Radio - AX25
    - ATM - Asynchronous Transfer Mode
    - ARCNet - Datapoint Corp., among others
    - FDDI - Fiber Distributed Data Interface
    - Frame Relay
    - Token Ring - IBM
    - X.25 - Slow, asynchronous
    - 802.11 - wireless LAN
    - Bluetooth - wireless

In keeping with its UNIX orientation, Linux gives strong support to the sockets and datagram mechanisms. They were included in the 1.0 release in 1994. This mechanism was introduced to the UNIX world with BSD 4.3 UNIX. The network interfaces and mechanisms were discussed more in Chapter 15.

Disk scheduling

In Chapter 14 we discussed the many options that OSs have for scheduling operations on disk drives, for example, when to move to the next track and which track to move to. One of the strengths of Linux that has been emphasized in this chapter is its modularity. This modularity allows replacement of individual modules in Linux with a different implementation that is more appropriate for a particular situation. The scheduling of disk operations is a good example. While the default scheduler is generally fair and performs quite well, the overall performance of any particular system depends greatly on the type of processing that is being done. Web servers, for example, place very different demands on a system than does a database server. Accordingly, several different disk schedulers are available to fit certain situations better than others. Historically the default disk request scheduler in Linux has been C-LOOK. It treats the disk like a cylinder, starting at one end of the drive and processing operations in order as it goes. When it reaches the end of the queue of operations it moves the head all the way back to the other end without processing any requests and begins processing the operations that piled up after the head had passed them by on the last scan. Later releases of Linux have begun to incorporate more advanced scheduling algorithms.

The recent history of disk schedulers in Linux demonstrates how having a replaceable module was used to great advantage. As was mentioned, the disk scheduler in Linux was basically a C-LOOK scheduler that merely merged requests in the direction of the seek. It was noted that this sometimes caused very poor performance of requests that were very far away from the bulk of the other requests. In order to improve the performance of such requests the scheduler was modified such that each new request was given a deadline. If the deadline for a request drew near, then it would be serviced immediately. This algorithm gave better performance in certain situations.

Unfortunately, applications that do a lot of reading tend to use synchronous I/O. Typically they read a block, process it a bit, and issue a read for the next block. While the processing was going on, the head was moved to another part of the drive and the next block could not be read until much later. In order to improve the performance of such applications, a new **anticipatory scheduler** was introduced in Version 2.6. This scheduler is basically C-LOOK, but when performing a read, this scheduler would delay moving the head away from the block read for a short time (a few milliseconds) on the theory that the application might shortly issue a new read for the next block. It performed well in some cases such as compilation, but was miserable in others, primarily interactive tasks. This poor performance was caused by not keeping the seeking mechanism busy all the time.

So yet another scheduler was released. It is known as complete fair queuing scheduler, or **CFQ scheduler.** CFQ places synchronous requests into separate queues for each process and allocates time slices for each of the queues to access the disk. The length of the time slice and the number of requests a queue is allowed to submit depends on an I/O priority assigned to the process. Asynchronous requests are batched together into separate queues for each priority. CFQ does not do anticipatory IO scheduling, but it gives good throughput for the system as a whole by allowing a process queue to idle at the end of synchronous I/O, thereby "anticipating" further close I/O from that process. The CFQ scheduler was released as part of the 2.6.18 kernel. It is the default scheduler in kernel releases.

Since no scheduler is optimum for all circumstances, there are presently four schedulers available for Linux:

- Noop Scheduler
- Anticipatory IO Scheduler ("as scheduler")
- Deadline Scheduler
- Complete Fair Queuing Scheduler ("cfq scheduler")

One can change schedulers by setting the kernel option 'elevator' at boot time. You can set it to one of "as," "cfq," "deadline," or "noop." In addition, some of the schedulers have parameters that can be tuned at runtime.

19.6 GUI PROGRAMMING

When UNIX was created, very little computing work was done in a graphics mode. Instead, many users connected to the computer with a terminal that was basically a typewriter (or Teletype), a printer with a keyboard built in. When CRT terminals came into use they normally displayed text only, much like the printer terminals then being used. Terminals that supported graphics might cost as much as the computer that they were connected to. As a result, UNIX kernels do not assume that the user interface is a graphical user interface (GUI). Instead, if a GUI is desired, it must be provided as a facility apart from the OS kernel. The **X-Window** system was created to provide a mechanism to display graphics in UNIX. The X-Window system is a platform-independent, client/server-based protocol for displaying graphics. A block diagram of the components of the X-Window system is seen in Figure 19.5. The naming of the

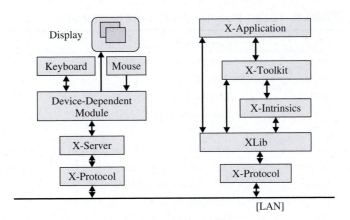

FIGURE 19.5
X-Windows.

components can be somewhat confusing today—the system where the graphics are viewed is called an X-Window server and the system where the graphics are generated is called an X-Window client. Both the server and the client can be running on the same machine as they often are in a Linux PC environment, or they can be different systems on opposite sides of the world, connected through a network.

The X-Window (or **X11**) protocol requires a third component to actually display windows, menus, boxes, and scroll bars, which may be drawn however the manager determines. This component is called a **window manager.** The window manager determines the way the interface looks and how the user interacts with it—the so-called **look-and-feel.** Running an X-Window server and window manager on a single machine provides a familiar GUI. There are currently two very popular window managers in the Linux world—the **Kool Desktop Environment** (**KDE**) and **GNU Network Object Model Environment** (**GNOME**). Both of these window managers are found in most Linux distributions, and occasionally they include other managers that are not as popular. Since Linux applications most often use the X-Windows API to draw on the system, programs that work with any one manager usually work correctly with any other windows manager as well. However, dialog boxes, menus, scroll bars, and moving between windows may appear differently to the user. So, for example, the Apple Mac OS version X is built on a UNIX kernel but the window manager looks and works like the prior releases of the Mac OS. A drawback to having the window manager as an external component is that there may be multiple, different GUI interfaces, so books and training materials will need to be customized for each. While this might not matter so much to an individual, it is a problem for institutions of all kinds who have to support many users who may choose different managers.

With UNIX this is not a problem confined only to GUI interfaces. Traditionally, UNIX commands are given to the OS by typing them on a line in a textual command interpreter, or shell. The UNIX text-oriented shell is a separate external module, just as are the GUIs. In the case of UNIX there were quite a few of them. See Table 19.2.

Different shells were sometimes only slightly different from one another, but some were very different in the way that they could be programmed, assist in helping users complete commands, and keeping and repeating command histories, among

TABLE 19.2   Popular UNIX and Linux Shells

Shell	Comments
KSH	Linux version of Korn shell
TCSH	Turbo C shell
BASH	Bourne Again shell
CSH	Linux version of C shell
ASH	
ZSH	Advanced command-line editing—not for scripting
Bourne	Enhanced original shell
Korn	Originated with AT&T and System V
C	UC Berkeley
SH	The original UNIX shell
rc	Plan 9 from Bell Labs
es	RC-like syntax with Scheme semantics
eshell	Emacs
CLISP	CommonLisp

other things. These differences made choosing a shell a very personal decision. It also made the life of help desk personnel more complicated and limited the ability of one user to help another.

19.7 NETWORKING

The **network interface** (NET) module of the OS provides access to several networking standards and a variety of network hardware.

19.7.1 Network layering

The networking model used in the Linux OS is based on the standard TCP/IP model. Since the physical interface is implemented by the network interface card (NIC), Linux generally ignores the Physical layer, so the model only shows three service layers and the Application layer. See Figure 19.6. The three service layers were also shown in Figure 19.2. Often OS developers create each network protocol layer in total isolation. The result is often that high overhead is caused by excessive copying of messages from layer to layer as the successive layers add headers and sometimes trailers to the message. Linux avoids this problem by allocating the space for a message in a buffer called a socket buffer, or **skbuff.** An skbuff contains pointers to locations in a contiguous block of memory that stores the whole packet. When data is passed from one layer to a lower layer, the header of the lower layer is added to the data, and likewise, the header of the lower layer is stripped off when data is passed from a lower layer to an upper layer. When an skbuff is allocated, Linux will calculate the amount of memory including the maximum length of the headers of various layers needed by the packet. The initial message is put into the middle of the buffer, leaving room for the headers from lower layers.

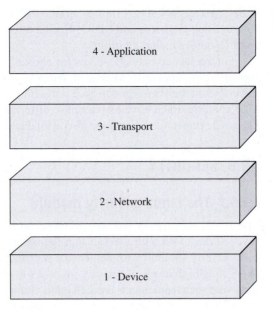

FIGURE 19.6
The Linux Network layer model.

So when a packet is passed between layers the only need is to set the pointers that indicate the new location of the start of the header or trailer of the corresponding skbuff.

19.7.2 Connection super-server

Linux uses a super-server called **inetd,** which listens on many ports used by common IP services such as HTTP, POP3, and Telnet. When an IP packet arrives on one of these port numbers, inetd launches a selected server program. For services that are not used frequently this mechanism uses memory more efficiently, as the specific servers run only when needed. Also, no network code is required in the applications, since inetd connects the sockets directly to the stdin, stdout, and stderr functions of the server process. For protocols that have more frequent use, a dedicated server that handles the server requests directly would be used instead.

19.7.3 SAMBA

Since Linux presently exists in a world dominated by Microsoft OS software, a great deal of effort goes into making Linux systems work well with Microsoft products. We briefly touched on file systems that support present and past Microsoft file system formats. We also mentioned a few networking protocols that Linux offers support for. But one server package dominates in the networking area—Samba.

Samba is a server that implements many Microsoft services and protocols, including SMB (Server Message Block), CIFS (Common Internet File System), DCE/RPC (Distributed Computing Environment/Remote Procedure Calls), MSRPC, a WINS server (a NetBIOS Name Server, NBNS), NetBIOS over TCP/IP (NBT), the Network Neighborhood protocols, the NT Domain protocols including NT Domain Logons, a Secure Accounts Manager (SAM) database, Local Security Authority

(LSA) service, NT-style printing service (SPOOLSS), NTLM, and Active Directory Logon using Kerberos and LDAP. Samba also uses these protocols to see and share local resources including printers.

Samba sets up network shares for chosen Linux directories (including subdirectories). These appear to Microsoft Windows users just as folders. Linux users can either mount the shares or can access the files with a utility program that acts like an FTP program. Each directory can have different access privileges aside from normal Linux file protections. Samba is also available on most other UNIX-variant systems.

19.8 SECURITY

19.8.1 The Linux security module

The Linux community has been divided on the issue of security. The crux of the division has to do with the fact that the security community is itself divided about how security should be implemented. A primary consideration with security is that supporting high levels of security involve substantial resources, obviously including hardware such as memory and CPU utilization but also administrative and user time to set it up and use it correctly. If high levels of security are not needed in a particular installation, then those resources should not have to be spent. The solution in Linux has been the inclusion of a module called the **Linux security module,** or **LSM.** It consists of a set of hooks that a specific security implementation can attach itself to in order to perform authorization checks when objects are accessed.

There are several different security systems that have been designed to run under Linux using the LSM hooks. The most well known is **Security-Enhanced Linux (SELinux)**, which provides a secure access control mechanism based on the trust (clearance) level of the individual requesting access. Others include **AppArmor (Application Armor)**, **Linux Intrusion Detection System, BSD Secure Levels,** and **Commercial IP Security Option (CIPSO).** As of release 2.6 of Linux, none of these modules had prevailed over the others, so the LSM approach continues to be supported.

19.8.2 Networking security

Because the source code for Linux is freely available it is often used as the OS of choice both for security analysts and hackers. As a result, there are many tools for both hacking and security protection available for Linux.

Port scanners are software packages that try to determine what services are running on a target machine. Generally they will try to make a connection to each possible port on the machine. Based on the results of this attempt a hacker may be able to tell if the machine is vulnerable to a known exploit. Port scanners can be set to attack a single machine, a group of machines, or all machines on a network. There are many software packages that do port scanning. **Nmap, SATAN, ISS,** and **SAINT** are some of the better known ones.

There are also **stealth port scanners.** These scanners use a low-level interface to create TCP or UDP packets that do not correctly conform to the protocol. For example, a TCP packet with the ACK bit set will likely get through a packet-filtering firewall because it looks like part of an established connection. If such a packet is received on a port that had no established session with the sender, then the TCP software will respond with an appropriate message and the hacker can assume that there is a process that is reading that port.

TCP Wrapper (tcpd) is used to filter network access to IP services run on Linux or other UNIX-like variants. When IP services are started by a super-server like **inetd** the TCP wrapper program is invoked to check the source of the connection. It supports filtering on host or subnet IP addresses or names. In addition, these IP services can be linked to an **ident** service. This service will first query the source IP address on TCP port 113. It will expect a query reply that identifies the source system. Only if the reply is received and matched against a database will the connection be allowed. Most network service programs can be directly linked with the library that does the filtering. This method is used by services that operate without being started by a super-server, or by any service that handles multiple connections. Otherwise, only the first connection attempt would get checked against the database by tcpd.

19.9 SYMMETRIC MULTIPROCESSING

With SMP the OS can be running on more than one CPU at one time. As was discussed in Chapter 6, the two (or more) instances of the running OS must be prevented from changing the same data structure at the same time by using locks. Early releases of the Linux SMP support used a single lock for the entire kernel, the so-called **Big Kernel Lock.** This was not very efficient, since many times the different instances of the OS would not be manipulating the same data structures at all. So later releases have begun replacing those references to that one lock with references to more localized locks. Some references to the Big Lock still remain as of version 2.6, but the multiprocessor performance is greatly improved over prior versions. The Linux kernel also uses spin-locks on a special read–write type of semaphore that allows multiple readers but only one writer at a time, when a structure is read mostly. For example, the table of network devices changes only very rarely but is read frequently, so allowing multiple readers is beneficial. When a change needs to be made to the table, then locking all the readers out briefly while it is changed by only one writer is not a frequent problem.

19.10 OTHER LINUX VARIANTS

Since the source code for Linux is readily available, there are several variants of Linux that have been created for special purposes. Two special areas are versions for real-time applications and for embedding Linux in small systems with limited resources.

19.10.1 Real-time Linux

The normal Linux OS is not a hard real-time OS. This is true for most OSs. A hard real-time system guarantees that real deadlines are met, for example that a process or thread will be run in the next 50 milliseconds. Hard real-time systems preclude many of the mechanisms that have evolved for traditional OSs, mechanisms that use stochastic techniques and try to be fair in providing services to processes. Hard real-time systems need to establish deadlines for events and for the servicing of requests and the normal OS mechanisms do not allow us to provide such deadline support. Embedded applications are also important, where a computer is a controlling component in a piece of equipment rather than a general-purpose computing tool. Such embedded applications are often real-time systems as well. This means that there is a considerable overlap between embedded Linux implementations and real-time Linux implementations.

There are two main schools of thought about how to make a real-time system out of Linux. Some of the implementations of real-time Linux use a small real-time OS (**RTOS**) as a host OS and they run a version of the Linux kernel that runs as a single thread in the host OS kernel at a background or idle priority. In other words, when there is no real-time process to run, then any normal Linux applications can run. This model is known as **RTLinux.** The other school uses the Linux kernel but modifies it heavily to include only scheduling mechanisms that allow the support of a real-time API. These mechanisms would include at least the process scheduler and the disk scheduler and probably the networking protocol stack. This **real-time application interface** model is also known as **RTAI.** There are also other interesting approaches that do not fit either of these categories. Deciding on the correct package to use for a project could be quite complex. Fortunately there is **real-time Linux common API,** an open source API that allows programmers to code to a common API when using either RTLinux or RTAI. Table 19.3 lists some embedded and real-time implementations of Linux.

19.10.2 Embedded Linux

Linux has also been modified to run in very limited environments. Such environments include platforms like those discussed in the chapter on the Palm OS, but it also include devices like microwave ovens and home heating controls where the user environment is very limited. The open source and modular nature of Linux make it ideal for such situations. However, there are many issues that must be resolved in using Linux as an OS in such systems:

- These devices typically have no secondary memory and thus don't really need paged memory. But standard Linux presumes that these exist. So one modification that is often found in embedded Linux systems is the removal of paged memory hardware support requirements. They also need no caching management system or features like memory mapped files.
- The very limited user interface is also significant because Linux does not presume a GUI. Rather, the GUI is an add-on and the standard interface is a command line. Even this may be too strong an assumption for a microwave where the display might be limited to an LCD panel that can only display a few digits. Some embedded Linux systems are found in complex devices such as small routers. These devices now often support the HTTP protocol and can be managed by a remote browser.
- Process scheduling in Linux typically uses the concept of "interactiveness" to promote the priority of a process that is interacting with a user. But in an embedded system there is no elaborate, interactive user interface. There may be a small display and a few buttons that can be handled quite adequately with some real-time processes or normal interrupt handlers. So the process scheduler may be a stripped-down version that does not incorporate dynamic priority changes.

TABLE 19.3 Common Linux Variants

Commercial platforms:

FSMLabs: RTLinuxpro - RTCore - a hard real-time platform that runs Linux as an idle thread.

Lineo Solutions: uLinux - hard real-time Linux kernel - targets consumer electronics devices.

LynuxWorks: BlueCat - time-critical handling of interrupts and other hardware operations - implements Linux kernel as a thread.

MontaVista Software: Real-Time Solutions for Linux - MontaVista Linux for embedded and real-time applications - includes a preemptable Linux kernel.

Concurrent Computer Corp.: RedHawk - a Linux-based RTOS kernel for multiprocessor systems - uses **CPU shielding** - processors can be designated as locked out from Linux so hard real-time processes execute on a shielded CPU with guaranteed interrupt response time.

REDSonic: REDICE-Linux - a real-time Linux kernel with extra preemption points that allow RTAI support and quality of service (QoS) guarantees.

TimeSys: TimeSys Reservations - dynamically installed kernel modules extend a Linux RTOS. Reservations retain a fixed amount of CPU and network bandwidth for a specific process or set of processes.

Open-source implementations:

Accelerated Technology - provides embedded developers with a real-time operating systems (RTOS).

ADEOS - provides a hardware abstraction layer that allows a real-time kernel and a general-purpose kernel to coexist. Supports dual-kernel hard real-time Linux environments like RTLinux or RTAI free from technology patent.

ART Linux - a real-time extension to the 2.2 Linux kernel.

Flight Linux - a real-time variation designed for onboard spacecraft use.

KURT—The KU Real-Time Linux - a real-time Linux kernel developed at the University of Kansas.

Linux/RK - a "resource kernel" enhancement to Linux based on a loadable kernel module that provides timely, guaranteed, and enforced access to system resources for applications. Development based at Carnegie Mellon University.

OnCore's Linux for Real-Time™ - allows embedded designers to pick a memory footprint and performance model appropriate to the problem.

RED-Linux - a real-time version of Linux; based at the University of California, Irvine.

RTAI - real-time application interface, a comprehensive real-time API usable both for uniprocessors and SMPs. Allows control of real-time processes from user space - soft real-time with fine-grained process scheduling. **AtomicRTAI** is a small-footprint (single floppy) version.

RTLinux - a "hard real-time" mini OS runs Linux as its lowest priority preemptable user thread so real-time threads and interrupt handlers are never delayed by non-real-time operations. Supports user-level real-time programming. **MiniRTL** is a small-footprint version.

RedIce Linux - RedIce Linux allows RTAI and RED-Linux to run concurrently, enabling real-time jobs requiring very low latency and hard real-time user applications with complete Linux kernel support to run under one structure.

19.11 SUMMARY

This chapter is one of several case studies of real OSs showing how they implement several standard OS features. This chapter discussed such features in a multiuser OS, Linux. We started this chapter with a discussion of the process scheduling mechanisms and followed it with a rundown on the virtual memory management by the OS necessitated by supporting potentially many users doing very different processes. We then gave an overview of the support of files in Linux and the many different file systems supported because of the unusual history of Linux, followed by coverage of the I/O functions that the OS provides. We then briefly discussed the implementation of the GUI. Sections on networking and security were also provided. Next, we touched on the subject of multiprocessor support under Linux, and finally we addressed some variations of Linux that have resulted from its being used in situations where an OS such as Linux would not normally be found such as hard real-time and embedded environments.

BIBLIOGRAPHY

Bovet, D. P., and M. Cesate, *Understanding the Linux Kernel,* 2nd ed., Sebastopol, CA: O'Reilly & Associates, Inc., 2003.

Gorman, M., *Understanding the Linux Virtual Memory Manager.* Upper Saddle River, NJ: Prentice Hall, 2004.

Love, R., *Linux Kernel Development.* Indianapolis, IN: Sams Publishing, 2004.

Stevens, R., *Advanced Programming in the UNIX Environment.* Boston, MA: Addison-Wesley, 1992.

Stevens, R., *Unix Network Programming.* Upper Saddle River, NJ: Prentice Hall, 1990.

Yaghmour, K., *Building Embedded Systems.* Sebastopol, CA: O'Reilly & Associates, Inc., 2003.

WEB RESOURCES

http://www.linux.org (the home of Linux kernel development)

http://www.kernel.org (a repository of historic kernel sources)

http://www.tldp.org (the Linux Documentation Project)

REVIEW QUESTIONS

19.1 What was the specific objective of the redesign of the scheduler for Linux 2.6?

19.2 True or false? In the Linux scheduler the real-time process queues are serviced in a FIFO manner.

19.3 Briefly describe SMP load balancing.

19.4 True or false? Linux uses a standard demand paging virtual memory manager.

19.5 What is the buddy system?

19.6 True or false? Linux offers only a simple file system derived from MINIX.

19.7 True or false? One of the main contributions of Linux is that it uses a unique disc scheduling algorithm not found in other OSs.

19.8 How does Linux provide protection for files belonging to different users?

19.9 In the Windows NT OS family the GUI is intrinsic to the OS. How is a GUI provided in Linux?

19.10 What does Linux do to keep from having excessive buffer copying when passing messages down through the layers of the networking architecture?

19.11 On a multiprocessor system the Linux kernel can be executing on multiple CPUs at the same time. When it is necessary for the kernel to enter a critical section it can't just call the OS to WAIT because it is the OS. What does it do instead?

19.12 Real-time OSs have some timing requirements that are ignored by most OSs. There are many

commercial and open source variants of Linux. We described two different approaches to supporting real-time requirements under Linux. One approach involved heavily modifying the Linux kernel process scheduling module. The other approach was conceptually cleaner and simpler. Briefly describe that approach.

19.13 What is the Big Kernel Lock and what is happening to it?

Chapter 20

Palm OS: A Class Case Study

In this chapter:

20.1 OVERVIEW

In Chapter 4 we discussed some elements of the Palm operating system. That discussion was mainly limited to issues that arose as we studied the more complex design goals of this OS compared to the ones studied before it. This chapter is nominally about the Palm OS versions prior to version 5. This OS represented a particular niche in the hierarchy of OSs that was described in Part 2 of this text. As such there is not a great deal more that can be said about this OS that was not covered in Chapter 4. So this chapter starts with a series of sections that parallel the other two case study chapters and provide some details that were not relevant to Chapter 4. But other material is added here that helps place this OS in the computer industry as it is evolving today. We discuss some aspects of programming such platforms and the trends of the applications that are developing in the industry.

We begin this chapter with a brief restatement of the type of environment that the Palm OS is designed for in Section 20.2. Sections 20.3 through 20.5 briefly summarize the related points of Chapter 4. Section 20.6 then discusses several developments that have occurred in the area of the input/output subsystems in the Palm OS beyond the fundamental things we covered in Chapter 4. These features are typical of new hand-held platforms. Sections 20.7 and 20.8 also summarize related sections of Chapter 4. Section 20.9 explains the nature of the cross-development systems needed to develop programs for such a limited environment. PDAs, cell phones, and multimedia players were originally different sorts of devices, but these platforms are currently undergoing a merger. So Section 20.10 discusses how software is evolving in these platforms. It also touches on some of the developments in later releases of the Palm OS. We conclude with a chapter summary in Section 20.11.

20.2 THE MULTI-PROCESS OS ENVIRONMENT

The Palm OS and its environment were discussed in Chapter 4, but they are reviewed here for convenience. The Palm OS is designed for a very specific type of environment. There are several characteristics of this environment that restricted the design of the OS. The environment characteristics are briefly outlined in Table 20.1.

The primary characteristic of the Palm OS is the small screen size. This means that the user is only interacting with one program at a time so that applications assume that their window fills the entire screen at all times except for small notice boxes that may pop up in front of the main window.

Although later models sometimes included disk drives, especially as an add-on feature, the initial machines did not include them and the OS design assumes that all programs reside in primary memory. The lack of a keyboard means that the OS must provide for handwriting recognition. This feature is a real-time application, so a real-time kernel underlies the Palm OS. User applications, however, are not real time and are single threaded. The resulting OS design choices are listed in Table 20.2.

TABLE 20.1   **Unusual Characteristics of the Palm Platform**

Small screen size

No secondary storage

No text keyboard—touch screen

Limited power for better battery life

Slow CPU to reduce power

Limited primary memory

TABLE 20.2   **Unusual Characteristics of the Palm OS**

Programs never stop

No demand paging (virtual memory) or disk caching

Single-window GUI

Multiple text input options

Real-time OS tasks but non-real-time applications

No application multithreading

20.3 PALM PROCESS SCHEDULING

20.3.1 Real-time tasks

The process scheduler in the Palm OS is a preemptive multitasking priority scheduler. It will dynamically determine which task that is ready has the highest priority and it will interrupt the running of a less important task to run a more important one that becomes ready. The underlying OS is a real-time kernel for support of handwriting recognition, but user application programs cannot access these functions. Handwriting recognition is divided into two parts: stylus tracking and character recognition. The stylus tracking task processes interrupts from the stylus using a standard interrupt mechanism. When the stylus tracking determines that the stylus has changed direction, stopped, or is no longer touching the screen, it will calculate a vector describing the movement and will pass this information on to another task that is running, the character (graffiti) recognizer. If this routine recognizes a character, then it will pass this information on to the OS so that it can decide what to do with the character. Usually the character will be passed to the application that has the focus to be placed on a control on the current form where the user is entering text. Of course, the character might be a control character instead of a text character and the application may then be given a message telling it about the event. If the screen touch is not in the graffiti area, then the OS must detect screen taps on form buttons or pass the information on to the application—perhaps it is a drawing tool, for example.

20.3.2 Other tasks

Only a single-user application has the focus, and that application is most likely waiting for user input as just described. But it is normal for Palm systems to have background communication functions running such as telephony, database synchronization, Bluetooth connection to local devices such as headphones, and Internet access for browsing and email. In addition, certain user features such as searching for a name will invoke a search function in applications that do not currently have the focus. Tasks that do not have the focus will be running in an event loop waiting for signals about events requesting them to do some work. The Palm scheduler module will see that each application gets some time to do its work.

20.4 PALM MEMORY MANAGEMENT

Processes in the Palm OS are always resident in primary memory. Once a process has begun running it never really stops. It may lose the focus, in which case it will not be running anymore, but it is still there waiting to be selected from the menu again and resume execution.

The memory manager in the Palm OS treats a large block of a primary memory as a heap. As memory is allocated and freed on the heap, the eventual result is external fragmentation. This requires occasional compaction to aggregate larger blocks of memory. To facilitate this, items in memory are addressed indirectly through a memory pointer table (MPT). Thus, when the memory manager moves an item, it merely updates the MPT entry that points to the item. The details of this mechanism were covered extensively in Chapter 4.

20.5 FILE SUPPORT

The Palm OS programmer's documentation refers to "databases," but these are actually random access flat files. They are accessed by an "index" value that is a 16-bit integer. Records are of variable length and can be resized dynamically, and added and deleted. The file manager maintains an index for each database giving the current location in memory of each record in that database. A database must fit entirely within a single memory card.

20.6 INPUT/OUTPUT SUBSYSTEMS

Early Palm devices were merely used as PDAs. As was mentioned, these systems have evolved to cover many additional functions including games, cell phones, Web browsers, and media players. The initial Palm releases had limited functionality in the audio area in particular, and these have been enhanced significantly through the various releases. In addition, the platform evolution has also seen advances in communication and networking functions. This section discusses the audio functions. The networking functions are covered in a later section in order to maintain a parallel structure with the other case study chapters.

20.6.1 Audio I/O

The continuing development of technology has led to a rising interest in portable music devices. In addition, the advanced games that users want to have on these machines needed enhanced audio features. The initial sound support in the Palm OS was limited to short sounds for alerts and a few noises for games. Later versions added support for a low-level implementation of a **musical instrument device interface** (MIDI) so that more elaborate musical sounds could be created by an application. This led to a number of interesting applications for musicians to use a Palm OS device as a simple musical tool, such as a tone generator and a metronome. Later versions of the platform also added more advanced sound support, allowing these devices to be used as cell phones and to play music files. Later they also added the ability to perform voice recording and playback—audio notes to oneself—and the recording and sending of audio to other cell phones.

20.6.2 Stream I/O

For purposes of ease of programming, the Palm OS also includes a version of file streams similar to the **stdin/stdout** functions available in most C language libraries. These functions use the database structure discussed in the File Support section but allow easier porting of some applications to the Palm OS.

20.6.3 RAM disk driver

The underlying OS is designed to be used in embedded systems where there is commonly no secondary memory. But many applications are developed to run from a standard file system–style interface. Therefore, the AMX OS comes with a predefined RAM "disk" driver that uses a portion of RAM to emulate a disk drive. This allowed the Palm OS to readily define a RAM drive as a DOS-formatted floppy drive so that porting applications to the Palm were easier and programmers did not have to learn a separate interface to use the system.

20.6.4 Cameras

The development of low-cost, high-resolution CMOS image sensor technology has meant that many cell phones and PDAs now include cameras. Moreover, since larger memories are now available, the cameras can even record video files as well as static images. So now these devices are capable of transmitting image and video files in addition to audio files.

20.6.5 Communication circuits

Bluetooth and 802.11 Wi-fi communication circuits are now available and have been incorporated in the latest Palm devices. These allow other synchronization pathways but also a merging of the PDA and cell phone device classes and to Internet access devices such as the Blackberry™.

20.7 GUI PROGRAMMING

The GUI environment on the Palm platform was extensively covered in Chapter 4. The principle factors that distinguish this platform are the small screen size and limited memory. As a result of the small screen size, the Palm system does not support tiling the forms of applications. (The Palm OS uses the term "form" for a normal window.) Pop-up boxes from a single application are allowed but the pop-up boxes must be closed before the application can continue. (The Palm OS calls these boxes windows.) The limited Palm memory led to the development of specific windows that can be created by Palm applications merely by filling in specific data structures and calling OS routines. The OS will then take on the task of displaying the window and closing it when the user selects an option.

20.8 NETWORK PROGRAMMING

20.8.1 Personal data synchronization

It is natural that a portable device would need to have strong support for communication protocols. Since the Palm devices were initially envisioned as PDAs, the most important communication application was synchronizing with a PC so that the data in the handheld unit could be backed up. Accordingly the initial interfaces provided with the Palm OS were low-level drivers for serial, infrared, and USB ports. At the same time there was a higher-level interface provided for writing applications for synchronization personal information such as contact lists and appointment calendars. A consortium of interested vendors was created known as the Versit Consortium. They have defined a set of standards concerning **personal data interchange (PDI)** that include standards for a **vCard,** an electronic business card, and **vCalendar,** an electronic calendar and scheduling exchange format. These standards are now maintained by the Internet Mail Consortium. The Palm OS includes a library that allows an application to open a PDI stream as either a reader or a writer to facilitate the development of synchronization applications.

20.8.2 Other data synchronization

Some users will be concerned with developing custom applications that go beyond traditional PDA applications. They may have specific data files that need to be synchronized between a Palm application and a similar application on another platform. So the Palm OS provides **exchange libraries,** which act as plug-ins to an OS module called the Exchange Manager. They allow Palm OS applications to import and export data records without being concerned with the transport mechanism. For example, one exchange library always available to Palm Powered™ handhelds implements the IrDA protocol, IrOBEX. This allows applications to beam objects by way of infrared from one Palm Powered handheld to another. Similar exchange libraries exist for other hardware ports and other protocols such as the **SMS (short message service)** library, email protocols, and the Bluetooth library.

20.8.3 Internet applications

During the last several years the Internet has risen in popularity to the point where it is almost mandatory that handheld units be able to access many of the popular features found there. In particular, these include accessing World Wide Web (WWW) sites as well as the email protocol already mentioned. Accordingly, more protocol stacks and APIs have been added to the Palm OS to support networking applications. The first addition was the widely used and well-known lower-level **Berkeley Sockets** API. This interface allows a programmer to connect to services on other systems using a variety of protocols without having to implement that protocol in the application. The interface included with the Palm OS allows either TCP (connection-oriented) or UDP (connectionless) communications.

The second level of protocol supported in the Palm OS includes support for Application layer protocols such hyperText Transport Protocol (HTTP), the protocol used for the WWW. This protocol is used by Web browser and Web service applications for Palm devices. There are some interesting problems to be solved when developing a browser for a Palm unit because initially few websites are developed with the very small screen space of a handheld unit in mind. However, current HTML attributes allow a Web server to determine that a browser is running on a mobile platform and to adjust its output to fit.

TABLE 20.3   Telephony API Service Sets

Service set	Functionality
Basic	Functions always available
Configuration	Configure phones including SMS
Data	Data call handling
Emergency calls	Emergency call handling
Information	Retrieve information about the current phone
Network	Network-oriented services, including authorized networks, current network, signal level, and search mode information
OEM	Allow manufacturers to add features to the Telephony Manager and provide a new set of functions for a device
Phone book	Access the Subscriber Identity Module (SIM) and address book
Power	Power supply–level functions
Security	Provide PIN code management and related services for phone and SIM security-related features
Short Message Service	Enable reading, sending, and deleting of short messages
Sound	Phone sound management, including the playing of key tones and muting
Speech calls	Handle the sending and receiving of speech calls; also includes Dual-tone multi-frequency (DTMF) signaling

20.8.4 Telephony applications

In Section 20.10 we discuss the current merging of PDA devices with cellular telephones. The Palm Telephony Manager provides a set of functions that allow an application to access a variety of telephony services. The telephony API organizes the functions in groups called service sets. Each service set contains a related set of functions that may or may not be available on a particular mobile device or network. One of the API functions allows the application to find out if a given service set is supported in the current environment. A list of some of the more common service sets is shown in Table 20.3.

20.9 PROGRAMMING ENVIRONMENTS

The resources available on a computer designed to run the Palm OS are usually not sufficient to develop software. The Palm OS programming website suggests that programs designed for a Palm-based system be designed to support only a minimum amount of data entry. This suggestion is made partly because of the difficulty of inputting data with the handwriting recognition, but also because of the very limited screen display. Instead, Palm suggests that the user should mainly input data on a desktop system and use the Palm system for referencing the data. Furthermore, once a program is running on the Palm OS there would be no simple way of getting any debugging information displayed and the environment is obviously not well suited for the entry and editing of program source code. Moreover, there rarely are printers attached to Palm systems and as was noted before, the CPUs are very slow and there is generally limited RAM and rarely any secondary storage. Most program development is therefore done on another system, a concept known as cross-platform development.

There is a wide variety of languages and tools for development of software for the Palm OS. Some is available from Palm itself and others are available from third parties. These include commercial integrated development environments (IDEs) such as CodeWarrior™ from Metrowerks and free tools such as PRC-Tools, which is a gcc-based compiler tool chain for building Palm OS applications in C or C++. Tools that are supplied by Palm include a Software Development Kit (SDK) that includes the headers, libraries, and tools for Palm OS platform development on Windows, Linux, and the Mac OS. It also includes a version of the Palm OS running in native X-86 code on a Windows machine. This emulation offers an easy way to test applications destined for the Palm OS for compatibility. Compilers are also available for developing applications in other languages, including Visual Basic, Pascal, Forth, Smalltalk, and Java.

An essential feature is a package that Palm calls an Emulator. This is a software package that emulates the hardware of the various models of Palm OS platform devices on Windows, Linux, or Mac OS computers. Since various platforms have different features available in their ROM, ROM images for use with the Palm OS Emulator are available to emulate each desired model.

Once a program has been developed with the cross-platform tools, it can be installed on a Palm device using the synchronization tools included with Palm PDAs that are available for the various cross-development platforms.

20.10 SIMILAR SYSTEMS AND CURRENT DEVELOPMENTS

One of the difficulties facing authors who write about computer science is that the state of the industry changes so rapidly that a book is not reflective of the latest developments even on the day it is printed. Operating Systems are no exception. There have been rapid developments in the hardware systems used for the Palm OS and others of its ilk discussed in this chapter. In addition, a different functional view has captured the minds of the public and the vendors that have forced some changes in the OS. As a result, other OSs that were developed for this different view have some features that are more complex than the Palm OS described here. But then, so do later versions of the Palm OS.

In this section we describe some features found in other OSs for small systems. We mostly mention the Symbian OS. This OS is developed by Symbian Ltd. It is a descendant of Psion's EPOC OS and runs only on ARM processors. Symbian is a consortium of manufacturers of cell phones.

20.10.1 New functional models

In addition to the use of more advanced CPUs, the basic functions of small handheld systems have also evolved in the last few years. At the beginning of this century the products in this area were mostly envisioned as either PDAs or cell phones. In PDAs the applications were things like phone and address books, appointment calendars, calculators, memo pads, to-do lists, specialized data bases, and an occasional specialized application. In cell phones the main application was the phone book or contact list. In either case, these were primarily standalone applications that required occasional connection to another computer for purposes of synchronization, backup, and loading new applications. In the cell phone the actual telephone application was a real-time task that was considered to be a fundamental function of the device rather than a separate application. These cell phones were closed systems in that installation of additional applications was not part of the design.

Lately, however, a new model has evolved for handheld devices. This evolution has come about partly because of the revolution in the availability of communications technology and ubiquitous connectivity. The devices are now positioned as mobile communications platforms—but as much more than just replacements for cell phones. The main feature that distinguishes a cell phone from a PDA is that PDAs are turned on, used for some single function and then turned off, while a cellular phone is normally left on most of the time and is continuously connected to the network and waiting for incoming calls. In addition to waiting for calls, a cellular phone does other work to manage the connection such as keeping the time synchronized and conversing with the cellular network so that if a cell phone is turned on the network knows where it is. In order for the PDA functions to be used while the cell phone is handling the network connection, the OSs for these mobile communicating devices have to incorporate multiple active tasks at the same time. In a pure PDA device such as the original Palm products, the OS provided only a few separate tasks so that handwriting recognition and synchronization could take place while a **user interface (UI)** application was also running. (You may recall the screens are so small that there is no room for more than one UI application to be executing at a time.) However, there was no provision for applications to provide any separate background function such as managing the connection to a cellular network and checking for incoming calls. As a result, these OSs all have added more features to support application multithreading. More importantly, applications can now start a thread as part of a background task in addition to the single foreground UI thread. An example of the utility of such a feature would be that a service can be built that will handle multiple TCP/IP connections at the same time, so that several TCP/IP-based applications can all be running at the same time using a single TCP/IP multithreaded service. The TCP/IP service will be running as a "user" application rather than as part of the OS kernel. Another important example is a Web browser. When a page is fetched from a server, the images and other included items are not automatically sent. The browser must parse the initial page and then individually request each referenced element. The browser must be able to continue to work on displaying the main page for the user while the other elements are being fetched from the server. This gives the user some immediate access to the contents and a smoother browsing experience.

As in the case of the cellular phone connectivity, other applications can benefit from these background tasks without having control of the UI. Some of the more obvious ones are playing an audio file, downloading new audio files to play, instant messaging, and having an email program connect to a server to check for new email. Other, less obvious background functions exist as well, such as synchronizing changes to distributed databases and updating installed software. These new tasks help cell-phone manufacturers to differentiate their products from one another. In addition, users are asking for these features because they are beginning to value the instant access to information through messaging, email, and the World Wide Web. In order to provide these features, these devices have incorporated advanced hardware components to handle the multiple communication streams, multimedia streams, and so forth. The OSs have had to improve as well. Not only can applications start many threads and set different priorities for each thread, they have new mechanisms to synchronize between the threads and with other processes, to share memory segments with other processes, to communicate with other processes, and to protect databases.

20.10.2 Advanced communication models

Other advanced facilities being provided by the OSs now include encryption and other security mechanisms, new Data Link layer modules such as Bluetooth and 802.11x, and APIs so that new user applications can easily access these OS functions. As the cost of bandwidth from communication services continues to decrease, we are beginning to see more and more intense multimedia applications. The near term projections of the marketplace include more streaming multimedia applications. These applications have heavy hard and soft real-time requirements. These small OSs will continue to evolve with the increasing requirements.

20.10.3 Thread scheduling

As discussed earlier, cell phones are used somewhat differently than PDAs. PDAs are generally turned off when not being used, but cell phones stay on all the time so that they can wait for incoming calls and keep the network updated about the location of the phone. In addition, the demands of the cellular technology are such that real-time tasks are needed to service the network. Accordingly, the scheduler used in the Symbian OS is a priority-based multithreading scheduler. Any application can be a "server" and can create multiple threads of execution within its address space. The Palm OS included a real-time scheduler because of the needs of the graffiti handwriting recognition program, but user applications were not able to create real-time tasks or threads. We discussed such schedulers in Chapter 8.

20.10.4 User interface reference design

The user interface (UI) for most PC systems is very flexible. Windows can fill the screen, shrink to a smaller size, move around, cover one another, and so on, depending on the whim of the user. These smaller systems, however, have simpler interfaces than personal computers do. Often the application assumes that its window fills the entire screen. There are generally three different types of UI in such devices. They roughly represent the classes of a cell phone, a PDA, and a handheld computer. The user interface class is an abstraction of the features that the members of each family have in common. These classes are summarized in Table 20.4.

The challenge for the OS designers and for application programmers is to write OSs and applications that will run on any of these different platforms without a major

TABLE 20.4   **Small Systems Device Families**

Cell phone	Small vertical screen
	Keyboard with digits and a few buttons
	Almost no user input
	Application has full screen
PDA	Larger vertical screen
	Stylus input and a few buttons
	Limited user data input
	Application has full screen
Advanced	Larger still horizontal screen
	Full QWERTY (usually) keyboard
	More extensive user input
	Application windows can overlap, etc.

rewrite. The desire for such portability forces system implementation into strict object-oriented designs in order to isolate the UI functions from the rest of the application. Industry estimates are that about 80% of an application can be isolated from the UI.

The rise of the popularity of the Internet have lead to the incorporation of several standard applications in these new devices. In particular, users want to send instant messages, work with their email, view (or listen to) streaming multimedia transmissions, browse the World Wide Web, and upload multimedia files to their websites. These small systems have very limited screen size, and Web pages are typically set up for at least 800 × 600 pixels. As a result, a browser on a cell phone has to work really hard to make an intelligent display of a larger Web page. Initially a separate standard was created for building Web pages intended to be viewed on a handheld system—**wireless markup language (WML),** a part of a larger standard, **wireless access protocol (WAP).** Later developments seem to indicate that standard browsers can be modified to display standard Web pages on handheld systems. This is an area of active research.

An additional protocol has been developed for sending short text messages when a phone call is not appropriate. For example, it might be used when the recipient is in a very noisy environment, in a lecture or arts performance, or in a meeting. IT can also be used for short queries where a complex interaction is not needed. This protocol is the short message service, or SMS. It allows the sending of messages up to 160 bytes long. It can be used similarly to **instant messaging (IM)** services on normal PCs, but IM is typically interactive while SMS typically uses one-way messages.

20.10.5 Location-aware applications

Another obvious but still interesting facet of these systems is that they move around with the user. After some time it became clear that there were some interesting applications that could be created if the application knew where the phone was. The initial impetus was probably the emergency location system that has been mandated for cell phones. In an emergency there is obviously a great benefit available if the cell phone can tell the emergency call handlers where the cell phone is located within a few tens of meters.

There are many other location-based applications that can be created as well. Since the cellular carriers in the United States were mandated to have the network able to locate the phone, they have decided to make lemonade out of those lemons by devising services that they can offer to their users (for a modest fee, of course) based on the current location of the phone. Where is the nearest pizza restaurant? Dial *1411 (or some similar special number) and a friendly operator will get your location from the network, ask what you are looking for, search a location-indexed database for the nearest Chinese restaurant, and give you the information. Some of the other obvious applications are general driving directions, traffic reports, and weather reports. Of course, these systems can also be computerized, eliminating the human operator.

An interesting question is, how does the phone (or the network) find out where the phone is? One answer is the federal GPS system. There are a few dozen satellites that are in orbit purely for this function. Initially they were installed for the benefit of the military, but since using the satellites merely involves listening to their broadcasts, it was impossible to keep civilian uses out forever. By locating several satellites at one time any device can determine its present location, including altitude. This is an extremely accurate mechanism, to within a few feet in many cases. However, the hardware costs are still somewhat high compared to most of the rest of the phone. Fortunately, there are at least two other ways to find the location of a phone. The first is just triangulation of the phone by the network. All the cells that can hear the phone will report the timing of the signals from the phone and the network will be able to locate the phone within a hundred feet or so. This is not accurate enough to drive a car, but it is usually accurate enough to locate the nearest post office, for example. The other location mechanism is for the network merely to report which cell is currently servicing the mobile device and perhaps a distance from the tower based on signal propagation times. Although this method is even less accurate than the triangulation, it is still accurate enough for many purposes.

20.10.6 Later Palm OS releases

Beginning with release 5 the Palm OS supports an ARM processor instead of the Motorola CPU used in previous platforms. Beginning with the 5.4 release the PAI came to be known as Garnet. The PalmSource company that had been spun off of Palm Inc. was purchased by a Access Co. Ltd. They have created a release of Linux with the Garnet API for use on mobile platforms. The latest release of Palm OS was version 6. It is named Cobalt.

20.11 SUMMARY

In this chapter, we discussed further the features and concepts of a simple modern OS—the Palm Operating System™ developed by Palm, Inc. This OS was developed for small handheld devices. Although this is a single-user system, it can concurrently run some OS processes and a small number of applications.

We started this chapter with a recap of the process scheduling and memory management functions of the OS. We then followed this by discussing several additional I/O subsystems in the Palm OS, GUI and network programming, and by explaining the process of developing programs for these limited environments using simulators and cross-compilers on larger systems. We continued with a discussion of some similar OSs for limited environments and how they differ from the Palm OS, including later versions of the Palm OS itself, actually a different OS for a different CPU. We further discussed some of the new types of applications emerging from the convergence of PDA and cell phone platforms.

BIBLIOGRAPHY

Exploring Palm OS: Palm OS File Formats, Document Number 3120-002. Sunnyvale, CA: PalmSource, Inc., 2004.

Exploring Palm OS: System Management, Document Number 3110-002. Sunnyvale, CA: PalmSource, Inc., 2004.

Palm OS Programmer's Companion, Volume 1, Document Number 3120-002. Sunnyvale, CA: Palm, Inc., 2001.

Palm OS Programmer's Companion, Volume 2, Communications, Document Number 3005-002. Sunnyvale, CA: Palm, Inc., 2001.

Palm OS® Programmer's API Reference, Document Number 3003-004. Sunnyvale, CA: Palm, Inc., 2001.

Rhodes, N., and McKeehan, J. *Palm Programming: The Developer's Guide.* Sebastopol, CA: O'Reilly & Associates, Inc., 2000.

SONY Clié, Personal Entertainment Organizer, Sony Corporation, 2001.

WEB RESOURCES

http://www.accessdevnet.com (ACCESS Linux Platform Development Suite)

http://www.freescale.com

http://www.freewarepalm.com (free Palm software)

http://www.freesoft.org/CIE/ (*Connected: An Internet Encyclopedia*)

http://www.imc.org/pdi/

http://oasis.palm.com/dev/palmos40-docs/memory%20architecture.html

http://www.palm.com (Palm home page)

http://www.palmsource.com/developers/

http://www.pocketgear.com/en_US/html/index.jsp (software for mobile devices)

http://prc-tools.sourceforge.net (programming tools supporting for Palm OS)

http://www.symbian.com (Symbian OS)

http://www.w3.org/Protocols/ (HTTP, primarily)

http://en.wikipedia.org/wiki/Graffiti_2 (article on Graffiti 2)

http://en.wikipedia.org/wiki/Palm_OS (history of the Palm OS versions)

REVIEW QUESTIONS

20.1 Since almost no websites are developed with the assumption that the screen size is 160 × 160 pixels, of what use is the HTTP protocol support?

20.2 What does a Palm device need a RAM disk driver for?

20.3 How does a programmer go about creating and testing programs for the kind of handheld platforms discussed in this chapter?

20.4 What are some of the new device types and features that have been added to the Palm platform since the earlier models and what sorts of applications do they facilitate?

20.5 What is a vCard?

20.6 What is a "location aware application?"

20.7 Describe the three different families of handheld systems.

20.8 One of the major differences between a cell phone and a PDA is that a PDA is turned off and on and a cell phone usually stays on most of the time. What major feature did this force to be included into OSs designed for cell phones?

Overview of Computer System and Architecture Concepts

In this appendix:

In this appendix, we give an overview of computer architecture concepts, with an emphasis on those concepts that are particularly relevant to OSs. Some readers will have already completed a course in computer organization or computer architecture, and hence will be familiar with these concepts. In this case, the appendix can provide a review of this material. For those who have not had a previous course in this topic, this appendix might be covered in detail, because the discussions of many OS concepts are based on the underlying computer architecture. The concepts presented here are needed throughout the presentation of OS concepts.

We start by giving a description of the major components of a typical computer system in Section A.1, and a discussion of the functions performed by each component. In Section A.2 we discuss the central processing unit and control concepts. Section A.3 outlines the ideas of memory and storage hierarchy, and Section A.4 describes the basic concepts of input/output systems. Section A.5 briefly discusses the role and characteristics of networks in modern computing. We then give a more detailed picture of typical computer system components in Section A.6. Finally, Section A.7 provides a summary.

A.1 TYPICAL COMPUTER SYSTEM COMPONENTS

Computer systems vary widely, based on their functionality and expected use. They include the following types of systems:

Personal desktop and notebook computers that are typically utilized by a single user at a time.

Large **server** computers that provide services to hundreds or thousands of users each day. These include Internet **Web servers** that store Web documents, **database servers** that store large databases, **file servers** that store and manage files for a network of computers, and application servers that run some specific application that provides a remotely accessed service.

Embedded computer systems, which are used in automobiles, aircraft, telephones, calculators, appliances, media players, game consoles, computer network units, and many other such devices. As CPU chips have become cheaper and cheaper we see them in more and more places. In the future we will see them in places that might be hard to imagine today.

Mobile wearable devices, cell phones, and PDAs (personal digital assistants) that are used for keeping appointment calendars, email, phone directories, and other information. Today these units are becoming hard to distinguish from personal computers as they become more and more powerful.

Hence, it is difficult to decide what a typical computer system would look like. However, it is traditionally accepted that most computer systems have three major components, as illustrated in Figure A.1. These are the processor or central processing unit, the memory unit, and the input/output units.[1] In addition to the three major components, network devices connect computer systems together and allow sharing of information and programs. Let us briefly describe the main functionality of each of these units.

The **central processing unit** (or **CPU**) is the circuitry that performs the computation and control logic required by a computer system. The **memory** is the component that stores both the data required by a computation and the actual commands that perform the computation. Memory is often organized into several levels, leading to a **storage hierarchy** of different types of storage devices, as we describe in Section A.3. The class of **input/output** (or **I/O**) units include two broad subclasses of devices based on their major functionality: input and output. Some devices can also be used for both input and output. **Input devices** are used to load data and program instructions into the memory unit from devices such as CD-ROMs or disks. They are also used to process input commands from a user through devices such as a keyboard or pointing device (e.g., a mouse or touchpad). **Output devices** are used to display data and information to the user through devices such as printers or

---

[1] At a more detailed level, the CPU is sometimes separated into two components: the control unit and the data path unit, as we discuss in the next section. Similarly, the input/output unit is sometimes separated into input devices and output devices.

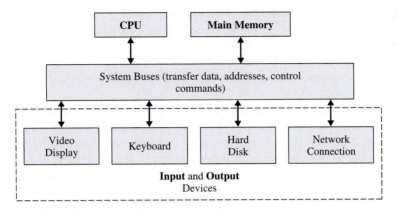

FIGURE A.1
Simplified diagram of the major computer system components.

video monitors, and to store data and programs on secondary storage devices such as various types of disks. Devices such as hard disk drives and CD-RW drives are used for *both input and output,* and hence are classified as **input/output devices.** Network devices can be considered as input/output devices but they are so special that they are best regarded as being something separate.

Disk devices in general (hard disk, floppy disk, CD, etc.) are considered as I/O devices if we consider a low-level hardware view of the computer system. If we take a more conceptual view of the roles they play, which is to store data and programs, then they can also be considered as part of the storage hierarchy of the computer system, as we discuss in Section A.3.

Another crucial component in many modern computer systems is the **network,** which is the hardware and software that allows the millions of computers and network devices in existence to communicate with one another. Networks can be formed from phone lines, fiber optic and other types of cables, satellites, wireless hubs, infrared devices, and other components. At the individual machine level, though, it is sometimes useful to consider the network as another type of input/output device, because its main functionality is to transfer data (such as files, text, pictures, commands, etc.) from one machine (as output) to another machine (as input). For computer users, the Internet is the most visible example of a network.

The following three sections discuss each of the three main computer system components—processor, memory, and input/output—in more detail. The network is discussed in Section A.5.

A.2   THE PROCESSOR OR CENTRAL PROCESSING UNIT

As was said before, the central processing unit, or CPU, is the hardware circuitry that performs the various arithmetic and logical operations. Each processor will have a particular **instruction set** that defines the operations that can be performed by the processor. These typically include integer arithmetic operations, comparison operations, transfer operations, control operations, and so on. A processor usually has a set of *registers* that hold the operations that are being executed as well as some of the data values or *operands* needed by these operations.[2] Other operands can be accessed directly from memory locations, depending on the design of the instruction set. We further elaborate on the use of registers and the types of operands later in this section.

Instruction sets can vary widely. Some processors are designed based on the **RISC** (reduced instruction set computer) philosophy, where only a few basic instruction types are directly implemented in hardware. These instructions are usually similar to one another in their design. One of the advantages of RISC is to reduce hardware complexity by having a limited set of instruction types and hence increase the speed of execution of the instructions. The most common RISC microprocessors are the HP Alpha series (no longer being manufactured, but historically significant), ARM-embedded processors, MIPS, the PIC microcontroller family, the Apple/IBM/Motorola PowerPC and related designs, and the Sun Microsystems SPARC family.

Other processors have a much larger instruction set implemented directly in hardware, with a variety of instruction types included in the instruction set. This approach is known as **CISC** (complex instruction set computer). A RISC processor typically has between 30 and 100 different instructions with a fixed instruction format of 32 bits. A CISC processor typically has between 120 and 400 different instructions. Examples of CISC processors are the IBM System/360, DEC VAX, DEC PDP-11, the Motorola 68000 family, and Intel x86 architecture–based processors and compatible CPUs.

Most of today's processors are not completely RISC or completely CISC. The two are really design philosophies that have evolved toward each other so much that there is no longer a clear distinction between the approaches to increasing performance and efficiency. Chips that use various RISC instruction sets have added more instructions and complexity so that now they are as complex as their CISC counterparts and the debate is mostly among marketing departments.

A.2.1 Instruction set architecture: The machine language

The instruction set architecture defines the **machine language** of the processor, which is the set of commands that the processor can directly execute. Each instruction is coded as a sequence of bits (a **bit string**) that can be decoded and executed by the processor. Instructions are stored in memory, and are typically executed in sequential order, except when a specific *transfer of control* is specified by some types of instructions. The instruction bit string is divided into several parts called **fields.** Although instruction formats can vary widely, some of the typical fields are the following:

The **opcode** (operation code) field specifies the particular operation to be executed.

---

[2] The registers that store data values can also be considered, at least conceptually, to be the top level of the storage hierarchy (see Section A.3), since they hold data and provide the fastest access time when accessed by the executing instructions. Physically they are part of the processor chip.

A **modifier field** is sometimes used to distinguish among different operations that have the same opcode and format—for example, integer addition and subtraction.

The **operand fields** specify the data values or addresses that are needed by each particular operation. Addresses can be either memory addresses or register addresses.

There are many different types of operands, and the way to interpret the meaning of each type of operand is called the **addressing mode.** We can distinguish between two main types of operands. The first type supplies a **data value** or the **address of a data value** needed by the operation. The second type provides the **address of an instruction,** and is used for changing the sequence of instruction execution by a **branch** or **jump** operation.

The most common addressing modes for **data** operands are the following:

Register addressing: The operand specifies a register location where the data that is needed or produced by the operation is stored.

Immediate addressing: The operand is a direct data value contained in one of the fields of the instruction bit string itself.

Base register addressing: The operand is stored in a memory location. The address of the memory location is calculated by adding the contents of a **base register** (which contains the address of a reference memory location) and a **displacement** or **offset.** The displacement can be a direct value in the instruction itself, or it could be the value in another register, called an **index register.**

Indirect addressing: The memory address of the data to be used as an operand is stored in a register or in another memory location. This is called *indirect addressing* because instead of pointing to the data to be used in an operation the instruction points to the address of the data, either in memory or in a register, and that address must first be accessed to get the actual data address needed.

The most common addressing modes for **instruction address** operands are the following:

PC-relative addressing: The memory address of the instruction is calculated by adding an offset to the contents of the **PC** (program counter) register, which holds the address of the next instruction to be executed. As in base register addressing, the offset can be a direct value in the instruction itself, or it could be the value in an index register.

Indirect addressing: The memory address of the instruction is stored in a register or in another memory location. As with indirect data addressing, instead of pointing to the address to be transferred to, the instruction points to the address of the address, either in memory or in a register, and that address must first be accessed to get the actual transfer address needed.

Some of these addressing modes are illustrated in Figure A.2.

The type of operation determines how to interpret the operands—whether as memory addresses or instruction addresses or direct data values or in some other way. RISC processors typically have a limited number of addressing modes, whereas CISC processors typically have a much larger variety of addressing modes.

We now illustrate some simple instruction formats and their addressing modes in Figure A.2.

FIGURE A.2
Illustrating some addressing modes and instruction formats.

FIGURE A.2(a)
Register addressing for add operation.

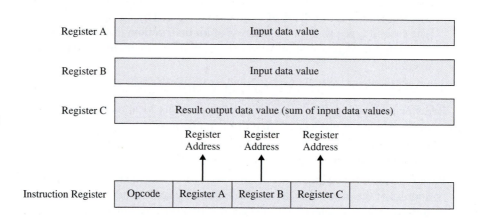

Figure A.2(a) illustrates an **add** operation which places the result of adding the contents of registers A and B into register C. Here the values to be added must first be loaded into registers A and B by previous instructions.

FIGURE A.2(b)
Register and immediate addressing for add operation.

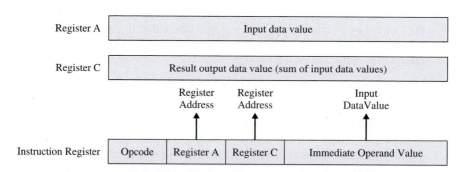

Figure A.2(b) shows an **add** operation where one of the operands is an immediate value stored in the instruction itself. This operation places the result of adding the contents of register A and the immediate operand value into register C.

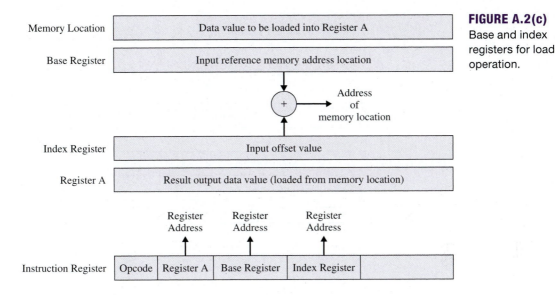

FIGURE A.2(c)
Base and index registers for load operation.

Figure A.2(c) illustrates a **load** operation that places a value from memory into register A. This instruction uses base register addressing mode to calculate the memory address. The values in the base and index registers are added, and their result is used as the memory address whose contents are loaded into the result register A.

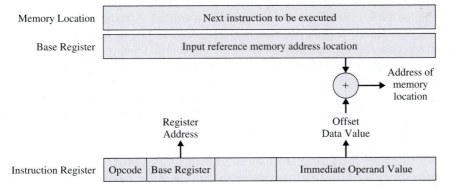

FIGURE A.2(d)
Immediate relative address for jump operation.

Figure A.2(d) shows an unconditional **jump** operation, which transfers control to an instruction other than the next instruction. It calculates the memory address of the next instruction based on a base register and an immediate value. The next instruction to be executed is in the memory address calculated by adding the base register contents to the immediate index value stored in the instruction itself.

FIGURE A.2(e)
Program counter
indexed addressing
for conditional
branch.

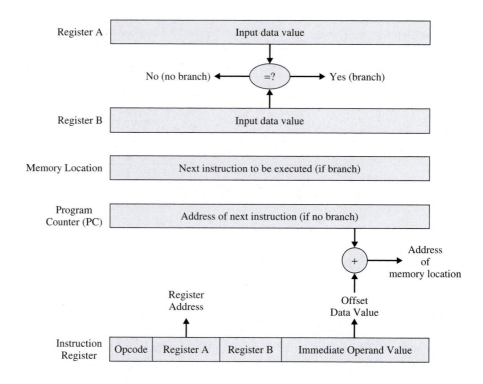

Figure A.2(e) shows a conditional **branch-on-equal** operation. The instruction first compares the values in registers A and B. If the values are equal, it transfers control to the instruction whose address is calculated by adding the contents of the program counter register (the next instruction address) to the immediate value in the instruction. Such an instruction can be used to control looping, for example.

In addition to different addressing modes—which determine how to interpret an operand location and value—many processors have two **execution modes. User mode** is used when a user or application program is executing. **Supervisory (or privileged) mode** is used when an OS kernel routine is executing. A special register in the processor determines which execution mode is being used. When in user mode, certain safeguards are incorporated during instruction execution. For example, memory protection is enabled in user mode to prohibit the program from accessing memory locations outside of the part of memory allocated to the user program. Certain privileged instructions are allowed to execute only when the system is in supervisory mode—for example, instructions that control I/O devices.

A.2.2 Components of a CPU

Figure A.3 is a simplified diagram that shows the typical components of a CPU. The **integer ALU** (arithmetic and logic unit) and the **floating point unit** include the hardware circuitry that performs instruction set operations. Most regular instructions are handled by the integer ALU, whereas floating-point arithmetic instructions are handled by the floating point unit, since such operations require more complex, highly specialized circuitry. The **control unit** usually includes the processor registers, as well as circuitry for controlling the sequencing of instruction execution, the interpretation of instruction codes and operands, and the execution of instructions using the ALU or floating point unit circuitry.

The **processor cache** shown in Figure A.3 is a memory component that is part of the processor chip, and holds instructions and data from main memory that are being used by the processor. (There may be other cache memories outside the CPU chip itself.) The cache is connected to main memory via a separate **memory bus.** The main memory is also connected to a main **system bus.** The control unit is connected to the I/O devices through the system bus as well. Another component is a **DMA** (direct memory access) controller. It allows for transfer of data directly from I/O devices to memory. We discuss the idea of caching in some detail in Section A.3.2 and covered DMA in Chapter 14.

A.2.3 Programs: Source, object, and executable

An **assembly language** is an alternate form of the machine language instructions that is easier to read (and write) by humans. In assembly language, each possible opcode is given a **mnemonic name**—a symbolic name to identify the instruction. The operands are shown as numbers or are also given names to identify program variables that are mapped to a memory address or register. A program that is written in a high-level programming language such as C++ (called the **source code**) is converted into a program in machine language (called the **object code**) by the programming language **compiler.** Such an object code program is then linked with other needed object code programs from program libraries and other program modules, creating an **executable code** program file. This is usually stored on disk as a binary file, and hence is sometimes called the **program binary** (or **bin**) file. The executable code is loaded into memory when needed, and the program instructions are executed in the desired sequence by the processor.

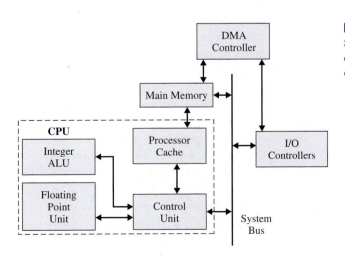

FIGURE A.3
Simplified diagram of typical CPU components.

Good programming language compilers should take advantage of the machine instruction set available when creating the object code. Hence, programmers who write compilers must study the instruction set architecture of each machine in detail in order to fully utilize its capabilities.

A.2.4 Processor registers, data path, and control

There are several types of registers that are part of the CPU. They are used by the processor circuitry in various ways. Some processors use **general-purpose** registers, where the same physical register may be used in many or all of the ways discussed below. In other processor designs some or all of the registers are **special-purpose** registers and can only be utilized for specific functions. The following are the most common uses of registers:

Instruction registers: These registers are used to hold the instructions that are being executed. They are directly connected to the control circuitry that interprets the opcode and operands when executing an instruction.

Program counter: Also known as the **instruction counter,** this register holds the address of the next instruction to be executed. It is initialized to the address of the first program instruction when the program is loaded into memory and is to start execution. The length of the current instruction is normally added to this register as the instruction is executed in order to fetch the next sequential instruction. Of course, branching or subroutine calls or other transfer of control may alter that sequence.

Data registers: These registers hold operands. Some data registers may be dedicated to hold operands of a certain data type; for example, a floating-point register could only hold a floating-point operand. Small CPUs may have only one main data register, typically called an **accumulator.** In some such cases there will be an additional register used for larger operands or remainders of division operations and generically called an **accumulator extension** register.

Address registers: These hold values of main memory addresses where operands or instructions are stored. They may hold absolute memory addresses, or relative memory addresses (offsets) that are added to a value in a **base register** to calculate an absolute address. Registers that hold relative addresses are called **index registers.**

Interrupt registers: These hold information about interrupt events that may have occurred, as we discuss shortly.

Program status registers: These hold control information needed by the CPU. Different machines may have any number of status registers and the contents vary wildly. Examples of the sort of control information that they hold include the following:

- Results of the last comparison operation (i.e., a > b, a = b or a < b)
- Processor status (i.e., whether it is in user or supervisory mode)
- Error status such as arithmetic overflow, divide by zero, etc.

Clock: The clock register is actually a timer that counts down to zero and causes an interrupt. This is known as a **clock** or **timer interrupt,** and can be set by the OS for various reasons. For example, in a multiuser system, the OS typically gives control to a user program for a limited amount of time known as the *time quantum.* By setting a timer interrupt, the OS can interrupt the user program if it is still running at the end of the time quantum and check to see if other programs are waiting to run on the processor. This interrupt may also be used to compute the actual date and time. A CPU usually has a privileged instruction that can only be executed by the OS to load a value into the clock register so that a user program cannot override the OS clock value.

Some registers can be set by user programs, and hence are known as **user-visible** registers. These usually include data, address, and instruction registers. Other registers can only be set by the processor or the OS kernel, such as status and interrupt registers. RISC processors typically have a large number of general-purpose registers because of their uniform instruction set design, whereas CISC processors often have both general-purpose and special-purpose registers. Some types of register use may require special-purpose registers; for example, interrupt registers, program status registers, and instruction registers.

The circuitry to identify the particular instruction (from the opcode) and to execute the instruction using the operands is connected to the instruction register. Since instruction execution involves the transfer of information (opcode, operands, etc.) from registers and memory through the hardware circuitry, it is sometimes referred to as the **data path** component of the processor. On the other hand, the circuitry that controls the fetching of the next instruction and handling of other events such as interrupts (see below) is referred to as the **control** component of the processor.

A.2.5 System timing

Another important component within each processor is the **system clock.** The operation of most logic circuits proceeds in synchronized steps. At the electronic level this is known as a system clock. (This should not be confused with the CPU register that is used by the OS for timing.) A system **clock cycle** is the fixed shortest time interval during which a processor action can occur. The speed of a processor is determined by how many cycles per second are generated by the system clock. A one-Gigacycle processor will have one billion clock cycles per second. The processor technology and the instruction set design are major factors that determine overall processor speed, because simple instructions take fewer clock cycles to complete than do complex instructions. That is considered one advantage of RISC machines, since the RISC instructions typically execute in a smaller number of clock cycles than will CISC instructions.

A.2.6 Instruction execution cycle and pipelining

It is customary to divide a typical instruction execution cycle into the following five phases:

Instruction Fetch: The instruction is fetched from memory into an instruction register.

Decode: The opcode is decoded and the input operand locations are determined.

Data Fetch: The operands are fetched from memory if necessary.

Execute: The operation is executed.

Write-back: The operation output results are stored in the appropriate locations.

Note that the instruction or the operands may be in a cache memory instead of the primary memory. For many simple instructions, each phase typically takes one clock cycle, although this may differ depending on the CPU, the type of instruction, and the addressing modes for the operands. A simple instruction would thus take five clock cycles from start to finish. In order to speed up program execution, most modern processors employ a strategy called **pipelining,** where successive instructions overlap their execution phases. For example, while one instruction is in its write-back phase, the next instruction would be in its execute phase, the following one in its data fetch phase, and so forth. This would work as long as all instructions are executed in sequential order so that their order of execution is known in advance by the processor. A speedup of instruction processing by a factor of five would be realized in this case.

A pipelining processor would have to include provisions for instructions that change the order of execution, such as *branch* and *jump* instructions. A jump will terminate one execution pipeline and start another at a different instruction location. Instructions that have gone through some steps of their execution cycle may have to be cancelled (undone) if a branch is determined after their execution cycle is started. It is also sometimes necessary to delay the pipeline if an instruction needs as its input an operand that is being produced by the previous instruction. Hence, the speedup actually achieved by pipelining must be estimated by averaging the speedup achieved by many different programs.

A.2.7 Interrupts

An important functionality included in the processor is the **interrupt.** This is particularly relevant to OSs, which use interrupts in various ways, as we see throughout this book. An interrupt is usually an **asynchronous event,** which is an event that can occur at any time, and is hence not synchronized with the system clock and with processor instruction execution cycle. The interrupt signals to the processor that it needs to handle a high-priority event. The processor hardware typically includes one or more **interrupt registers,** which are set by the interrupting event.

Whenever an instruction finishes executing, the control circuitry automatically checks to see whether any event has placed a value in an interrupt register. Hence, interrupts cannot be serviced *during instruction execution*—only between instructions.[3] If so, the **processor state**—which includes the contents of the program counter and any registers that will be used during interrupt processing—is saved into memory and a jump to execute the program code that handles interrupts is

---

[3] When pipelining is used, interrupts may be checked whenever an instruction completes its execution cycle. Provisions for undoing partially executed subsequent instructions by the processor would be needed.

performed. Once the interrupt handler is done, the system will normally restore the processor state and resume processing the user program from the point at which it was interrupted. The OS may switch to run another program if the interrupt caused the current program to be terminated or suspended.

While processing an interrupt, it is usually the case that lower priority or less important interrupts are disabled until interrupt handling is completed. The OS does this by setting an **interrupt disable** (or **interrupt mask**) register. Depending on the value in that register the system will not check for interrupts for lower priority interrupt levels. Hence, the OS can set this register before starting interrupt processing, and reset it back after completing the interrupt processing.

We can categorize the events that cause interrupts into hardware events and software events. In general, hardware interrupts are asynchronous and software interrupts are synchronous. Typical of the **hardware events** that can cause interrupts are the following:

Some I/O user action has occurred, such as mouse movement or mouse button click or keyboard input. The interrupt handler would retrieve the information about the I/O action, such as mouse coordinates or which character was input from the keyboard.

A disk I/O transfer was completed. The interrupt handler would check to see if other disk I/O operations were pending, and if so initiate the next disk I/O transfer to or from main memory.

A clock timer interrupt has occurred, which allows the OS to allocate the CPU to another program.

The **software events** that can cause interrupts may be further categorized into **traps,** which occur when a program error or violation happens, and **system calls,** which occur when a program requests services from the OS. (For historical reasons a system call interrupt is sometimes called a trap—somewhat confusing.) Some events that cause traps are the following:

A memory protection violation, for example, a program executing in user mode tries to access an area of memory outside of its allowed memory space.

An instruction protection violation, for example, a program executing in user mode attempts to execute an instruction reserved for supervisor mode.

An instruction error such as division by zero.

An arithmetic error such as a floating point overflow.

We discuss in detail how these events and other events that cause interrupts are handled by the OS throughout this book.

A.2.8 Microprogramming

In some computers complex instructions are implemented as sequences of basic instructions, often using the concept of **microprogramming.** A microprogram is a sequence of basic operations that implement a more complex operation. This sequence is stored in a special microprogram memory in the processor, so that it can be invoked when the complex instruction is to be executed. The microprograms are sometimes referred to as **firmware.** Some CPU architectures, usually CISC, use microprogramming while others do not.

A.2.9 Processor chip

Historically the CPU was built out of discrete components such as relays, tubes, transistors, or simple integrated circuits. In modern systems the whole processor is typically implemented as a single integrated circuit (chip). The **processor chip** includes the CPU, clock, registers, cache memory, and perhaps other circuitry depending on the particular processor design.

A.2.10 Multicore chips

In the last few years the manufacturers of CPU integrated circuits have concluded that the demand for ever faster CPUs is slacking off somewhat. They have begun to use the extra space on the chips to provide multiple CPUs in the package. There are various alternative designs regarding placement of cache memories, etc. We talk about these caches in the next section. Although this would appear to be a fairly trivial change, we see in the chapters on memory that it is not at all trivial for the OS. At the present time chips with four CPU cores are fairly common. Predictions call for up to 128 cores in the next few years.

It is difficult to write a program that can effectively use multiple CPUs at the same time. But most users have many programs running at the same time and having multiple CPUs to run them on will mean that they will all run faster. Furthermore, most users use only a few programs, and they are ones that have been highly developed and are prepared to use the multiple CPUs. Such programs include most of the programs we use the most—word processors, spreadsheets, browsers, and so on.

A.3 THE MEMORY UNIT AND STORAGE HIERARCHIES

A.3.1 Storage units: Bits, bytes, and words

The memory unit is the hardware that stores the program instructions and operands that are needed by the processor. The basic physical storage unit is a single **bit,** which stores a binary zero (0) or one (1) value. In modern systems, bits are grouped into **bytes** (8 bits), and bytes are grouped into **words** (typically 4 bytes or 8 bytes, though CPUs designed for embedded systems may have 1- or 2-byte words). Normally, the basic unit that will be transferred between the memory unit and the processor is a word. Typically there will be instructions that will allow loading or storing of a single byte or half word. In most systems each byte has a unique **memory address.** Given a particular memory address, the memory circuitry can locate that particular byte in memory. The word containing this byte can then be transferred to or from the processor. Memory bytes or words can also be transferred to or from input/output devices. In many cases, blocks of multiple words are transferred directly.

The word size is usually the standard size for processor registers. A 32-bit processor thus will have standard data items of 32 bits, or 4 bytes. On the other hand, 16-bit processors would have 16-bit data formats as many older PC processors had. Some processors have a 64-bit "double word" data size. At one time this was mostly found in large mainframe computers. Most processors currently are of the 32-bit variety, but today's PCs are switching to a 64-bit format. The size of many operands is also one word size (4 bytes), although some operands can be a single byte or 2 bytes or 8 bytes. The particular opcode will determine the type and size of each operand.

As the basic data word size has increased from 16 to 64 bits, the instruction formats have also increased in size, mainly so that larger memory addresses can be used. Instructions in CISC machines tend to be variable length since it takes only a few bits to specify a register but many to specify a memory address. Depending on the addressing mode, instructions specify anywhere from none to three memory addresses, so the instruction lengths will vary accordingly.

A.3.2 A storage hierarchy

Most current systems have several levels of storage, often referred to as the **storage hierarchy.** This is illustrated in Figure A.4. The traditional view of a storage hierarchy has three levels: primary, secondary, and tertiary storage. We discuss each of these next.

Primary storage consists of main memory and usually one or more cache memories. Even the processor registers are sometimes considered to be part of the main memory storage hierarchy. Hence, within primary storage, there can be several levels. If we consider the processor **registers** to be part of the memory hierarchy, they would be at the top level. At the next level is a high-speed low-capacity **cache memory,** which is usually included as part of the processor chip itself. There may be additional cache memories outside of the main CPU chip, each slower but larger than the previous level. At a still lower level, a lower-speed but higher-capacity **main memory** is included on one or more separate chips. The cache memory typically uses a

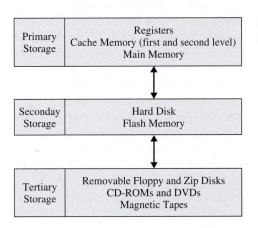

FIGURE A.4
A storage hierarchy.

hardware technology known as SRAM (static random access memory), whereas the main memory typically uses DRAM (dynamic random access memory) technology. SRAM technology is faster but more expensive than DRAM per unit of storage.[4]

Processor registers are faster to read or write than cache memory or main memory locations. For example, a register-to-register copy may take a single clock cycle in a RISC processor, whereas a register-to-cache transfer may take two clock cycles, and a register-to-memory transfer might take three or four clock cycles.

The cache memory is often divided into two parts: the **data cache** (for storing operands) and the **instruction cache** (for storing instructions). In some cases there are distinct cache parts for applications in user mode and the kernel in supervisor mode. Transfer of bytes between the cache and processor is several times faster than that between the main memory and the cache. Hence, the goal is to keep in the cache the data and instructions currently being used. This job is the responsibility of the cache management circuitry in the processor, but program design can affect the ability of the hardware to cache the needed instructions and data.

Memory capacity is usually measured in Kilobytes (KB or 1,024 bytes), Megabytes (MB or 1,048,576 bytes), Gigabytes (GB or 1,073,741,824 bytes), and even Terabytes (TB or 1,099,511,627,776 bytes). Since cache is more expensive than main memory it has a much smaller capacity. Many processors have two caches: a level-1 or **L1 cache** on the processor chip and an external level-2 or **L2 cache** outside the processor. A few processors have a third **L3 cache** that is also outside the CPU. The higher-level caches are faster than the lower-level caches but are more expensive and hold less information.

The **memory bus** is the hardware component that handles the transfer of data between main memory (on the memory chip) and cache memory (on the processor chip). Cache memory sizes often are in the 64-KB to several Megabyte range, whereas main memory capacity is typically in the 32-MB to 4-GB range. These numbers continue to grow rapidly, though.

A.3.3 Secondary storage: Hard disk

The next level in the storage hierarchy is typically a **magnetic disk hard-drive** storage component or simply **hard disk,** which is slower than main memory but has a much higher capacity and lower cost per Megabyte. Hard disk capacity typically ranges between 10-GB to 1-TB or higher, but again these numbers continue to grow rapidly. A hard disk is a part of most standalone computer systems, but is often not included in embedded systems that are used in various devices such as PDAs, music players, telephones, cars, home appliances, and so on. Traditionally, the registers, cache memories, and main memory together are referred to as **primary storage,** whereas the hard disk is referred to as **secondary storage.** Every system must have a primary storage component.

An important distinction between primary and secondary storage is called **storage volatility.** In a **volatile memory,** memory content is lost when electric power

---

[4] Memory, processor, and disk technologies are always changing, so newer technologies may come in use at any time. We will not discuss further how different types of memories are actually built at the hardware level, since this is not directly relevant to our presentation.

is turned off. In **nonvolatile memory,** content is not lost when power is turned off. Most main memory systems are volatile, whereas most secondary storage systems are nonvolatile. Hence, the disk also serves as a backup storage medium in case of system crashes due to power failure.[5]

At the hardware level, transfer of data between primary and secondary storage involves an I/O device controller, which we discuss in Section A.4. Device controllers often have a storage component to hold data being transferred between the disks and main memory. This storage component is called the **disk cache** or **controller cache.**

This cache is needed because the controller typically has its own processor and clock that are not synchronized with the clock of the CPU. Once the CPU initiates a transfer operation, it leaves the actual control of the transfer to the I/O controller—while the CPU continues with program execution. Hence, main memory is being accessed by both the CPU and the device controllers. Because requests to access memory by the CPU are given higher priority, memory access by the controller may be delayed. The controller cache prevents the loss of data because of such delays by acting as a buffer storage when transferring data from disks and other secondary storage devices to main memory. Controller caches also exist in I/O controllers for some types of tertiary storage devices such as floppy disks and CDs, which we describe next. This type of data transfer between an I/O controller and main memory may make use of DMA technology (direct memory access), which we discussed in Chapter 14.

A.3.4 Tertiary and offline storage: Removable discs and tapes

Additional levels of the storage hierarchy exist in many computer systems, such as various types of magnetic tape storage for backup, sometimes referred to as tertiary storage or offline storage. In addition, various types of rotating memories (floppy disk, CD-ROM, CD-RW, DVD, etc.)[6] are used as storage media to hold information. The information stored on removable media is generally either too large to fit on secondary storage or is not usually needed frequently or immediately, so it is not permanently kept on the hard disk. So this data is not usually available within the computer system as is the case with cache memory, main memory, and hard disk, which are referred to as **online storage** because they are available as soon as the computer system is turned on.

Removable media units can be automated so that the drive can select from among many individual media that are inserted into the drive. Examples include automated tape libraries or optical disc jukeboxes. In this case they are properly referred to as **tertiary storage.** Removable media storage units that are not automated are usually called **offline storage,** because the storage media (floppy disk, DVD, CD-ROM, tape) must be manually loaded before the data on the media can be accessed. Tertiary and offline storage devices can also be viewed as input/output devices (see Section A.4).

---

[5] Historically, main memories were not necessarily volatile. Magnetic core primary memory in particular would retain its contents even with the power turned off.

[6] CD-ROM stands for compact disc-read only memory; CD-RW stands for compact disc-read write; and DVD stands for digital video disc.

A.3.5 **Managing the storage hierarchy**

Transfer between the various levels of the storage hierarchy is usually done in units of multiple bytes or **blocks** of bytes. The block size between main memory and cache memory is typically in the range of 16 bytes (four words) to 256 bytes (64 words), whereas the block size between hard disk and main memory is typically in the 4-KB to 16-KB range or even higher. The main reason for transferring blocks instead of single bytes or single words is to improve performance by reducing overall transfer time. Especially with tapes there is a large overhead to start and stop the tape move-ment. So transferring larger blocks with each read or write is much more efficient than transferring smaller blocks. Similarly, positioning a tape or disk to access the needed information is quite slow. Transferring more data at one time means that fewer such positioning operations are needed.

Performance is also improved by taking advantage of the *locality principle,* which states that programs tend to access a small portion of their instructions and operands in any short time interval. This locality characteristic has been shown to exist in most programs, and has two components:

Temporal locality: This characteristic states that a program that accesses certain memory addresses may soon access them again. An example is that instructions within a loop may be accessed repeatedly within a short period of time.

Spatial locality: This characteristic states that if a program accesses certain memory addresses, it may soon access other words that are stored nearby. For example, instructions are typically stored and accessed sequentially. Another example is that a program may process operands (data) that are stored consecutively—for example, accessing consecutive array elements or sequentially scanning through a block of text that is being edited.

If multiple words that are stored in spatial proximity in a block are loaded into cache memory, then access to subsequent words when needed will be quite fast since they will already be in the cache. These are known as **cache hits.** On the other hand, if these subsequent words are never accessed, the cost of loading them into the cache will be wasted. When instructions or operands are referenced that are not in cache memory, the system will try to locate them in main memory and transfer them to the cache. These are known as a **cache misses.**

If the words that caused a cache miss are not in main memory, they have to be located on hard disk and transferred to main memory, and the needed part is then transferred to cache. Hence, it is necessary to find an appropriate block size that reduces the access cost per unit of storage. Generally, the cost of transferring *n* con-secutive bytes or words between one level and the next in a single transfer is much lower than transferring them using multiple transfers. This is particularly true for transfer between hard disk and main memory, and is also true to a lesser extent for transfer between main memory and cache memory. As we will see, a major part of the memory management component of an OS is to attempt to optimize these types of transfers. In general, the OS handles transfers between hard disk and primary memory, and the CPU hardware handles memory-to-cache transfers.

A.3.6 **Memory protection**

Another aspect of main memory that is particularly relevant to OSs is the memory protection component. When an executing program references a memory location, the OS needs to make sure that this location is part of the **address space** for that program. It should not allow an application program to make references to memory locations that are being used by other programs or by the OS itself. This protects the OS and other user programs and data from being corrupted by an erroneous or malicious program.

One technique for memory protection is to use a pair of registers, the **base register** and **limit register.** This is illustrated in Figure A.5. Before a program starts execution, the OS sets those registers to delimit the addresses in memory that contain the program address space. Setting the contents of the base and limit registers are privileged instructions that can only be used when the CPU is in supervisory mode in the OS kernel. Once the OS sets the execution mode to user mode and transfers control to the user program, the base and limit registers cannot be changed. Any reference to memory locations outside this range causes a hardware interrupt that indicates an invalid memory reference. The OS will reset the base and limit registers whenever it transfers execution to another program.

In many modern systems a more complex scheme is used. Memory is divided into equal-sized **memory pages.** Typical memory page sizes range from 512 bytes to 4 KB. This technique uses **page tables,** which are data structures that refer to the particular memory pages that can be accessed by the executing user program. Only those memory locations referenced through the page table are accessible to the program. The page table is implemented through hardware support in the processor itself. The commands to load the contents of the page table would be privileged instructions that can only be executed by the OS in supervisory mode in the kernel. We discussed this and other memory protection techniques in detail in Chapters 10 and 11.

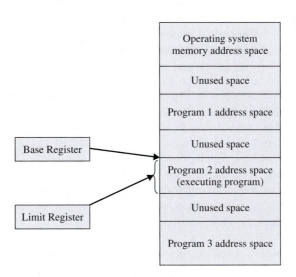

FIGURE A.5

A memory protection mechanism using base and limit registers.

A.4 INPUT AND OUTPUT

The input and output systems are the components that connect the main memory and the processor to other devices. These are sometimes called **I/O devices** or **peripheral devices.**

A.4.1 Types of I/O devices

I/O devices can be divided into four broad categories: user interface devices, storage devices, network devices, and devices that the computer is controlling.

> **User interface I/O devices:** These are employed for user interaction with the computer system. Devices for direct interaction between a user and a system include keyboards, pointing devices (such as mouse, trackball, touch screen, or pad), joysticks, microphones (voice or sound input), other similar components for *input,* and video monitors, speakers (voice or sound output), and the like for *output.* Other I/O devices allow indirect interaction, such as digital cameras and scanners for video or image input, and printers and plotters for hard copy or film output.

> **Storage I/O devices:** These are used for *storing information* and hence are considered as both input/output devices and as part of the storage hierarchy. They include magnetic disks (hard or floppy), optical discs/DVD, magnetic tape, flash memory chips, and so on.

> **Network I/O devices:** These are devices that connect a computer system to a network, and include analog telephone modems, DSL (digital subscriber line) connections, cable modems, and wired cables. In addition, wireless connections such as infrared or Bluetooth are becoming quite common. They may use a wireless network card installed in a computer or device to connect to a wireless hub, which in turn connects to the network, or they may connect devices directly to a computer.

> **Controlled devices:** Computers are often used to control noncomputing devices. Examples include motors, heating and air conditioning, light displays, and so on. Embedded computer systems also fit into this category.

As we can see, there are a wide variety of I/O devices, and new devices are frequently being introduced. To deal with this proliferation of I/O devices, efforts were undertaken to standardize single interfaces that can be used with different types of I/O devices. One such standard is the USB (Universal Serial Bus) 2.0 standard, which allows I/O transmission rates of 480 million bps (bits per second), and is hence suitable for connecting everything from keyboards to digital video cameras or external disk hard drives. Another standard is IEEE 1394, which also allows transmission rates of up to 400 million bps and is used for the same sorts of devices. This interface is also known by two proprietary names, FireWire™ from Apple and i.Link™ from Sony. FireWire is somewhat more efficient than USB for higher-speed devices and is commonly used for video cameras. It has also been selected as the standard connection interface for audio/visual component communication and control.

A.4.2 Device controllers and device drivers

A **device controller** is a component that interfaces an I/O device to the computer processor and memory. Device controllers frequently contain their own processor, which has a specialized instruction set that is used by device manufacturers to write programs that control the I/O devices. A device controller will also have a **command set,** which is the set of commands that the OS can send to the controller across one of the system buses to control the I/O device. These commands are generally restricted to being used only by OS **device drivers,** and are usually not accessible to application or systems programmers. Many device controllers also have a memory component known as controller cache (see Section A.3.3).

Standard device controllers such as USB and FireWire can be used to connect to any type of I/O device that supports the standard. On the other hand, some specialized device controllers—such as disk controllers or graphics video controllers—can only connect to a single type of I/O device for which it was designed.[7] The controller handles the interfacing with the I/O device and may use its memory to either buffer or cache the data as it is being transferred from or to the computer primary memory. The command set of the controller will include commands that initiate input or output operations. For example, a hard disk controller would have commands to initiate a read-block command for a particular disk block address, while providing the address of the computer memory buffer that will hold the block. Figure A.6 is a simplified diagram to illustrate these concepts.

At the computer side, the OS typically handles all interactions with the device controllers. As was mentioned, the parts of the OS that interact with the device controllers and handle I/O are called the **device drivers.** Each device driver will be programmed to handle the low-level hardware commands and details of a particular device controller. The device driver will present an abstract and uniform view of the device to the rest of the OS.

---

[7] In some cases, a controller is limited further to a subset of a certain type of device; for example, an ATA controller only works with ATA disk drives rather than all types of disk drives. Sometimes the controller will only work with devices from a single manufacturer or even only with a specific model.

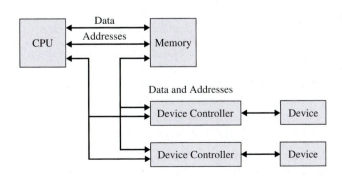

FIGURE A.6

How I/O devices connect to memory and the CPU through device controllers.

A.4.3 Other categorizations of I/O devices and connections

There are other ways to categorize I/O devices. One categorization is to divide them into groups based on the type of connection to the computer. I/O devices are typically connected to the memory and CPU at the hardware connection level using either serial or parallel physical connections (usually cables). A **serial** connection transfers bits serially over a single wire, whereas a **parallel** connection typically transfers 8 bits (or more) at a time in parallel over multiple wires. Interfaces to simple I/O devices such as keyboard, mouse, or modem typically use serial connections, whereas higher-speed devices such as some hard disk SCSI (small computer system interface) connections use parallel cables. USB and FireWire controllers use serial cables, but the cables are high grade and shielded, and this permits the high data transfer speeds of these controllers.

Another higher-level categorization of I/O devices is into **block devices** that transfer multiple bytes at a time versus **character devices** that transfer single characters or bytes. Disks are a good example of block devices, whereas a keyboard is an example of a character device.

A third categorization is whether the connection is wired through a cable or wireless. Wireless connections are being used increasingly to connect portable computers to the network or to output devices such as printers.

A.5 THE NETWORK

Many computers are connected to some kind of network. At an abstract level, one may consider a network connection to be similar to the way that a computer's CPU and memory can be connected to I/O devices. However, the network allows the computer to be connected to other computers, as well as other devices connected to the network. This connectivity allows users to access functions and information on other computers and to use devices that their own computer does not have. It also allows for exchange of information among processes running on different computers.

A.5.1 Client-server versus peer-to-peer versus multitier models

One common way to look at network interaction is through the **client–server model.** Here, one computer—typically where the user is located—is called the **client.** The client can access one or more **server** computers to access information or other functions that the server provides. Servers might include any of the following:

- database servers that contain large amounts of information
- Web servers that allow the client to access documents on the Internet
- printer servers that allow the user to print on various printers
- file servers that manage user files
- email servers for storing and forwarding email
- servers that support application such as word processing or spreadsheets

Another model for network interaction is the **peer-to-peer model** in which the computers are considered to be equals. For example, the computers could be cooperating toward solving a large computing problem that has been designed to run in a distributed manner over multiple computers on the network.

As distributed systems have evolved it has become necessary to have more complex models than these. Large applications are frequently designed in **multiple tiers.** In a typical three-tier design there will be a front-end that is responsible for the user interface, a middle tier that contains the main logic for the application—often called the business rules—and a database tier that is responsible for all the data storage for the application. In Chapter 17 we discussed the reasons why these more complex architectures have evolved. These models are discussed in greater length in Chapter 15 on networking and Chapters 7 and 17 on distributed processing systems.

A.5.2 Network controllers, routers, and name servers

Similar to the manner in which a computer interacts with a device controller that controls an I/O device, the CPU and memory connect to a network through a **network interface controller,** or **NIC.** At the hardware level there are various types of network connections of varying speed, and new technologies for connections are being introduced all the time. Some of the common hardware devices and technologies that connect computers to a network are modems, Ethernet, DSL, cable modems, and several wireless techniques.

At the Physical level, it is useful to distinguish between two types of connections used to build a network: wired and wireless. Hardware for wired networks includes cables or optical fibers of different types, network gateways, routers, switches, hubs, and other similar components. Wireless network components include satellites, base stations for wireless connections, wireless hubs, infrared and Bluetooth ports, and so on.

The network can route a message from its source to its destination through the use of **bridges, switching devices,** or **routers.** To manage the complexity it is common to divide a network within an organization into subnetworks, each connecting a small number of computers via a local area network (LAN). These subnetworks are connected to one another through local routers, which then connect to a regional router, which then connects to the rest of the global network through one or more additional Internet routers.

In the case of the Internet, every computer on the network has a numeric IP (Internet protocol) address (such as 192.168.2.1), which uniquely identifies that computer, and allows the network to route messages addressed to that IP address. Computers also have unique names, such as ourserver.example.com. Specialized servers called **domain name servers** (DNS) have databases that can find a computer's numeric IP address when given its name. The other specialized computers that connect the network, namely the routers and switching devices, can then find a path through the network to deliver a message to the destination computer based on the numeric IP address or the **media access control** (**MAC**) address of the destination. These devices use specific network protocols at various levels to physically deliver the message. Figure A.7 shows a simplified diagram to illustrate these concepts. The techniques for doing this routing and switching are covered in Chapter 15.

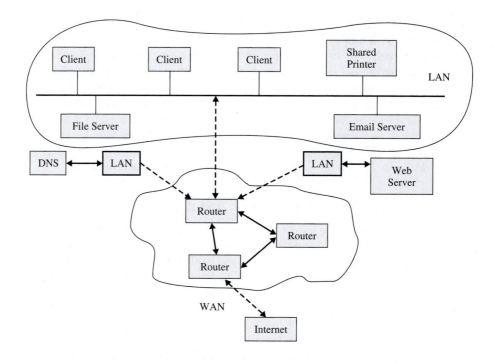

A.5.3 Types of networks

We conclude this brief introduction to networks with a traditional characterization of the types of networks.[8]

Local area networks (**LAN**s) are networks that normally connect computers within a limited geographical area, say a group of offices or one building or a number of adjacent buildings within an organization. These networks are primarily built of cables that run through and between the buildings, possibly with switches or routers connecting, say, the various networks on each floor or in each cluster of adjacent offices. Increasingly, wireless access points are being used that allow the connection of a computer with a wireless network card to the local area network.

Wide area networks (**WAN**s), on the other hand, generally refer to networks that connect computers over a large geographical area. These use phone lines, fiber optic cables, satellites, and other connections to connect the thousands of local area networks to one another, and hence to allow global connectivity of computers.

Mobile networks are made up of thousands of telecommunications towers and control systems that operate as fixed base stations, which are then connected to local or wide area networks. Mobile devices such as cellular phones or handheld computers or PDAs can connect to a nearby base station, which connects it to the rest of the network, and to other parts of the global network.

---

[8] The technical distinction between a LAN and a WAN is somewhat different. See Chapter 15 for details.

A.6 A MORE DETAILED PICTURE

We conclude this appendix with Figure A.8, which presents a more detailed picture to illustrate how various system components that we discussed throughout this appendix are connected to one another.

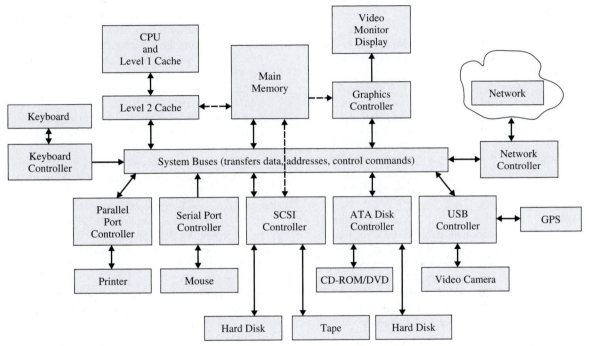

FIGURE A.8 A diagram to illustrate a computer system in some additional detail.

A.7 SUMMARY

In this appendix, we gave an overview of the basic components of a computer system. We started with a simple overview and a diagram of typical computer system components, and concluded with a more detailed—though still simplified—diagram. In between, we devoted one section to each of the main components of modern-day computers: the processor or CPU, memory and storage hierarchy, I/O devices, and the network. From the discussion, it should be clear that there is overlap between these categories. For example, hard disks can be considered as both an I/O device or as part of the storage hierarchy, and the network interface to a computer can also be abstracted to look like I/O devices. However, the traditional division is useful for structuring our discussion and presentation of computer systems and OSs.

BIBLIOGRAPHY

Belady, L. A., R. P. Parmelee, and C. A. Scalzi, "The IBM History of Memory Management Technology," *IBM Journal of Research and Development,* Vol. 25, No. 5, September 1981, pp. 491–503.

Brown, G. E., et al., "Operating System Enhancement through Firmware," *SIGMICRO Newsletter,* Vol. 8, September 1977, pp. 119–133.

Bucci, G., G. Neri, and F. Baldassarri, "MP80: A Microprogrammed CPU with a Microcoded Operating System Kernel," *Computer,* October 1981, pp. 81–90.

Chow, F., S. Correll, M. Himelstein, E. Killian, and L. Weber, "How Many Addressing Modes Are Enough?" *Proceedings of the Second International Conference on Architectural Support for Programming Languages and Operating Systems,* Palo Alto, CA, October 5–8, 1987, pp. 117–122.

Davidson, S., and B. D. Shriver, "An Overview of Firmware Engineering," *Computer,* May 1978, pp. 21–31.

DeRosa, J., R. Glackemeyer, and T. Knight, "Design and Implementation of the VAX 8600 Pipeline," *Computer,* Vol. 18, No. 5, May 1985, pp. 38–50.

Elmer-DeWitt, P., and L. Mondi, "Hardware, Software, Vaporware," *Time,* February 3, 1986, p. 51.

Fenner, J. N., J. A. Schmidt, H. A. Halabi, and D. P. Agrawal, "MASCO: The Design of a Microprogrammed Processor," *Computer,* Vol. 18, No. 3, March 1985, pp. 41–53.

Foley, J. D., "Interfaces for Advanced Computing," *Scientific American,* Vol. 257, No. 4, October 1987, pp. 126–135.

Foster, C. C., and T. Iberall, *Computer Architecture,* 3rd ed., New York: Van Nostrand Reinhold, 1985.

Fox, E. R., K. J. Kiefer, R. F. Vangen, and S. P. Whalen, "Reduced Instruction Set Architecture for a GaAs Microprocessor System," *Computer,* Vol. 19, Issue 10, October 1986, pp. 71–81.

Hunt, J. G., "Interrupts," *Software—Practice and Experience,* Vol. 10, No. 7, July 1980, pp. 523–530.

Leonard, T. E., ed., *VAX Architecture Reference Manual.* Bedford, MA: Digital Press, 1987.

Lilja, D. J., "Reducing the Branch Penalty in Pipelined Processors," *Computer,* Vol. 21, No. 7, July 1988, pp. 47–53.

Mallach, E. G., "Emulator Architecture," *Computer,* Vol. 8, August 1975, pp. 24–32.

Patterson, D. A., "Reduced Instruction Set Computers," *Communications of the ACM,* Vol. 28, No. 1, January 1985, pp. 8–21.

Patterson, D., and J. Hennessy, *Computer Organization and Design,* 3rd ed., San Francisco, CA: Morgan Kaufmann, 2004.

Patterson, D. A., and R. S. Piepho, "Assessing RISCs in High- Level Language Support," *IEEE Micro,* Vol. 2, No. 4, November 1982, pp. 9–19.

Patton, C. P., "Microprocessors: Architecture and Applications," *IEEE Computer,* Vol. 18, No. 6, June 1985, pp. 29–40.

Pohm, A. V., and T. A. Smay, "Computer Memory Systems," *Computer,* October 1981, pp. 93–110.

Rauscher, T. G., and P. N. Adams, "Microprogramming: A Tutorial and Survey of Recent Developments," *IEEE Transactions on Computers,* Vol. C-29, No. 1, January 1980, pp. 2–20.

Smith, A. J.; "Cache Memories," *ACM Computing Surveys,* Vol. 14, No. 3, September 1982, pp. 473–530.

WEB RESOURCES

http://books.elsevier.com/companions/1558606041/ (Hennessy and Patterson)

http://en.wikipedia.org/wiki/Cache

REVIEW QUESTIONS

A.1 What are the two major classes of CPU design?

A.2 What is the importance of the instruction set architecture to a discussion of the design and development of OSs?

A.3 Why is a system hardware timer important to an OS?

A.4 What is the purpose of an interrupt?

A.5 What is the significance of multicore CPU chips?

A.6 True or false? Primary storage in computers is always made up of electronic memory circuits.

A.7 It is hard to overemphasize the importance of caching to the performance of an OS.
  a. What is the purpose of a cache?
  b. What theory underlies its function?

A.8 In theory we could make the cache between secondary storage and primary storage as big as the secondary storage. This would have the advantage of having much smaller latency. Why do we not do this?

A.9 What is the purpose of memory protection?

A.10 What is the purpose of having device controllers?

A.11 In order to help us discuss and understand large complex topics such as I/O devices, we can view the subject as a space with many dimensions. We first discussed a broad division of I/O devices according to the purpose of the device. What were the three broad purposes that were discussed? Give some examples of each class.

A.12 We also divided the I/O device space into those interfaces that were general-purpose interfaces and those that were for specific device types. Give some examples of each class.

A.13 DMA controllers cause many fewer interrupts per block transferred to or from a device than do controllers, which do not use DMA. Other than obviously freeing up the CPU to do other things, why do we need controllers that use DMA?

A.14 What is the function of a device driver and how do we configure OSs with the correct drivers?

A.15 What facility is used to translate computer names such as omega.example.com to IP addresses for use in the Internet?

Index